NOT GUILTY-ish

Rick Kirkman

Jerry Scott

Collection

NO.
40

Andrews McMeel
PUBLISHING®

Baby Blues® is distributed internationally by Andrews McMeel Syndication.

Not Guilty-ish copyright © 2023 by Baby Blues Partnership. All rights reserved. Printed in China. No part of this book may be used or reproduced in any manner whatsoever without written permission except in the case of reprints in the context of reviews.

Andrews McMeel Publishing
a division of Andrews McMeel Universal
1130 Walnut Street, Kansas City, Missouri 64106

www.andrewsmcmeel.com

23 24 25 26 27 SDB 10 9 8 7 6 5 4 3 2 1

ISBN: 978-1-5248-8094-1

Library of Congress Control Number: 2023932685

Editor: Lucas Wetzel
Designer/Art Director: Julie Barnes
Production Manager: Chadd Keim
Production Editor: Julie Railsback

Find Baby Blues® on the Web at www.babyblues.com.

ATTENTION: SCHOOLS AND BUSINESSES
Andrews McMeel books are available at quantity discounts with bulk purchase for educational, business, or sales promotional use. For information, please e-mail the Andrews McMeel Publishing Special Sales Department: sales@amuniversal.com.

To Mary and Peggy, from your boys.

—Rick and Jerry

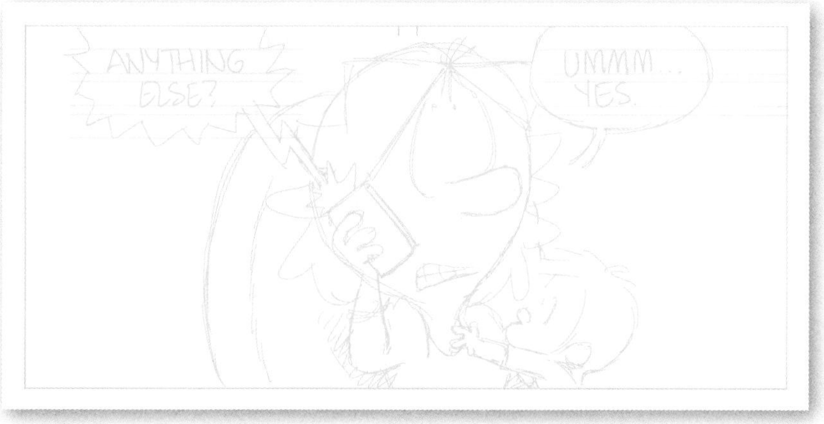
ANYTHING ELSE?
UMMM... YES.

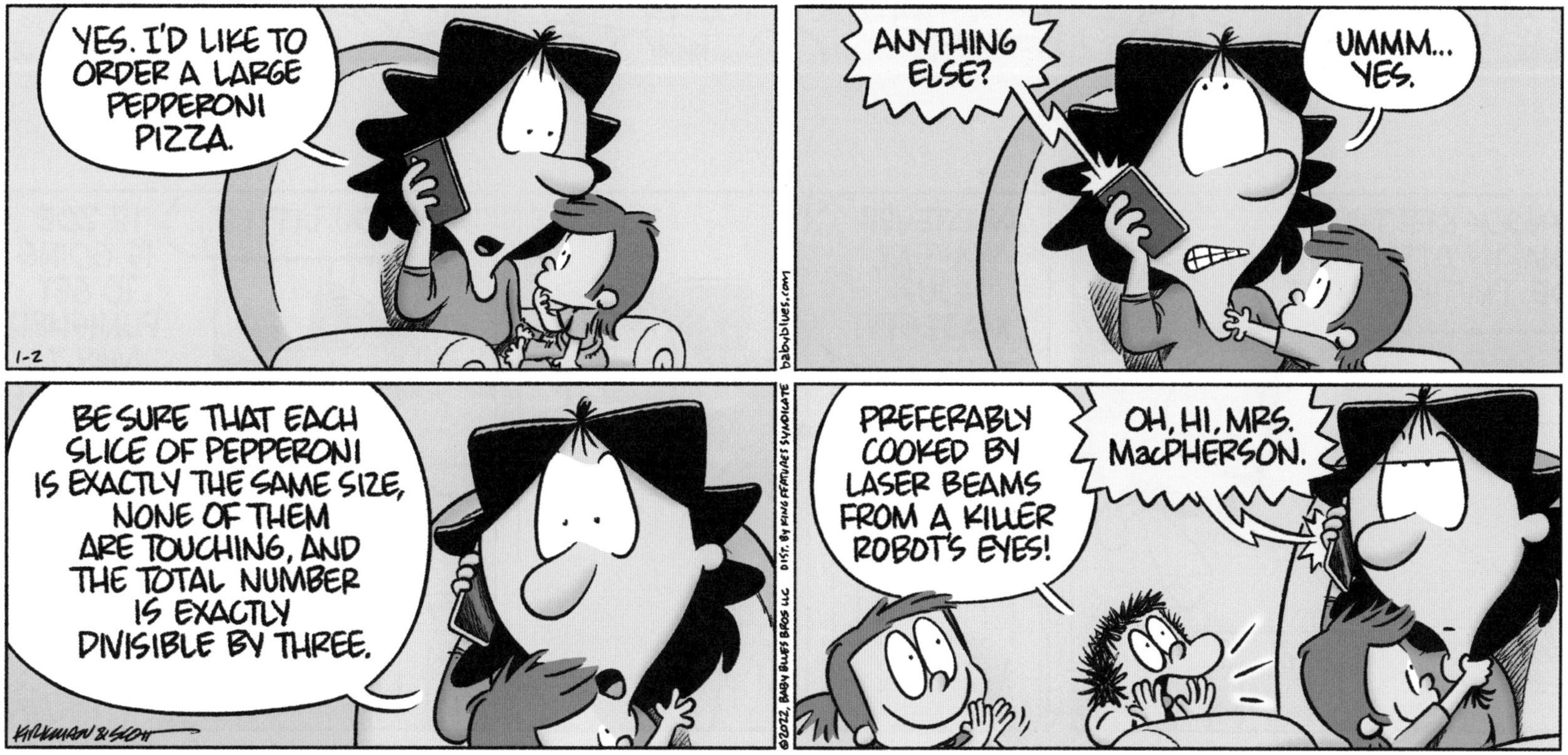
YES. I'D LIKE TO ORDER A LARGE PEPPERONI PIZZA.
1-2
ANYTHING ELSE?
UMMM... YES.
babyblues.com
BE SURE THAT EACH SLICE OF PEPPERONI IS EXACTLY THE SAME SIZE, NONE OF THEM ARE TOUCHING, AND THE TOTAL NUMBER IS EXACTLY DIVISIBLE BY THREE.
KIRKMAN & SCOTT
©2022, BABY BLUES BROS LLC DIST. BY KING FEATURES SYNDICATE
PREFERABLY COOKED BY LASER BEAMS FROM A KILLER ROBOT'S EYES!
OH, HI, MRS. MacPHERSON.

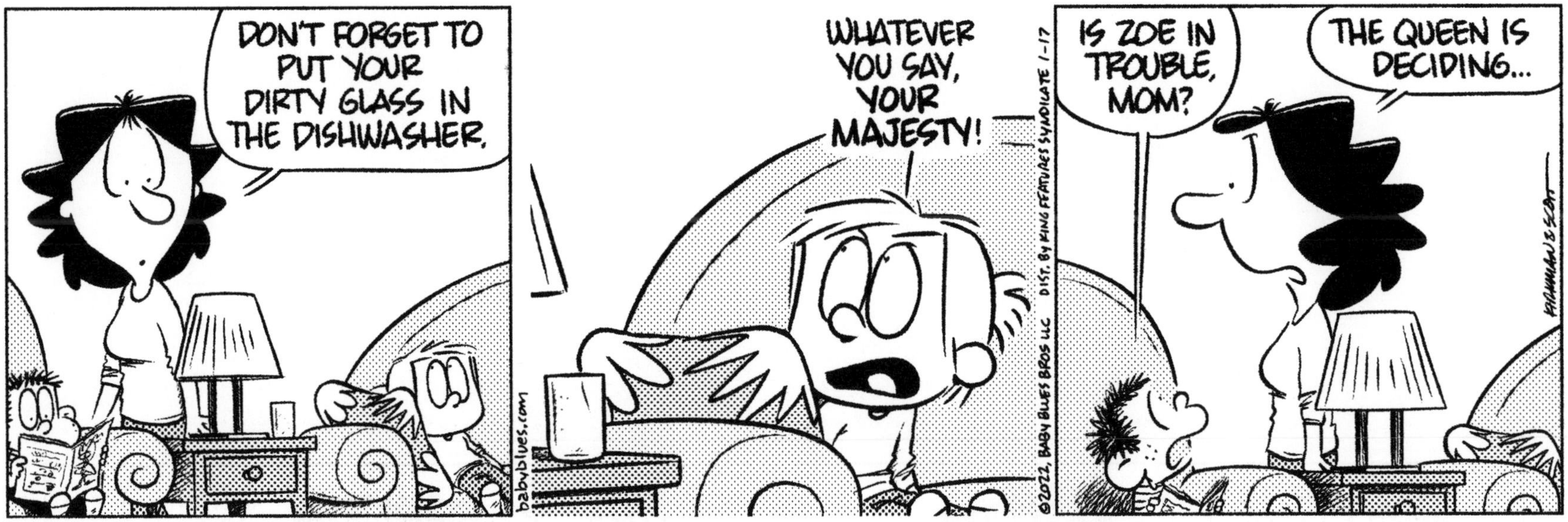
DON'T FORGET TO PUT YOUR DIRTY GLASS IN THE DISHWASHER.
babyblues.com
WHATEVER YOU SAY, YOUR MAJESTY!
©2022, BABY BLUES BROS LLC DIST. BY KING FEATURES SYNDICATE 1-17
IS ZOE IN TROUBLE, MOM?
THE QUEEN IS DECIDING...

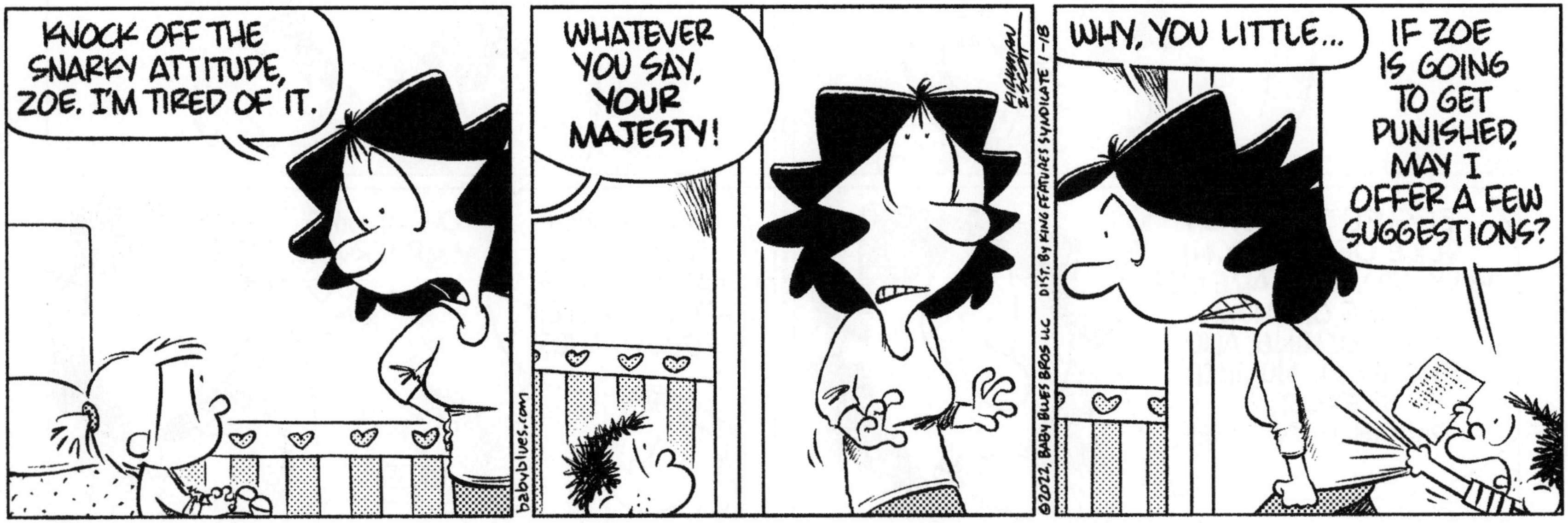
KNOCK OFF THE SNARKY ATTITUDE, ZOE. I'M TIRED OF IT.
babyblues.com
WHATEVER YOU SAY, YOUR MAJESTY!
©2022, BABY BLUES BROS LLC DIST. BY KING FEATURES SYNDICATE 1-18
WHY, YOU LITTLE...
IF ZOE IS GOING TO GET PUNISHED, MAY I OFFER A FEW SUGGESTIONS?

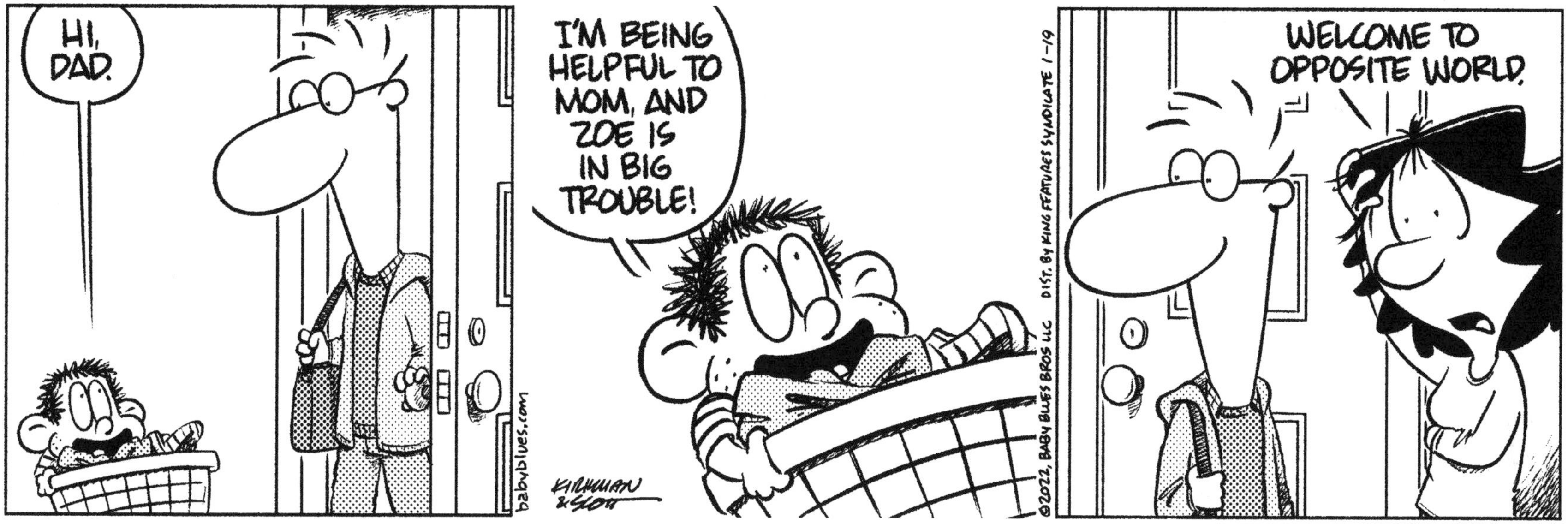
HI, DAD.
I'M BEING HELPFUL TO MOM, AND ZOE IS IN BIG TROUBLE!
WELCOME TO OPPOSITE WORLD.
babyblues.com
KIRKMAN & SCOTT
©2022, BABY BLUES BROS LLC DIST. BY KING FEATURES SYNDICATE 1-19

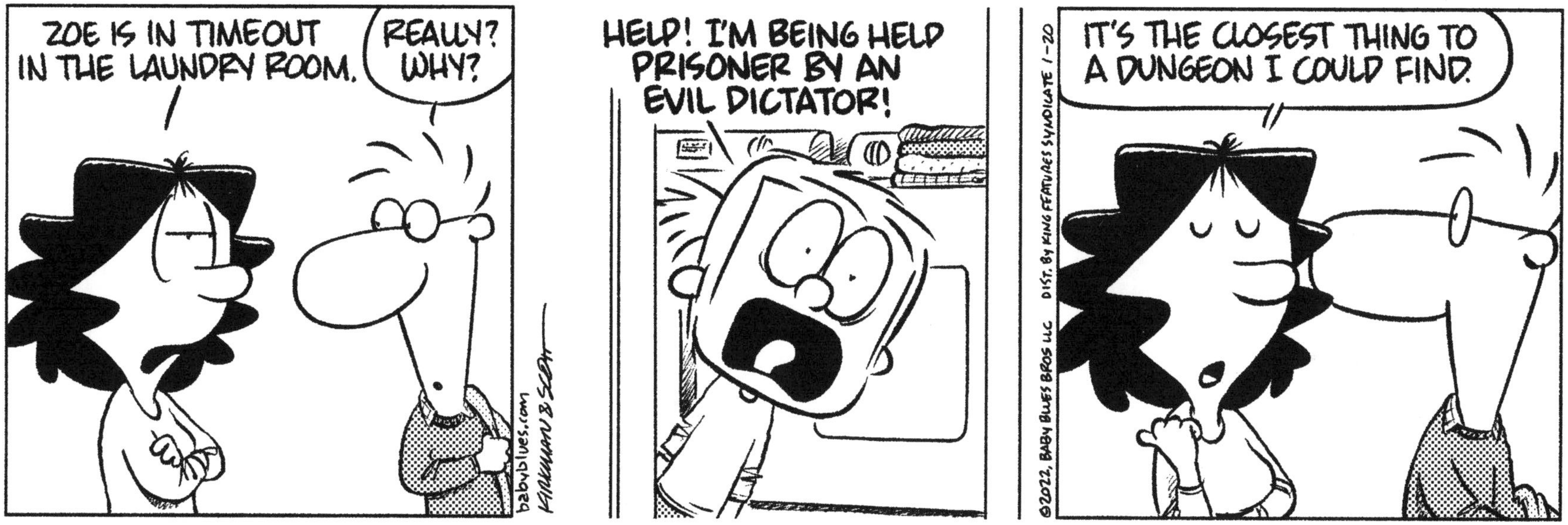
ZOE IS IN TIMEOUT IN THE LAUNDRY ROOM.
REALLY? WHY?
HELP! I'M BEING HELD PRISONER BY AN EVIL DICTATOR!
IT'S THE CLOSEST THING TO A DUNGEON I COULD FIND.
babyblues.com
KIRKMAN & SCOTT
©2022, BABY BLUES BROS LLC DIST. BY KING FEATURES SYNDICATE 1-20

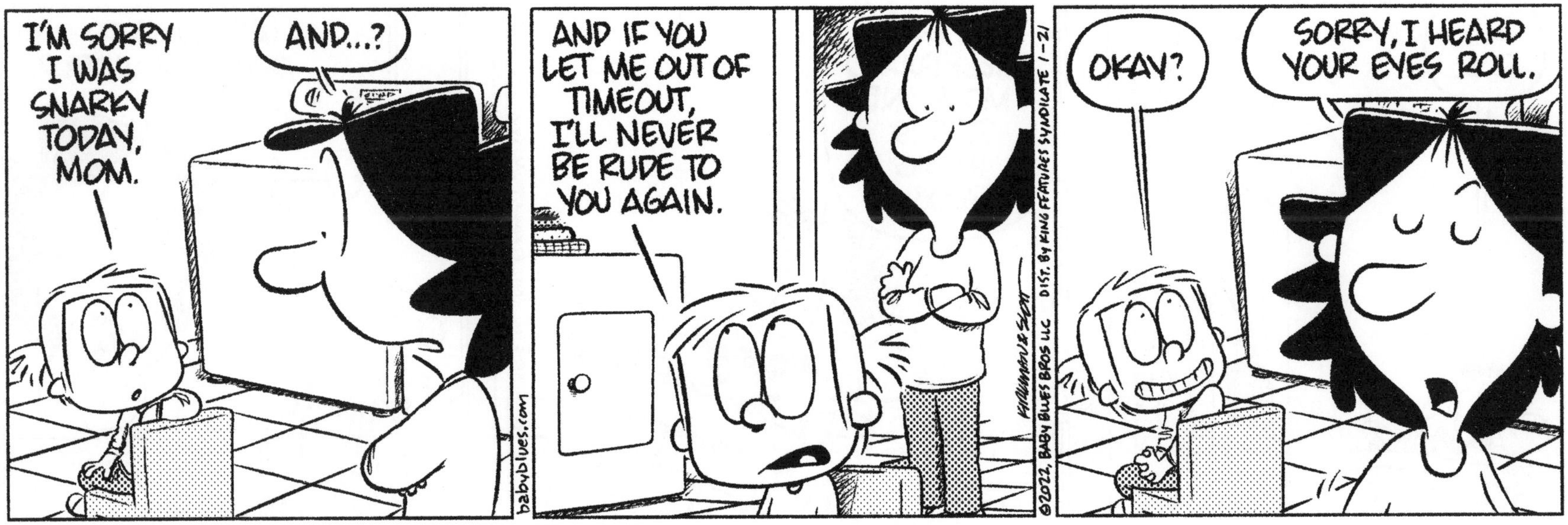
I'M SORRY I WAS SNARKY TODAY, MOM.
AND...?
babyblues.com
AND IF YOU LET ME OUT OF TIMEOUT, I'LL NEVER BE RUDE TO YOU AGAIN.
©2022, BABY BLUES BROS LLC DIST. BY KING FEATURES SYNDICATE 1-21
KIRKMAN & SCOTT
OKAY?
SORRY, I HEARD YOUR EYES ROLL.

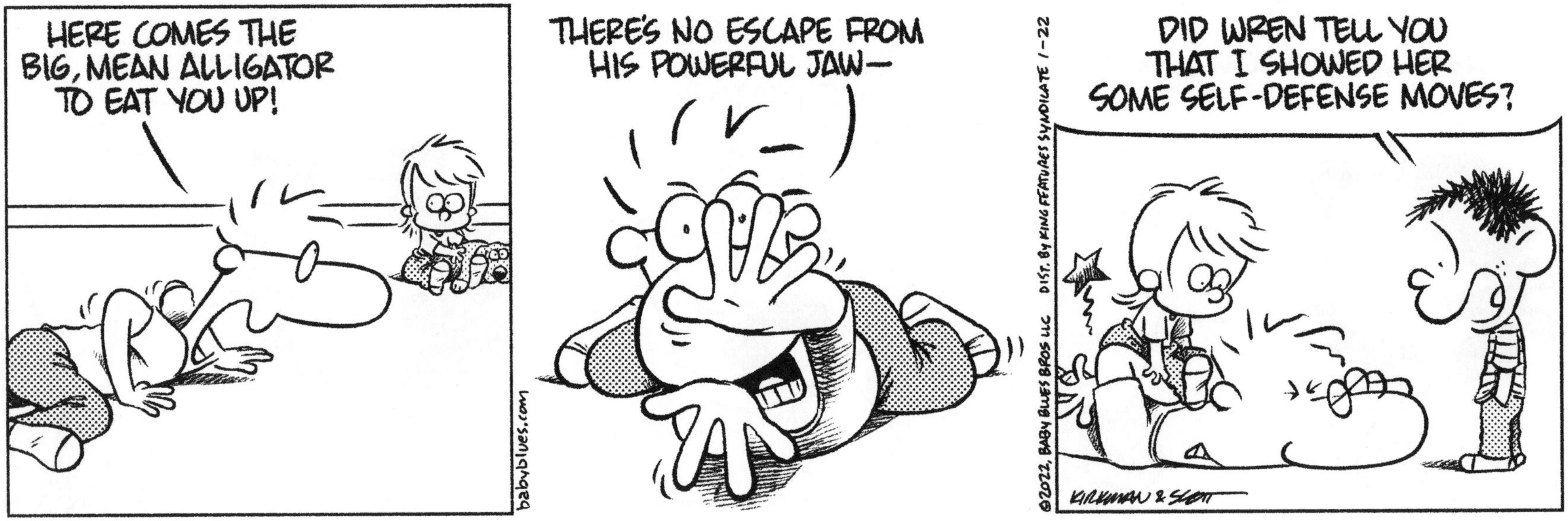
HERE COMES THE BIG, MEAN ALLIGATOR TO EAT YOU UP!
babyblues.com
THERE'S NO ESCAPE FROM HIS POWERFUL JAW—
©2022, BABY BLUES BROS LLC DIST. BY KING FEATURES SYNDICATE 1-22
DID WREN TELL YOU THAT I SHOWED HER SOME SELF-DEFENSE MOVES?
KIRKMAN & SCOTT

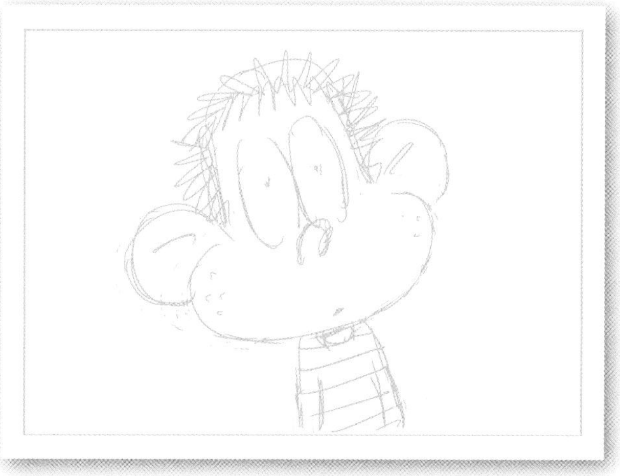

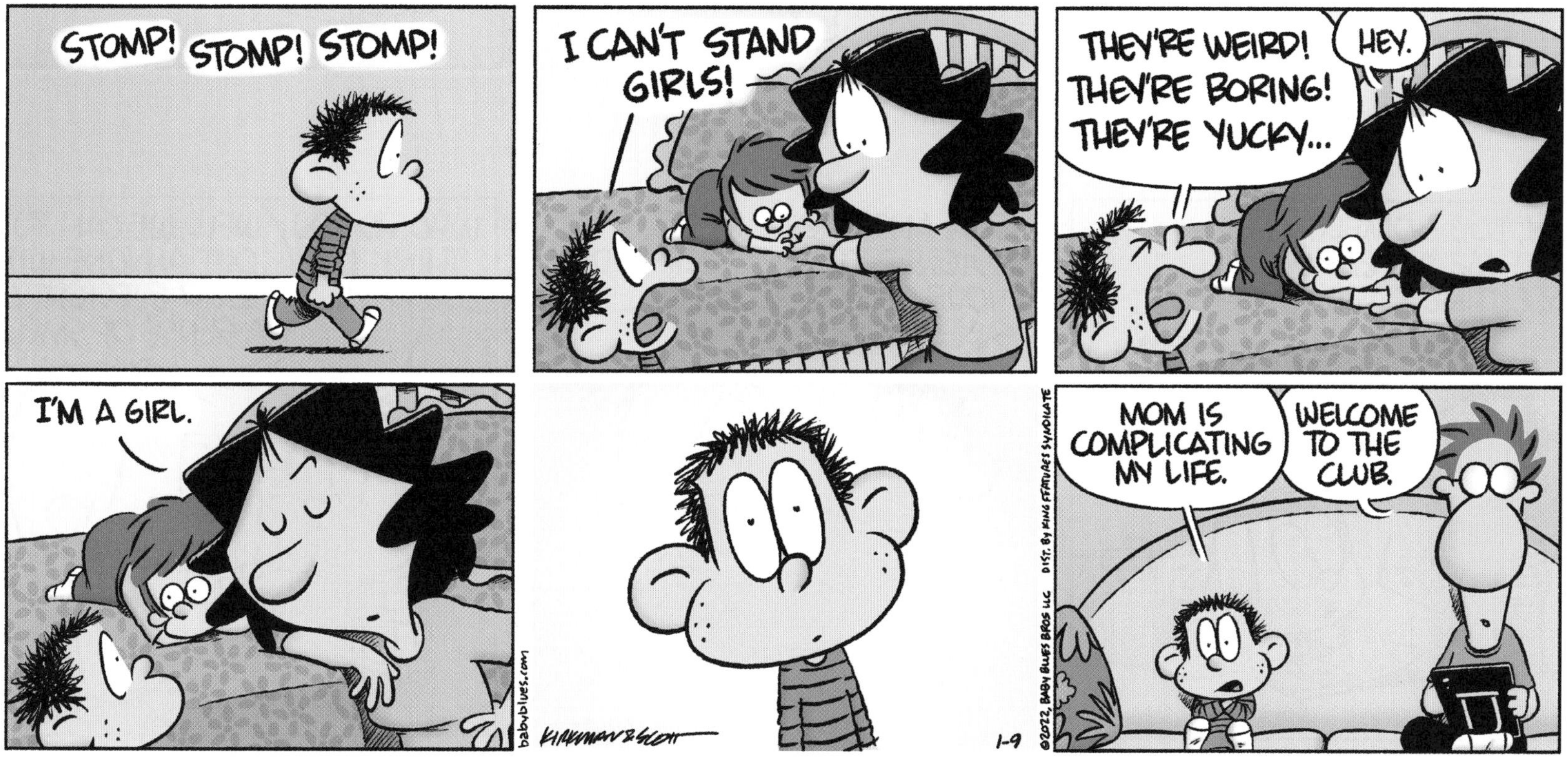
STOMP! STOMP! STOMP!
I CAN'T STAND GIRLS!
THEY'RE WEIRD! THEY'RE BORING! THEY'RE YUCKY...
HEY.
I'M A GIRL.
MOM IS COMPLICATING MY LIFE.
WELCOME TO THE CLUB.
babyblues.com
1-9
©2022, BABY BLUES BROS LLC DIST. BY KING FEATURES SYNDICATE

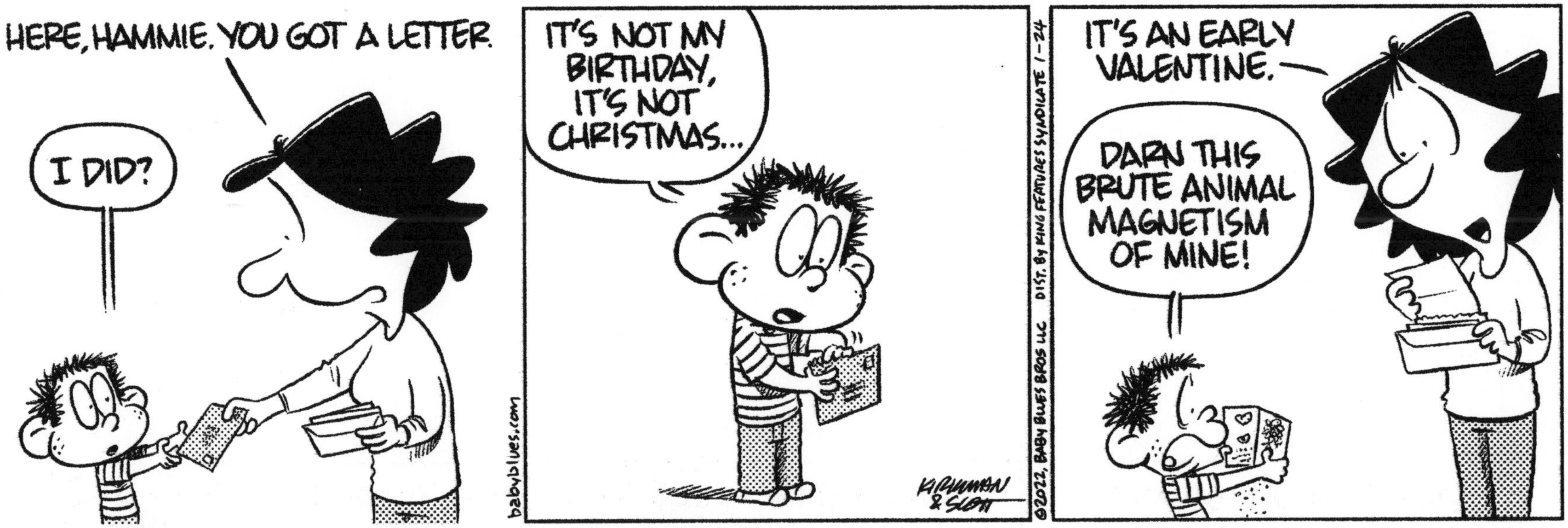
HERE, HAMMIE. YOU GOT A LETTER.
I DID?
IT'S NOT MY BIRTHDAY, IT'S NOT CHRISTMAS...
IT'S AN EARLY VALENTINE.
DARN THIS BRUTE ANIMAL MAGNETISM OF MINE!
babyblues.com
KIRKMAN & SCOTT
©2022, BABY BLUES BROS LLC DIST. BY KING FEATURES SYNDICATE 1-24

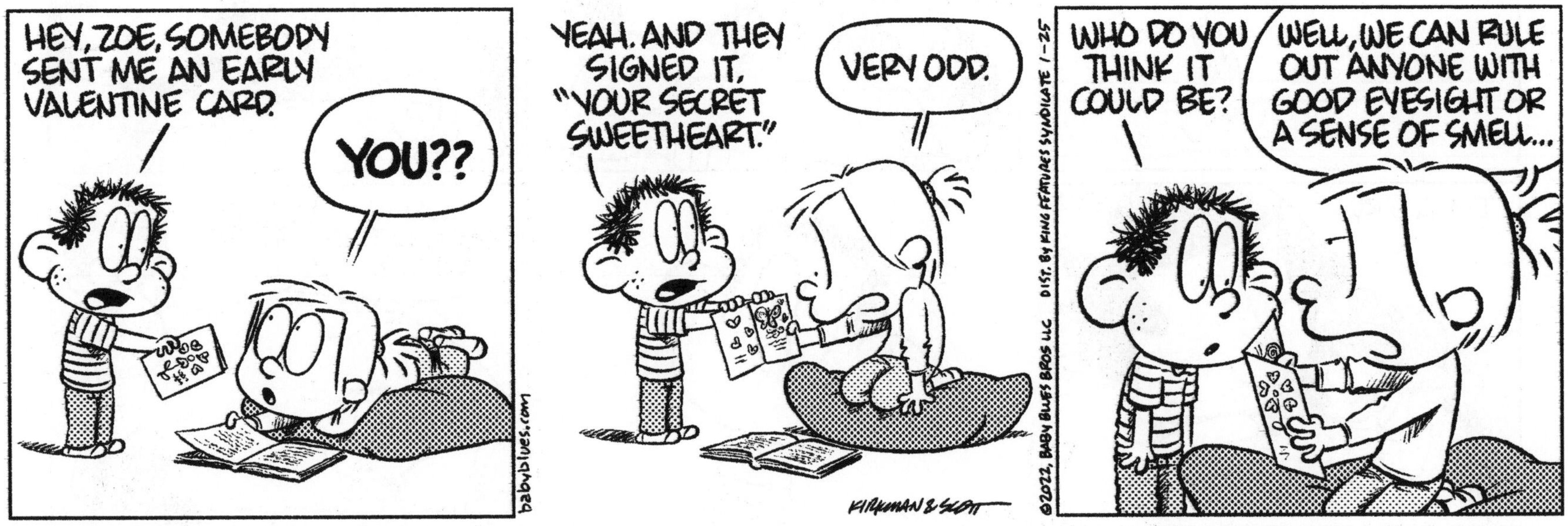
HEY, ZOE, SOMEBODY SENT ME AN EARLY VALENTINE CARD.
YOU??
YEAH. AND THEY SIGNED IT, "YOUR SECRET SWEETHEART."
VERY ODD.
WHO DO YOU THINK IT COULD BE?
WELL, WE CAN RULE OUT ANYONE WITH GOOD EYESIGHT OR A SENSE OF SMELL...
babyblues.com
KIRKMAN & SCOTT
©2022, BABY BLUES BROS LLC DIST. BY KING FEATURES SYNDICATE 1-25

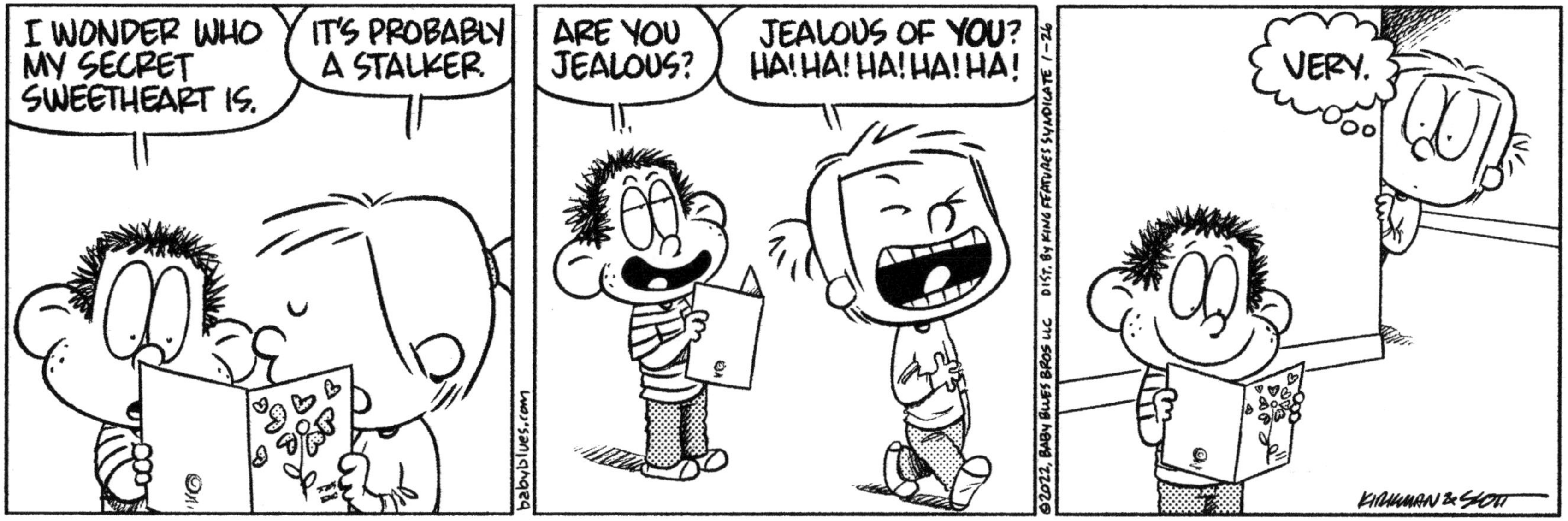
I WONDER WHO MY SECRET SWEETHEART IS.
IT'S PROBABLY A STALKER.
babyblues.com
ARE YOU JEALOUS?
JEALOUS OF YOU? HA! HA! HA! HA! HA!
©2022, BABY BLUES BROS LLC DIST. BY KING FEATURES SYNDICATE 1-26
VERY.
KIRKMAN & SCOTT

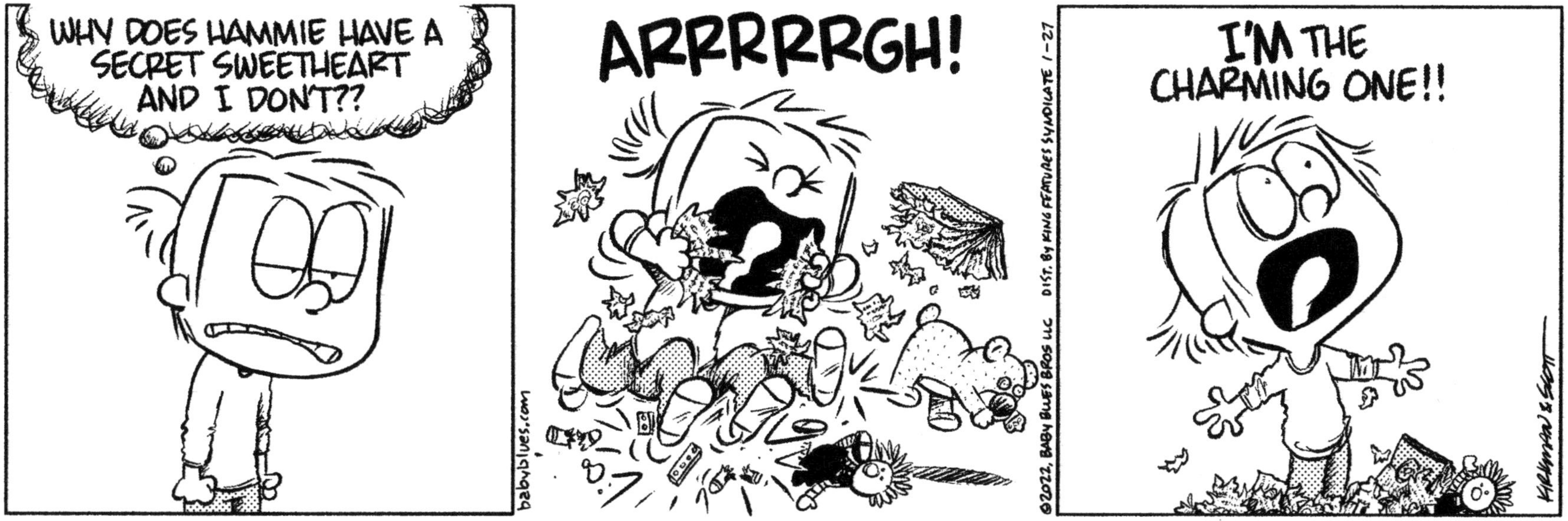
WHY DOES HAMMIE HAVE A SECRET SWEETHEART AND I DON'T??
babyblues.com
ARRRRRGH!
©2022, BABY BLUES BROS LLC DIST. BY KING FEATURES SYNDICATE 1-27
I'M THE CHARMING ONE!!
KIRKMAN & SCOTT

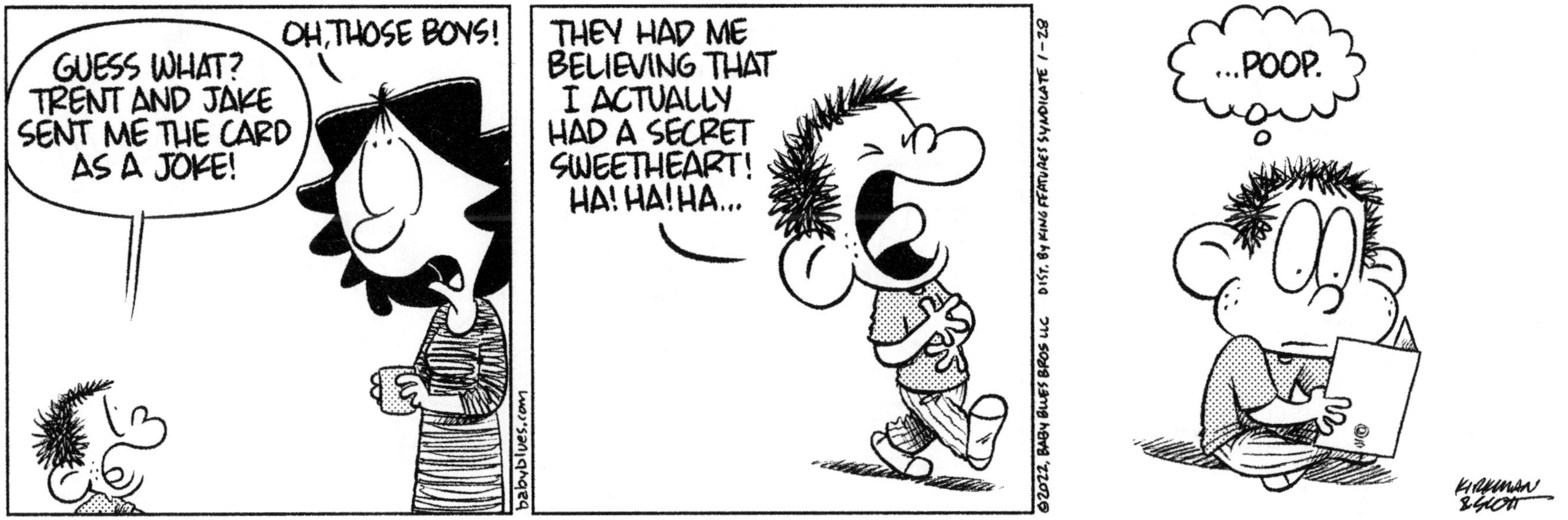
GUESS WHAT? TRENT AND JAKE SENT ME THE CARD AS A JOKE!
OH, THOSE BOYS!
babyblues.com
THEY HAD ME BELIEVING THAT I ACTUALLY HAD A SECRET SWEETHEART! HA! HA! HA...
©2022, BABY BLUES BROS LLC DIST. BY KING FEATURES SYNDICATE 1-28
...POOP.
KIRKMAN & SCOTT

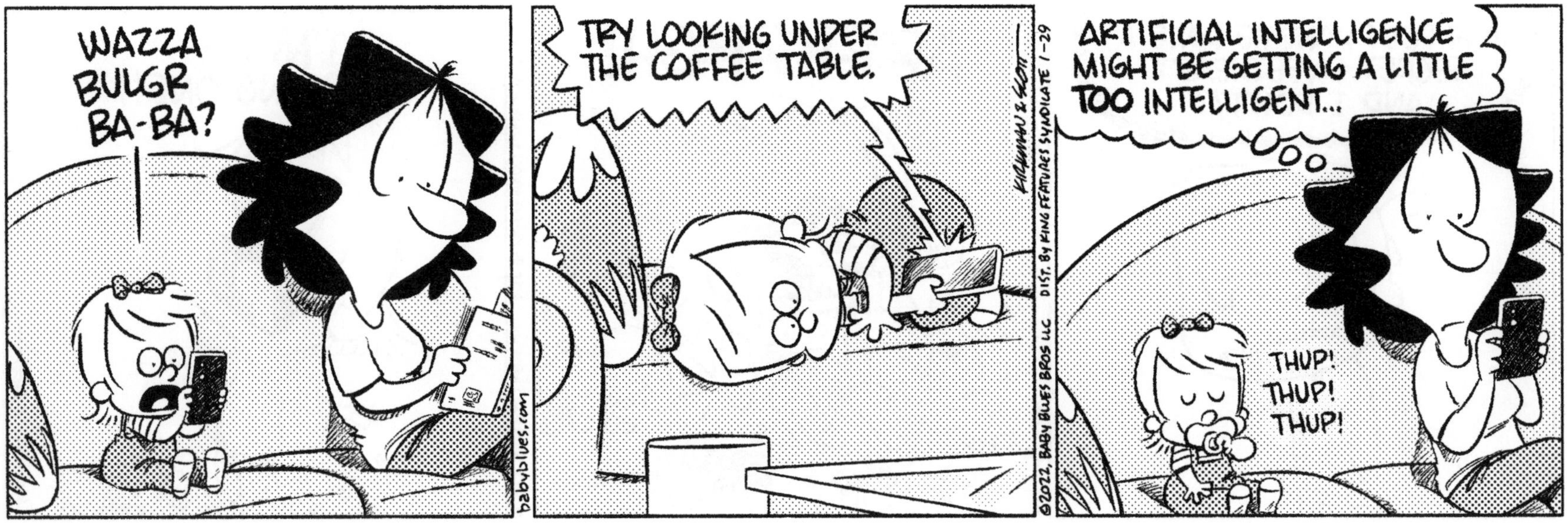
WAZZA BULGR BA-BA?
babyblues.com
TRY LOOKING UNDER THE COFFEE TABLE.
KIRKMAN & SCOTT
©2022, BABY BLUES BROS LLC DIST. BY KING FEATURES SYNDICATE 1-29
ARTIFICIAL INTELLIGENCE MIGHT BE GETTING A LITTLE TOO INTELLIGENT...
THUP! THUP! THUP!

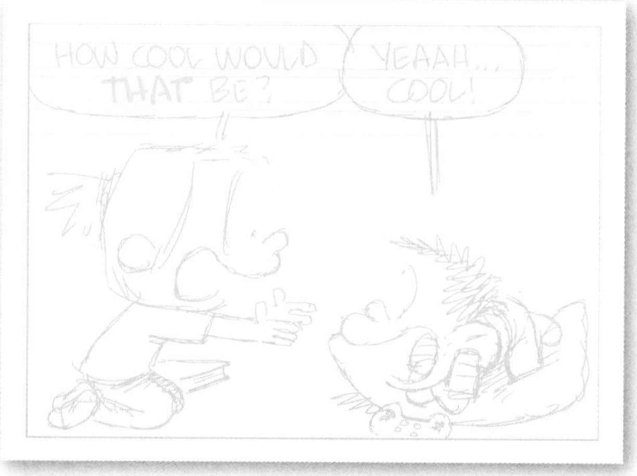
HOW COOL WOULD THAT BE?
YEAAH... COOL!

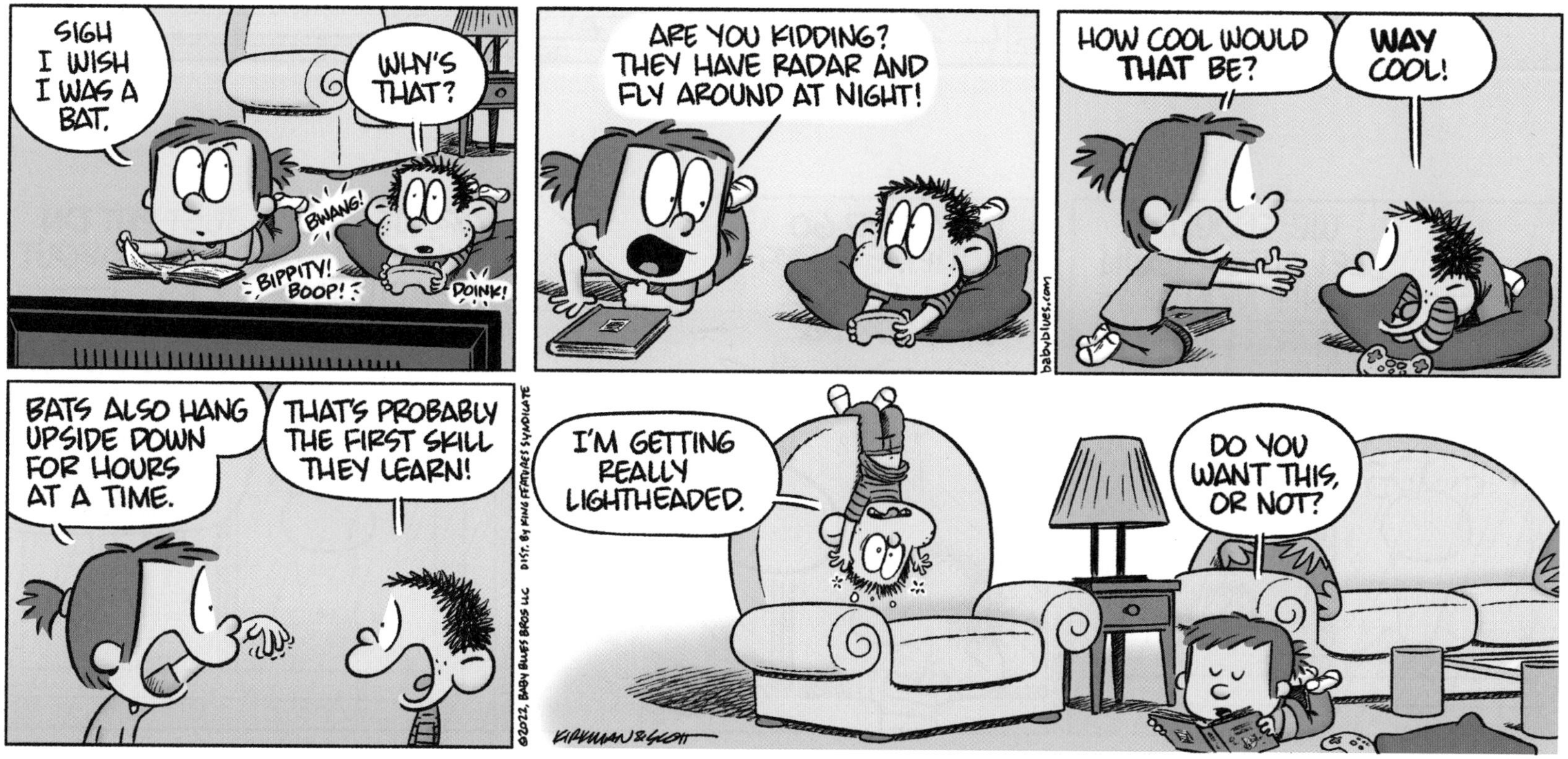
SIGH I WISH I WAS A BAT.
WHY'S THAT?
BWANG!
BIPPITY! BOOP!
DOINK!
ARE YOU KIDDING? THEY HAVE RADAR AND FLY AROUND AT NIGHT!
HOW COOL WOULD THAT BE?
WAY COOL!
babyblues.com
BATS ALSO HANG UPSIDE DOWN FOR HOURS AT A TIME.
THAT'S PROBABLY THE FIRST SKILL THEY LEARN!
©2022, BABY BLUES BROS LLC DIST. BY KING FEATURES SYNDICATE
I'M GETTING REALLY LIGHTHEADED.
DO YOU WANT THIS, OR NOT?
KIRKMAN & SCOTT

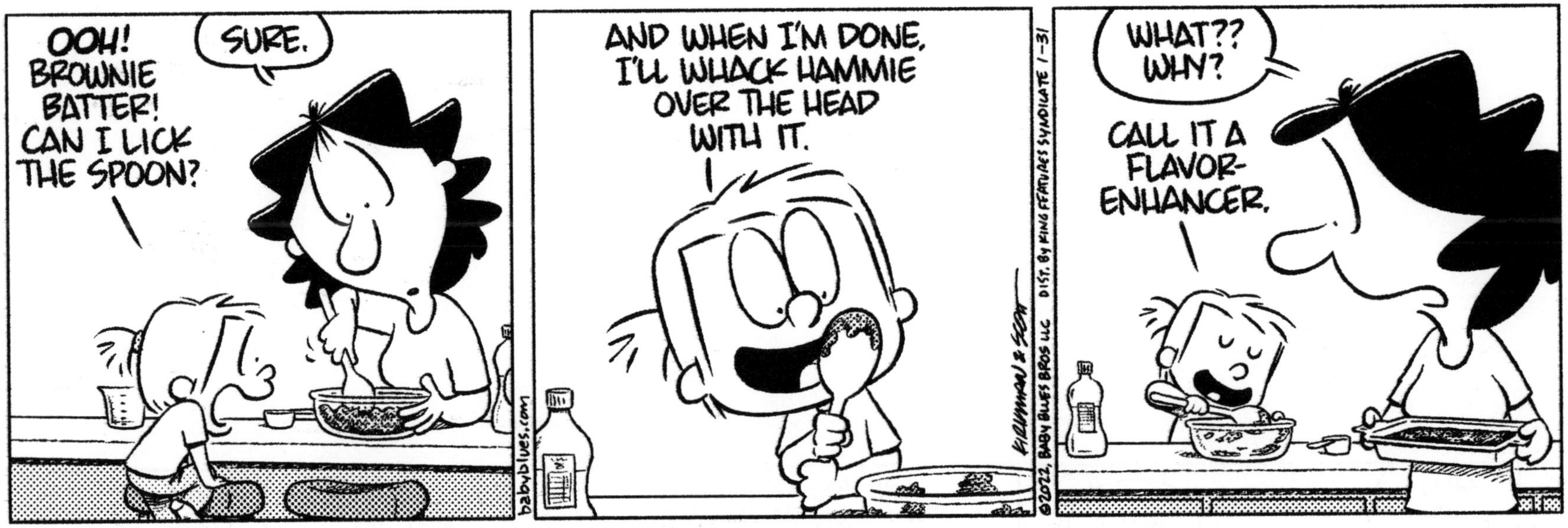
OOH! BROWNIE BATTER! CAN I LICK THE SPOON?
SURE.
babyblues.com
AND WHEN I'M DONE, I'LL WHACK HAMMIE OVER THE HEAD WITH IT.
KIRKMAN & SCOTT
©2022, BABY BLUES BROS LLC DIST. BY KING FEATURES SYNDICATE 1-31
WHAT?? WHY?
CALL IT A FLAVOR-ENHANCER.

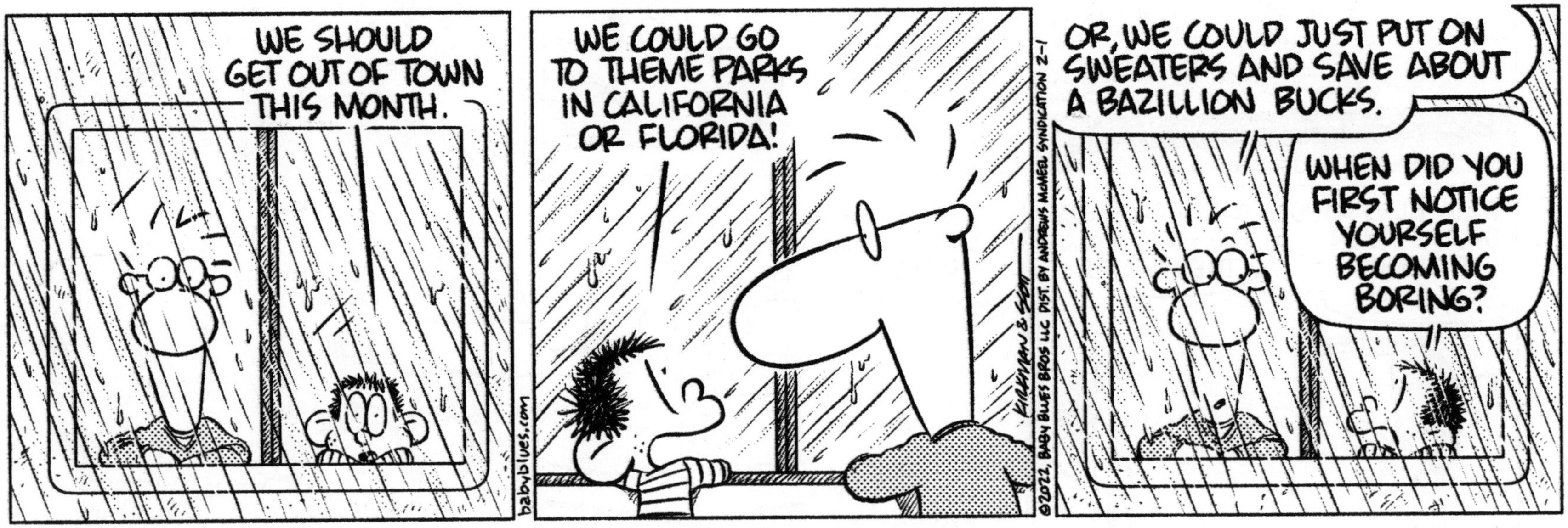
WE SHOULD GET OUT OF TOWN THIS MONTH.
babyblues.com
WE COULD GO TO THEME PARKS IN CALIFORNIA OR FLORIDA!
KIRKMAN & SCOTT
©2022, BABY BLUES BROS LLC DIST. BY ANDREWS MCMEEL SYNDICATION 2-1
OR, WE COULD JUST PUT ON SWEATERS AND SAVE ABOUT A BAZILLION BUCKS.
WHEN DID YOU FIRST NOTICE YOURSELF BECOMING BORING?

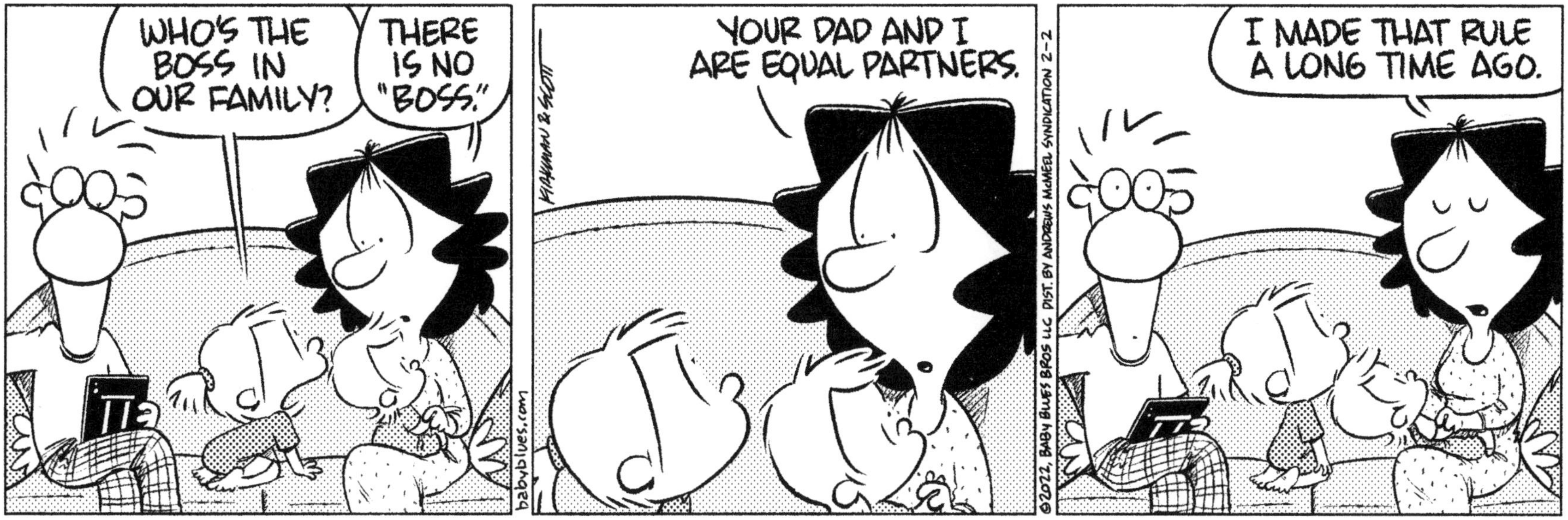
WHO'S THE BOSS IN OUR FAMILY?
THERE IS NO "BOSS."
KIRKMAN & SCOTT
babyblues.com
YOUR DAD AND I ARE EQUAL PARTNERS.
©2022, BABY BLUES BROS LLC DIST. BY ANDREWS MCMEEL SYNDICATION 2-2
I MADE THAT RULE A LONG TIME AGO.

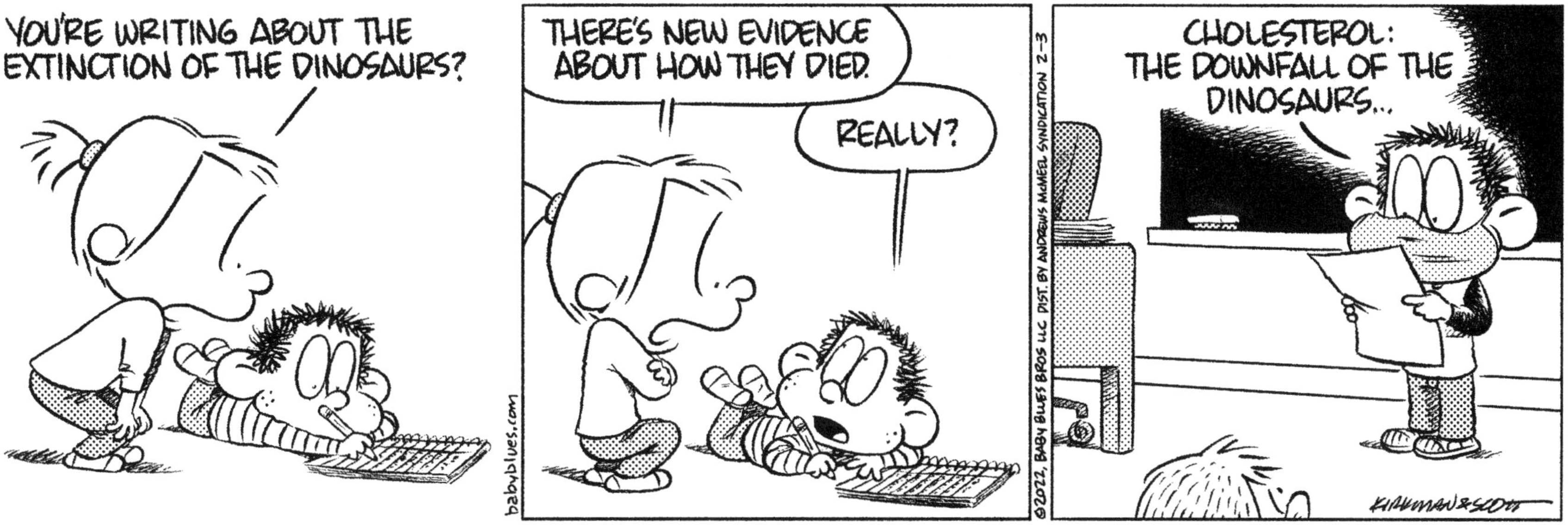
YOU'RE WRITING ABOUT THE EXTINCTION OF THE DINOSAURS?
babyblues.com
THERE'S NEW EVIDENCE ABOUT HOW THEY DIED.
REALLY?
©2022, BABY BLUES BROS LLC DIST. BY ANDREWS MCMEEL SYNDICATION 2-3
CHOLESTEROL: THE DOWNFALL OF THE DINOSAURS...
KIRKMAN & SCOTT

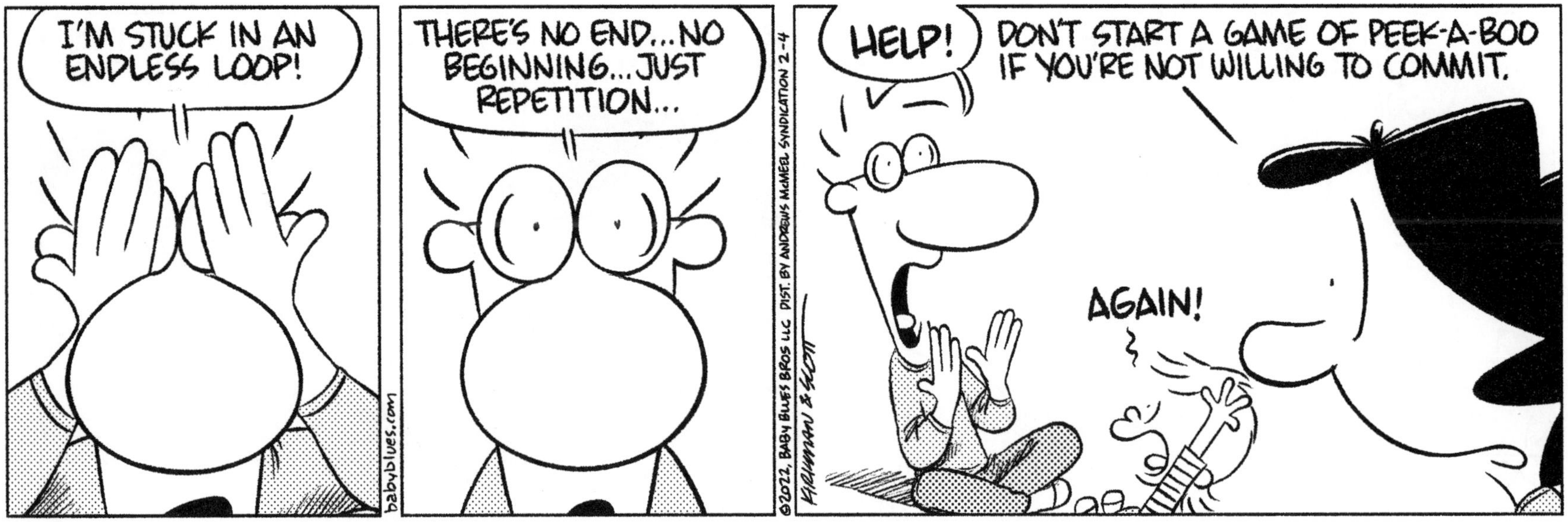
I'M STUCK IN AN ENDLESS LOOP!
babyblues.com
THERE'S NO END...NO BEGINNING...JUST REPETITION...
©2022, BABY BLUES BROS LLC DIST. BY ANDREWS McMEEL SYNDICATION 2-4
HELP!
DON'T START A GAME OF PEEK-A-BOO IF YOU'RE NOT WILLING TO COMMIT.
AGAIN!

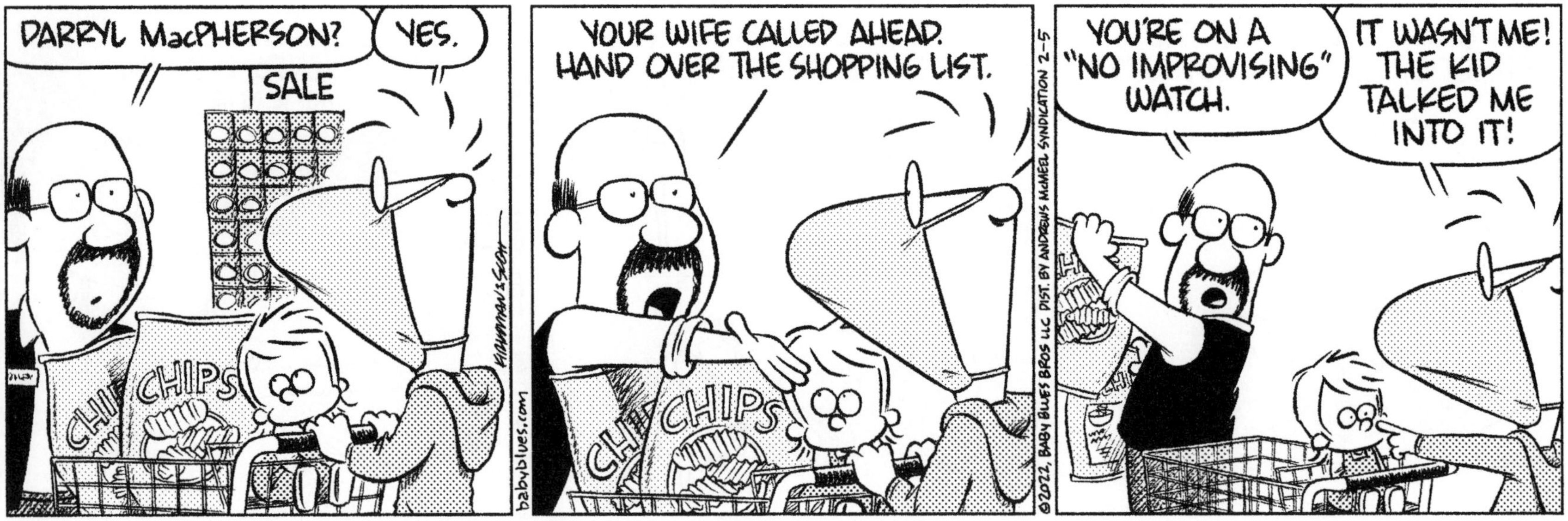
DARRYL MacPHERSON?
YES.
SALE
CHIPS
babyblues.com
YOUR WIFE CALLED AHEAD. HAND OVER THE SHOPPING LIST.
CHIPS
©2022, BABY BLUES BROS LLC DIST. BY ANDREWS McMEEL SYNDICATION 2-5
YOU'RE ON A "NO IMPROVISING" WATCH.
IT WASN'T ME! THE KID TALKED ME INTO IT!

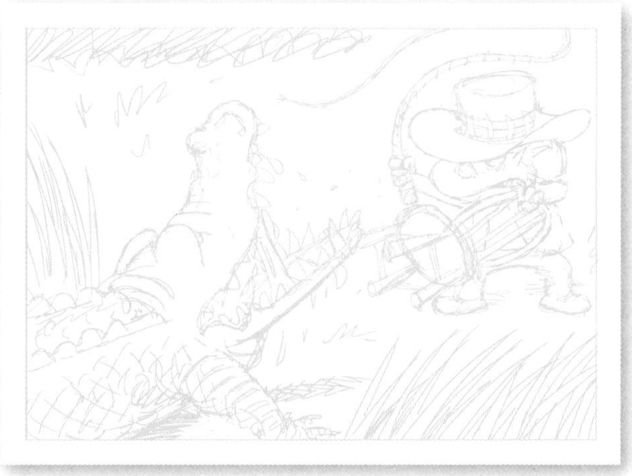

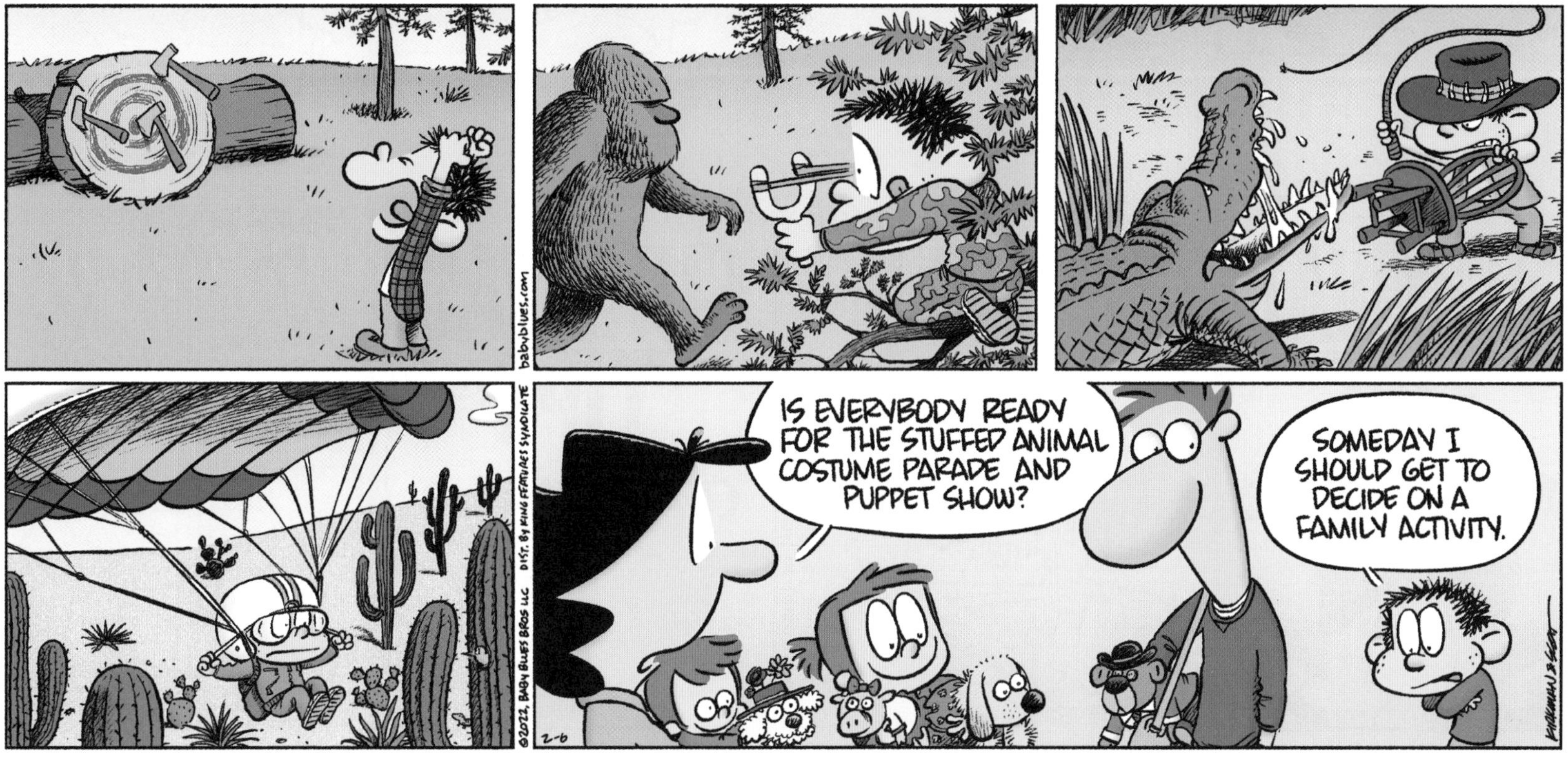
babyblues.com
©2022, BABY BLUES BROS LLC DIST. BY KING FEATURES SYNDICATE
2-6
IS EVERYBODY READY FOR THE STUFFED ANIMAL COSTUME PARADE AND PUPPET SHOW?
SOMEDAY I SHOULD GET TO DECIDE ON A FAMILY ACTIVITY.

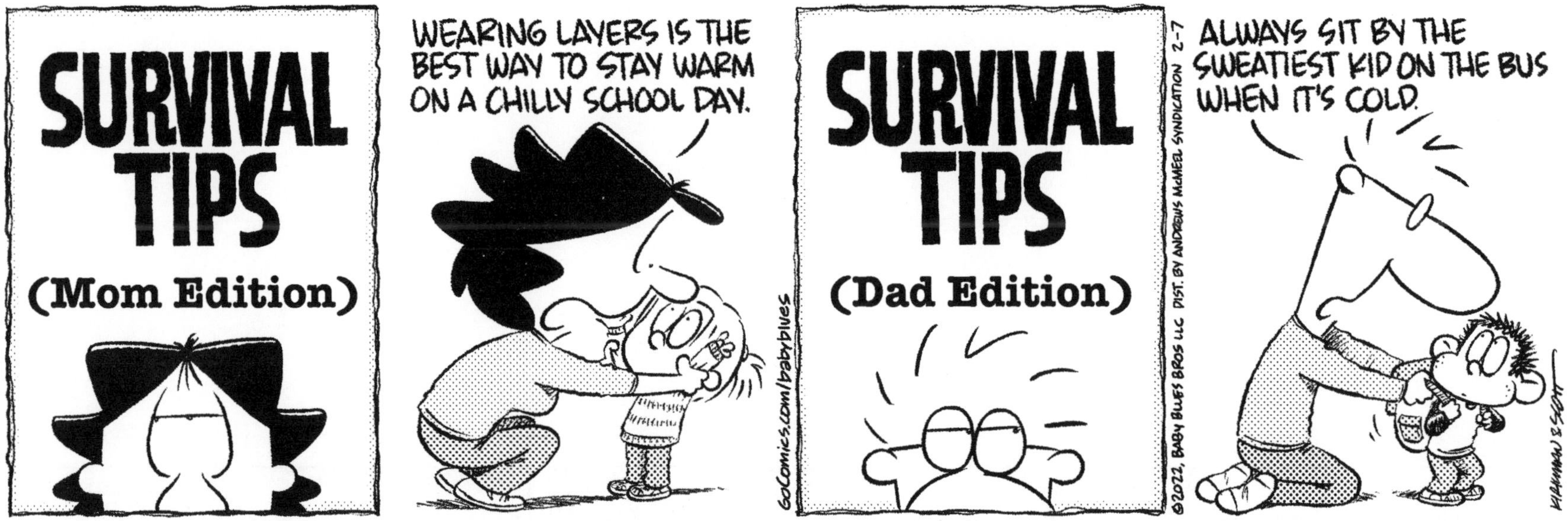
SURVIVAL TIPS
(Mom Edition)
WEARING LAYERS IS THE BEST WAY TO STAY WARM ON A CHILLY SCHOOL DAY.
GoComics.com/babyblues
SURVIVAL TIPS
(Dad Edition)
©2022, BABY BLUES BROS LLC DIST. BY ANDREWS McMEEL SYNDICATION 2-7
ALWAYS SIT BY THE SWEATIEST KID ON THE BUS WHEN IT'S COLD.
KIRKMAN & SCOTT

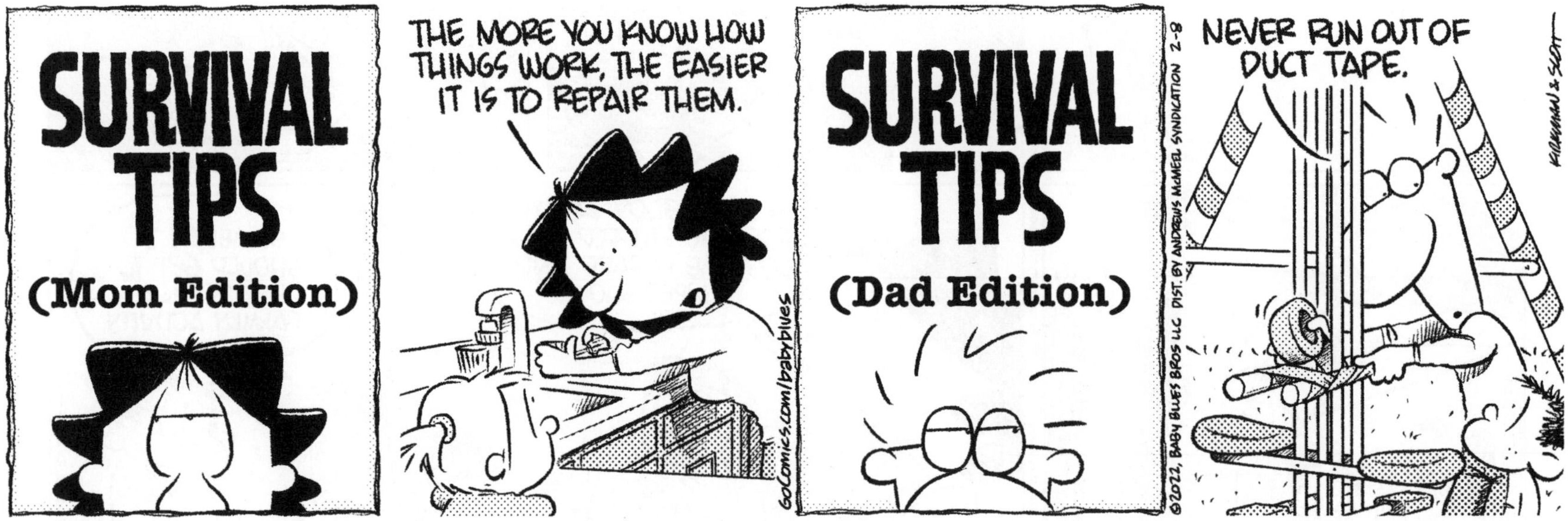
SURVIVAL TIPS
(Mom Edition)
THE MORE YOU KNOW HOW THINGS WORK, THE EASIER IT IS TO REPAIR THEM.
GoComics.com/babyblues
SURVIVAL TIPS
(Dad Edition)
©2022, BABY BLUES BROS LLC DIST. BY ANDREWS McMEEL SYNDICATION 2-8
NEVER RUN OUT OF DUCT TAPE.
KIRKMAN & SCOTT

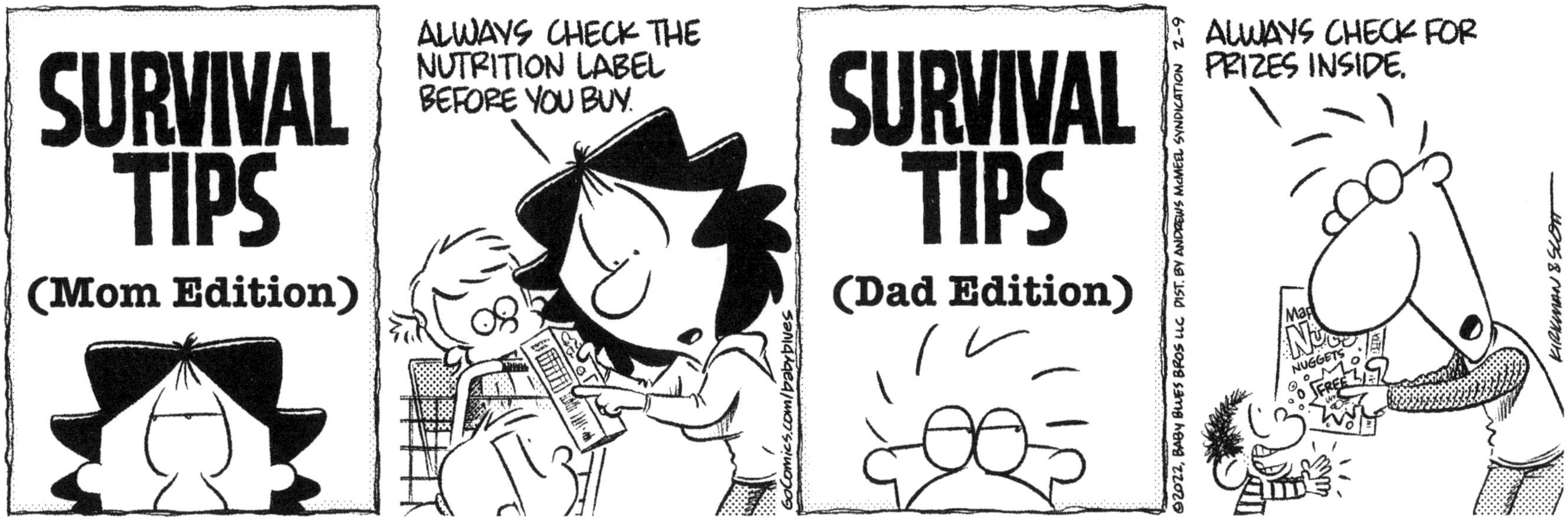
SURVIVAL TIPS
(Mom Edition)
ALWAYS CHECK THE NUTRITION LABEL BEFORE YOU BUY.
SURVIVAL TIPS
(Dad Edition)
ALWAYS CHECK FOR PRIZES INSIDE.
NUGGETS
FREE
GoComics.com/babyblues
©2022, BABY BLUES BROS LLC DIST. BY ANDREWS McMEEL SYNDICATION 2-9
KIRKMAN & SCOTT

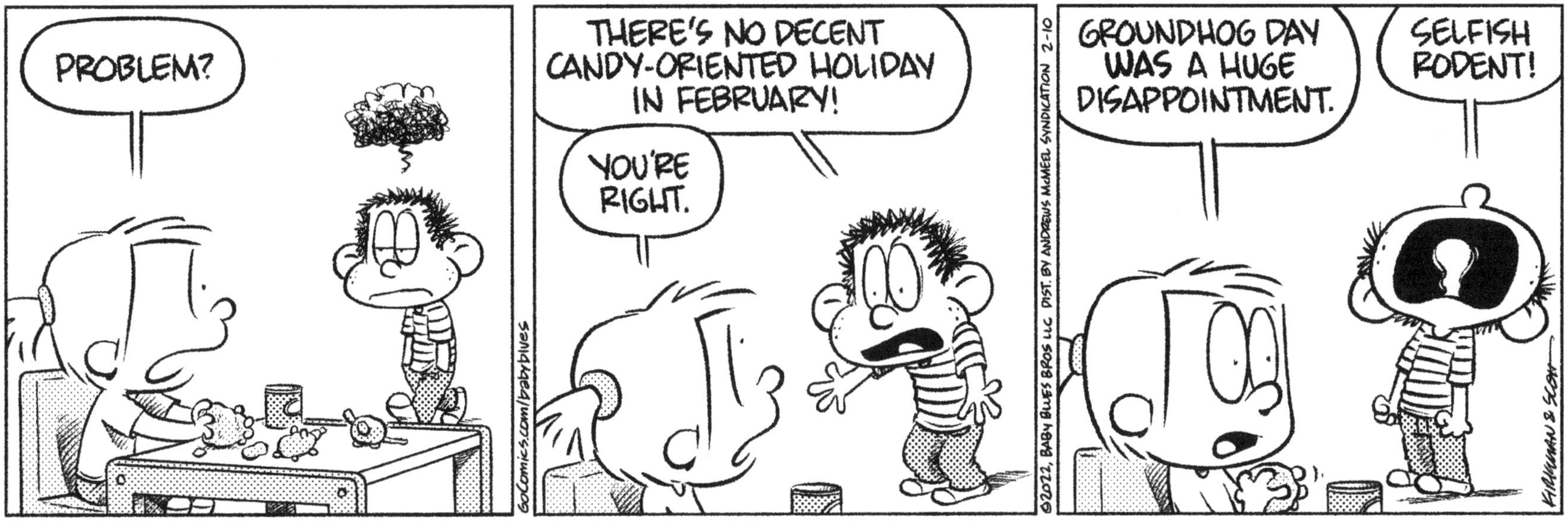
PROBLEM?
THERE'S NO DECENT CANDY-ORIENTED HOLIDAY IN FEBRUARY!
YOU'RE RIGHT.
GROUNDHOG DAY WAS A HUGE DISAPPOINTMENT.
SELFISH RODENT!
GoComics.com/babyblues
©2022, BABY BLUES BROS LLC DIST. BY ANDREWS McMEEL SYNDICATION 2-10
KIRKMAN & SCOTT

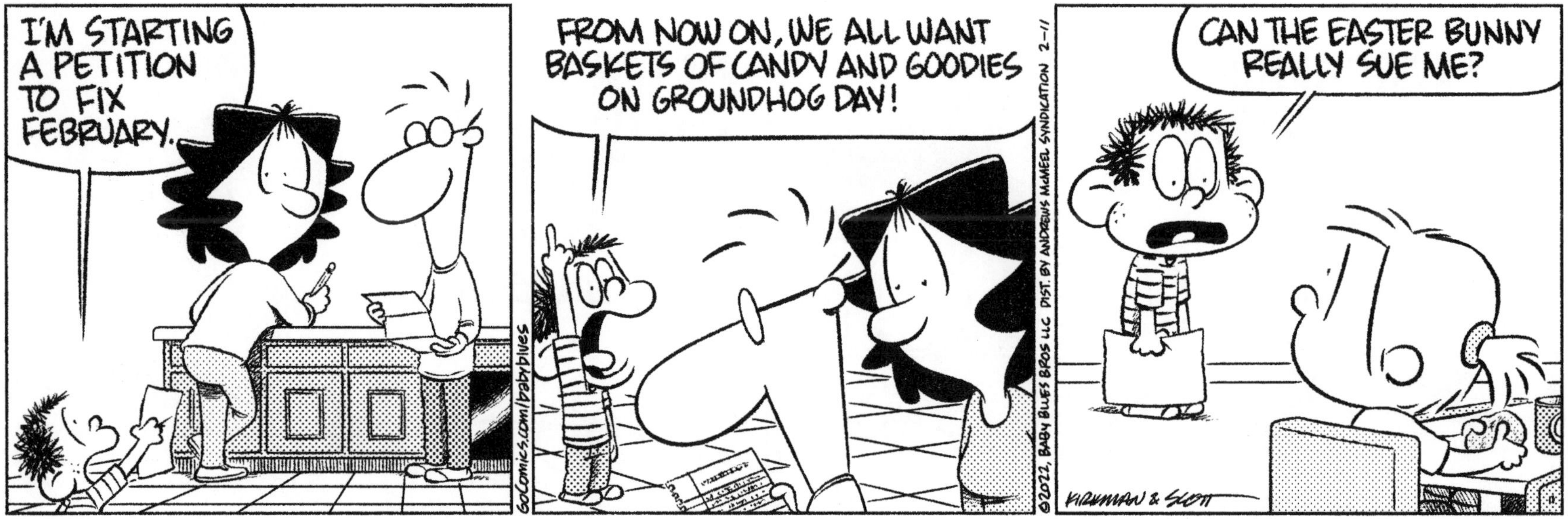
I'M STARTING A PETITION TO FIX FEBRUARY.
GoComics.com/babyblues
FROM NOW ON, WE ALL WANT BASKETS OF CANDY AND GOODIES ON GROUNDHOG DAY!
©2022, BABY BLUES BROS LLC DIST. BY ANDREWS McMEEL SYNDICATION 2-11
CAN THE EASTER BUNNY REALLY SUE ME?
KIRKMAN & SCOTT

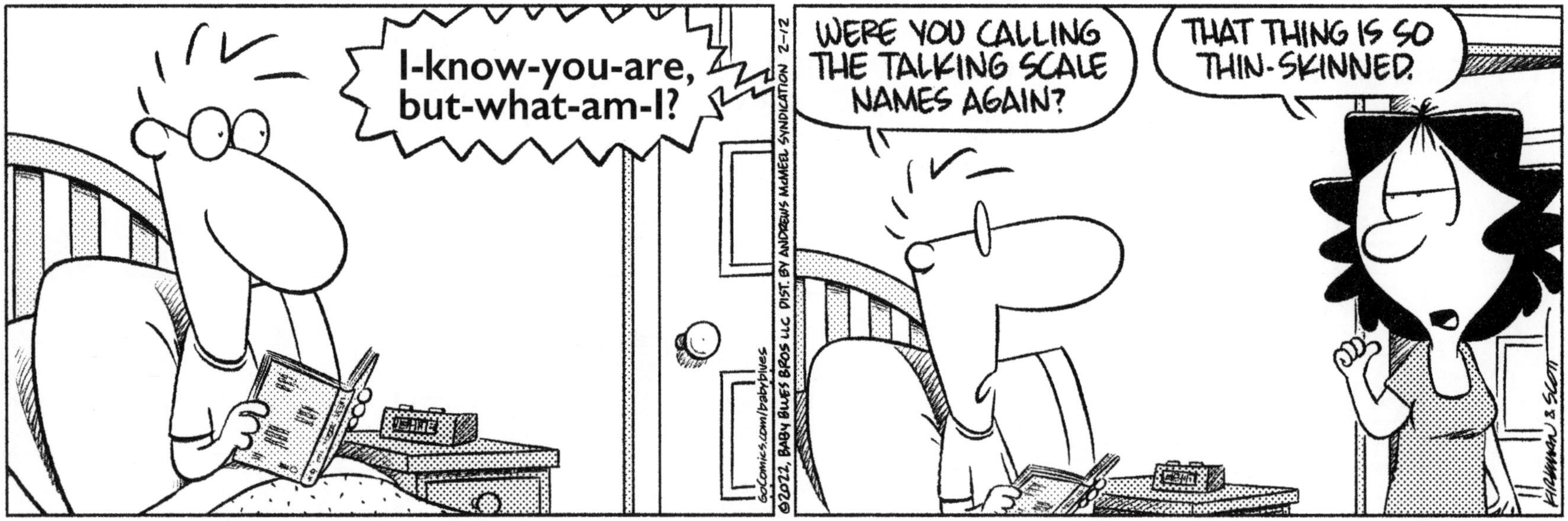
I-know-you-are, but-what-am-I?
GoComics.com/babyblues
©2022, BABY BLUES BROS LLC DIST. BY ANDREWS McMEEL SYNDICATION 2-12
WERE YOU CALLING THE TALKING SCALE NAMES AGAIN?
THAT THING IS SO THIN-SKINNED.
KIRKMAN & SCOTT

THESE STAMP PADS MAKE
EACH VALENTINE A WORK OF ART!
Happy Valentines Day

HOW'S IT GOING, HAMMIE?
ALMOST DONE!
babyblues.com
THIS WAS A GREAT IDEA, ZOE!
THANKS!
©2022, BABY BLUES BROS LLC DIST. BY KING FEATURES SYNDICATE
THESE STAMP PADS MAKE EACH VALENTINE A WORK OF ART!
Happy Valentines Day
WHO KNEW YOU COULD BE SO CREATIVE WITH THUMBPRINTS?
WAIT...
Happy Valentines Day
2-13
KIRKMAN & SCOTT
...DID YOU SAY THUMBPRINTS?

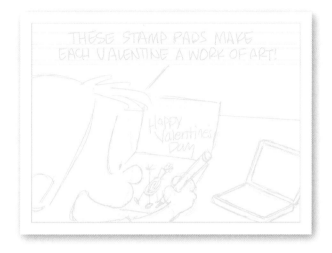

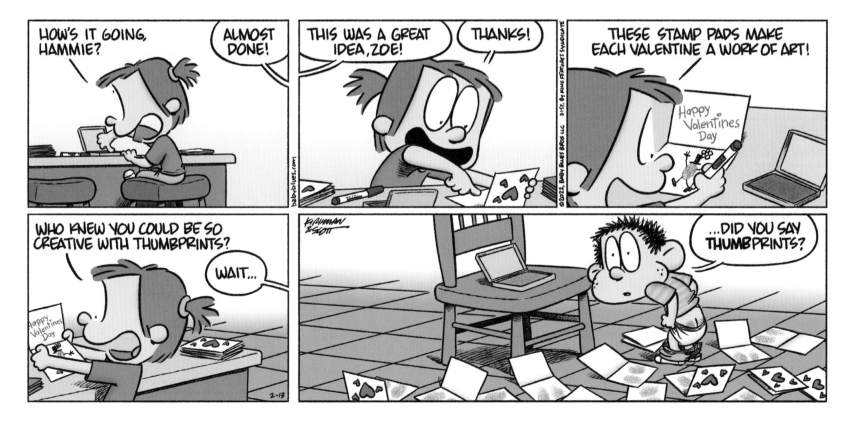

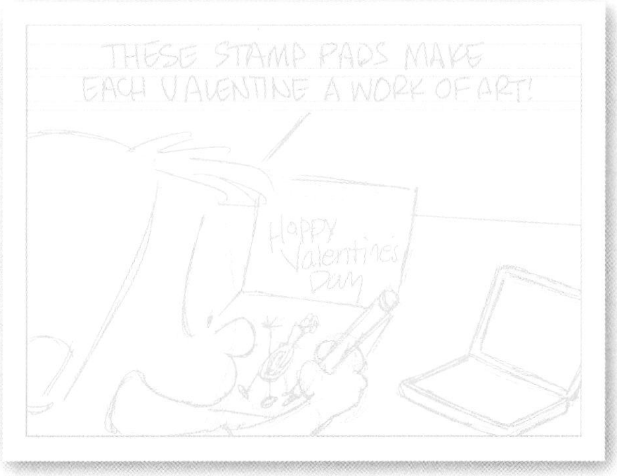

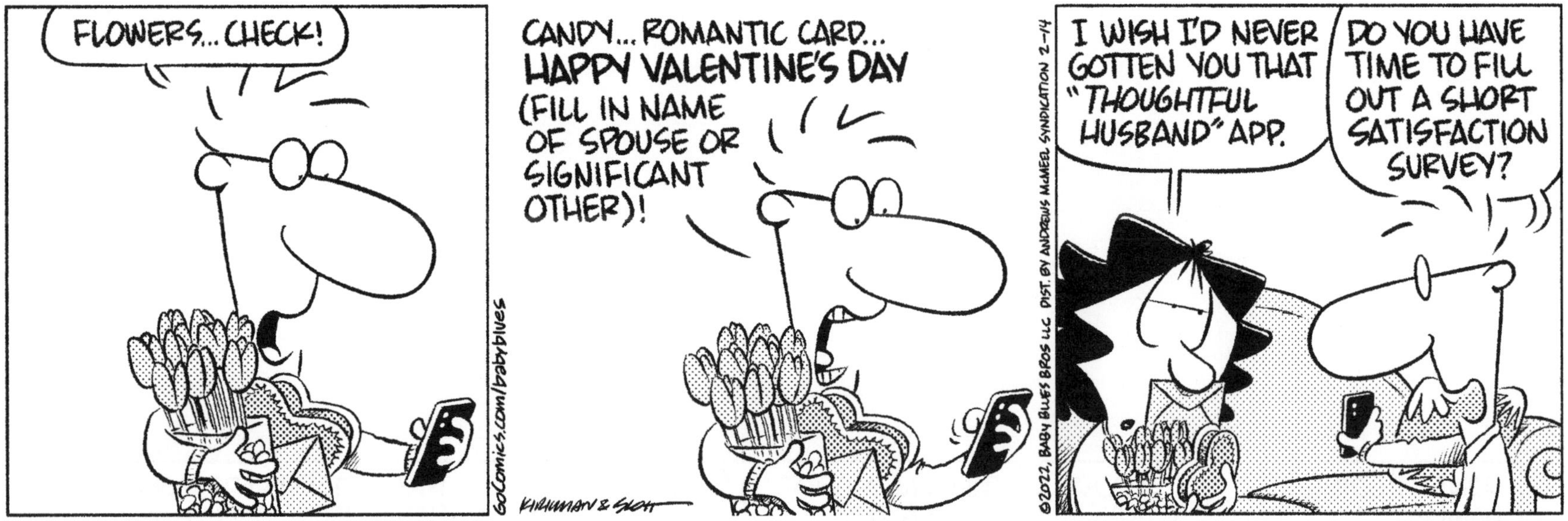
FLOWERS... CHECK!
CANDY... ROMANTIC CARD... HAPPY VALENTINE'S DAY (FILL IN NAME OF SPOUSE OR SIGNIFICANT OTHER)!
I WISH I'D NEVER GOTTEN YOU THAT "THOUGHTFUL HUSBAND" APP.
DO YOU HAVE TIME TO FILL OUT A SHORT SATISFACTION SURVEY?
GoComics.com/babyblues
KIRKMAN & SCOTT
©2022, BABY BLUES BROS LLC DIST. BY ANDREWS McMEEL SYNDICATION 2-14

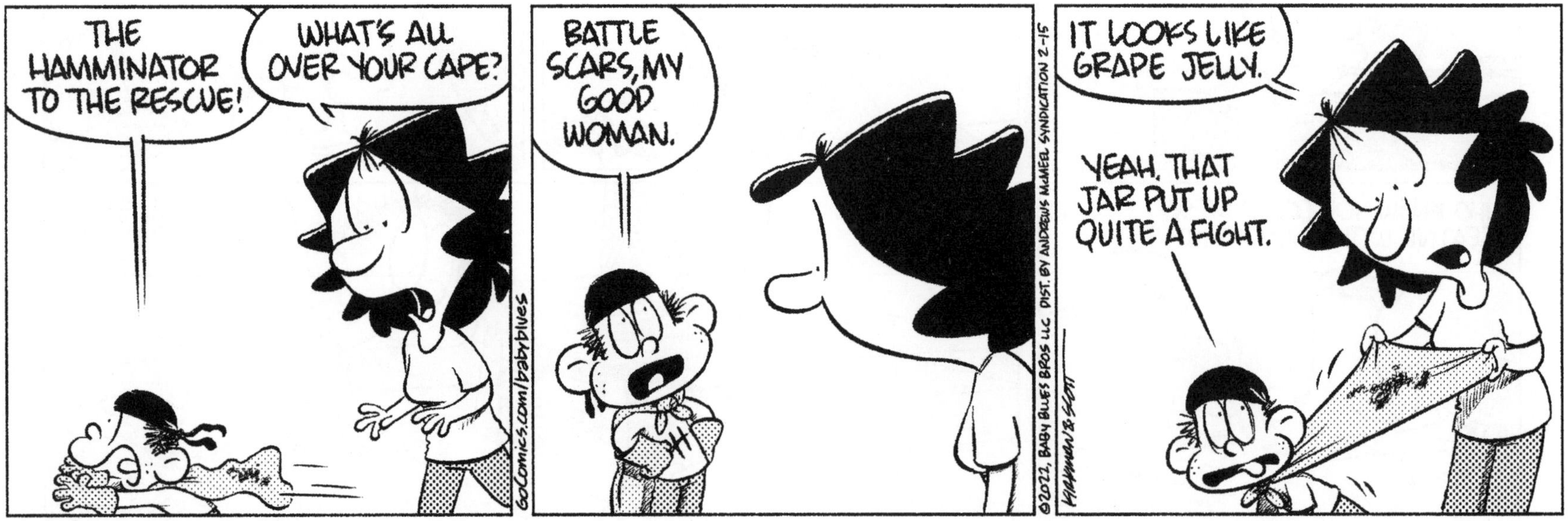
THE HAMMINATOR TO THE RESCUE!
WHAT'S ALL OVER YOUR CAPE?
BATTLE SCARS, MY GOOD WOMAN.
IT LOOKS LIKE GRAPE JELLY.
YEAH, THAT JAR PUT UP QUITE A FIGHT.
GoComics.com/babyblues
KIRKMAN & SCOTT
©2022, BABY BLUES BROS LLC DIST. BY ANDREWS McMEEL SYNDICATION 2-15

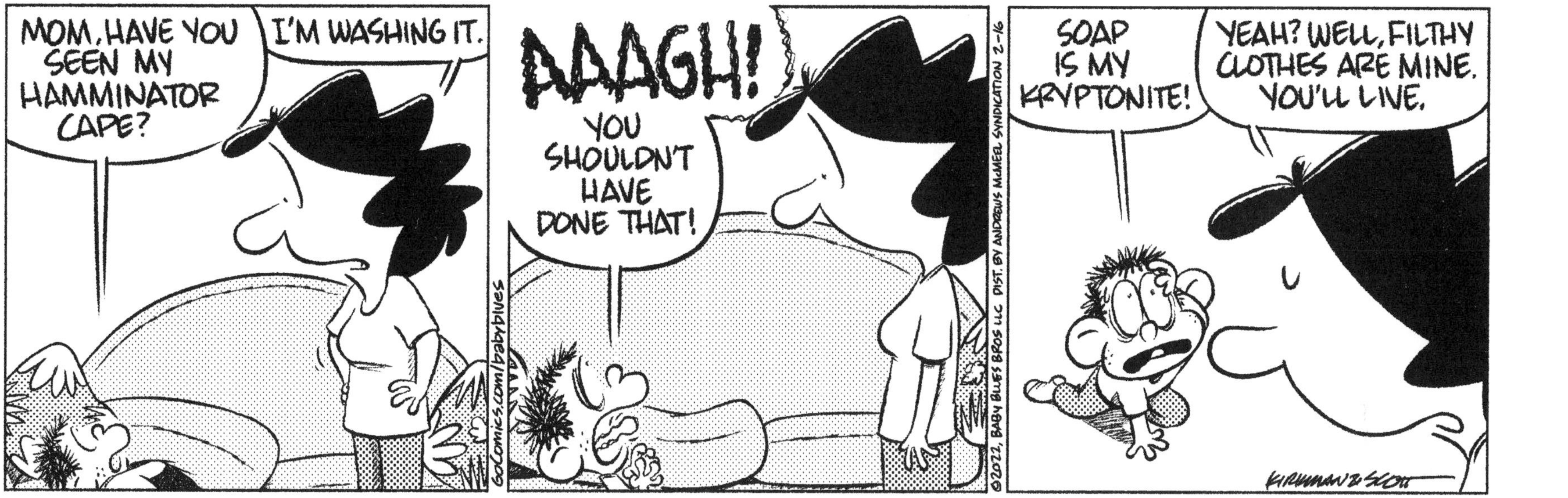
MOM, HAVE YOU SEEN MY HAMMINATOR CAPE?
I'M WASHING IT.
AAAGH!
YOU SHOULDN'T HAVE DONE THAT!
SOAP IS MY KRYPTONITE!
YEAH? WELL, FILTHY CLOTHES ARE MINE. YOU'LL LIVE.
GoComics.com/babyblues
©2022, BABY BLUES BROS LLC DIST. BY ANDREWS McMEEL SYNDICATION 2-16
KIRKMAN & SCOTT

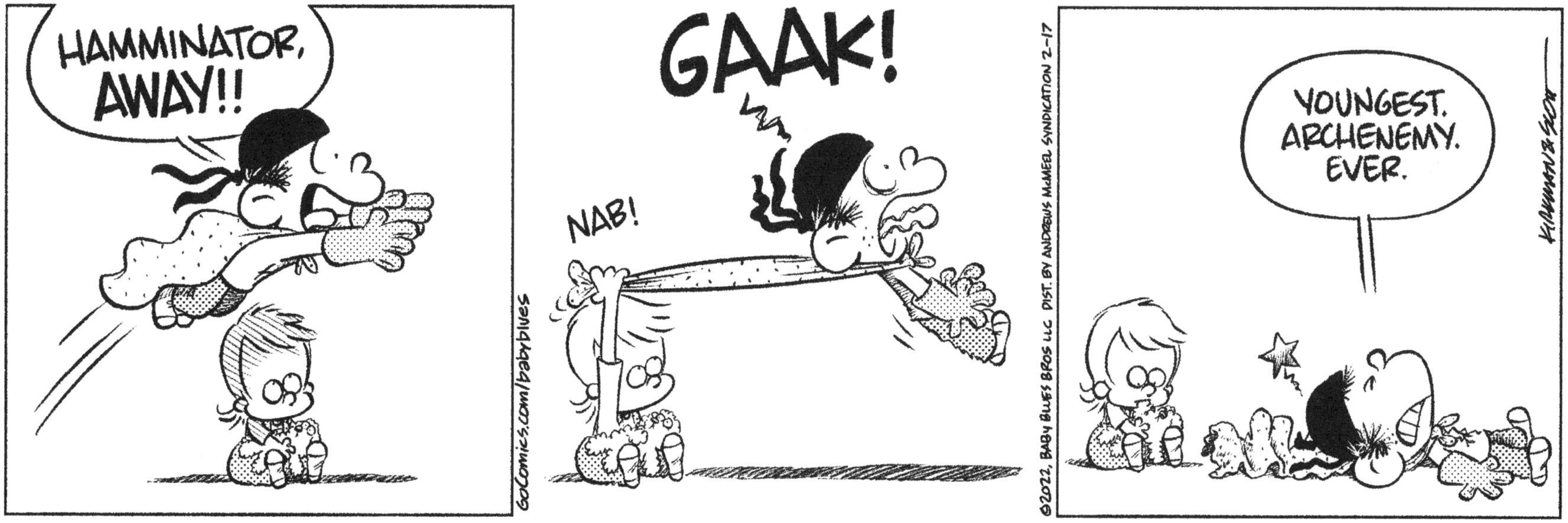
HAMMINATOR, AWAY!!
GAAK!
NAB!
YOUNGEST. ARCHENEMY. EVER.
GoComics.com/babyblues
©2022, BABY BLUES BROS LLC DIST. BY ANDREWS McMEEL SYNDICATION 2-17
KIRKMAN & SCOTT

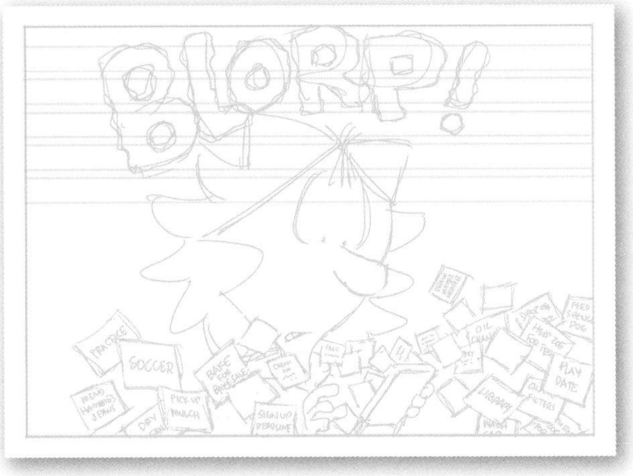
BLORP!

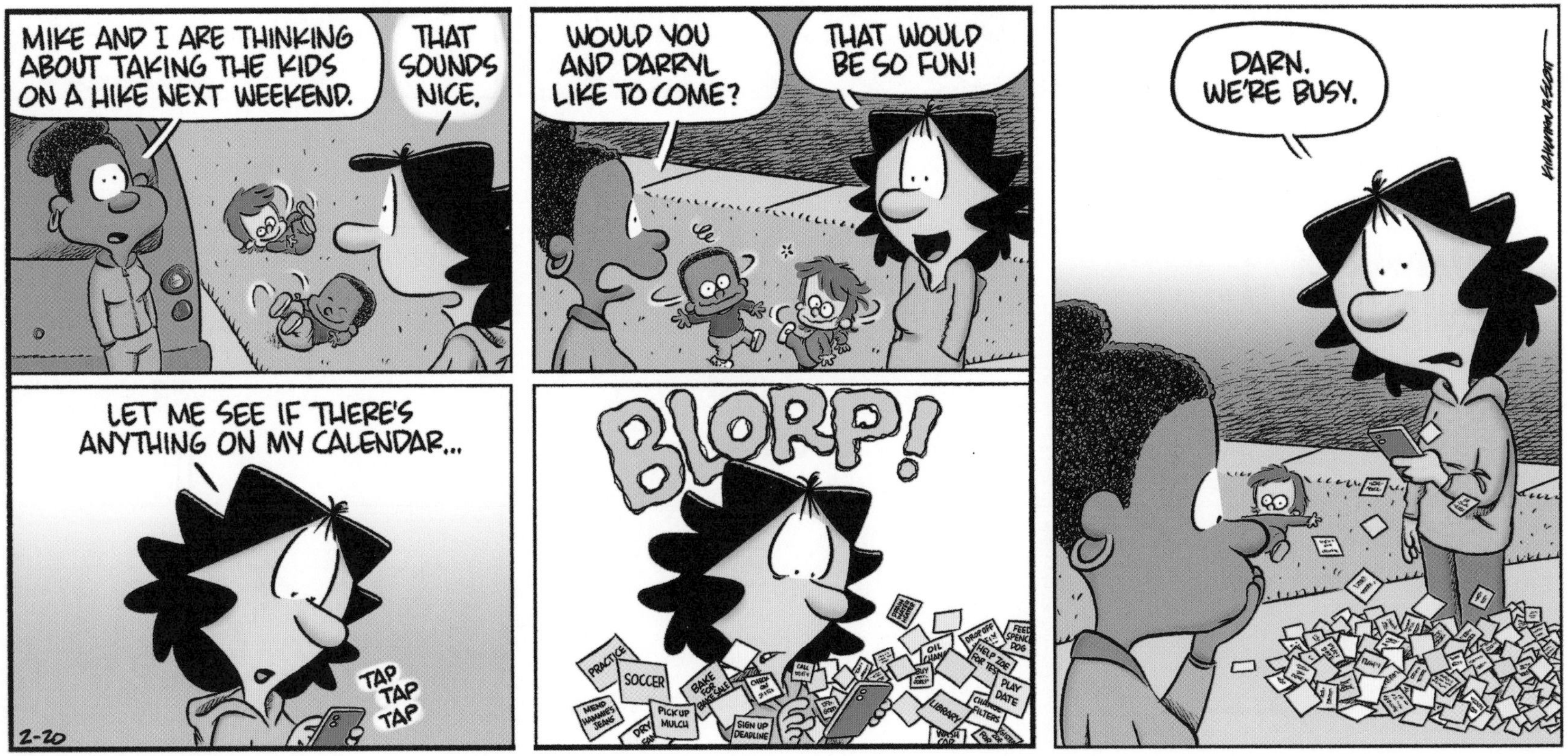
MIKE AND I ARE THINKING ABOUT TAKING THE KIDS ON A HIKE NEXT WEEKEND.
THAT SOUNDS NICE.
WOULD YOU AND DARRYL LIKE TO COME?
THAT WOULD BE SO FUN!
LET ME SEE IF THERE'S ANYTHING ON MY CALENDAR...
TAP TAP TAP
2-20
BLORP!
PRACTICE
SOCCER
PICK UP MULCH
SIGN UP DEADLINE
PLAY DATE
LIBRARY
DARN. WE'RE BUSY.

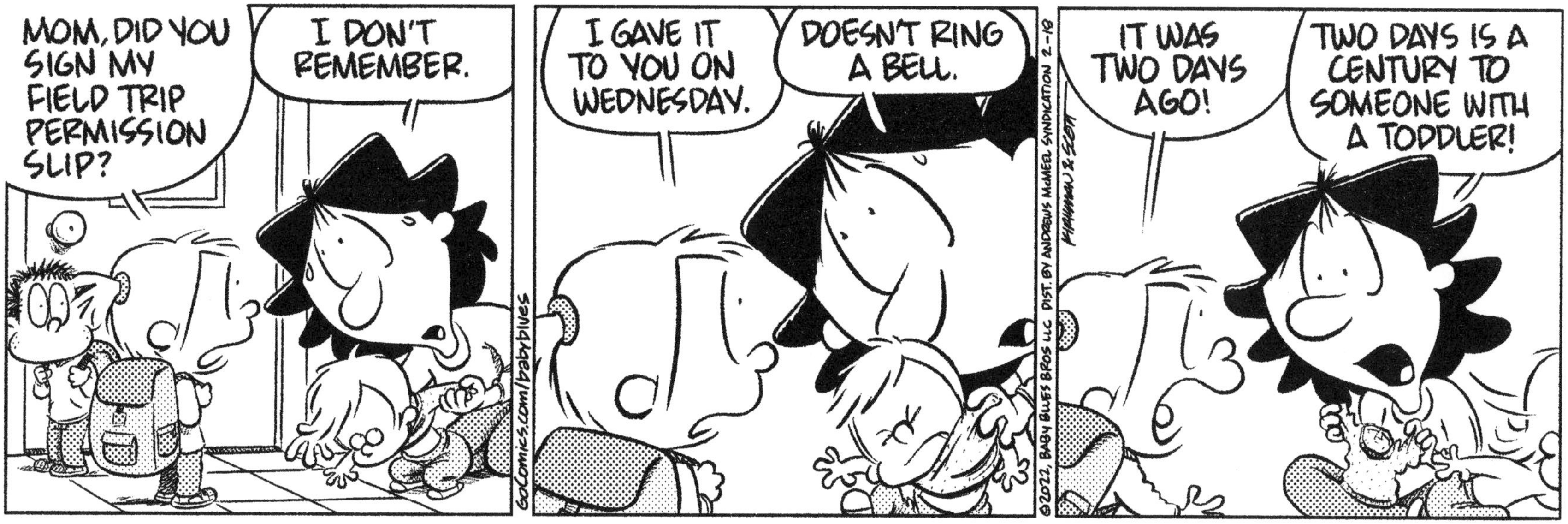
MOM, DID YOU SIGN MY FIELD TRIP PERMISSION SLIP?
I DON'T REMEMBER.
GoComics.com/babyblues
I GAVE IT TO YOU ON WEDNESDAY.
DOESN'T RING A BELL.
©2022, BABY BLUES BROS LLC DIST. BY ANDREWS McMEEL SYNDICATION 2-18
KIRKMAN & SCOTT
IT WAS TWO DAYS AGO!
TWO DAYS IS A CENTURY TO SOMEONE WITH A TODDLER!

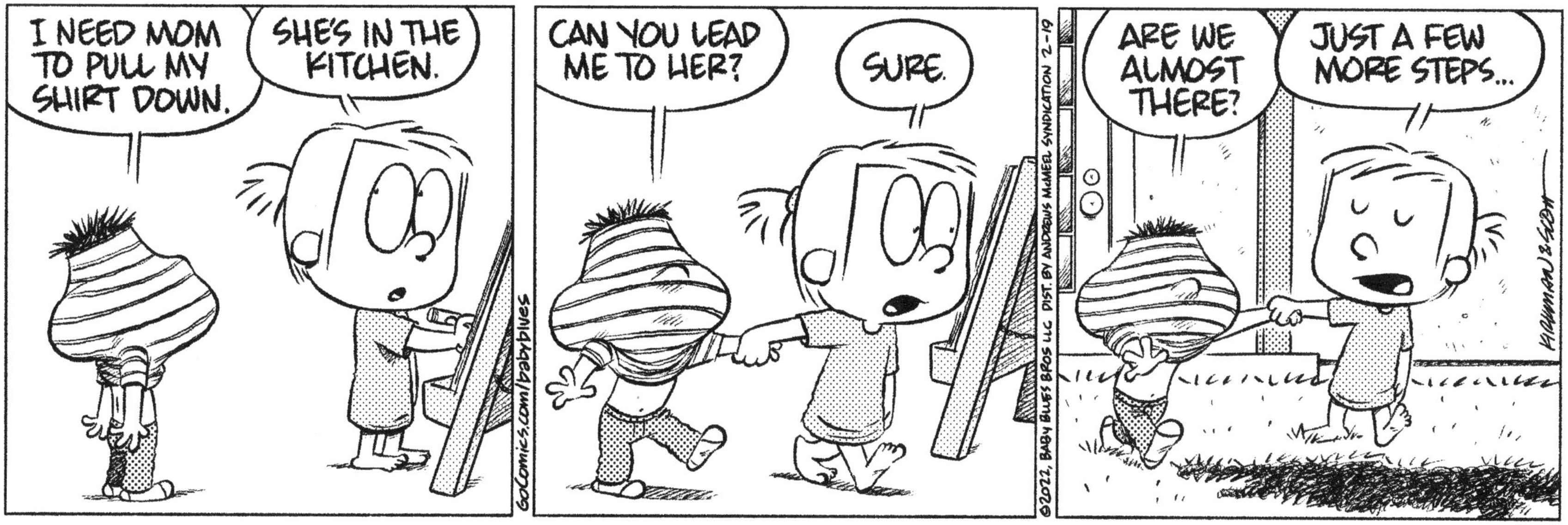
I NEED MOM TO PULL MY SHIRT DOWN.
SHE'S IN THE KITCHEN.
GoComics.com/babyblues
CAN YOU LEAD ME TO HER?
SURE.
©2022, BABY BLUES BROS LLC DIST. BY ANDREWS McMEEL SYNDICATION 2-19
ARE WE ALMOST THERE?
JUST A FEW MORE STEPS...
KIRKMAN & SCOTT

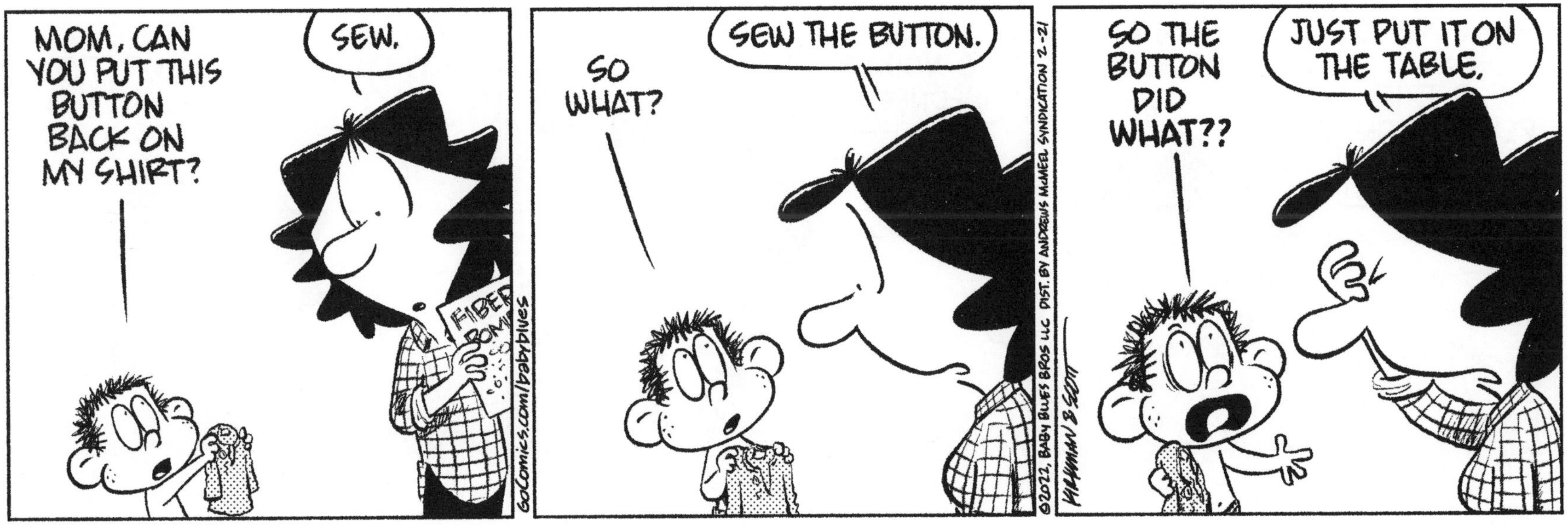
MOM, CAN YOU PUT THIS BUTTON BACK ON MY SHIRT?
SEW.
FIBER BOMBS
GoComics.com/babyblues
SO WHAT?
SEW THE BUTTON.
©2022, BABY BLUES BROS LLC DIST. BY ANDREWS McMEEL SYNDICATION 2-21
KIRKMAN & SCOTT
SO THE BUTTON DID WHAT??
JUST PUT IT ON THE TABLE.

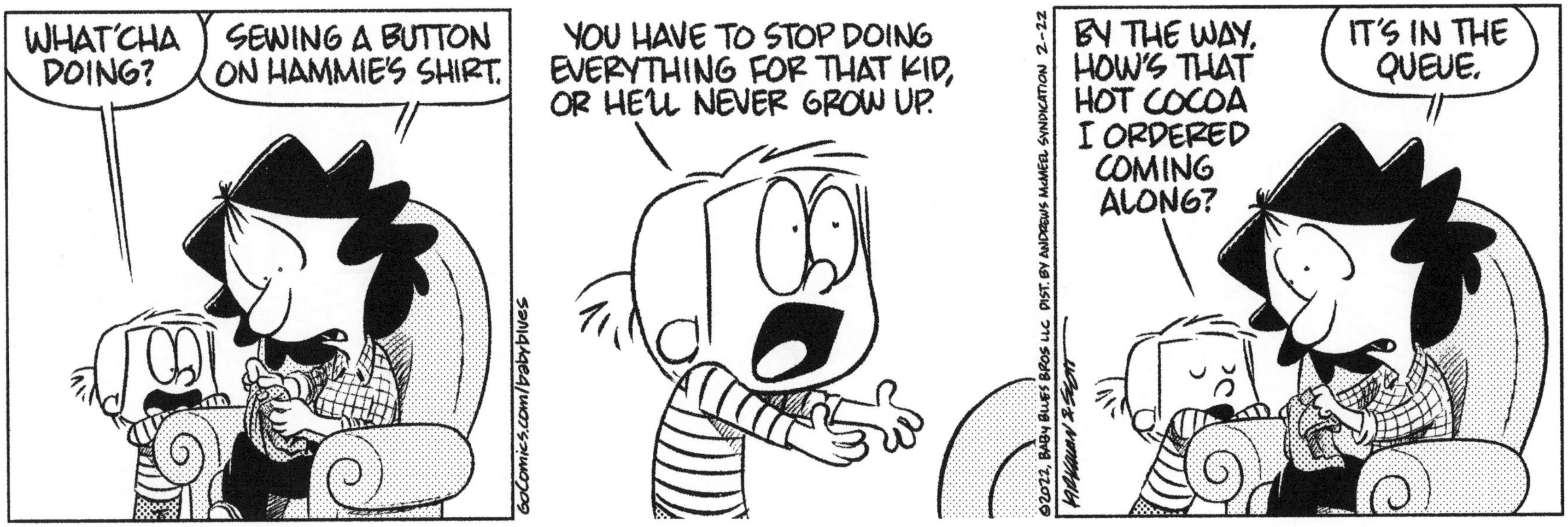
WHAT'CHA DOING?
SEWING A BUTTON ON HAMMIE'S SHIRT.
GoComics.com/babyblues
YOU HAVE TO STOP DOING EVERYTHING FOR THAT KID, OR HE'LL NEVER GROW UP.
©2022, BABY BLUES BROS LLC DIST. BY ANDREWS McMEEL SYNDICATION 2-22
KIRKMAN & SCOTT
BY THE WAY, HOW'S THAT HOT COCOA I ORDERED COMING ALONG?
IT'S IN THE QUEUE.

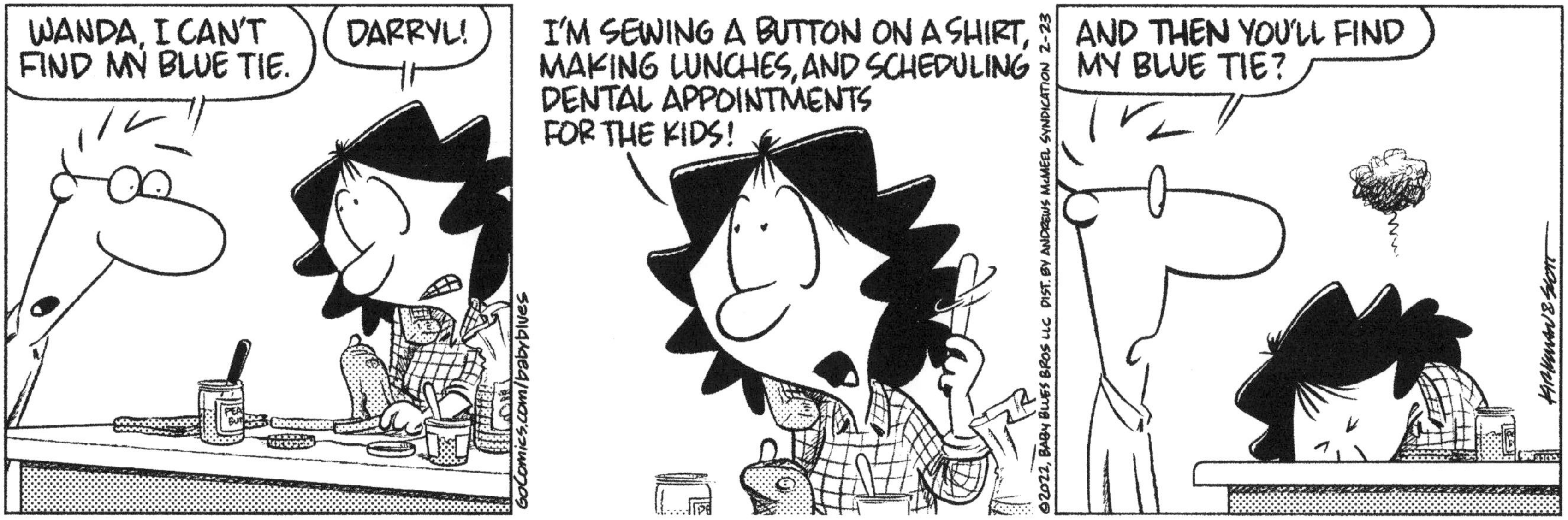
WANDA, I CAN'T FIND MY BLUE TIE.
DARRYL!
I'M SEWING A BUTTON ON A SHIRT, MAKING LUNCHES, AND SCHEDULING DENTAL APPOINTMENTS FOR THE KIDS!
AND THEN YOU'LL FIND MY BLUE TIE?
GoComics.com/babyblues
©2022, BABY BLUES BROS LLC DIST. BY ANDREWS McMEEL SYNDICATION 2-23
KIRKMAN & SCOTT

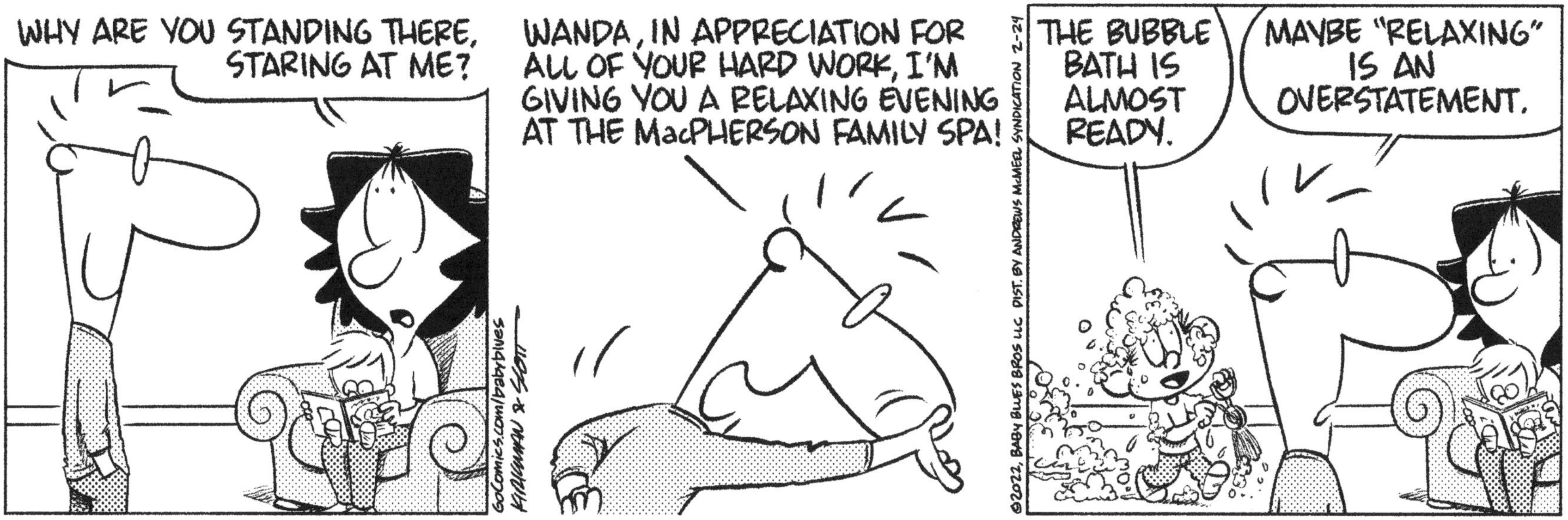
WHY ARE YOU STANDING THERE, STARING AT ME?
GoComics.com/babyblues
KIRKMAN & SCOTT
WANDA, IN APPRECIATION FOR ALL OF YOUR HARD WORK, I'M GIVING YOU A RELAXING EVENING AT THE MacPHERSON FAMILY SPA!
©2022, BABY BLUES BROS LLC DIST. BY ANDREWS McMEEL SYNDICATION 2-24
THE BUBBLE BATH IS ALMOST READY.
MAYBE "RELAXING" IS AN OVERSTATEMENT.

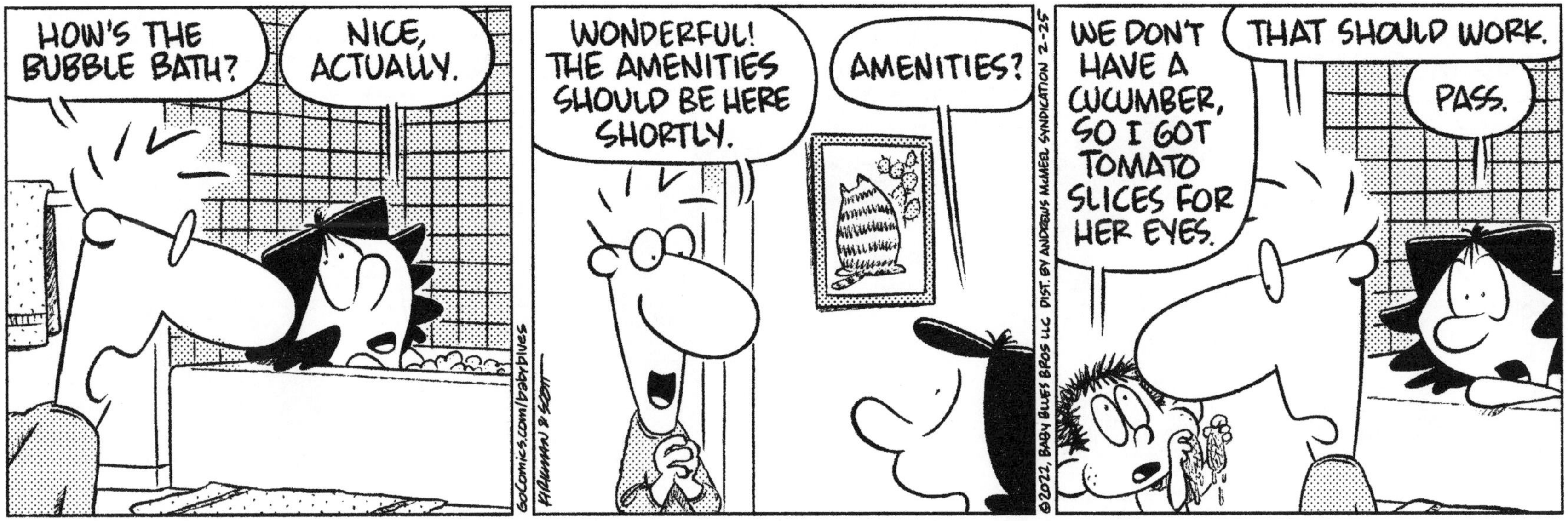
HOW'S THE BUBBLE BATH?
NICE, ACTUALLY.
GoComics.com/babyblues
KIRKMAN & SCOTT
WONDERFUL! THE AMENITIES SHOULD BE HERE SHORTLY.
AMENITIES?
©2022, BABY BLUES BROS LLC DIST. BY ANDREWS McMEEL SYNDICATION 2-25
WE DON'T HAVE A CUCUMBER, SO I GOT TOMATO SLICES FOR HER EYES.
THAT SHOULD WORK.
PASS.

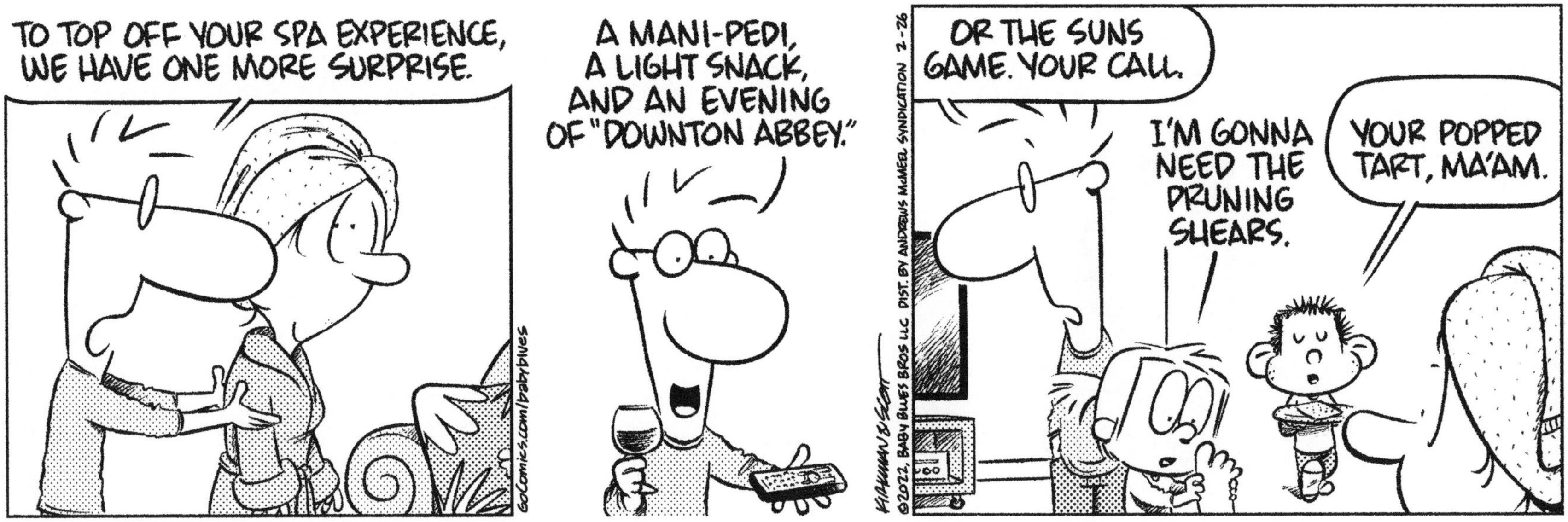
TO TOP OFF YOUR SPA EXPERIENCE, WE HAVE ONE MORE SURPRISE.
GoComics.com/babyblues
A MANI-PEDI, A LIGHT SNACK, AND AN EVENING OF "DOWNTON ABBEY."
KIRKMAN & SCOTT
©2022, BABY BLUES BROS LLC DIST. BY ANDREWS McMEEL SYNDICATION 2-26
OR THE SUNS GAME. YOUR CALL.
I'M GONNA NEED THE PRUNING SHEARS.
YOUR POPPED TART, MA'AM.

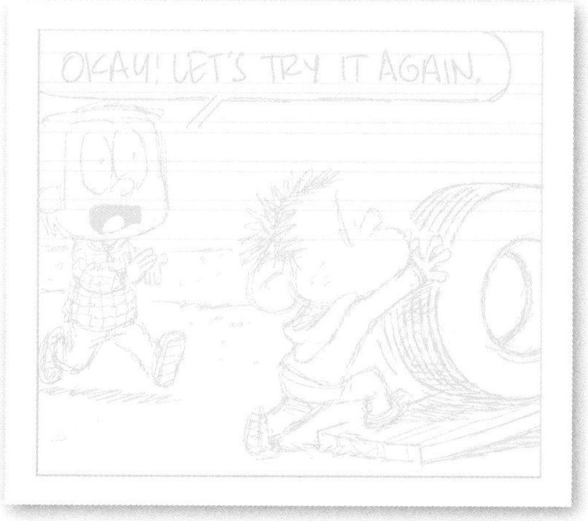
OKAY! LET'S TRY IT AGAIN.

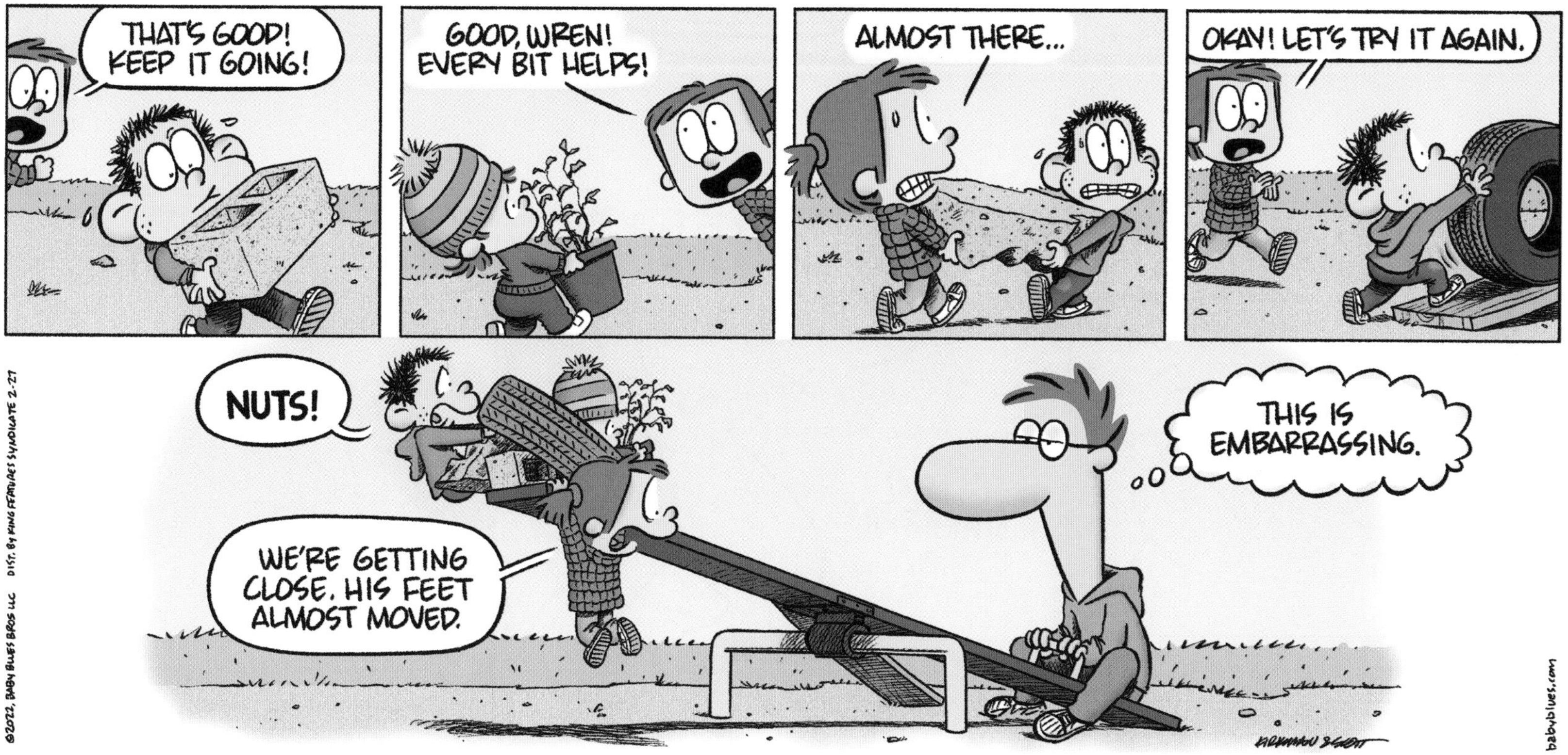
THAT'S GOOD! KEEP IT GOING!
GOOD, WREN! EVERY BIT HELPS!
ALMOST THERE...
OKAY! LET'S TRY IT AGAIN.
NUTS!
WE'RE GETTING CLOSE. HIS FEET ALMOST MOVED.
THIS IS EMBARRASSING.
©2022, BABY BLUES BROS LLC DIST. BY KING FEATURES SYNDICATE 2-27
babyblues.com

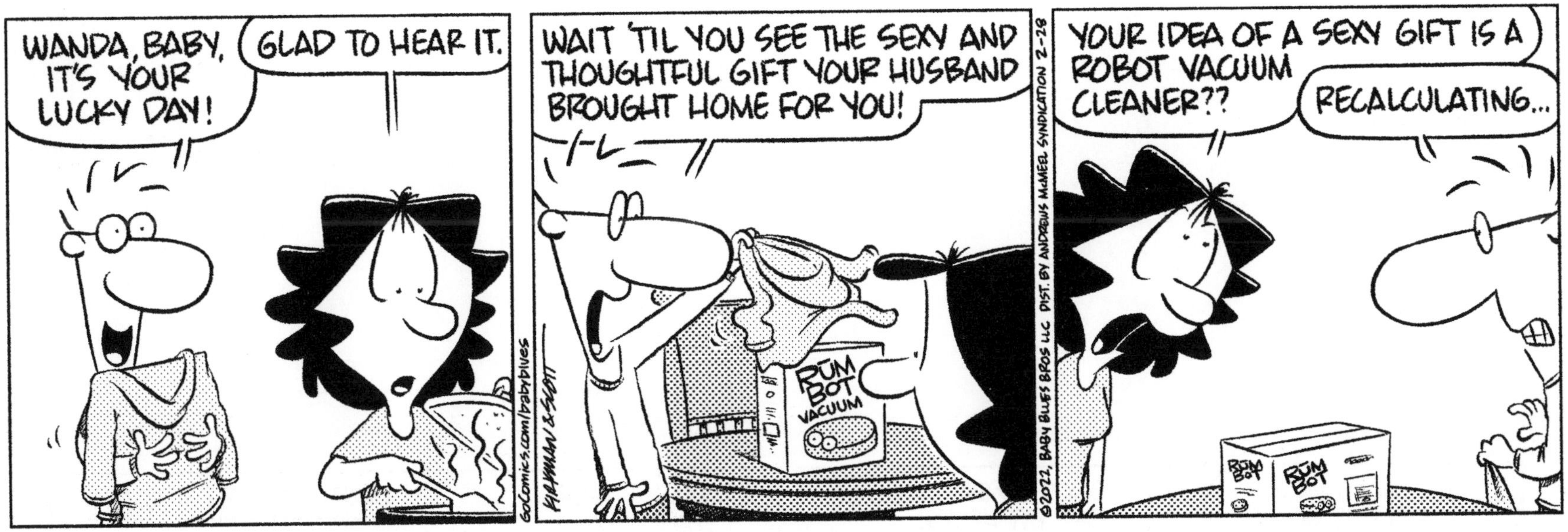
WANDA, BABY, IT'S YOUR LUCKY DAY!
GLAD TO HEAR IT.
GoComics.com/babyblues
KIRKMAN & SCOTT
WAIT 'TIL YOU SEE THE SEXY AND THOUGHTFUL GIFT YOUR HUSBAND BROUGHT HOME FOR YOU!
RŪMBOT VACUUM
©2022, BABY BLUES BROS LLC DIST. BY ANDREWS McMEEL SYNDICATION 2-28
YOUR IDEA OF A SEXY GIFT IS A ROBOT VACUUM CLEANER??
RECALCULATING...
RŪMBOT
RŪMBOT

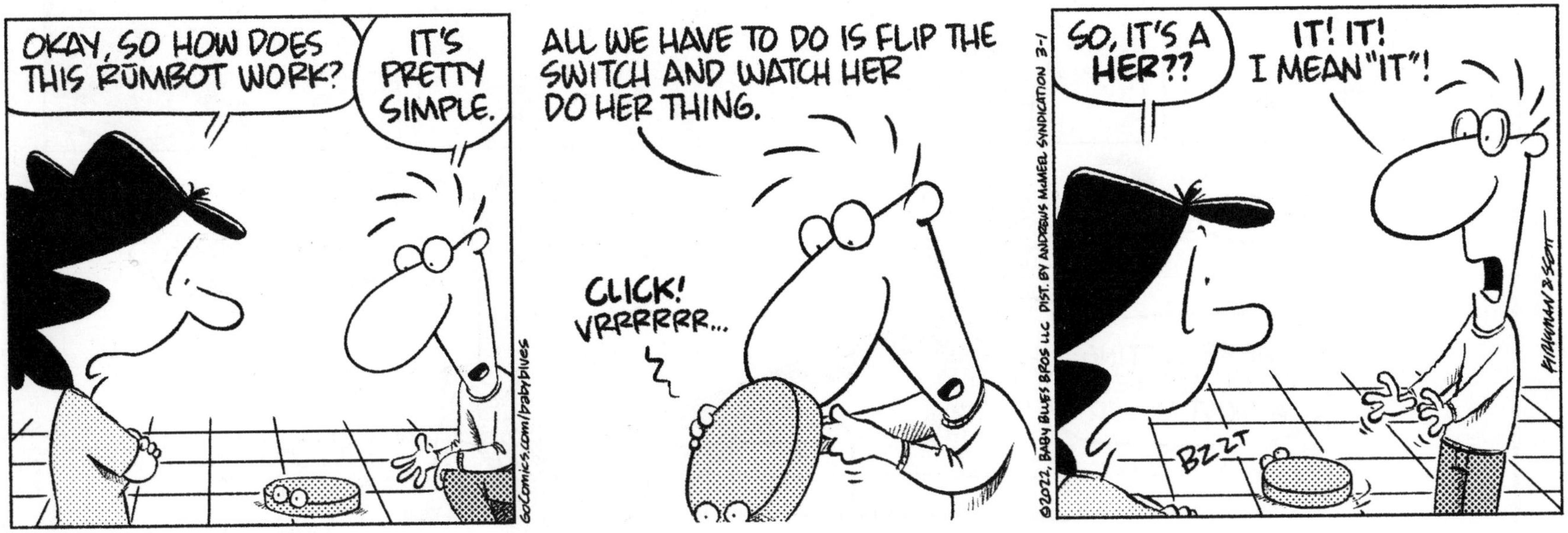
OKAY, SO HOW DOES THIS RŪMBOT WORK?
IT'S PRETTY SIMPLE.
GoComics.com/babyblues
ALL WE HAVE TO DO IS FLIP THE SWITCH AND WATCH HER DO HER THING.
CLICK! VRRRRRR...
©2022, BABY BLUES BROS LLC DIST. BY ANDREWS McMEEL SYNDICATION 3-1
SO, IT'S A HER??
IT! IT! I MEAN "IT"!
BZZT
KIRKMAN & SCOTT

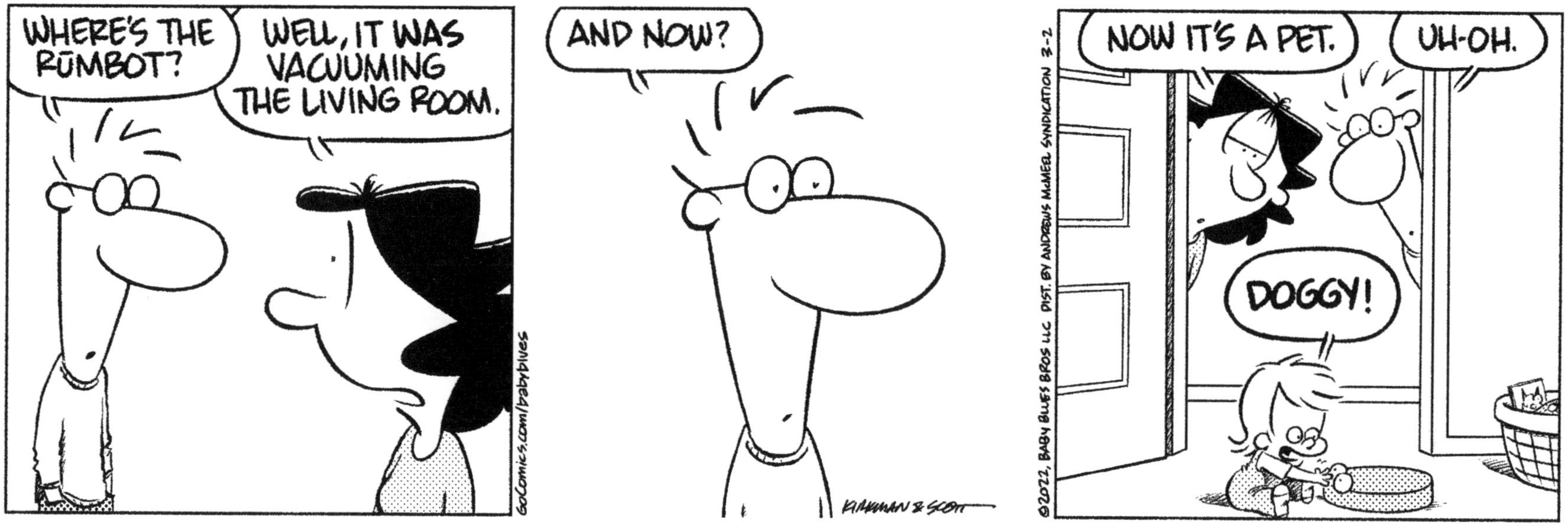
WHERE'S THE RŪMBOT?
WELL, IT WAS VACUUMING THE LIVING ROOM.
GoComics.com/babyblues
AND NOW?
KIRKMAN & SCOTT
©2022, BABY BLUES BROS LLC DIST. BY ANDREWS McMEEL SYNDICATION 3-2
NOW IT'S A PET.
UH-OH.
DOGGY!

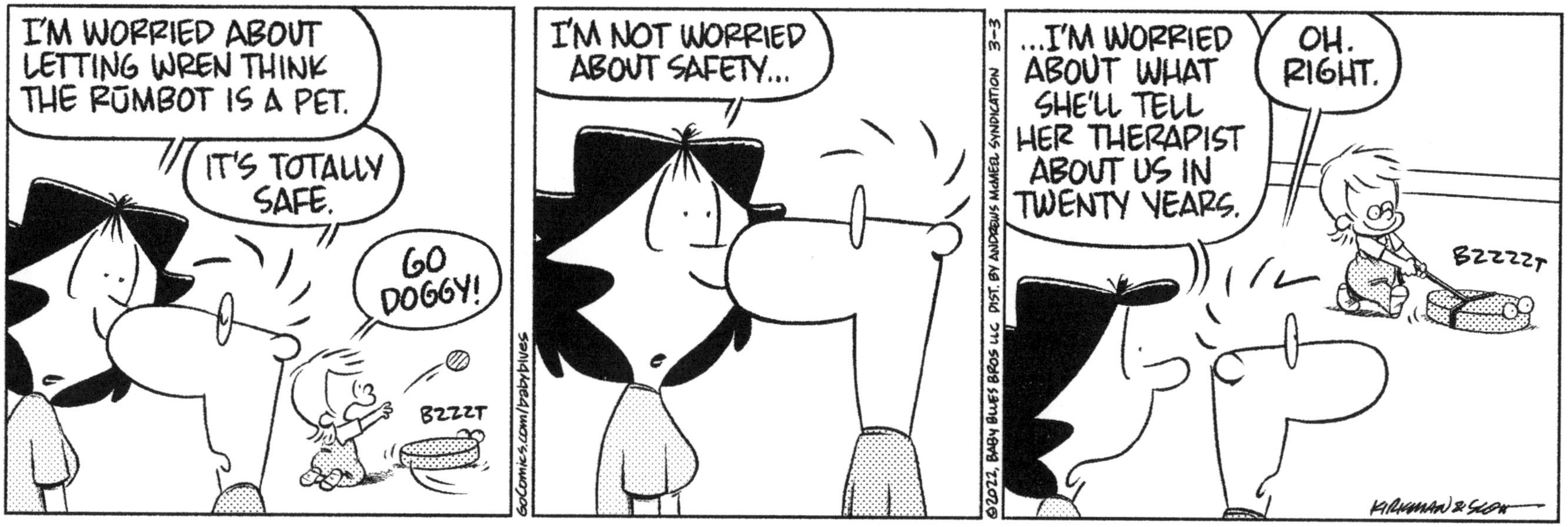
I'M WORRIED ABOUT LETTING WREN THINK THE RŪMBOT IS A PET.
IT'S TOTALLY SAFE.
GO DOGGY!
BZZZT
GoComics.com/babyblues
I'M NOT WORRIED ABOUT SAFETY...
©2022, BABY BLUES BROS LLC DIST. BY ANDREWS McMEEL SYNDICATION 3-3
...I'M WORRIED ABOUT WHAT SHE'LL TELL HER THERAPIST ABOUT US IN TWENTY YEARS.
OH. RIGHT.
BZZZZZT
KIRKMAN & SCOTT

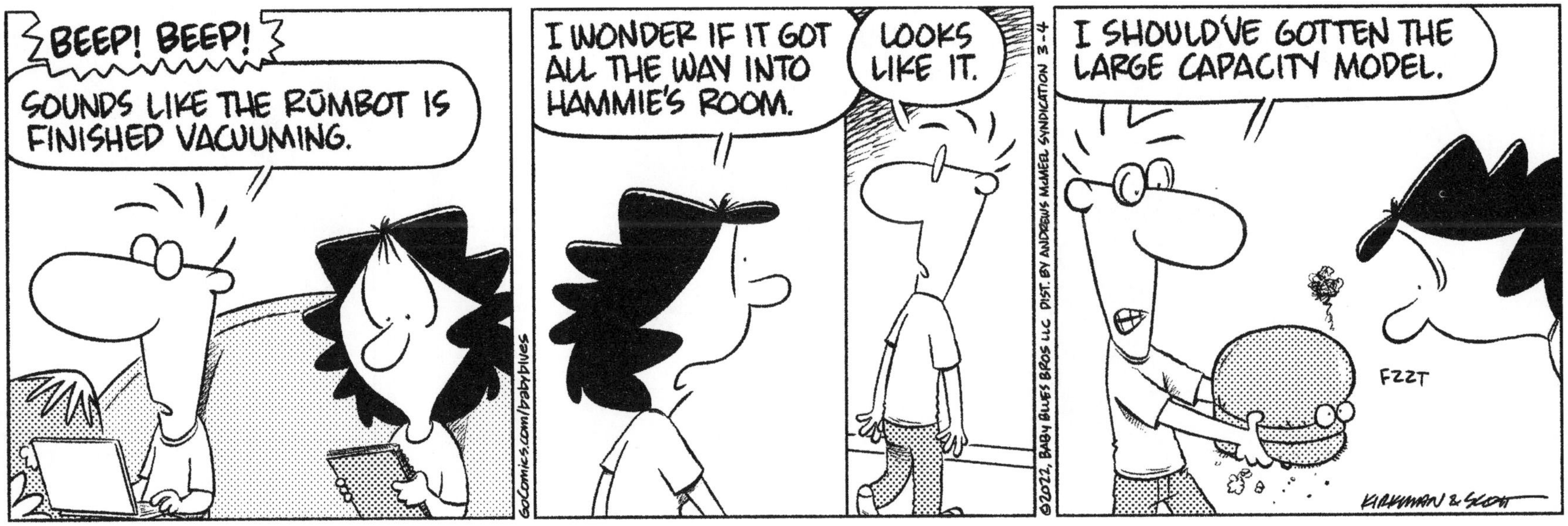
BEEP! BEEP!
SOUNDS LIKE THE RŪMBOT IS FINISHED VACUUMING.
GoComics.com/babyblues
I WONDER IF IT GOT ALL THE WAY INTO HAMMIE'S ROOM.
LOOKS LIKE IT.
©2022, BABY BLUES BROS LLC DIST. BY ANDREWS McMEEL SYNDICATION 3-4
I SHOULD'VE GOTTEN THE LARGE CAPACITY MODEL.
FZZT
KIRKMAN & SCOTT

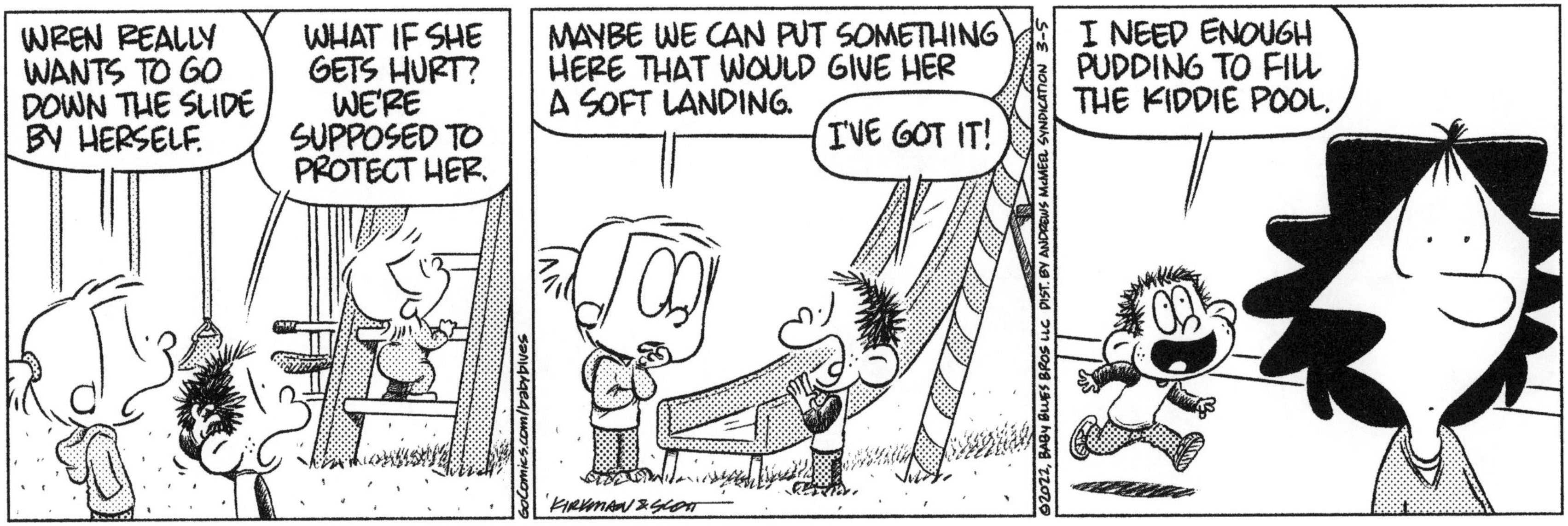
WREN REALLY WANTS TO GO DOWN THE SLIDE BY HERSELF.
WHAT IF SHE GETS HURT? WE'RE SUPPOSED TO PROTECT HER.
GoComics.com/babyblues
MAYBE WE CAN PUT SOMETHING HERE THAT WOULD GIVE HER A SOFT LANDING.
I'VE GOT IT!
KIRKMAN & SCOTT
©2022, BABY BLUES BROS LLC DIST. BY ANDREWS McMEEL SYNDICATION 3-5
I NEED ENOUGH PUDDING TO FILL THE KIDDIE POOL.

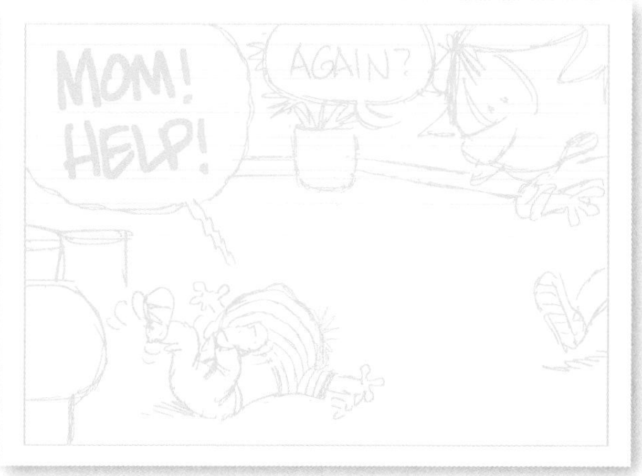
MOM! HELP!
AGAIN?

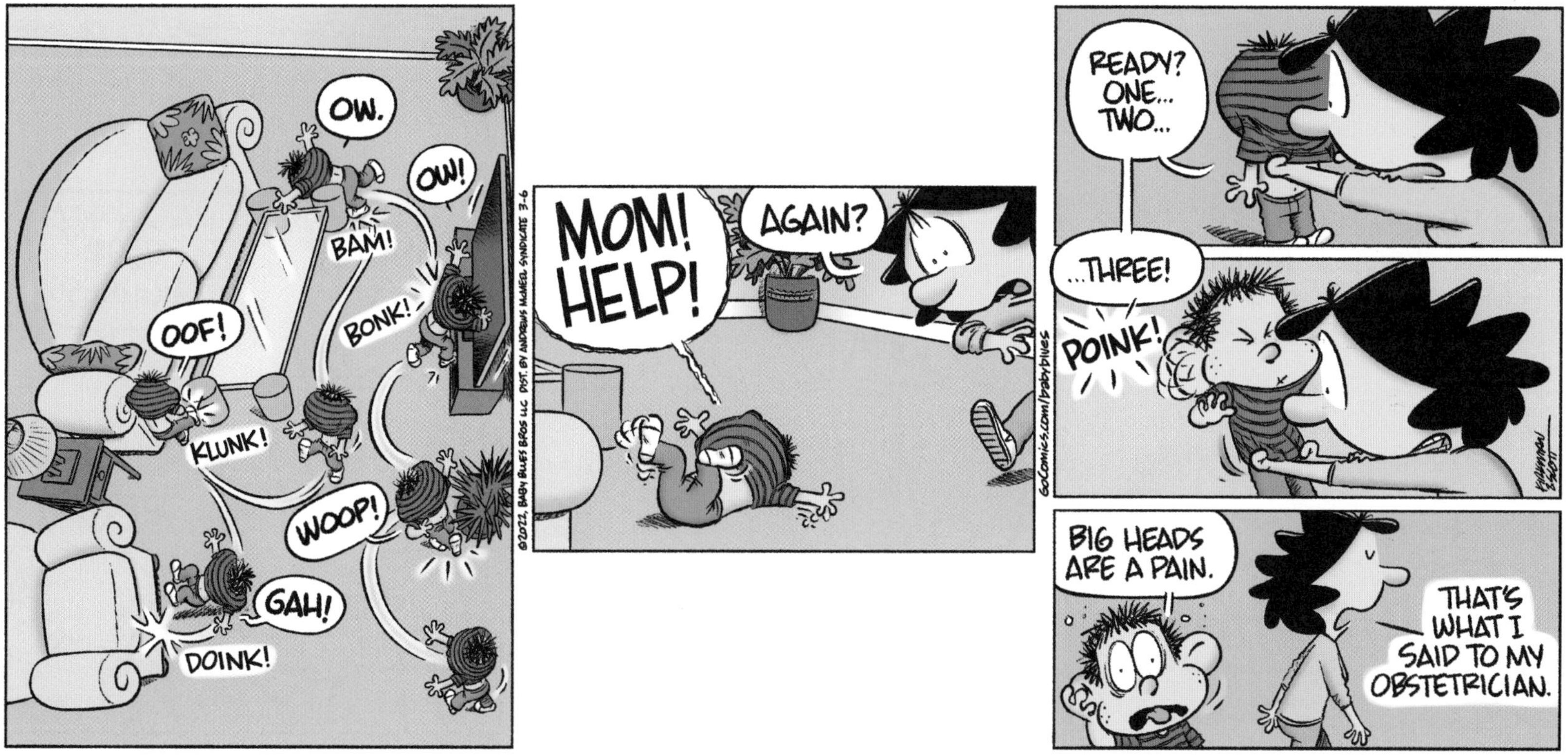
OW.
OW!
BAM!
BONK!
OOF!
KLUNK!
WOOP!
GAH!
DOINK!
©2022, BABY BLUES BROS LLC DIST. BY ANDREWS MCMEEL SYNDICATE 3-6
MOM! HELP!
AGAIN?
GoComics.com/babyblues
READY? ONE... TWO...
...THREE!
POINK!
BIG HEADS ARE A PAIN.
THAT'S WHAT I SAID TO MY OBSTETRICIAN.

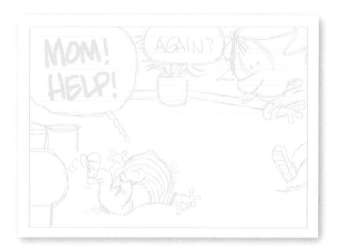

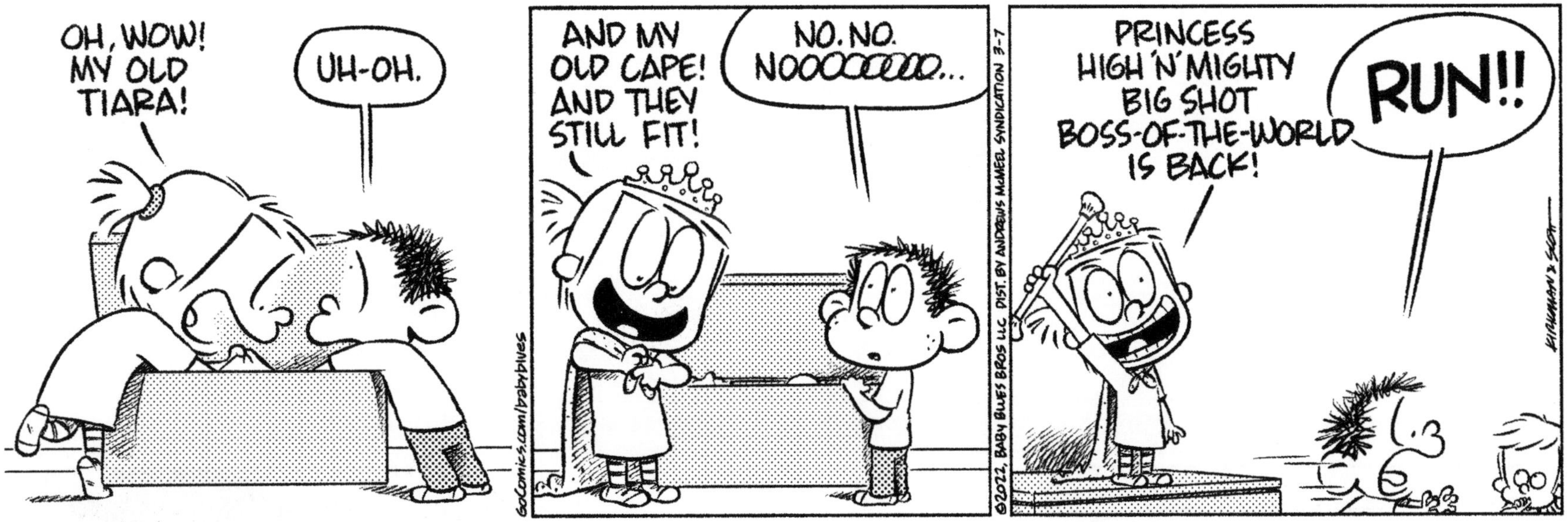
OH, WOW! MY OLD TIARA!
UH-OH.
GoComics.com/babyblues
AND MY OLD CAPE! AND THEY STILL FIT!
NO. NO. NOOOOOOOO...
©2022, BABY BLUES BROS LLC DIST. BY ANDREWS McMEEL SYNDICATION 3-7
PRINCESS HIGH 'N' MIGHTY BIG SHOT BOSS-OF-THE-WORLD IS BACK!
RUN!!
KIRKMAN & SCOTT

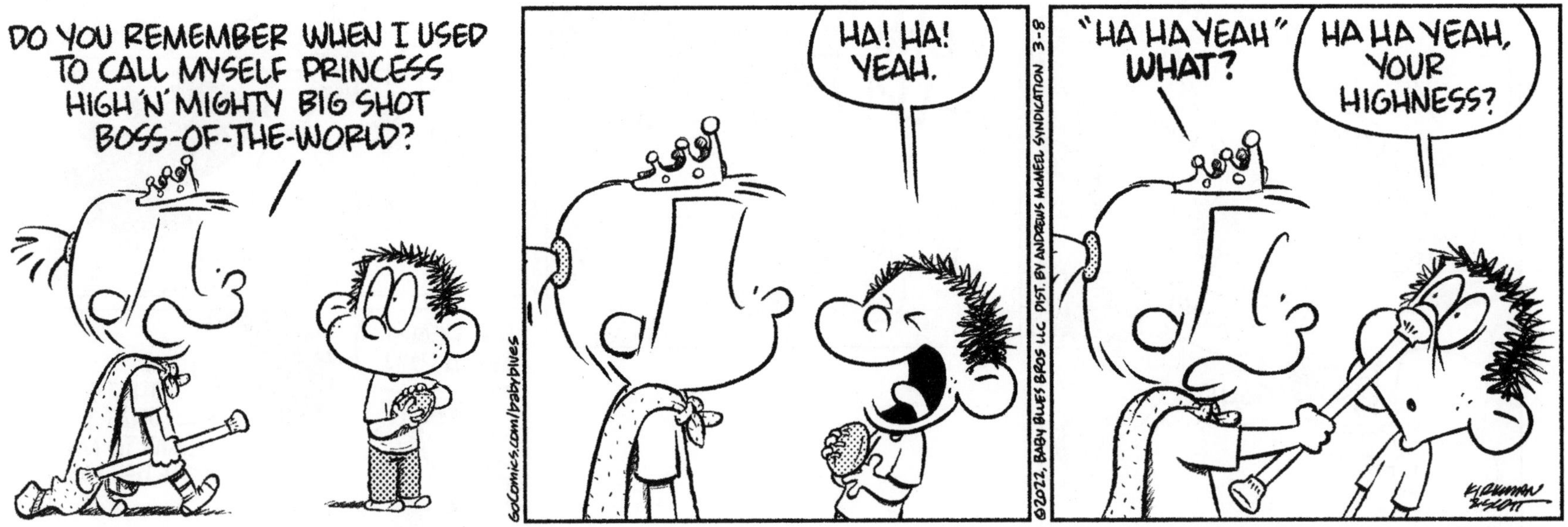
DO YOU REMEMBER WHEN I USED TO CALL MYSELF PRINCESS HIGH 'N' MIGHTY BIG SHOT BOSS-OF-THE-WORLD?
GoComics.com/babyblues
HA! HA! YEAH.
©2022, BABY BLUES BROS LLC DIST. BY ANDREWS McMEEL SYNDICATION 3-8
"HA HA YEAH" WHAT?
HA HA YEAH, YOUR HIGHNESS?
KIRKMAN & SCOTT

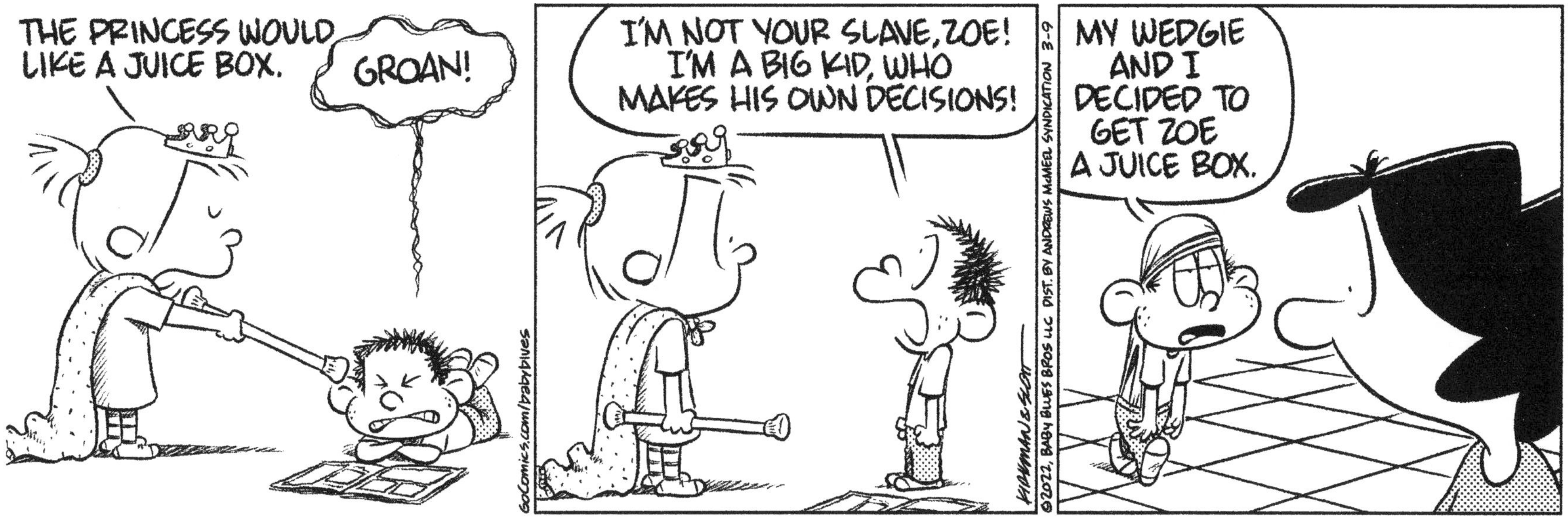
THE PRINCESS WOULD LIKE A JUICE BOX.
GROAN!
I'M NOT YOUR SLAVE, ZOE! I'M A BIG KID, WHO MAKES HIS OWN DECISIONS!
MY WEDGIE AND I DECIDED TO GET ZOE A JUICE BOX.
GoComics.com/babyblues
©2022, BABY BLUES BROS LLC DIST. BY ANDREWS McMEEL SYNDICATION 3-9
KIRKMAN & SCOTT

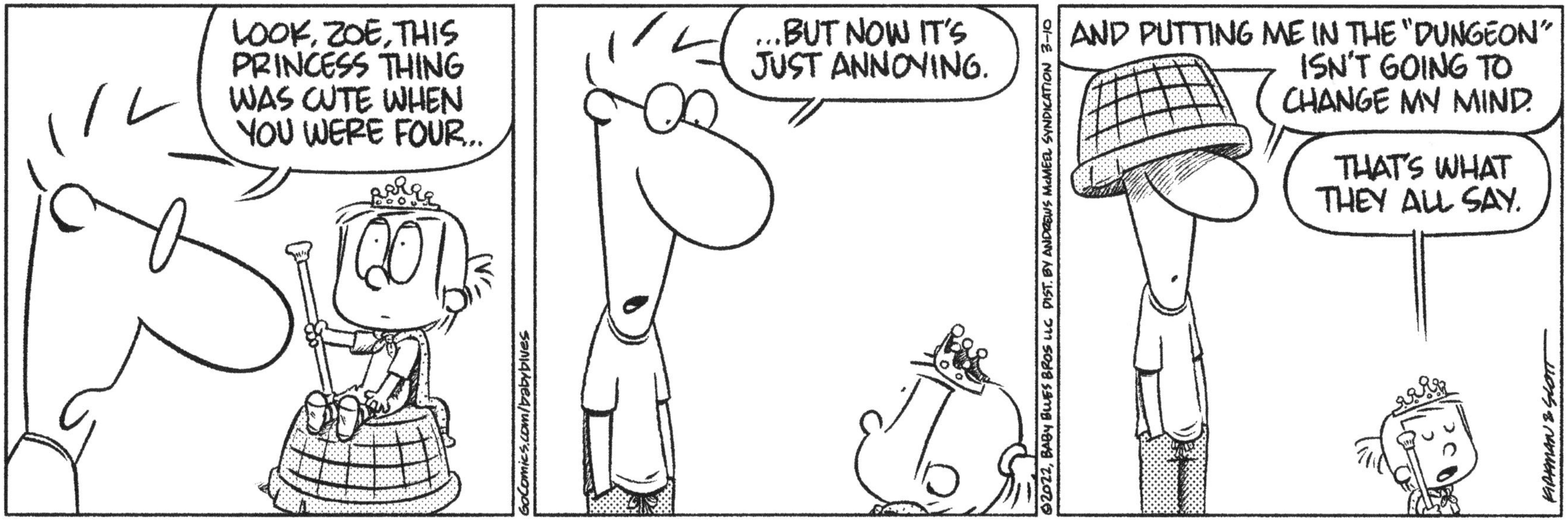
LOOK, ZOE, THIS PRINCESS THING WAS CUTE WHEN YOU WERE FOUR...
...BUT NOW IT'S JUST ANNOYING.
AND PUTTING ME IN THE "DUNGEON" ISN'T GOING TO CHANGE MY MIND.
THAT'S WHAT THEY ALL SAY.
GoComics.com/babyblues
©2022, BABY BLUES BROS LLC DIST. BY ANDREWS McMEEL SYNDICATION 3-10
KIRKMAN & SCOTT

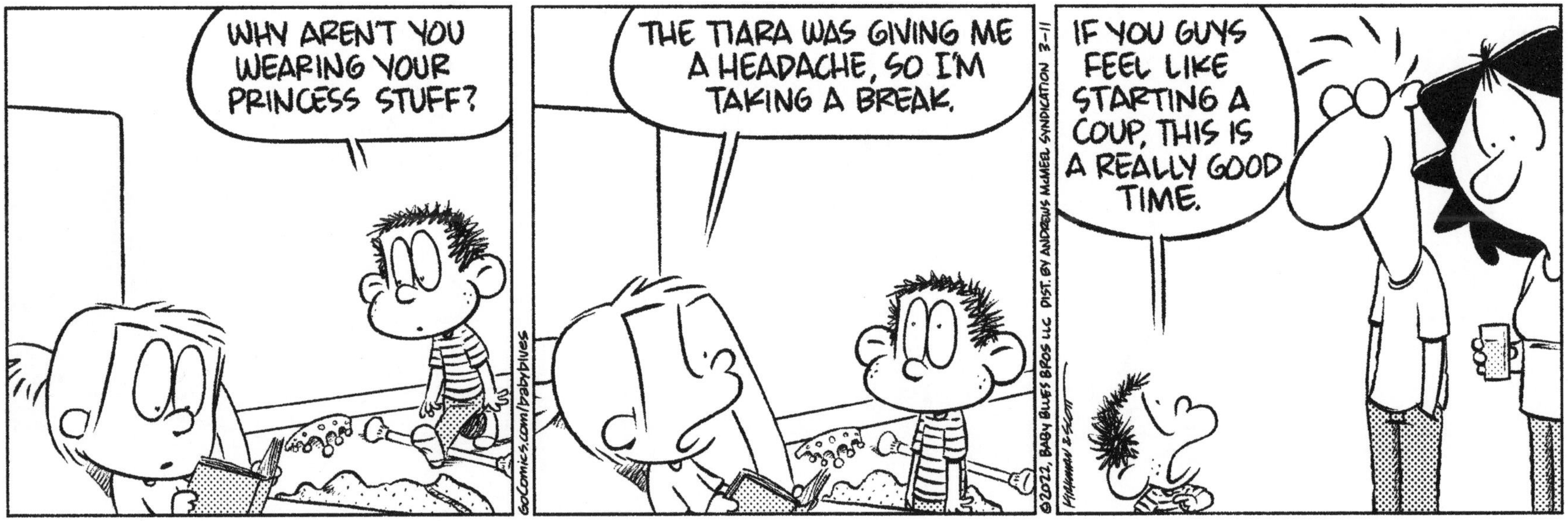
WHY AREN'T YOU WEARING YOUR PRINCESS STUFF?
GoComics.com/babyblues
THE TIARA WAS GIVING ME A HEADACHE, SO I'M TAKING A BREAK.
©2022, BABY BLUES BROS LLC DIST. BY ANDREWS McMEEL SYNDICATION 3-11
IF YOU GUYS FEEL LIKE STARTING A COUP, THIS IS A REALLY GOOD TIME.

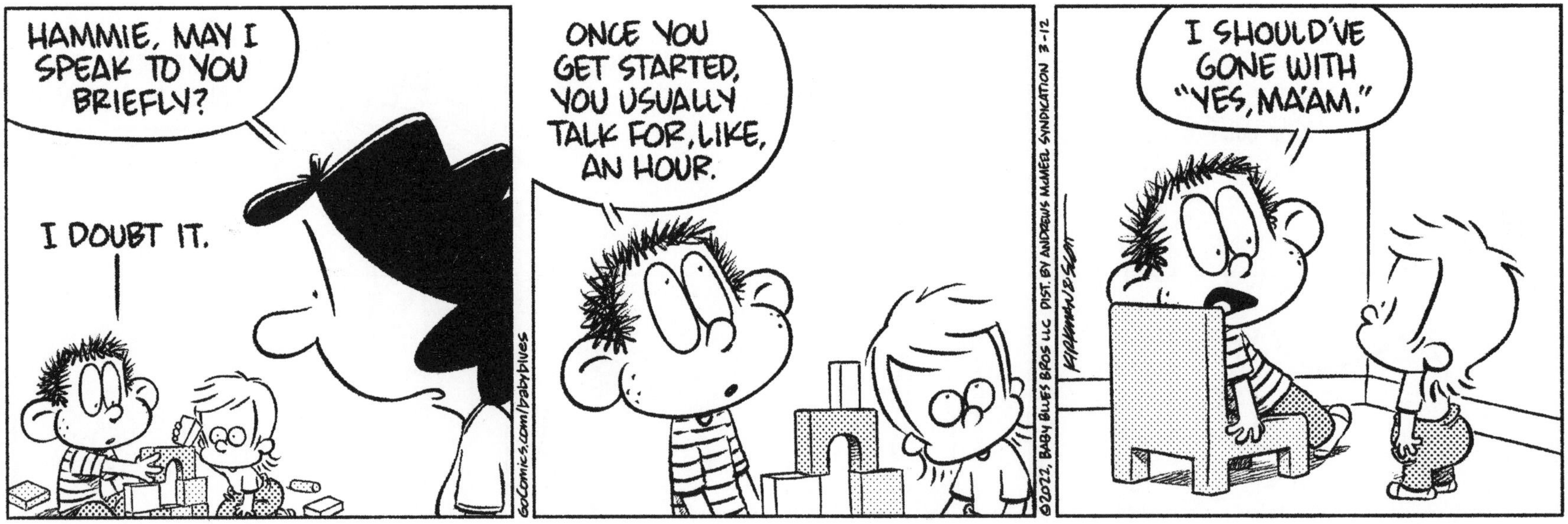
HAMMIE, MAY I SPEAK TO YOU BRIEFLY?
I DOUBT IT.
GoComics.com/babyblues
ONCE YOU GET STARTED, YOU USUALLY TALK FOR, LIKE, AN HOUR.
©2022, BABY BLUES BROS LLC DIST. BY ANDREWS McMEEL SYNDICATION 3-12
I SHOULD'VE GONE WITH "YES, MA'AM."

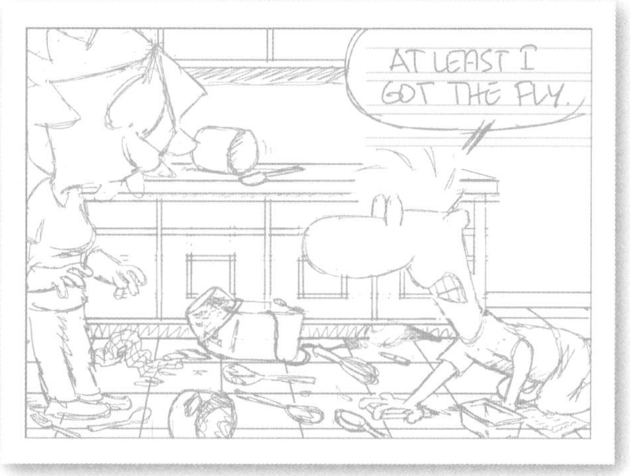
AT LEAST I GOT THE FLY.

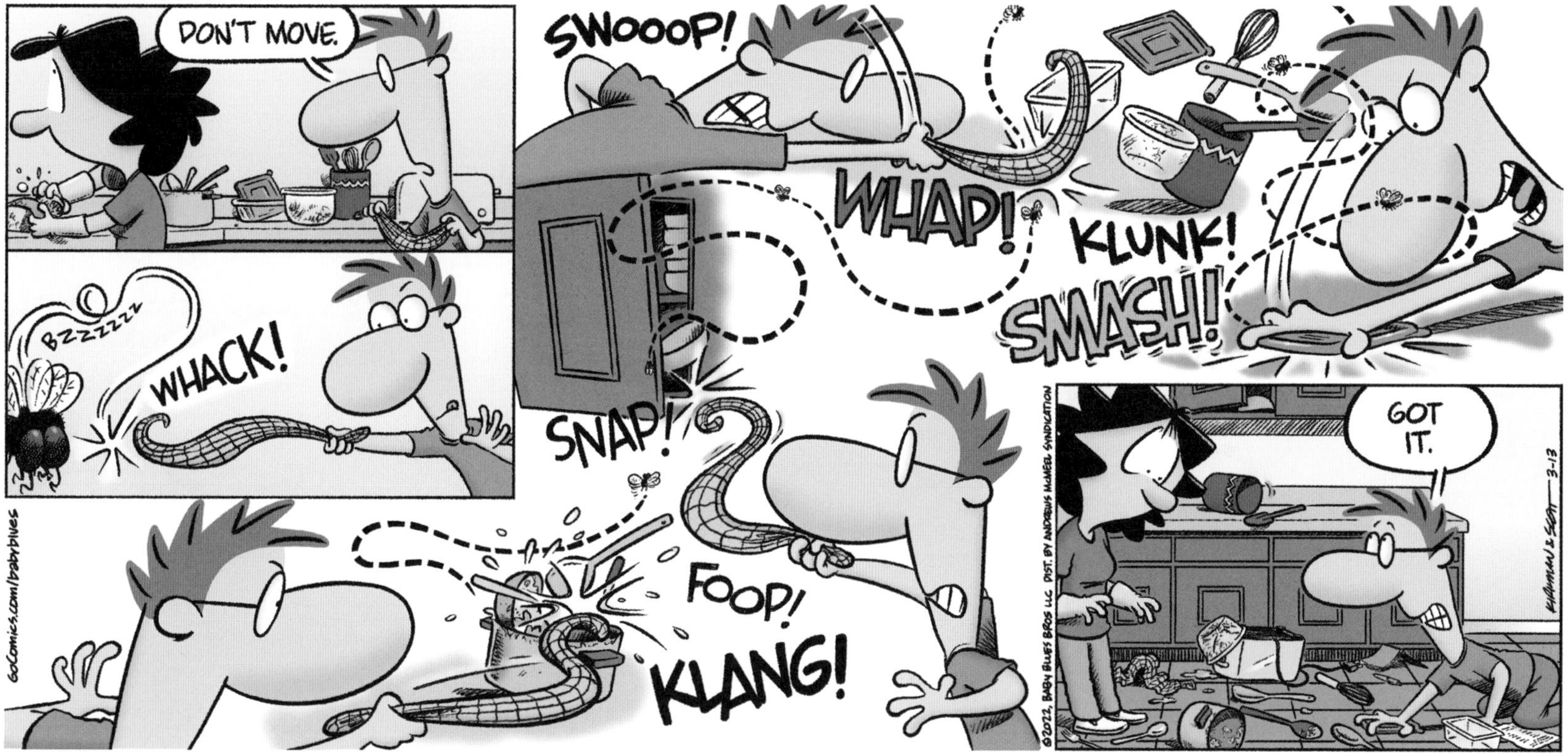
DON'T MOVE.
BZZZZZZ
WHACK!
GoComics.com/babyblues
SWOOOP!
WHAP!
KLUNK!
SMASH!
SNAP!
FOOP!
KLANG!
©2022, BABY BLUES BROS LLC DIST. BY ANDREWS McMEEL SYNDICATION
GOT IT.
3-13

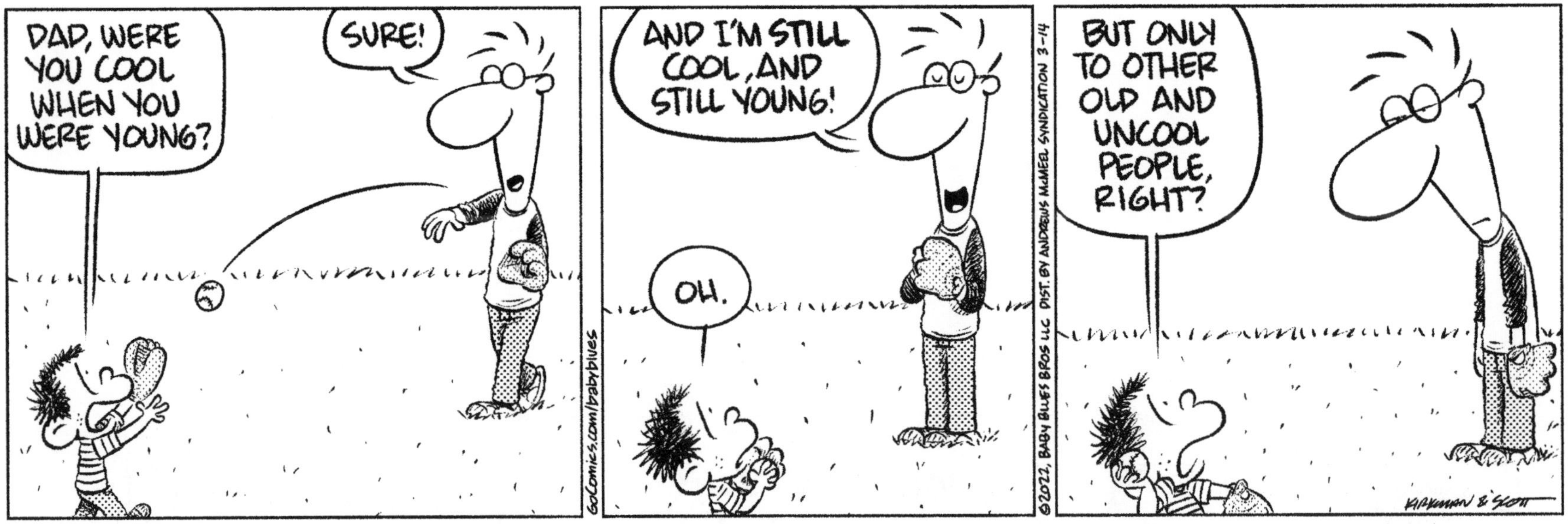
DAD, WERE YOU COOL WHEN YOU WERE YOUNG?
SURE!
AND I'M STILL COOL, AND STILL YOUNG!
OH.
BUT ONLY TO OTHER OLD AND UNCOOL PEOPLE, RIGHT?
GoComics.com/babyblues
©2022, BABY BLUES BROS LLC DIST. BY ANDREWS McMEEL SYNDICATION 3-14
KIRKMAN & SCOTT

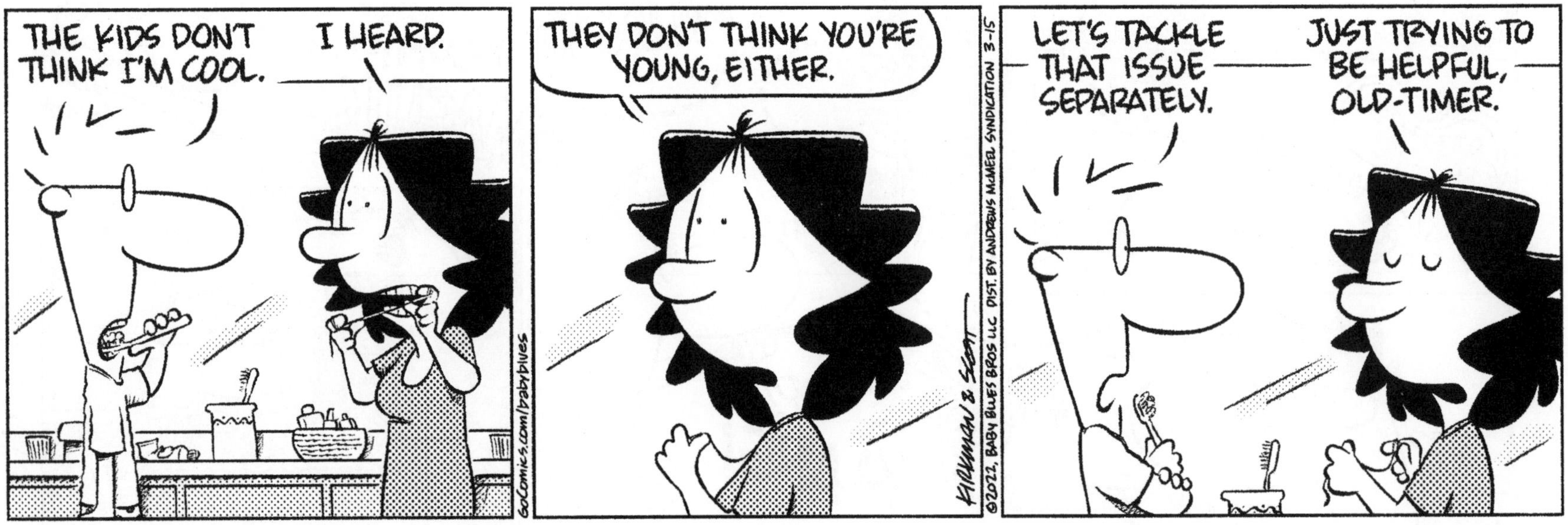
THE KIDS DON'T THINK I'M COOL.
I HEARD.
THEY DON'T THINK YOU'RE YOUNG, EITHER.
LET'S TACKLE THAT ISSUE SEPARATELY.
JUST TRYING TO BE HELPFUL, OLD-TIMER.
GoComics.com/babyblues
©2022, BABY BLUES BROS LLC DIST. BY ANDREWS McMEEL SYNDICATION 3-15
KIRKMAN & SCOTT

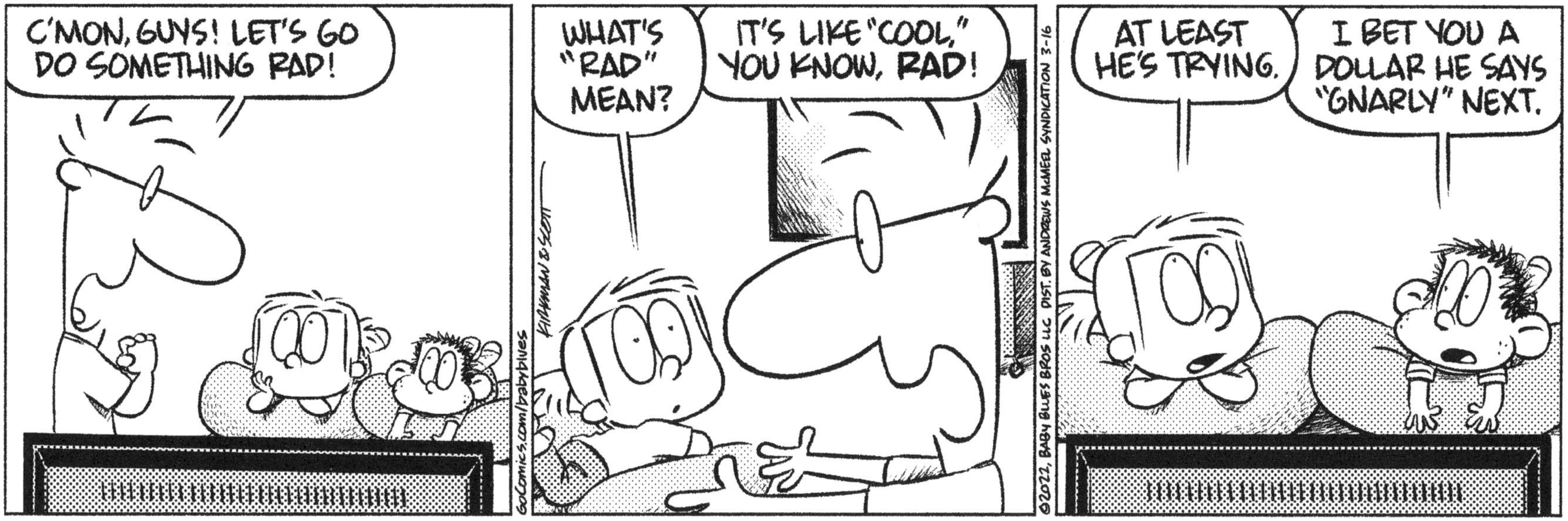
C'MON, GUYS! LET'S GO DO SOMETHING RAD!
WHAT'S "RAD" MEAN?
IT'S LIKE "COOL," YOU KNOW, RAD!
AT LEAST HE'S TRYING.
I BET YOU A DOLLAR HE SAYS "GNARLY" NEXT.
GoComics.com/babyblues
KIRKMAN & SCOTT
©2022, BABY BLUES BROS LLC DIST. BY ANDREWS McMEEL SYNDICATION 3-16

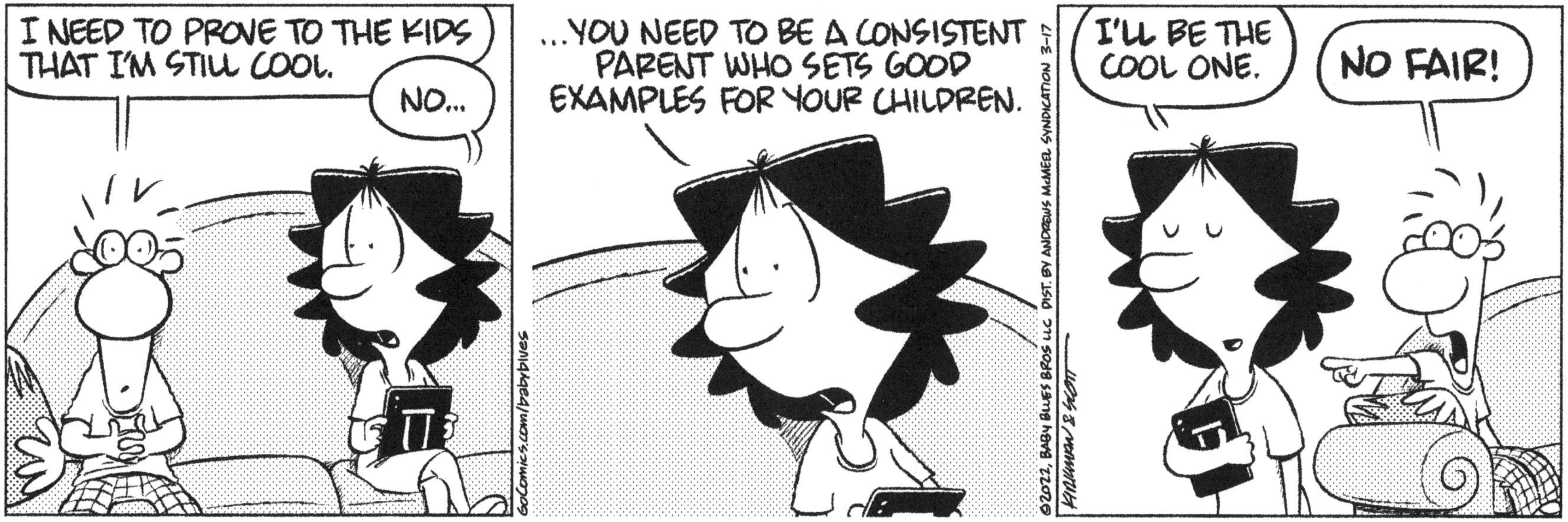
I NEED TO PROVE TO THE KIDS THAT I'M STILL COOL.
NO...
...YOU NEED TO BE A CONSISTENT PARENT WHO SETS GOOD EXAMPLES FOR YOUR CHILDREN.
I'LL BE THE COOL ONE.
NO FAIR!
GoComics.com/babyblues
©2022, BABY BLUES BROS LLC DIST. BY ANDREWS McMEEL SYNDICATION 3-17
KIRKMAN & SCOTT

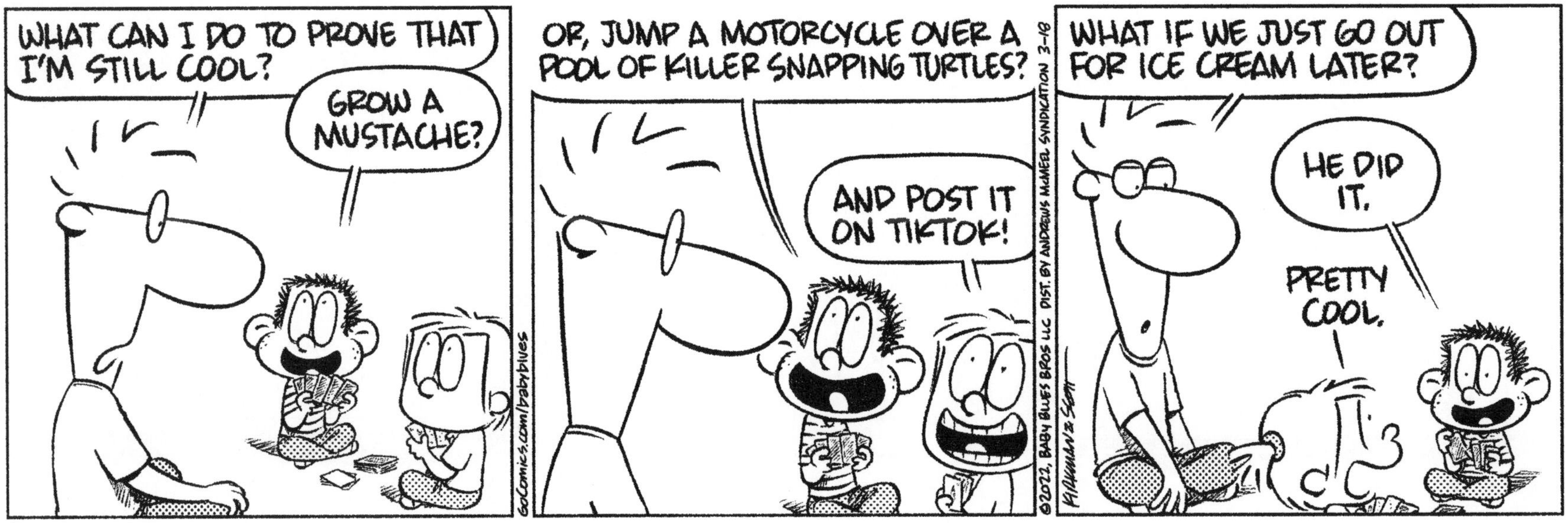
WHAT CAN I DO TO PROVE THAT I'M STILL COOL?
GROW A MUSTACHE?
GoComics.com/babyblues
OR, JUMP A MOTORCYCLE OVER A POOL OF KILLER SNAPPING TURTLES?
AND POST IT ON TIKTOK!
©2022, BABY BLUES BROS LLC DIST. BY ANDREWS McMEEL SYNDICATION 3-18
WHAT IF WE JUST GO OUT FOR ICE CREAM LATER?
HE DID IT.
PRETTY COOL.

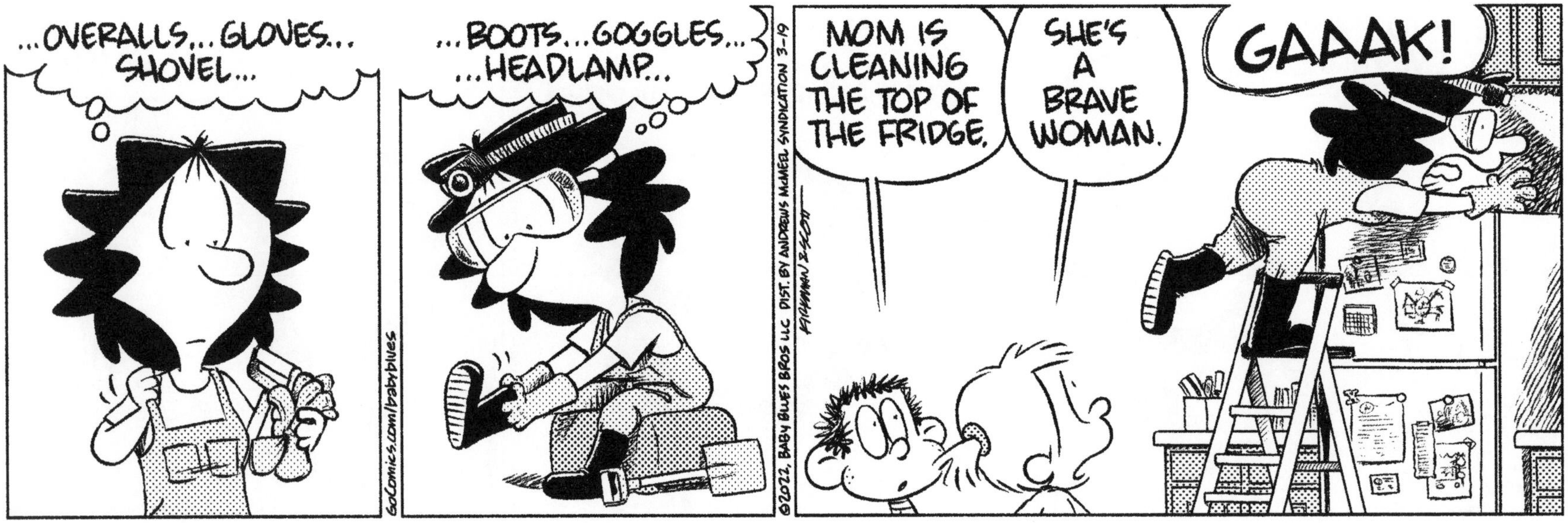
...OVERALLS... GLOVES... SHOVEL...
GoComics.com/babyblues
...BOOTS...GOGGLES... ...HEADLAMP...
©2022, BABY BLUES BROS LLC DIST. BY ANDREWS McMEEL SYNDICATION 3-19
MOM IS CLEANING THE TOP OF THE FRIDGE.
SHE'S A BRAVE WOMAN.
GAAAK!

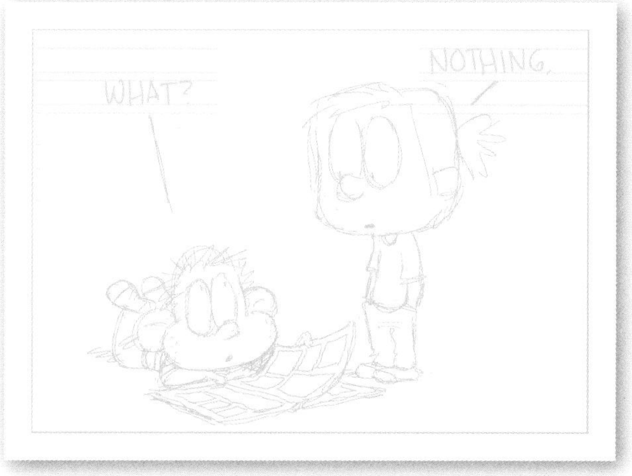
WHAT?
NOTHING.

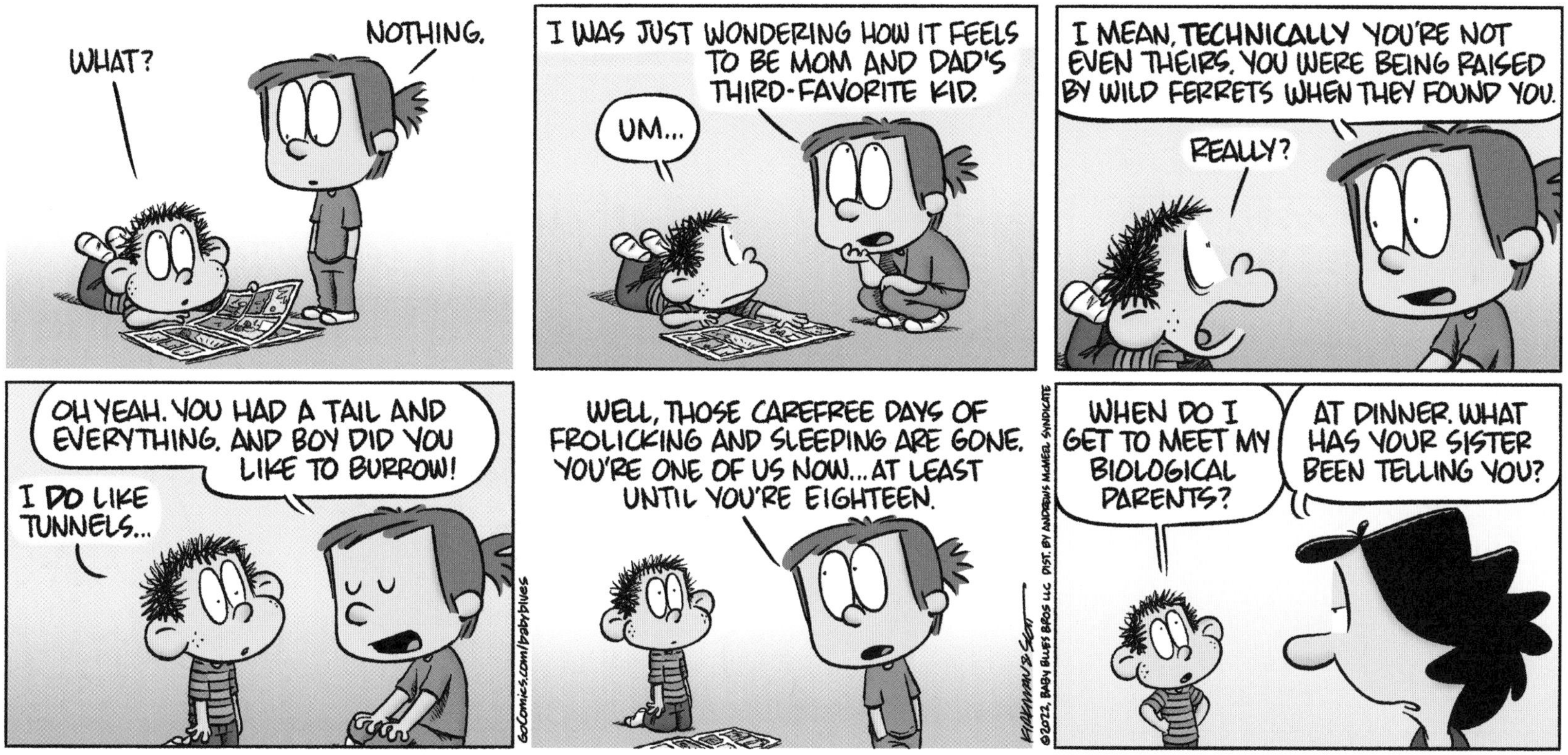
WHAT?
NOTHING.
I WAS JUST WONDERING HOW IT FEELS TO BE MOM AND DAD'S THIRD-FAVORITE KID.
UM...
I MEAN, TECHNICALLY YOU'RE NOT EVEN THEIRS. YOU WERE BEING RAISED BY WILD FERRETS WHEN THEY FOUND YOU.
REALLY?
OH YEAH. YOU HAD A TAIL AND EVERYTHING. AND BOY DID YOU LIKE TO BURROW!
I DO LIKE TUNNELS...
GoComics.com/babyblues
WELL, THOSE CAREFREE DAYS OF FROLICKING AND SLEEPING ARE GONE. YOU'RE ONE OF US NOW...AT LEAST UNTIL YOU'RE EIGHTEEN.
KIRKMAN & SCOTT
©2022, BABY BLUES BROS LLC DIST. BY ANDREWS MCMEEL SYNDICATE
WHEN DO I GET TO MEET MY BIOLOGICAL PARENTS?
AT DINNER. WHAT HAS YOUR SISTER BEEN TELLING YOU?

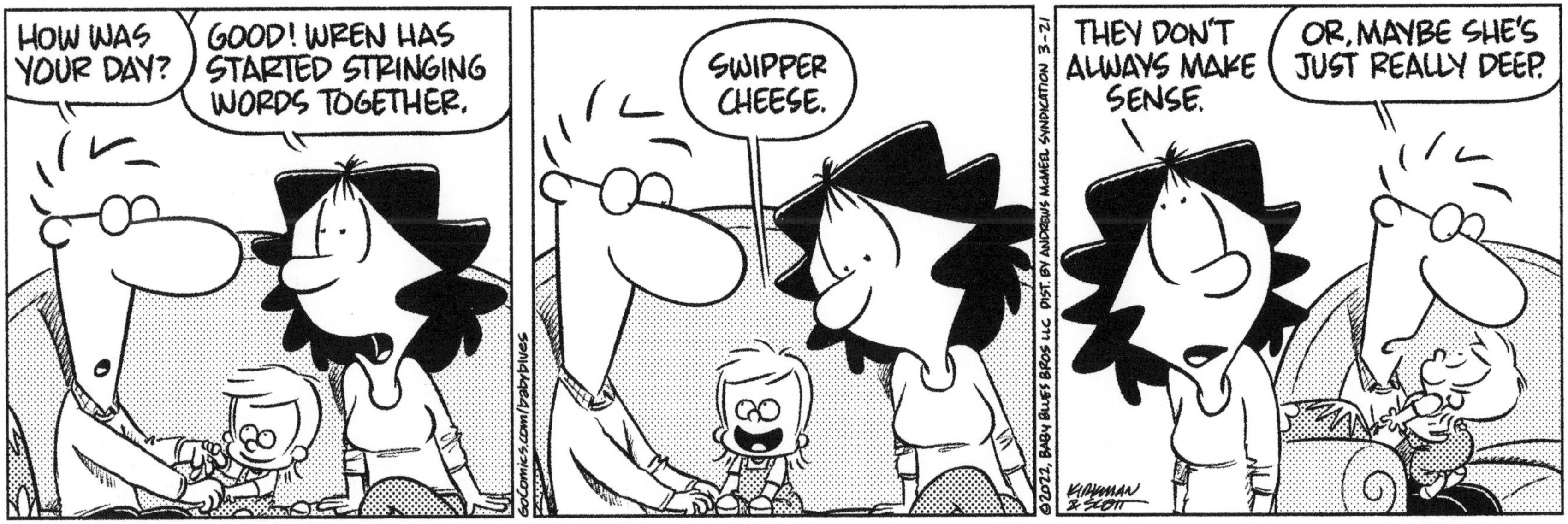
HOW WAS YOUR DAY?
GOOD! WREN HAS STARTED STRINGING WORDS TOGETHER.
SWIPPER CHEESE.
THEY DON'T ALWAYS MAKE SENSE.
OR, MAYBE SHE'S JUST REALLY DEEP.
GoComics.com/babyblues
©2022, BABY BLUES BROS LLC DIST. BY ANDREWS McMEEL SYNDICATION 3-21
KIRKMAN & SCOTT

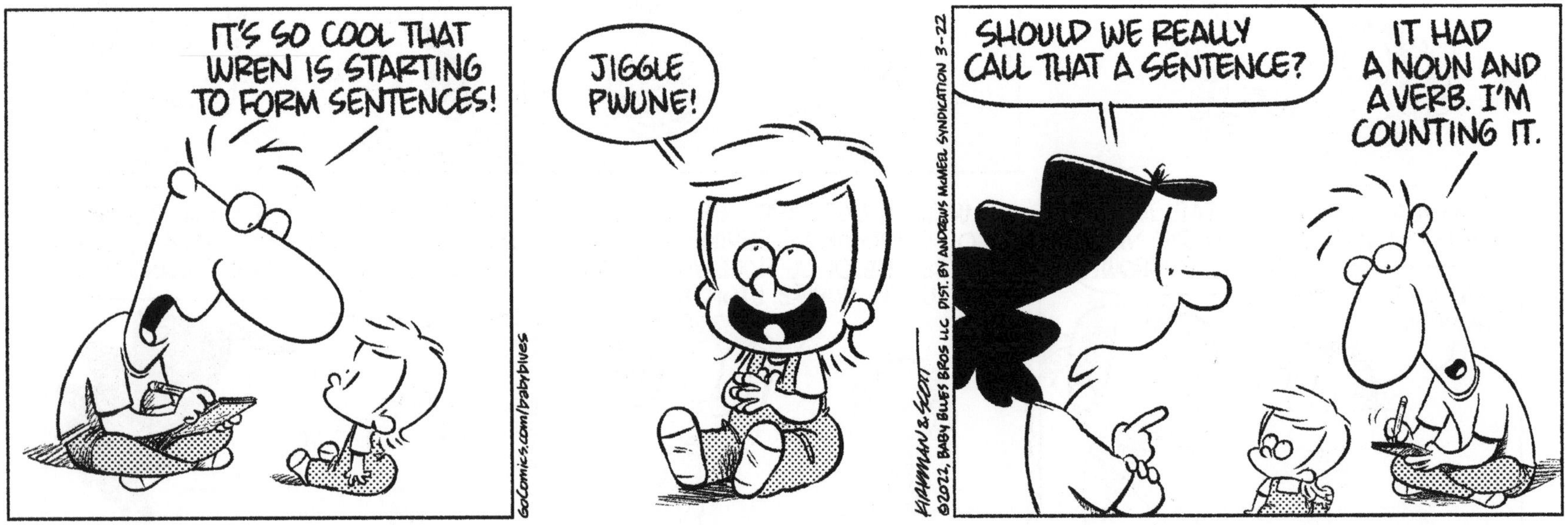
IT'S SO COOL THAT WREN IS STARTING TO FORM SENTENCES!
JIGGLE PWUNE!
SHOULD WE REALLY CALL THAT A SENTENCE?
IT HAD A NOUN AND A VERB. I'M COUNTING IT.
GoComics.com/babyblues
©2022, BABY BLUES BROS LLC DIST. BY ANDREWS McMEEL SYNDICATION 3-22
KIRKMAN & SCOTT

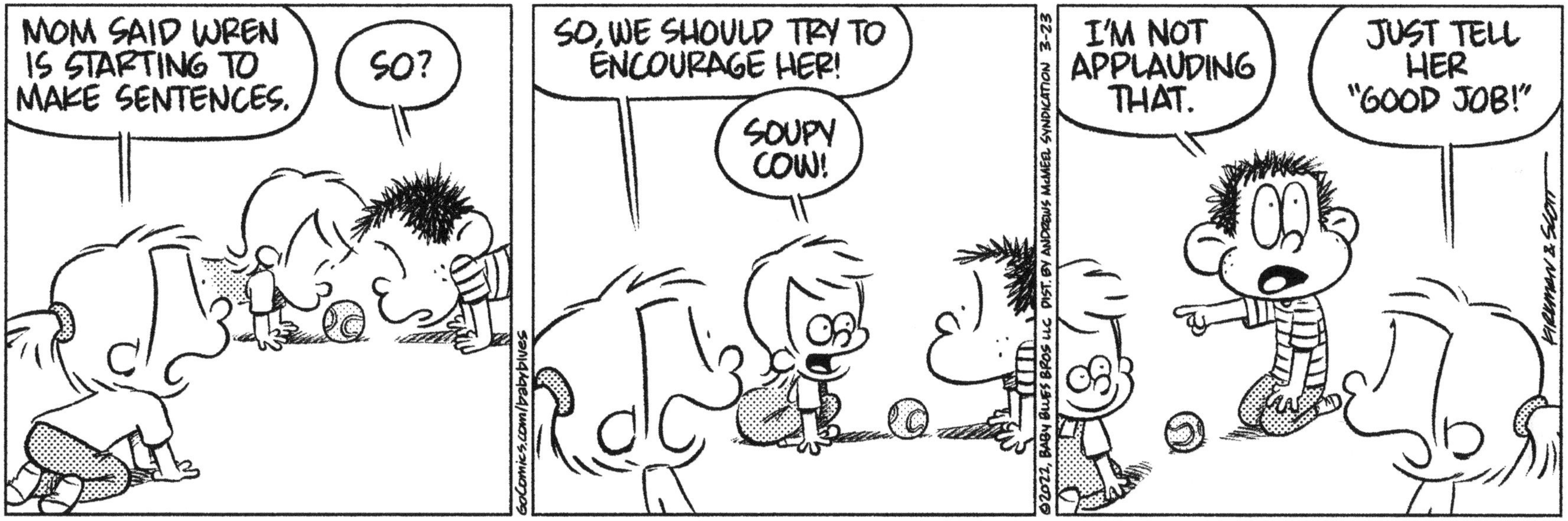
MOM SAID WREN IS STARTING TO MAKE SENTENCES.
SO?
gocomics.com/babyblues
SO, WE SHOULD TRY TO ENCOURAGE HER!
SOUPY COW!
©2022, BABY BLUES BROS LLC DIST. BY ANDREWS McMEEL SYNDICATION 3-23
I'M NOT APPLAUDING THAT.
JUST TELL HER "GOOD JOB!"
KIRKMAN & SCOTT

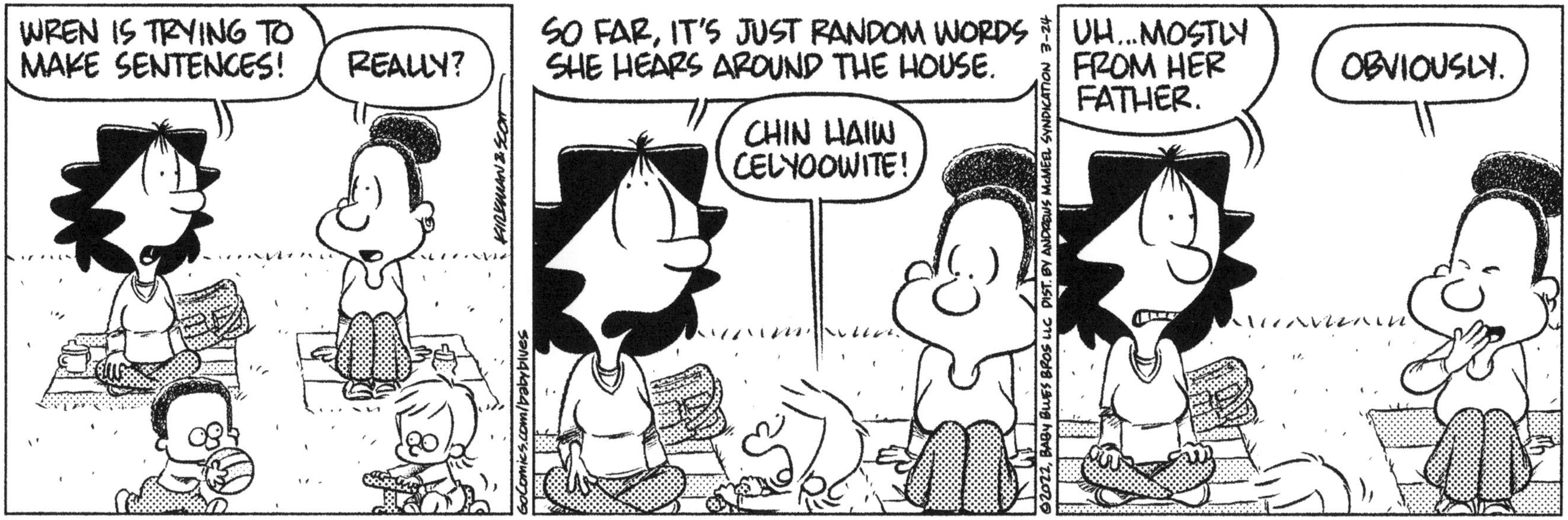
WREN IS TRYING TO MAKE SENTENCES!
REALLY?
KIRKMAN & SCOTT
gocomics.com/babyblues
SO FAR, IT'S JUST RANDOM WORDS SHE HEARS AROUND THE HOUSE.
CHIN HAIW CELYOOWITE!
©2022, BABY BLUES BROS LLC DIST. BY ANDREWS McMEEL SYNDICATION 3-24
UH...MOSTLY FROM HER FATHER.
OBVIOUSLY.

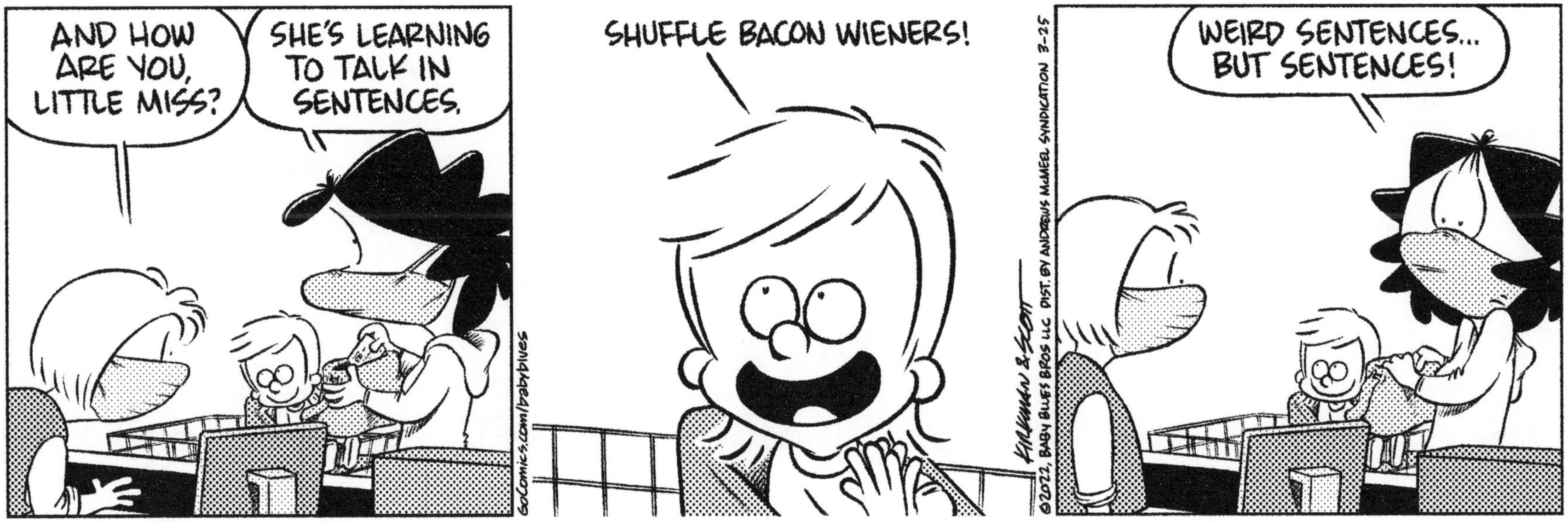
AND HOW ARE YOU, LITTLE MISS?
SHE'S LEARNING TO TALK IN SENTENCES.
GoComics.com/babyblues
SHUFFLE BACON WIENERS!
KIRKMAN & SCOTT
©2022, BABY BLUES BROS LLC DIST. BY ANDREWS McMEEL SYNDICATION 3-25
WEIRD SENTENCES... BUT SENTENCES!

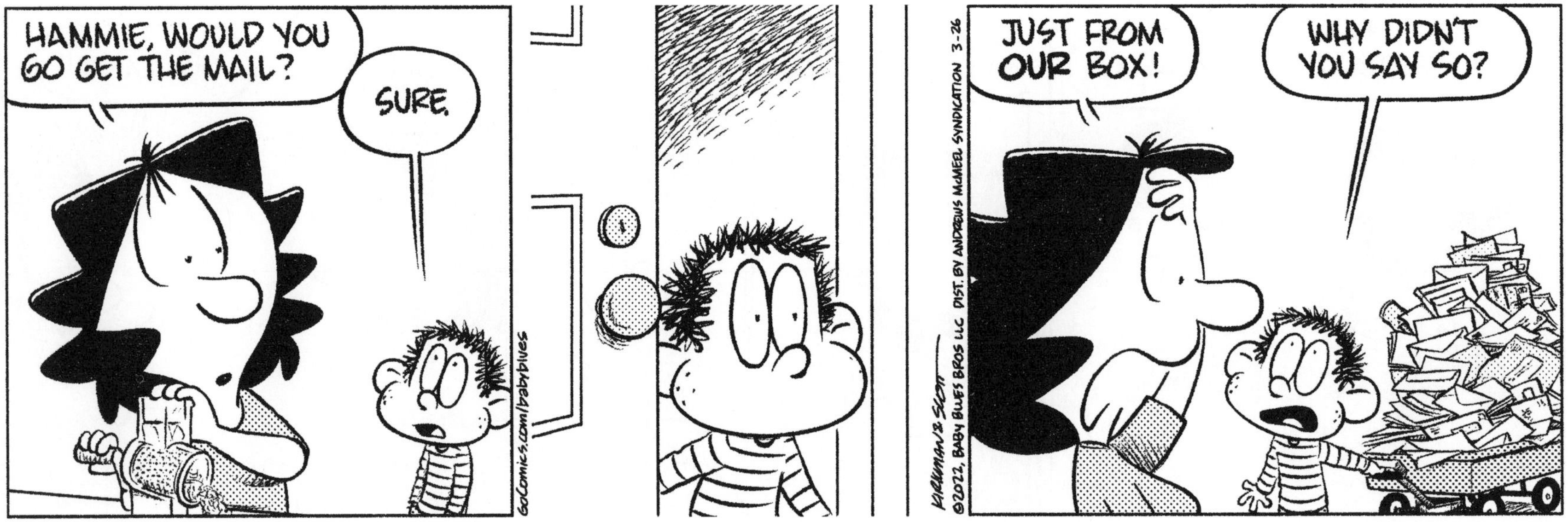
HAMMIE, WOULD YOU GO GET THE MAIL?
SURE.
GoComics.com/babyblues
KIRKMAN & SCOTT
©2022, BABY BLUES BROS LLC DIST. BY ANDREWS McMEEL SYNDICATION 3-26
JUST FROM OUR BOX!
WHY DIDN'T YOU SAY SO?

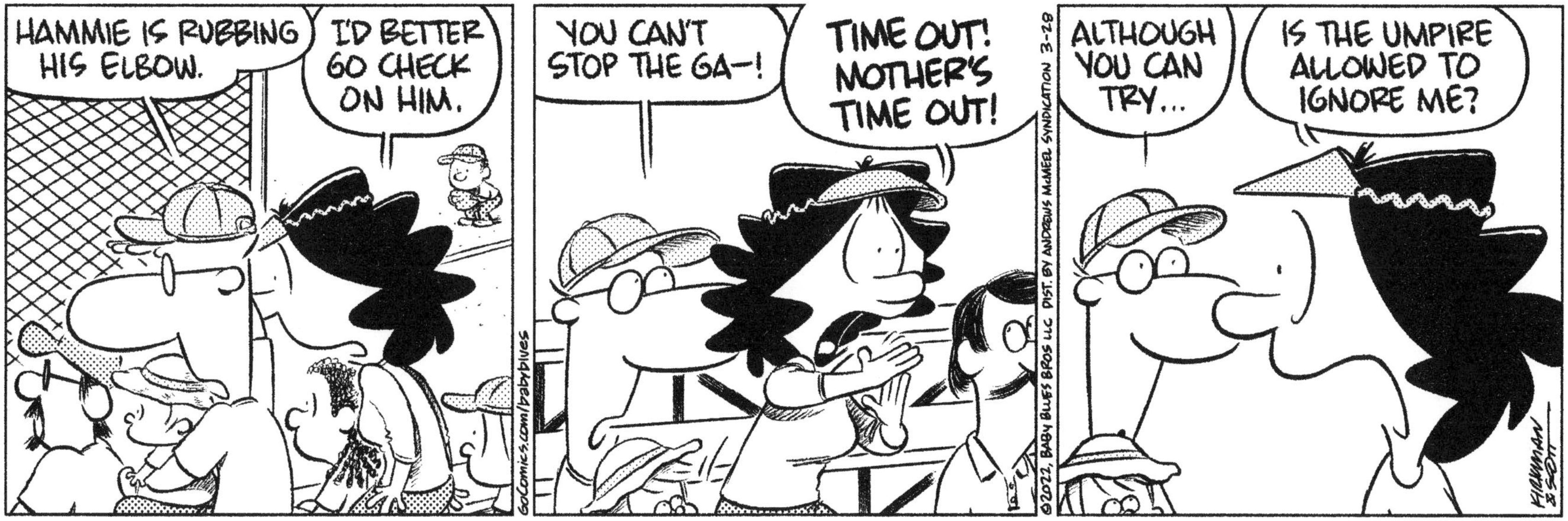
HAMMIE IS RUBBING HIS ELBOW.
I'D BETTER GO CHECK ON HIM.
GoComics.com/babyblues
YOU CAN'T STOP THE GA—!
TIME OUT! MOTHER'S TIME OUT!
©2022, BABY BLUES BROS LLC DIST. BY ANDREWS McMEEL SYNDICATION 3-28
ALTHOUGH YOU CAN TRY...
IS THE UMPIRE ALLOWED TO IGNORE ME?
KIRKMAN & SCOTT

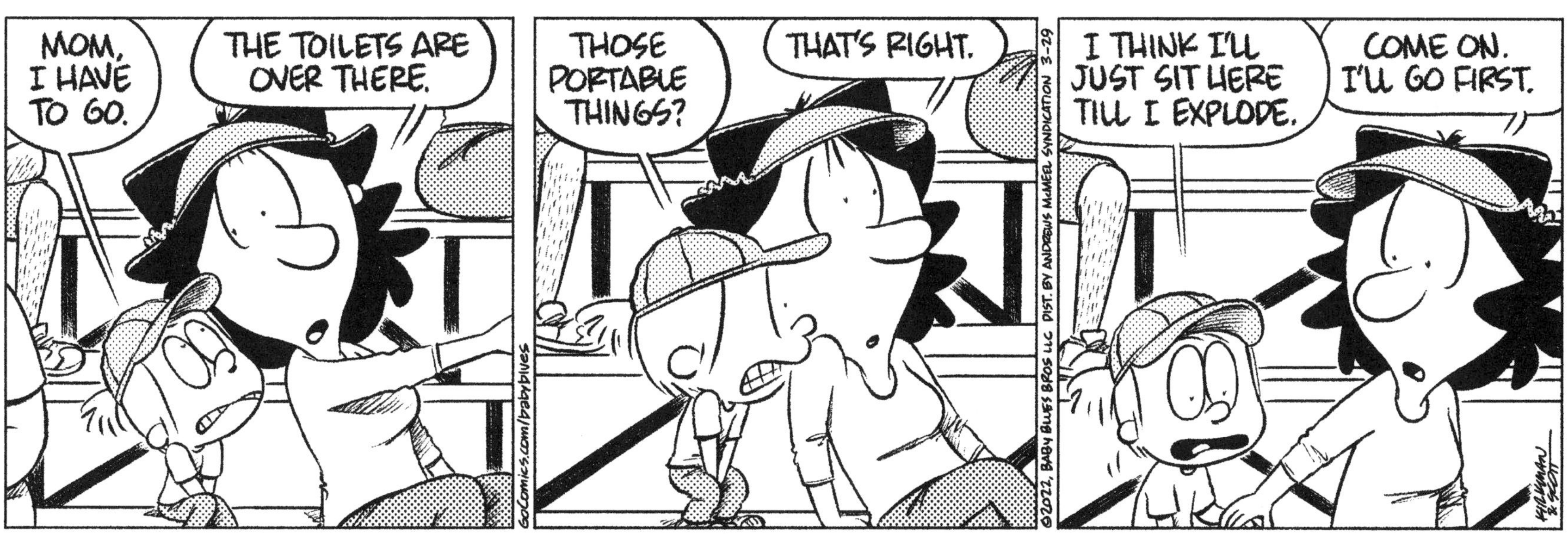
MOM, I HAVE TO GO.
THE TOILETS ARE OVER THERE.
GoComics.com/babyblues
THOSE PORTABLE THINGS?
THAT'S RIGHT.
©2022, BABY BLUES BROS LLC DIST. BY ANDREWS McMEEL SYNDICATION 3-29
I THINK I'LL JUST SIT HERE TILL I EXPLODE.
COME ON. I'LL GO FIRST.
KIRKMAN & SCOTT

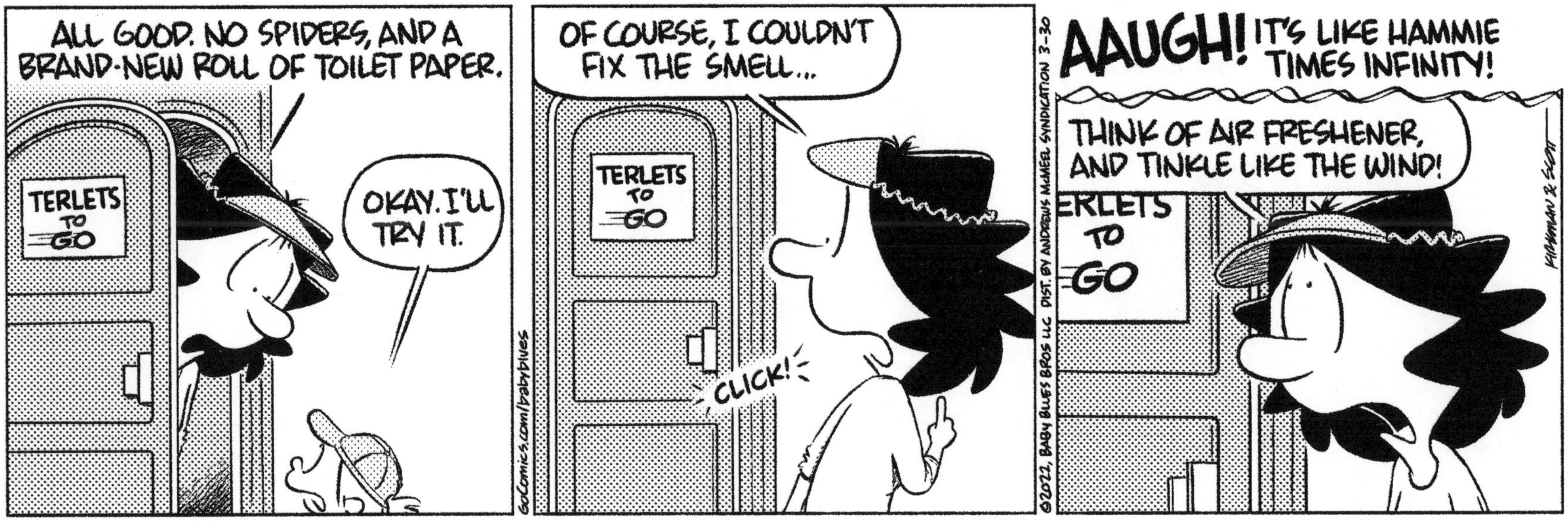
ALL GOOD. NO SPIDERS, AND A BRAND-NEW ROLL OF TOILET PAPER.
TERLETS TO GO
OKAY. I'LL TRY IT.
GoComics.com/babyblues
OF COURSE, I COULDN'T FIX THE SMELL...
TERLETS TO GO
CLICK!
©2022, BABY BLUES BROS LLC DIST. BY ANDREWS McMEEL SYNDICATION 3-30
AAUGH! IT'S LIKE HAMMIE TIMES INFINITY!
THINK OF AIR FRESHENER, AND TINKLE LIKE THE WIND!
ERLETS TO GO
KIRKMAN & SCOTT

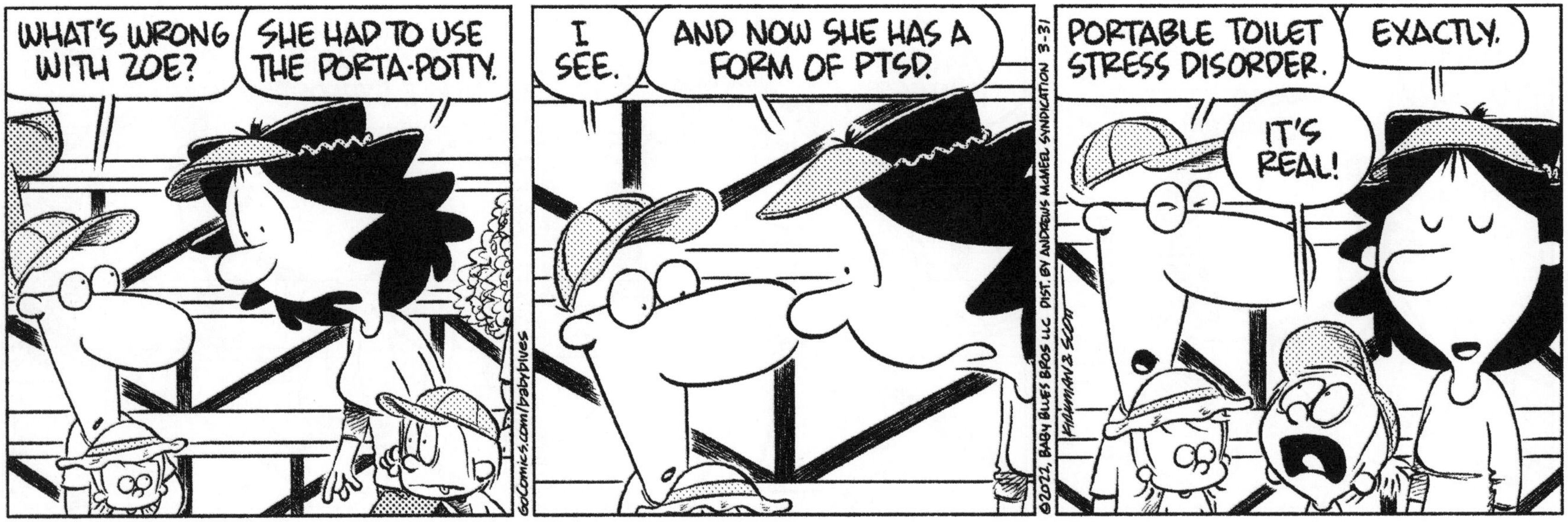
WHAT'S WRONG WITH ZOE?
SHE HAD TO USE THE PORTA-POTTY.
GoComics.com/babyblues
I SEE.
AND NOW SHE HAS A FORM OF PTSD.
©2022, BABY BLUES BROS LLC DIST. BY ANDREWS McMEEL SYNDICATION 3-31
KIRKMAN & SCOTT
PORTABLE TOILET STRESS DISORDER.
EXACTLY.
IT'S REAL!

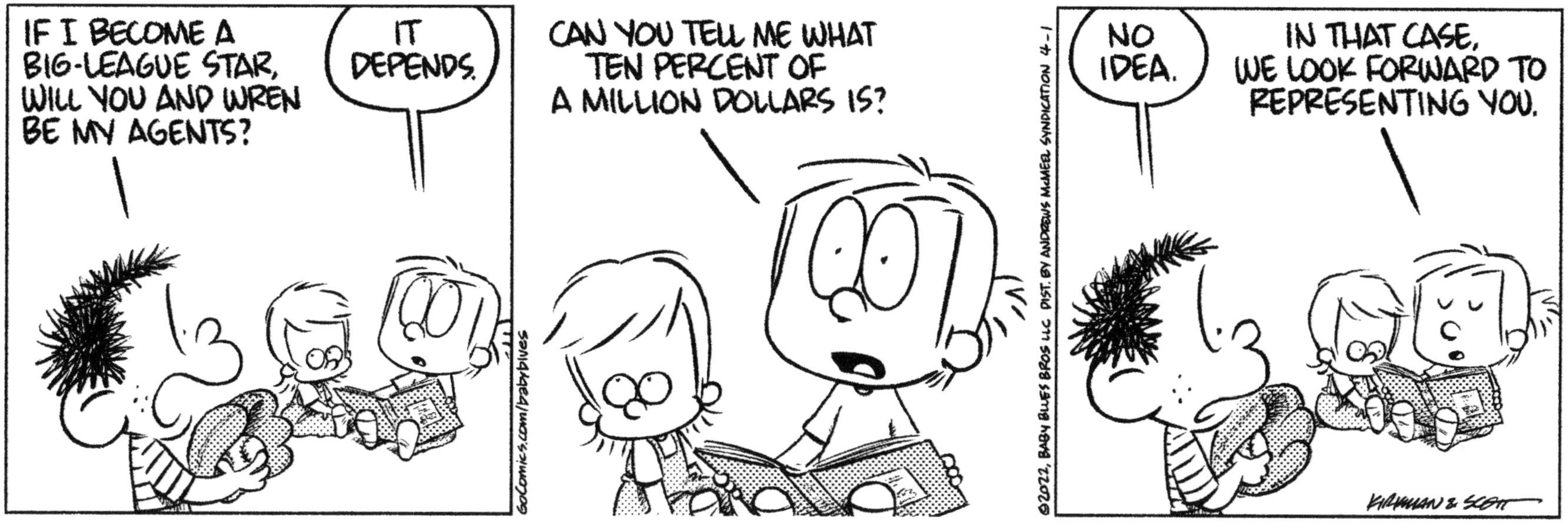
IF I BECOME A BIG-LEAGUE STAR, WILL YOU AND WREN BE MY AGENTS?
IT DEPENDS.
GoComics.com/babyblues
CAN YOU TELL ME WHAT TEN PERCENT OF A MILLION DOLLARS IS?
©2022, BABY BLUES BROS LLC DIST. BY ANDREWS McMEEL SYNDICATION 4-1
NO IDEA.
IN THAT CASE, WE LOOK FORWARD TO REPRESENTING YOU.
KIRKMAN & SCOTT

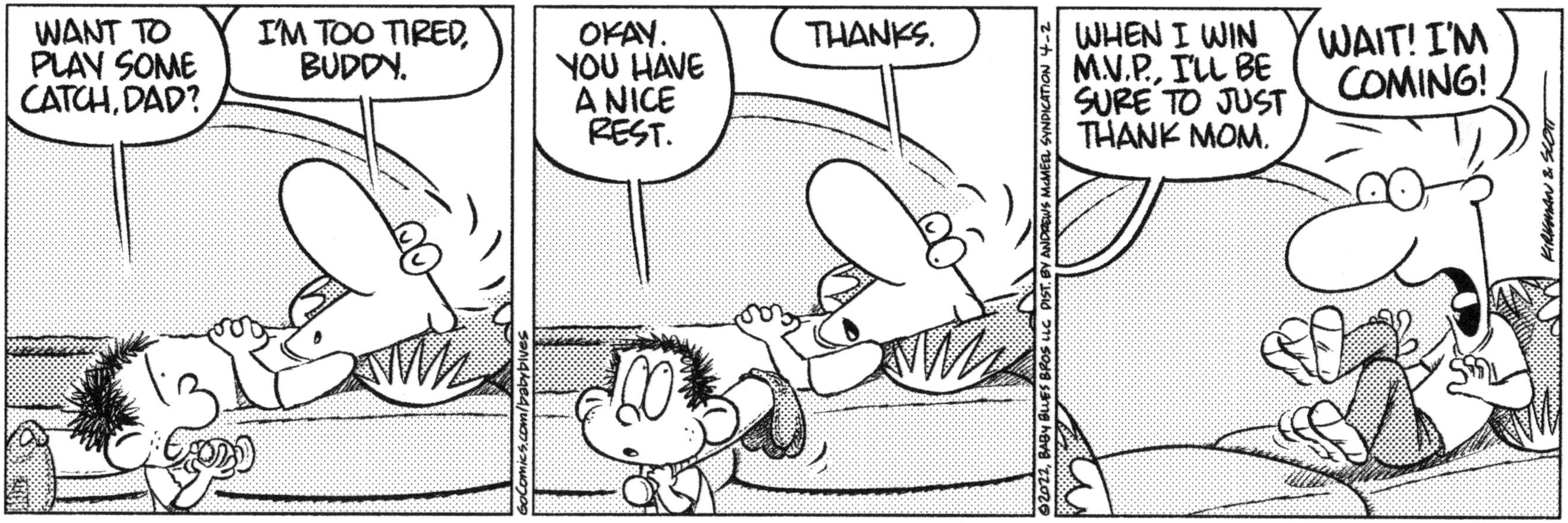
WANT TO PLAY SOME CATCH, DAD?
I'M TOO TIRED, BUDDY.
GoComics.com/babyblues
OKAY. YOU HAVE A NICE REST.
THANKS.
©2022, BABY BLUES BROS LLC DIST. BY ANDREWS McMEEL SYNDICATION 4-2
WHEN I WIN M.V.P., I'LL BE SURE TO JUST THANK MOM.
WAIT! I'M COMING!
KIRKMAN & SCOTT

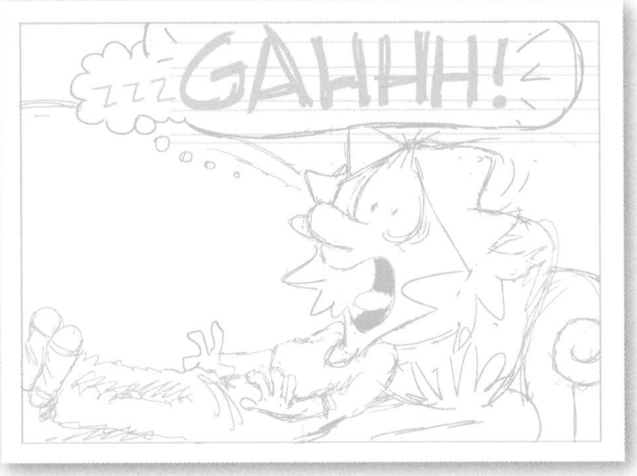
ZZZ GAHHH!

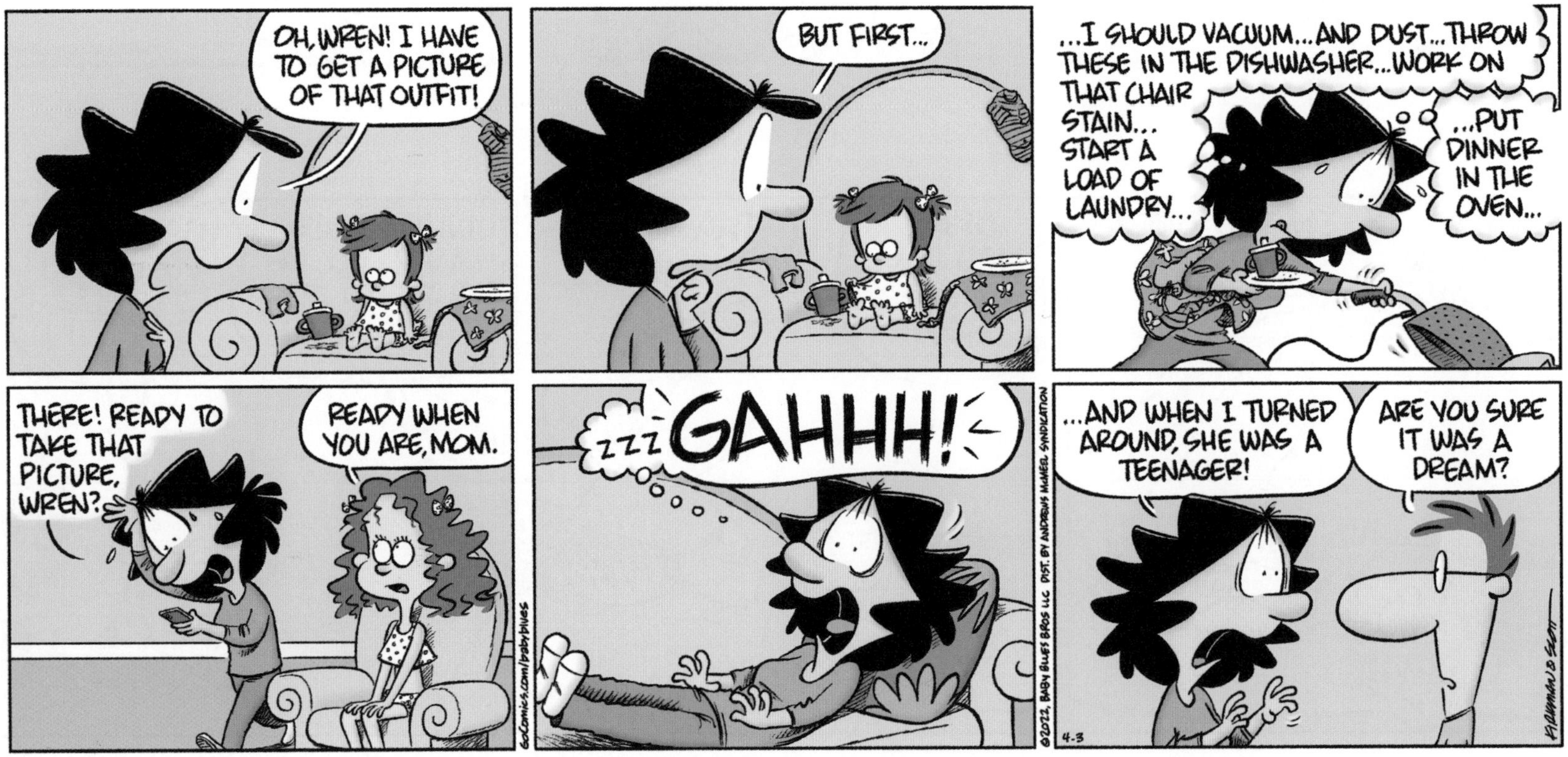
OH, WREN! I HAVE TO GET A PICTURE OF THAT OUTFIT!
BUT FIRST...
...I SHOULD VACUUM...AND DUST...THROW THESE IN THE DISHWASHER...WORK ON THAT CHAIR STAIN... START A LOAD OF LAUNDRY...
...PUT DINNER IN THE OVEN...
THERE! READY TO TAKE THAT PICTURE, WREN?
READY WHEN YOU ARE, MOM.
GoComics.com/babyblues
ZZZ GAHHH!
©2022, BABY BLUES BROS LLC DIST. BY ANDREWS McMEEL SYNDICATION
4-3
...AND WHEN I TURNED AROUND, SHE WAS A TEENAGER!
ARE YOU SURE IT WAS A DREAM?
KIRKMAN & SCOTT

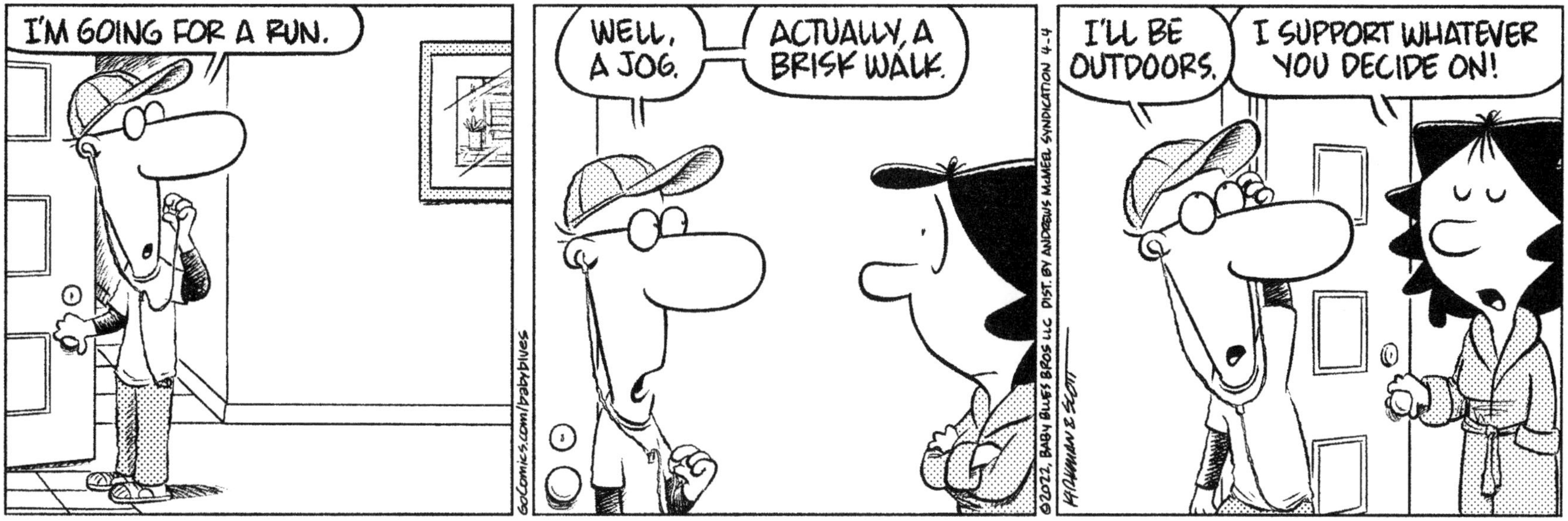
I'M GOING FOR A RUN.
WELL, A JOG.
ACTUALLY, A BRISK WALK.
I'LL BE OUTDOORS.
I SUPPORT WHATEVER YOU DECIDE ON!
GoComics.com/babyblues
©2022, BABY BLUES BROS LLC DIST. BY ANDREWS MCMEEL SYNDICATION 4-4
KIRKMAN & SCOTT

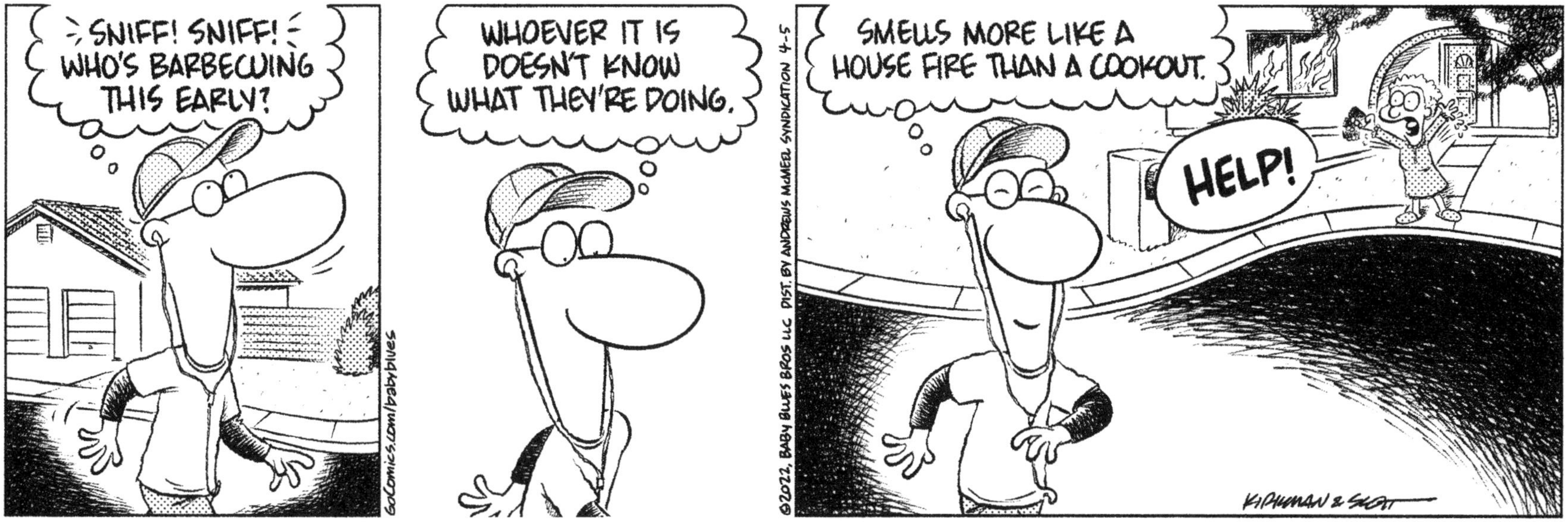
SNIFF! SNIFF! WHO'S BARBECUING THIS EARLY?
WHOEVER IT IS DOESN'T KNOW WHAT THEY'RE DOING.
SMELLS MORE LIKE A HOUSE FIRE THAN A COOKOUT.
HELP!
GoComics.com/babyblues
©2022, BABY BLUES BROS LLC DIST. BY ANDREWS MCMEEL SYNDICATION 4-5
KIRKMAN & SCOTT

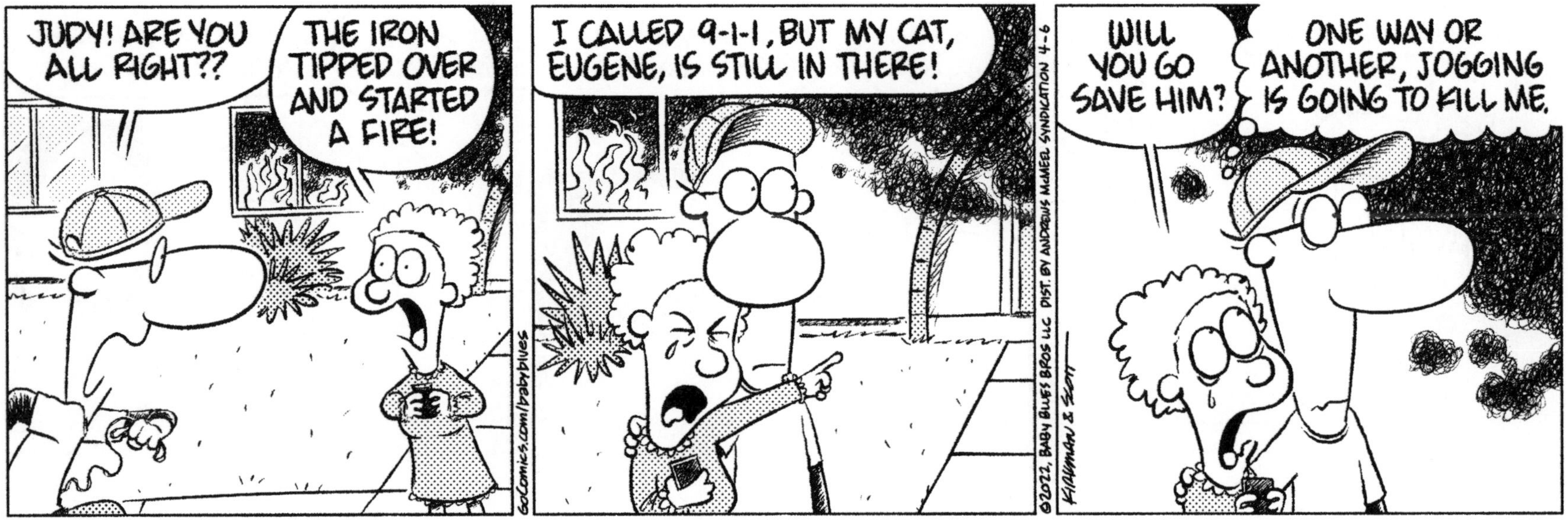
JUDY! ARE YOU ALL RIGHT??
THE IRON TIPPED OVER AND STARTED A FIRE!
GoComics.com/babyblues
I CALLED 9-1-1, BUT MY CAT, EUGENE, IS STILL IN THERE!
©2022, BABY BLUES BROS LLC DIST. BY ANDREWS McMEEL SYNDICATION 4-6
KIRKMAN & SCOTT
WILL YOU GO SAVE HIM?
ONE WAY OR ANOTHER, JOGGING IS GOING TO KILL ME.

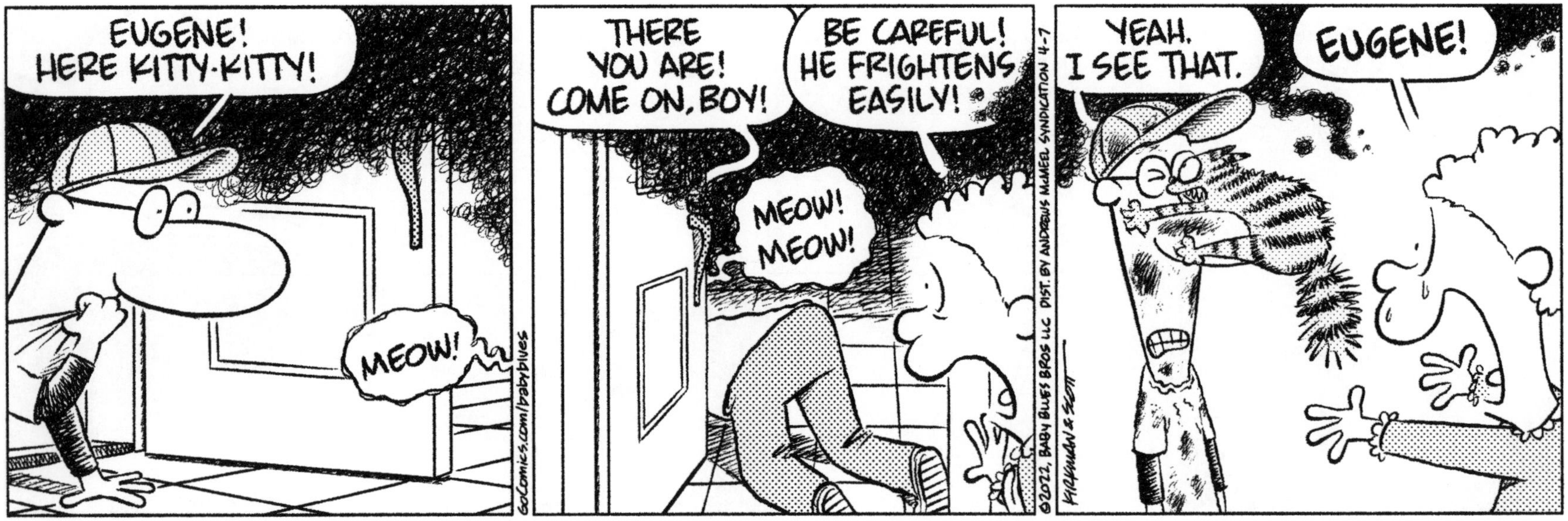
EUGENE! HERE KITTY-KITTY!
MEOW!
GoComics.com/babyblues
THERE YOU ARE! COME ON, BOY!
BE CAREFUL! HE FRIGHTENS EASILY!
MEOW! MEOW!
©2022, BABY BLUES BROS LLC DIST. BY ANDREWS McMEEL SYNDICATION 4-7
KIRKMAN & SCOTT
YEAH. I SEE THAT.
EUGENE!

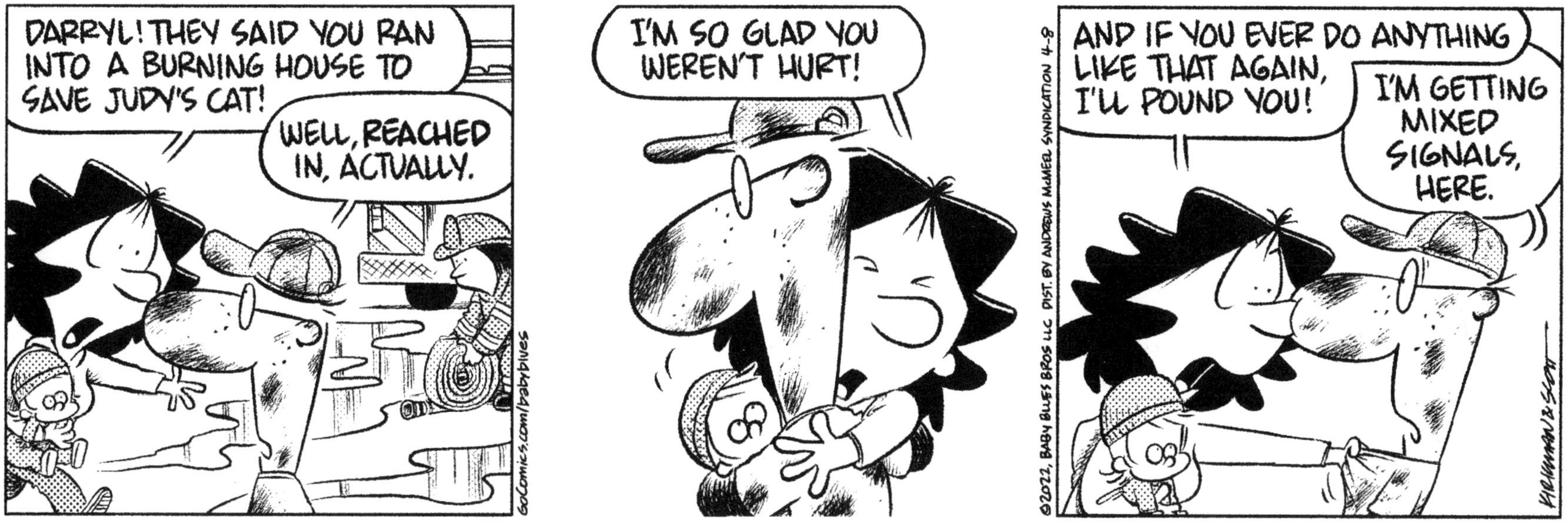
DARRYL! THEY SAID YOU RAN INTO A BURNING HOUSE TO SAVE JUDY'S CAT!
WELL, REACHED IN, ACTUALLY.
GoComics.com/babyblues
I'M SO GLAD YOU WEREN'T HURT!
©2022, BABY BLUES BROS LLC DIST. BY ANDREWS McMEEL SYNDICATION 4-8
AND IF YOU EVER DO ANYTHING LIKE THAT AGAIN, I'LL POUND YOU!
I'M GETTING MIXED SIGNALS, HERE.
KIRKMAN & SCOTT

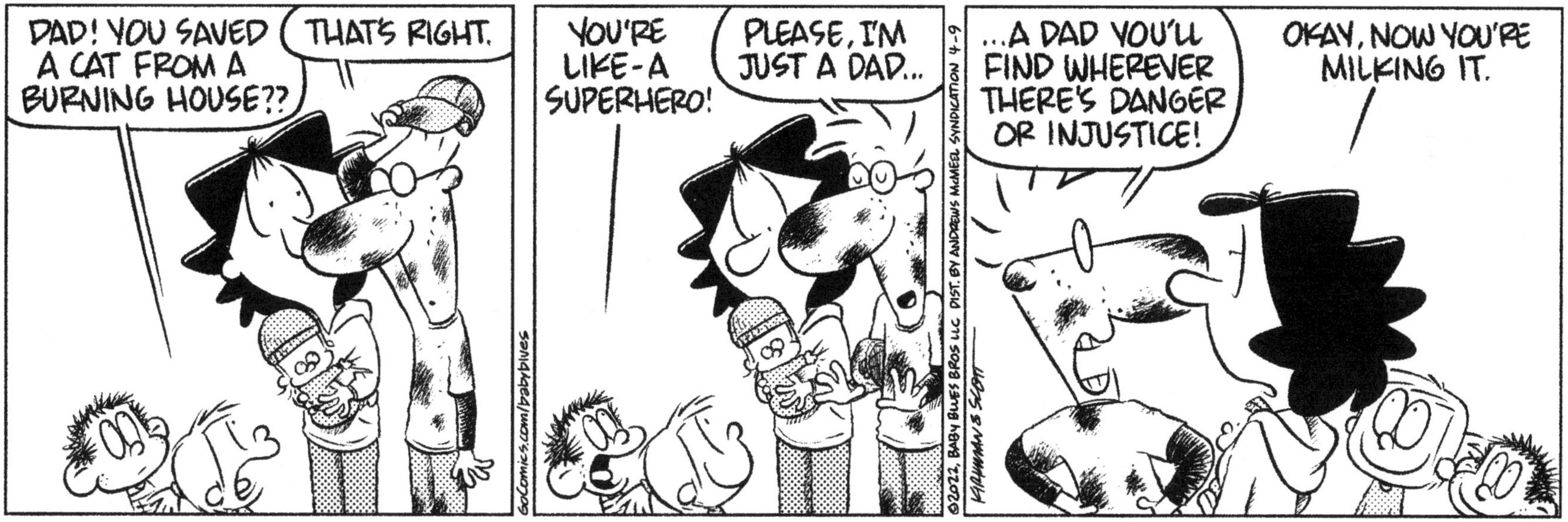
DAD! YOU SAVED A CAT FROM A BURNING HOUSE??
THAT'S RIGHT.
GoComics.com/babyblues
YOU'RE LIKE-A SUPERHERO!
PLEASE, I'M JUST A DAD...
©2022, BABY BLUES BROS LLC DIST. BY ANDREWS McMEEL SYNDICATION 4-9
KIRKMAN & SCOTT
...A DAD YOU'LL FIND WHEREVER THERE'S DANGER OR INJUSTICE!
OKAY, NOW YOU'RE MILKING IT.

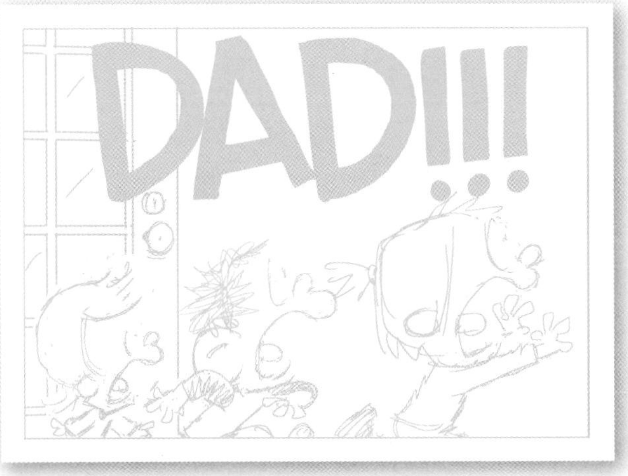
DAD!!!

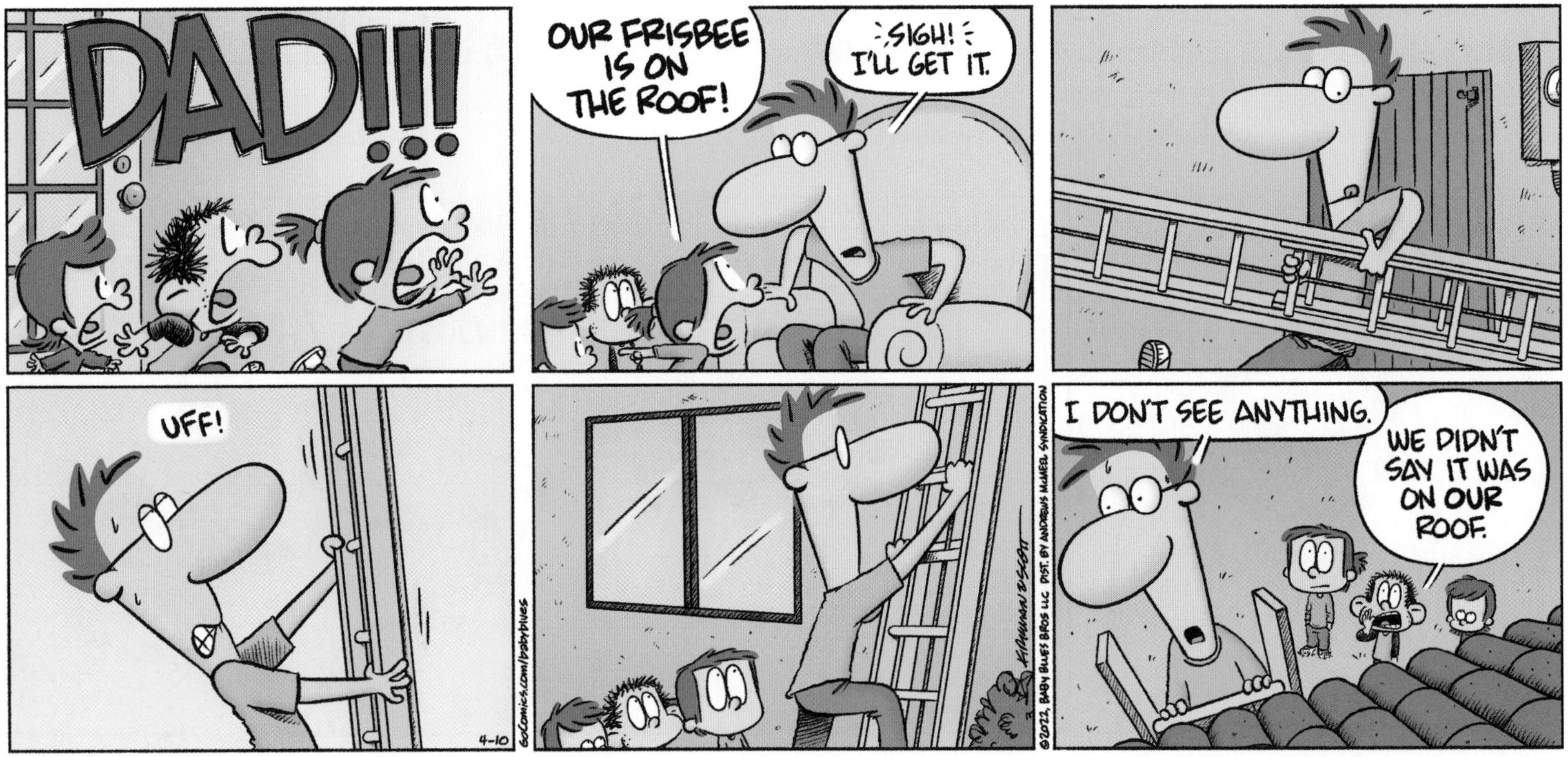
DAD!!!
OUR FRISBEE IS ON THE ROOF!
SIGH! I'LL GET IT.
UFF!
4-10
GoComics.com/babyblues
KIRKMAN & SCOTT
©2022, BABY BLUES BROS LLC DIST. BY ANDREWS McMEEL SYNDICATION
I DON'T SEE ANYTHING.
WE DIDN'T SAY IT WAS ON OUR ROOF.

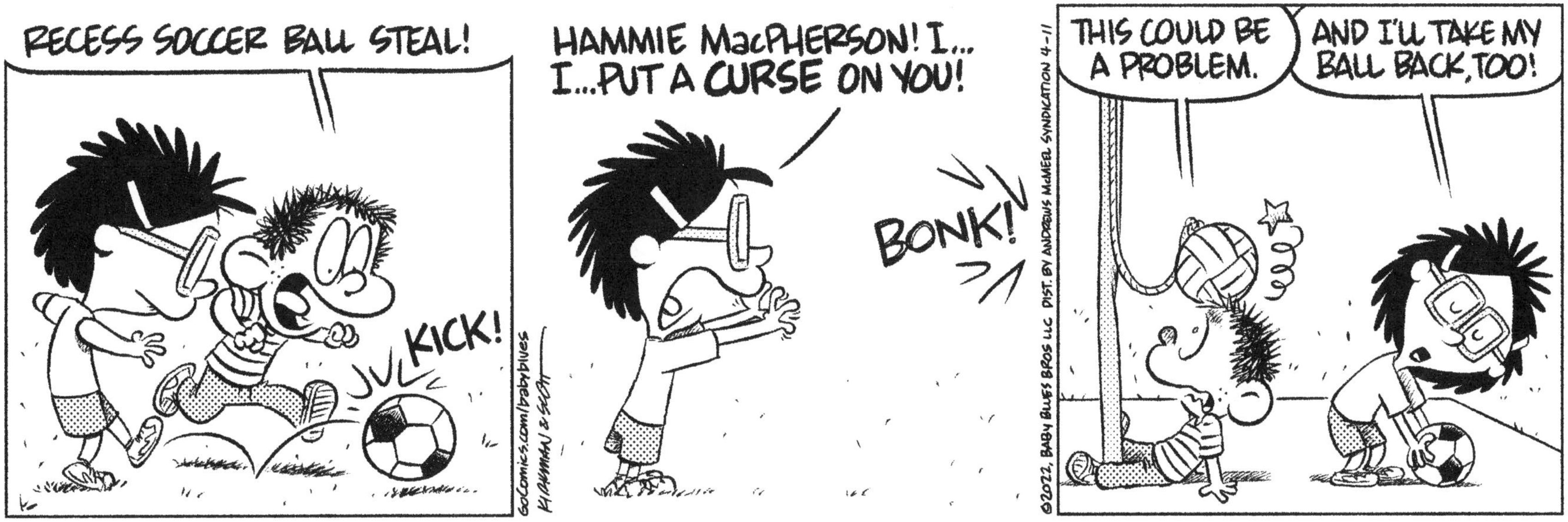
RECESS SOCCER BALL STEAL!
KICK!
GoComics.com/babyblues
KIRKMAN & SCOTT
HAMMIE MacPHERSON! I... I...PUT A CURSE ON YOU!
BONK!
©2022, BABY BLUES BROS LLC DIST. BY ANDREWS McMEEL SYNDICATION 4-11
THIS COULD BE A PROBLEM.
AND I'LL TAKE MY BALL BACK, TOO!

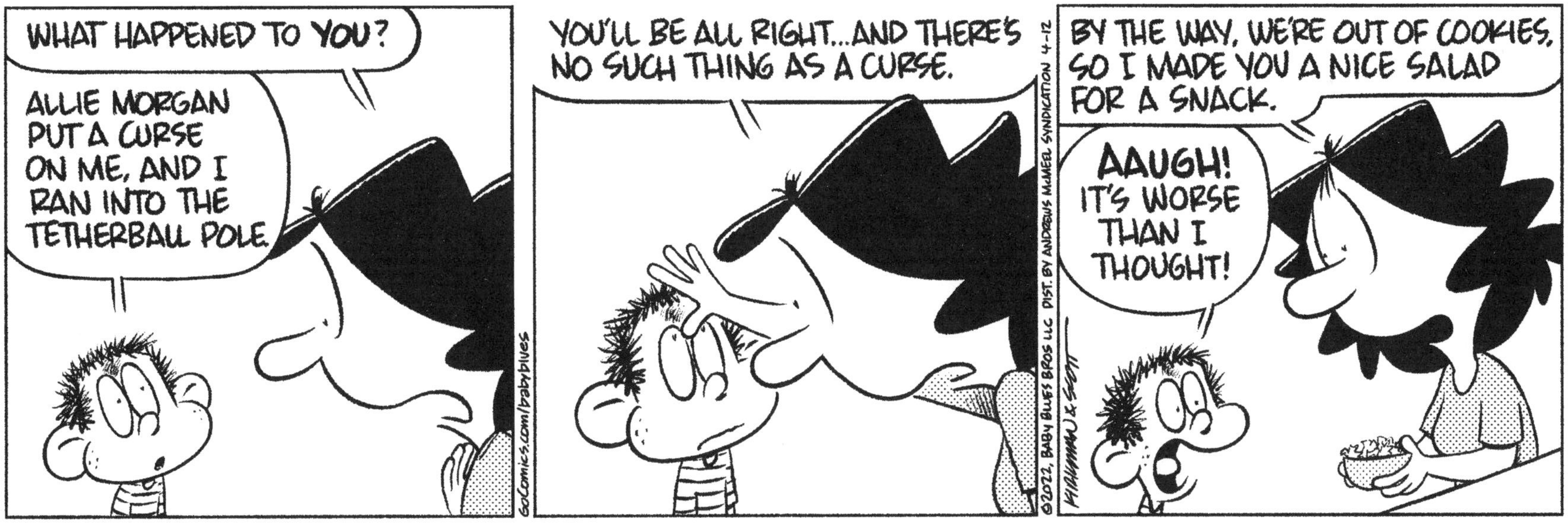
WHAT HAPPENED TO YOU?
ALLIE MORGAN PUT A CURSE ON ME, AND I RAN INTO THE TETHERBALL POLE.
GoComics.com/babyblues
YOU'LL BE ALL RIGHT...AND THERE'S NO SUCH THING AS A CURSE.
©2022, BABY BLUES BROS LLC DIST. BY ANDREWS McMEEL SYNDICATION 4-12
KIRKMAN & SCOTT
BY THE WAY, WE'RE OUT OF COOKIES, SO I MADE YOU A NICE SALAD FOR A SNACK.
AAUGH! IT'S WORSE THAN I THOUGHT!

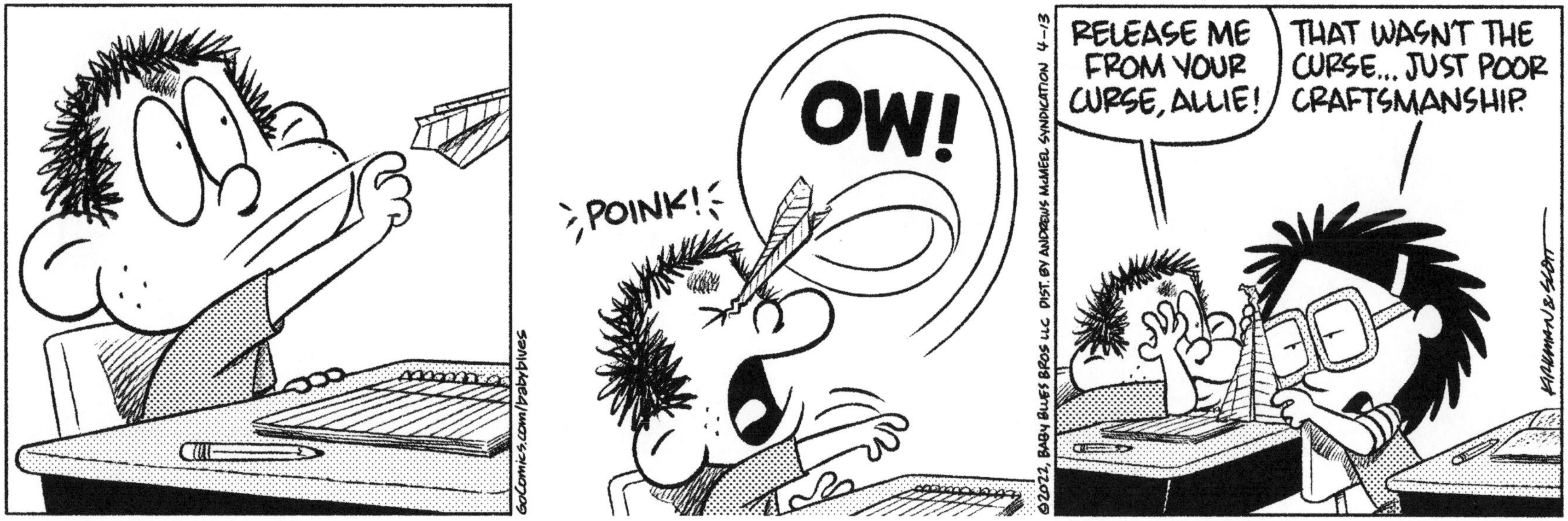
POINK!
OW!
RELEASE ME FROM YOUR CURSE, ALLIE!
THAT WASN'T THE CURSE... JUST POOR CRAFTSMANSHIP.
GoComics.com/babyblues
©2022, BABY BLUES BROS LLC DIST. BY ANDREWS McMEEL SYNDICATION 4-13
KIRKMAN & SCOTT

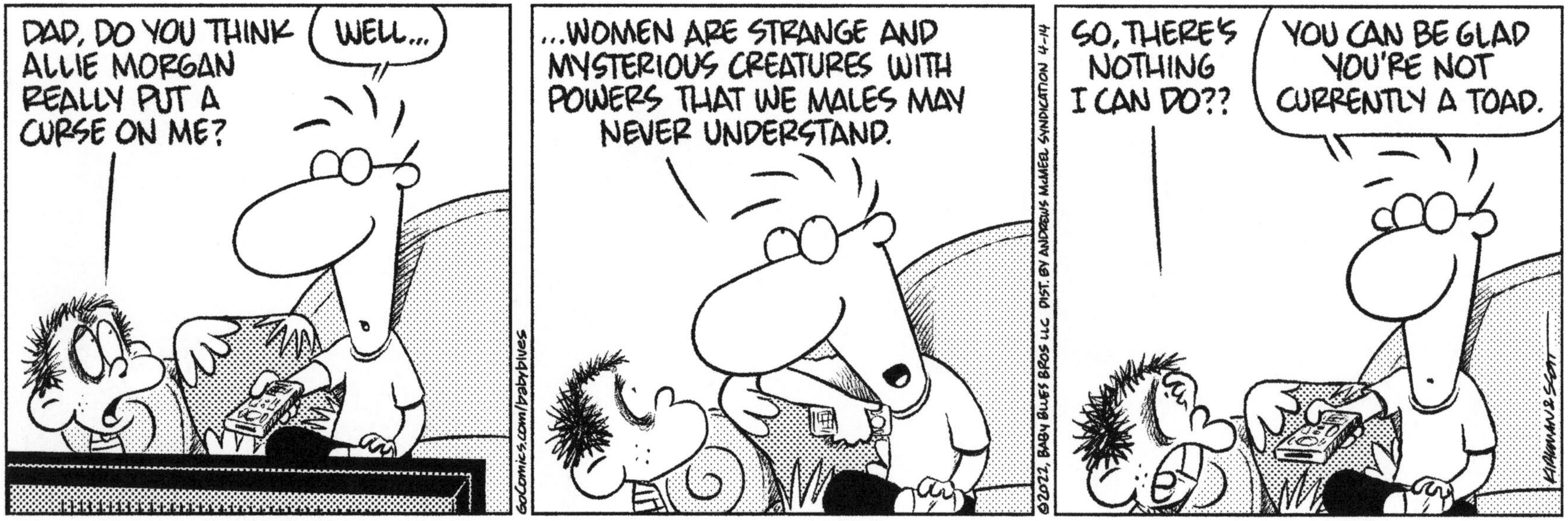
DAD, DO YOU THINK ALLIE MORGAN REALLY PUT A CURSE ON ME?
WELL...
...WOMEN ARE STRANGE AND MYSTERIOUS CREATURES WITH POWERS THAT WE MALES MAY NEVER UNDERSTAND.
SO, THERE'S NOTHING I CAN DO??
YOU CAN BE GLAD YOU'RE NOT CURRENTLY A TOAD.
GoComics.com/babyblues
©2022, BABY BLUES BROS LLC DIST. BY ANDREWS McMEEL SYNDICATION 4-14
KIRKMAN & SCOTT

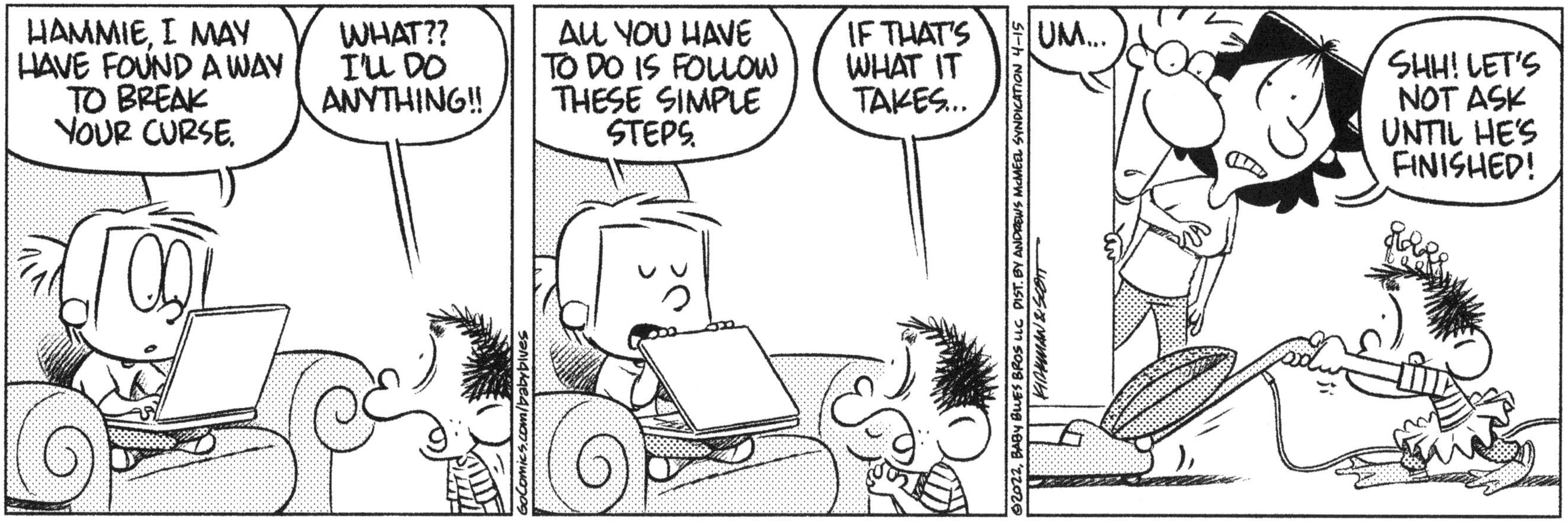
HAMMIE, I MAY HAVE FOUND A WAY TO BREAK YOUR CURSE.
WHAT?? I'LL DO ANYTHING!!
GoComics.com/babyblues
ALL YOU HAVE TO DO IS FOLLOW THESE SIMPLE STEPS.
IF THAT'S WHAT IT TAKES...
©2022, BABY BLUES BROS LLC DIST. BY ANDREWS McMEEL SYNDICATION 4-15
KIRKMAN & SCOTT
UM...
SHH! LET'S NOT ASK UNTIL HE'S FINISHED!

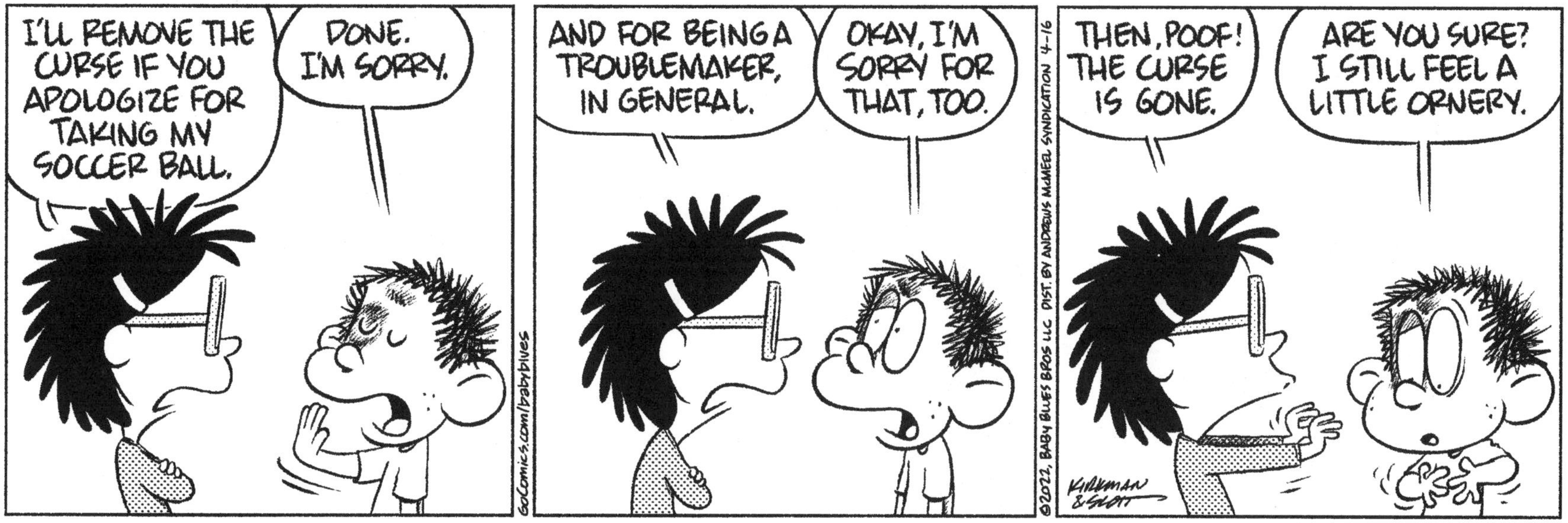
I'LL REMOVE THE CURSE IF YOU APOLOGIZE FOR TAKING MY SOCCER BALL.
DONE. I'M SORRY.
GoComics.com/babyblues
AND FOR BEING A TROUBLEMAKER, IN GENERAL.
OKAY, I'M SORRY FOR THAT, TOO.
©2022, BABY BLUES BROS LLC DIST. BY ANDREWS McMEEL SYNDICATION 4-16
KIRKMAN & SCOTT
THEN, POOF! THE CURSE IS GONE.
ARE YOU SURE? I STILL FEEL A LITTLE ORNERY.

I KNOW JUST WHERE I'M
GOING TO PUT THESE!

HAPPY EASTER, MOM!
TULIPS! I LOVE TULIPS!
GoComics.com/babyblues
KISS! KISS! YOU'RE SUCH A DEAR! AND YOU'RE SUCH A DEAR!
©2022, BABY BLUES BROS LLC DIST. BY ANDREWS McMEEL SYNDICATION
I KNOW JUST WHERE I'M GOING TO PUT THESE!
HALF OF MY TULIPS ARE GONE!!
MAYBE A COUPLE OF "DEAR" GOT TO THEM...
KIRKMAN & SCOTT
4-17

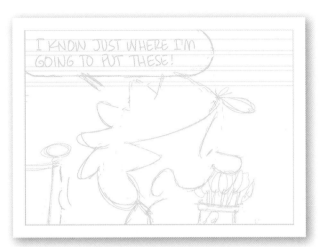

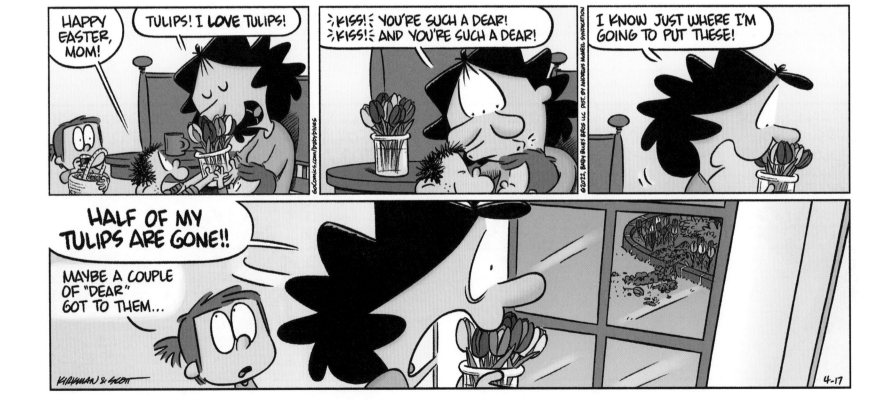

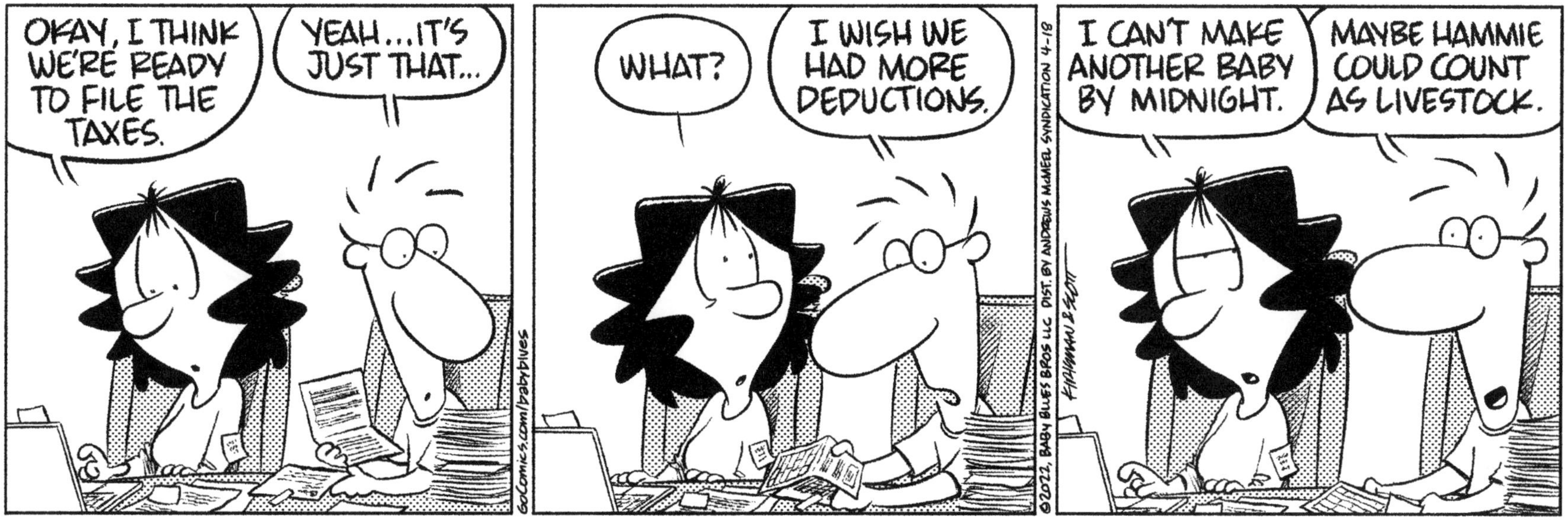
OKAY, I THINK WE'RE READY TO FILE THE TAXES.
YEAH...IT'S JUST THAT...
WHAT?
I WISH WE HAD MORE DEDUCTIONS.
I CAN'T MAKE ANOTHER BABY BY MIDNIGHT.
MAYBE HAMMIE COULD COUNT AS LIVESTOCK.
GoComics.com/babyblues
©2022, BABY BLUES BROS LLC DIST. BY ANDREWS McMEEL SYNDICATION 4-18
KIRKMAN & SCOTT

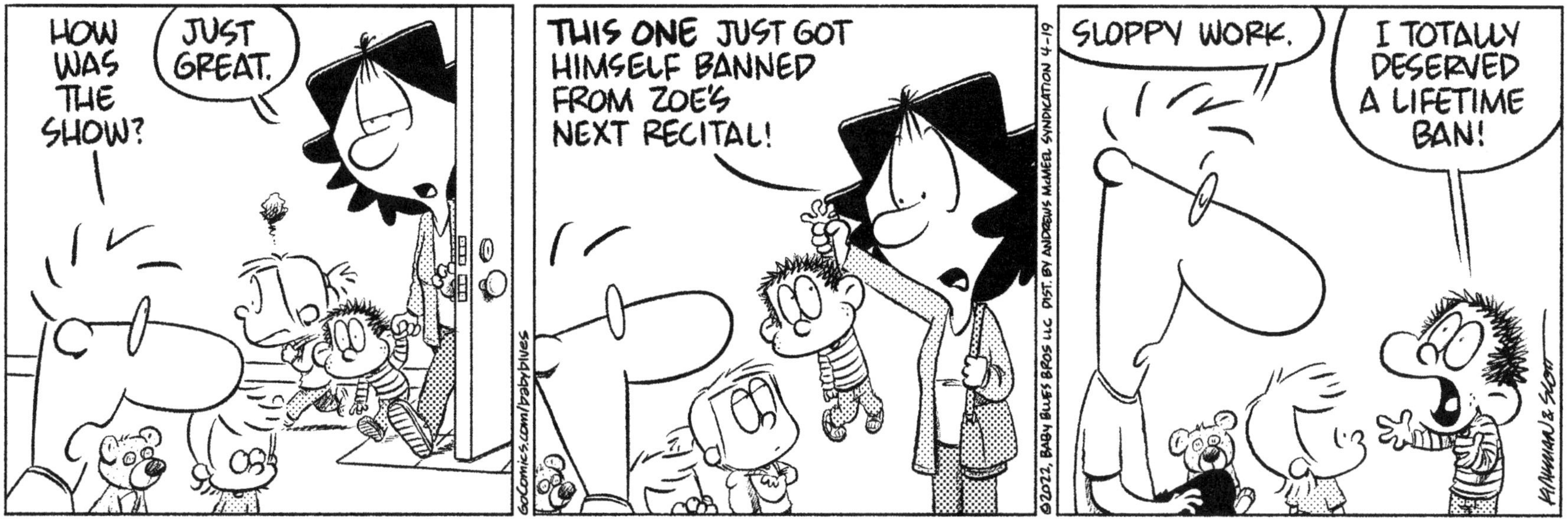
HOW WAS THE SHOW?
JUST GREAT.
THIS ONE JUST GOT HIMSELF BANNED FROM ZOE'S NEXT RECITAL!
SLOPPY WORK.
I TOTALLY DESERVED A LIFETIME BAN!
GoComics.com/babyblues
©2022, BABY BLUES BROS LLC DIST. BY ANDREWS McMEEL SYNDICATION 4-19
KIRKMAN & SCOTT

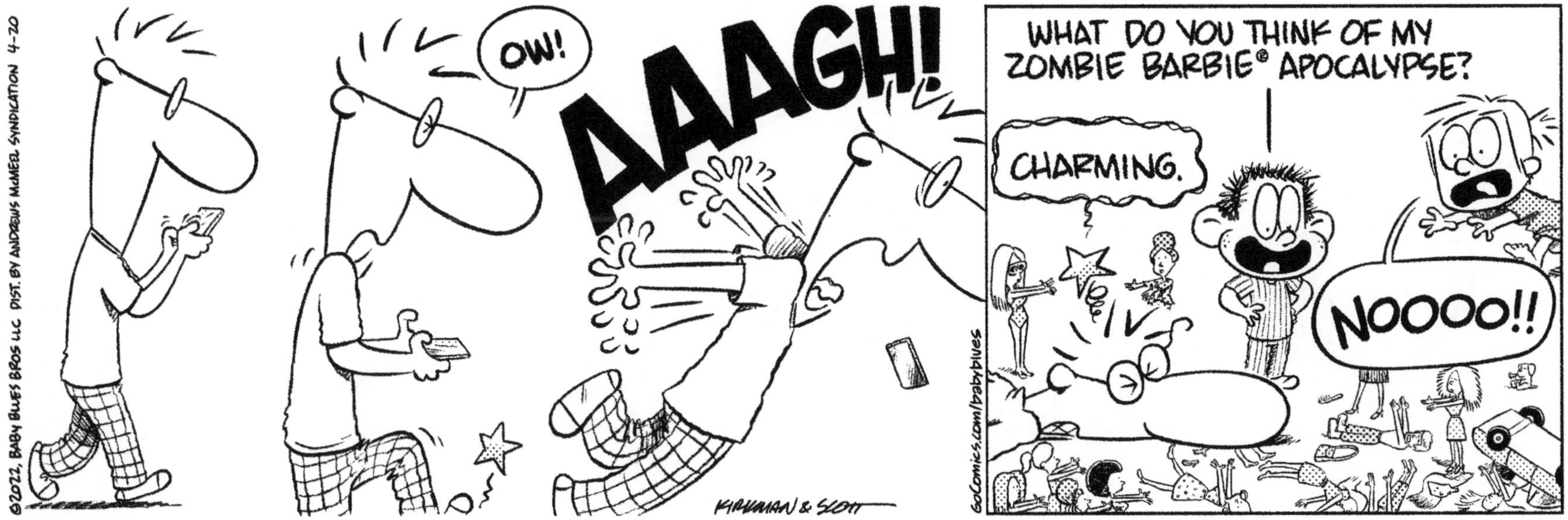
©2022, BABY BLUES BROS LLC DIST. BY ANDREWS McMEEL SYNDICATION 4-20
OW!
AAAGH!
KIRKMAN & SCOTT
GoComics.com/babyblues
WHAT DO YOU THINK OF MY ZOMBIE BARBIE® APOCALYPSE?
CHARMING.
NOOOO!!

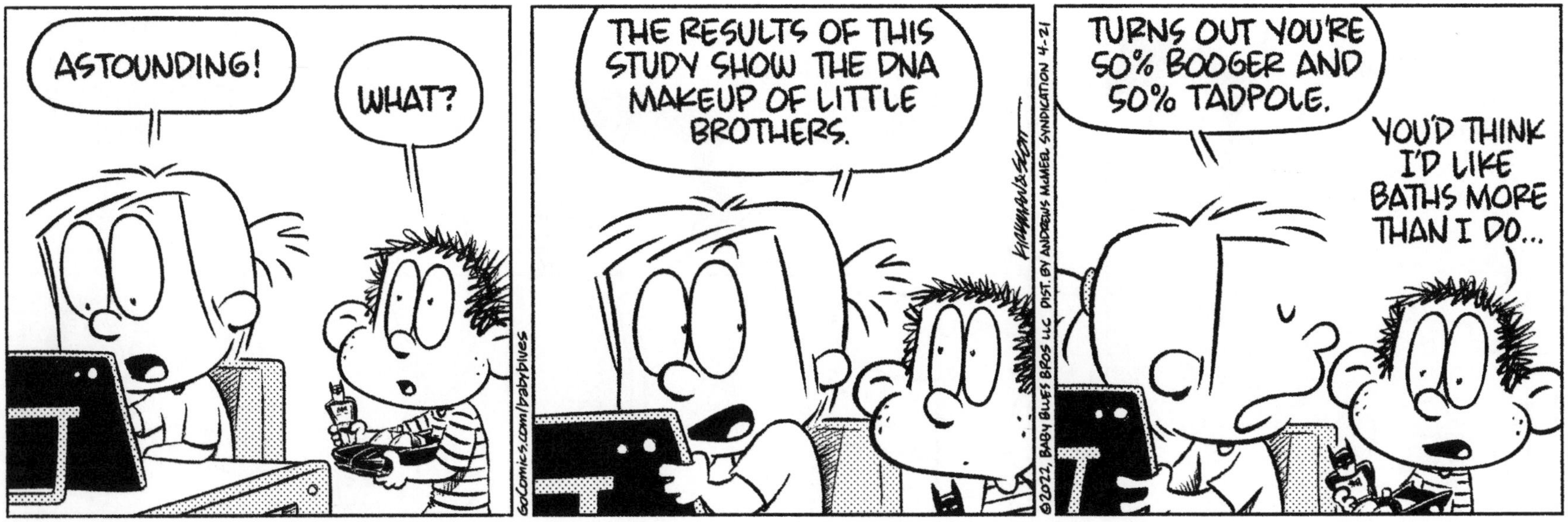
ASTOUNDING!
WHAT?
GoComics.com/babyblues
THE RESULTS OF THIS STUDY SHOW THE DNA MAKEUP OF LITTLE BROTHERS.
KIRKMAN & SCOTT
©2022, BABY BLUES BROS LLC DIST. BY ANDREWS McMEEL SYNDICATION 4-21
TURNS OUT YOU'RE 50% BOOGER AND 50% TADPOLE.
YOU'D THINK I'D LIKE BATHS MORE THAN I DO...

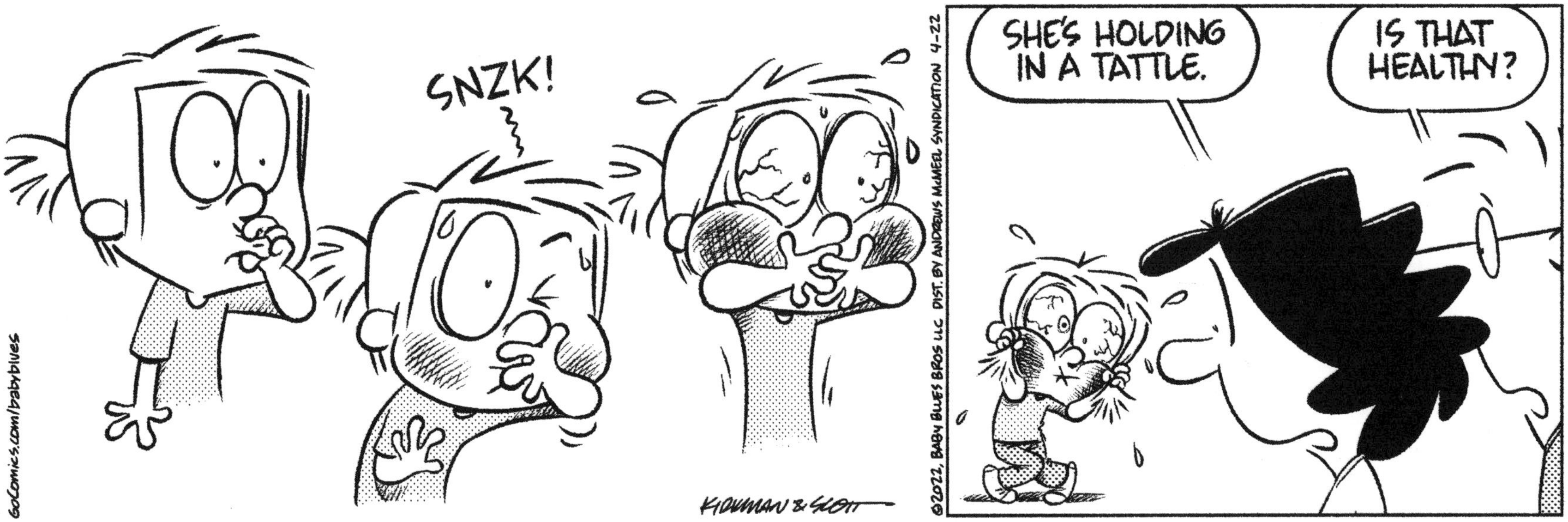
GoComics.com/babyblues
SNZK!
KIRKMAN & SCOTT
©2022, BABY BLUES BROS LLC DIST. BY ANDREWS McMEEL SYNDICATION 4-22
SHE'S HOLDING IN A TATTLE.
IS THAT HEALTHY?

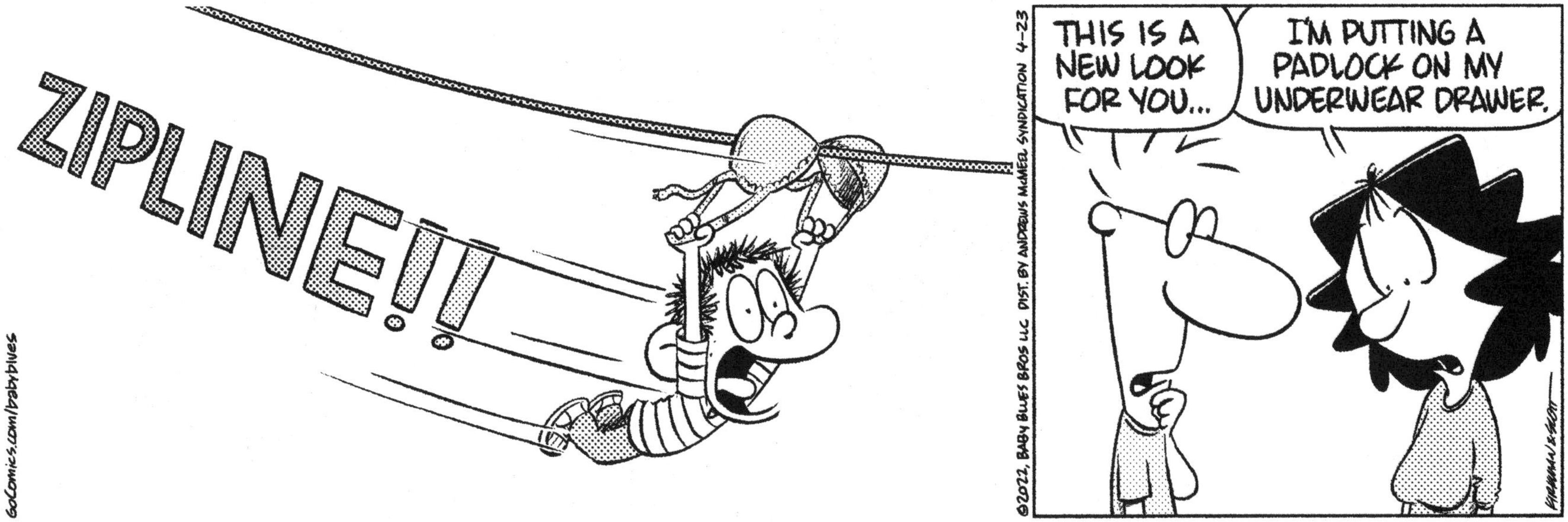
GoComics.com/babyblues
ZIPLINE!!
©2022, BABY BLUES BROS LLC DIST. BY ANDREWS McMEEL SYNDICATION 4-23
THIS IS A NEW LOOK FOR YOU...
I'M PUTTING A PADLOCK ON MY UNDERWEAR DRAWER.

OOH! YOU KNOW WHAT GOES GOOD WITH THIS? ALMONDS!
I'LL GO GET SOME.

I'M GOING TO THE KITCHEN. DO YOU WANT ANYTHING?
NO. I'LL JUST HAVE A NIBBLE OF WHATEVER YOU'RE HAVING.
4-24
GoComics.com/babyblues
WHAT DID YOU GET?
KETTLE CORN.
©2022, BABY BLUES BROS LLC DIST. BY ANDREWS McMEEL SYNDICATION
OOH! YOU KNOW WHAT GOES GOOD WITH THIS? ALMONDS!
I'LL GO GET SOME.
PLUS CINNAMON! AND CHOCOLATE CHIPS! AND A GLASS OF MILK!
AND SOME MORE KETTLE CORN?
NO, THANKS. I'M STUFFED.

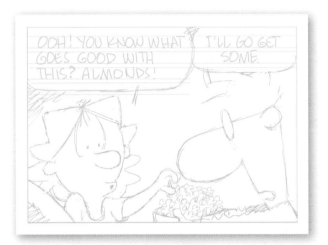

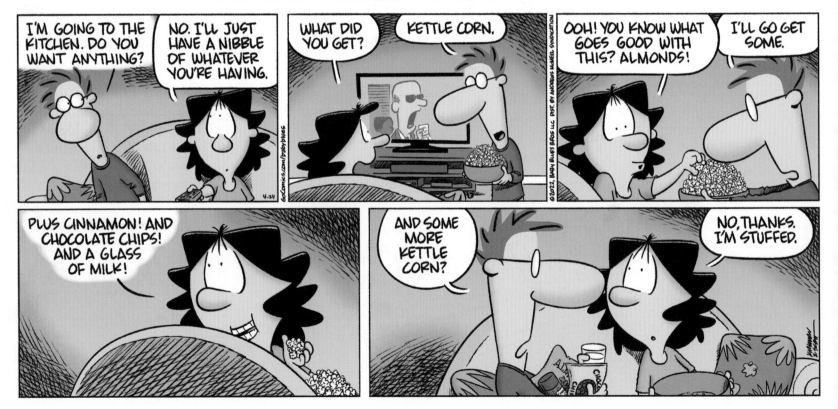

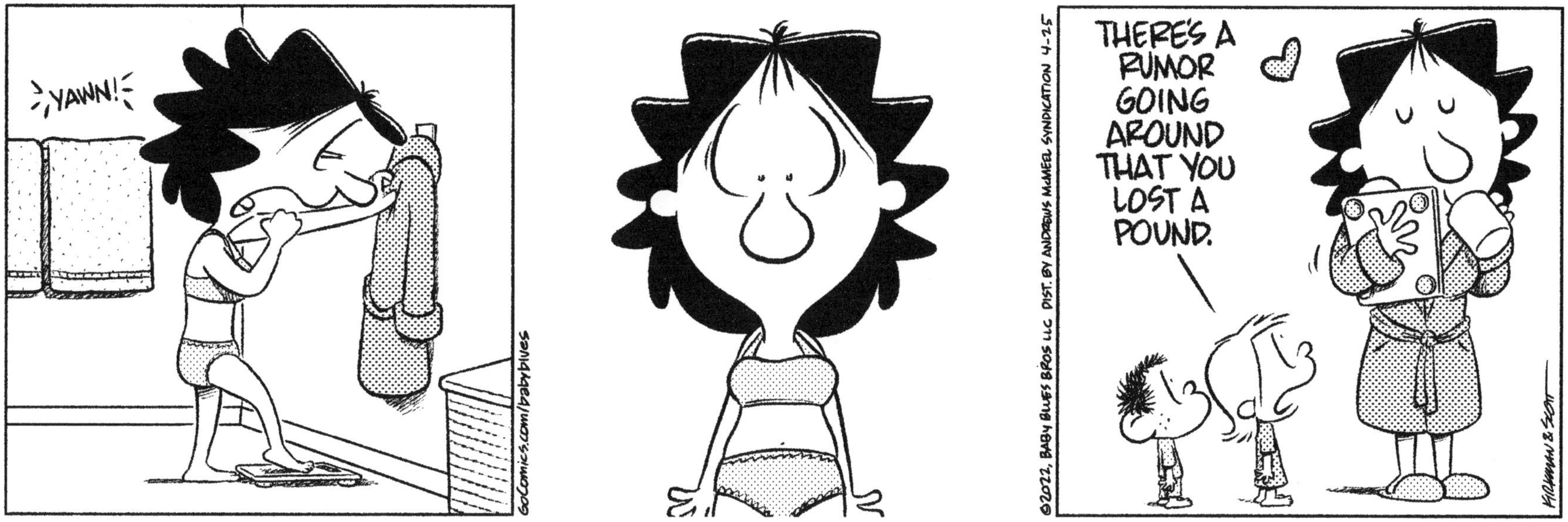
YAWN!
GoComics.com/babyblues
©2022, BABY BLUES BROS LLC DIST. BY ANDREWS McMEEL SYNDICATION 4-25
THERE'S A RUMOR GOING AROUND THAT YOU LOST A POUND.
KIRKMAN & SCOTT

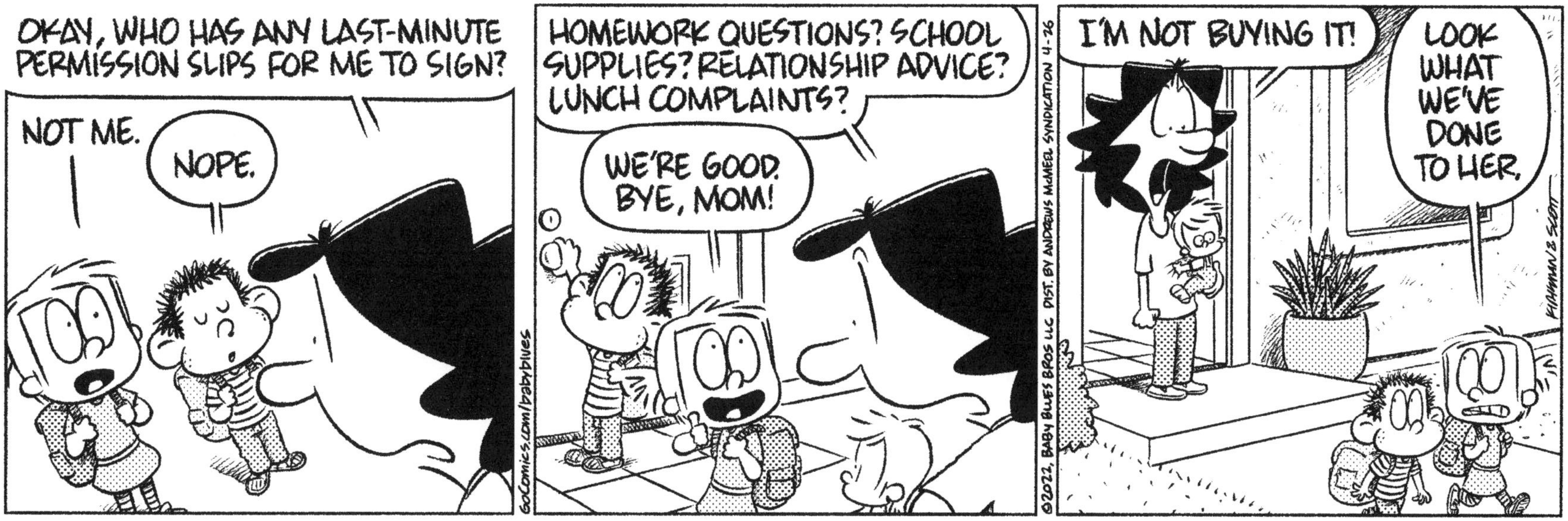
OKAY, WHO HAS ANY LAST-MINUTE PERMISSION SLIPS FOR ME TO SIGN?
NOT ME.
NOPE.
GoComics.com/babyblues
HOMEWORK QUESTIONS? SCHOOL SUPPLIES? RELATIONSHIP ADVICE? LUNCH COMPLAINTS?
WE'RE GOOD. BYE, MOM!
©2022, BABY BLUES BROS LLC DIST. BY ANDREWS McMEEL SYNDICATION 4-26
I'M NOT BUYING IT!
LOOK WHAT WE'VE DONE TO HER.
KIRKMAN & SCOTT

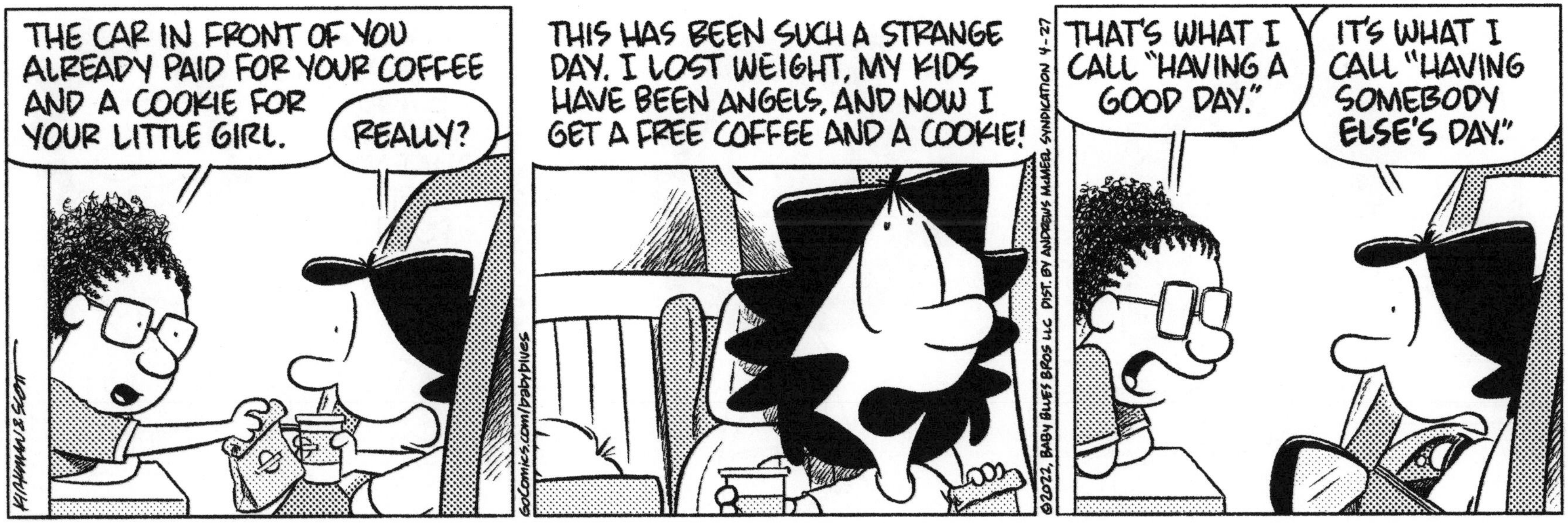
THE CAR IN FRONT OF YOU ALREADY PAID FOR YOUR COFFEE AND A COOKIE FOR YOUR LITTLE GIRL.
REALLY?
KIRKMAN & SCOTT
GoComics.com/babyblues
THIS HAS BEEN SUCH A STRANGE DAY. I LOST WEIGHT, MY KIDS HAVE BEEN ANGELS, AND NOW I GET A FREE COFFEE AND A COOKIE!
©2022, BABY BLUES BROS LLC DIST. BY ANDREWS McMEEL SYNDICATION 4-27
THAT'S WHAT I CALL "HAVING A GOOD DAY."
IT'S WHAT I CALL "HAVING SOMEBODY ELSE'S DAY."

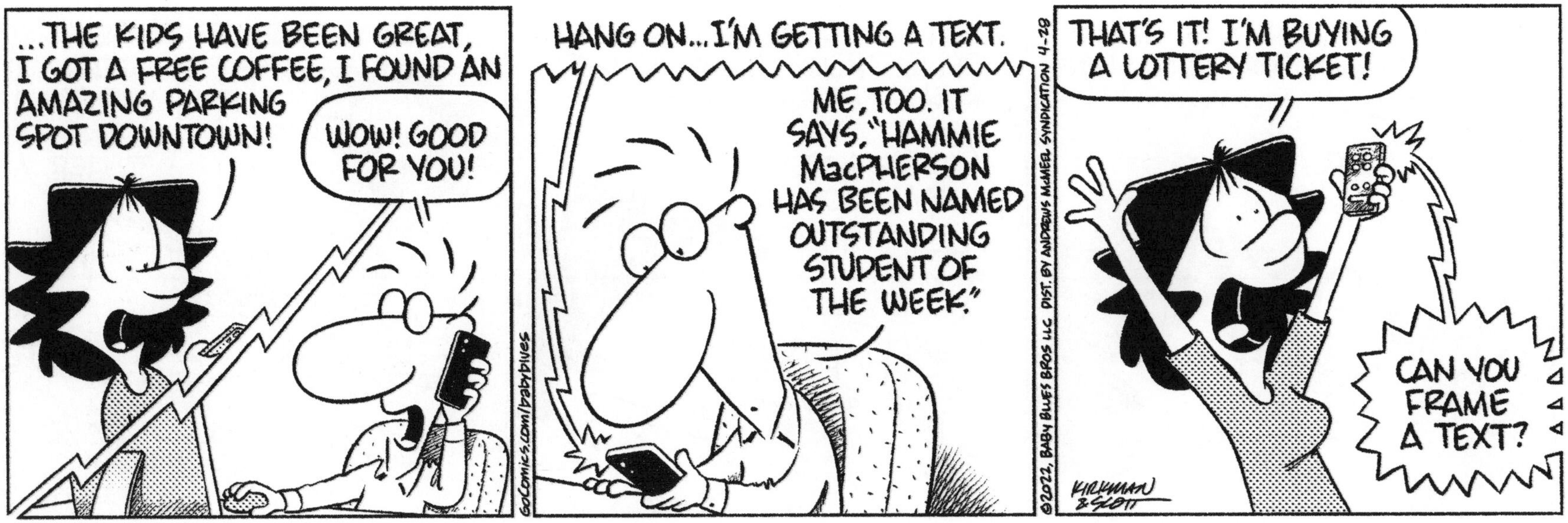
...THE KIDS HAVE BEEN GREAT, I GOT A FREE COFFEE, I FOUND AN AMAZING PARKING SPOT DOWNTOWN!
WOW! GOOD FOR YOU!
GoComics.com/babyblues
HANG ON... I'M GETTING A TEXT.
ME, TOO. IT SAYS, "HAMMIE MacPHERSON HAS BEEN NAMED OUTSTANDING STUDENT OF THE WEEK."
©2022, BABY BLUES BROS LLC DIST. BY ANDREWS McMEEL SYNDICATION 4-28
THAT'S IT! I'M BUYING A LOTTERY TICKET!
CAN YOU FRAME A TEXT?
KIRKMAN & SCOTT

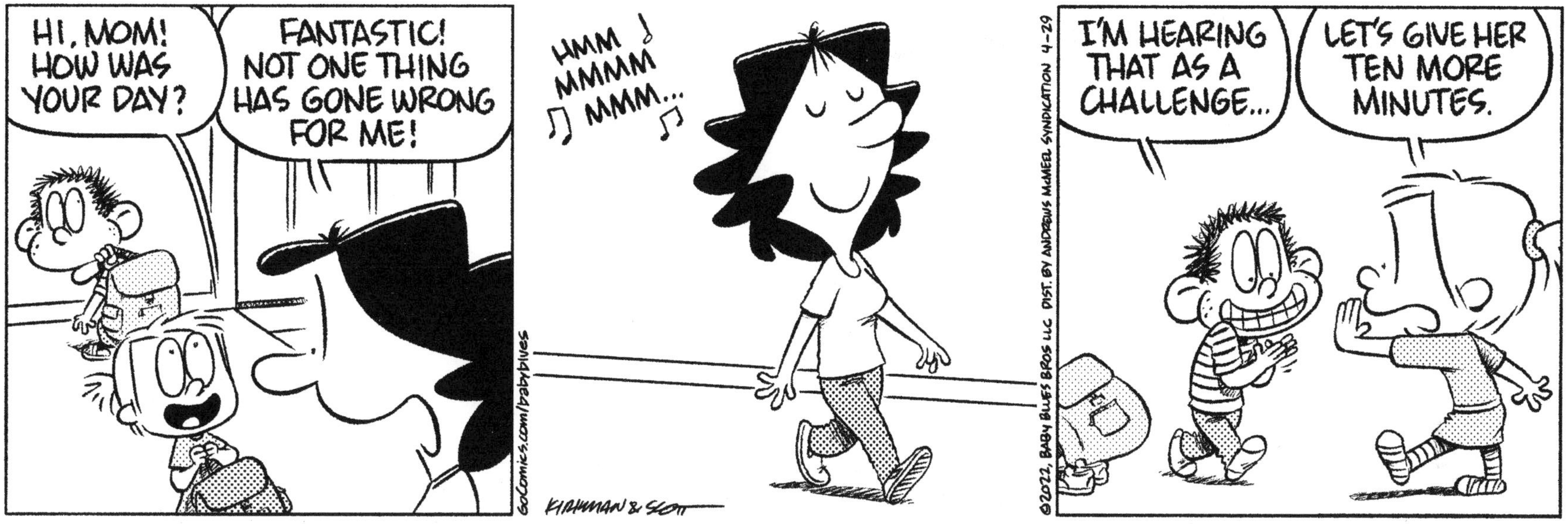
HI, MOM! HOW WAS YOUR DAY?
FANTASTIC! NOT ONE THING HAS GONE WRONG FOR ME!
HMM MMMM MMM...
I'M HEARING THAT AS A CHALLENGE...
LET'S GIVE HER TEN MORE MINUTES.
KIRKMAN & SCOTT
GoComics.com/babyblues
©2022, BABY BLUES BROS LLC DIST. BY ANDREWS McMEEL SYNDICATION 4-29

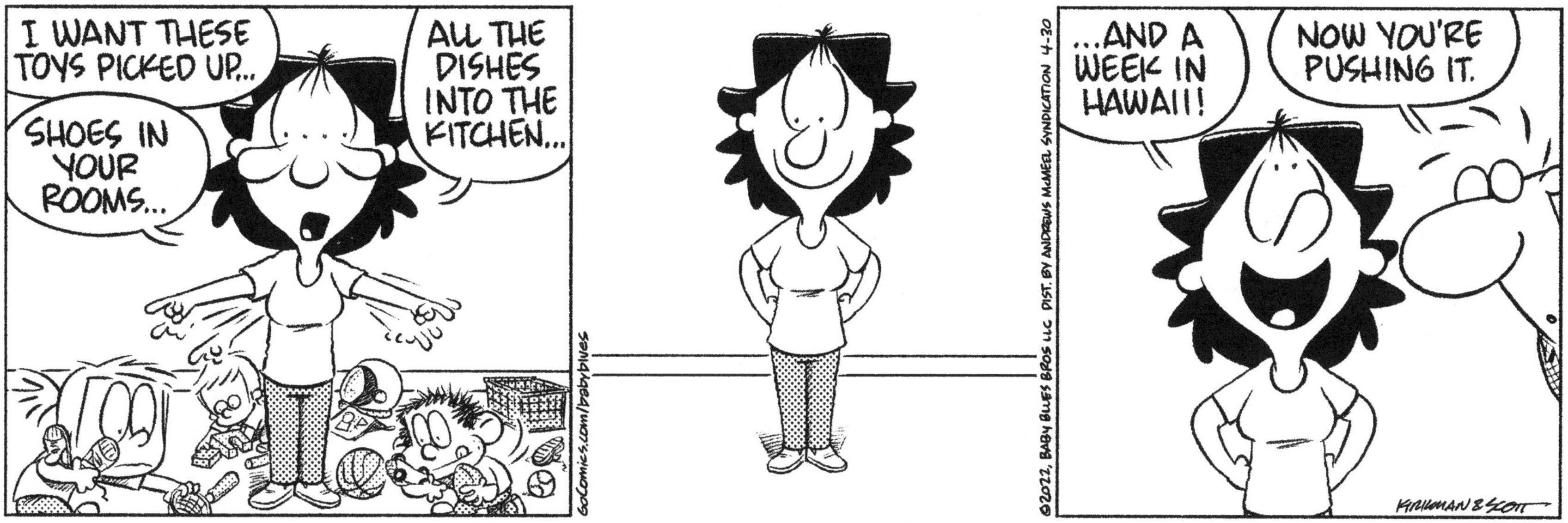
I WANT THESE TOYS PICKED UP...
SHOES IN YOUR ROOMS...
ALL THE DISHES INTO THE KITCHEN...
...AND A WEEK IN HAWAII!
NOW YOU'RE PUSHING IT.
KIRKMAN & SCOTT
GoComics.com/babyblues
©2022, BABY BLUES BROS LLC DIST. BY ANDREWS McMEEL SYNDICATION 4-30

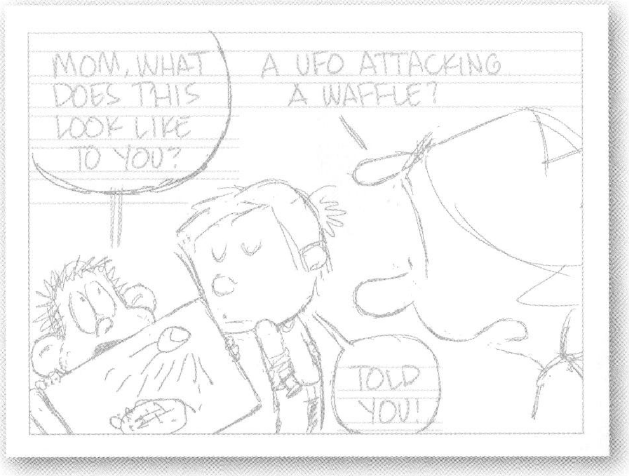
MOM, WHAT DOES THIS LOOK LIKE TO YOU?
A UFO ATTACKING A WAFFLE?
TOLD YOU!

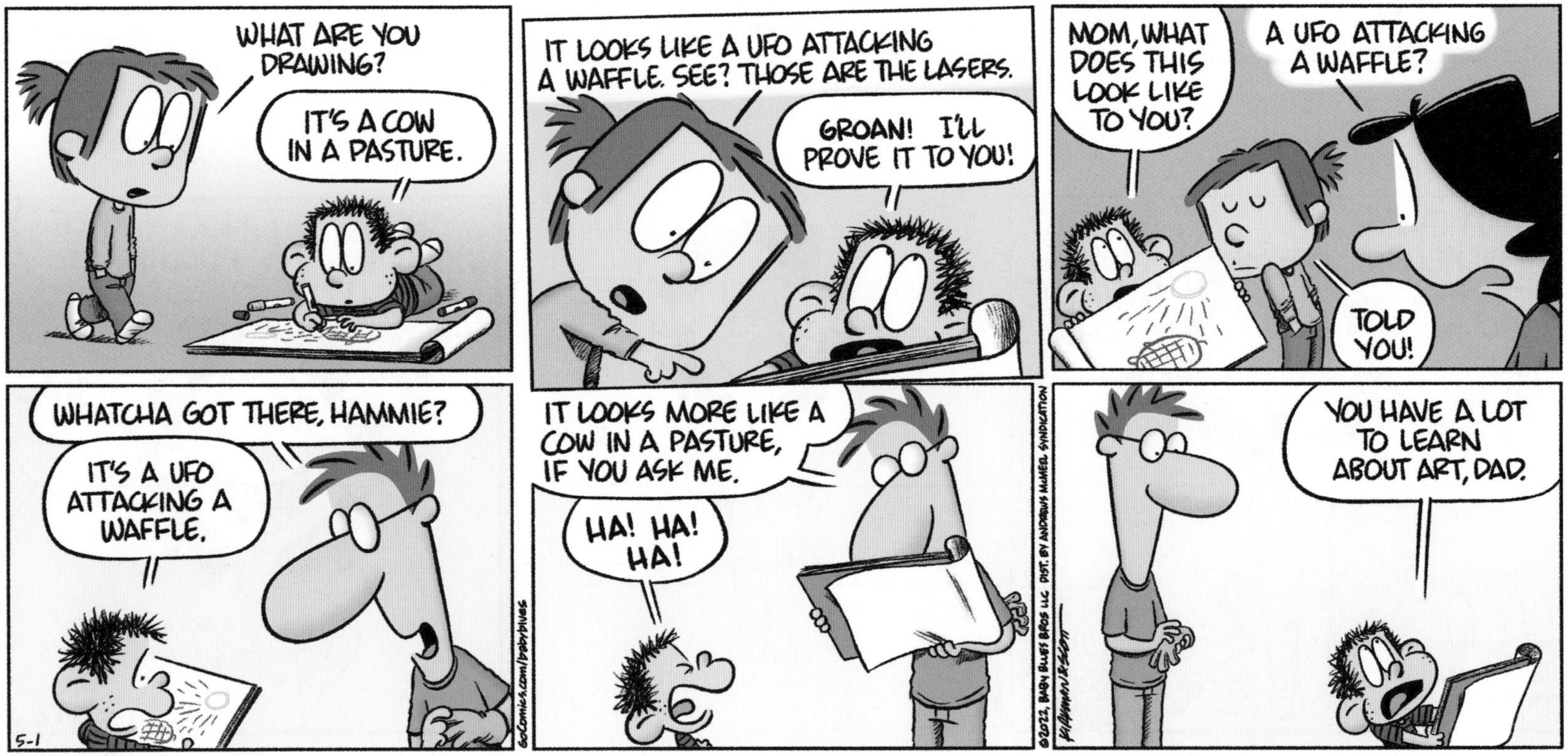
WHAT ARE YOU DRAWING?
IT'S A COW IN A PASTURE.
IT LOOKS LIKE A UFO ATTACKING A WAFFLE. SEE? THOSE ARE THE LASERS.
GROAN! I'LL PROVE IT TO YOU!
MOM, WHAT DOES THIS LOOK LIKE TO YOU?
A UFO ATTACKING A WAFFLE?
TOLD YOU!
WHATCHA GOT THERE, HAMMIE?
IT'S A UFO ATTACKING A WAFFLE.
5-1
GoComics.com/babyblues
IT LOOKS MORE LIKE A COW IN A PASTURE, IF YOU ASK ME.
HA! HA! HA!
©2022, BABY BLUES BROS LLC DIST. BY ANDREWS MCMEEL SYNDICATION
YOU HAVE A LOT TO LEARN ABOUT ART, DAD.

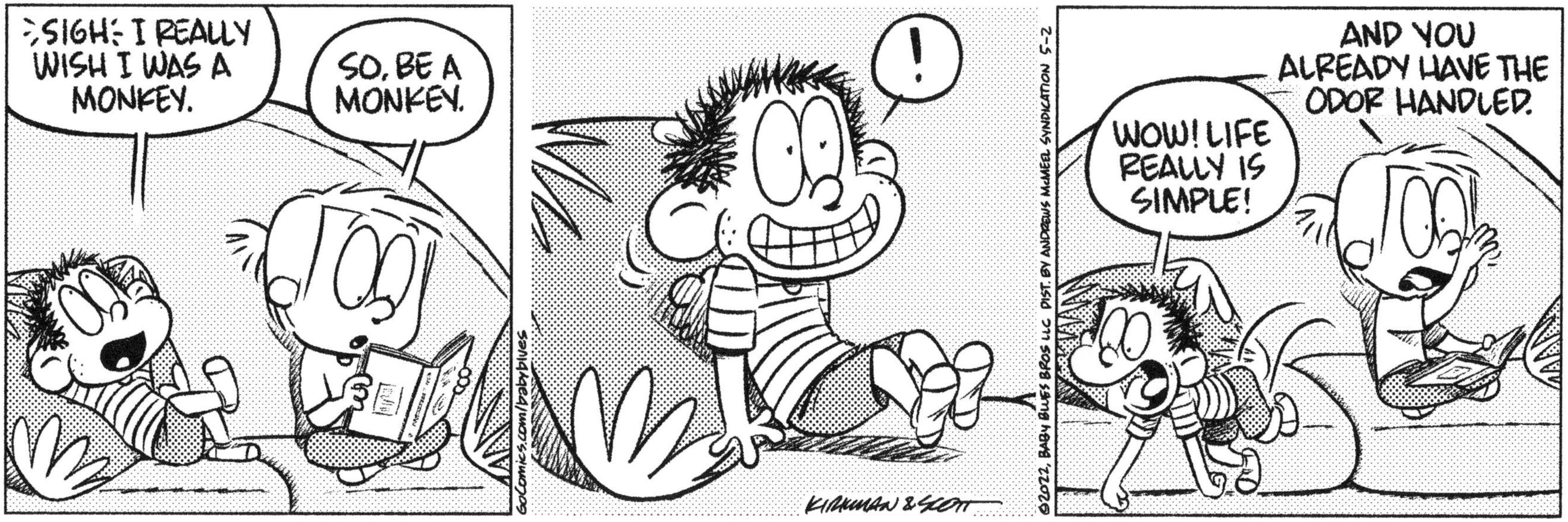
:SIGH: I REALLY WISH I WAS A MONKEY.
SO, BE A MONKEY.
!
WOW! LIFE REALLY IS SIMPLE!
AND YOU ALREADY HAVE THE ODOR HANDLED.
GoComics.com/babyblues
KIRKMAN & SCOTT
©2022, BABY BLUES BROS LLC DIST. BY ANDREWS McMEEL SYNDICATION 5-2

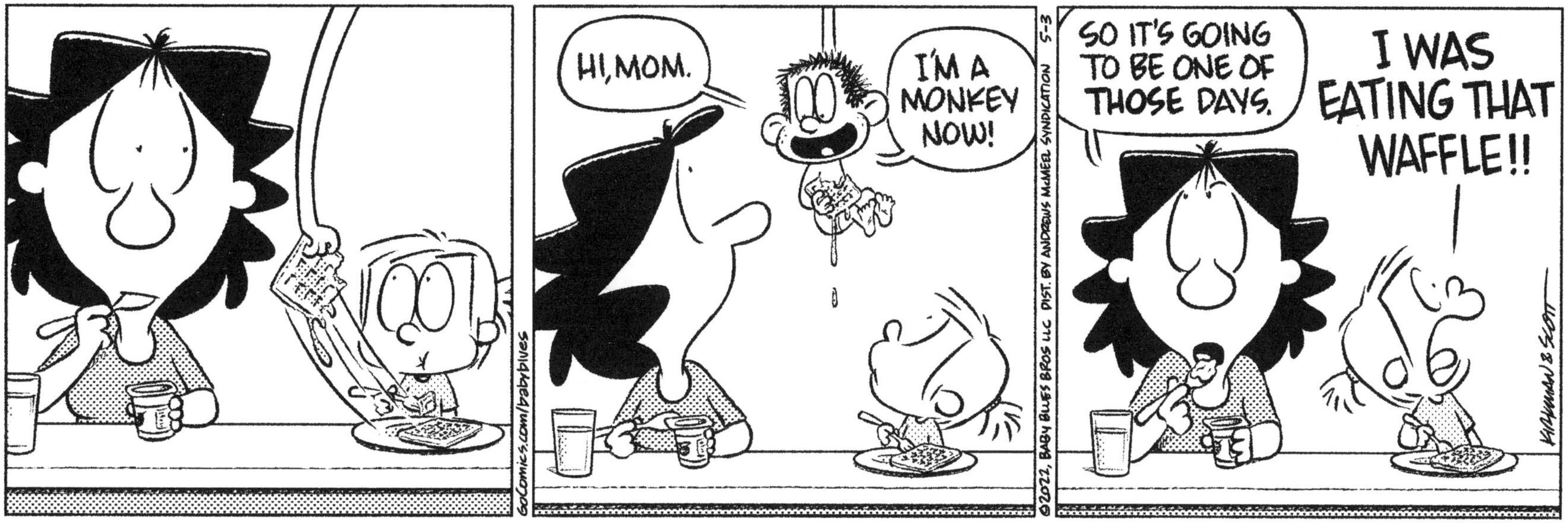
HI, MOM.
I'M A MONKEY NOW!
SO IT'S GOING TO BE ONE OF THOSE DAYS.
I WAS EATING THAT WAFFLE!!
GoComics.com/babyblues
©2022, BABY BLUES BROS LLC DIST. BY ANDREWS McMEEL SYNDICATION 5-3
KIRKMAN & SCOTT

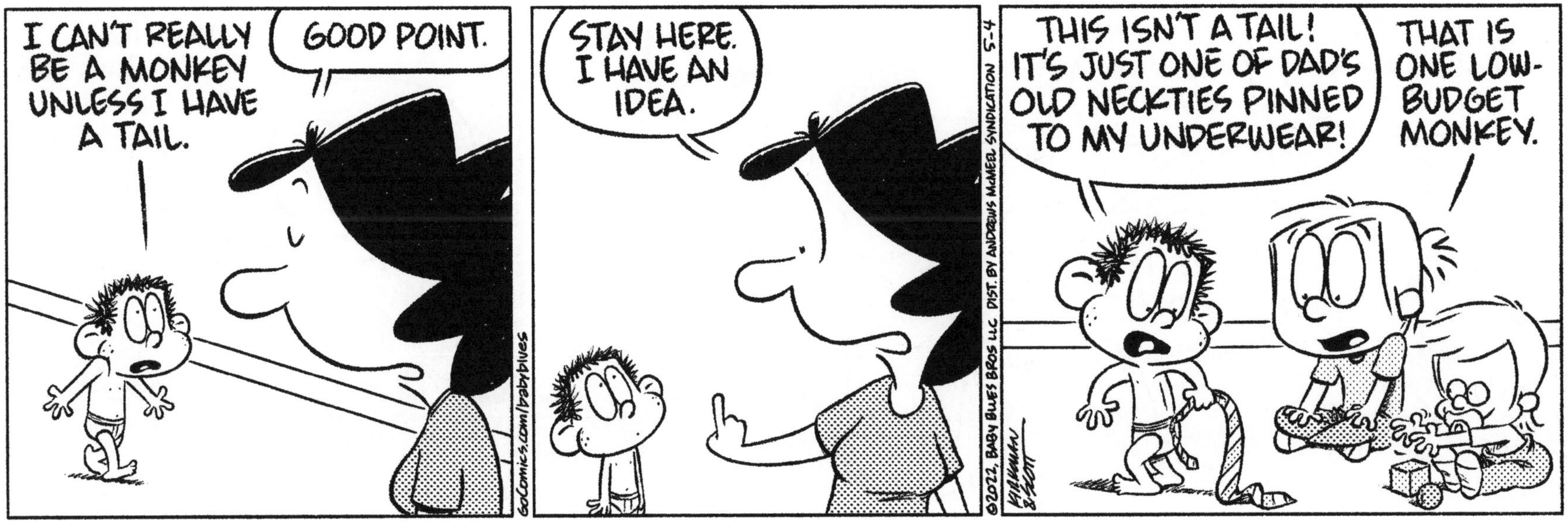
I CAN'T REALLY BE A MONKEY UNLESS I HAVE A TAIL.
GOOD POINT.
GoComics.com/babyblues
STAY HERE. I HAVE AN IDEA.
©2022, BABY BLUES BROS LLC DIST. BY ANDREWS McMEEL SYNDICATION 5-4
THIS ISN'T A TAIL! IT'S JUST ONE OF DAD'S OLD NECKTIES PINNED TO MY UNDERWEAR!
THAT IS ONE LOW-BUDGET MONKEY.
KIRKMAN & SCOTT

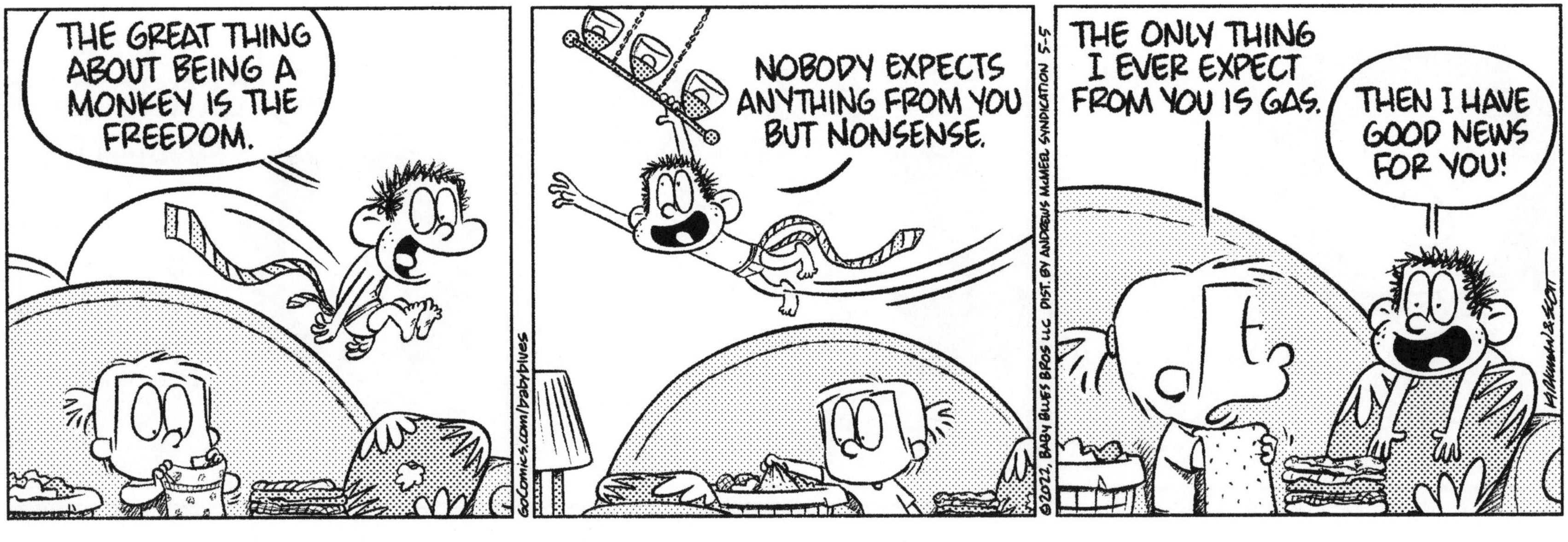
THE GREAT THING ABOUT BEING A MONKEY IS THE FREEDOM.
GoComics.com/babyblues
NOBODY EXPECTS ANYTHING FROM YOU BUT NONSENSE.
©2022, BABY BLUES BROS LLC DIST. BY ANDREWS McMEEL SYNDICATION 5-5
THE ONLY THING I EVER EXPECT FROM YOU IS GAS.
THEN I HAVE GOOD NEWS FOR YOU!
KIRKMAN & SCOTT

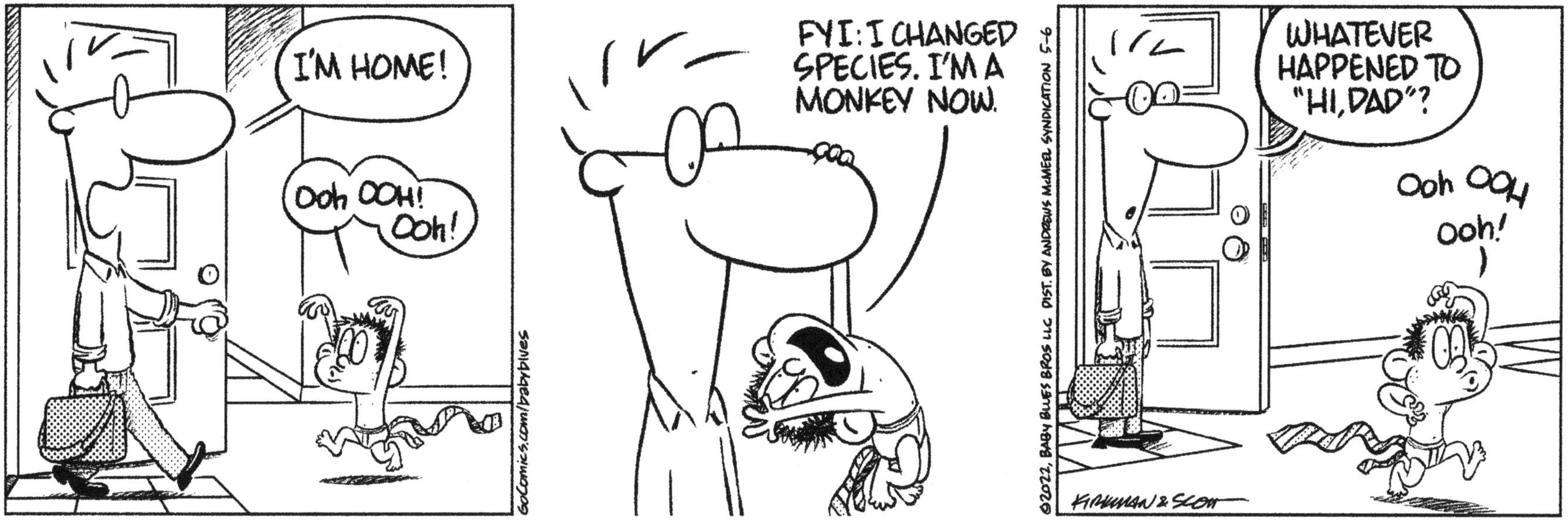
I'M HOME!
Ooh OOH! Ooh!
GoComics.com/babyblues
FYI: I CHANGED SPECIES. I'M A MONKEY NOW.
©2022, BABY BLUES BROS LLC. DIST. BY ANDREWS McMEEL SYNDICATION 5-6
WHATEVER HAPPENED TO "HI, DAD"?
Ooh OOH ooh!
KIRKMAN & SCOTT

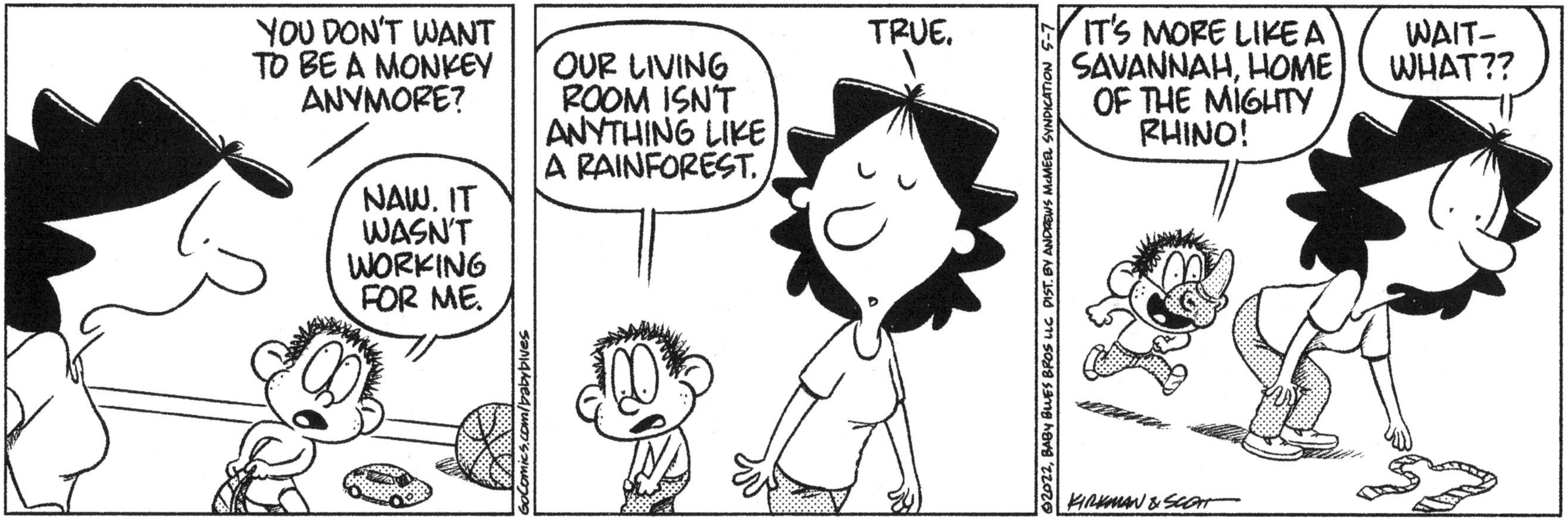
YOU DON'T WANT TO BE A MONKEY ANYMORE?
NAW. IT WASN'T WORKING FOR ME.
GoComics.com/babyblues
OUR LIVING ROOM ISN'T ANYTHING LIKE A RAINFOREST.
TRUE.
©2022, BABY BLUES BROS LLC. DIST. BY ANDREWS McMEEL SYNDICATION 5-7
IT'S MORE LIKE A SAVANNAH, HOME OF THE MIGHTY RHINO!
WAIT- WHAT??
KIRKMAN & SCOTT

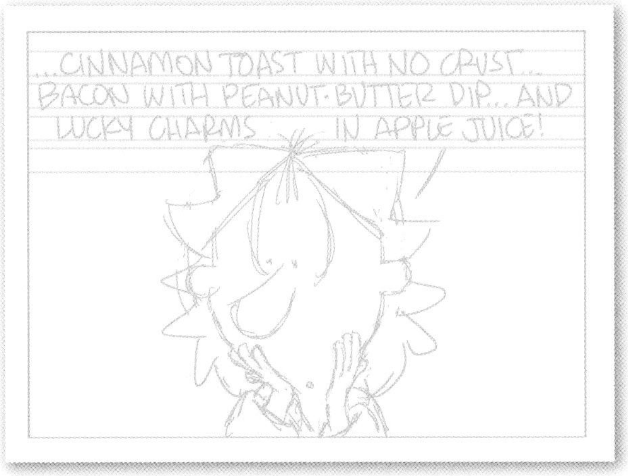
...CINNAMON TOAST WITH NO CRUST...
BACON WITH PEANUT-BUTTER DIP... AND
LUCKY CHARMS IN APPLE JUICE!

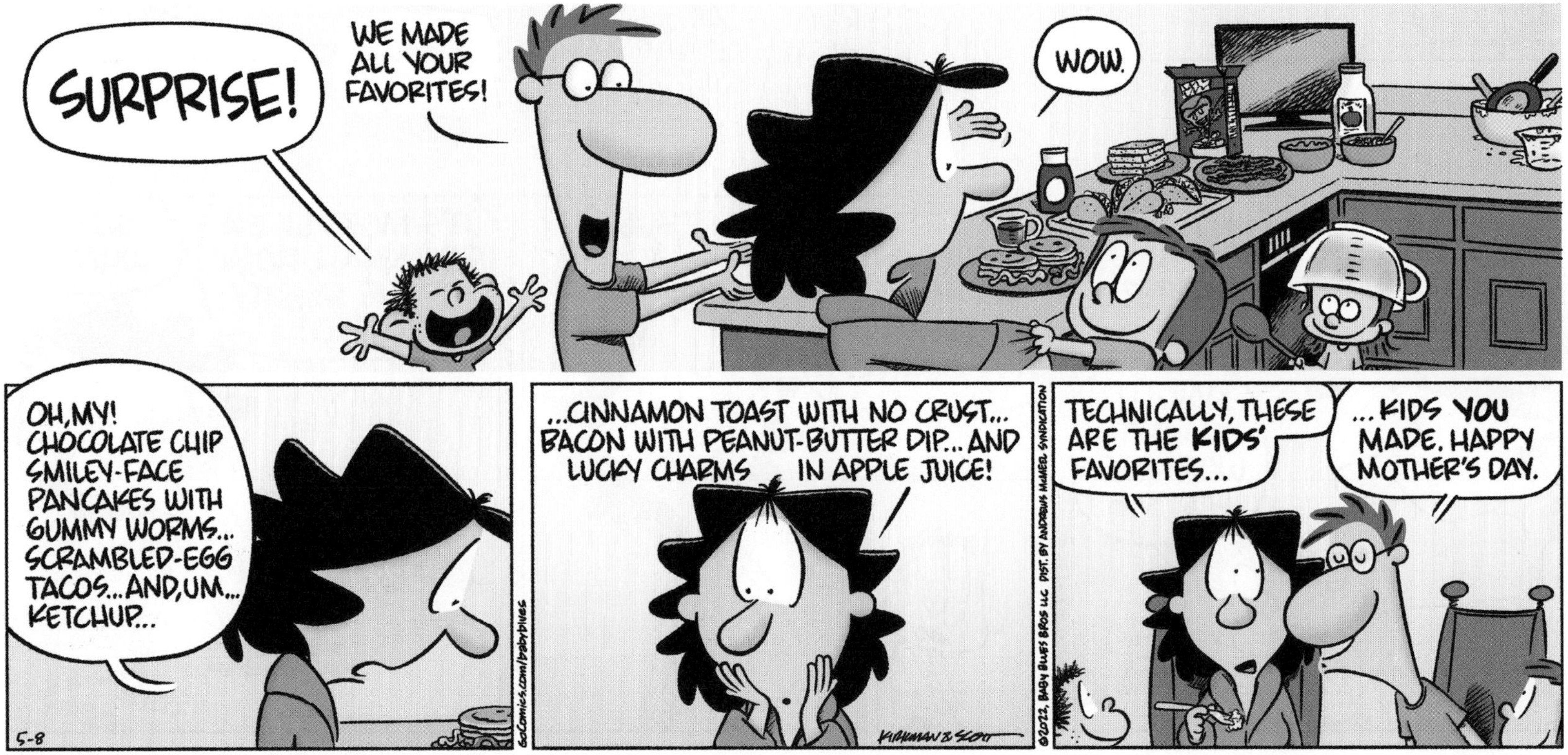
SURPRISE!
WE MADE ALL YOUR FAVORITES!
WOW.
OH, MY! CHOCOLATE CHIP SMILEY-FACE PANCAKES WITH GUMMY WORMS... SCRAMBLED-EGG TACOS... AND, UM... KETCHUP...
5-8
GoComics.com/babyblues
...CINNAMON TOAST WITH NO CRUST... BACON WITH PEANUT-BUTTER DIP... AND LUCKY CHARMS IN APPLE JUICE!
KIRKMAN & SCOTT
©2022, BABY BLUES BROS LLC DIST. BY ANDREWS MCMEEL SYNDICATION
TECHNICALLY, THESE ARE THE KIDS' FAVORITES...
...KIDS YOU MADE. HAPPY MOTHER'S DAY.

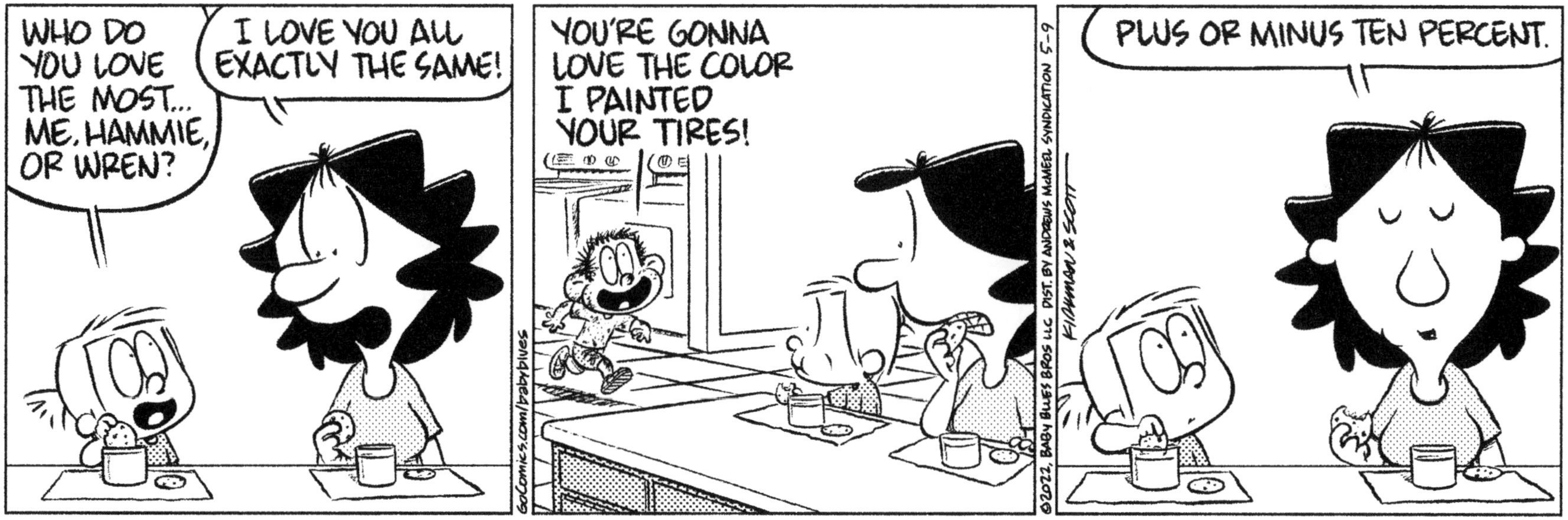
WHO DO YOU LOVE THE MOST... ME, HAMMIE, OR WREN?
I LOVE YOU ALL EXACTLY THE SAME!
GoComics.com/babyblues
YOU'RE GONNA LOVE THE COLOR I PAINTED YOUR TIRES!
5-9
©2022, BABY BLUES BROS LLC DIST. BY ANDREWS McMEEL SYNDICATION
KIRKMAN & SCOTT
PLUS OR MINUS TEN PERCENT.

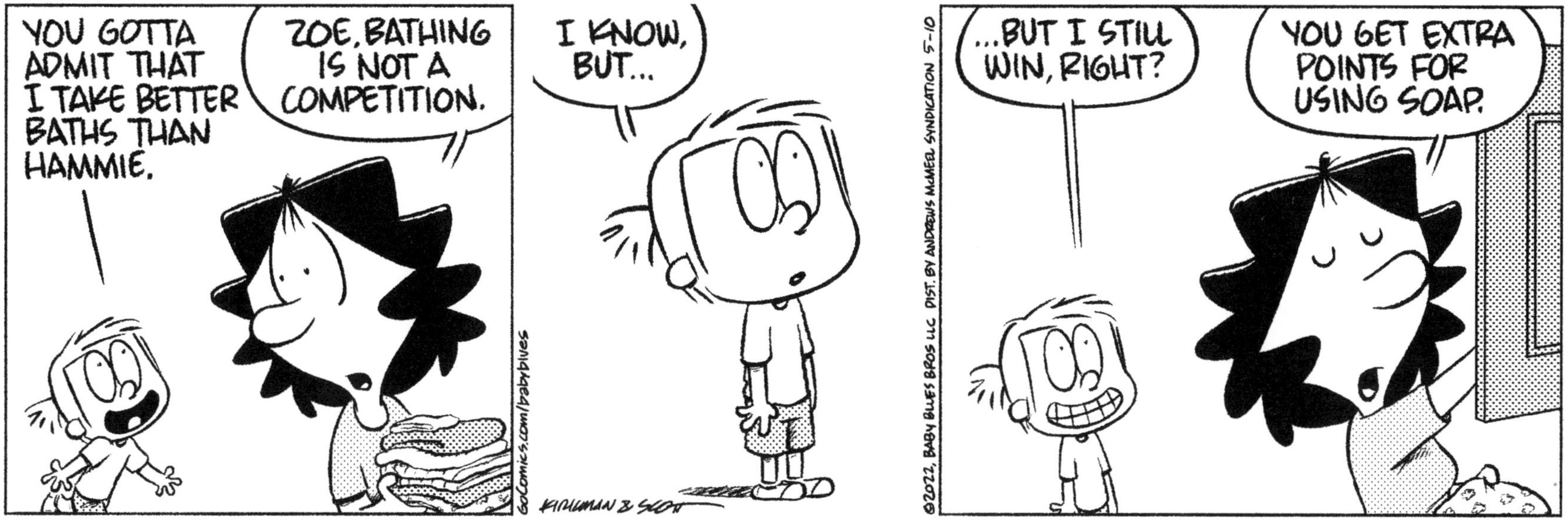
YOU GOTTA ADMIT THAT I TAKE BETTER BATHS THAN HAMMIE.
ZOE, BATHING IS NOT A COMPETITION.
GoComics.com/babyblues
I KNOW, BUT...
KIRKMAN & SCOTT
5-10
©2022, BABY BLUES BROS LLC DIST. BY ANDREWS McMEEL SYNDICATION
...BUT I STILL WIN, RIGHT?
YOU GET EXTRA POINTS FOR USING SOAP.

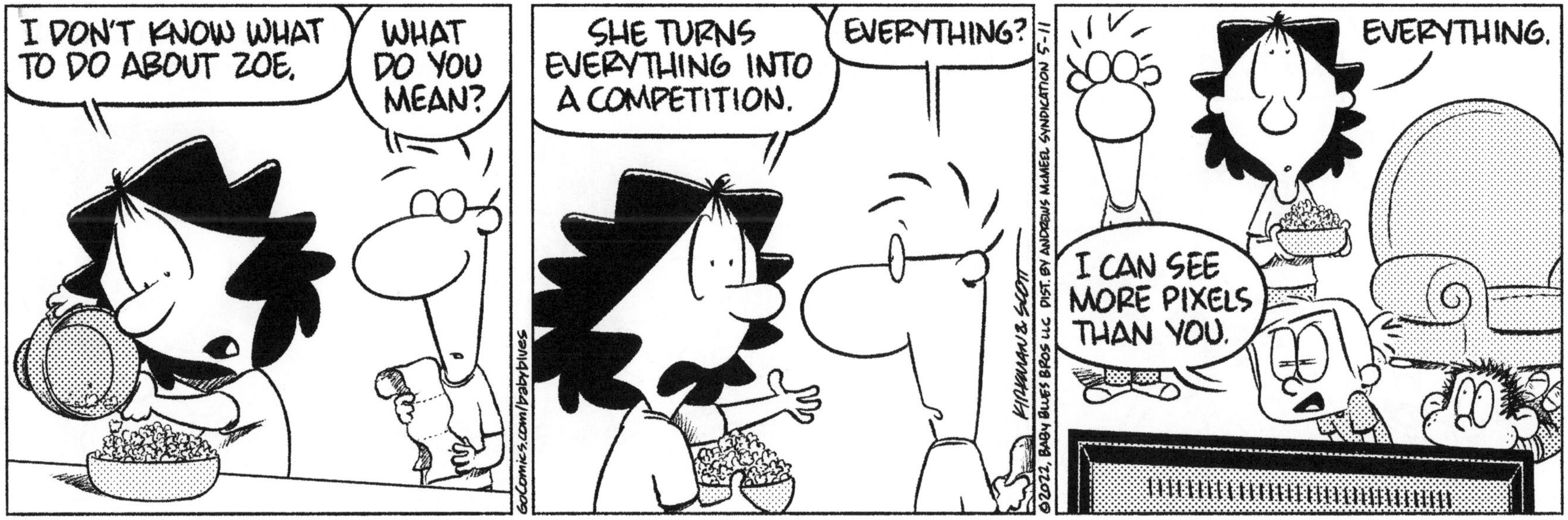
I DON'T KNOW WHAT TO DO ABOUT ZOE.
WHAT DO YOU MEAN?
GoComics.com/babyblues
SHE TURNS EVERYTHING INTO A COMPETITION.
EVERYTHING?
©2022, BABY BLUES BROS LLC DIST. BY ANDREWS McMEEL SYNDICATION 5-11
KIRKMAN & SCOTT
EVERYTHING.
I CAN SEE MORE PIXELS THAN YOU.

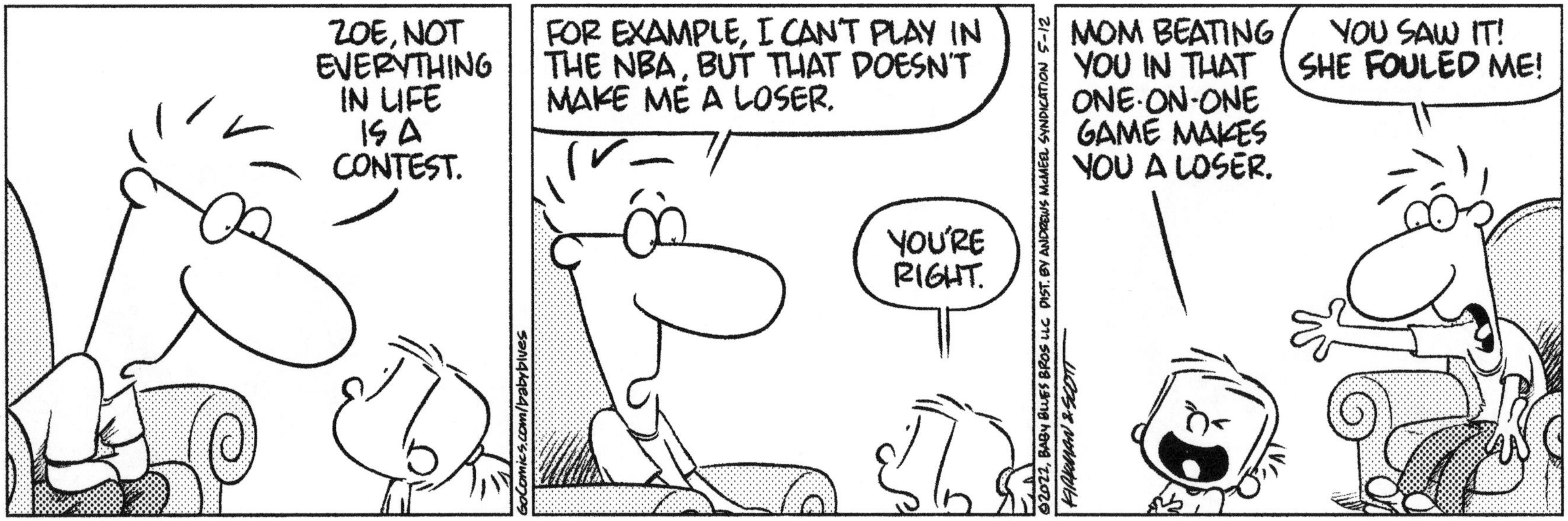
ZOE, NOT EVERYTHING IN LIFE IS A CONTEST.
GoComics.com/babyblues
FOR EXAMPLE, I CAN'T PLAY IN THE NBA, BUT THAT DOESN'T MAKE ME A LOSER.
YOU'RE RIGHT.
©2022, BABY BLUES BROS LLC DIST. BY ANDREWS McMEEL SYNDICATION 5-12
KIRKMAN & SCOTT
MOM BEATING YOU IN THAT ONE-ON-ONE GAME MAKES YOU A LOSER.
YOU SAW IT! SHE **FOULED** ME!

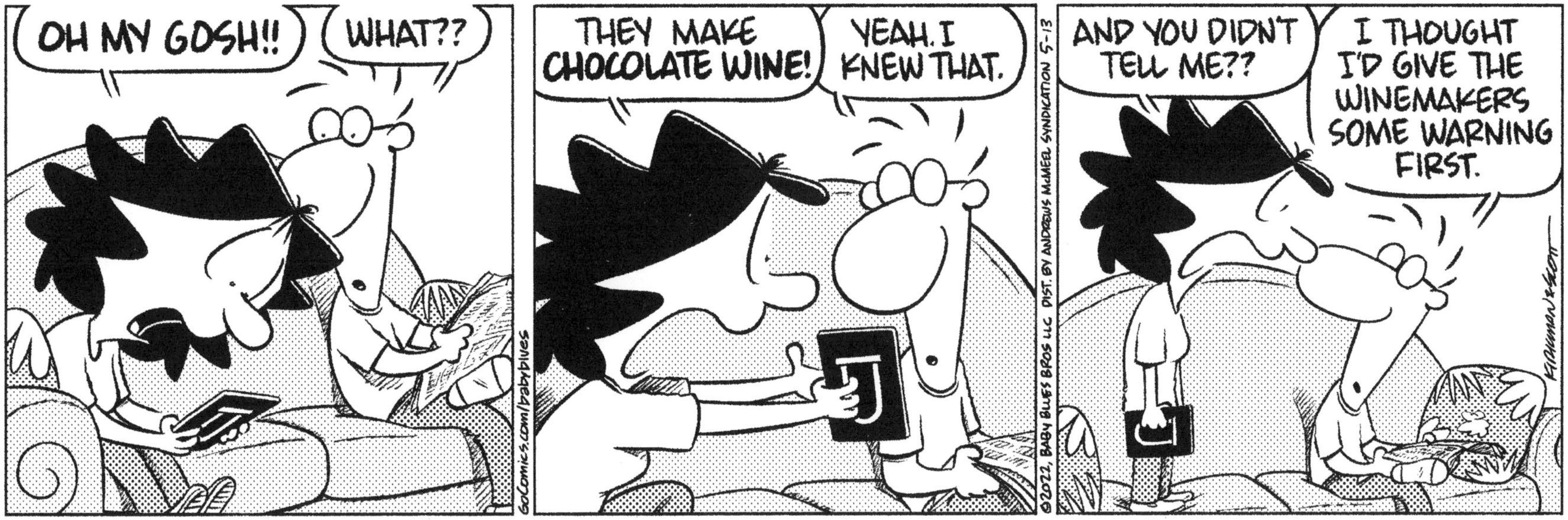
OH MY GOSH!!
WHAT??
GoComics.com/babyblues
THEY MAKE CHOCOLATE WINE!
YEAH. I KNEW THAT.
©2022, BABY BLUES BROS LLC DIST. BY ANDREWS McMEEL SYNDICATION 5-13
AND YOU DIDN'T TELL ME??
I THOUGHT I'D GIVE THE WINEMAKERS SOME WARNING FIRST.
KIRKMAN & SCOTT

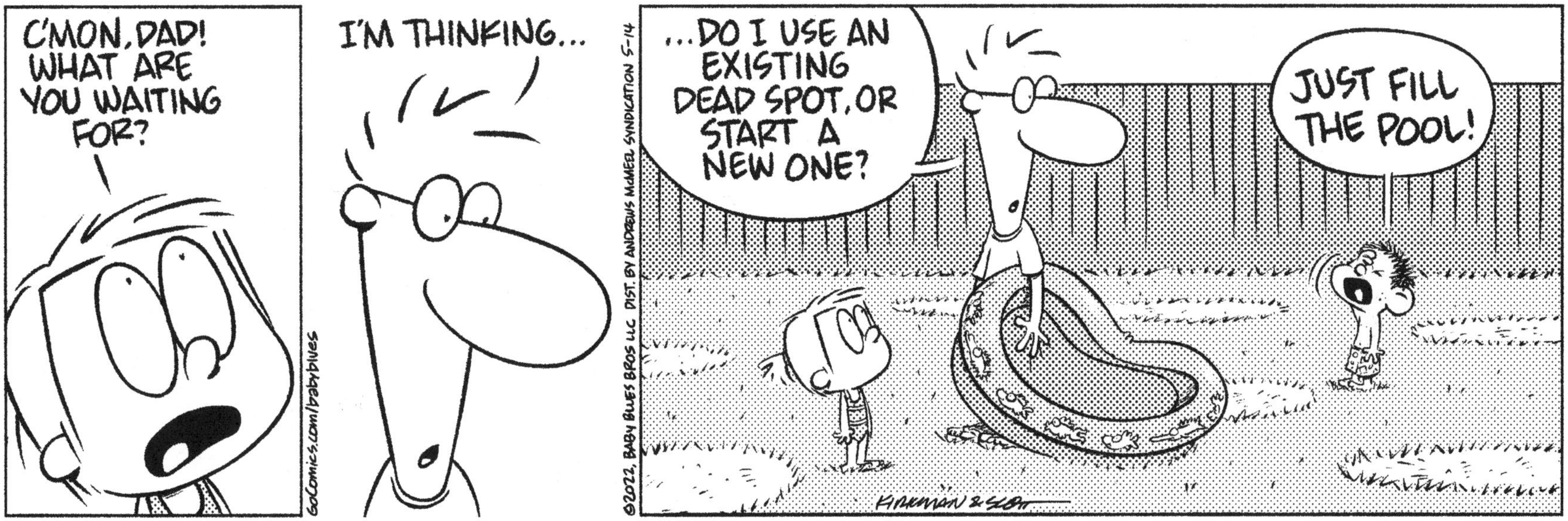
C'MON, DAD! WHAT ARE YOU WAITING FOR?
GoComics.com/babyblues
I'M THINKING...
©2022, BABY BLUES BROS LLC DIST. BY ANDREWS McMEEL SYNDICATION 5-14
...DO I USE AN EXISTING DEAD SPOT, OR START A NEW ONE?
JUST FILL THE POOL!
KIRKMAN & SCOTT

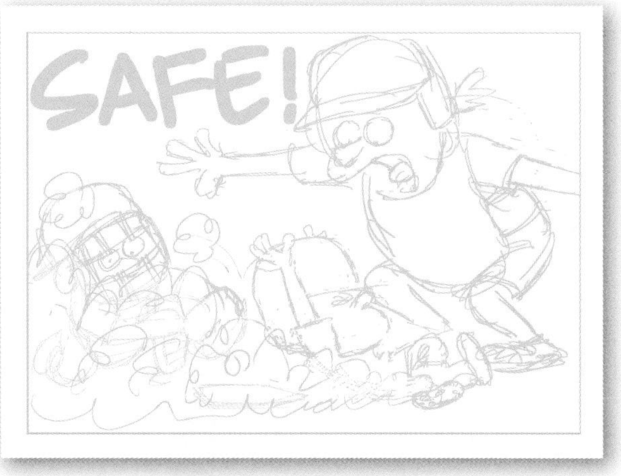
SAFE!

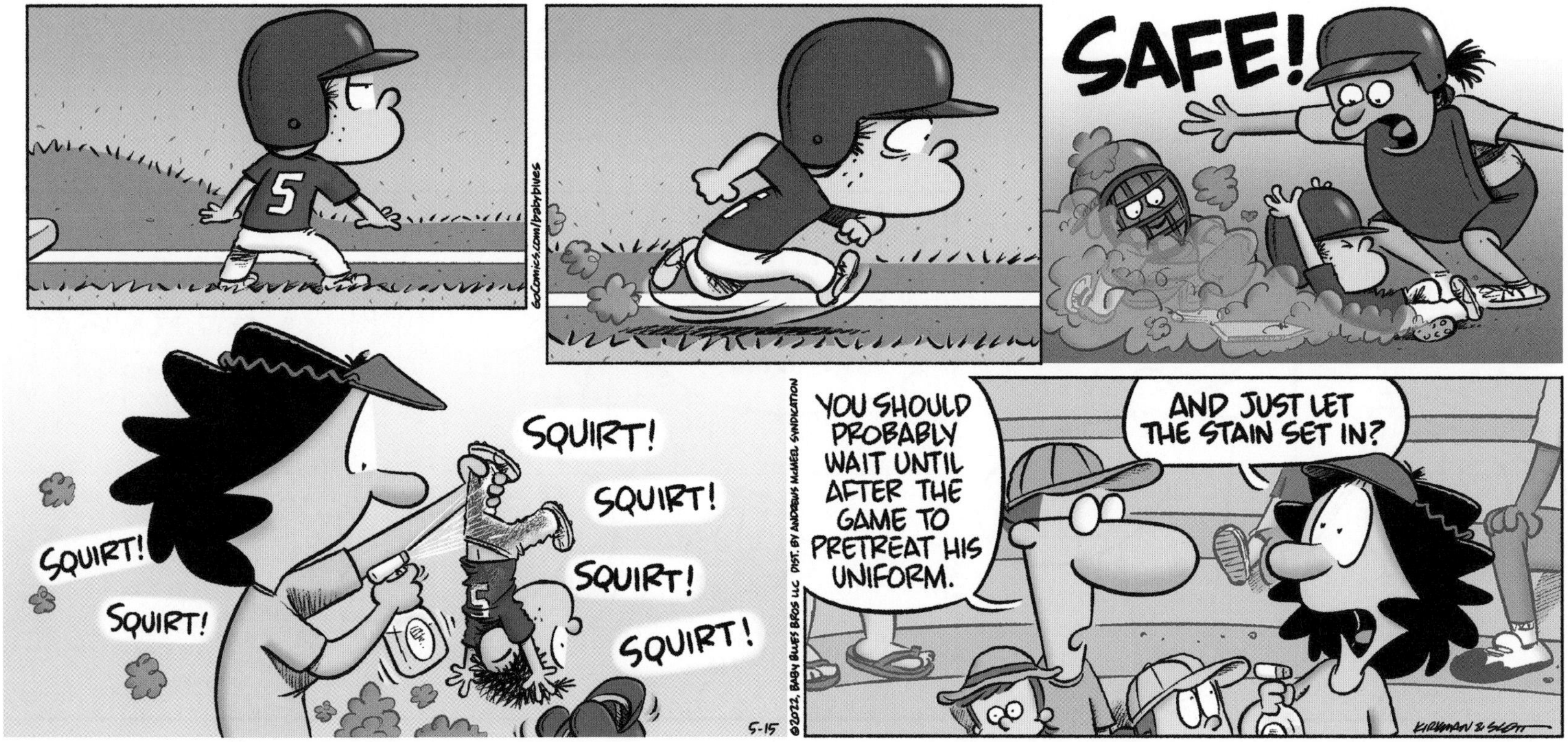
GoComics.com/babyblues
SAFE!
SQUIRT!
SQUIRT!
SQUIRT!
SQUIRT!
SQUIRT!
SQUIRT!
5-15
©2022, BABY BLUES BROS LLC. DIST. BY ANDREWS McMEEL SYNDICATION
YOU SHOULD PROBABLY WAIT UNTIL AFTER THE GAME TO PRETREAT HIS UNIFORM.
AND JUST LET THE STAIN SET IN?
KIRKMAN & SCOTT

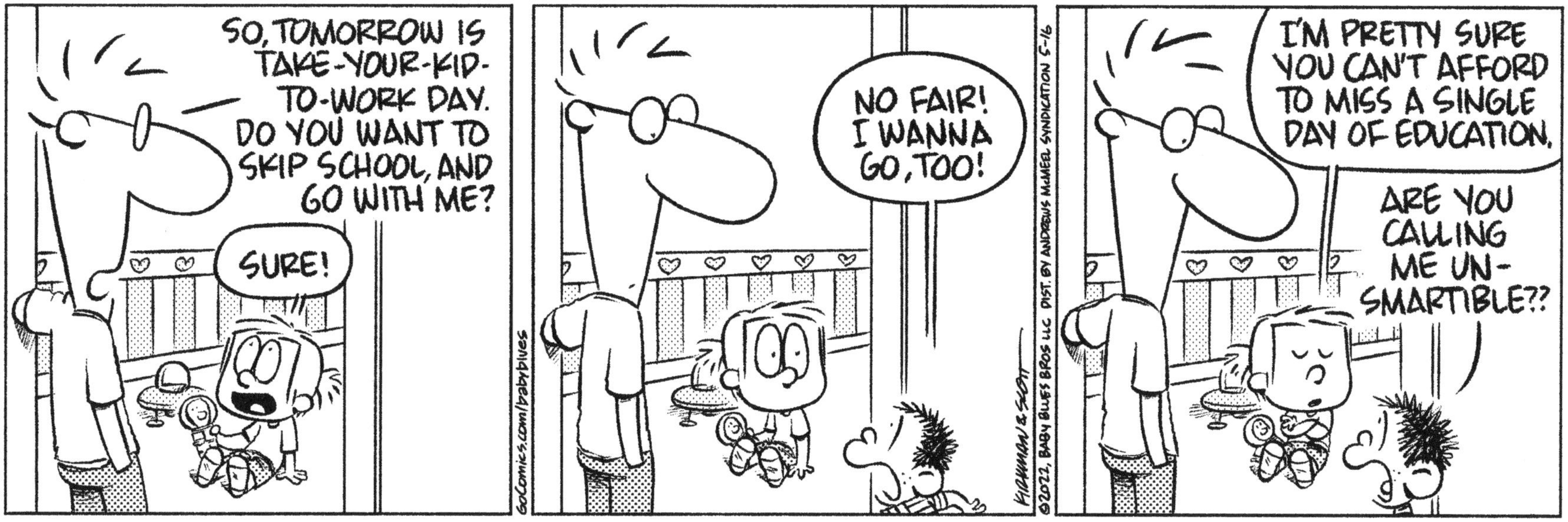
SO, TOMORROW IS TAKE-YOUR-KID-TO-WORK DAY. DO YOU WANT TO SKIP SCHOOL, AND GO WITH ME?
SURE!
GoComics.com/babyblues
NO FAIR! I WANNA GO, TOO!
©2022, BABY BLUES BROS LLC DIST. BY ANDREWS MCMEEL SYNDICATION 5-16
KIRKMAN & SCOTT
I'M PRETTY SURE YOU CAN'T AFFORD TO MISS A SINGLE DAY OF EDUCATION.
ARE YOU CALLING ME UN-SMARTIBLE??

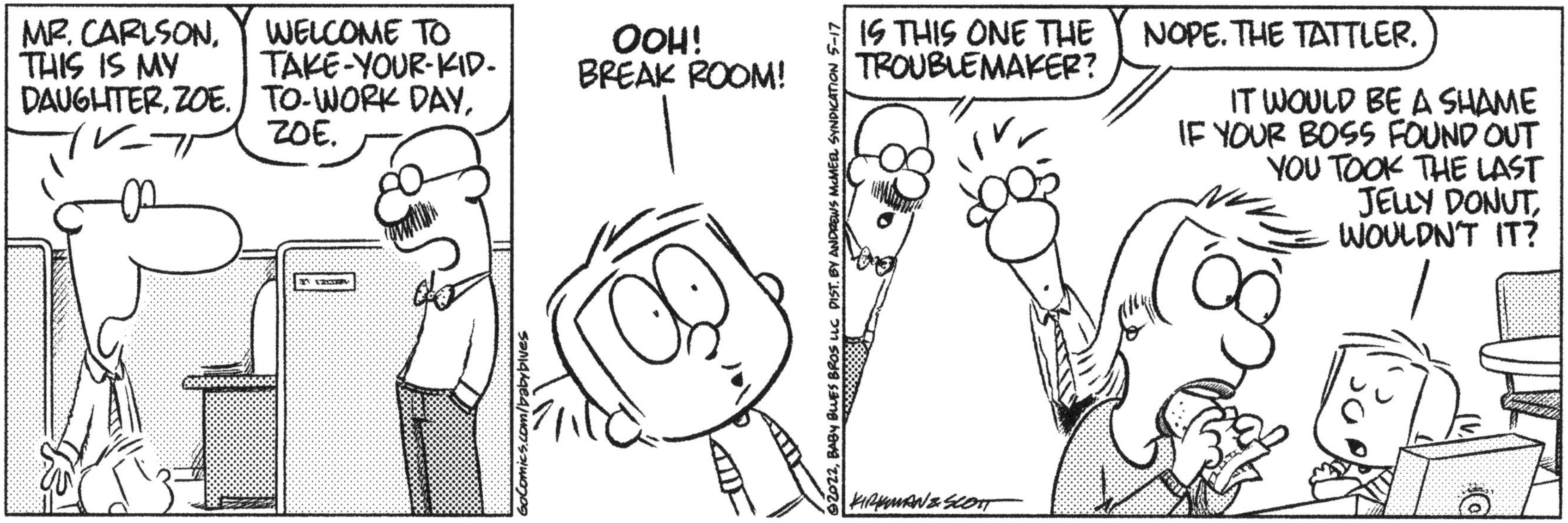
MR. CARLSON, THIS IS MY DAUGHTER, ZOE.
WELCOME TO TAKE-YOUR-KID-TO-WORK DAY, ZOE.
GoComics.com/babyblues
OOH! BREAK ROOM!
©2022, BABY BLUES BROS LLC DIST. BY ANDREWS MCMEEL SYNDICATION 5-17
IS THIS ONE THE TROUBLEMAKER?
NOPE. THE TATTLER.
IT WOULD BE A SHAME IF YOUR BOSS FOUND OUT YOU TOOK THE LAST JELLY DONUT, WOULDN'T IT?
KIRKMAN & SCOTT

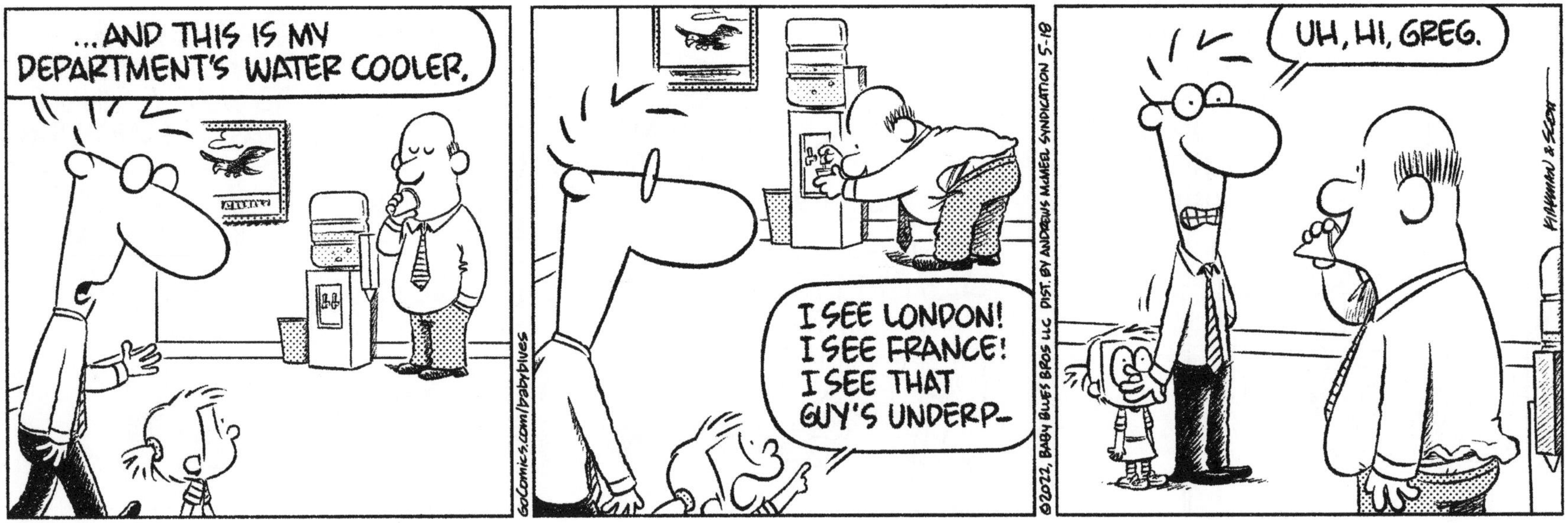
...AND THIS IS MY DEPARTMENT'S WATER COOLER.
I SEE LONDON! I SEE FRANCE! I SEE THAT GUY'S UNDERP–
UH, HI, GREG.
GoComics.com/babyblues
©2022, BABY BLUES BROS LLC DIST. BY ANDREWS MCMEEL SYNDICATION 5-18
KIRKMAN & SCOTT

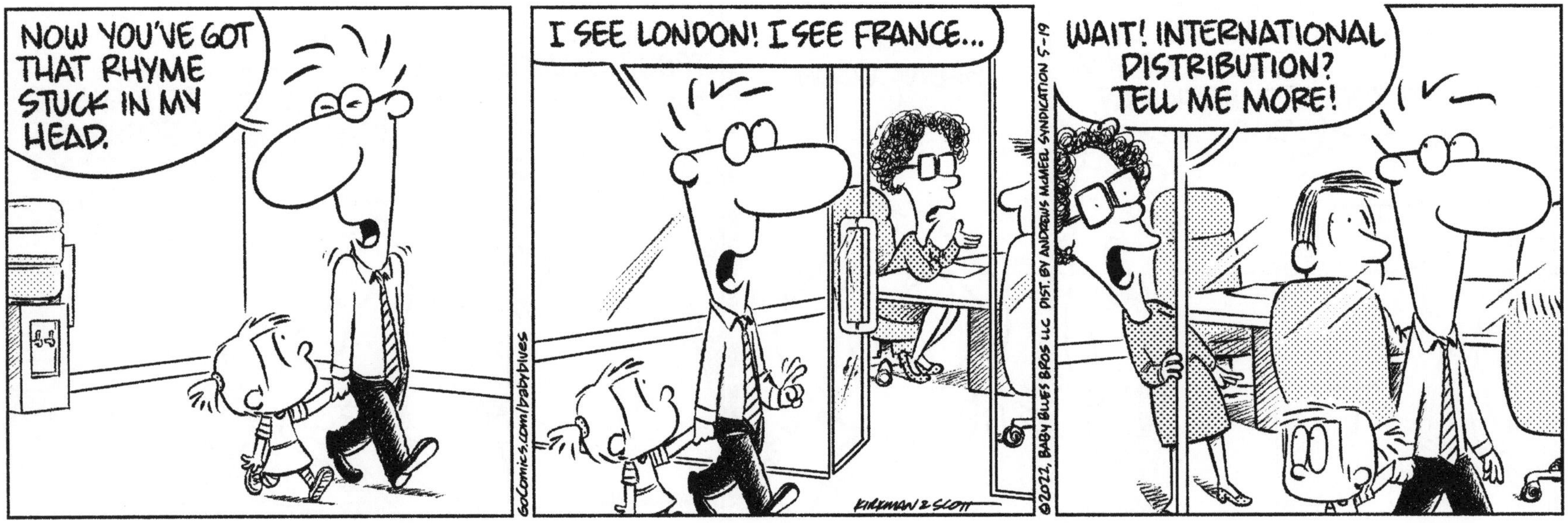
NOW YOU'VE GOT THAT RHYME STUCK IN MY HEAD.
I SEE LONDON! I SEE FRANCE...
WAIT! INTERNATIONAL DISTRIBUTION? TELL ME MORE!
GoComics.com/babyblues
©2022, BABY BLUES BROS LLC DIST. BY ANDREWS MCMEEL SYNDICATION 5-19
KIRKMAN & SCOTT

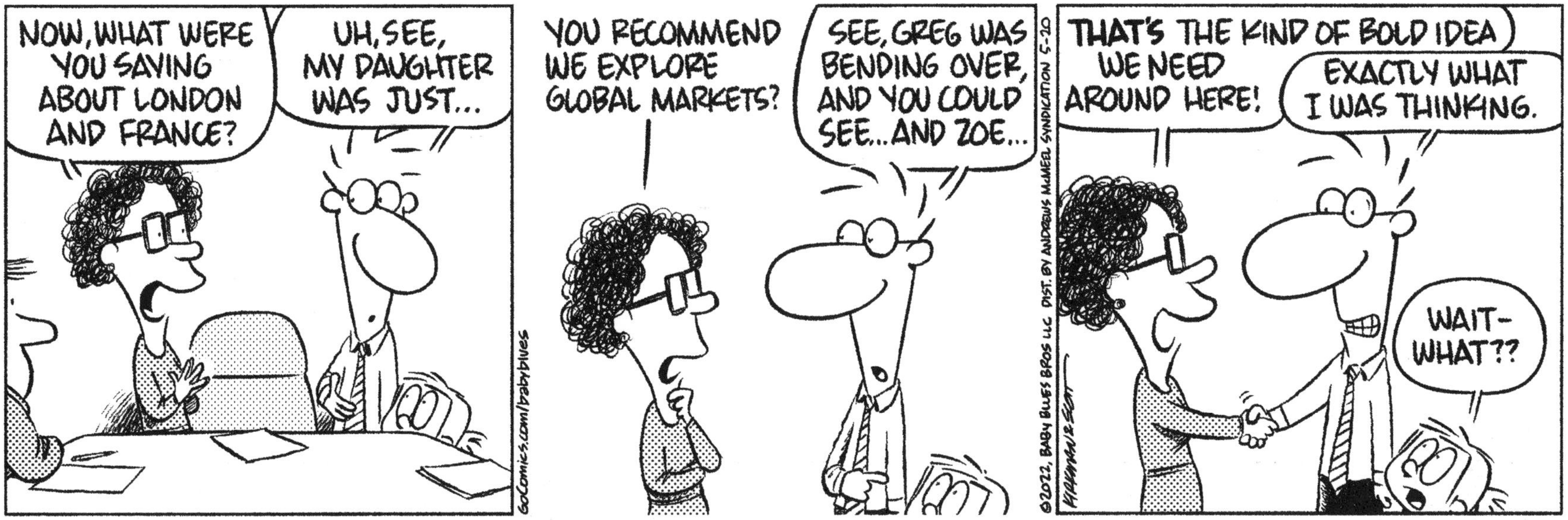
NOW, WHAT WERE YOU SAYING ABOUT LONDON AND FRANCE?
UH, SEE, MY DAUGHTER WAS JUST...
YOU RECOMMEND WE EXPLORE GLOBAL MARKETS?
SEE, GREG WAS BENDING OVER, AND YOU COULD SEE...AND ZOE...
THAT'S THE KIND OF BOLD IDEA WE NEED AROUND HERE!
EXACTLY WHAT I WAS THINKING.
WAIT-WHAT??
GoComics.com/babyblues
©2022, BABY BLUES BROS LLC DIST. BY ANDREWS McMEEL SYNDICATION 5-20

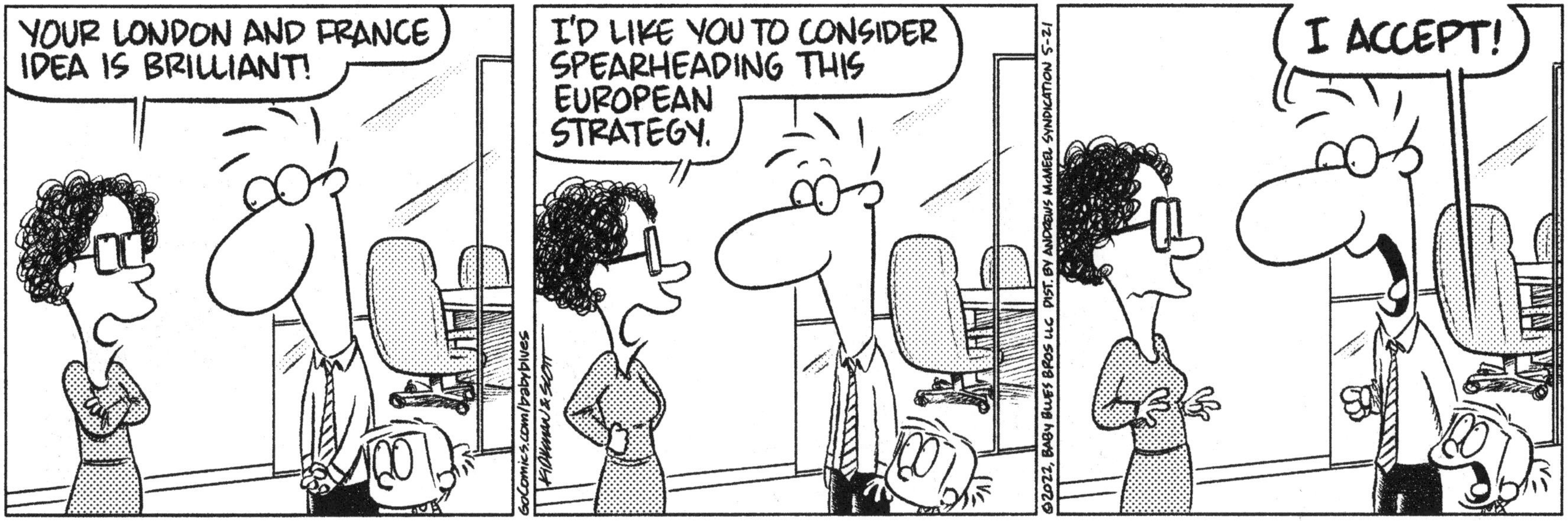
YOUR LONDON AND FRANCE IDEA IS BRILLIANT!
I'D LIKE YOU TO CONSIDER SPEARHEADING THIS EUROPEAN STRATEGY.
I ACCEPT!
GoComics.com/babyblues
©2022, BABY BLUES BROS LLC DIST. BY ANDREWS McMEEL SYNDICATION 5-21

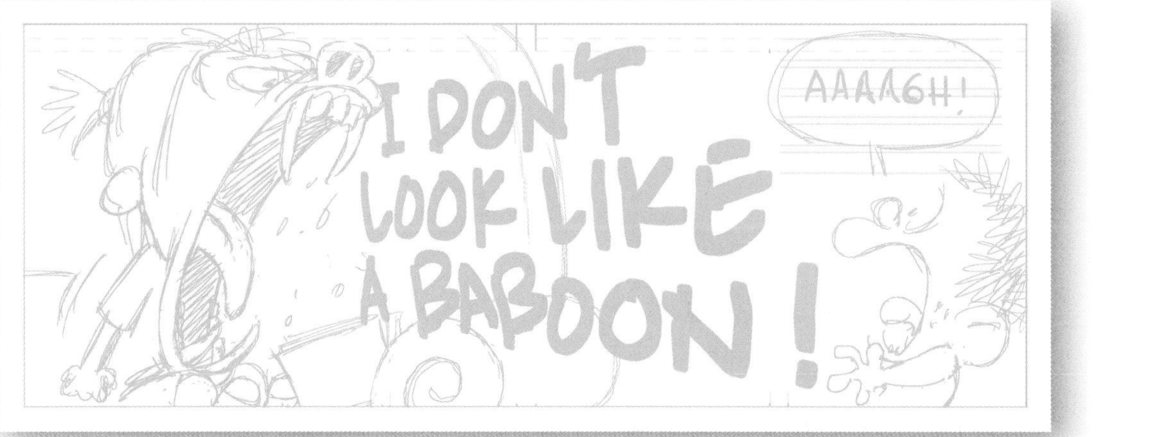
I DON'T LOOK LIKE A BABOON!
AAAAGH!

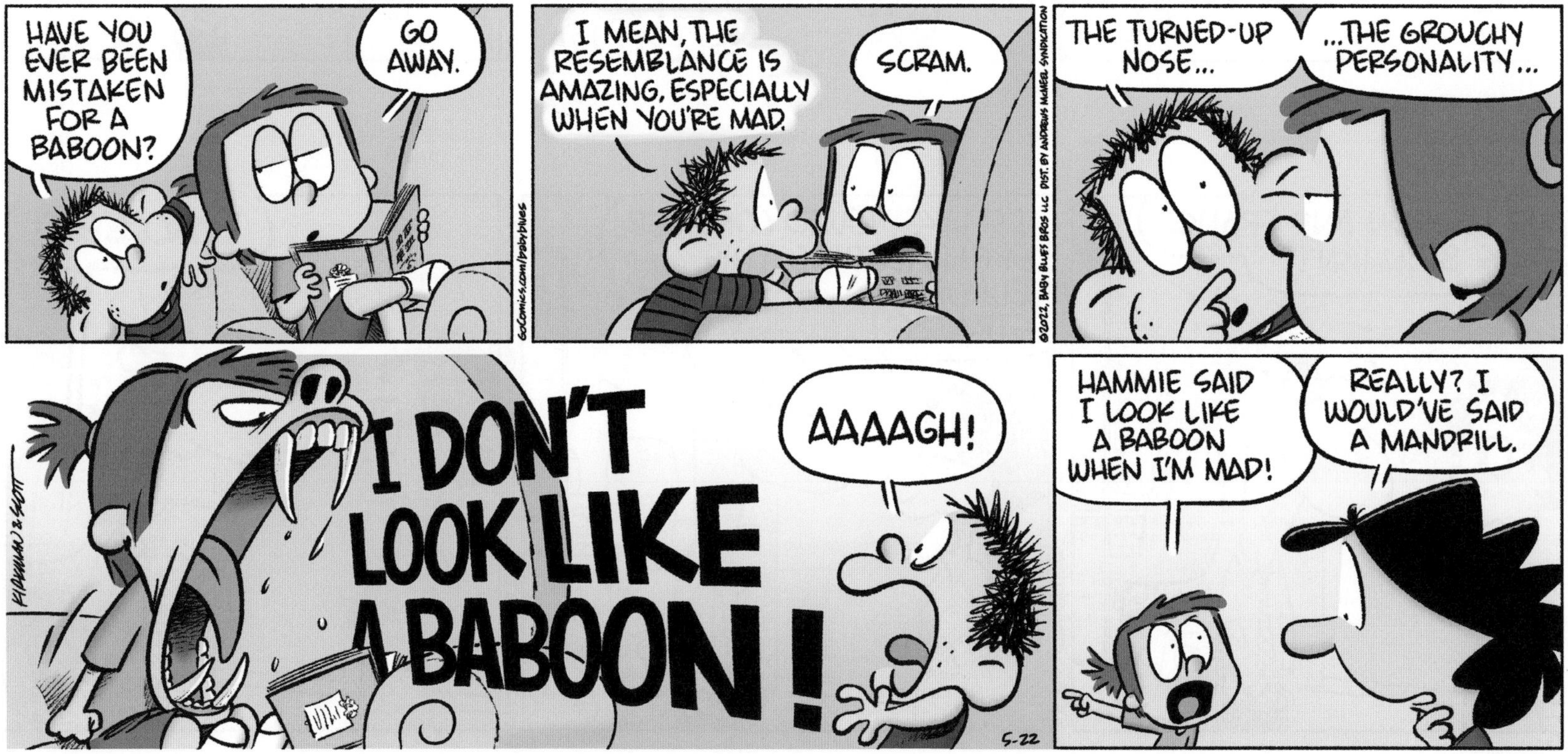
HAVE YOU EVER BEEN MISTAKEN FOR A BABOON?
GO AWAY.
GoComics.com/babyblues
I MEAN, THE RESEMBLANCE IS AMAZING, ESPECIALLY WHEN YOU'RE MAD.
SCRAM.
©2022, BABY BLUES BROS LLC DIST. BY ANDREWS MCMEEL SYNDICATION
THE TURNED-UP NOSE...
...THE GROUCHY PERSONALITY...
KIRKMAN & SCOTT
I DON'T LOOK LIKE A BABOON!
AAAAGH!
5-22
HAMMIE SAID I LOOK LIKE A BABOON WHEN I'M MAD!
REALLY? I WOULD'VE SAID A MANDRILL.

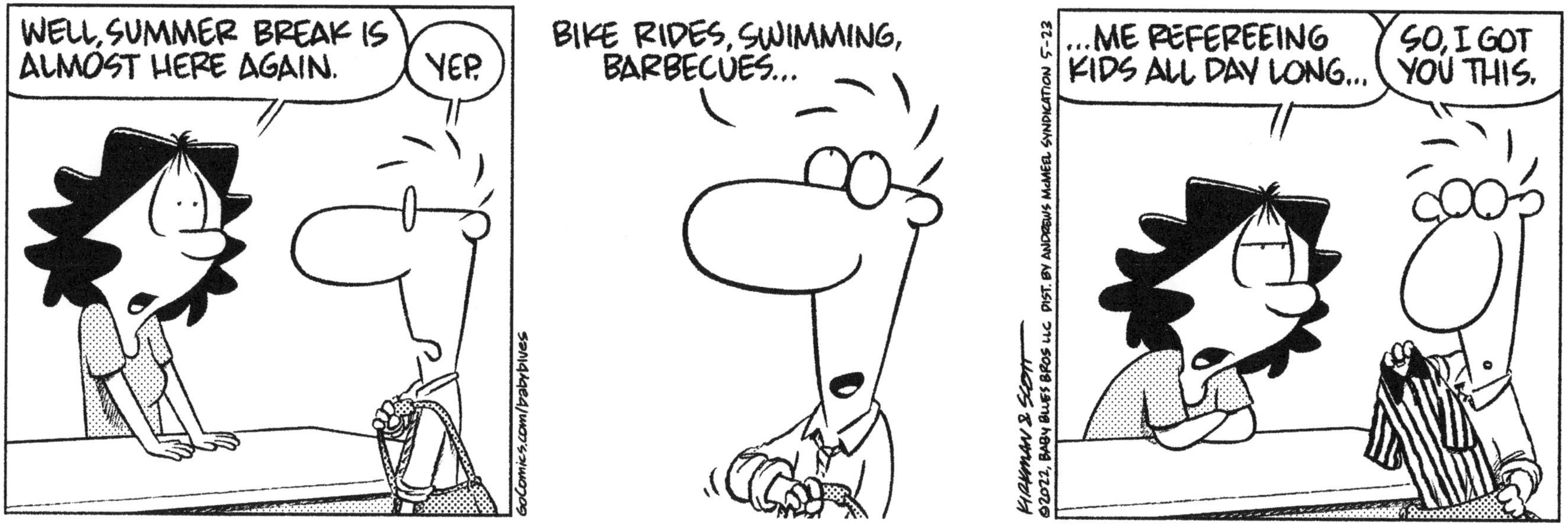
WELL, SUMMER BREAK IS ALMOST HERE AGAIN.
YEP.
BIKE RIDES, SWIMMING, BARBECUES...
...ME REFEREEING KIDS ALL DAY LONG...
SO, I GOT YOU THIS.
GoComics.com/babyblues
KIRKMAN & SCOTT
©2022, BABY BLUES BROS LLC DIST. BY ANDREWS McMEEL SYNDICATION 5-23

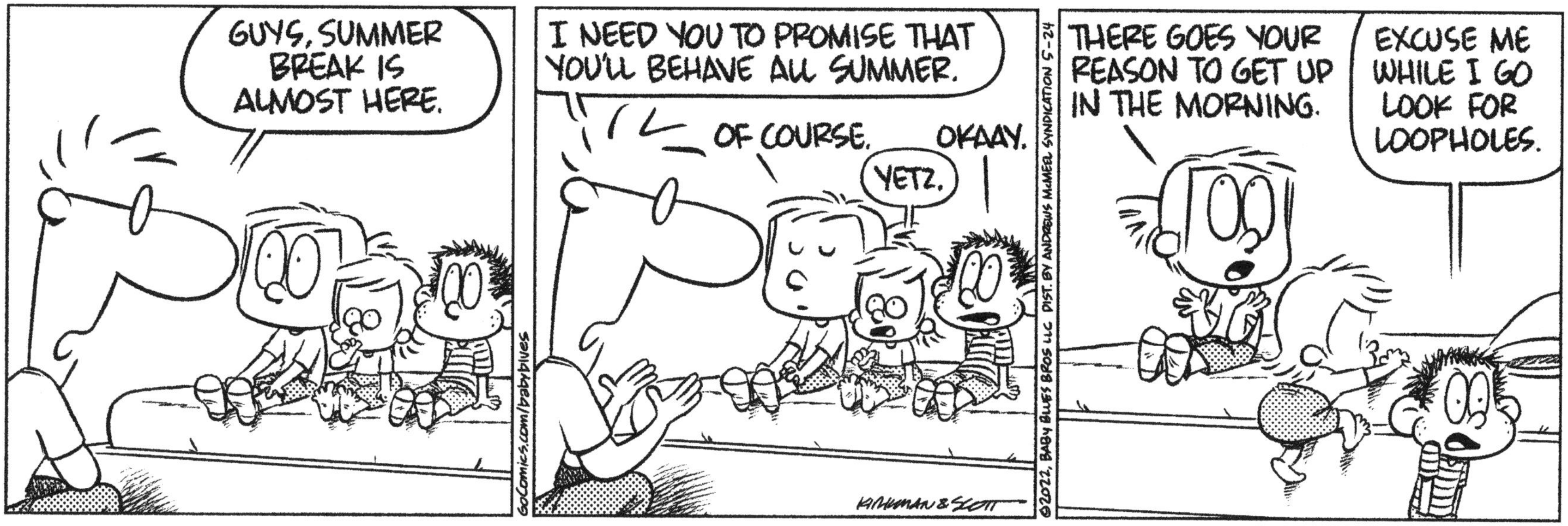
GUYS, SUMMER BREAK IS ALMOST HERE.
I NEED YOU TO PROMISE THAT YOU'LL BEHAVE ALL SUMMER.
OF COURSE.
YETZ.
OKAAY.
THERE GOES YOUR REASON TO GET UP IN THE MORNING.
EXCUSE ME WHILE I GO LOOK FOR LOOPHOLES.
GoComics.com/babyblues
KIRKMAN & SCOTT
©2022, BABY BLUES BROS LLC DIST. BY ANDREWS McMEEL SYNDICATION 5-24

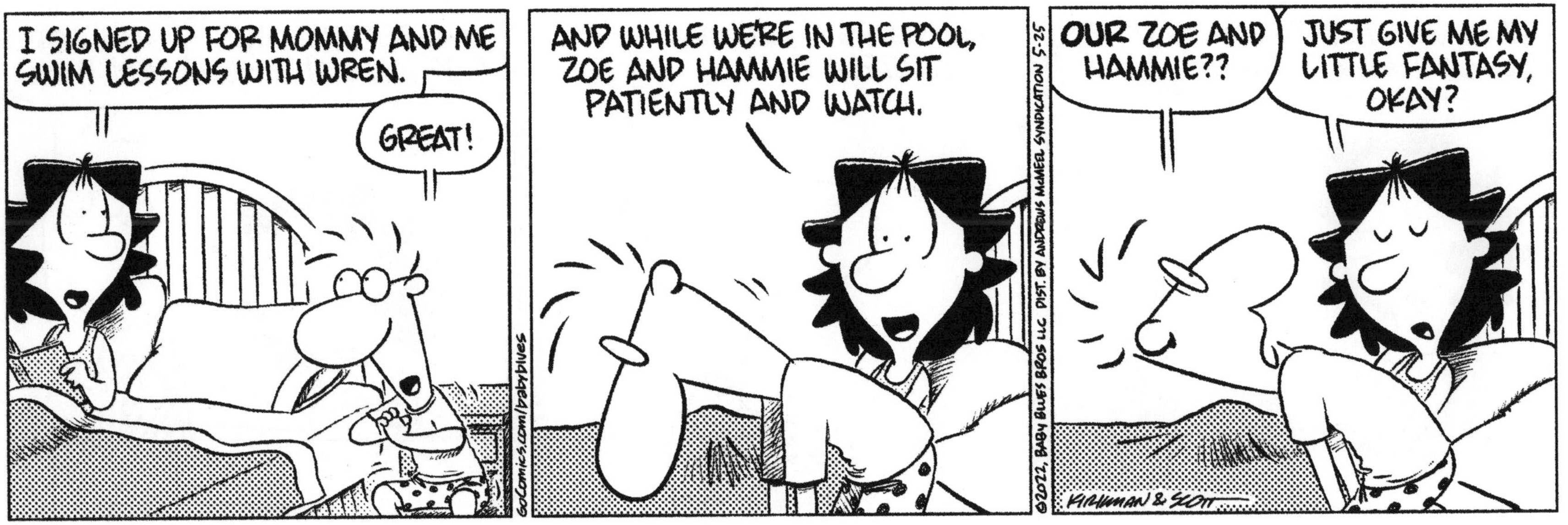
I SIGNED UP FOR MOMMY AND ME SWIM LESSONS WITH WREN.
GREAT!
GoComics.com/babyblues
AND WHILE WE'RE IN THE POOL, ZOE AND HAMMIE WILL SIT PATIENTLY AND WATCH.
©2022, BABY BLUES BROS LLC DIST. BY ANDREWS McMEEL SYNDICATION 5-25
OUR ZOE AND HAMMIE??
JUST GIVE ME MY LITTLE FANTASY, OKAY?
KIRKMAN & SCOTT

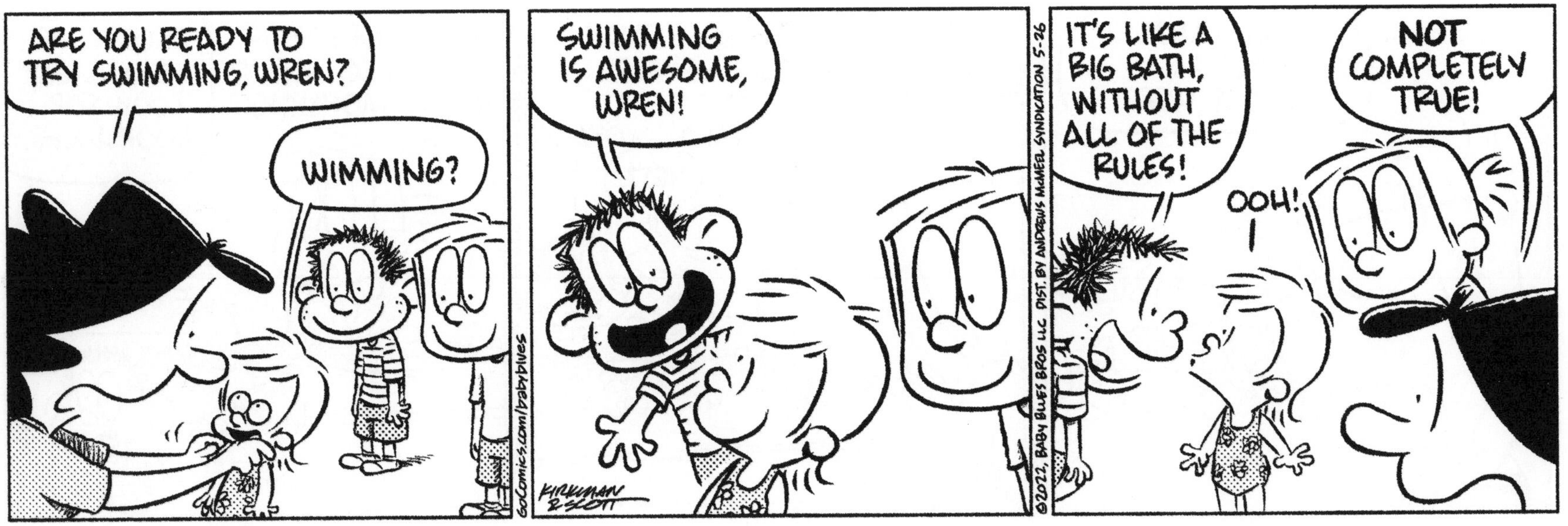
ARE YOU READY TO TRY SWIMMING, WREN?
WIMMING?
GoComics.com/babyblues
SWIMMING IS AWESOME, WREN!
KIRKMAN & SCOTT
©2022, BABY BLUES BROS LLC DIST. BY ANDREWS McMEEL SYNDICATION 5-26
IT'S LIKE A BIG BATH, WITHOUT ALL OF THE RULES!
OOH!
NOT COMPLETELY TRUE!

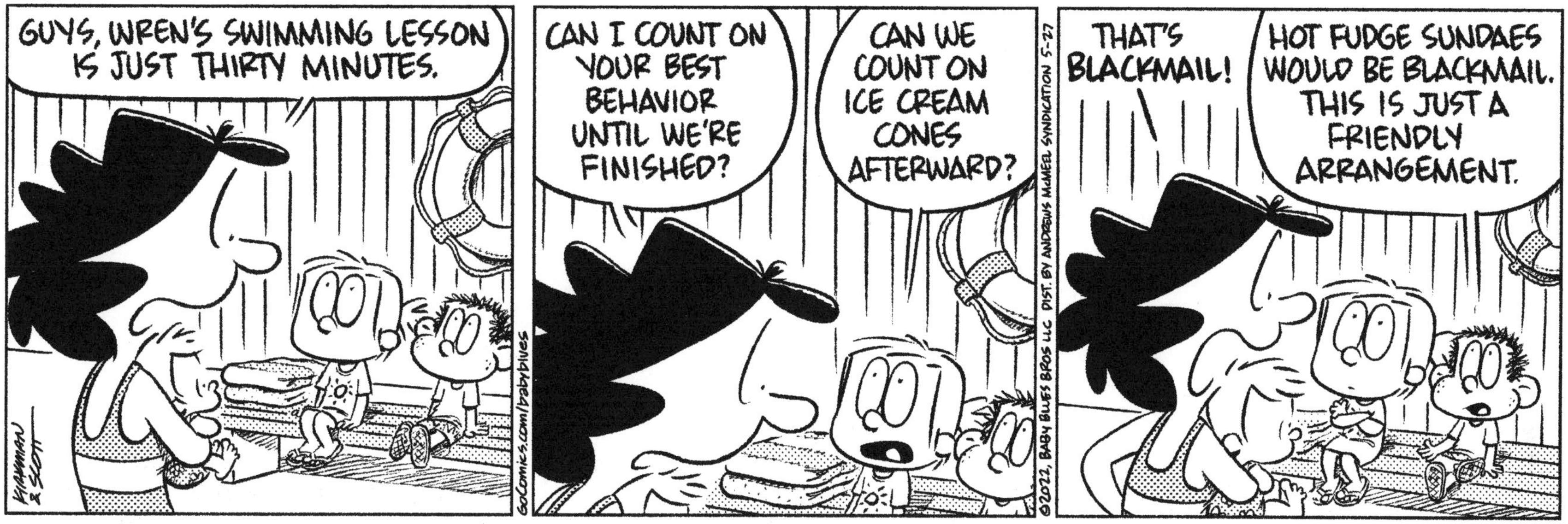
GUYS, WREN'S SWIMMING LESSON IS JUST THIRTY MINUTES.
CAN I COUNT ON YOUR BEST BEHAVIOR UNTIL WE'RE FINISHED?
CAN WE COUNT ON ICE CREAM CONES AFTERWARD?
THAT'S BLACKMAIL!
HOT FUDGE SUNDAES WOULD BE BLACKMAIL. THIS IS JUST A FRIENDLY ARRANGEMENT.
KIRKMAN & SCOTT
GoComics.com/babyblues
©2022, BABY BLUES BROS LLC DIST. BY ANDREWS McMEEL SYNDICATION 5-27

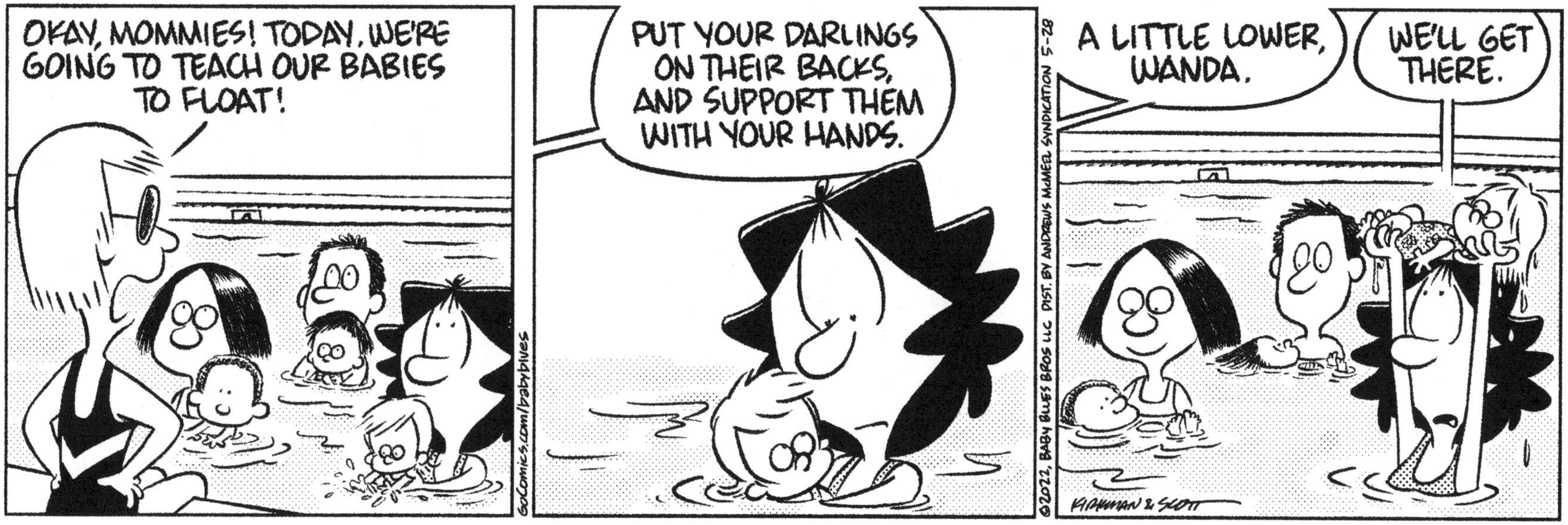
OKAY, MOMMIES! TODAY, WE'RE GOING TO TEACH OUR BABIES TO FLOAT!
PUT YOUR DARLINGS ON THEIR BACKS, AND SUPPORT THEM WITH YOUR HANDS.
A LITTLE LOWER, WANDA.
WE'LL GET THERE.
GoComics.com/babyblues
©2022, BABY BLUES BROS LLC DIST. BY ANDREWS McMEEL SYNDICATION 5-28
KIRKMAN & SCOTT

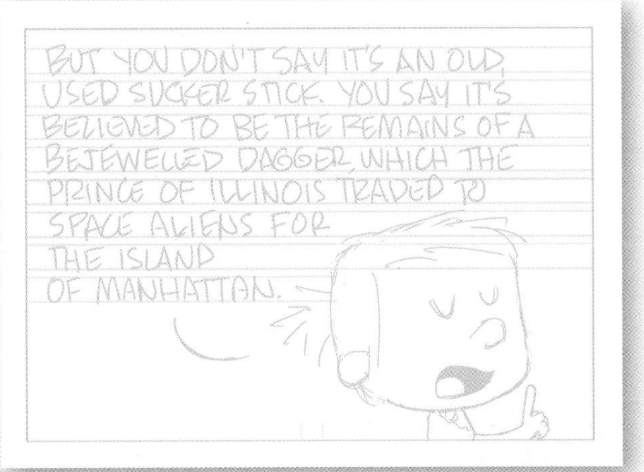
BUT YOU DON'T SAY IT'S AN OLD, USED SUCKER STICK. YOU SAY IT'S BELIEVED TO BE THE REMAINS OF A BEJEWELLED DAGGER, WHICH THE PRINCE OF ILLINOIS TRADED TO SPACE ALIENS FOR THE ISLAND OF MANHATTAN.

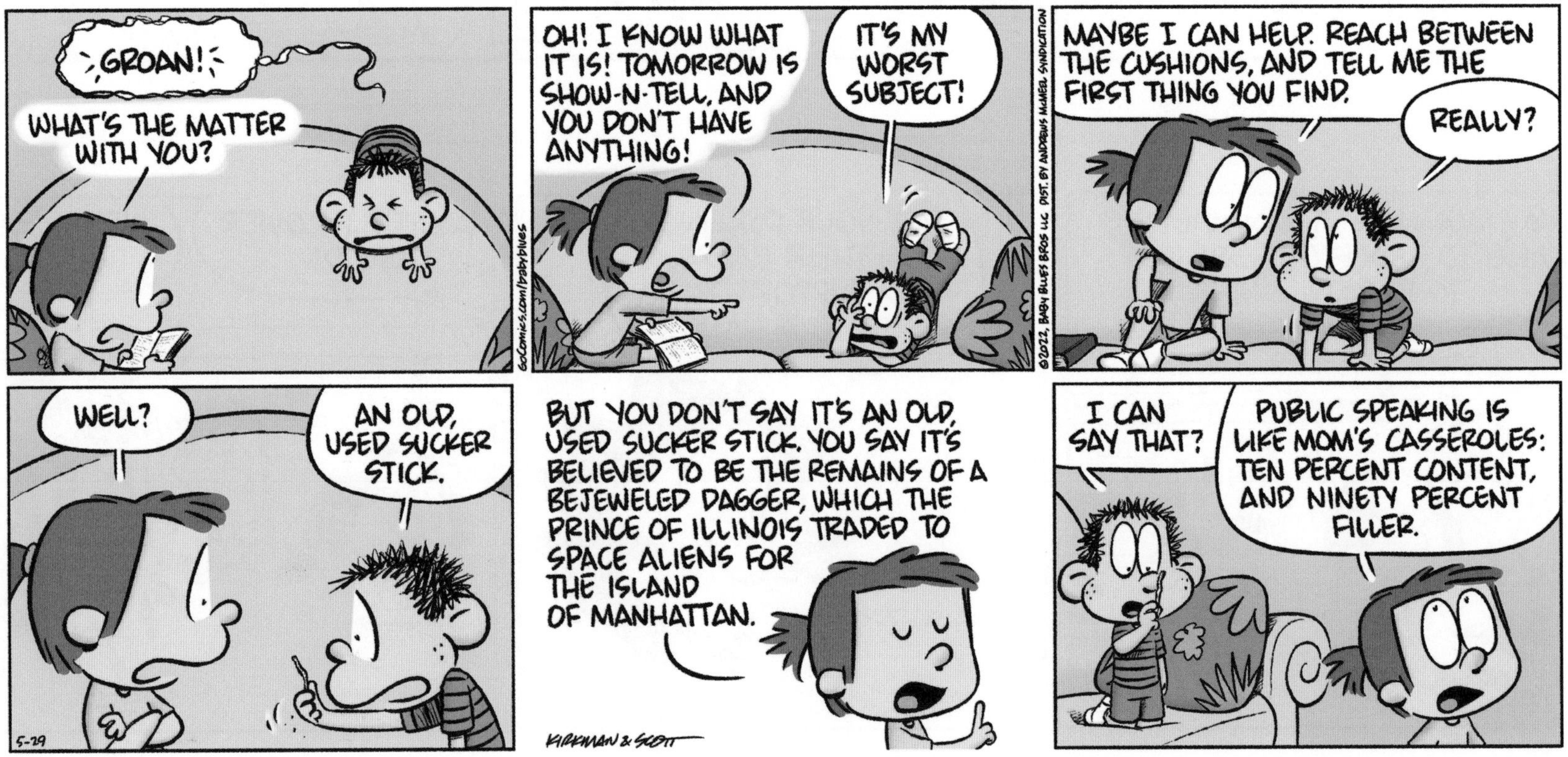
GROAN!
WHAT'S THE MATTER WITH YOU?
OH! I KNOW WHAT IT IS! TOMORROW IS SHOW-N-TELL, AND YOU DON'T HAVE ANYTHING!
IT'S MY WORST SUBJECT!
GoComics.com/babyblues
©2022, BABY BLUES BROS LLC. DIST. BY ANDREWS McMEEL SYNDICATION
MAYBE I CAN HELP. REACH BETWEEN THE CUSHIONS, AND TELL ME THE FIRST THING YOU FIND.
REALLY?
WELL?
AN OLD, USED SUCKER STICK.
5-29
BUT YOU DON'T SAY IT'S AN OLD, USED SUCKER STICK. YOU SAY IT'S BELIEVED TO BE THE REMAINS OF A BEJEWELED DAGGER, WHICH THE PRINCE OF ILLINOIS TRADED TO SPACE ALIENS FOR THE ISLAND OF MANHATTAN.
KIRKMAN & SCOTT
I CAN SAY THAT?
PUBLIC SPEAKING IS LIKE MOM'S CASSEROLES: TEN PERCENT CONTENT, AND NINETY PERCENT FILLER.

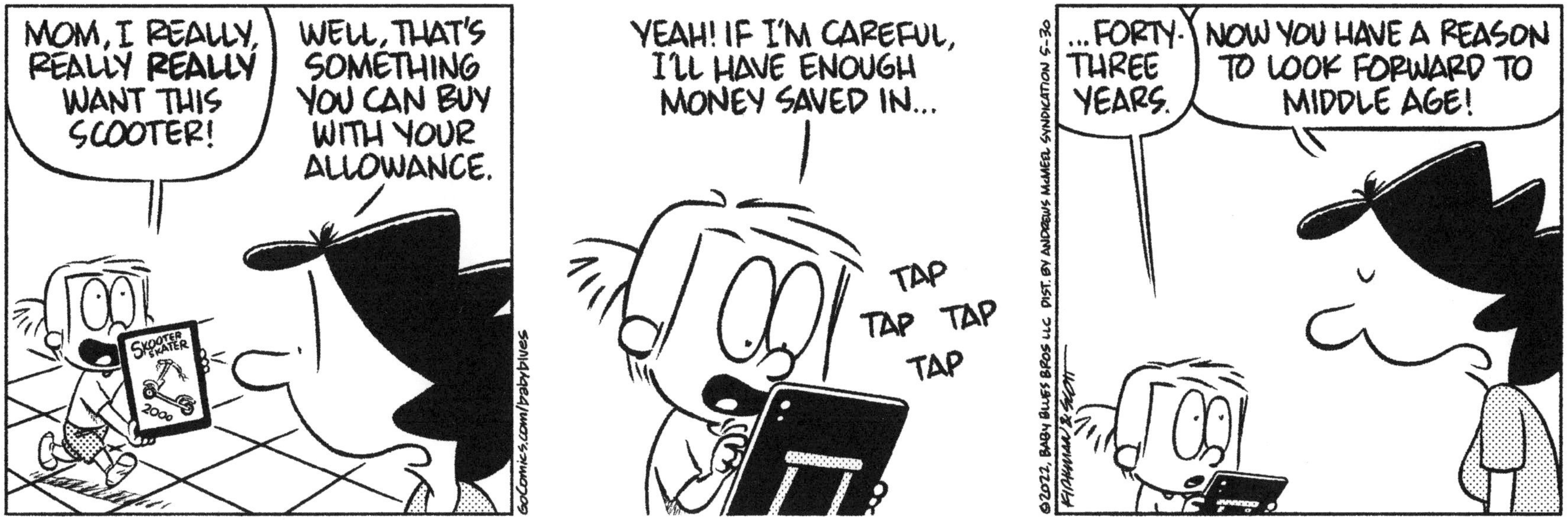
MOM, I REALLY, REALLY **REALLY** WANT THIS SCOOTER!
WELL, THAT'S SOMETHING YOU CAN BUY WITH YOUR ALLOWANCE.
SKOOTER SKATER 2000
GoComics.com/babyblues
YEAH! IF I'M CAREFUL, I'LL HAVE ENOUGH MONEY SAVED IN...
TAP TAP TAP TAP
...FORTY-THREE YEARS.
NOW YOU HAVE A REASON TO LOOK FORWARD TO MIDDLE AGE!
©2022, BABY BLUES BROS LLC DIST. BY ANDREWS McMEEL SYNDICATION 5-30
KIRKMAN & SCOTT

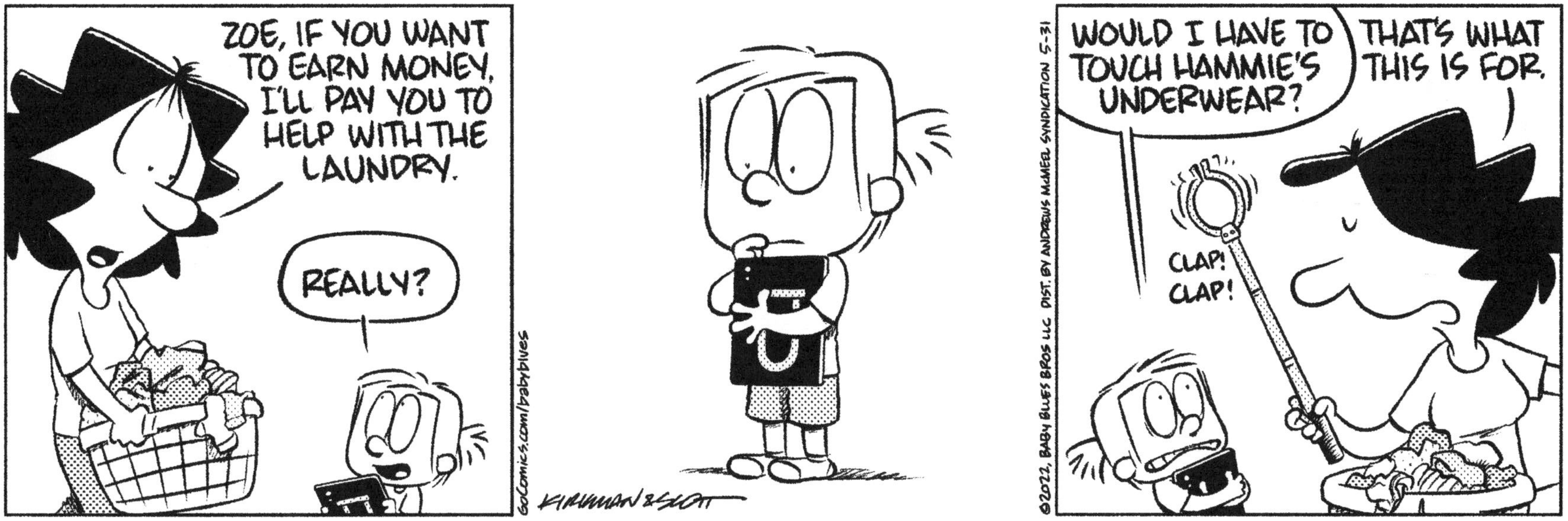
ZOE, IF YOU WANT TO EARN MONEY, I'LL PAY YOU TO HELP WITH THE LAUNDRY.
REALLY?
GoComics.com/babyblues
KIRKMAN & SCOTT
WOULD I HAVE TO TOUCH HAMMIE'S UNDERWEAR?
THAT'S WHAT THIS IS FOR.
CLAP! CLAP!
©2022, BABY BLUES BROS LLC DIST. BY ANDREWS McMEEL SYNDICATION 5-31

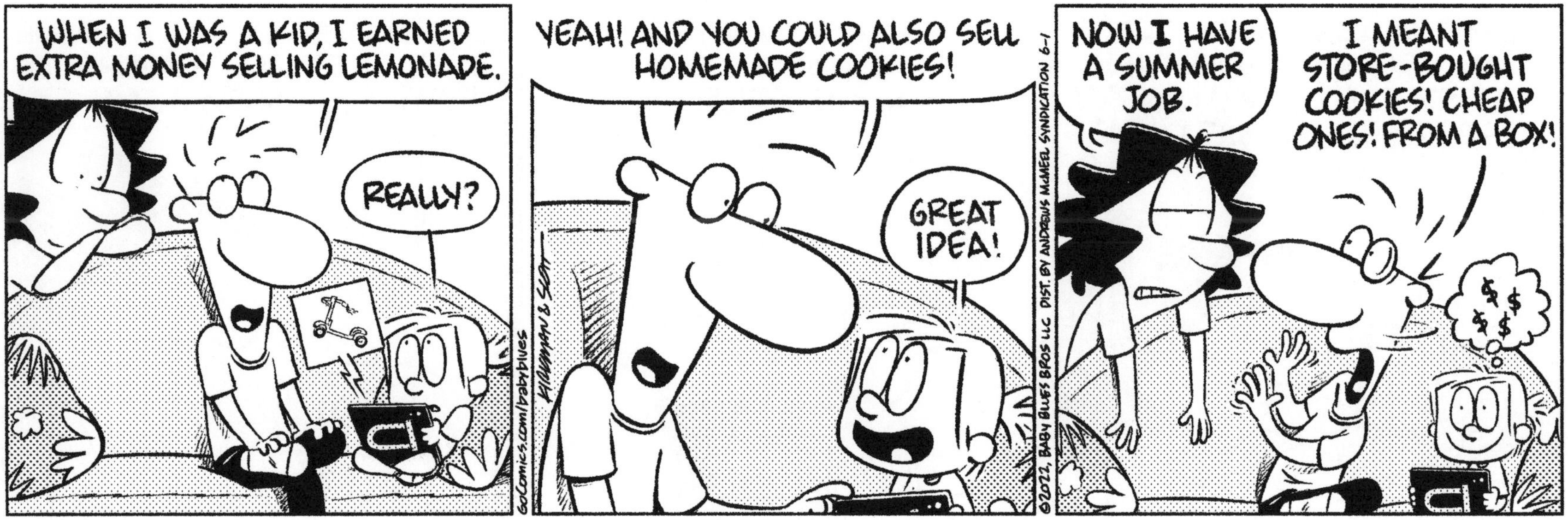
WHEN I WAS A KID, I EARNED EXTRA MONEY SELLING LEMONADE.
REALLY?
gocomics.com/babyblues
KIRKMAN & SCOTT
YEAH! AND YOU COULD ALSO SELL HOMEMADE COOKIES!
GREAT IDEA!
©2022, BABY BLUES BROS LLC DIST. BY ANDREWS MCMEEL SYNDICATION 6-1
NOW I HAVE A SUMMER JOB.
I MEANT STORE-BOUGHT COOKIES! CHEAP ONES! FROM A BOX!
$ $ $ $

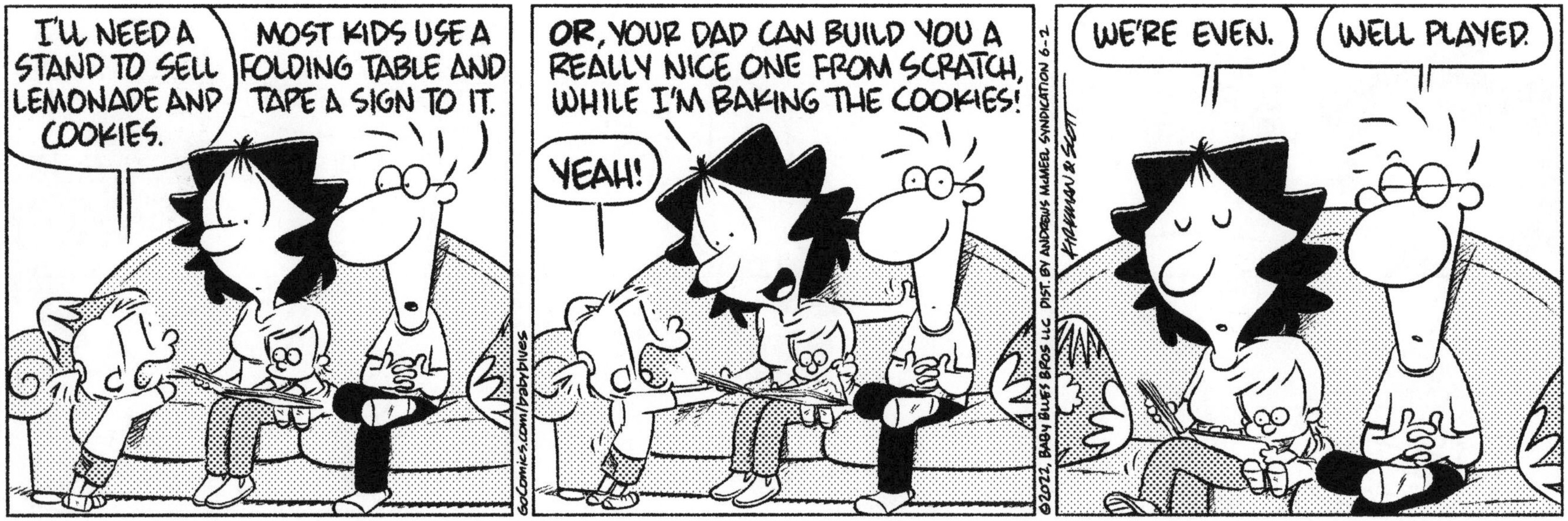
I'LL NEED A STAND TO SELL LEMONADE AND COOKIES.
MOST KIDS USE A FOLDING TABLE AND TAPE A SIGN TO IT.
gocomics.com/babyblues
OR, YOUR DAD CAN BUILD YOU A REALLY NICE ONE FROM SCRATCH, WHILE I'M BAKING THE COOKIES!
YEAH!
©2022, BABY BLUES BROS LLC DIST. BY ANDREWS MCMEEL SYNDICATION 6-2
KIRKMAN & SCOTT
WE'RE EVEN.
WELL PLAYED.

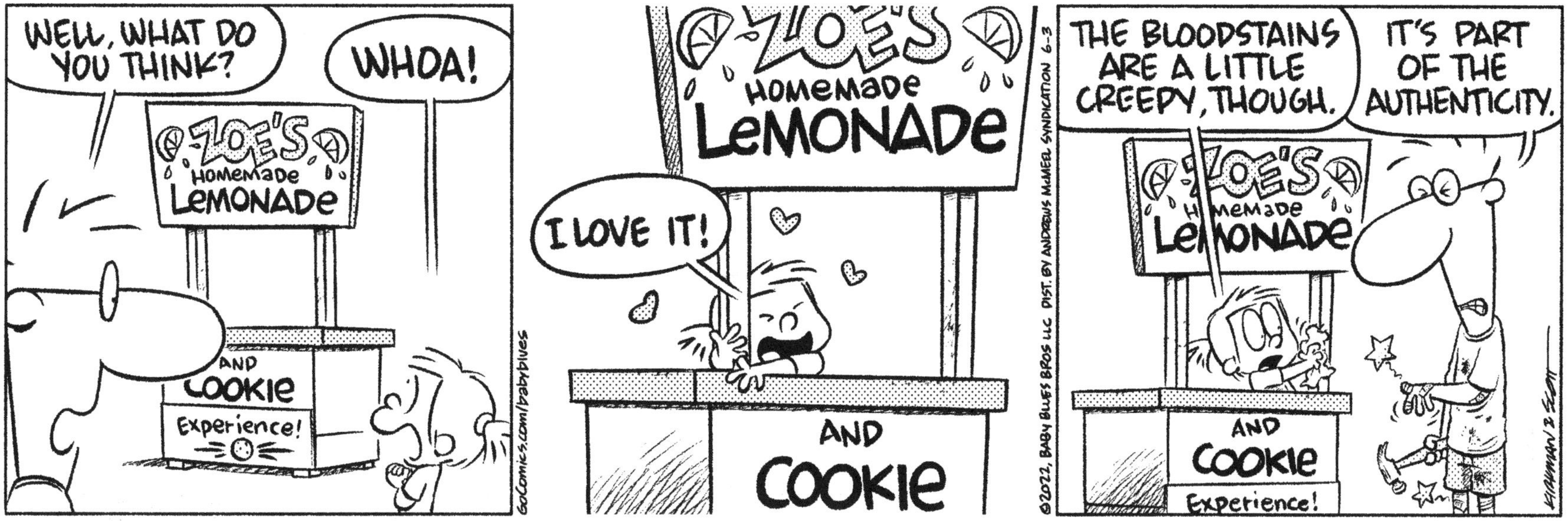
WELL, WHAT DO YOU THINK?
WHOA!
ZOE'S HOMEMADE LEMONADE
AND COOKIE Experience!
GoComics.com/babyblues
I LOVE IT!
ZOE'S HOMEMADE LEMONADE
AND COOKIE
©2022, BABY BLUES BROS LLC DIST. BY ANDREWS McMEEL SYNDICATION 6-3
THE BLOODSTAINS ARE A LITTLE CREEPY, THOUGH.
IT'S PART OF THE AUTHENTICITY.
ZOE'S HOMEMADE LEMONADE
AND COOKIE Experience!
KIRKMAN & SCOTT

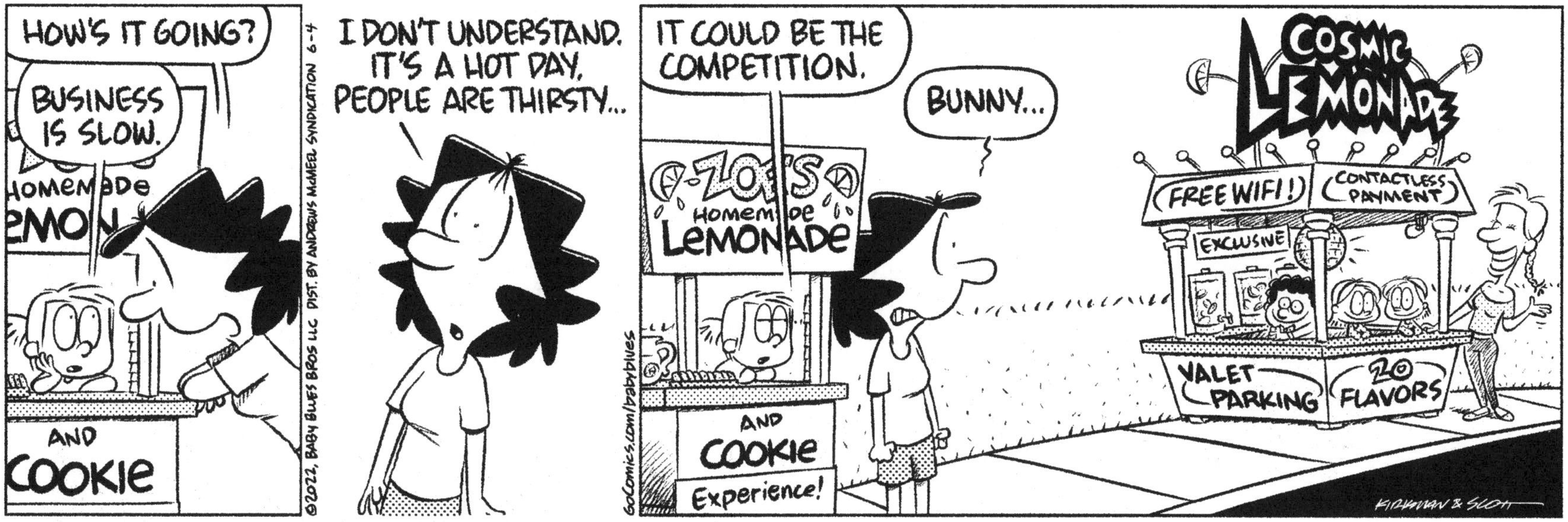
HOW'S IT GOING?
BUSINESS IS SLOW.
AND COOKIE
©2022, BABY BLUES BROS LLC DIST. BY ANDREWS McMEEL SYNDICATION 6-4
I DON'T UNDERSTAND. IT'S A HOT DAY, PEOPLE ARE THIRSTY...
IT COULD BE THE COMPETITION.
BUNNY...
ZOE'S HOMEMADE LEMONADE
AND COOKIE Experience!
COSMIC LEMONADE
FREE WIFI!
CONTACTLESS PAYMENT
EXCLUSIVE
VALET PARKING
20 FLAVORS
GoComics.com/babyblues
KIRKMAN & SCOTT

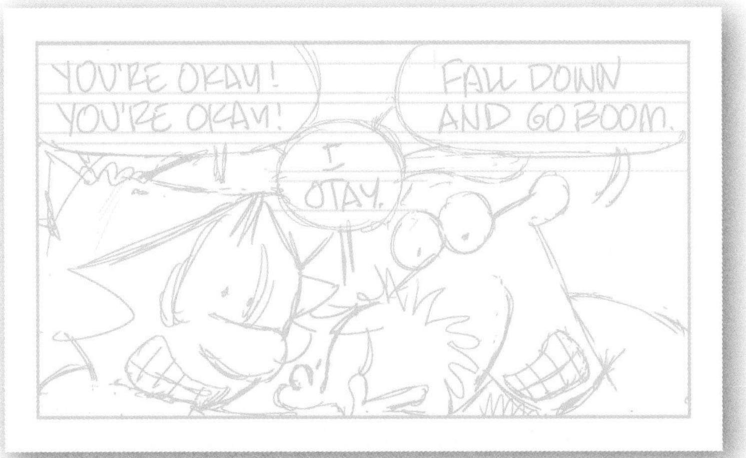
YOU'RE OKAY! YOU'RE OKAY!
FALL DOWN AND GO BOOM.
I OTAY.

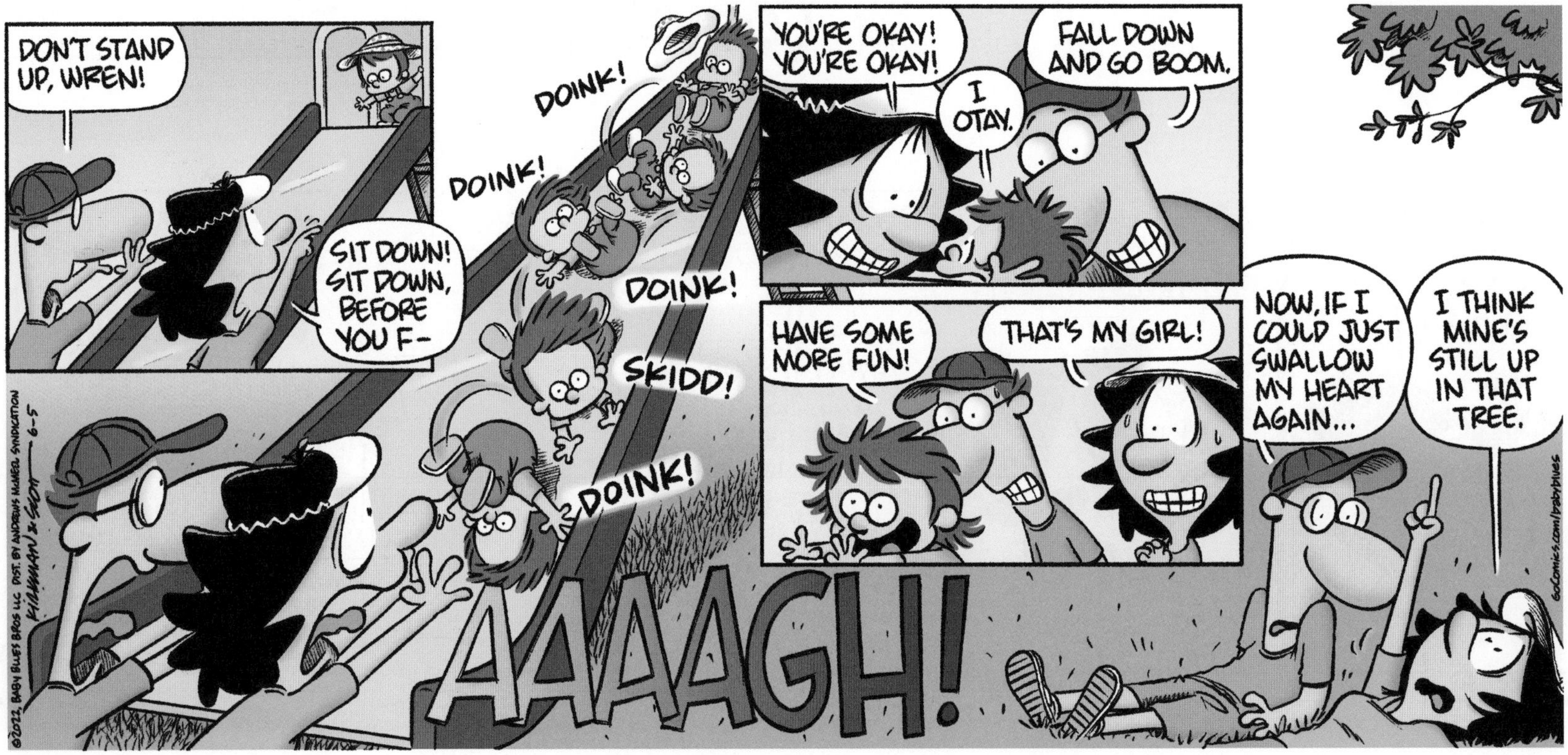
DON'T STAND UP, WREN!
SIT DOWN! SIT DOWN, BEFORE YOU F–
DOINK!
DOINK!
DOINK!
SKIDD!
DOINK!
AAAAGH!
YOU'RE OKAY! YOU'RE OKAY!
I OTAY.
FALL DOWN AND GO BOOM.
HAVE SOME MORE FUN!
THAT'S MY GIRL!
NOW, IF I COULD JUST SWALLOW MY HEART AGAIN...
I THINK MINE'S STILL UP IN THAT TREE.
©2022, BABY BLUES BROS LLC. DIST. BY ANDREWS MCMEEL SYNDICATION
GoComics.com/BabyBlues

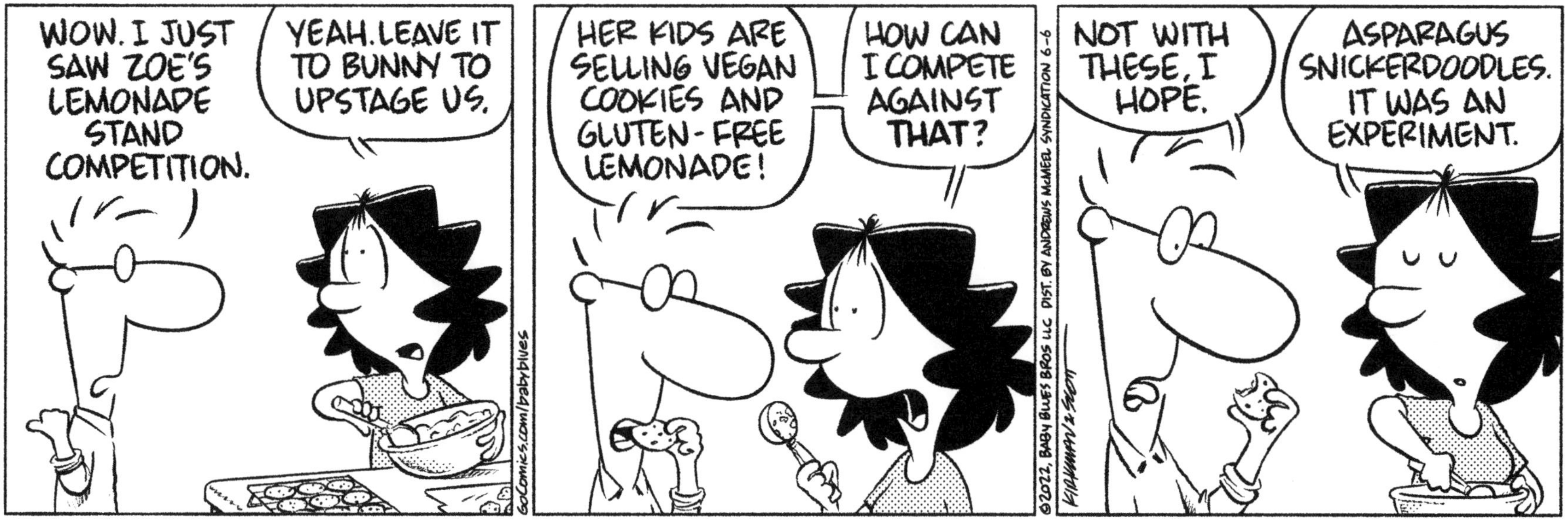
WOW. I JUST SAW ZOE'S LEMONADE STAND COMPETITION.
YEAH. LEAVE IT TO BUNNY TO UPSTAGE US.
GoComics.com/babyblues
HER KIDS ARE SELLING VEGAN COOKIES AND GLUTEN-FREE LEMONADE!
HOW CAN I COMPETE AGAINST THAT?
©2022, BABY BLUES BROS LLC DIST. BY ANDREWS McMEEL SYNDICATION 6-6
KIRKMAN & SCOTT
NOT WITH THESE, I HOPE.
ASPARAGUS SNICKERDOODLES. IT WAS AN EXPERIMENT.

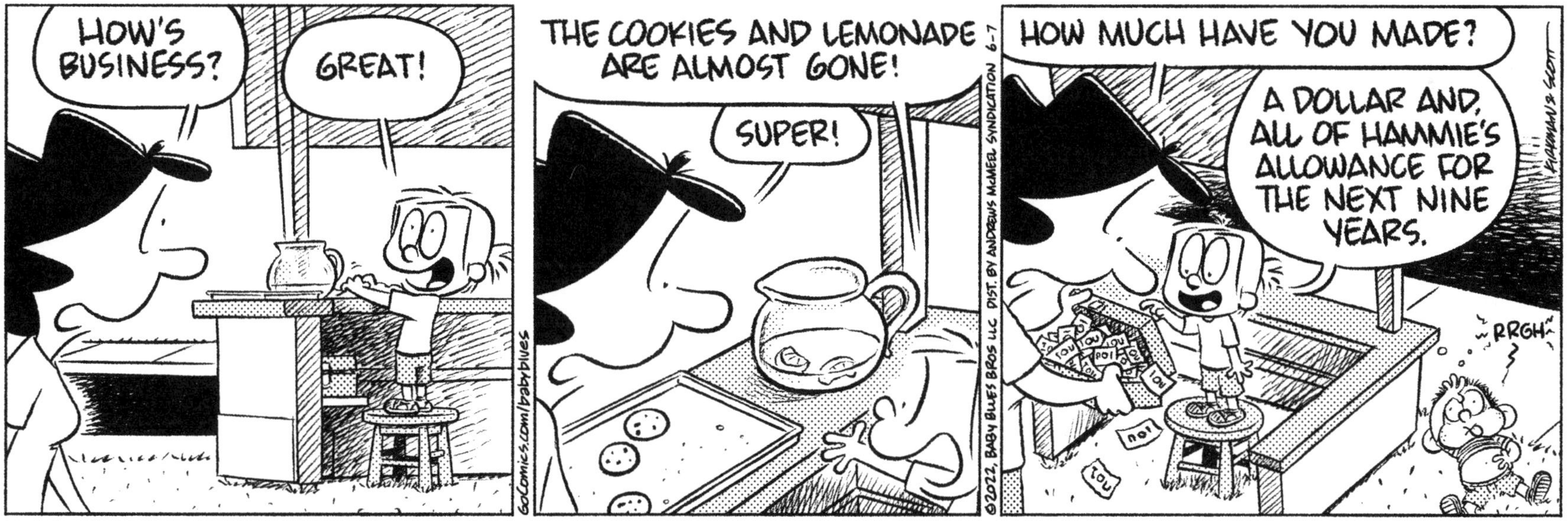
HOW'S BUSINESS?
GREAT!
GoComics.com/babyblues
THE COOKIES AND LEMONADE ARE ALMOST GONE!
SUPER!
©2022, BABY BLUES BROS LLC DIST. BY ANDREWS McMEEL SYNDICATION 6-7
HOW MUCH HAVE YOU MADE?
A DOLLAR AND ALL OF HAMMIE'S ALLOWANCE FOR THE NEXT NINE YEARS.
KIRKMAN & SCOTT
RRGH

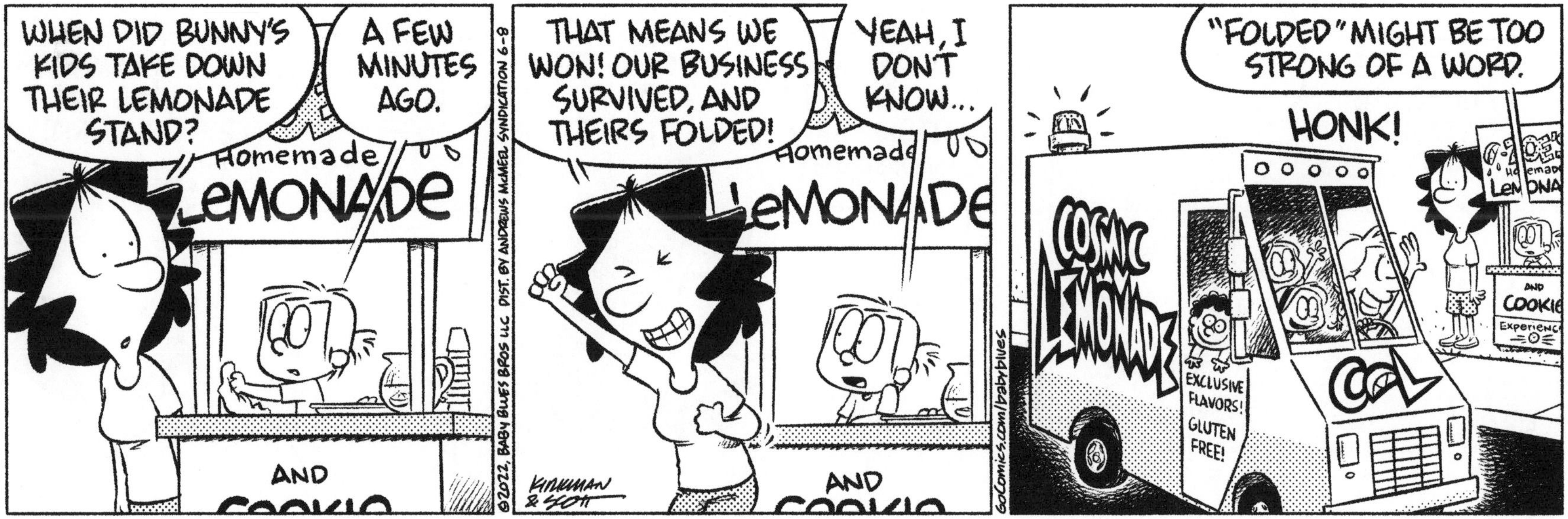
WHEN DID BUNNY'S KIDS TAKE DOWN THEIR LEMONADE STAND?
A FEW MINUTES AGO.
Homemade LEMONADE
AND
©2022, BABY BLUES BROS LLC DIST. BY ANDREWS McMEEL SYNDICATION 6-8
THAT MEANS WE WON! OUR BUSINESS SURVIVED, AND THEIRS FOLDED!
YEAH, I DON'T KNOW...
KIRKMAN & SCOTT
Homemade LEMONADE
AND
GoComics.com/babyblues
"FOLDED" MIGHT BE TOO STRONG OF A WORD.
HONK!
COSMIC LEMONADE
EXCLUSIVE FLAVORS!
GLUTEN FREE!
AND COOKIE
Experience

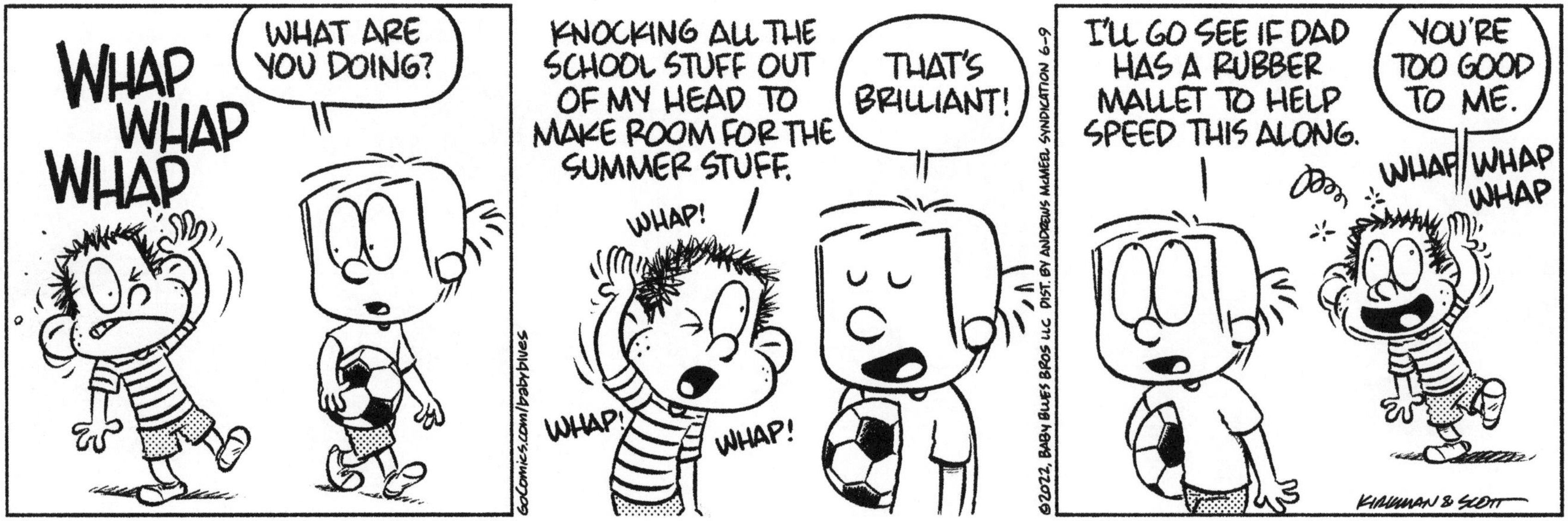
WHAP WHAP WHAP
WHAT ARE YOU DOING?
GoComics.com/babyblues
KNOCKING ALL THE SCHOOL STUFF OUT OF MY HEAD TO MAKE ROOM FOR THE SUMMER STUFF.
WHAP!
WHAP!
WHAP!
THAT'S BRILLIANT!
©2022, BABY BLUES BROS LLC DIST. BY ANDREWS McMEEL SYNDICATION 6-9
I'LL GO SEE IF DAD HAS A RUBBER MALLET TO HELP SPEED THIS ALONG.
YOU'RE TOO GOOD TO ME.
WHAP WHAP WHAP
KIRKMAN & SCOTT

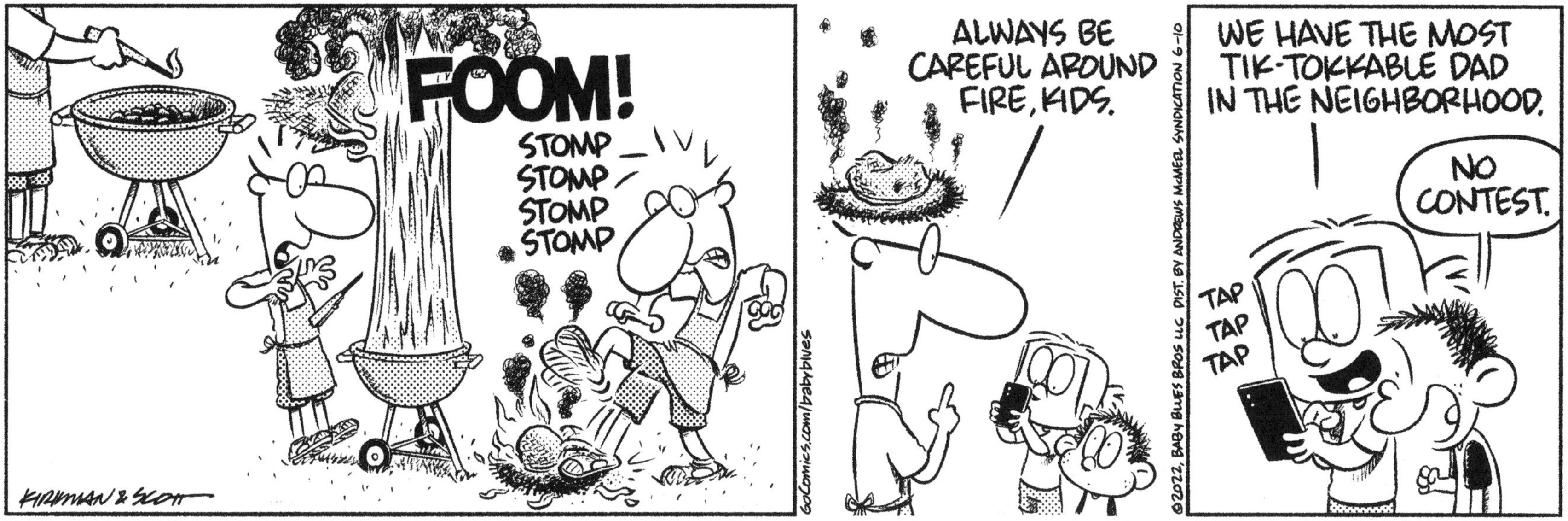
FOOM!
STOMP
STOMP
STOMP
STOMP
ALWAYS BE CAREFUL AROUND FIRE, KIDS.
WE HAVE THE MOST TIK-TOKKABLE DAD IN THE NEIGHBORHOOD.
NO CONTEST.
TAP
TAP
TAP
KIRKMAN & SCOTT
GoComics.com/babyblues
©2022, BABY BLUES BROS LLC DIST. BY ANDREWS McMEEL SYNDICATION 6-10

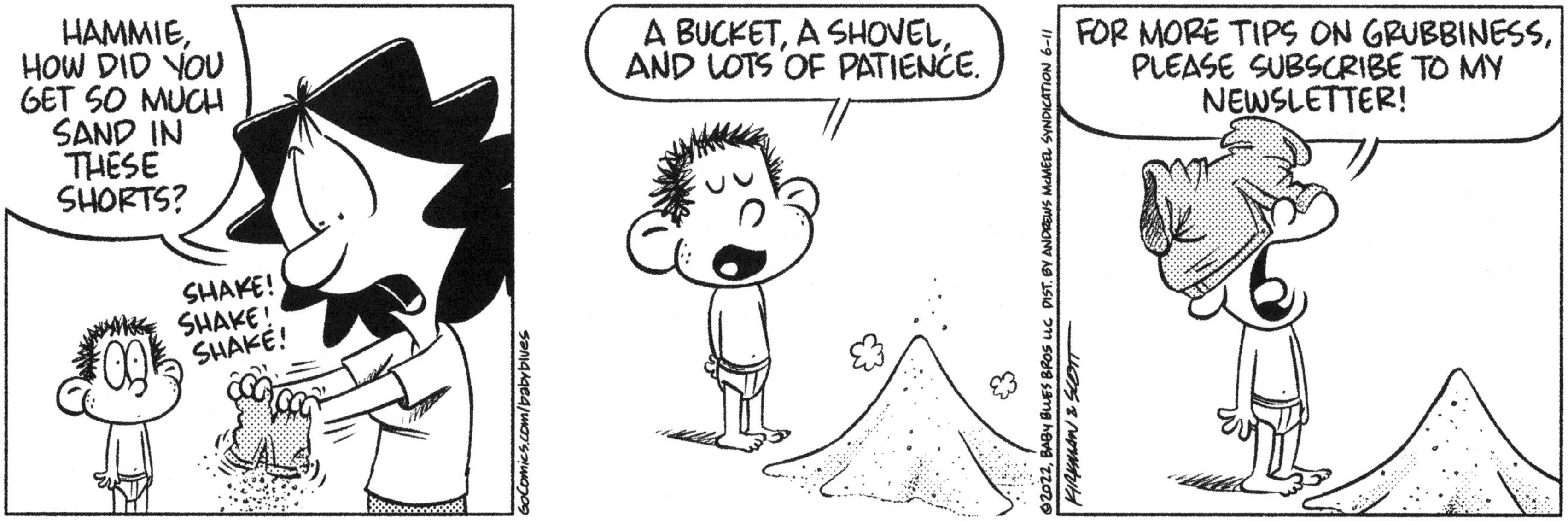
HAMMIE, HOW DID YOU GET SO MUCH SAND IN THESE SHORTS?
SHAKE! SHAKE! SHAKE!
A BUCKET, A SHOVEL, AND LOTS OF PATIENCE.
FOR MORE TIPS ON GRUBBINESS, PLEASE SUBSCRIBE TO MY NEWSLETTER!
GoComics.com/babyblues
©2022, BABY BLUES BROS LLC DIST. BY ANDREWS McMEEL SYNDICATION 6-11
KIRKMAN & SCOTT

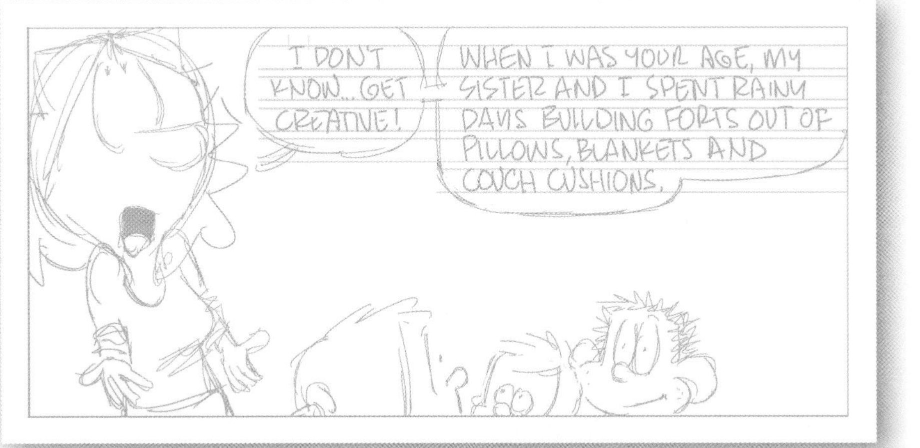
I DON'T KNOW... GET CREATIVE!
WHEN I WAS YOUR AGE, MY SISTER AND I SPENT RAINY DAYS BUILDING FORTS OUT OF PILLOWS, BLANKETS AND COUCH CUSHIONS.

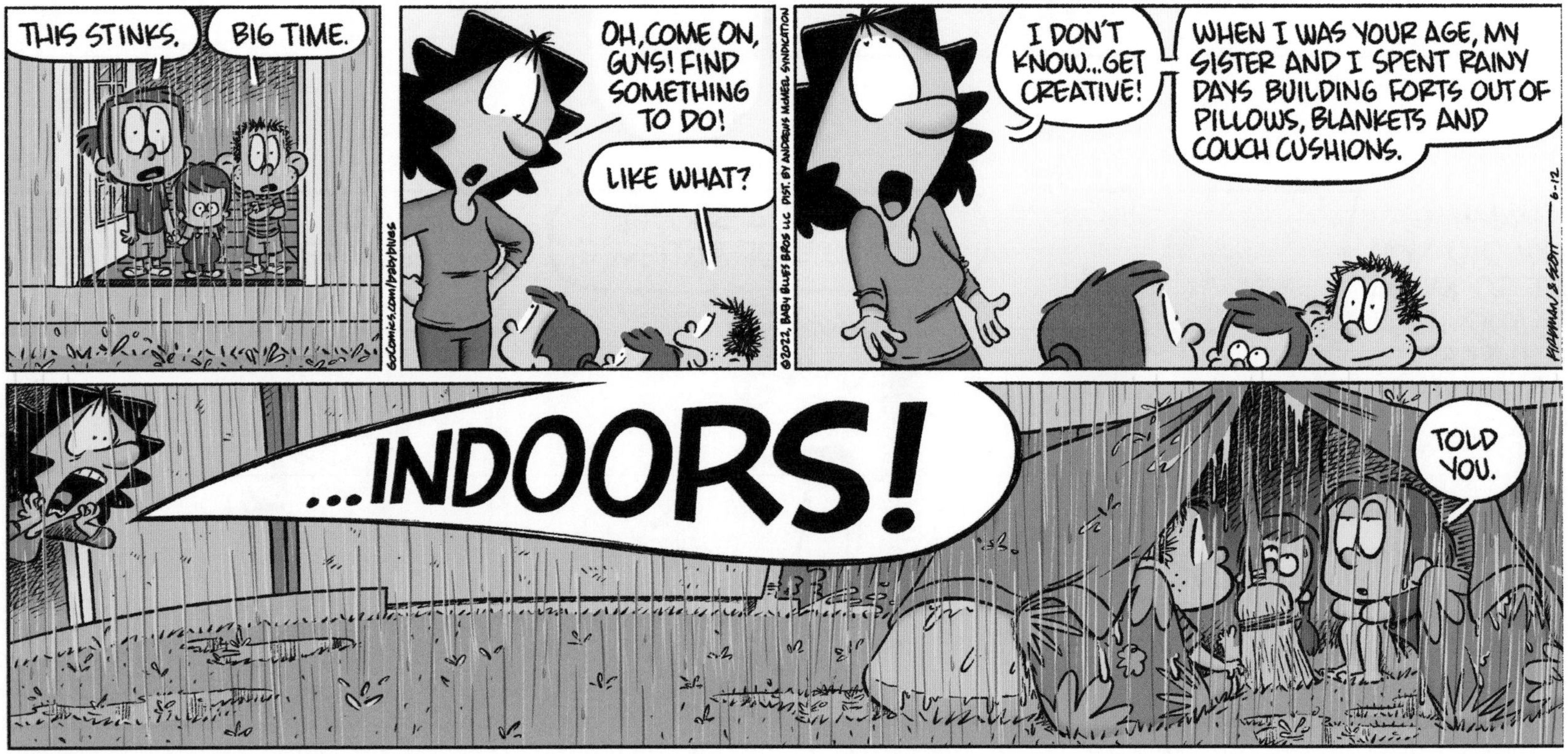
THIS STINKS.
BIG TIME.
OH, COME ON, GUYS! FIND SOMETHING TO DO!
LIKE WHAT?
GoComics.com/babyblues
©2022, BABY BLUES BROS LLC DIST. BY ANDREWS MCMEEL SYNDICATION
I DON'T KNOW...GET CREATIVE!
WHEN I WAS YOUR AGE, MY SISTER AND I SPENT RAINY DAYS BUILDING FORTS OUT OF PILLOWS, BLANKETS AND COUCH CUSHIONS.
6-12
KIRKMAN & SCOTT
...INDOORS!
TOLD YOU.

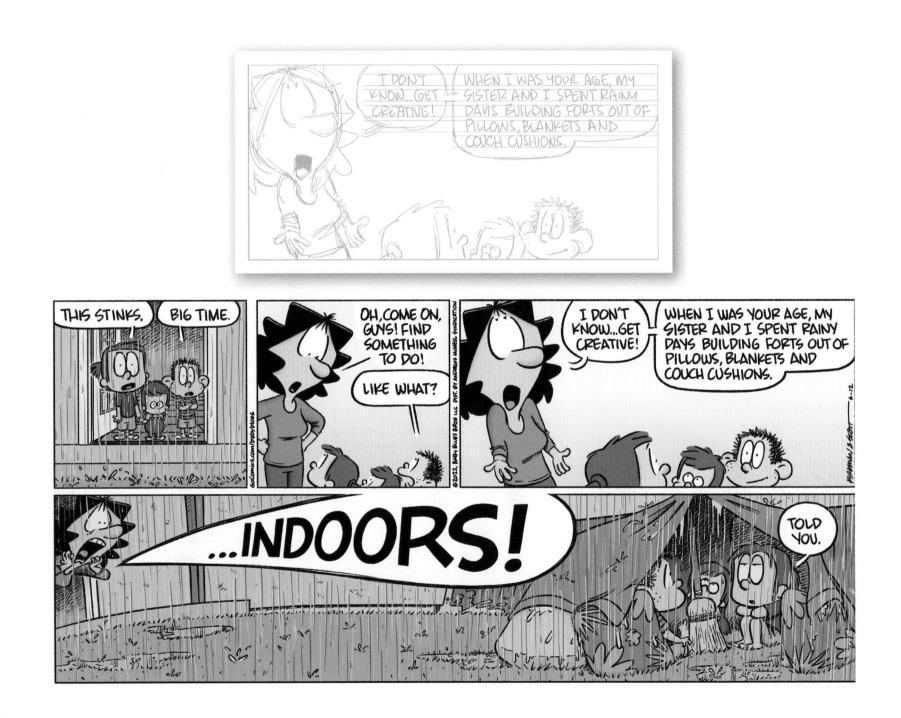

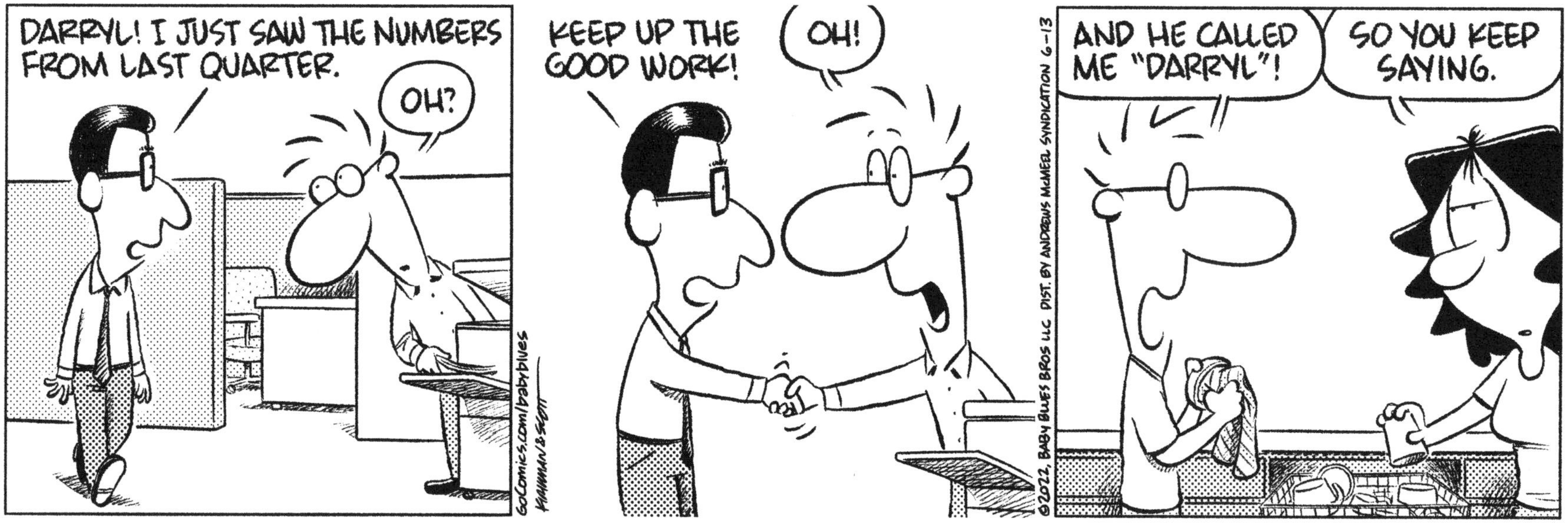
DARRYL! I JUST SAW THE NUMBERS FROM LAST QUARTER.
OH?
GOCOMICS.COM/BABYBLUES
KIRKMAN & SCOTT
KEEP UP THE GOOD WORK!
OH!
©2022, BABY BLUES BROS LLC DIST. BY ANDREWS MCMEEL SYNDICATION 6-13
AND HE CALLED ME "DARRYL"!
SO YOU KEEP SAYING.

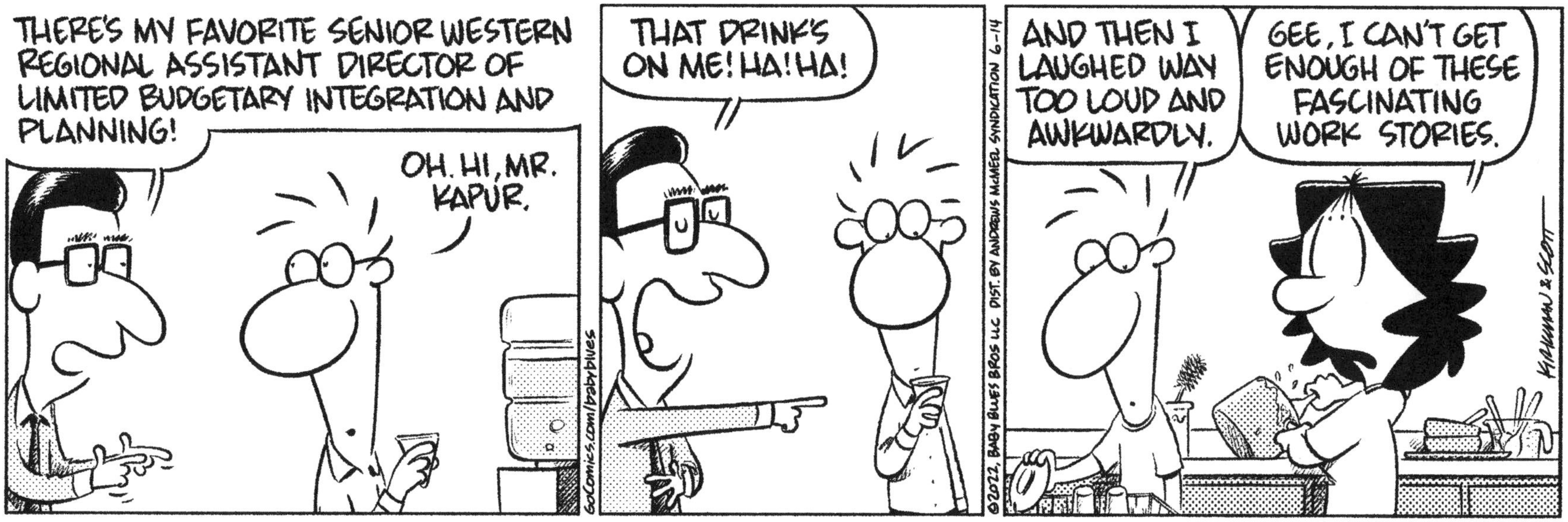
THERE'S MY FAVORITE SENIOR WESTERN REGIONAL ASSISTANT DIRECTOR OF LIMITED BUDGETARY INTEGRATION AND PLANNING!
OH. HI, MR. KAPUR.
GOCOMICS.COM/BABYBLUES
THAT DRINK'S ON ME! HA! HA!
©2022, BABY BLUES BROS LLC DIST. BY ANDREWS MCMEEL SYNDICATION 6-14
AND THEN I LAUGHED WAY TOO LOUD AND AWKWARDLY.
GEE, I CAN'T GET ENOUGH OF THESE FASCINATING WORK STORIES.
KIRKMAN & SCOTT

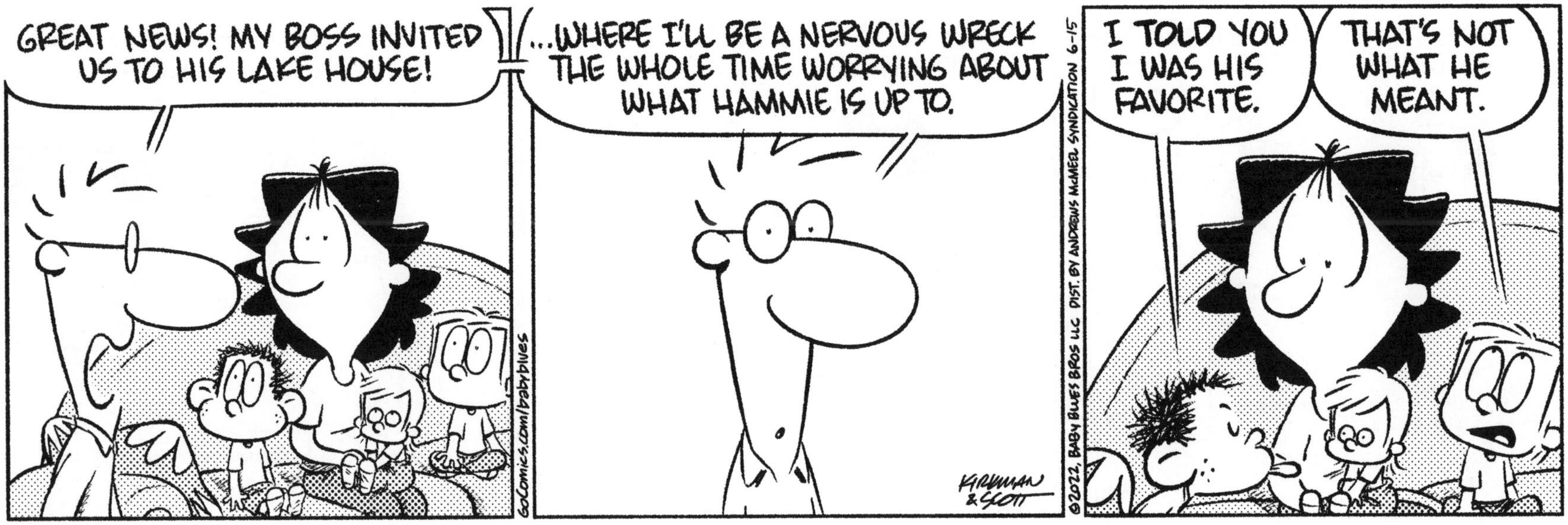

GREAT NEWS! MY BOSS INVITED US TO HIS LAKE HOUSE!
GoComics.com/babyblues
...WHERE I'LL BE A NERVOUS WRECK THE WHOLE TIME WORRYING ABOUT WHAT HAMMIE IS UP TO.
KIRKMAN & SCOTT
©2022, BABY BLUES BROS LLC DIST. BY ANDREWS McMEEL SYNDICATION 6-15
I TOLD YOU I WAS HIS FAVORITE.
THAT'S NOT WHAT HE MEANT.

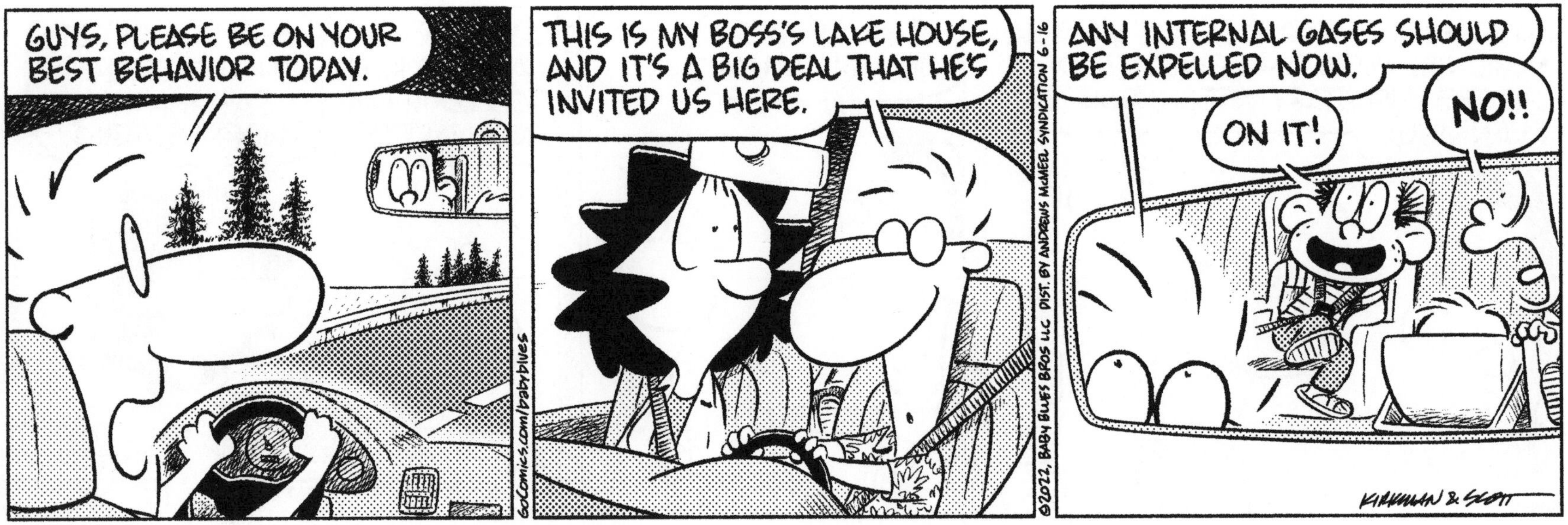

GUYS, PLEASE BE ON YOUR BEST BEHAVIOR TODAY.
GoComics.com/babyblues
THIS IS MY BOSS'S LAKE HOUSE, AND IT'S A BIG DEAL THAT HE'S INVITED US HERE.
©2022, BABY BLUES BROS LLC DIST. BY ANDREWS McMEEL SYNDICATION 6-16
ANY INTERNAL GASES SHOULD BE EXPELLED NOW.
ON IT!
NO!!
KIRKMAN & SCOTT

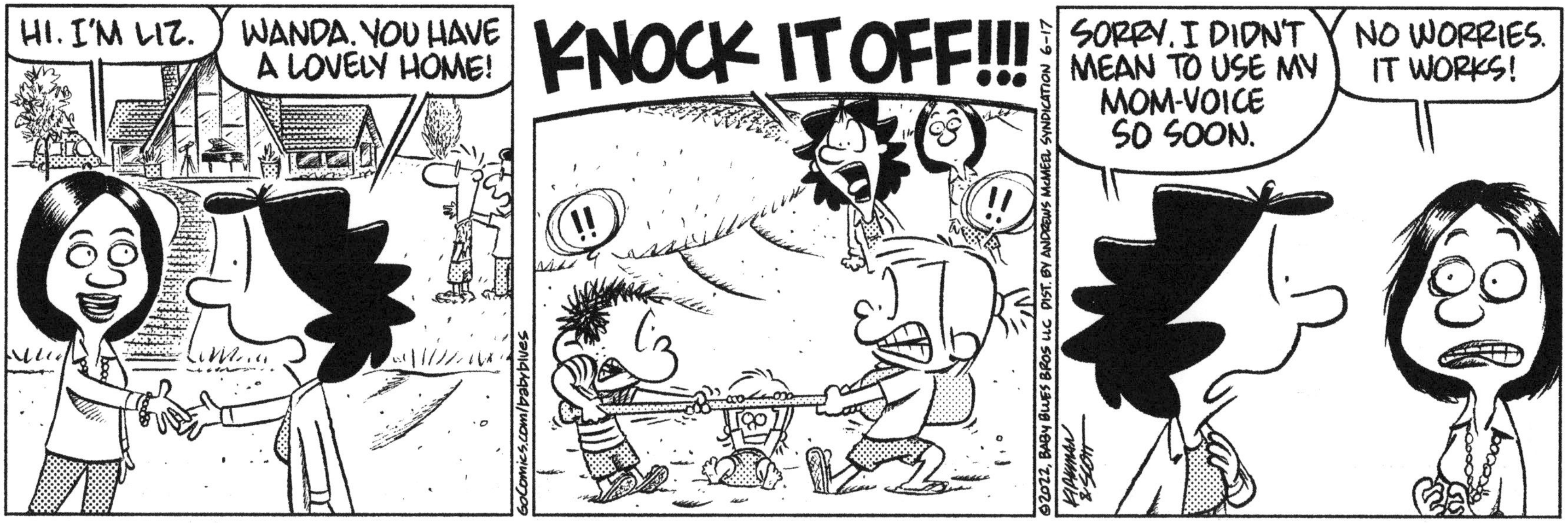
HI. I'M LIZ.
WANDA. YOU HAVE A LOVELY HOME!
GoComics.com/babyblues
KNOCK IT OFF!!!
!!
!!
©2022, BABY BLUES BROS LLC DIST. BY ANDREWS McMEEL SYNDICATION 6-17
SORRY. I DIDN'T MEAN TO USE MY MOM-VOICE SO SOON.
NO WORRIES. IT WORKS!
KIRKMAN & SCOTT

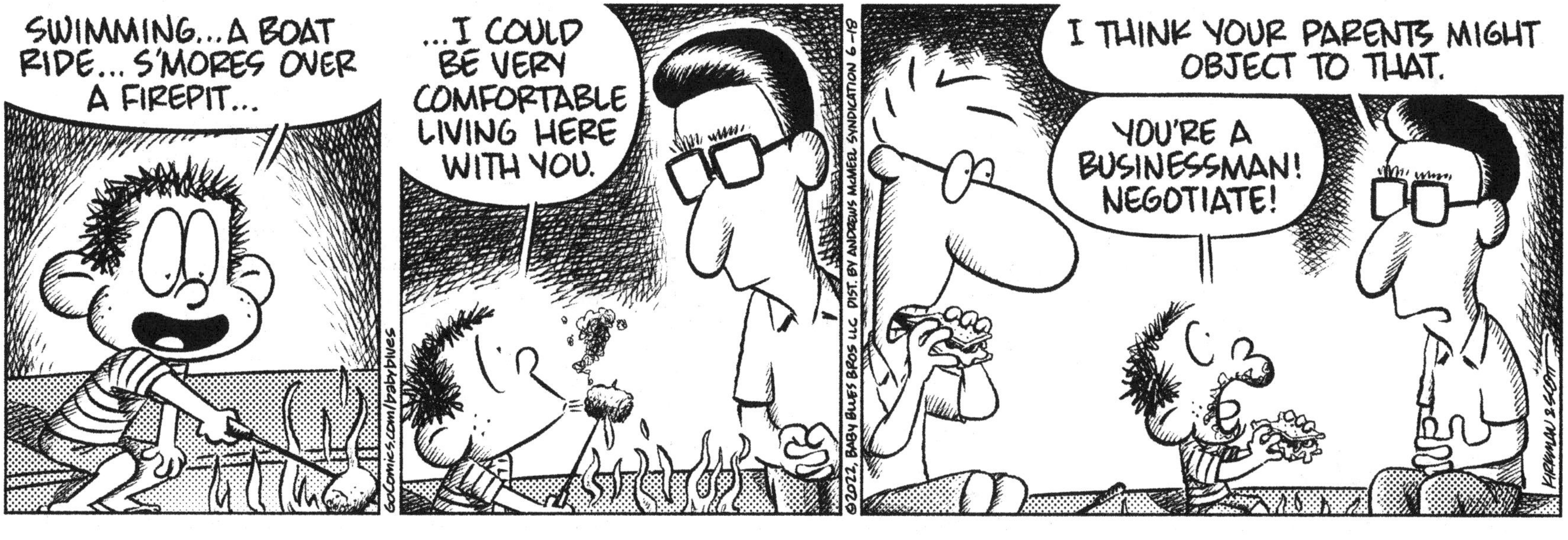
SWIMMING... A BOAT RIDE... S'MORES OVER A FIREPIT...
GoComics.com/babyblues
...I COULD BE VERY COMFORTABLE LIVING HERE WITH YOU.
©2022, BABY BLUES BROS LLC DIST. BY ANDREWS McMEEL SYNDICATION 6-18
I THINK YOUR PARENTS MIGHT OBJECT TO THAT.
YOU'RE A BUSINESSMAN! NEGOTIATE!
KIRKMAN & SCOTT

YEP.
YEP.

HAPPY FATHER'S DAY, DAD!
WELL, HAPPY FATHER'S DAY TO YOU, SON!
GoComics.com/babyblues
YEP.
YEP.
©2022, BABY BLUES BROS LLC DIST. BY ANDREWS MCMEEL SYNDICATION
HOW'S MOM?
GOOD.
GOOD. HOW ARE WANDA AND THE KIDS?
YEP.
YEP.
WELL, I SHOULD GO.
YEP.
THAT WAS A CONVERSATION??
THE APPLE DIDN'T FALL FAR FROM THE TREE...THEN, IT ROLLED BACK UP THE TRUNK AND REATTACHED ITSELF TO THE BRANCH.
BEST TALK EVER!
6-19

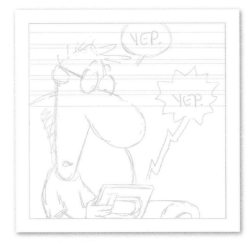

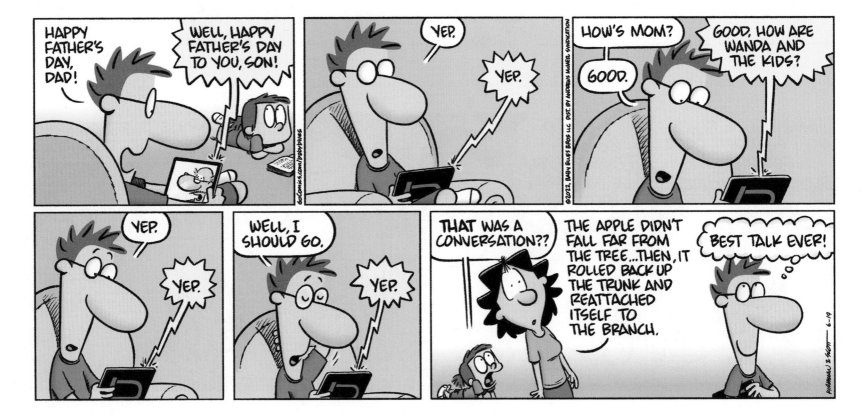

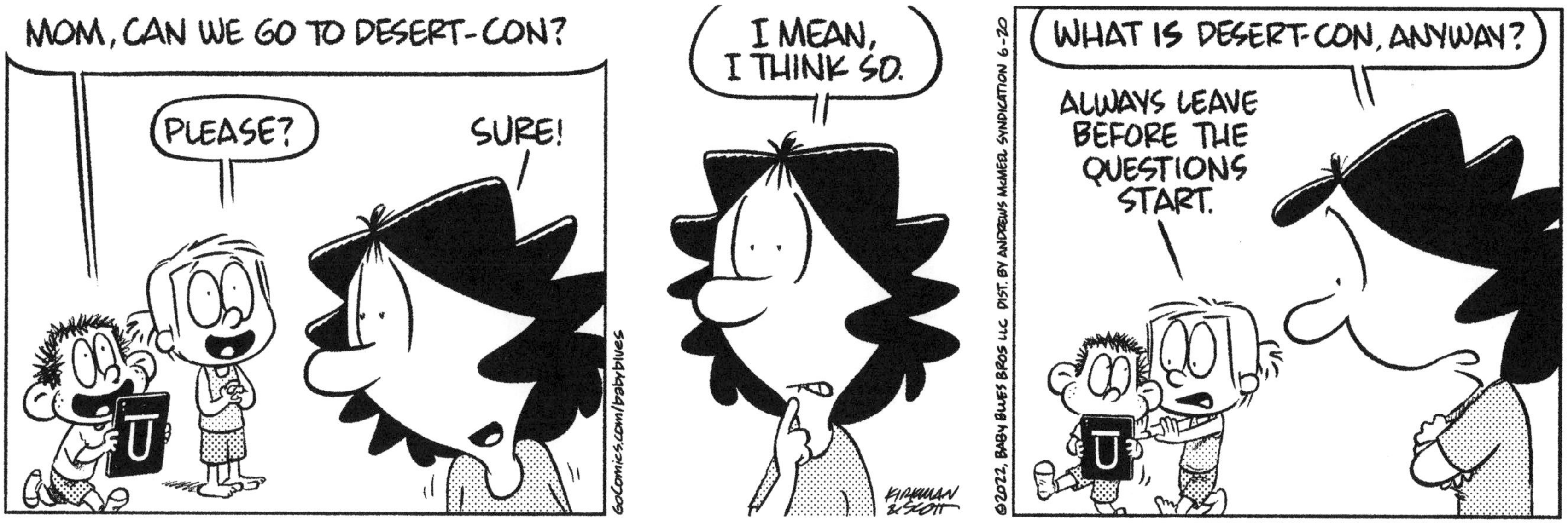
MOM, CAN WE GO TO DESERT-CON?
PLEASE?
SURE!
GoComics.com/babyblues
I MEAN, I THINK SO.
KIRKMAN & SCOTT
©2022, BABY BLUES BROS LLC DIST. BY ANDREWS MCMEEL SYNDICATION 6-20
WHAT IS DESERT-CON, ANYWAY?
ALWAYS LEAVE BEFORE THE QUESTIONS START.

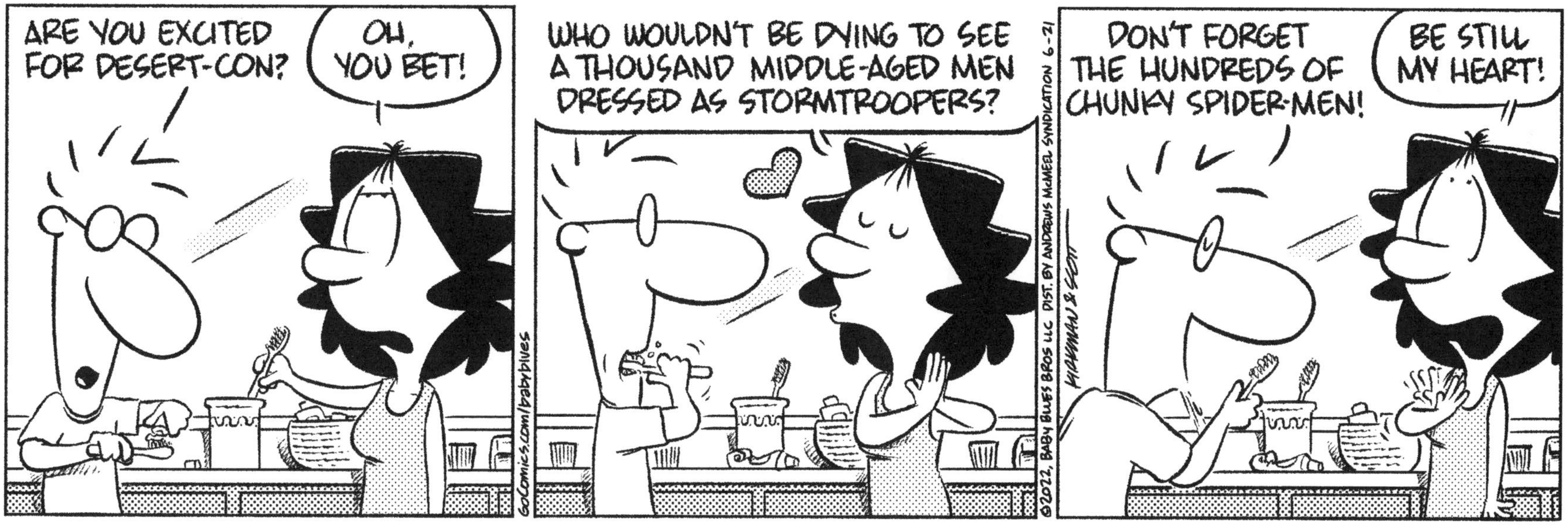
ARE YOU EXCITED FOR DESERT-CON?
OH, YOU BET!
GoComics.com/babyblues
WHO WOULDN'T BE DYING TO SEE A THOUSAND MIDDLE-AGED MEN DRESSED AS STORMTROOPERS?
©2022, BABY BLUES BROS LLC DIST. BY ANDREWS MCMEEL SYNDICATION 6-21
KIRKMAN & SCOTT
DON'T FORGET THE HUNDREDS OF CHUNKY SPIDER-MEN!
BE STILL MY HEART!

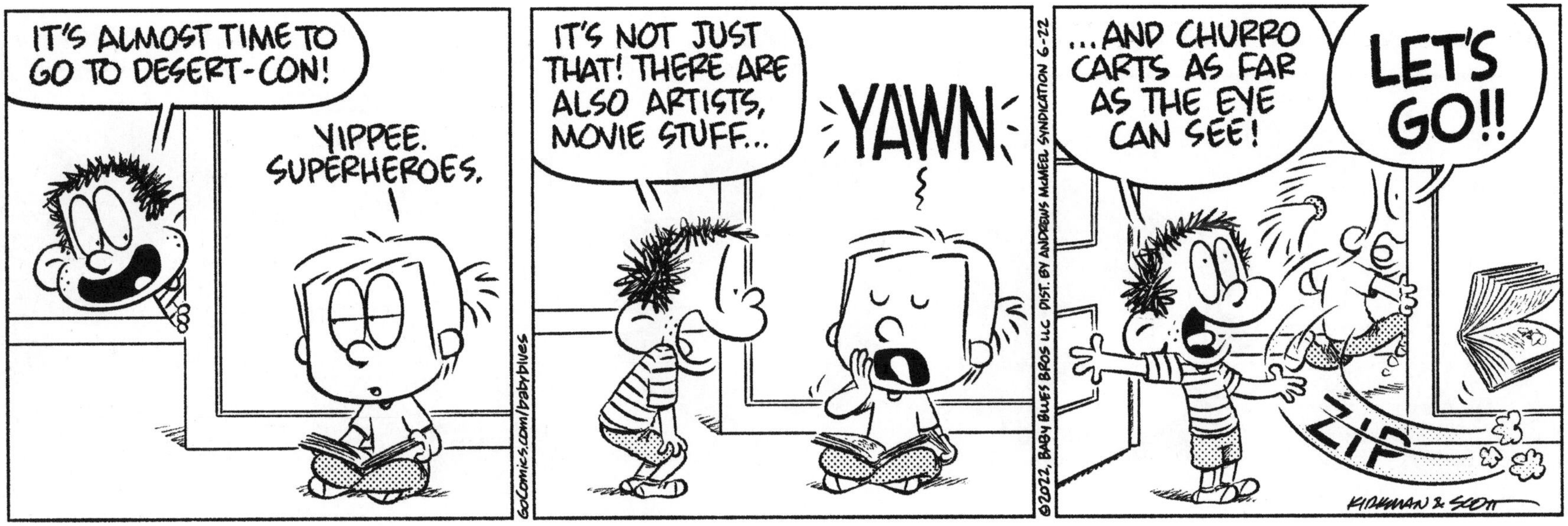
IT'S ALMOST TIME TO GO TO DESERT-CON!
YIPPEE. SUPERHEROES.
GoComics.com/babyblues
IT'S NOT JUST THAT! THERE ARE ALSO ARTISTS, MOVIE STUFF...
YAWN
©2022, BABY BLUES BROS LLC DIST. BY ANDREWS McMEEL SYNDICATION 6-22
...AND CHURRO CARTS AS FAR AS THE EYE CAN SEE!
LET'S GO!!
ZIP
KIRKMAN & SCOTT

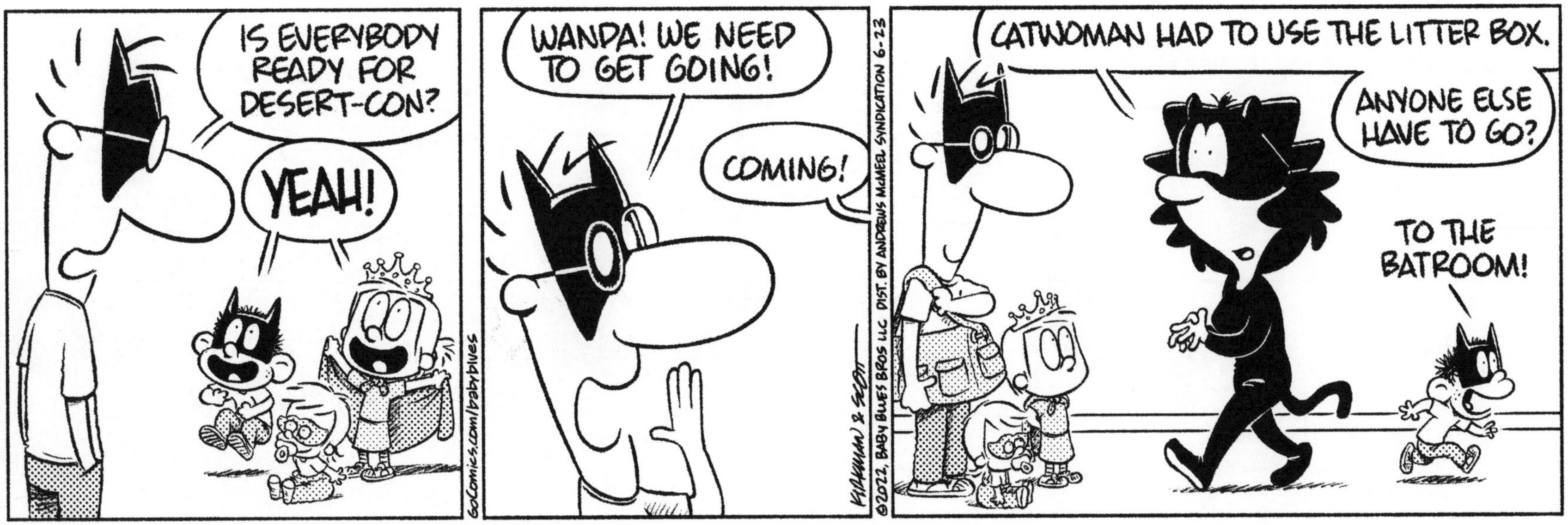
IS EVERYBODY READY FOR DESERT-CON?
YEAH!
GoComics.com/babyblues
WANDA! WE NEED TO GET GOING!
COMING!
KIRKMAN & SCOTT
©2022, BABY BLUES BROS LLC DIST. BY ANDREWS McMEEL SYNDICATION 6-23
CATWOMAN HAD TO USE THE LITTER BOX.
ANYONE ELSE HAVE TO GO?
TO THE BATROOM!

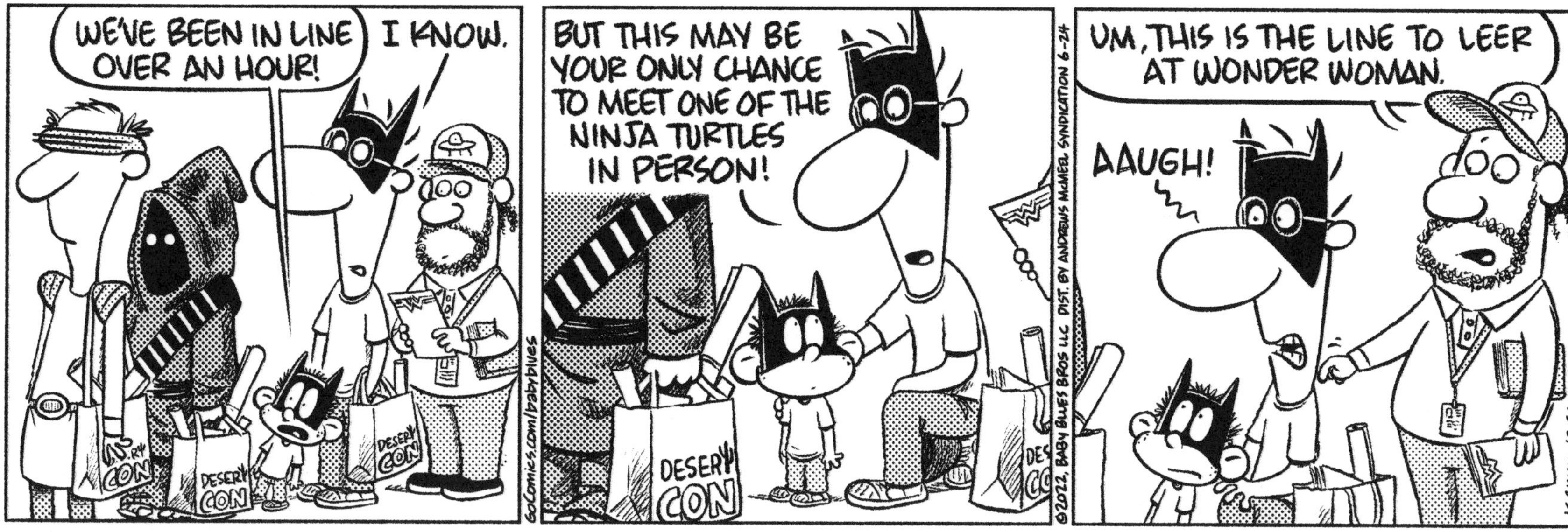
WE'VE BEEN IN LINE OVER AN HOUR!
I KNOW.
BUT THIS MAY BE YOUR ONLY CHANCE TO MEET ONE OF THE NINJA TURTLES IN PERSON!
UM, THIS IS THE LINE TO LEER AT WONDER WOMAN.
AAUGH!
DESERT CON
GoComics.com/babyblues
©2022, BABY BLUES BROS LLC DIST. BY ANDREWS McMEEL SYNDICATION 6-24
KIRKMAN & SCOTT

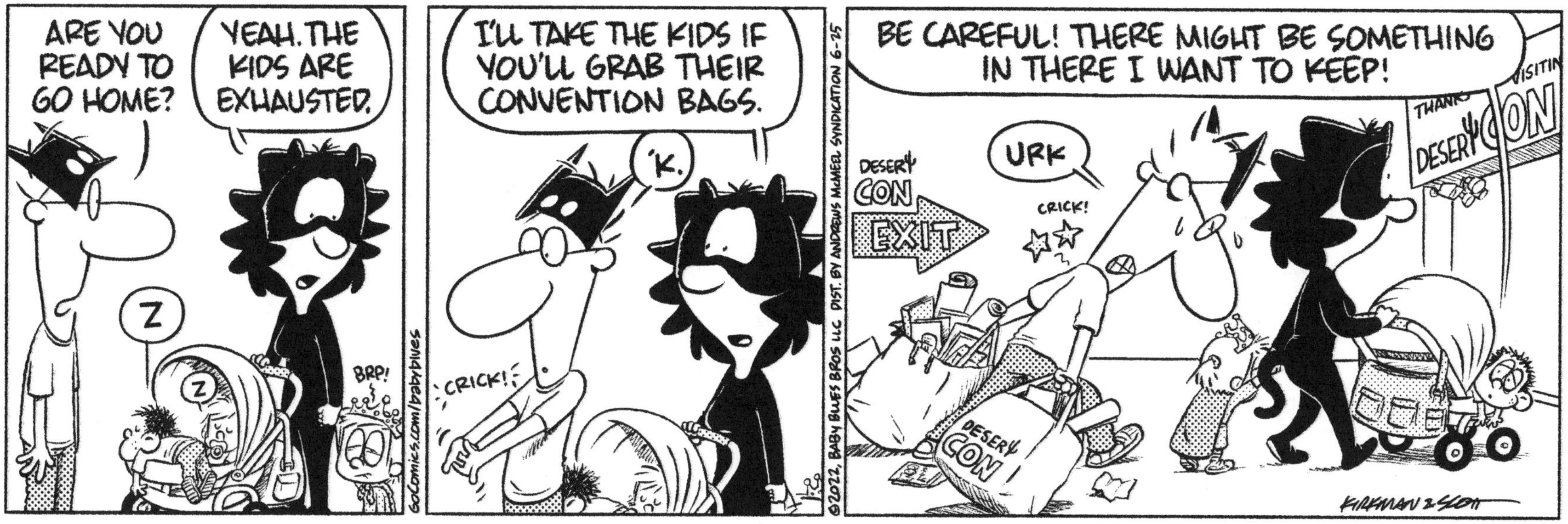
ARE YOU READY TO GO HOME?
YEAH. THE KIDS ARE EXHAUSTED.
Z
Z
BRP!
GoComics.com/babyblues
I'LL TAKE THE KIDS IF YOU'LL GRAB THEIR CONVENTION BAGS.
'K.
CRICK!
©2022, BABY BLUES BROS LLC DIST. BY ANDREWS McMEEL SYNDICATION 6-25
BE CAREFUL! THERE MIGHT BE SOMETHING IN THERE I WANT TO KEEP!
DESERT CON
EXIT
URK
CRICK!
KIRKMAN & SCOTT

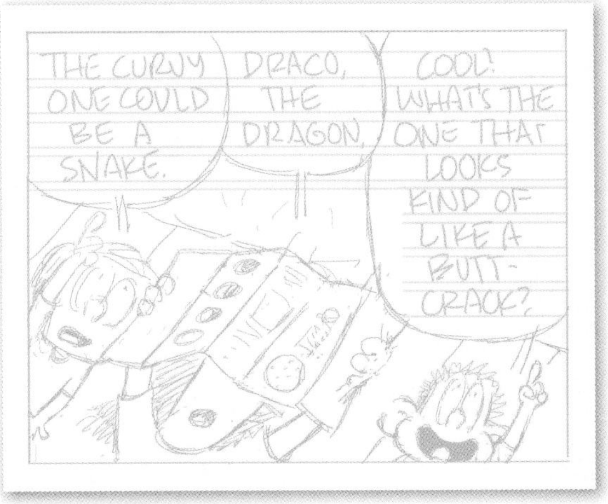
THE CURVY ONE COULD BE A SNAKE.
DRACO, THE DRAGON.
COOL! WHAT'S THE ONE THAT LOOKS KIND OF LIKE A BUTT-CRACK?

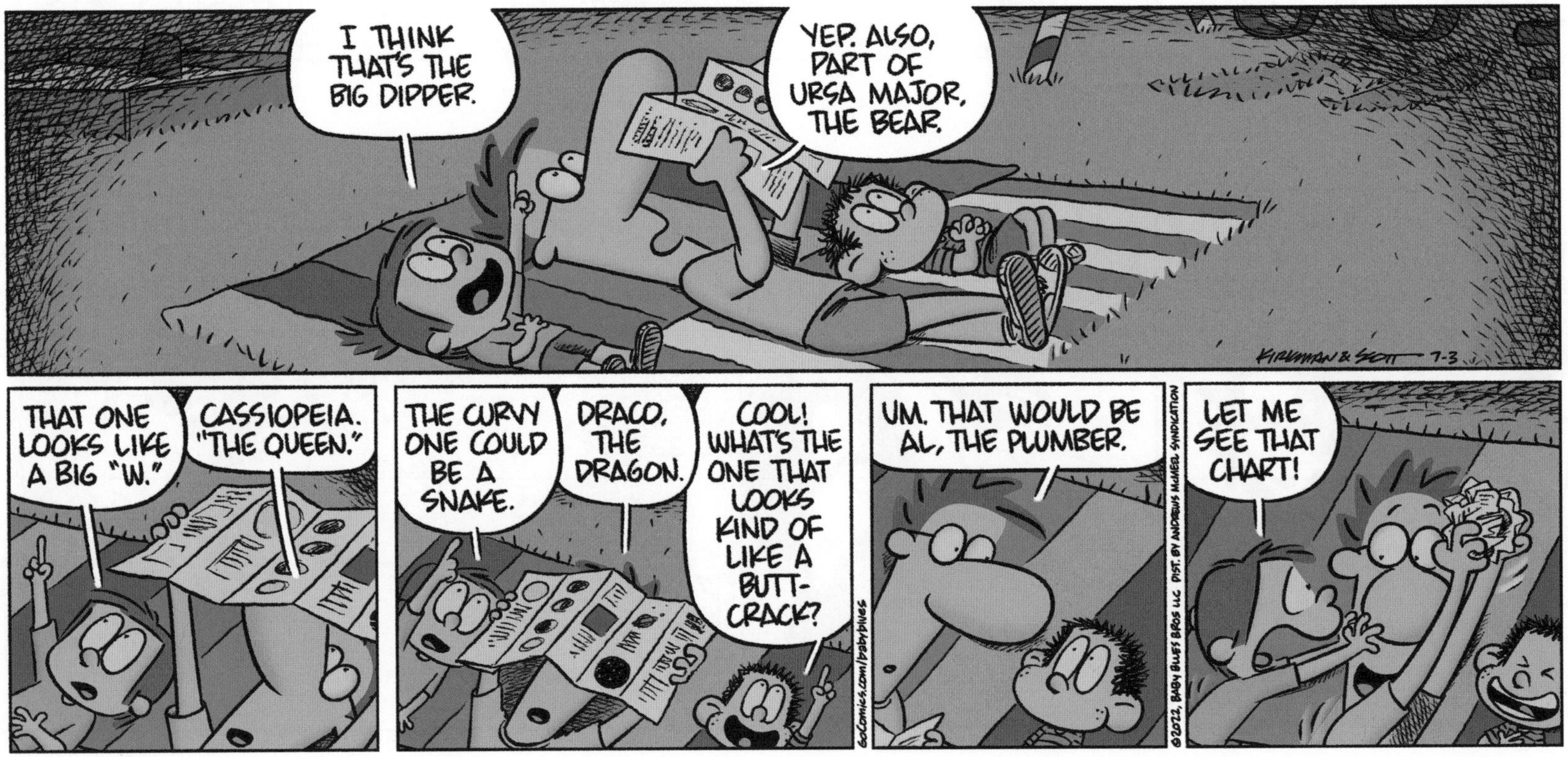
I THINK THAT'S THE BIG DIPPER.
YEP. ALSO, PART OF URSA MAJOR, THE BEAR.
KIRKMAN & SCOTT 7-3
THAT ONE LOOKS LIKE A BIG "W."
CASSIOPEIA. "THE QUEEN."
THE CURVY ONE COULD BE A SNAKE.
DRACO, THE DRAGON.
COOL! WHAT'S THE ONE THAT LOOKS KIND OF LIKE A BUTT-CRACK?
GoComics.com/babyblues
UM. THAT WOULD BE AL, THE PLUMBER.
©2022, BABY BLUES BROS LLC DIST. BY ANDREWS McMEEL SYNDICATION
LET ME SEE THAT CHART!

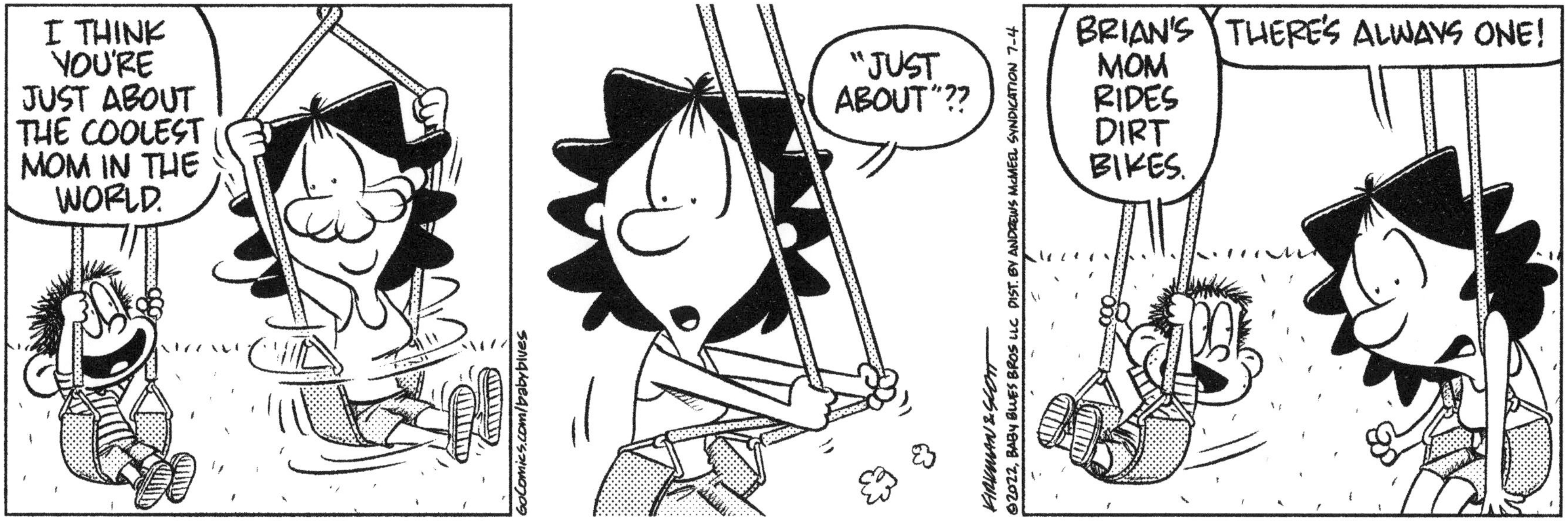
I THINK YOU'RE JUST ABOUT THE COOLEST MOM IN THE WORLD.
GoComics.com/babyblues
"JUST ABOUT"??
KIRKMAN & SCOTT
©2022, BABY BLUES BROS LLC DIST. BY ANDREWS McMEEL SYNDICATION 7-4
BRIAN'S MOM RIDES DIRT BIKES.
THERE'S ALWAYS ONE!

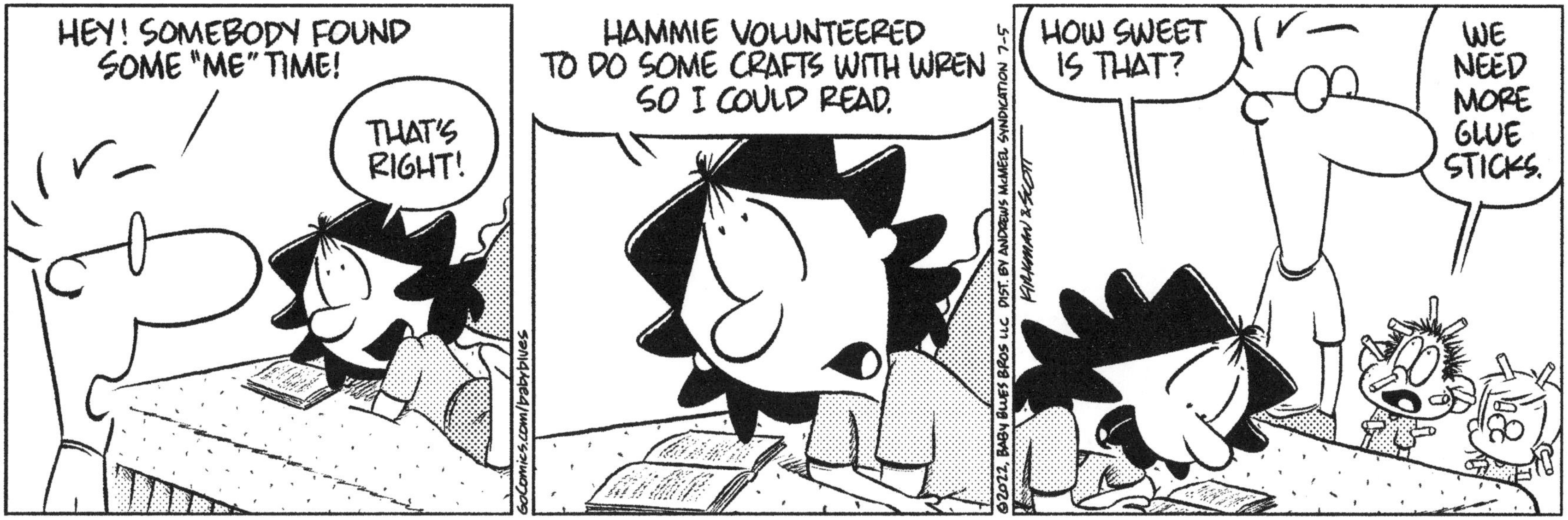
HEY! SOMEBODY FOUND SOME "ME" TIME!
THAT'S RIGHT!
GoComics.com/babyblues
HAMMIE VOLUNTEERED TO DO SOME CRAFTS WITH WREN SO I COULD READ.
KIRKMAN & SCOTT
©2022, BABY BLUES BROS LLC DIST. BY ANDREWS McMEEL SYNDICATION 7-5
HOW SWEET IS THAT?
WE NEED MORE GLUE STICKS.

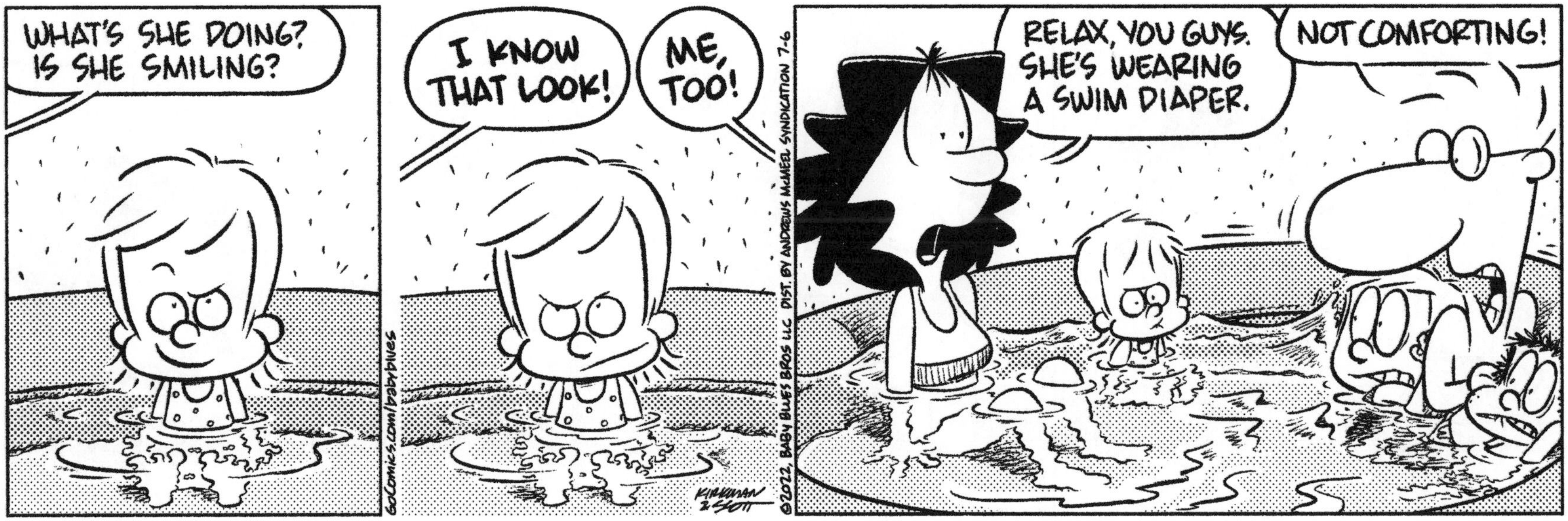
WHAT'S SHE DOING? IS SHE SMILING?
I KNOW THAT LOOK!
ME, TOO!
RELAX, YOU GUYS. SHE'S WEARING A SWIM DIAPER.
NOT COMFORTING!
GoComics.com/babyblues
KIRKMAN & SCOTT
©2022, BABY BLUES BROS LLC DIST. BY ANDREWS McMEEL SYNDICATION 7-6

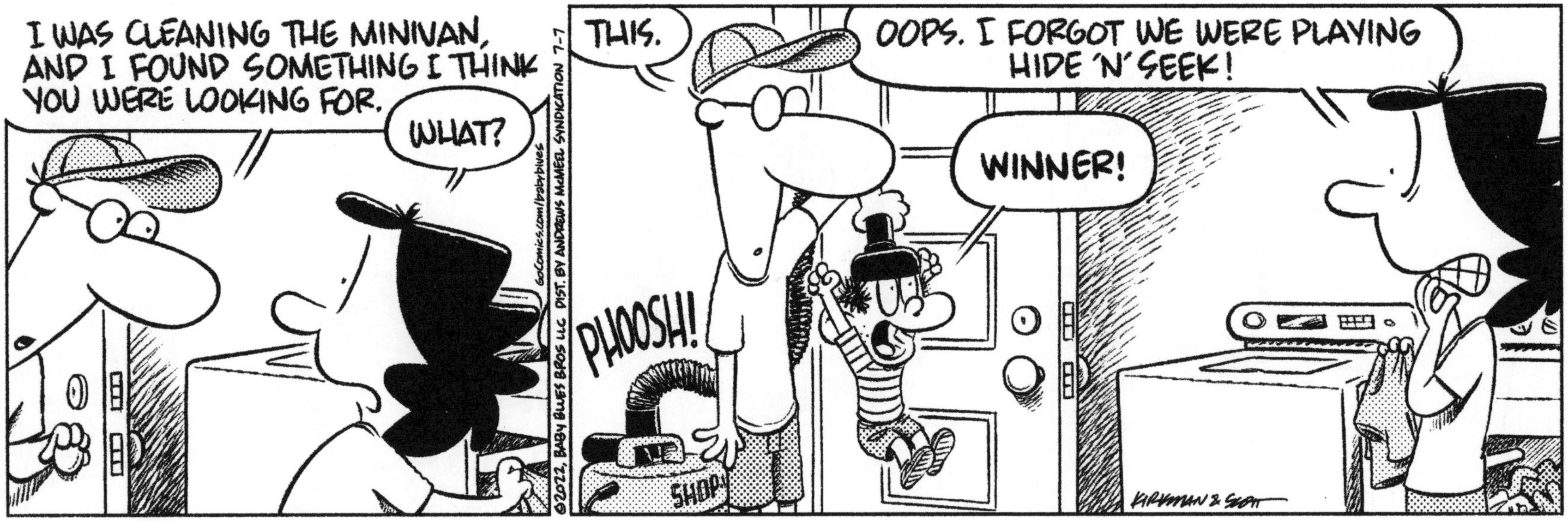
I WAS CLEANING THE MINIVAN, AND I FOUND SOMETHING I THINK YOU WERE LOOKING FOR.
WHAT?
THIS.
OOPS. I FORGOT WE WERE PLAYING HIDE 'N' SEEK!
WINNER!
PHOOSH!
SHOP
GoComics.com/babyblues
KIRKMAN & SCOTT
©2022, BABY BLUES BROS LLC DIST. BY ANDREWS McMEEL SYNDICATION 7-7

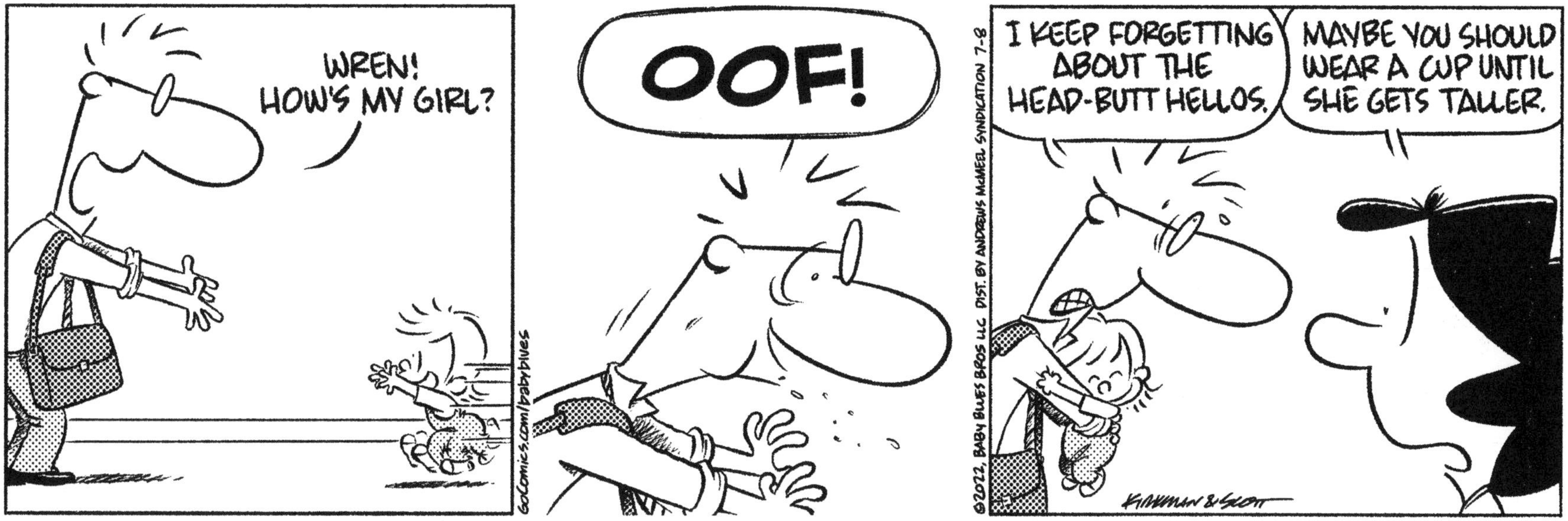
WREN! HOW'S MY GIRL?
gocomics.com/babyblues
OOF!
©2022, BABY BLUES BROS LLC DIST. BY ANDREWS MCMEEL SYNDICATION 7-8
I KEEP FORGETTING ABOUT THE HEAD-BUTT HELLOS.
MAYBE YOU SHOULD WEAR A CUP UNTIL SHE GETS TALLER.
KIRKMAN & SCOTT

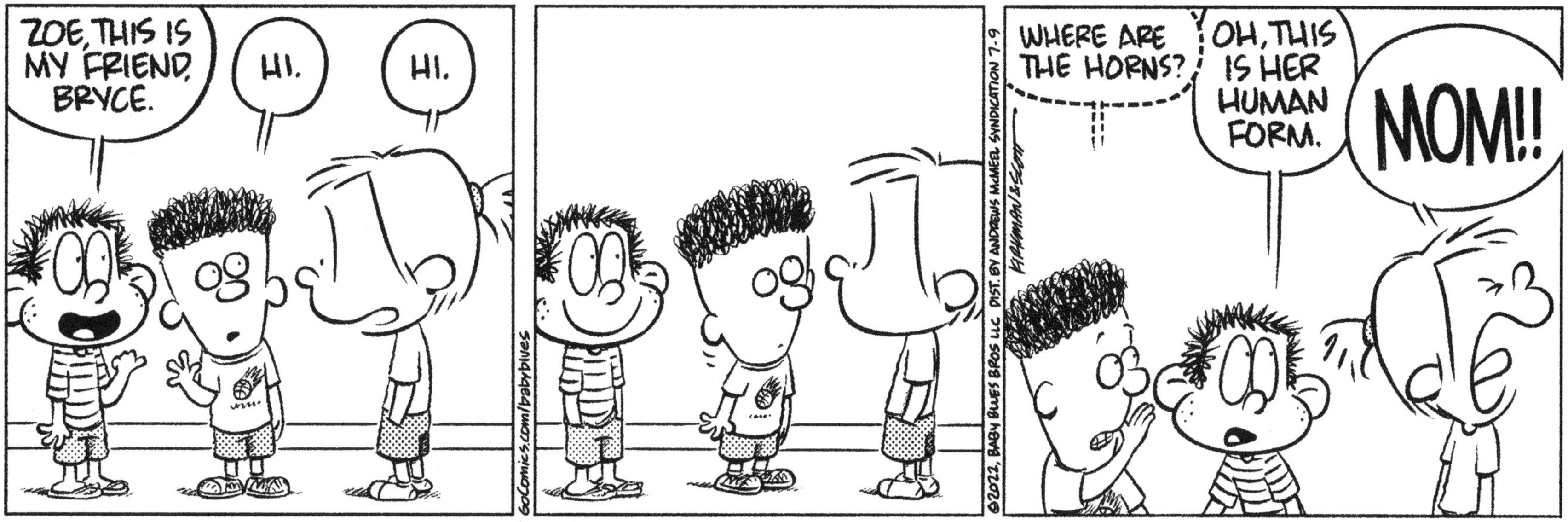
ZOE, THIS IS MY FRIEND, BRYCE.
HI.
HI.
gocomics.com/babyblues
©2022, BABY BLUES BROS LLC DIST. BY ANDREWS MCMEEL SYNDICATION 7-9
WHERE ARE THE HORNS?
OH, THIS IS HER HUMAN FORM.
MOM!!
KIRKMAN & SCOTT

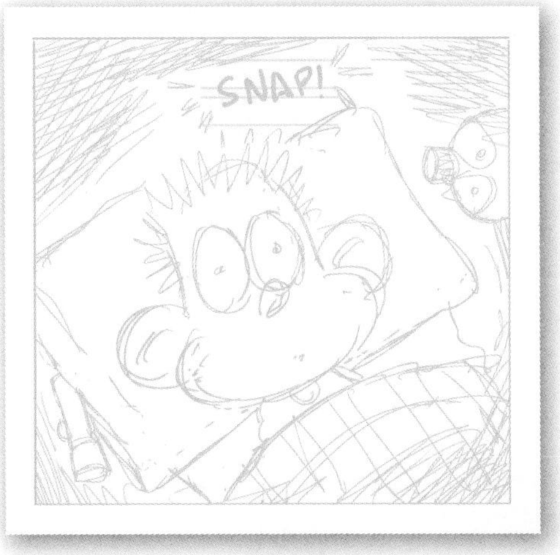
SNAP!

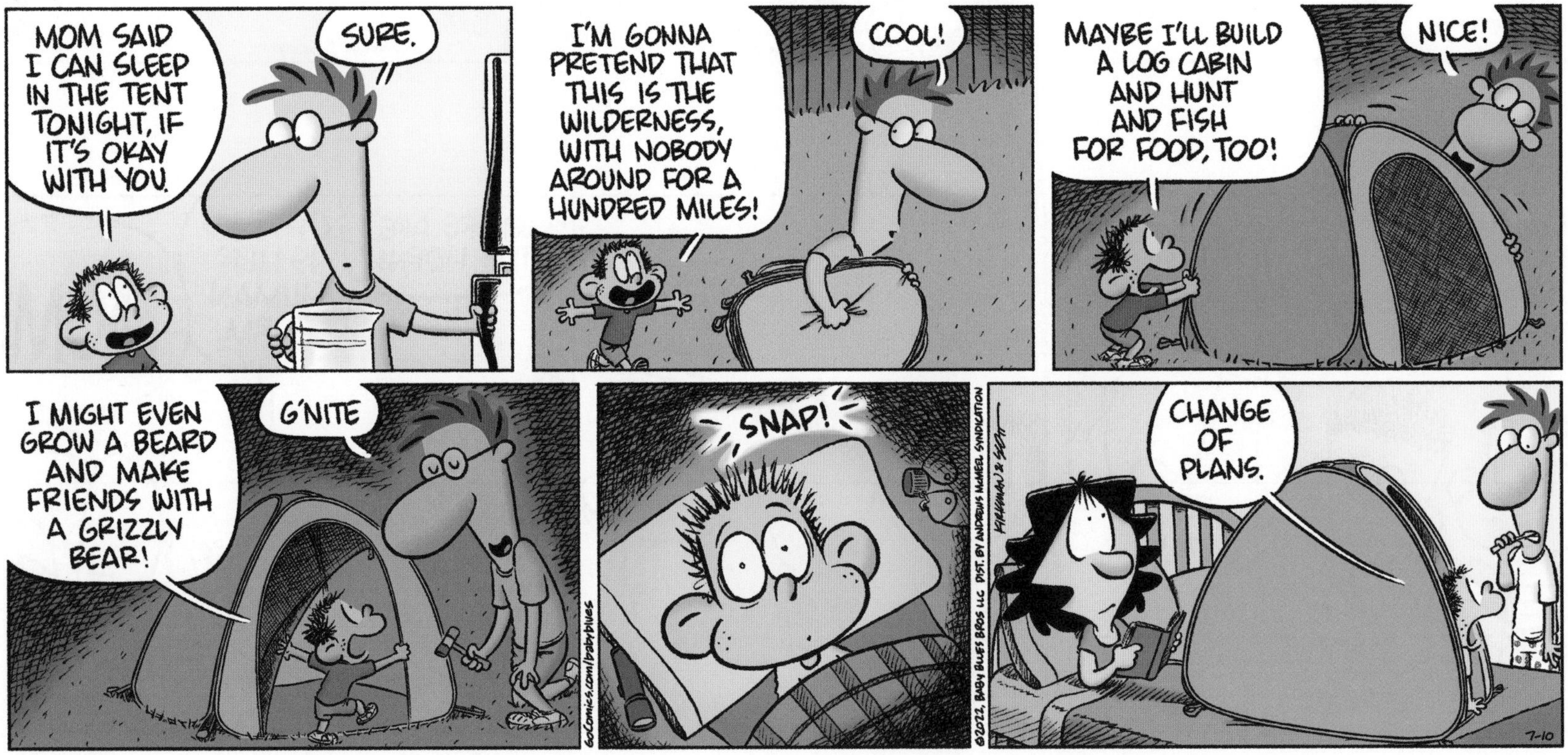
MOM SAID I CAN SLEEP IN THE TENT TONIGHT, IF IT'S OKAY WITH YOU.
SURE.
I'M GONNA PRETEND THAT THIS IS THE WILDERNESS, WITH NOBODY AROUND FOR A HUNDRED MILES!
COOL!
MAYBE I'LL BUILD A LOG CABIN AND HUNT AND FISH FOR FOOD, TOO!
NICE!
I MIGHT EVEN GROW A BEARD AND MAKE FRIENDS WITH A GRIZZLY BEAR!
G'NITE
GoComics.com/babyblues
SNAP!
©2022, BABY BLUES BROS LLC DIST. BY ANDREWS McMEEL SYNDICATION
KIRKMAN & SCOTT
CHANGE OF PLANS.
7-10

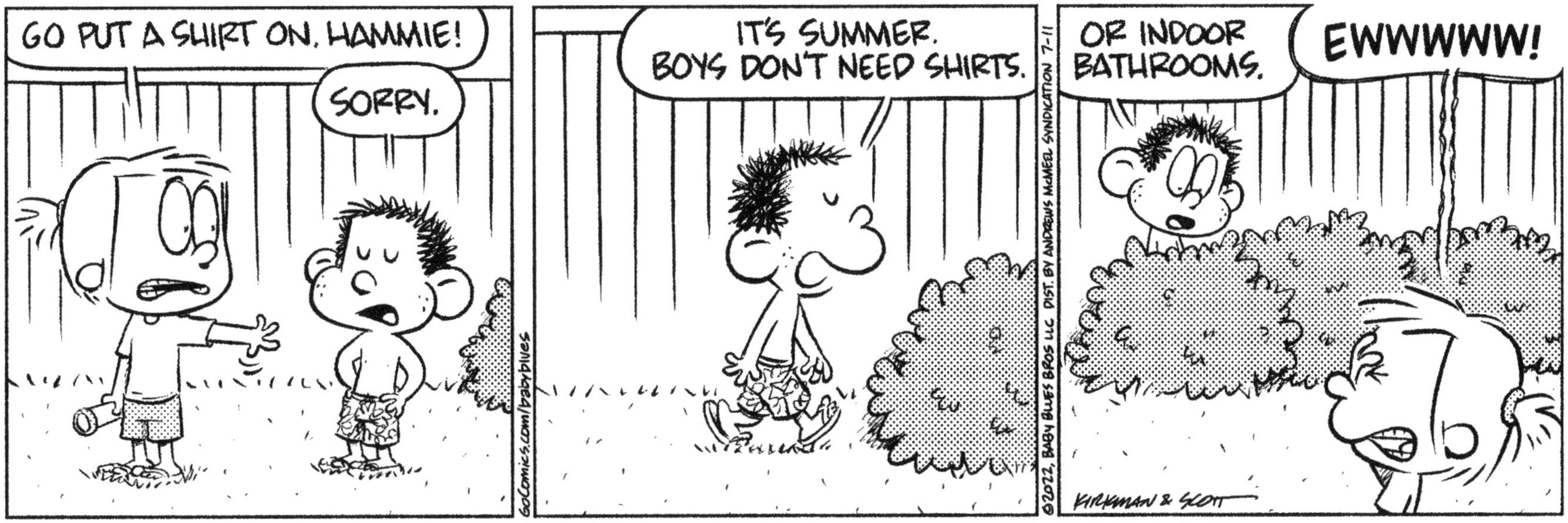
GO PUT A SHIRT ON, HAMMIE!
SORRY.
GoComics.com/babyblues
IT'S SUMMER. BOYS DON'T NEED SHIRTS.
©2022, BABY BLUES BROS LLC DIST. BY ANDREWS MCMEEL SYNDICATION 7-11
OR INDOOR BATHROOMS.
EWWWWW!
KIRKMAN & SCOTT

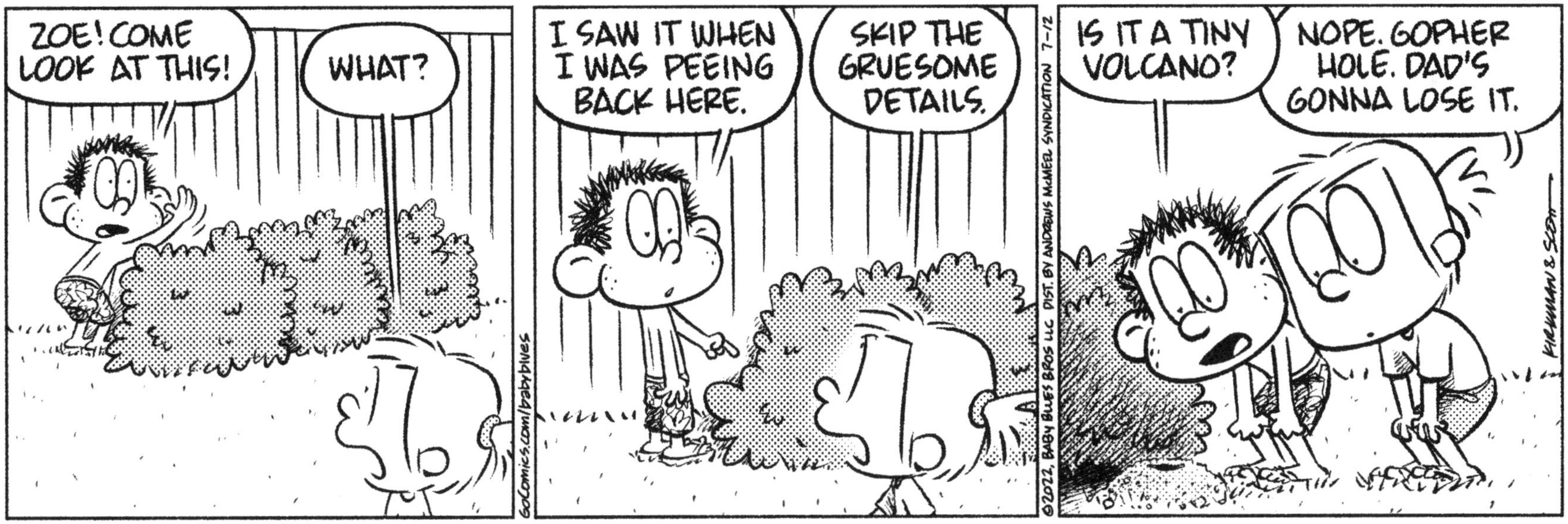
ZOE! COME LOOK AT THIS!
WHAT?
GoComics.com/babyblues
I SAW IT WHEN I WAS PEEING BACK HERE.
SKIP THE GRUESOME DETAILS.
©2022, BABY BLUES BROS LLC DIST. BY ANDREWS MCMEEL SYNDICATION 7-12
IS IT A TINY VOLCANO?
NOPE. GOPHER HOLE. DAD'S GONNA LOSE IT.
KIRKMAN & SCOTT

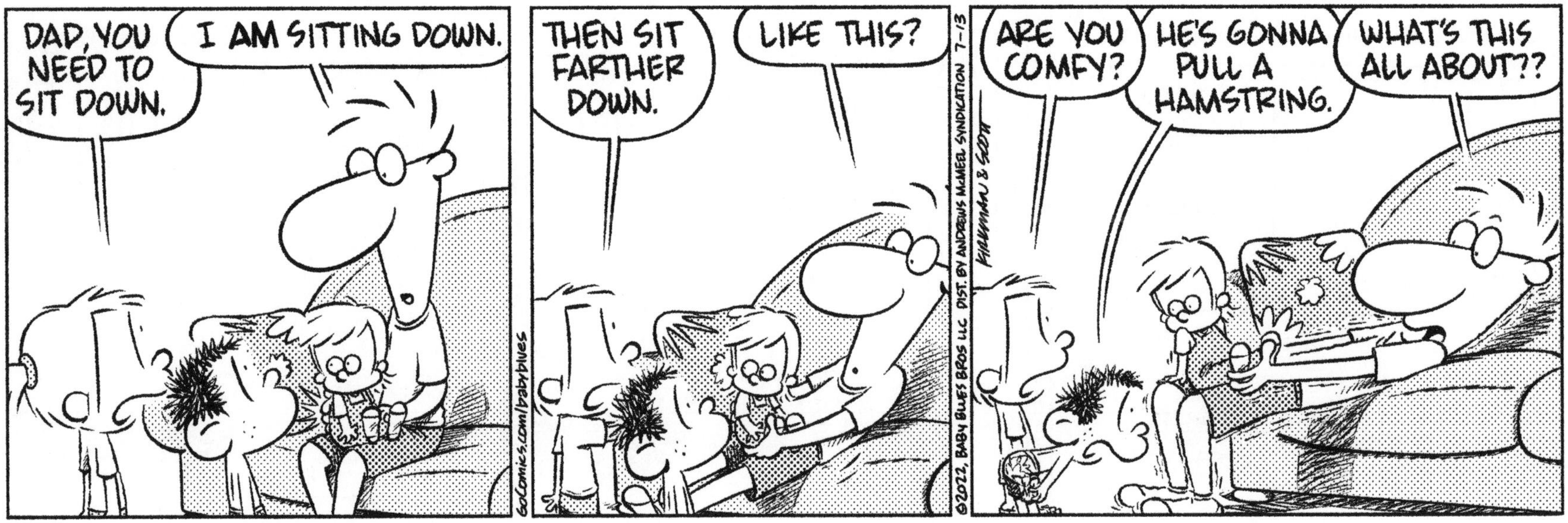
DAD, YOU NEED TO SIT DOWN.
I AM SITTING DOWN.
GoComics.com/babyblues
THEN SIT FARTHER DOWN.
LIKE THIS?
7-13
©2022, BABY BLUES BROS LLC DIST. BY ANDREWS McMEEL SYNDICATION
KIRKMAN & SCOTT
ARE YOU COMFY?
HE'S GONNA PULL A HAMSTRING.
WHAT'S THIS ALL ABOUT??

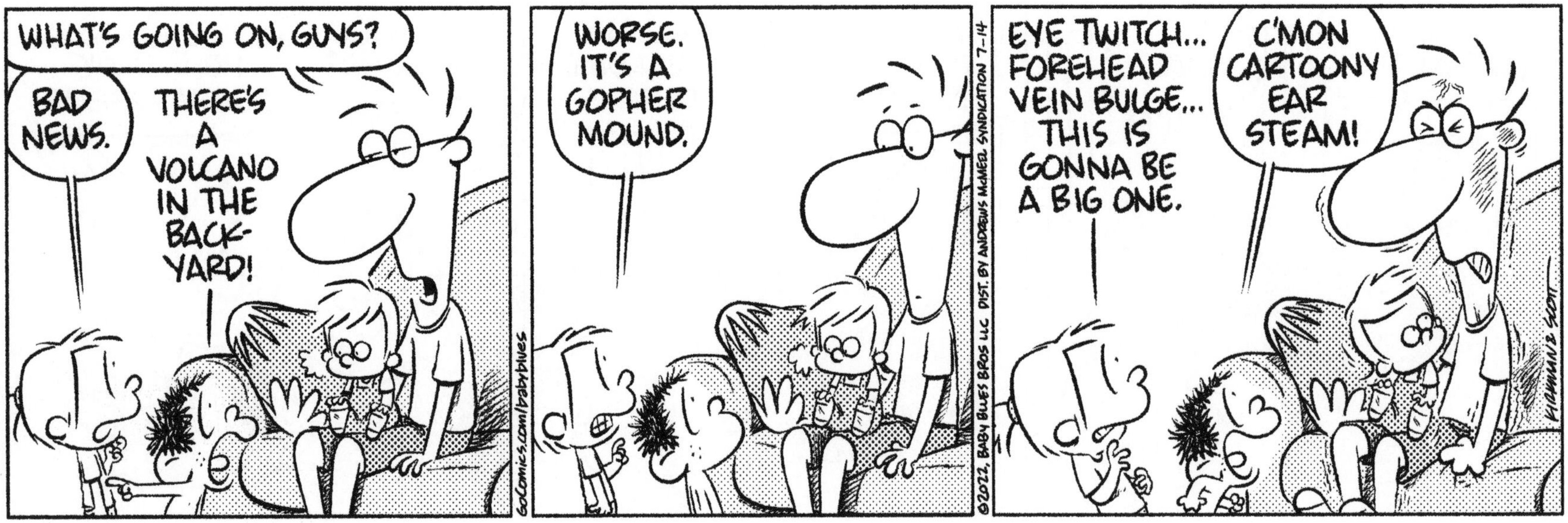
WHAT'S GOING ON, GUYS?
BAD NEWS.
THERE'S A VOLCANO IN THE BACK-YARD!
GoComics.com/babyblues
WORSE. IT'S A GOPHER MOUND.
7-14
©2022, BABY BLUES BROS LLC DIST. BY ANDREWS McMEEL SYNDICATION
EYE TWITCH... FOREHEAD VEIN BULGE... THIS IS GONNA BE A BIG ONE.
C'MON CARTOONY EAR STEAM!
KIRKMAN & SCOTT

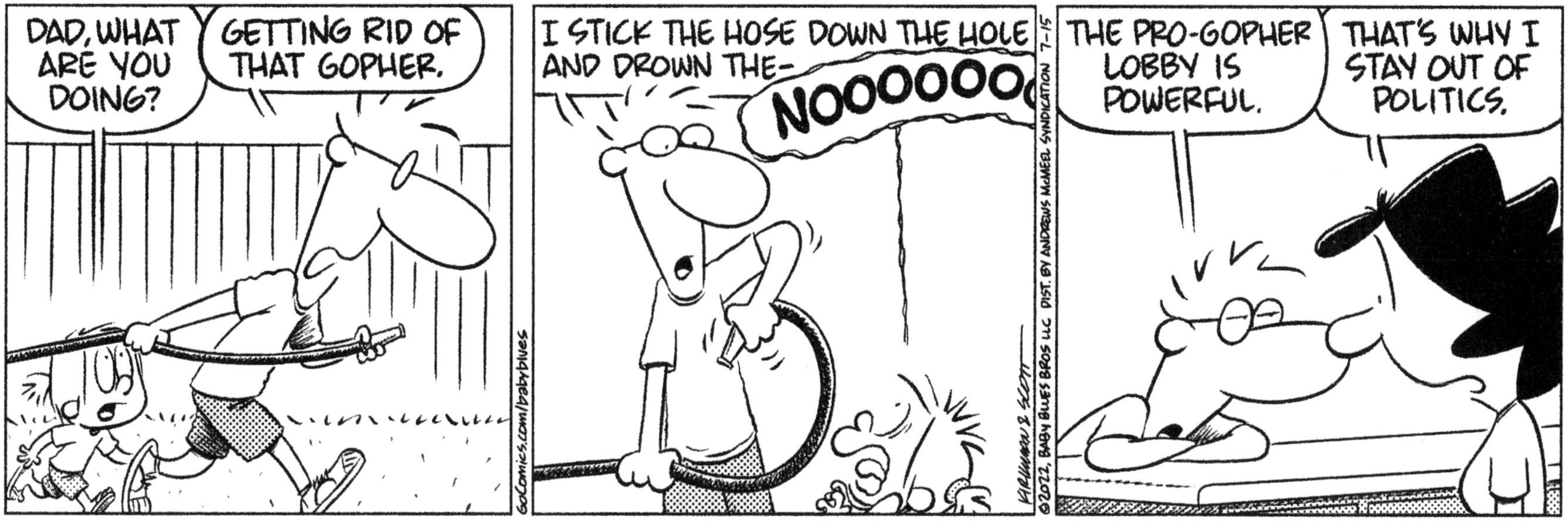
DAD, WHAT ARE YOU DOING?
GETTING RID OF THAT GOPHER.
GoComics.com/babyblues
I STICK THE HOSE DOWN THE HOLE AND DROWN THE-
NOOOOOO
©2022, BABY BLUES BROS LLC DIST. BY ANDREWS McMEEL SYNDICATION 7-15
KIRKMAN & SCOTT
THE PRO-GOPHER LOBBY IS POWERFUL.
THAT'S WHY I STAY OUT OF POLITICS.

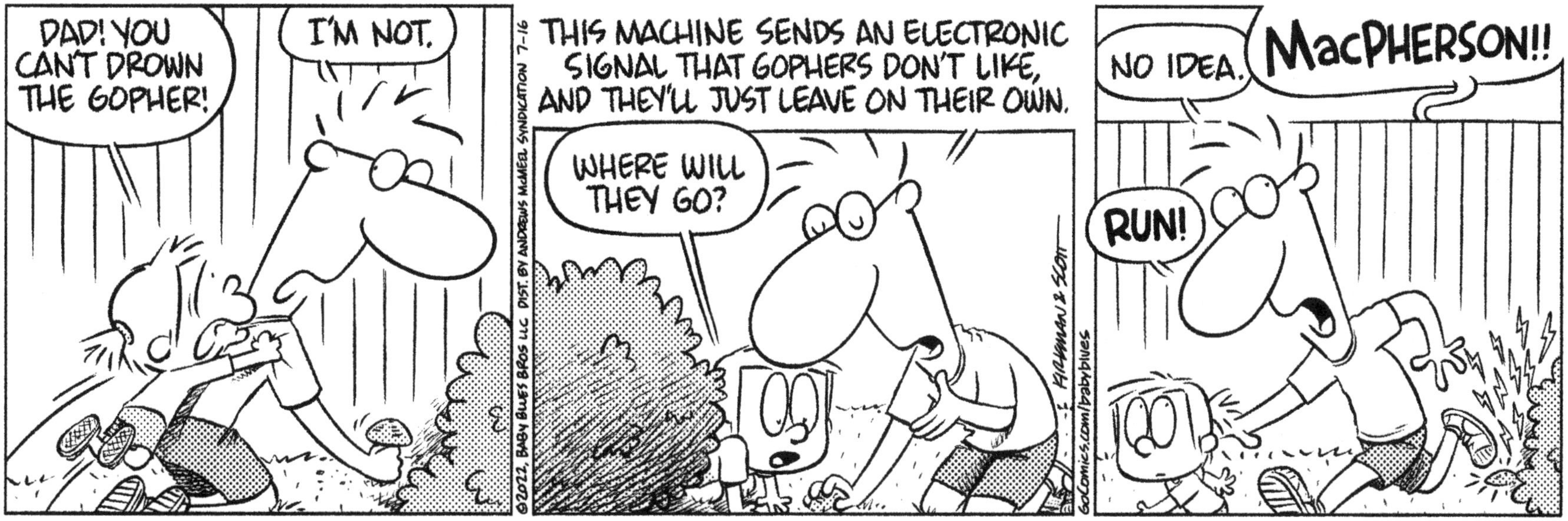
DAD! YOU CAN'T DROWN THE GOPHER!
I'M NOT.
©2022, BABY BLUES BROS LLC DIST. BY ANDREWS McMEEL SYNDICATION 7-16
THIS MACHINE SENDS AN ELECTRONIC SIGNAL THAT GOPHERS DON'T LIKE, AND THEY'LL JUST LEAVE ON THEIR OWN.
WHERE WILL THEY GO?
KIRKMAN & SCOTT
GoComics.com/babyblues
NO IDEA.
MacPHERSON!!
RUN!

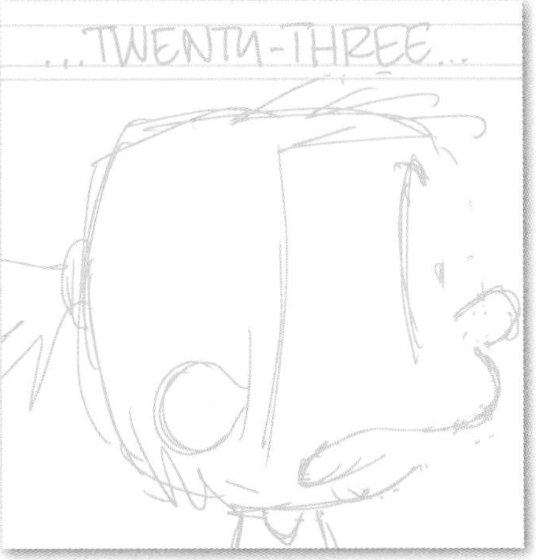
...TWENTY-THREE...

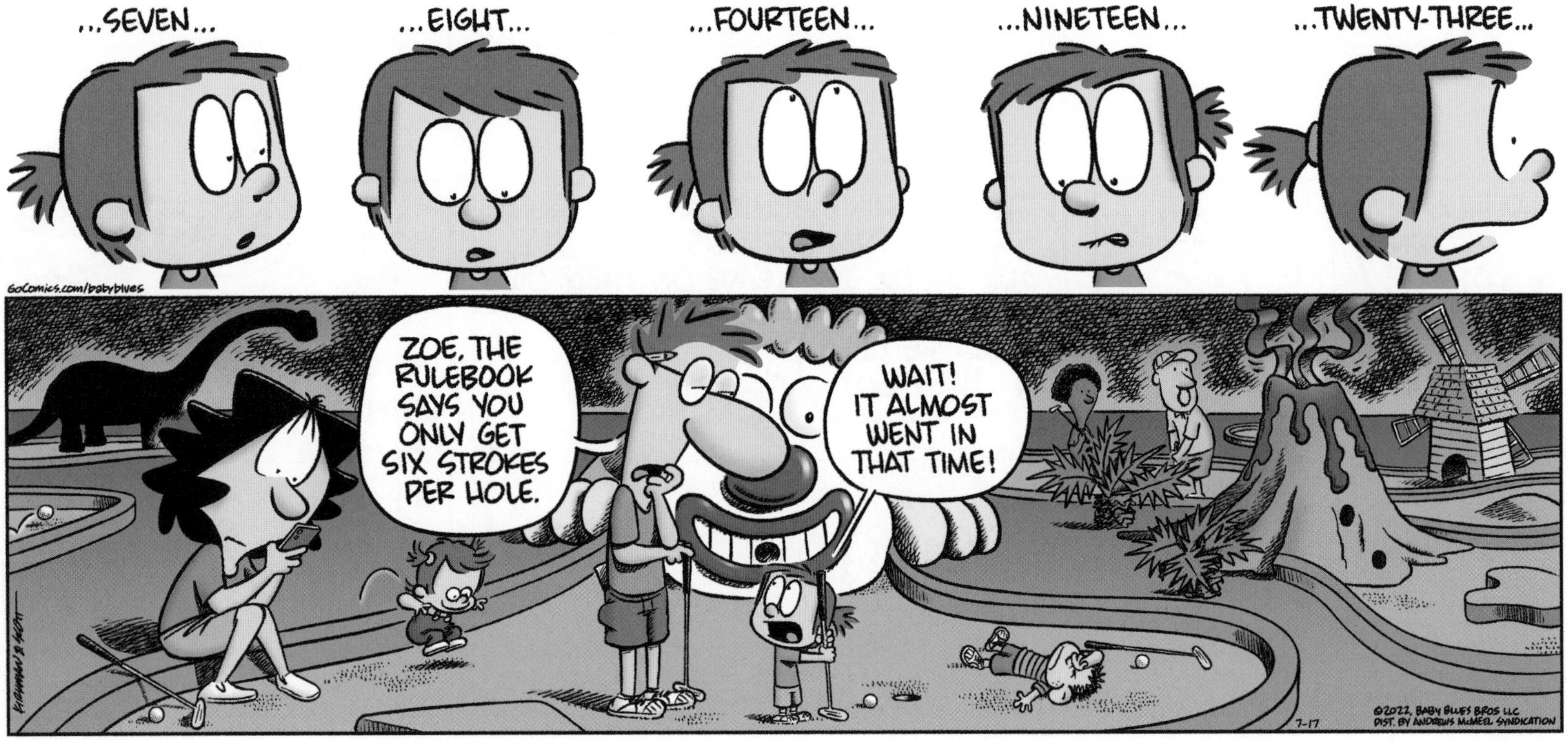
...SEVEN...
...EIGHT...
...FOURTEEN...
...NINETEEN...
...TWENTY-THREE...
GoComics.com/babyblues
ZOE, THE RULEBOOK SAYS YOU ONLY GET SIX STROKES PER HOLE.
WAIT! IT ALMOST WENT IN THAT TIME!
7-17
©2022, BABY BLUES BROS LLC
DIST. BY ANDREWS McMEEL SYNDICATION

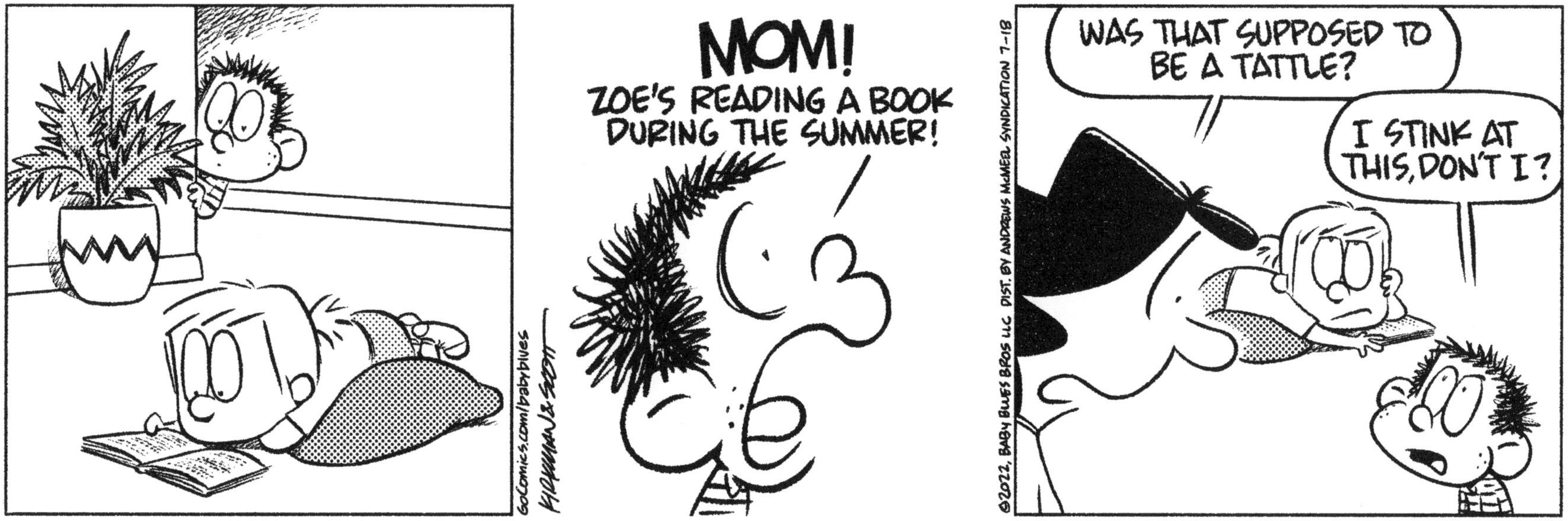
GoComics.com/babyblues
Kirkman & Scott
MOM!
ZOE'S READING A BOOK DURING THE SUMMER!
©2022, BABY BLUES BROS LLC DIST. BY ANDREWS McMEEL SYNDICATION 7-18
WAS THAT SUPPOSED TO BE A TATTLE?
I STINK AT THIS, DON'T I?

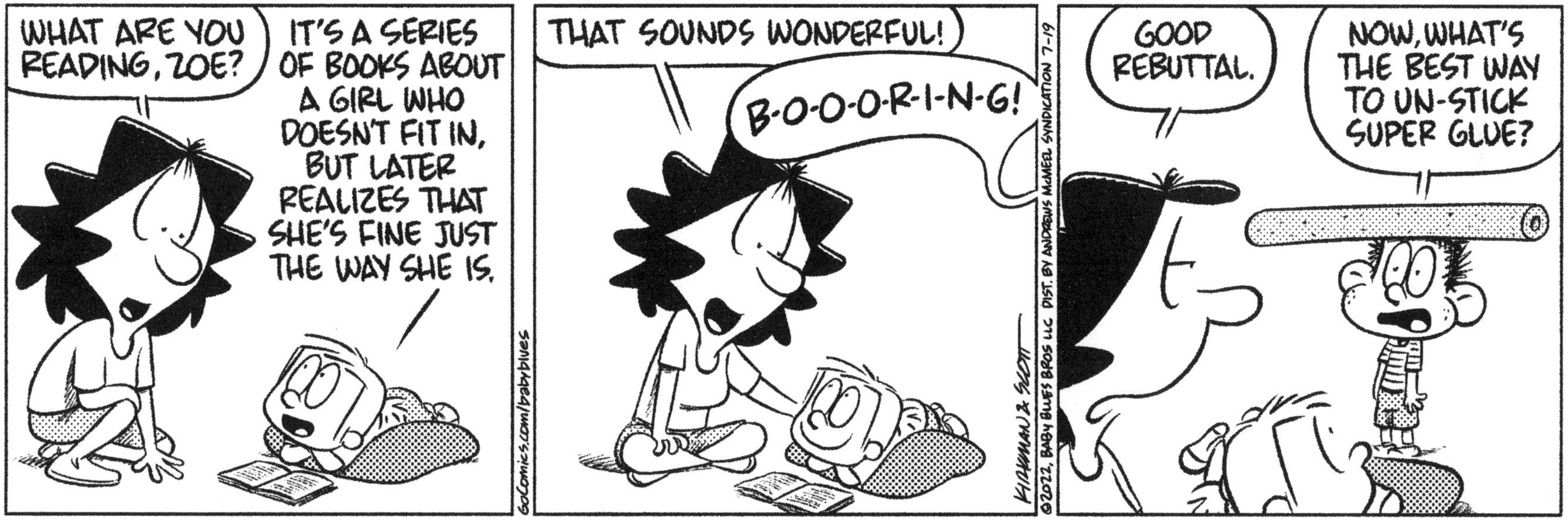
WHAT ARE YOU READING, ZOE?
IT'S A SERIES OF BOOKS ABOUT A GIRL WHO DOESN'T FIT IN, BUT LATER REALIZES THAT SHE'S FINE JUST THE WAY SHE IS.
GoComics.com/babyblues
THAT SOUNDS WONDERFUL!
B-O-O-O-R-I-N-G!
Kirkman & Scott
©2022, BABY BLUES BROS LLC DIST. BY ANDREWS McMEEL SYNDICATION 7-19
GOOD REBUTTAL.
NOW, WHAT'S THE BEST WAY TO UN-STICK SUPER GLUE?

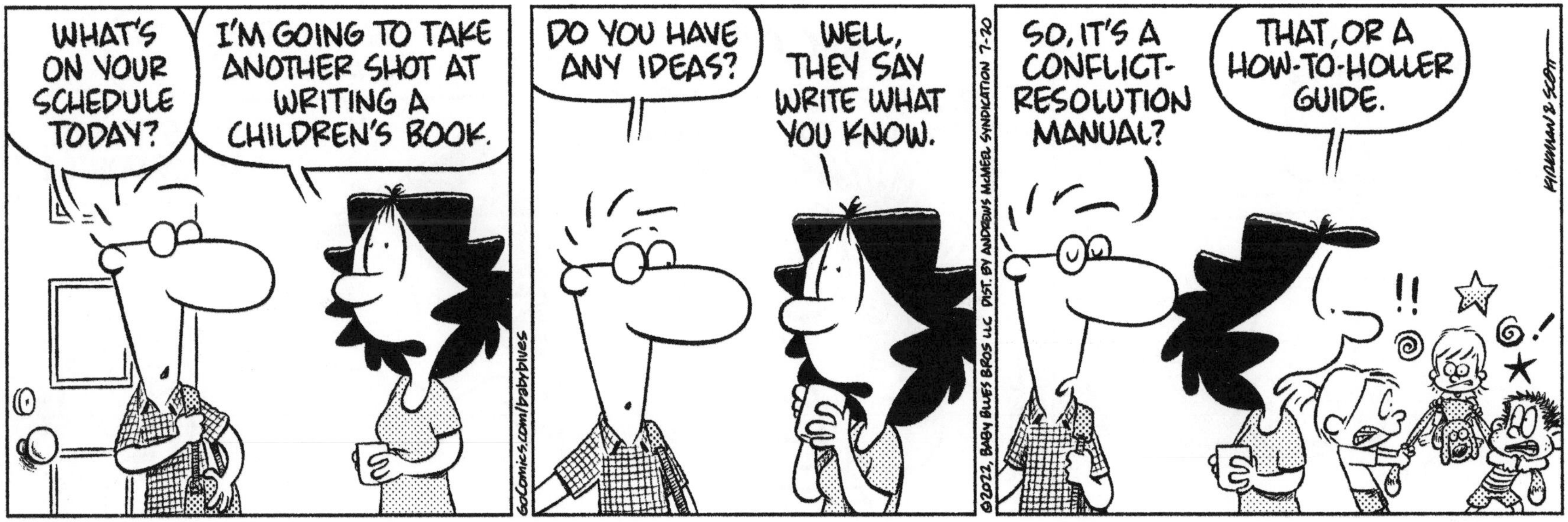
WHAT'S ON YOUR SCHEDULE TODAY?
I'M GOING TO TAKE ANOTHER SHOT AT WRITING A CHILDREN'S BOOK.
GoComics.com/babyblues
DO YOU HAVE ANY IDEAS?
WELL, THEY SAY WRITE WHAT YOU KNOW.
©2022, BABY BLUES BROS LLC DIST. BY ANDREWS McMEEL SYNDICATION 7-20
SO, IT'S A CONFLICT-RESOLUTION MANUAL?
THAT, OR A HOW-TO-HOLLER GUIDE.
KIRKMAN & SCOTT

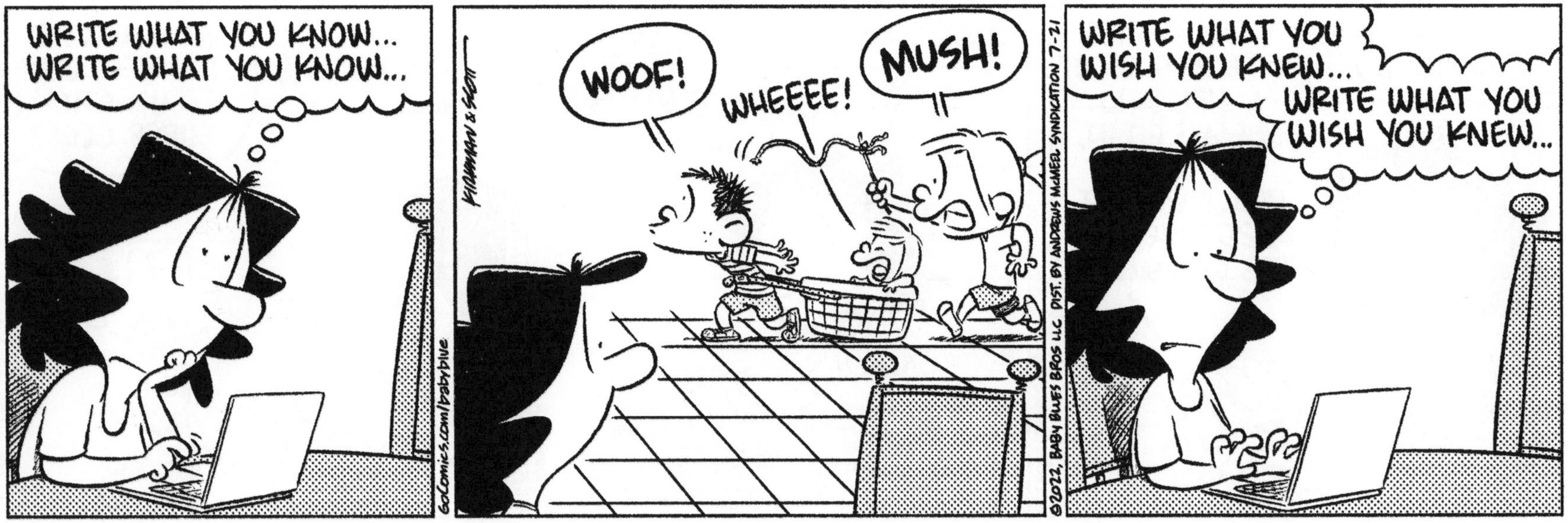
WRITE WHAT YOU KNOW... WRITE WHAT YOU KNOW...
GoComics.com/babyblues
KIRKMAN & SCOTT
WOOF!
WHEEEE!
MUSH!
©2022, BABY BLUES BROS LLC DIST. BY ANDREWS McMEEL SYNDICATION 7-21
WRITE WHAT YOU WISH YOU KNEW...
WRITE WHAT YOU WISH YOU KNEW...

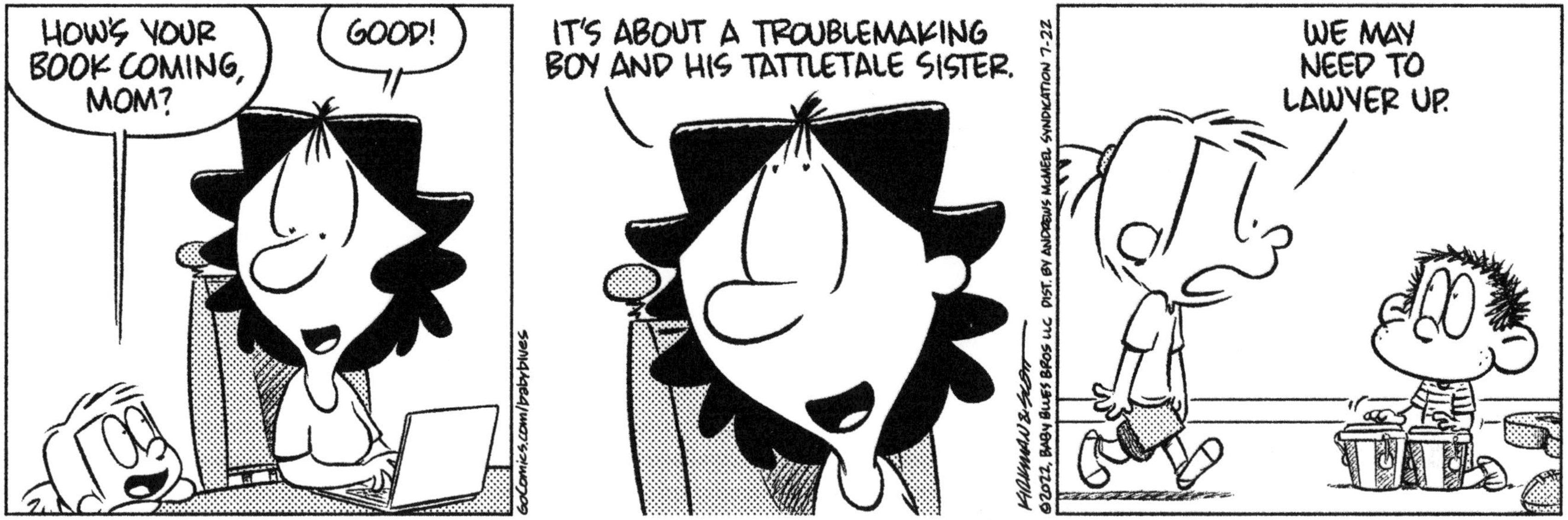
HOW'S YOUR BOOK COMING, MOM?
GOOD!
IT'S ABOUT A TROUBLEMAKING BOY AND HIS TATTLETALE SISTER.
WE MAY NEED TO LAWYER UP.
GoComics.com/babyblues
KIRKMAN & SCOTT
©2022, BABY BLUES BROS LLC DIST. BY ANDREWS MCMEEL SYNDICATION 7-22

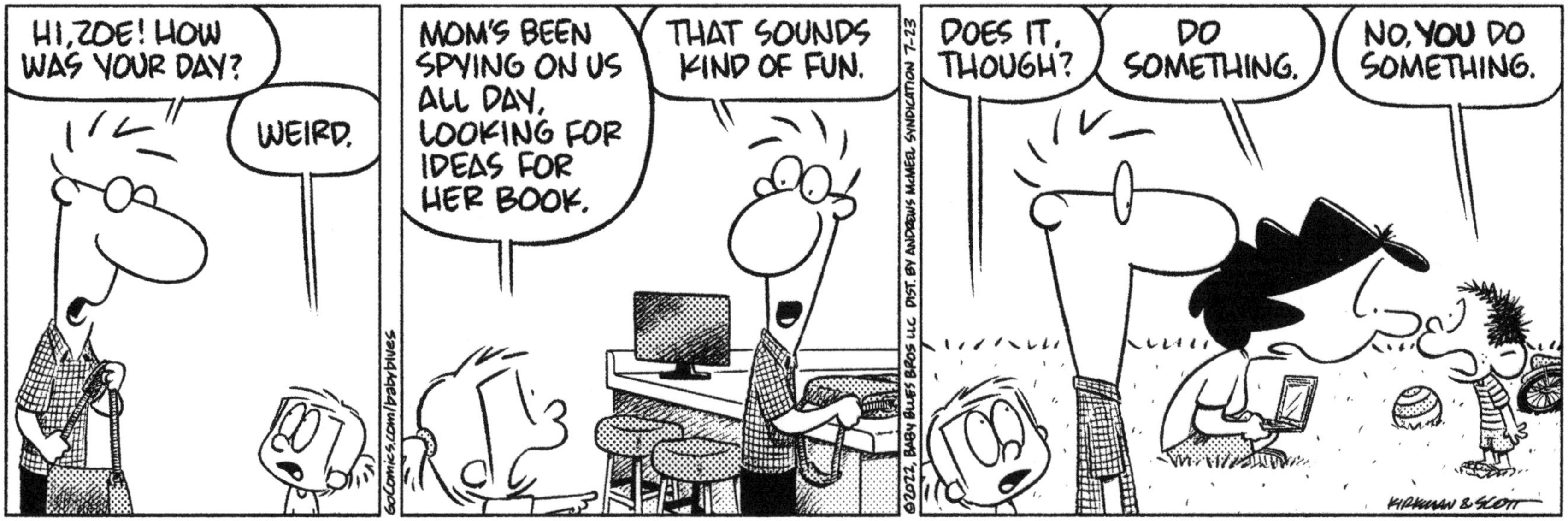
HI, ZOE! HOW WAS YOUR DAY?
WEIRD.
MOM'S BEEN SPYING ON US ALL DAY, LOOKING FOR IDEAS FOR HER BOOK.
THAT SOUNDS KIND OF FUN.
DOES IT, THOUGH?
DO SOMETHING.
NO, YOU DO SOMETHING.
GoComics.com/babyblues
©2022, BABY BLUES BROS LLC DIST. BY ANDREWS MCMEEL SYNDICATION 7-23
KIRKMAN & SCOTT

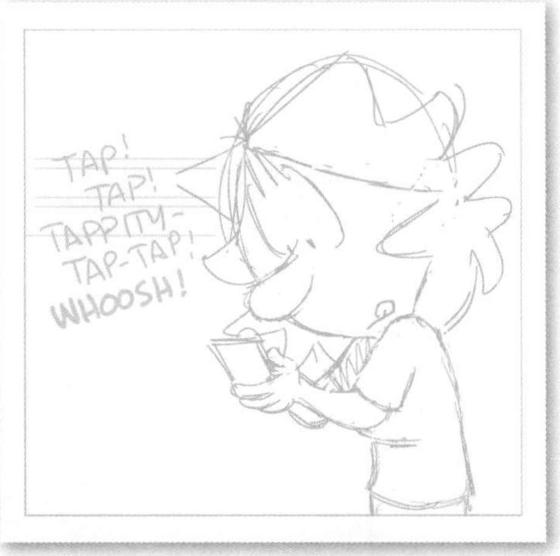
TAP!
TAP!
TAPPITY-
TAP-TAP!
WHOOSH!

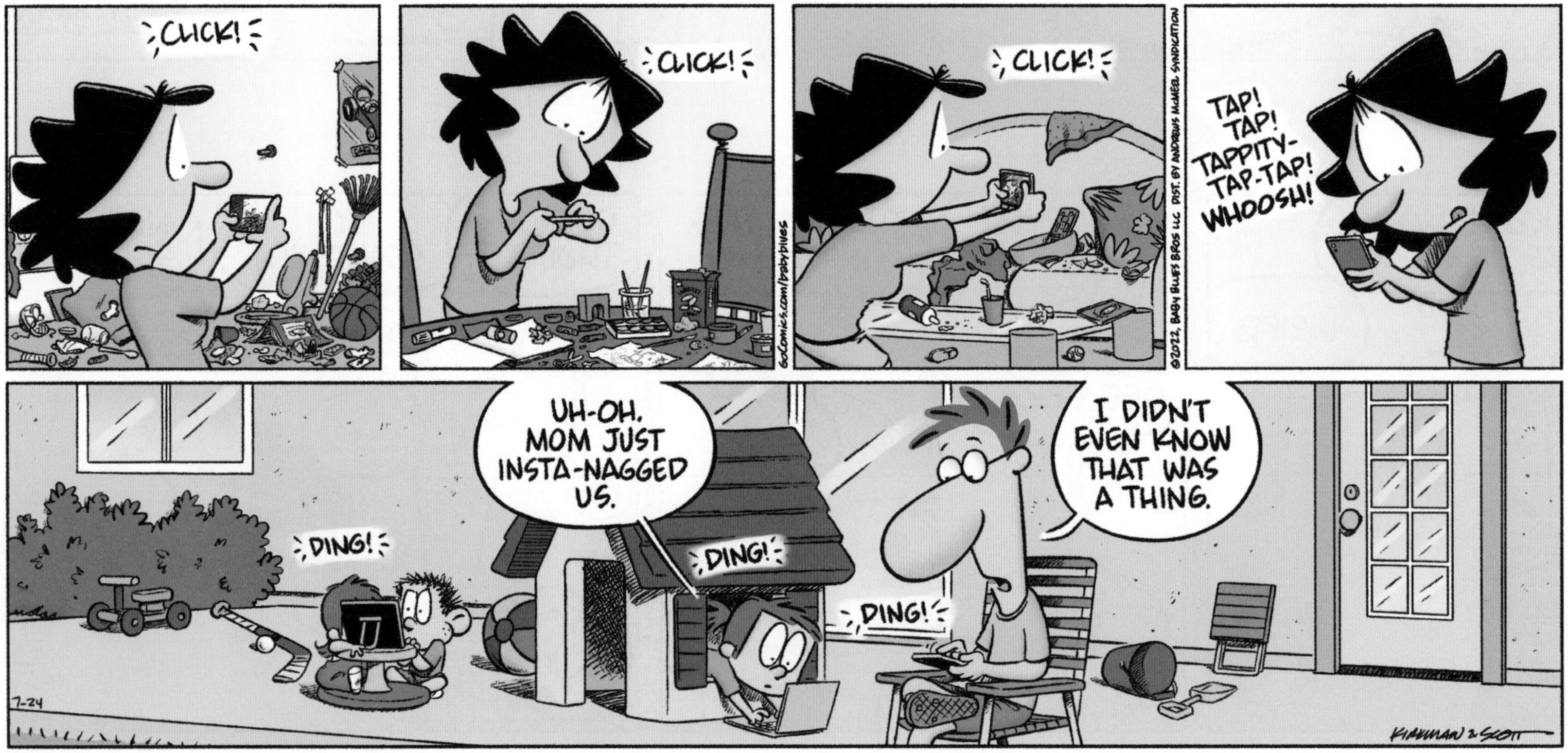
CLICK!
CLICK!
CLICK!
TAP! TAP! TAPPITY-TAP-TAP! WHOOSH!
UH-OH. MOM JUST INSTA-NAGGED US.
I DIDN'T EVEN KNOW THAT WAS A THING.
DING!
DING!
DING!
7-24
KIRKMAN & SCOTT
GoComics.com/babyblues
©2022, BABY BLUES BROS LLC DIST. BY ANDREWS MCMEEL SYNDICATION

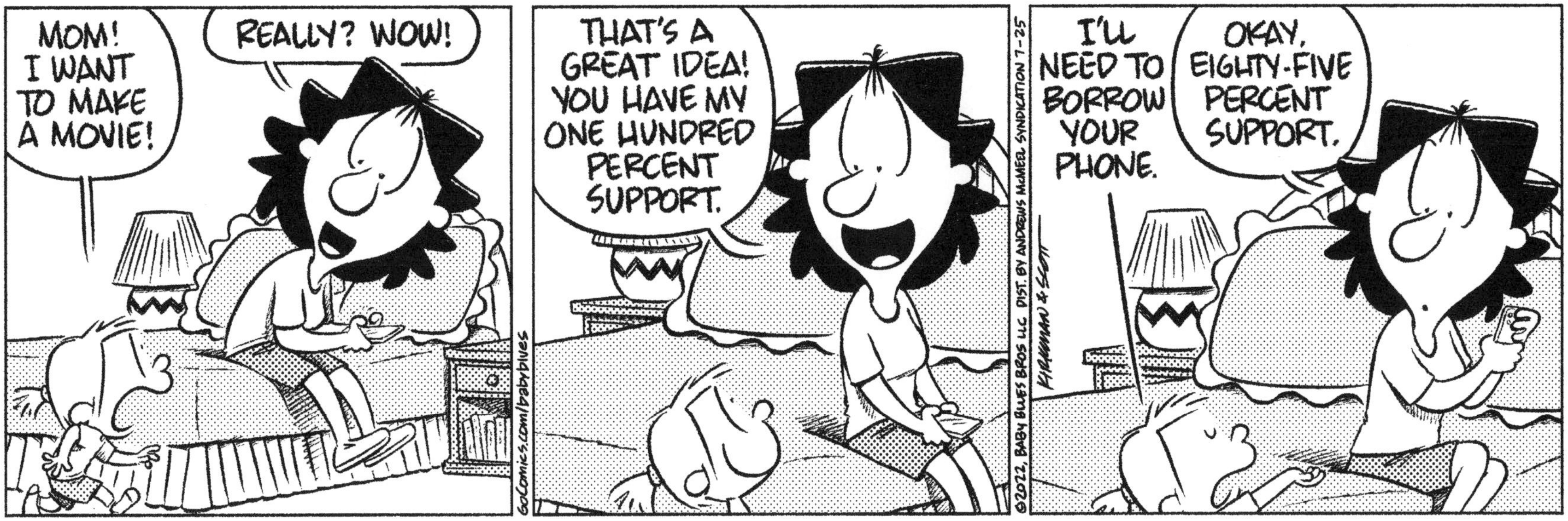
MOM! I WANT TO MAKE A MOVIE!
REALLY? WOW!
GoComics.com/babyblues
THAT'S A GREAT IDEA! YOU HAVE MY ONE HUNDRED PERCENT SUPPORT.
©2022, BABY BLUES BROS LLC DIST. BY ANDREWS MCMEEL SYNDICATION 7-25
KIRKMAN & SCOTT
I'LL NEED TO BORROW YOUR PHONE.
OKAY, EIGHTY-FIVE PERCENT SUPPORT.

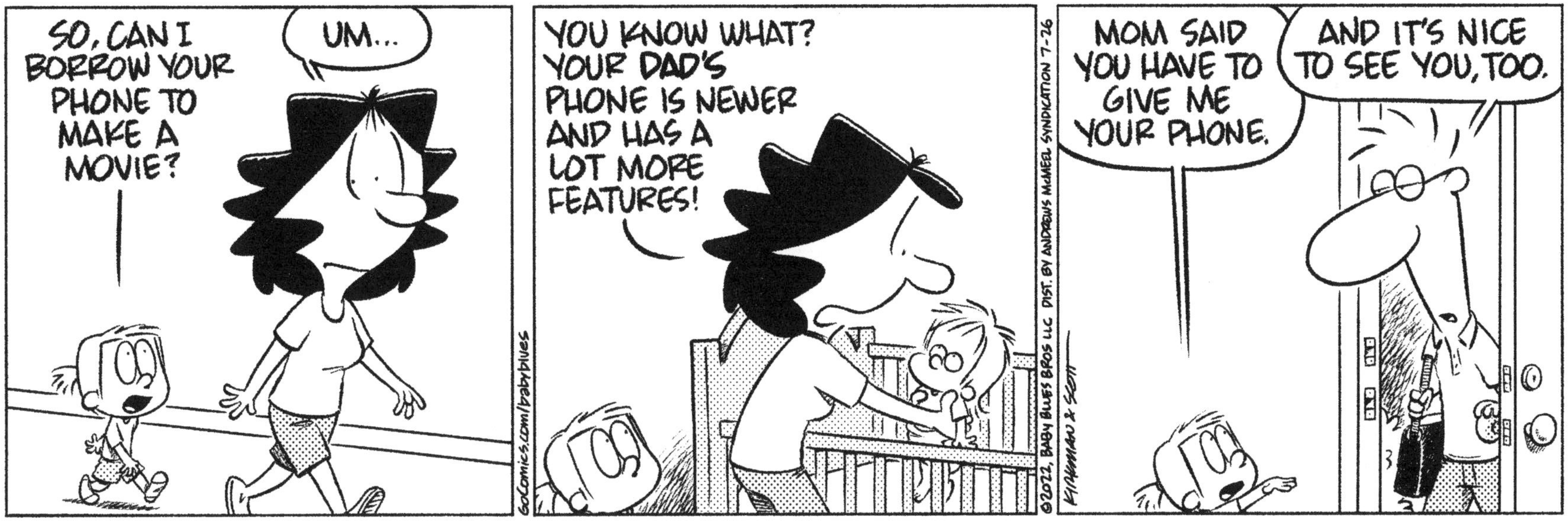
SO, CAN I BORROW YOUR PHONE TO MAKE A MOVIE?
UM...
GoComics.com/babyblues
YOU KNOW WHAT? YOUR DAD'S PHONE IS NEWER AND HAS A LOT MORE FEATURES!
©2022, BABY BLUES BROS LLC DIST. BY ANDREWS MCMEEL SYNDICATION 7-26
KIRKMAN & SCOTT
MOM SAID YOU HAVE TO GIVE ME YOUR PHONE.
AND IT'S NICE TO SEE YOU, TOO.

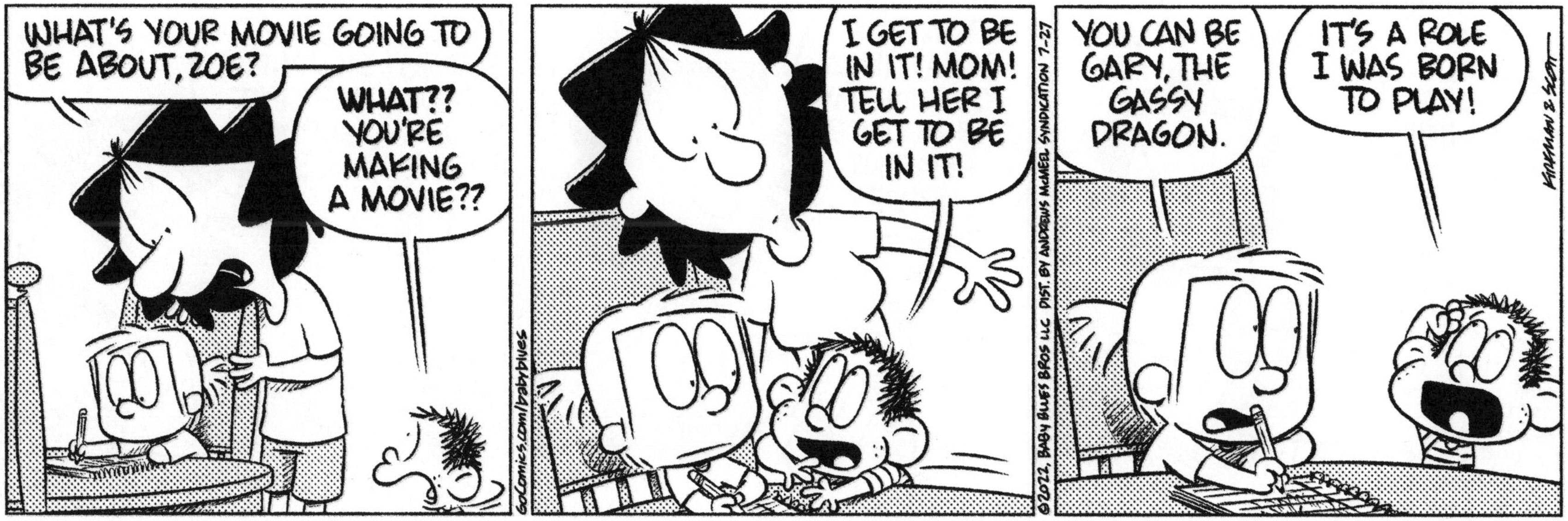
WHAT'S YOUR MOVIE GOING TO BE ABOUT, ZOE?
WHAT?? YOU'RE MAKING A MOVIE??
GoComics.com/babyblues
I GET TO BE IN IT! MOM! TELL HER I GET TO BE IN IT!
©2022, BABY BLUES BROS LLC DIST. BY ANDREWS McMEEL SYNDICATION 7-27
YOU CAN BE GARY, THE GASSY DRAGON.
IT'S A ROLE I WAS BORN TO PLAY!
KIRKMAN & SCOTT

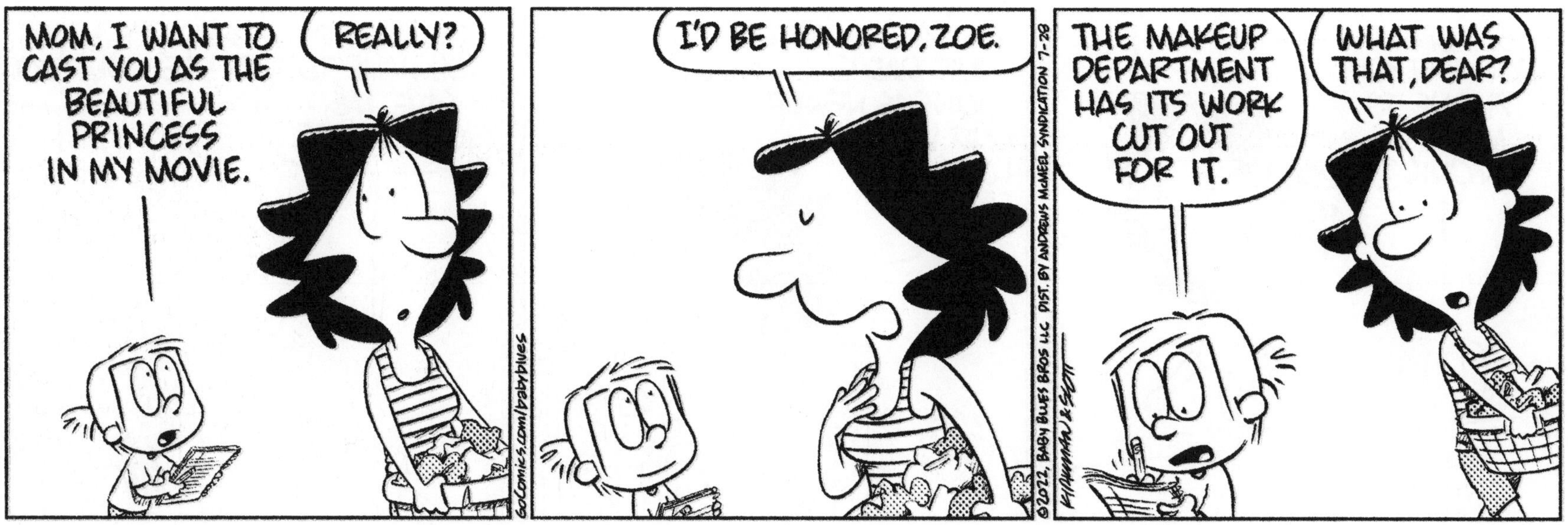
MOM, I WANT TO CAST YOU AS THE BEAUTIFUL PRINCESS IN MY MOVIE.
REALLY?
GoComics.com/babyblues
I'D BE HONORED, ZOE.
©2022, BABY BLUES BROS LLC DIST. BY ANDREWS McMEEL SYNDICATION 7-28
KIRKMAN & SCOTT
THE MAKEUP DEPARTMENT HAS ITS WORK CUT OUT FOR IT.
WHAT WAS THAT, DEAR?

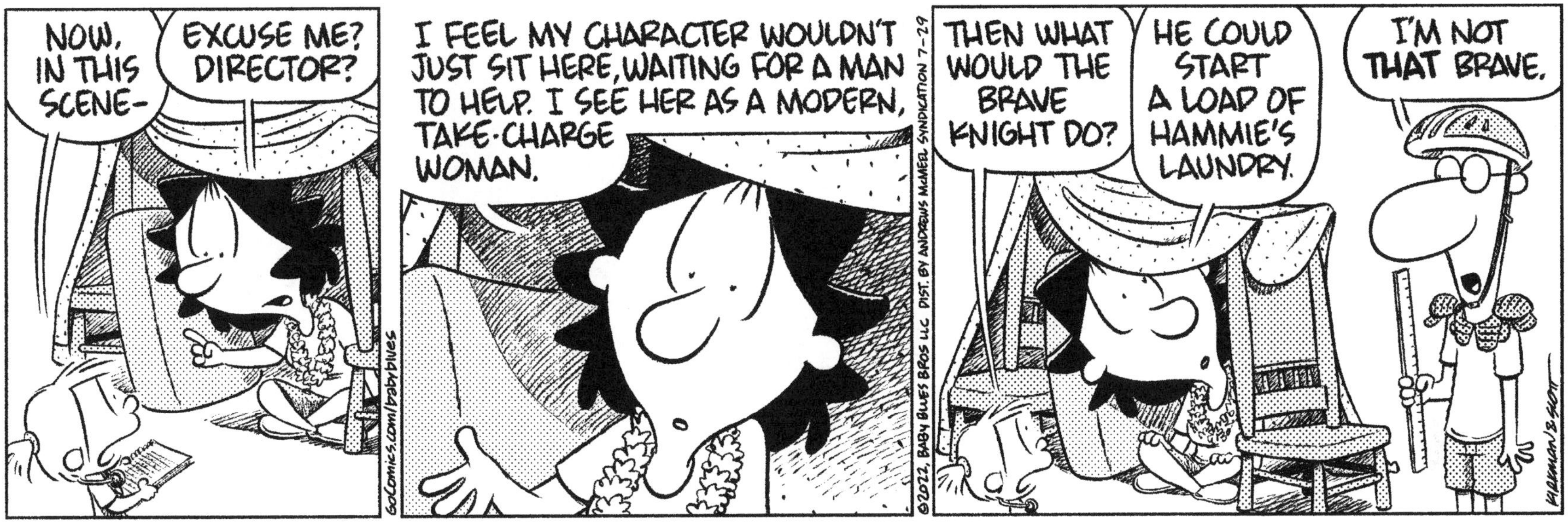
NOW, IN THIS SCENE-
EXCUSE ME? DIRECTOR?
GoComics.com/babyblues
I FEEL MY CHARACTER WOULDN'T JUST SIT HERE, WAITING FOR A MAN TO HELP. I SEE HER AS A MODERN, TAKE-CHARGE WOMAN.
©2022, BABY BLUES BROS LLC DIST. BY ANDREWS McMEEL SYNDICATION 7-29
THEN WHAT WOULD THE BRAVE KNIGHT DO?
HE COULD START A LOAD OF HAMMIE'S LAUNDRY.
I'M NOT THAT BRAVE.
KIRKMAN & SCOTT

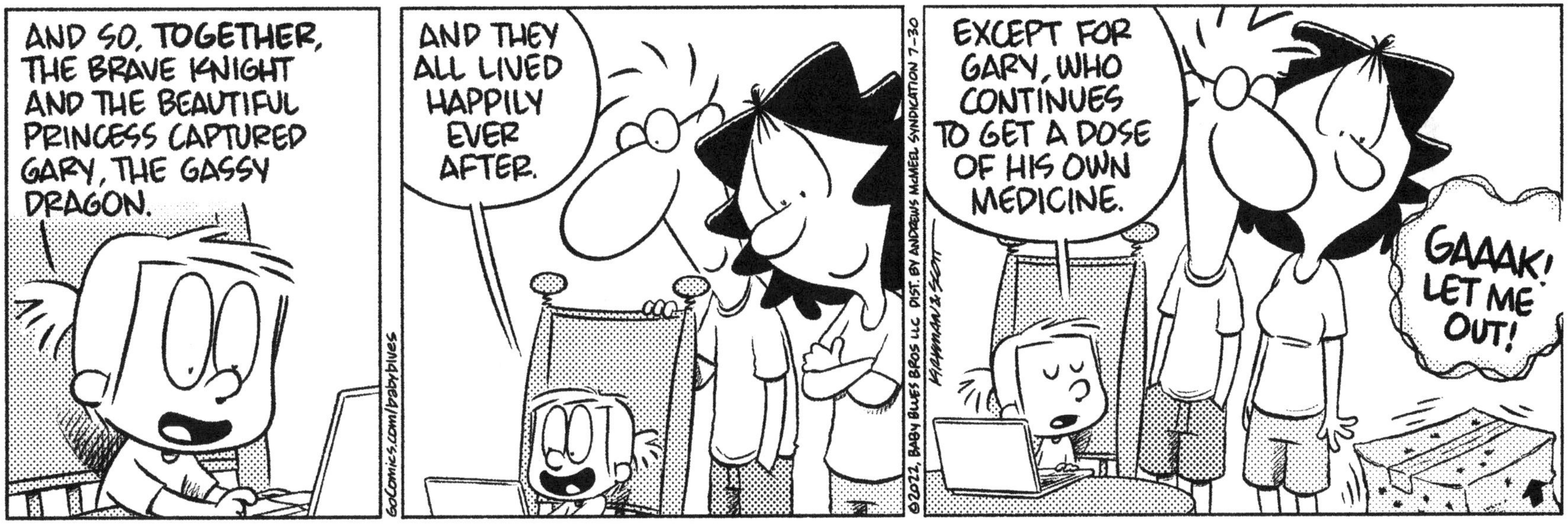
AND SO, TOGETHER, THE BRAVE KNIGHT AND THE BEAUTIFUL PRINCESS CAPTURED GARY, THE GASSY DRAGON.
GoComics.com/babyblues
AND THEY ALL LIVED HAPPILY EVER AFTER.
©2022, BABY BLUES BROS LLC DIST. BY ANDREWS McMEEL SYNDICATION 7-30
KIRKMAN & SCOTT
EXCEPT FOR GARY, WHO CONTINUES TO GET A DOSE OF HIS OWN MEDICINE.
GAAAK! LET ME OUT!

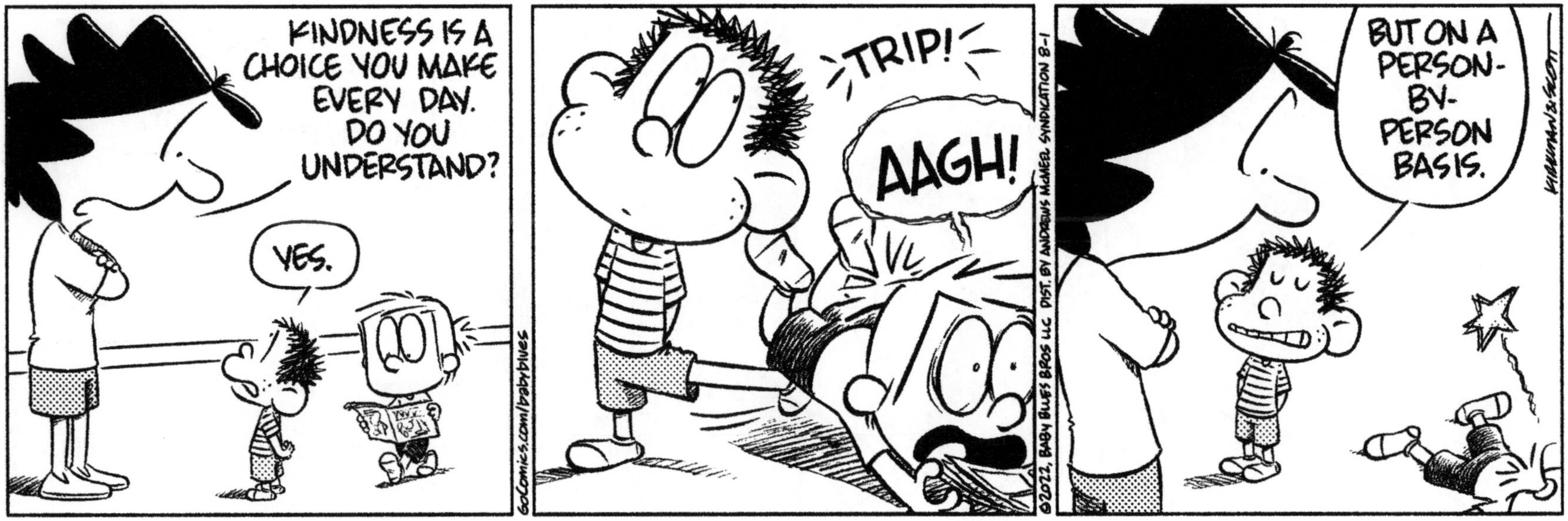
KINDNESS IS A CHOICE YOU MAKE EVERY DAY. DO YOU UNDERSTAND?
YES.
GoComics.com/babyblues
TRIP!
AAGH!
©2022, BABY BLUES BROS LLC DIST. BY ANDREWS McMEEL SYNDICATION 8-1
BUT ON A PERSON-BY-PERSON BASIS.
KIRKMAN & SCOTT

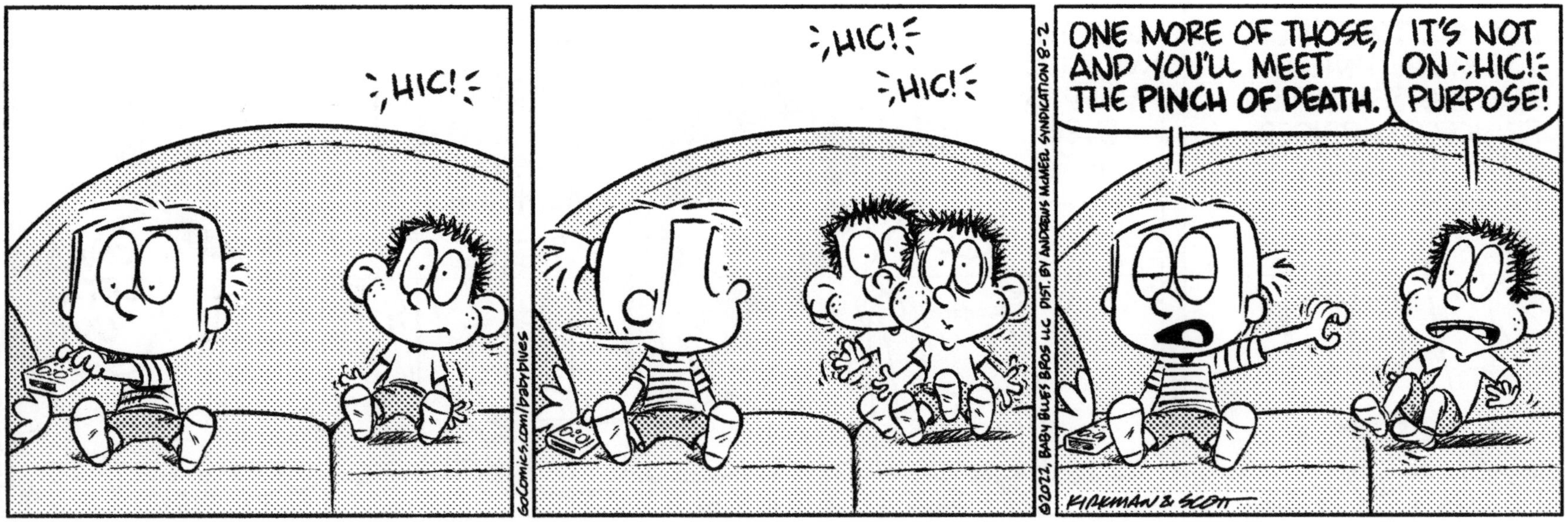
HIC!
GoComics.com/babyblues
HIC!
HIC!
©2022, BABY BLUES BROS LLC DIST. BY ANDREWS McMEEL SYNDICATION 8-2
ONE MORE OF THOSE, AND YOU'LL MEET THE PINCH OF DEATH.
IT'S NOT ON HIC! PURPOSE!
KIRKMAN & SCOTT

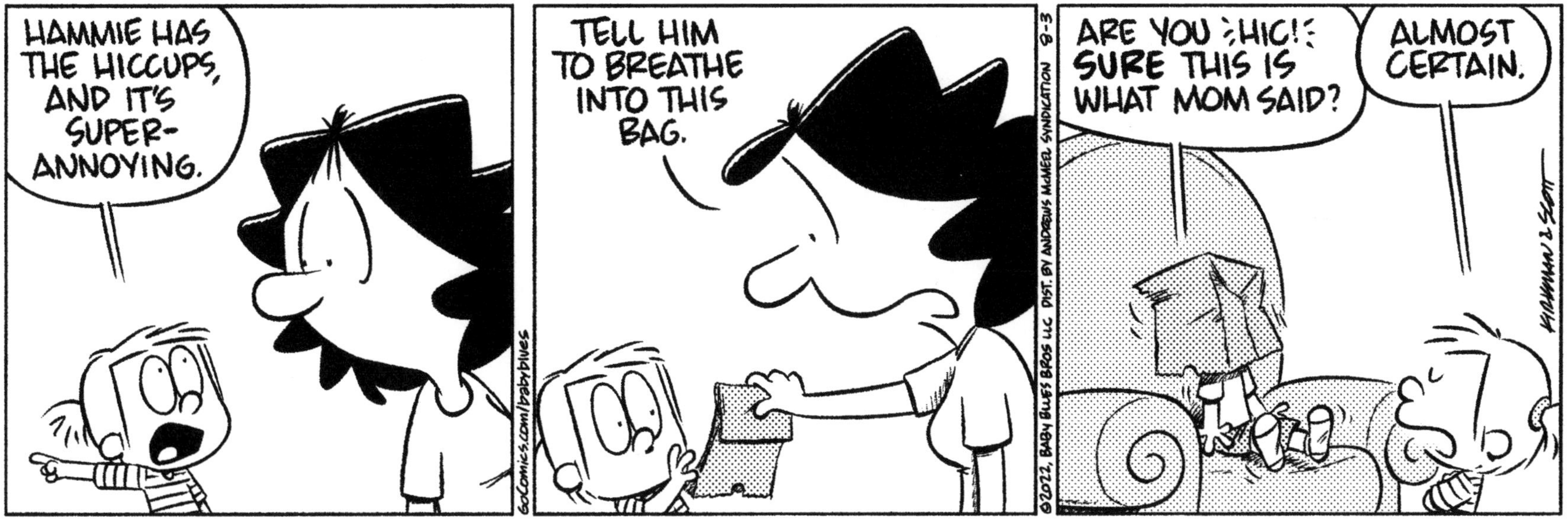
HAMMIE HAS THE HICCUPS, AND IT'S SUPER-ANNOYING.
TELL HIM TO BREATHE INTO THIS BAG.
ARE YOU HIC! SURE THIS IS WHAT MOM SAID?
ALMOST CERTAIN.
GoComics.com/babyblues
©2022, BABY BLUES BROS LLC DIST. BY ANDREWS McMEEL SYNDICATION 8-3
KIRKMAN & SCOTT

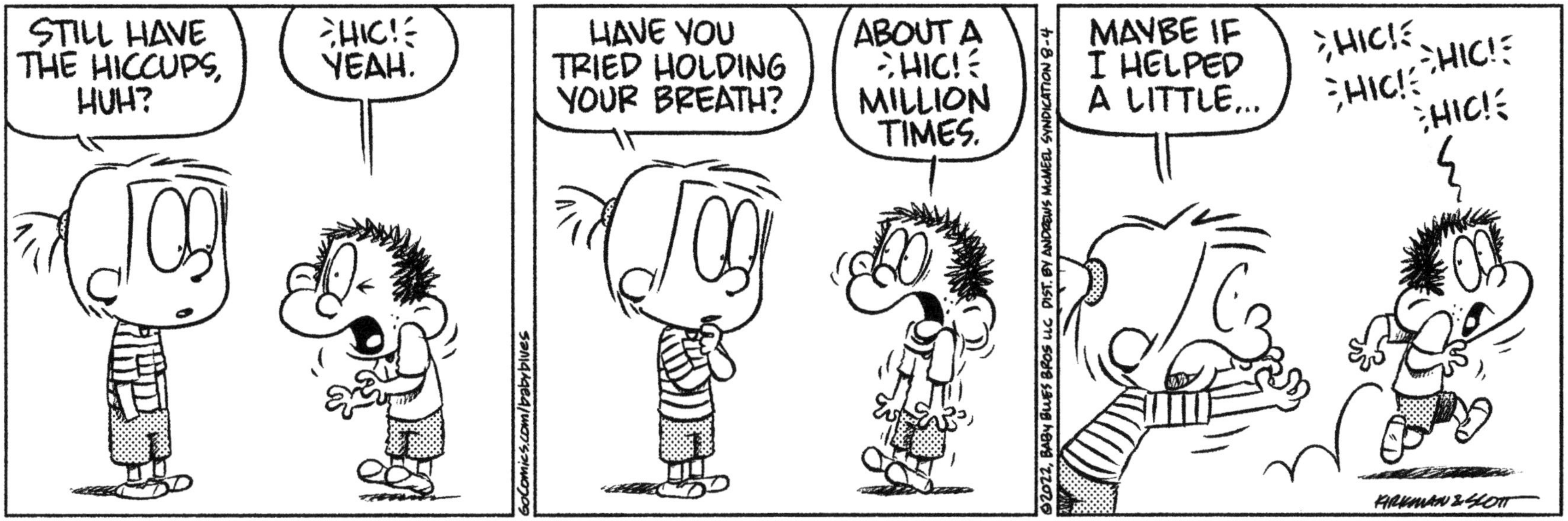
STILL HAVE THE HICCUPS, HUH?
HIC! YEAH.
HAVE YOU TRIED HOLDING YOUR BREATH?
ABOUT A HIC! MILLION TIMES.
MAYBE IF I HELPED A LITTLE...
HIC!
HIC!
HIC!
HIC!
GoComics.com/babyblues
©2022, BABY BLUES BROS LLC DIST. BY ANDREWS McMEEL SYNDICATION 8-4
KIRKMAN & SCOTT

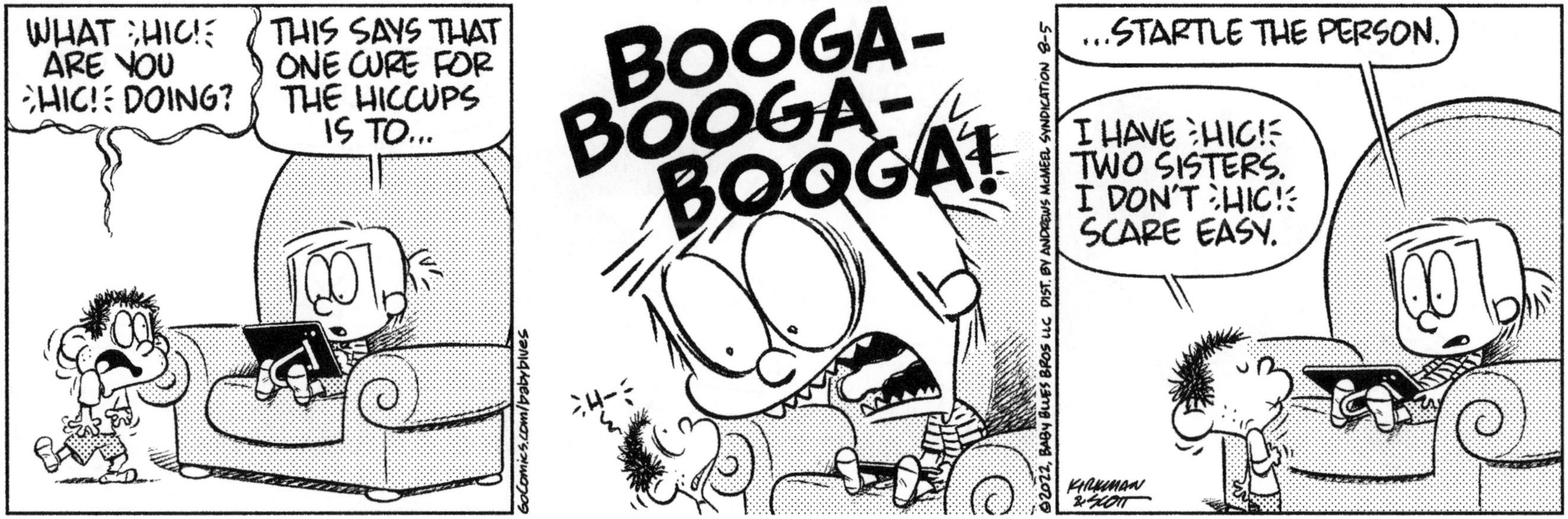
WHAT HIC! ARE YOU HIC! DOING?
THIS SAYS THAT ONE CURE FOR THE HICCUPS IS TO...
GoComics.com/babyblues
BOOGA-BOOGA-BOOGA!
H-
©2022, BABY BLUES BROS LLC DIST. BY ANDREWS McMEEL SYNDICATION 8-5
...STARTLE THE PERSON.
I HAVE HIC! TWO SISTERS. I DON'T HIC! SCARE EASY.
KIRKMAN & SCOTT

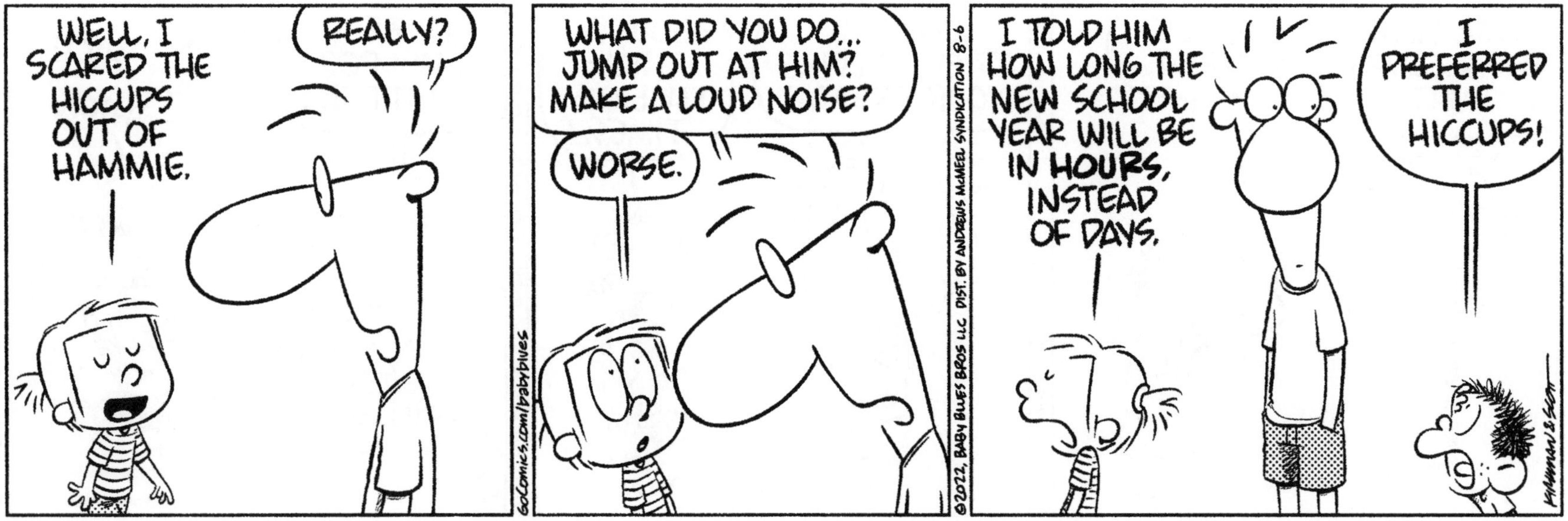
WELL, I SCARED THE HICCUPS OUT OF HAMMIE.
REALLY?
GoComics.com/babyblues
WHAT DID YOU DO... JUMP OUT AT HIM? MAKE A LOUD NOISE?
WORSE.
©2022, BABY BLUES BROS LLC DIST. BY ANDREWS McMEEL SYNDICATION 8-6
I TOLD HIM HOW LONG THE NEW SCHOOL YEAR WILL BE IN **HOURS**, INSTEAD OF DAYS.
I PREFERRED THE HICCUPS!
KIRKMAN & SCOTT

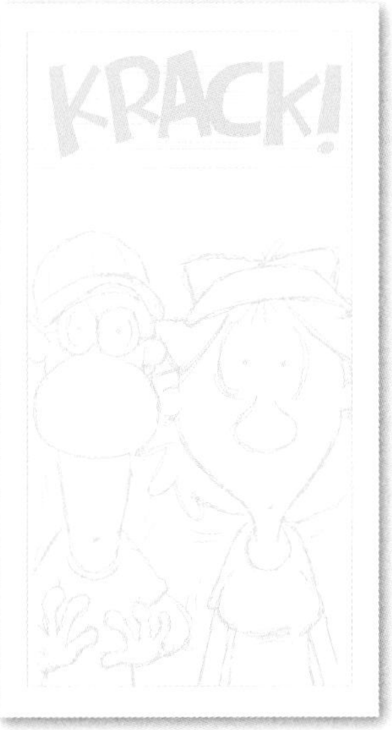
KRACK!

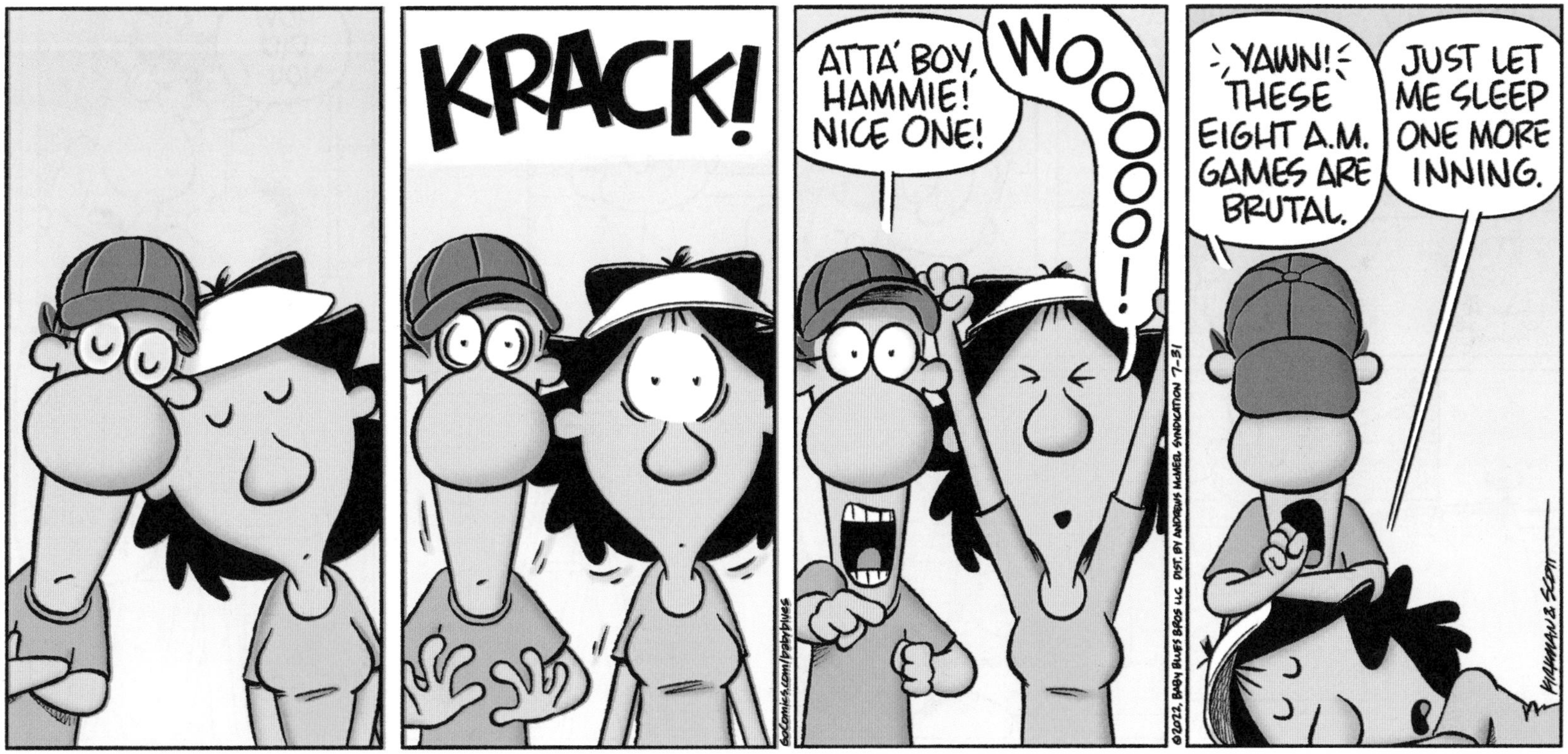
KRACK!
GoComics.com/babyblues
ATTA' BOY, HAMMIE! NICE ONE!
WOOOOOO!
©2022, BABY BLUES BROS LLC DIST. BY ANDREWS MCMEEL SYNDICATION 7-31
YAWN! THESE EIGHT A.M. GAMES ARE BRUTAL.
JUST LET ME SLEEP ONE MORE INNING.
KIRKMAN & SCOTT

WHERE'S DAD?
HE SAID HE WAS GOING TO FIND A QUIET SPOT TO READ.
OKAY, THANKS.
8-7
GoComics.com/babyblues
©2022, BABY BLUES BROS LLC DIST. BY ANDREWS McMEEL SYNDICATION
KIRKMAN & SCOTT
HOW DID YOU-?
PLEASE, I KNOW EVERY HIDING PLACE IN THIS HOUSE.

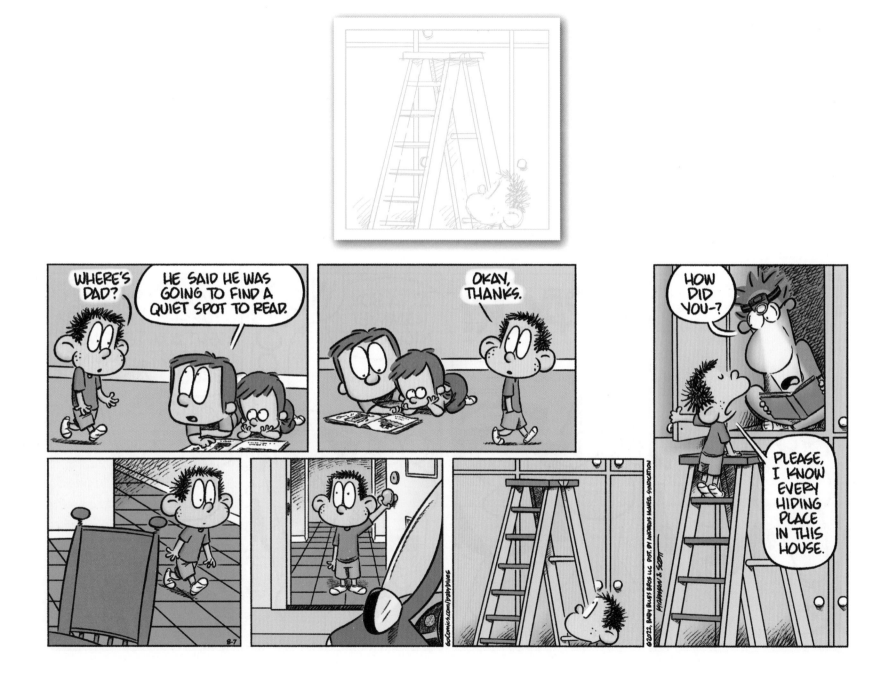

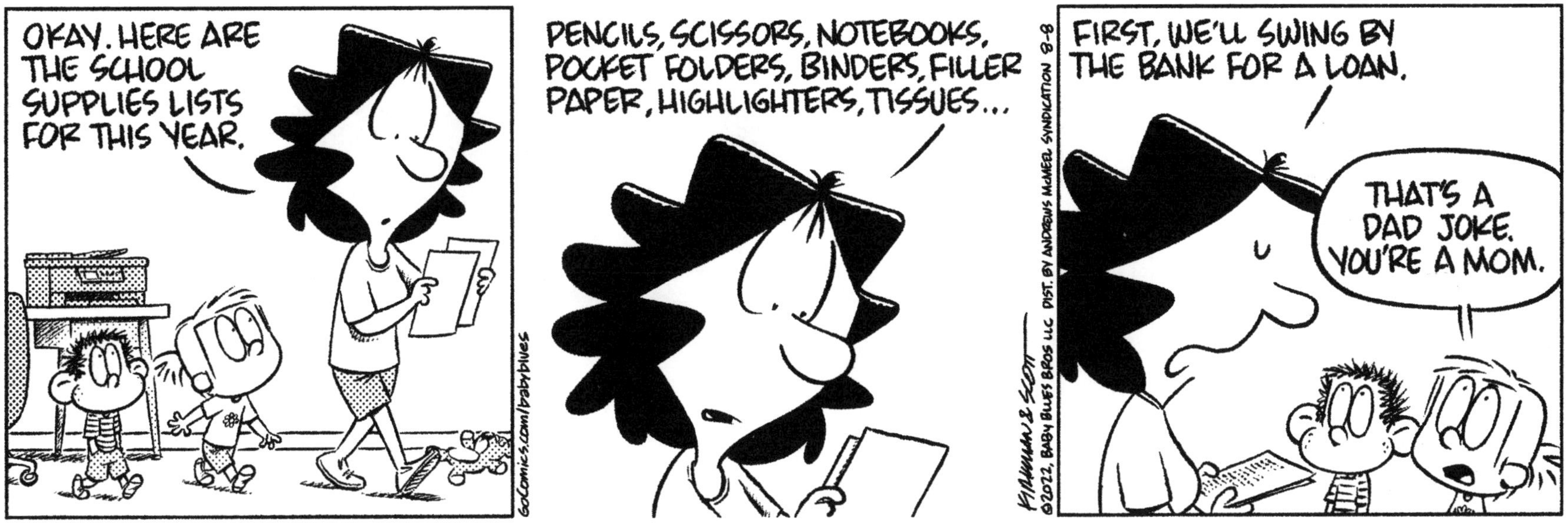
OKAY. HERE ARE THE SCHOOL SUPPLIES LISTS FOR THIS YEAR.
GoComics.com/babyblues
PENCILS, SCISSORS, NOTEBOOKS, POCKET FOLDERS, BINDERS, FILLER PAPER, HIGHLIGHTERS, TISSUES...
KIRKMAN & SCOTT
©2022, BABY BLUES BROS LLC DIST. BY ANDREWS MCMEEL SYNDICATION 8-8
FIRST, WE'LL SWING BY THE BANK FOR A LOAN.
THAT'S A DAD JOKE. YOU'RE A MOM.

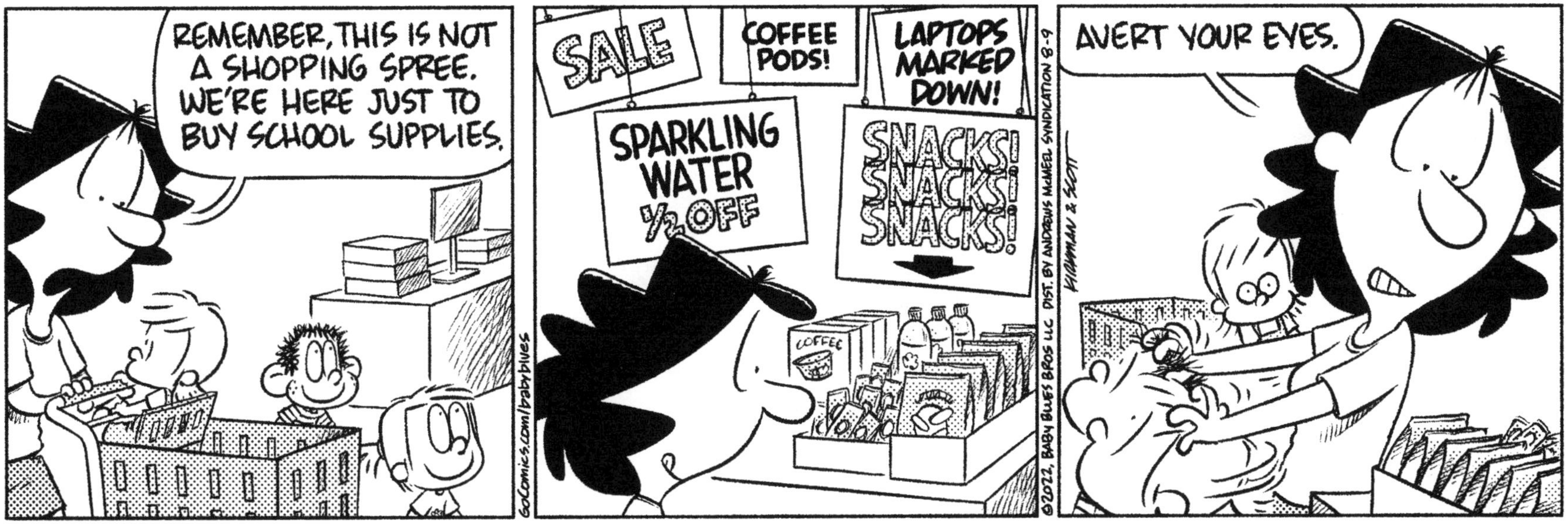
REMEMBER, THIS IS NOT A SHOPPING SPREE. WE'RE HERE JUST TO BUY SCHOOL SUPPLIES.
GoComics.com/babyblues
SALE
COFFEE PODS!
LAPTOPS MARKED DOWN!
SPARKLING WATER ½ OFF
SNACKS! SNACKS! SNACKS!
COFFEE
©2022, BABY BLUES BROS LLC DIST. BY ANDREWS MCMEEL SYNDICATION 8-9
KIRKMAN & SCOTT
AVERT YOUR EYES.

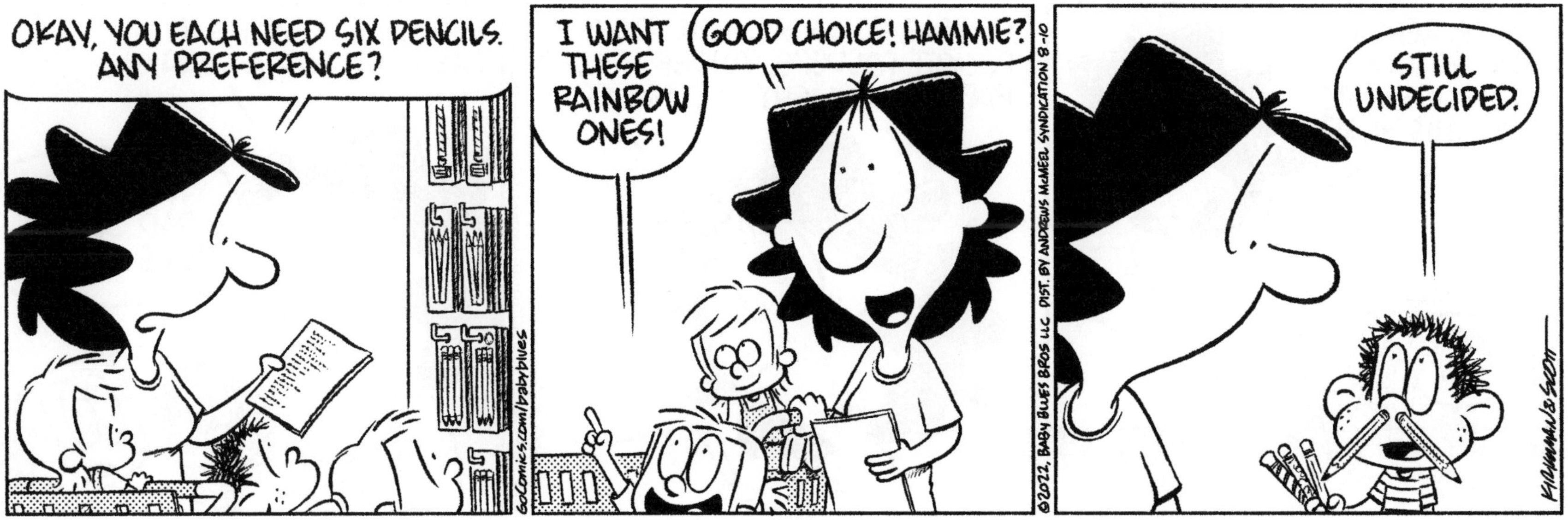
OKAY, YOU EACH NEED SIX PENCILS. ANY PREFERENCE?
GoComics.com/babyblues
I WANT THESE RAINBOW ONES!
GOOD CHOICE! HAMMIE?
©2022, BABY BLUES BROS LLC DIST. BY ANDREWS McMEEL SYNDICATION 8-10
STILL UNDECIDED.
KIRKMAN & SCOTT

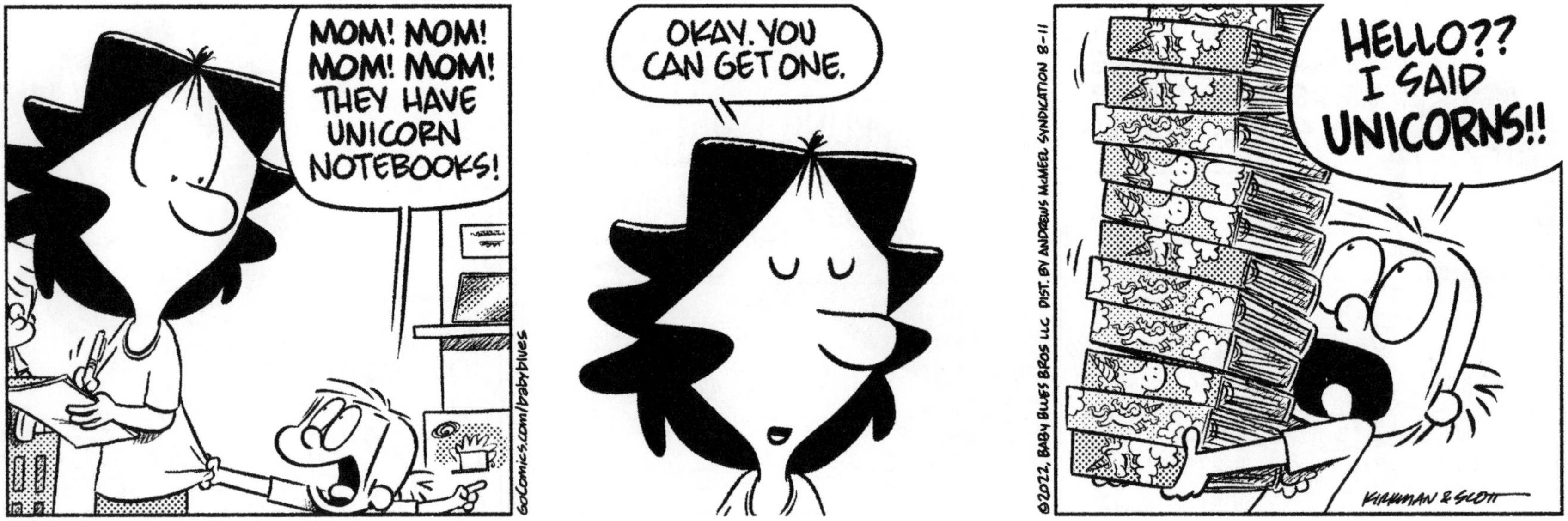
MOM! MOM! MOM! MOM! THEY HAVE UNICORN NOTEBOOKS!
GoComics.com/babyblues
OKAY. YOU CAN GET ONE.
©2022, BABY BLUES BROS LLC DIST. BY ANDREWS McMEEL SYNDICATION 8-11
HELLO?? I SAID UNICORNS!!
KIRKMAN & SCOTT

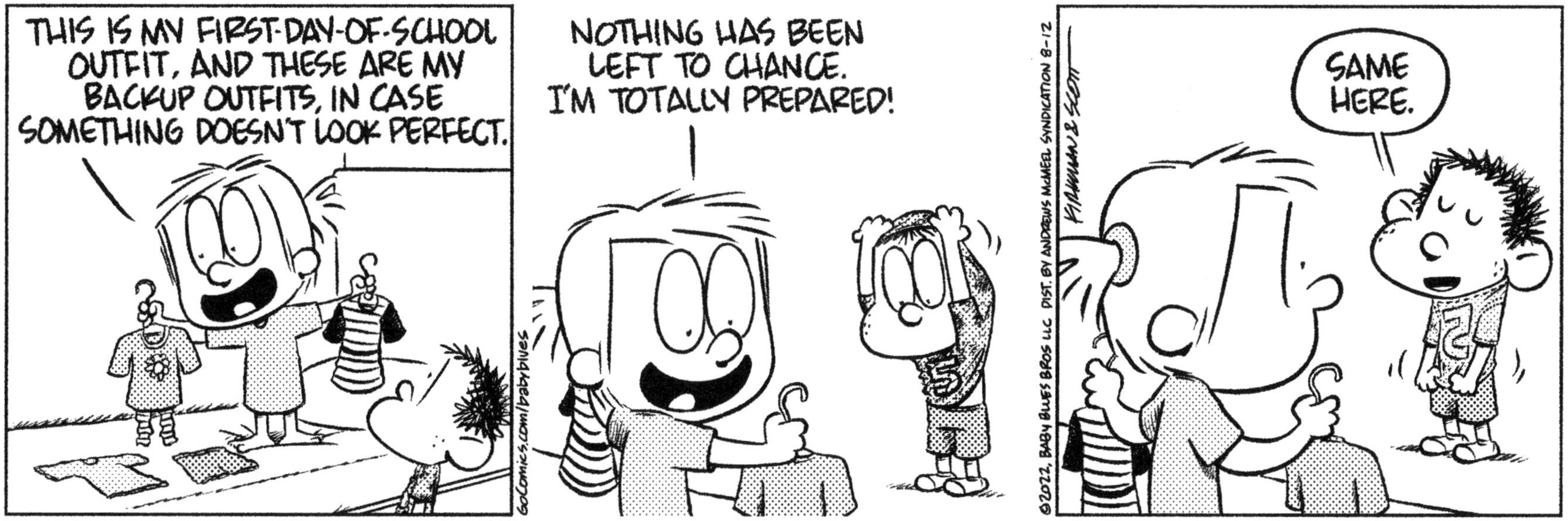
THIS IS MY FIRST-DAY-OF-SCHOOL OUTFIT, AND THESE ARE MY BACKUP OUTFITS, IN CASE SOMETHING DOESN'T LOOK PERFECT.
GoComics.com/babyblues
NOTHING HAS BEEN LEFT TO CHANCE. I'M TOTALLY PREPARED!
©2022, BABY BLUES BROS LLC DIST. BY ANDREWS MCMEEL SYNDICATION 8-12
KIRKMAN & SCOTT
SAME HERE.

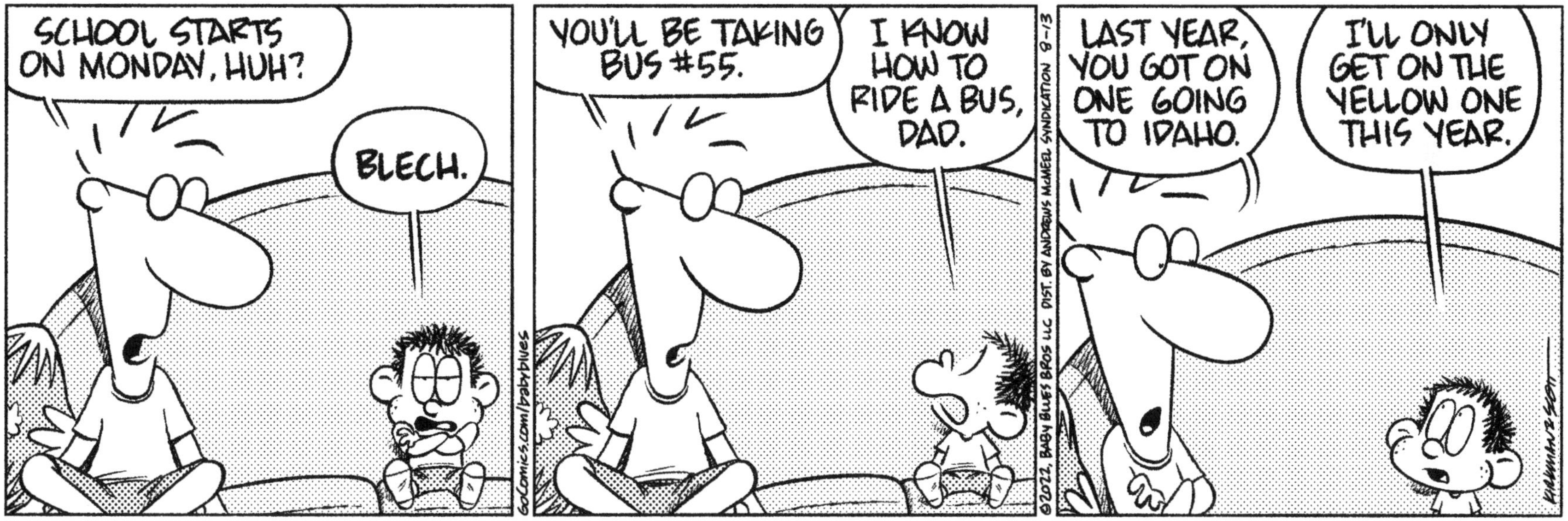
SCHOOL STARTS ON MONDAY, HUH?
BLECH.
GoComics.com/babyblues
YOU'LL BE TAKING BUS #55.
I KNOW HOW TO RIDE A BUS, DAD.
©2022, BABY BLUES BROS LLC DIST. BY ANDREWS MCMEEL SYNDICATION 8-13
LAST YEAR, YOU GOT ON ONE GOING TO IDAHO.
I'LL ONLY GET ON THE YELLOW ONE THIS YEAR.
KIRKMAN & SCOTT

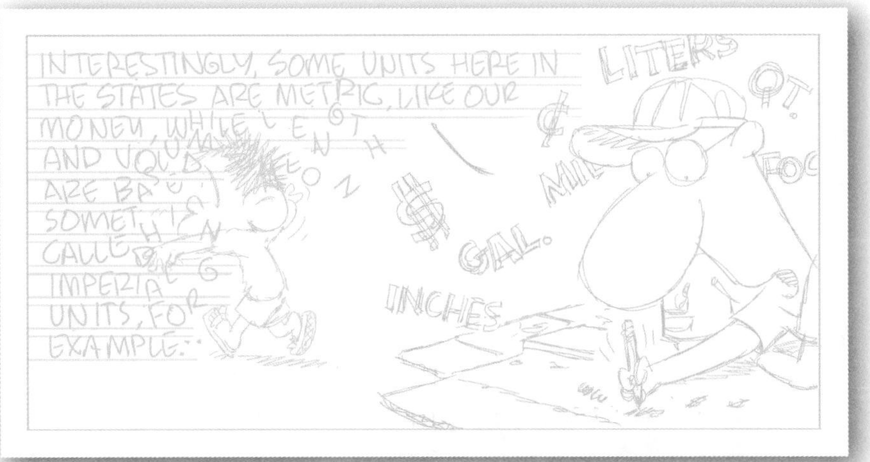

INTERESTINGLY, SOME UNITS HERE IN THE STATES ARE METRIC, LIKE OUR MONEY, WHILE
AND VOLU
ARE BA
SOMET
CALLE
IMPERIA
UNITS, FOR EXAMPLE.
LITERS
QT.
GAL.
INCHES

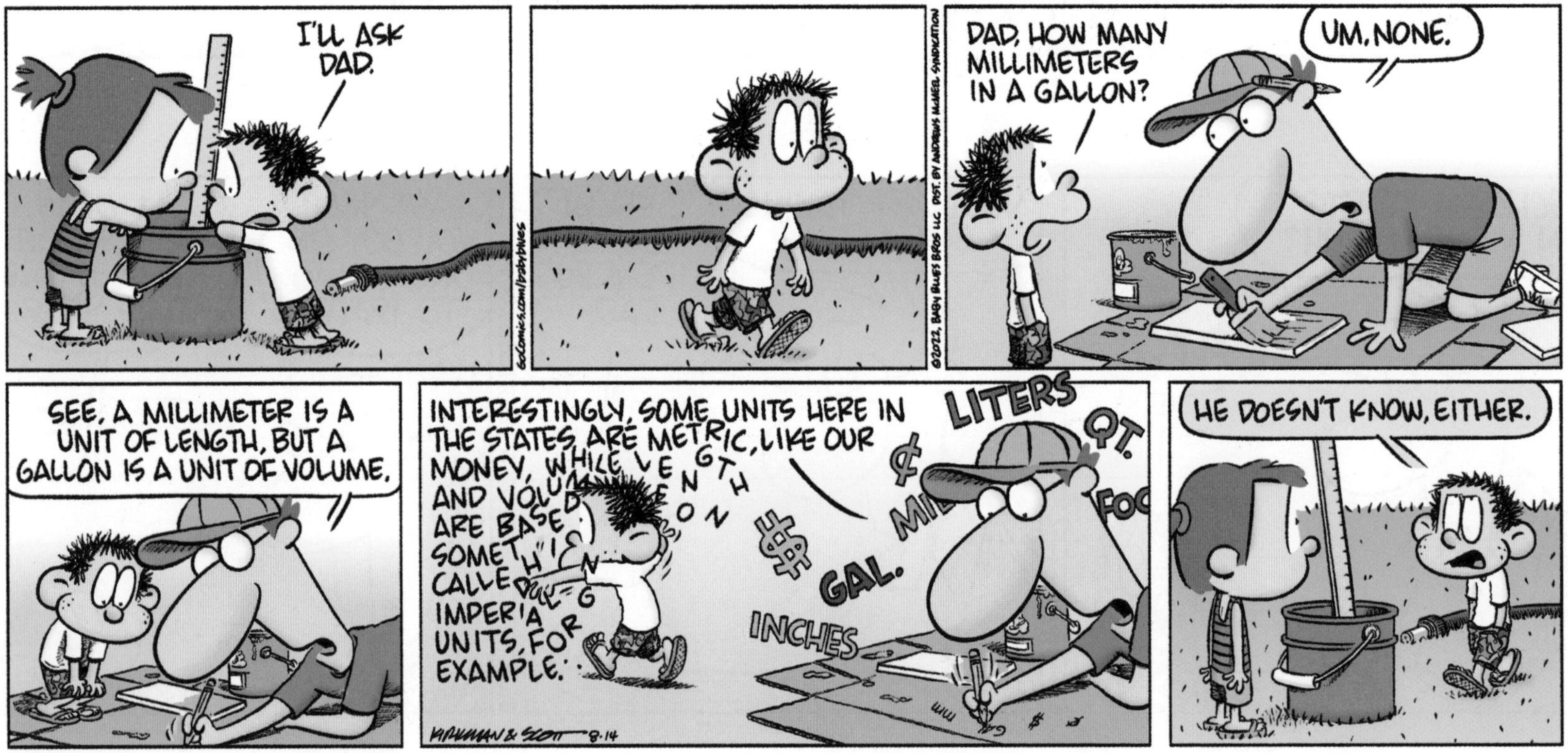

I'LL ASK DAD.
GoComics.com/babyblues
©2022, BABY BLUES BROS LLC DIST. BY ANDREWS McMEEL SYNDICATION
DAD, HOW MANY MILLIMETERS IN A GALLON?
UM, NONE.
SEE, A MILLIMETER IS A UNIT OF LENGTH, BUT A GALLON IS A UNIT OF VOLUME.
INTERESTINGLY, SOME UNITS HERE IN THE STATES ARE METRIC, LIKE OUR MONEY, WHILE LENGTH
AND VOLUME ARE BASED ON SOMETHING CALLED IMPERIAL UNITS, FOR EXAMPLE.
LITERS
QT.
GAL.
INCHES
KIRKMAN & SCOTT 8.14
HE DOESN'T KNOW, EITHER.

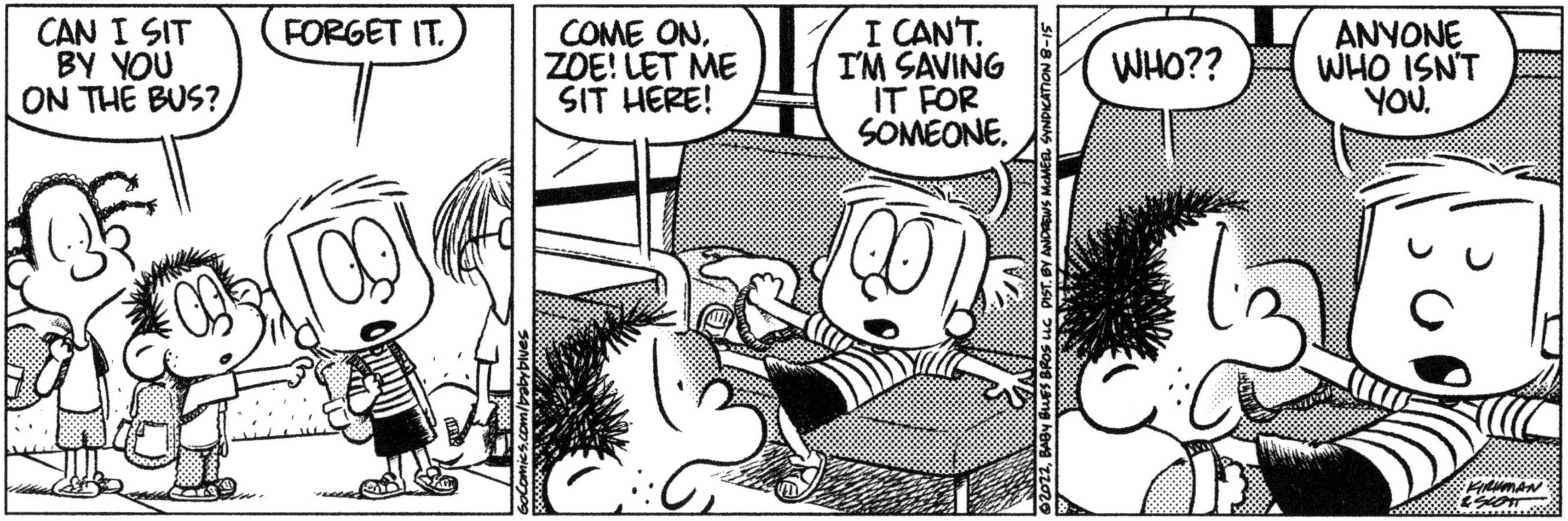
CAN I SIT BY YOU ON THE BUS?
FORGET IT.
goComics.com/babyblues
COME ON, ZOE! LET ME SIT HERE!
I CAN'T. I'M SAVING IT FOR SOMEONE.
©2022, BABY BLUES BROS LLC DIST. BY ANDREWS McMEEL SYNDICATION 8-15
WHO??
ANYONE WHO ISN'T YOU.
KIRKMAN & SCOTT

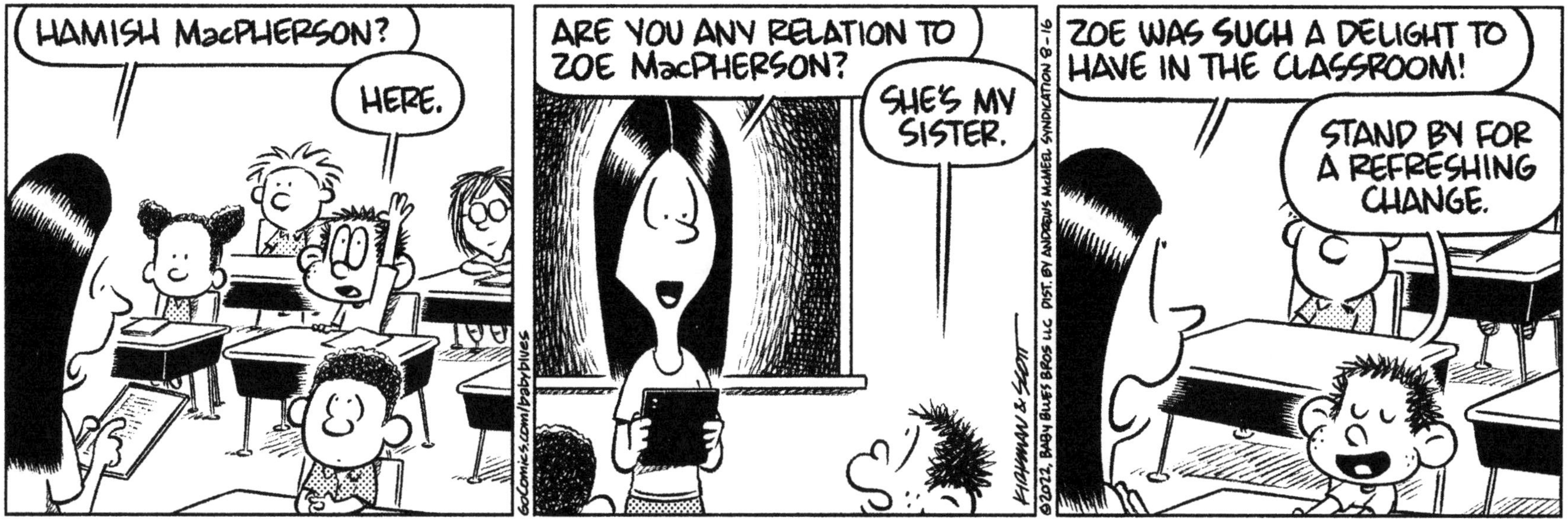
HAMISH MacPHERSON?
HERE.
goComics.com/babyblues
ARE YOU ANY RELATION TO ZOE MacPHERSON?
SHE'S MY SISTER.
KIRKMAN & SCOTT
©2022, BABY BLUES BROS LLC DIST. BY ANDREWS McMEEL SYNDICATION 8-16
ZOE WAS SUCH A DELIGHT TO HAVE IN THE CLASSROOM!
STAND BY FOR A REFRESHING CHANGE.

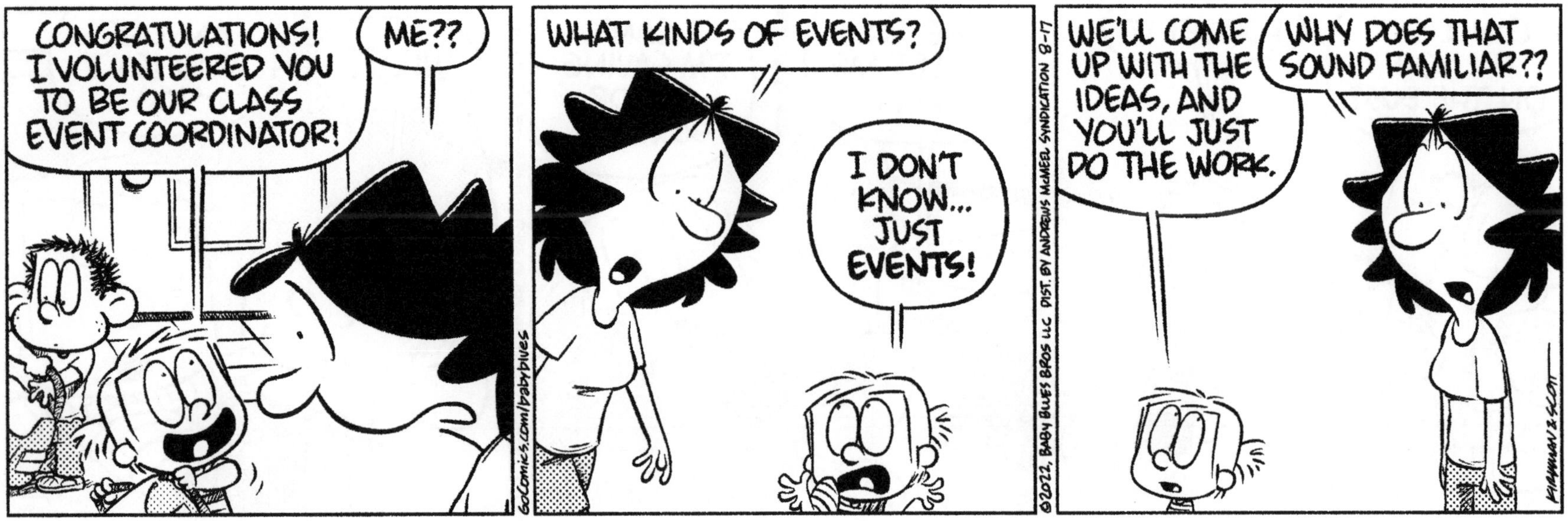
CONGRATULATIONS! I VOLUNTEERED YOU TO BE OUR CLASS EVENT COORDINATOR!
ME??
GoComics.com/babyblues
WHAT KINDS OF EVENTS?
I DON'T KNOW... JUST EVENTS!
©2022, BABY BLUES BROS LLC DIST. BY ANDREWS McMEEL SYNDICATION 8-17
WE'LL COME UP WITH THE IDEAS, AND YOU'LL JUST DO THE WORK.
WHY DOES THAT SOUND FAMILIAR??
KIRKMAN & SCOTT

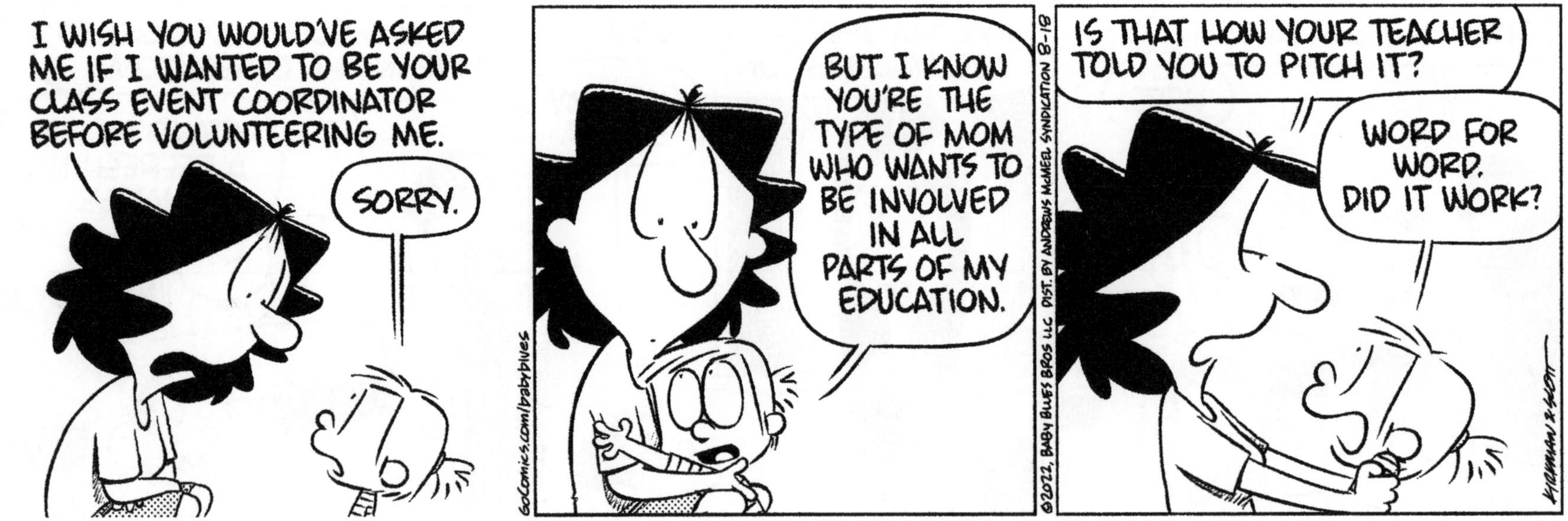
I WISH YOU WOULD'VE ASKED ME IF I WANTED TO BE YOUR CLASS EVENT COORDINATOR BEFORE VOLUNTEERING ME.
SORRY.
GoComics.com/babyblues
BUT I KNOW YOU'RE THE TYPE OF MOM WHO WANTS TO BE INVOLVED IN ALL PARTS OF MY EDUCATION.
©2022, BABY BLUES BROS LLC DIST. BY ANDREWS McMEEL SYNDICATION 8-18
IS THAT HOW YOUR TEACHER TOLD YOU TO PITCH IT?
WORD FOR WORD. DID IT WORK?
KIRKMAN & SCOTT

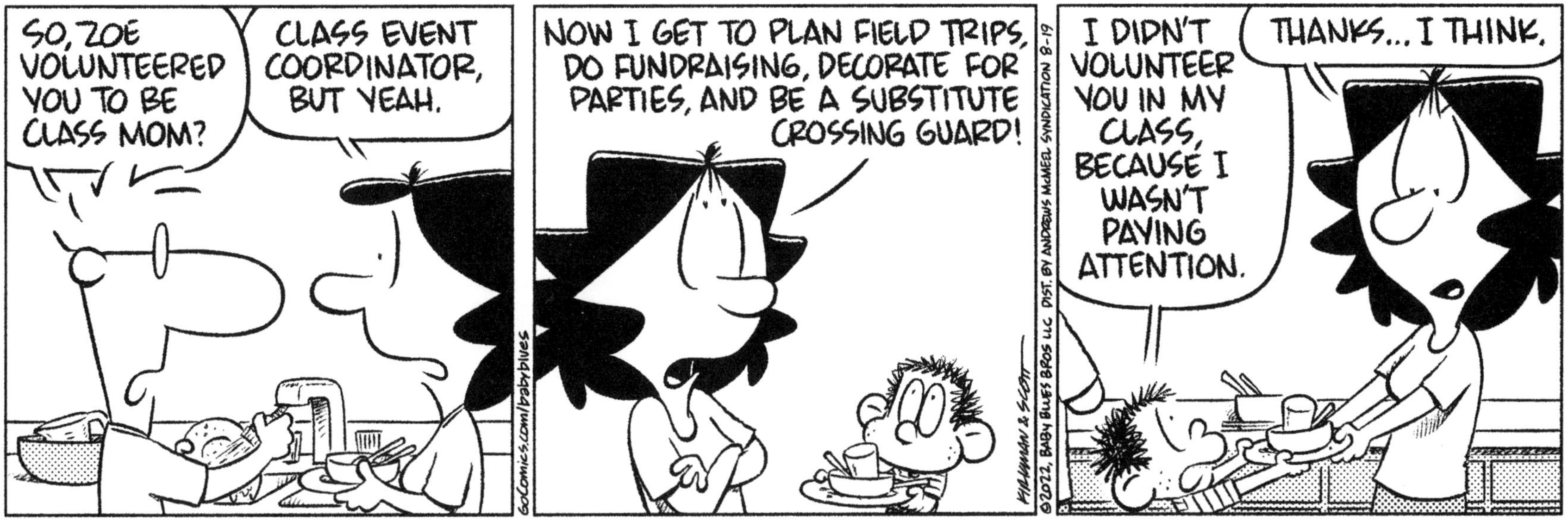
SO, ZOE VOLUNTEERED YOU TO BE CLASS MOM?
CLASS EVENT COORDINATOR, BUT YEAH.
GoComics.com/babyblues
NOW I GET TO PLAN FIELD TRIPS, DO FUNDRAISING, DECORATE FOR PARTIES, AND BE A SUBSTITUTE CROSSING GUARD!
KIRKMAN & SCOTT
©2022, BABY BLUES BROS LLC DIST. BY ANDREWS McMEEL SYNDICATION 8-19
I DIDN'T VOLUNTEER YOU IN MY CLASS, BECAUSE I WASN'T PAYING ATTENTION.
THANKS... I THINK.

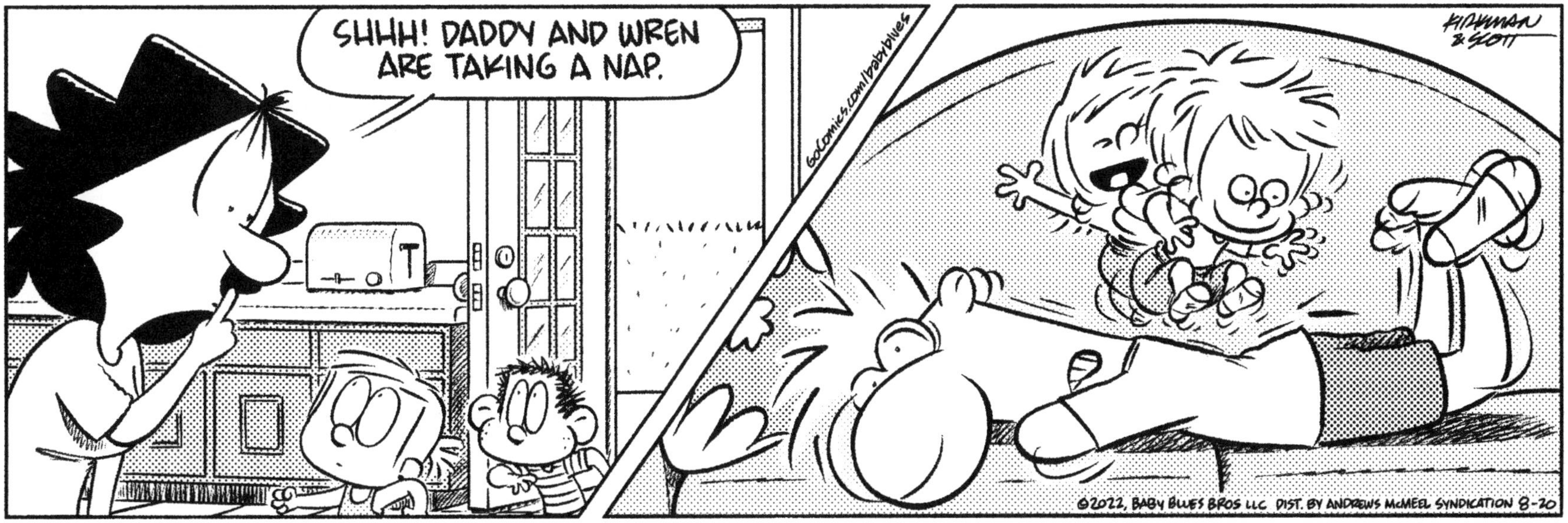
SHHH! DADDY AND WREN ARE TAKING A NAP.
GoComics.com/babyblues
KIRKMAN & SCOTT
©2022, BABY BLUES BROS LLC DIST. BY ANDREWS McMEEL SYNDICATION 8-20

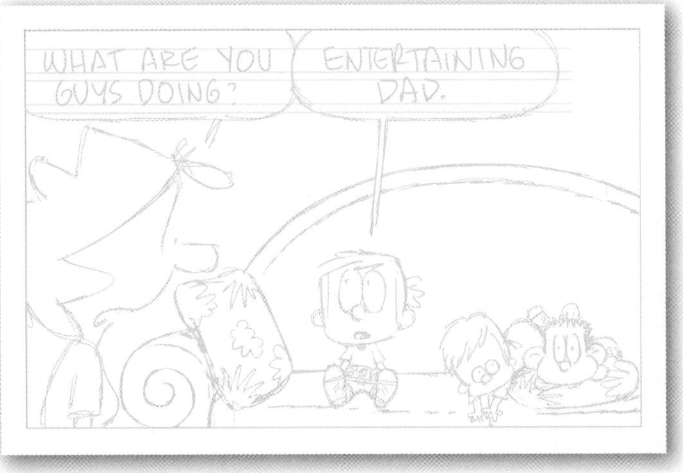
WHAT ARE YOU GUYS DOING?
ENTERTAINING DAD.

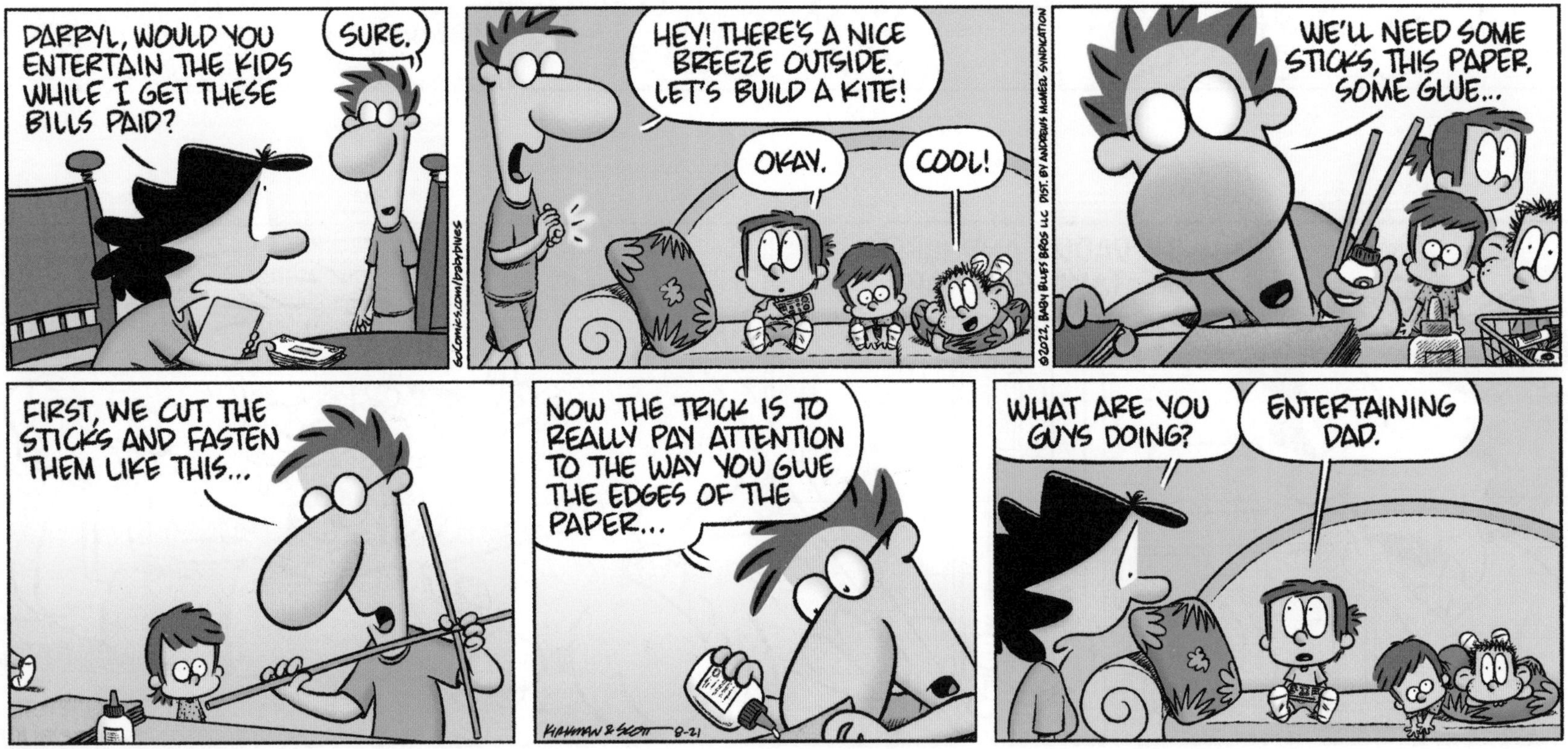
DARRYL, WOULD YOU ENTERTAIN THE KIDS WHILE I GET THESE BILLS PAID?
SURE.
GoComics.com/babyblues
HEY! THERE'S A NICE BREEZE OUTSIDE. LET'S BUILD A KITE!
OKAY.
COOL!
©2022, BABY BLUES BROS LLC DIST. BY ANDREWS McMEEL SYNDICATION
WE'LL NEED SOME STICKS, THIS PAPER, SOME GLUE...
FIRST, WE CUT THE STICKS AND FASTEN THEM LIKE THIS...
NOW THE TRICK IS TO REALLY PAY ATTENTION TO THE WAY YOU GLUE THE EDGES OF THE PAPER...
KIRKMAN & SCOTT 8-21
WHAT ARE YOU GUYS DOING?
ENTERTAINING DAD.

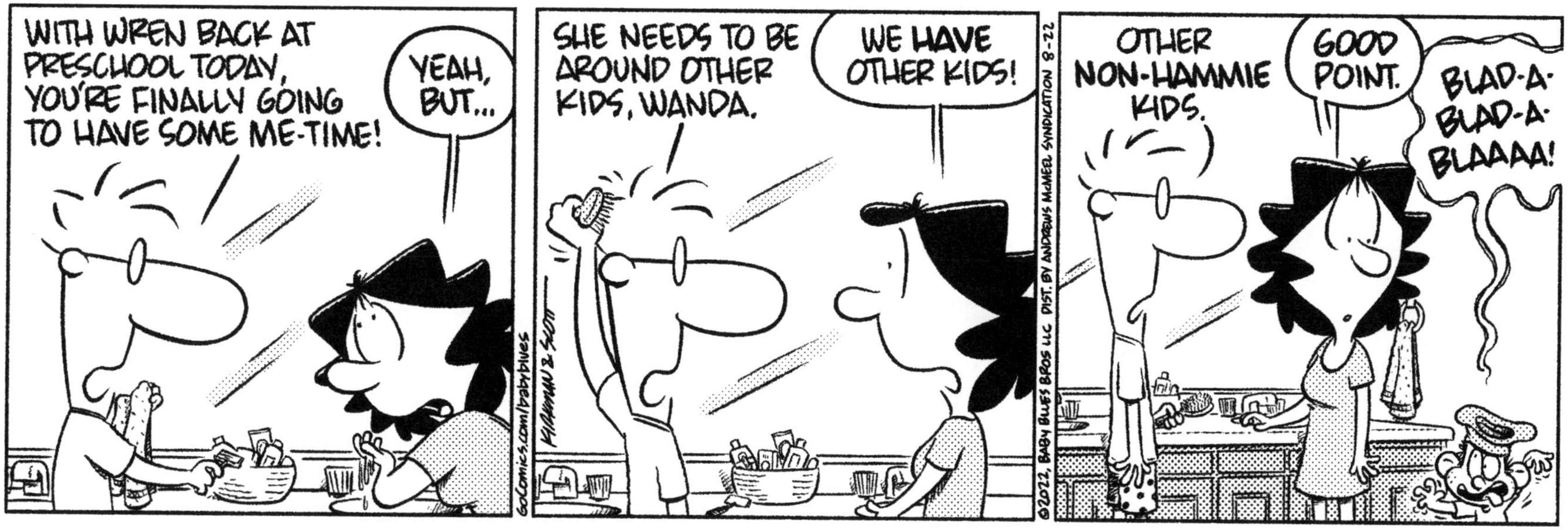
WITH WREN BACK AT PRESCHOOL TODAY, YOU'RE FINALLY GOING TO HAVE SOME ME-TIME!
YEAH, BUT...
SHE NEEDS TO BE AROUND OTHER KIDS, WANDA.
WE HAVE OTHER KIDS!
OTHER NON-HAMMIE KIDS.
GOOD POINT.
BLAD-A-BLAD-A-BLAAAA!
GoComics.com/babyblues
KIRKMAN & SCOTT
©2022, BABY BLUES BROS LLC DIST. BY ANDREWS McMEEL SYNDICATION 8-22

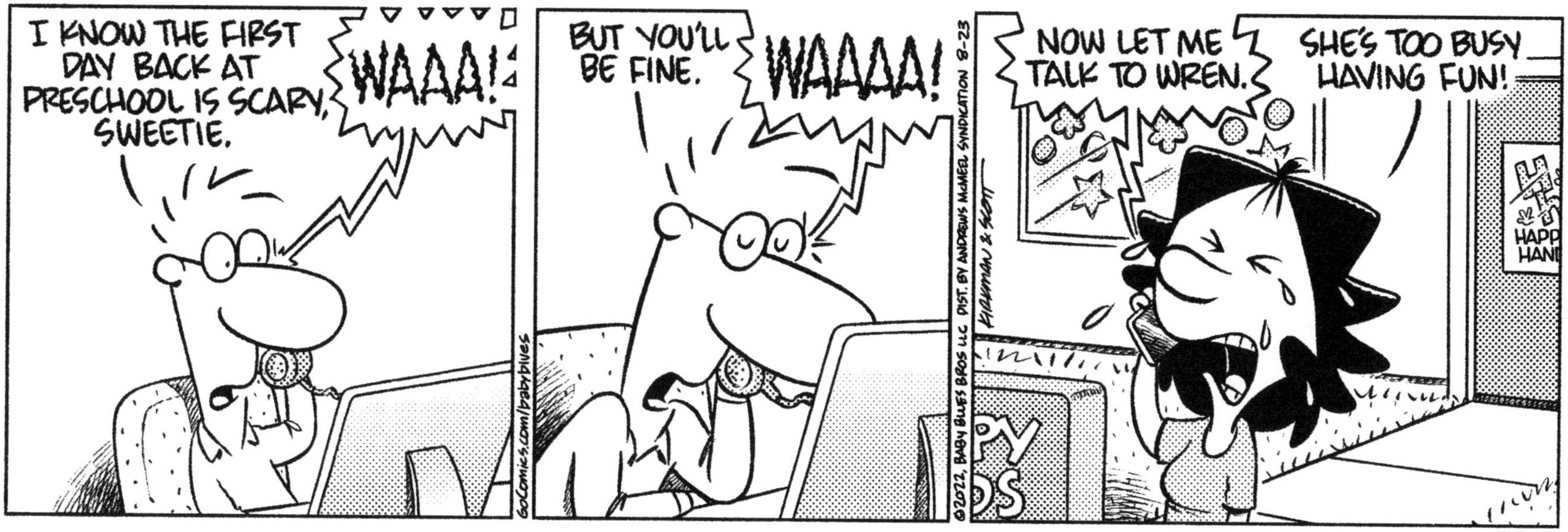
I KNOW THE FIRST DAY BACK AT PRESCHOOL IS SCARY, SWEETIE.
WAAA!
BUT YOU'LL BE FINE.
WAAAA!
NOW LET ME TALK TO WREN.
SHE'S TOO BUSY HAVING FUN!
GoComics.com/babyblues
©2022, BABY BLUES BROS LLC DIST. BY ANDREWS McMEEL SYNDICATION 8-23
KIRKMAN & SCOTT

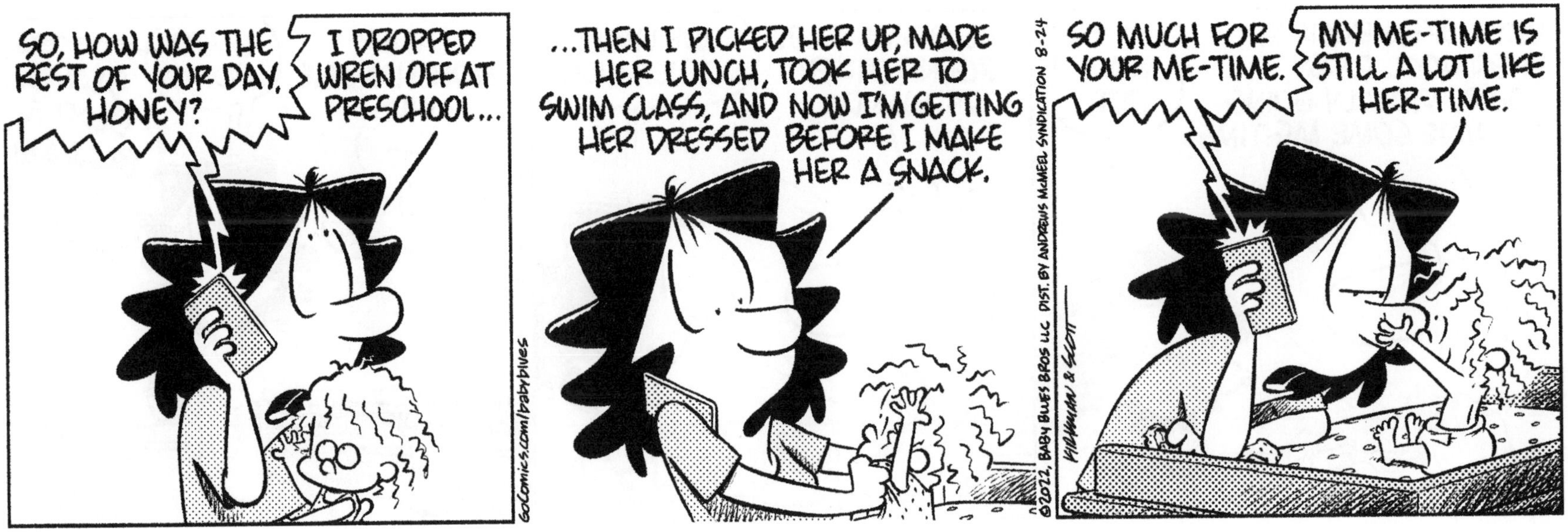
SO, HOW WAS THE REST OF YOUR DAY, HONEY?
I DROPPED WREN OFF AT PRESCHOOL...
gocomics.com/babyblues
...THEN I PICKED HER UP, MADE HER LUNCH, TOOK HER TO SWIM CLASS, AND NOW I'M GETTING HER DRESSED BEFORE I MAKE HER A SNACK.
©2022, BABY BLUES BROS LLC DIST. BY ANDREWS McMEEL SYNDICATION 8-24
KIRKMAN & SCOTT
SO MUCH FOR YOUR ME-TIME.
MY ME-TIME IS STILL A LOT LIKE HER-TIME.

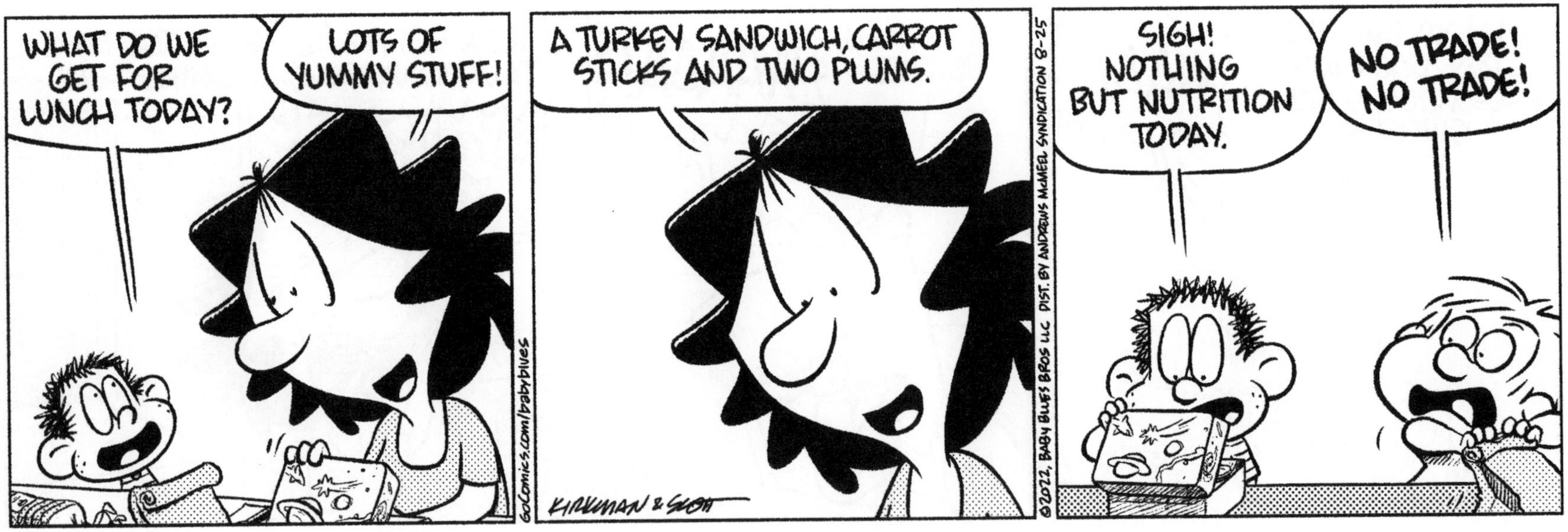
WHAT DO WE GET FOR LUNCH TODAY?
LOTS OF YUMMY STUFF!
gocomics.com/babyblues
A TURKEY SANDWICH, CARROT STICKS AND TWO PLUMS.
KIRKMAN & SCOTT
©2022, BABY BLUES BROS LLC DIST. BY ANDREWS McMEEL SYNDICATION 8-25
SIGH! NOTHING BUT NUTRITION TODAY.
NO TRADE! NO TRADE!

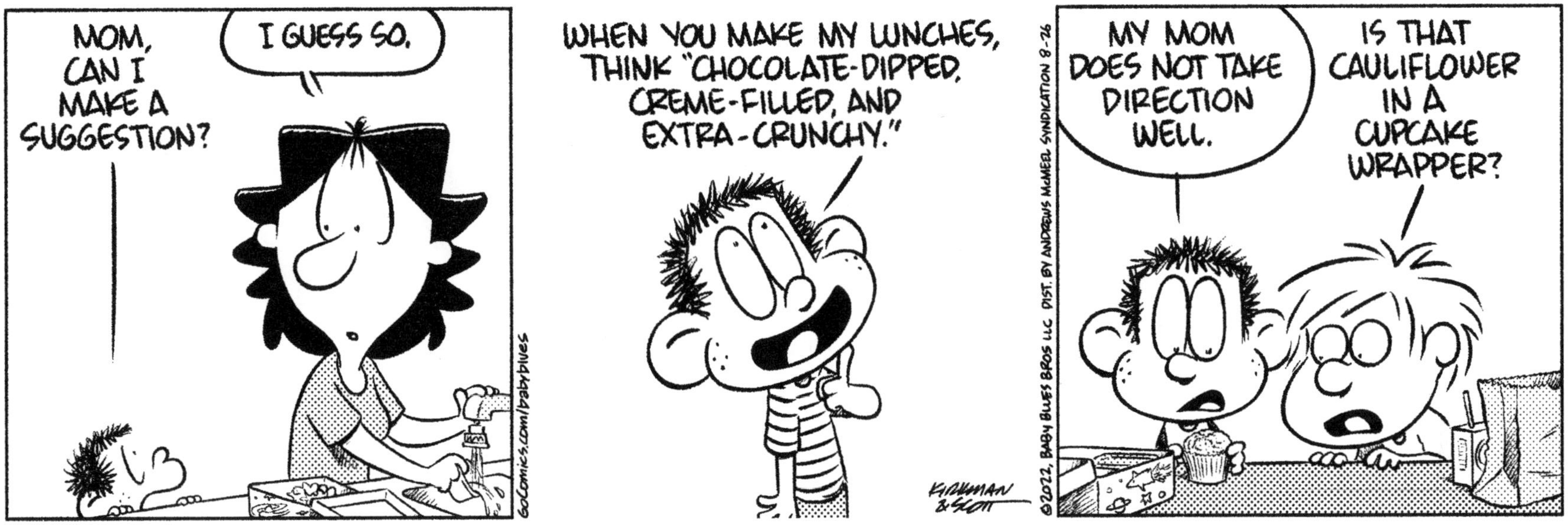
MOM, CAN I MAKE A SUGGESTION?
I GUESS SO.
WHEN YOU MAKE MY LUNCHES, THINK "CHOCOLATE-DIPPED, CREME-FILLED, AND EXTRA-CRUNCHY."
MY MOM DOES NOT TAKE DIRECTION WELL.
IS THAT CAULIFLOWER IN A CUPCAKE WRAPPER?
GoComics.com/babyblues
©2022, BABY BLUES BROS LLC DIST. BY ANDREWS McMEEL SYNDICATION 8-26
KIRKMAN & SCOTT

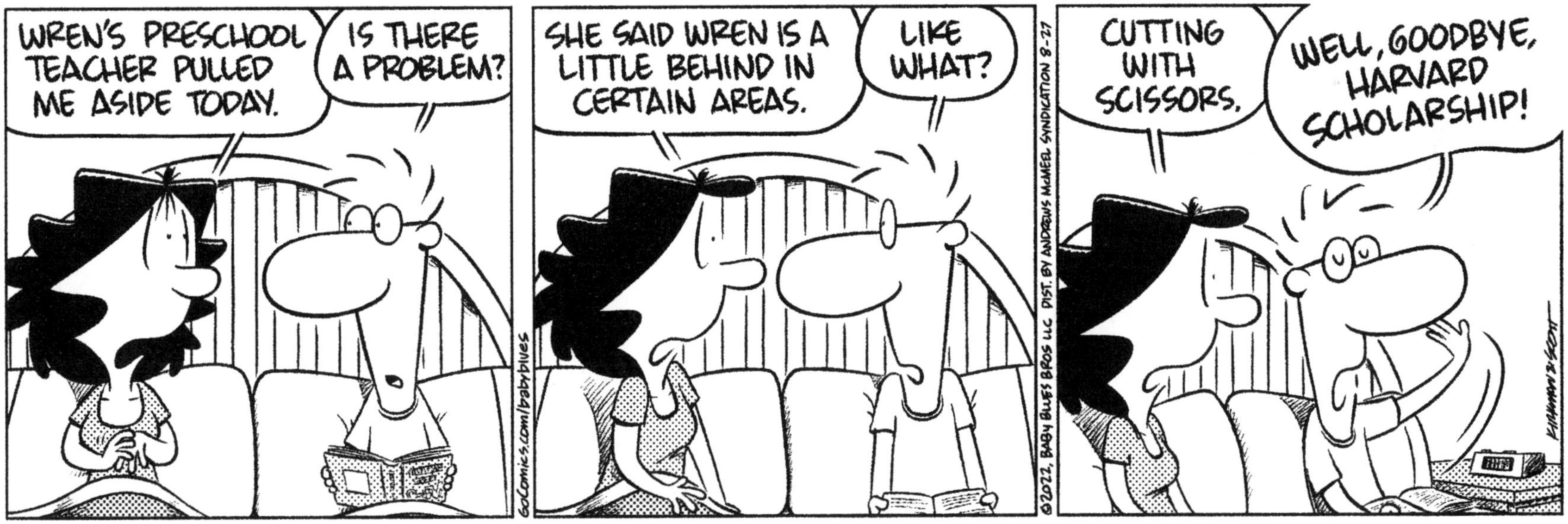
WREN'S PRESCHOOL TEACHER PULLED ME ASIDE TODAY.
IS THERE A PROBLEM?
SHE SAID WREN IS A LITTLE BEHIND IN CERTAIN AREAS.
LIKE WHAT?
CUTTING WITH SCISSORS.
WELL, GOODBYE, HARVARD SCHOLARSHIP!
GoComics.com/babyblues
©2022, BABY BLUES BROS LLC DIST. BY ANDREWS McMEEL SYNDICATION 8-27
KIRKMAN & SCOTT

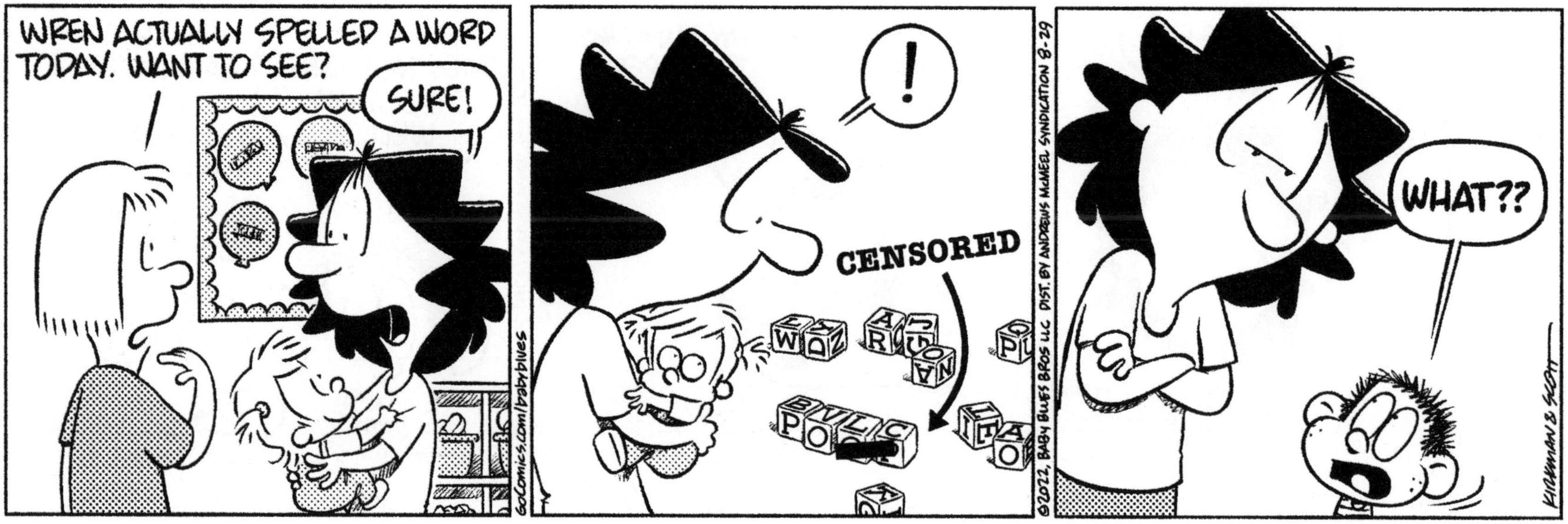
WREN ACTUALLY SPELLED A WORD TODAY. WANT TO SEE?
SURE!
!
CENSORED
WHAT??
GoComics.com/babyblues
©2022, BABY BLUES BROS LLC DIST. BY ANDREWS MCMEEL SYNDICATION 8-29
KIRKMAN & SCOTT

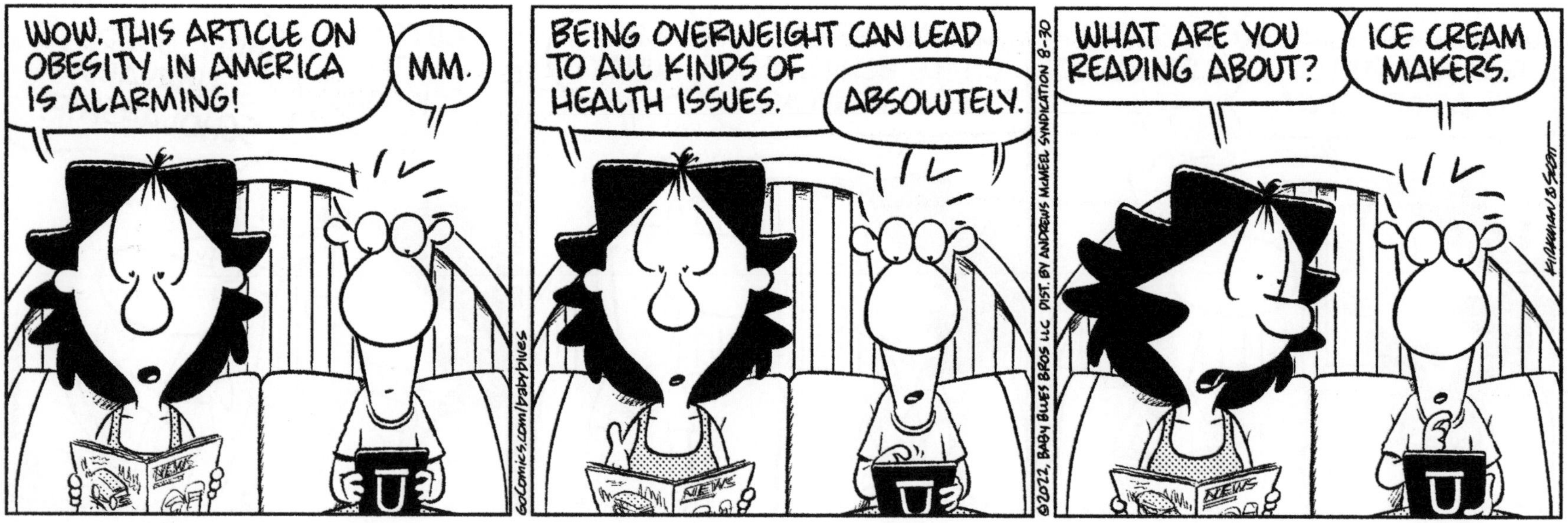
WOW. THIS ARTICLE ON OBESITY IN AMERICA IS ALARMING!
MM.
BEING OVERWEIGHT CAN LEAD TO ALL KINDS OF HEALTH ISSUES.
ABSOLUTELY.
WHAT ARE YOU READING ABOUT?
ICE CREAM MAKERS.
NEWS
GoComics.com/babyblues
©2022, BABY BLUES BROS LLC DIST. BY ANDREWS MCMEEL SYNDICATION 8-30
KIRKMAN & SCOTT

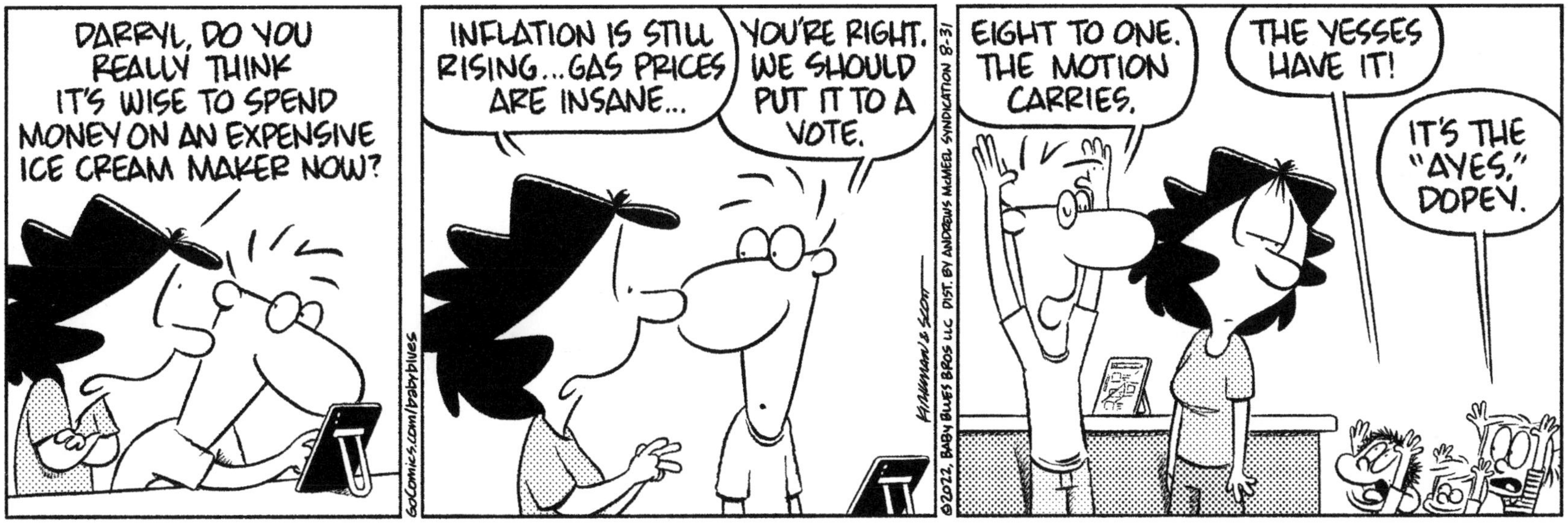
DARRYL, DO YOU REALLY THINK IT'S WISE TO SPEND MONEY ON AN EXPENSIVE ICE CREAM MAKER NOW?
INFLATION IS STILL RISING...GAS PRICES ARE INSANE...
YOU'RE RIGHT. WE SHOULD PUT IT TO A VOTE.
EIGHT TO ONE. THE MOTION CARRIES.
THE YESSES HAVE IT!
IT'S THE "AYES," DOPEY.
GoComics.com/babyblues
©2022, BABY BLUES BROS LLC DIST. BY ANDREWS McMEEL SYNDICATION 8-31
KIRKMAN & SCOTT

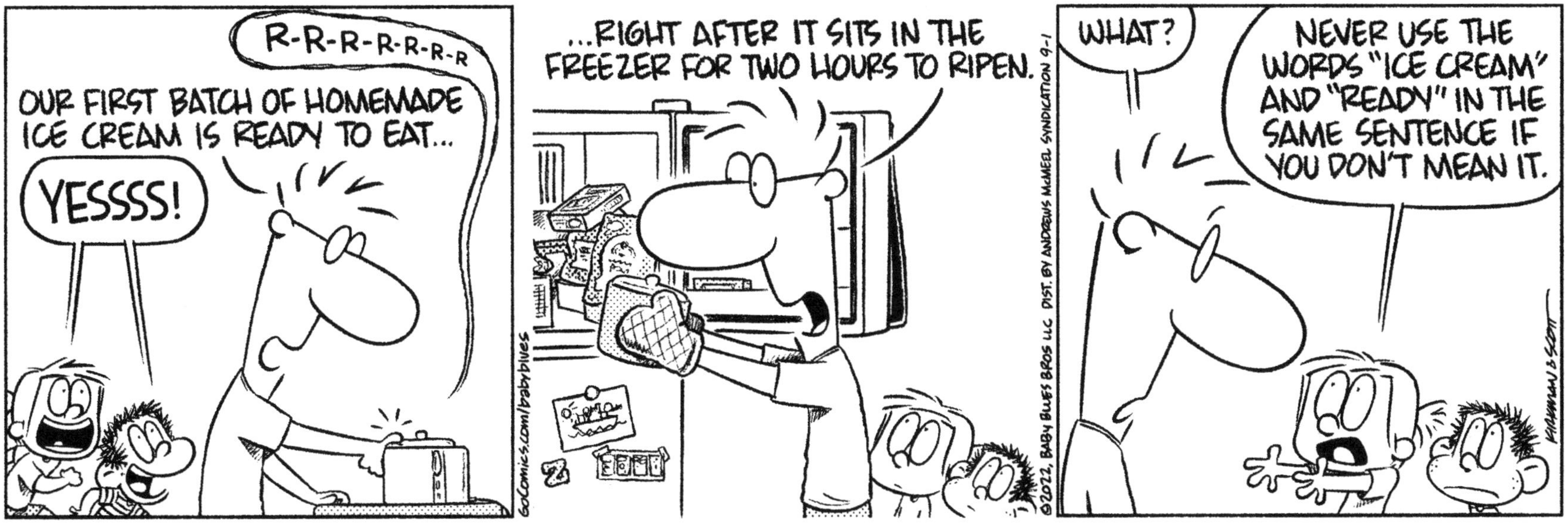
R-R-R-R-R-R-R-R
OUR FIRST BATCH OF HOMEMADE ICE CREAM IS READY TO EAT...
YESSSS!
...RIGHT AFTER IT SITS IN THE FREEZER FOR TWO HOURS TO RIPEN.
WHAT?
NEVER USE THE WORDS "ICE CREAM" AND "READY" IN THE SAME SENTENCE IF YOU DON'T MEAN IT.
GoComics.com/babyblues
©2022, BABY BLUES BROS LLC DIST. BY ANDREWS McMEEL SYNDICATION 9-1
KIRKMAN & SCOTT

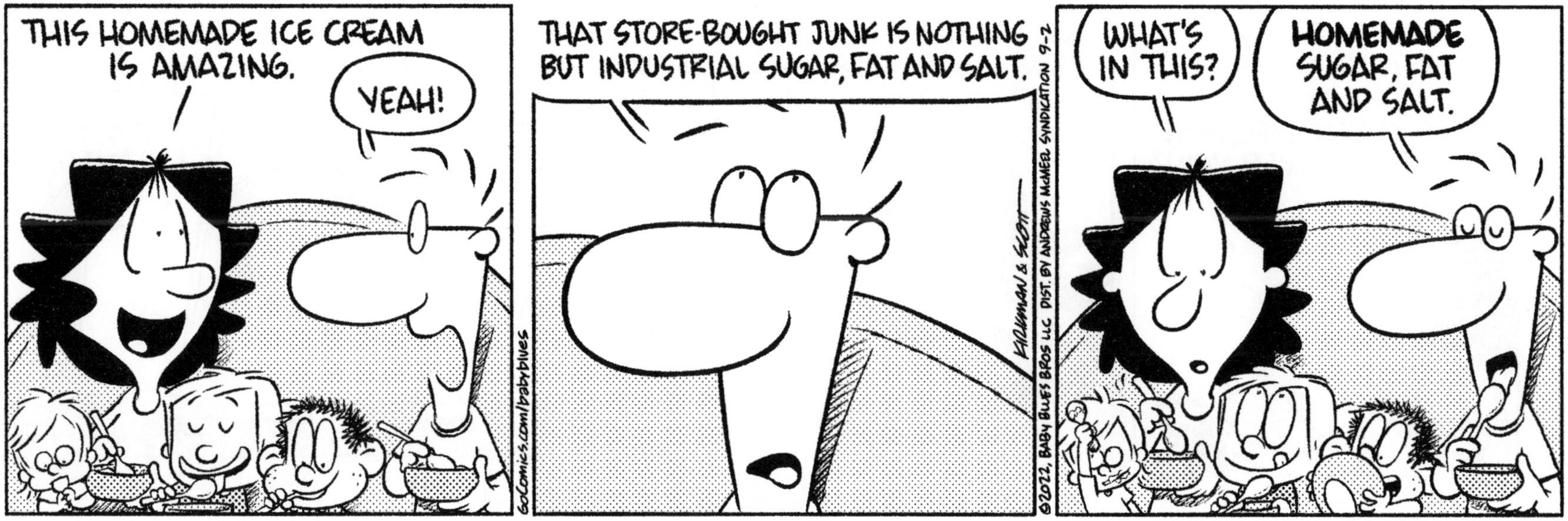
THIS HOMEMADE ICE CREAM IS AMAZING.
YEAH!
GoComics.com/babyblues
THAT STORE-BOUGHT JUNK IS NOTHING BUT INDUSTRIAL SUGAR, FAT AND SALT.
KIRKMAN & SCOTT
©2022, BABY BLUES BROS LLC DIST. BY ANDREWS McMEEL SYNDICATION 9-2
WHAT'S IN THIS?
HOMEMADE SUGAR, FAT AND SALT.

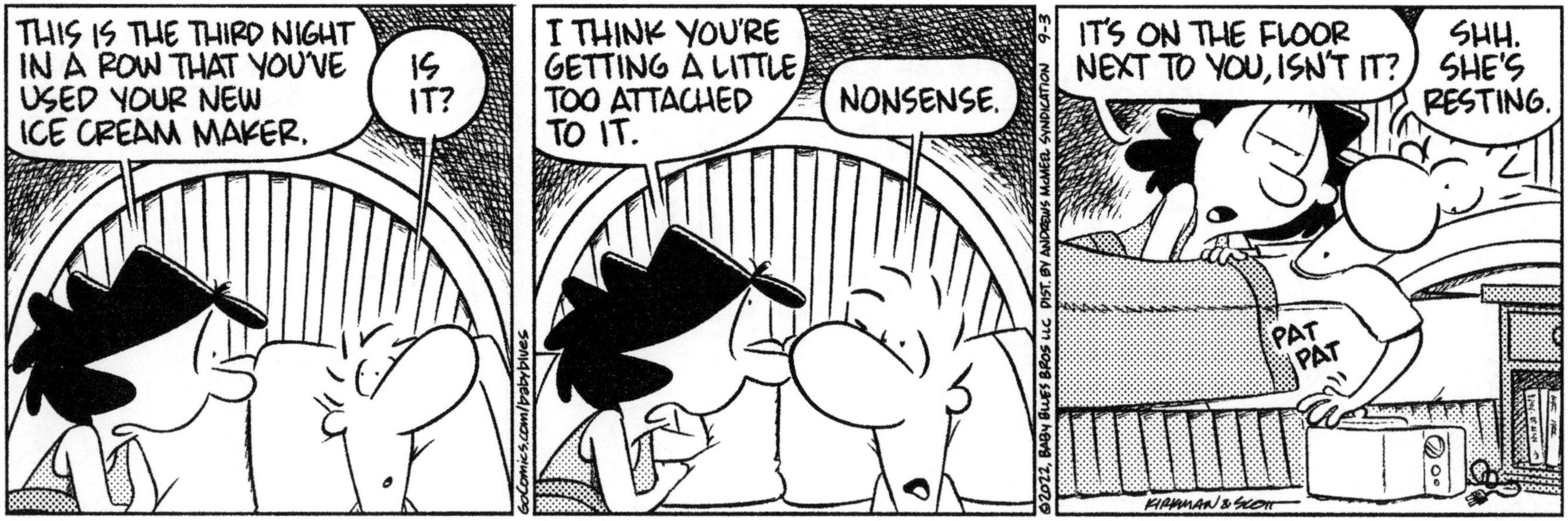
THIS IS THE THIRD NIGHT IN A ROW THAT YOU'VE USED YOUR NEW ICE CREAM MAKER.
IS IT?
GoComics.com/babyblues
I THINK YOU'RE GETTING A LITTLE TOO ATTACHED TO IT.
NONSENSE.
©2022, BABY BLUES BROS LLC DIST. BY ANDREWS McMEEL SYNDICATION 9-3
IT'S ON THE FLOOR NEXT TO YOU, ISN'T IT?
SHH. SHE'S RESTING.
PAT PAT
KIRKMAN & SCOTT

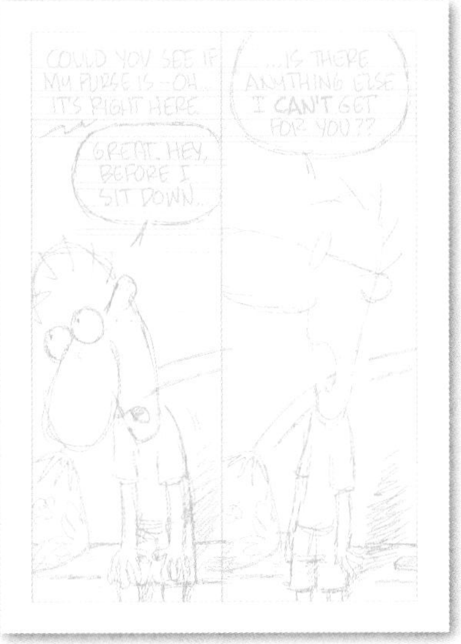
COULD YOU SEE IF MY PURSE IS–OH IT'S RIGHT HERE
GREAT. HEY, BEFORE I SIT DOWN...
...IS THERE ANYTHING ELSE I CAN'T GET FOR YOU??

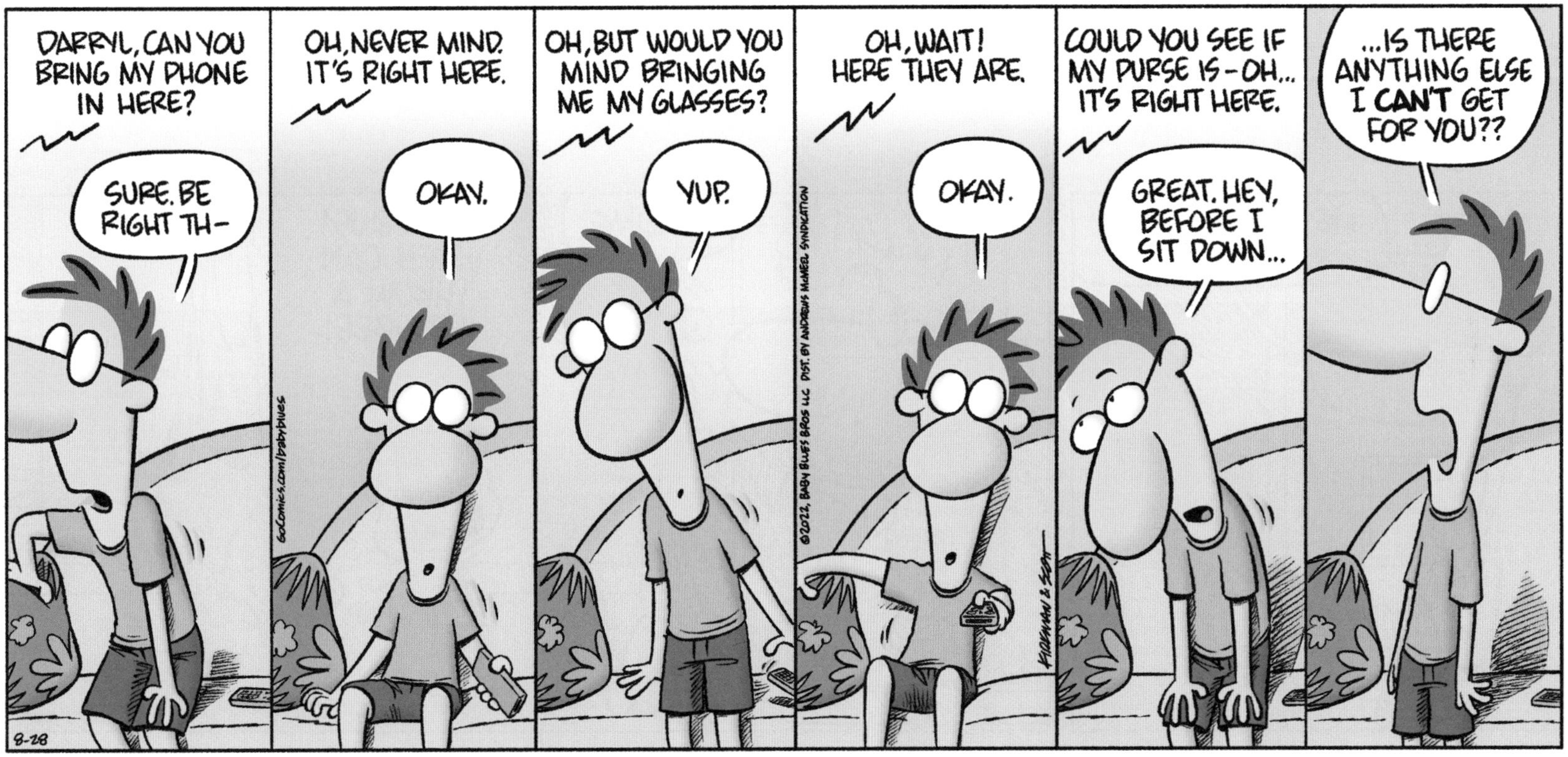
DARRYL, CAN YOU BRING MY PHONE IN HERE?
SURE. BE RIGHT TH–
8-28
OH, NEVER MIND. IT'S RIGHT HERE.
OKAY.
GoComics.com/babyblues
OH, BUT WOULD YOU MIND BRINGING ME MY GLASSES?
YUP.
©2022, BABY BLUES BROS LLC DIST. BY ANDREWS MCMEEL SYNDICATION
OH, WAIT! HERE THEY ARE.
OKAY.
KIRKMAN & SCOTT
COULD YOU SEE IF MY PURSE IS–OH... IT'S RIGHT HERE.
GREAT. HEY, BEFORE I SIT DOWN...
...IS THERE ANYTHING ELSE I **CAN'T** GET FOR YOU??

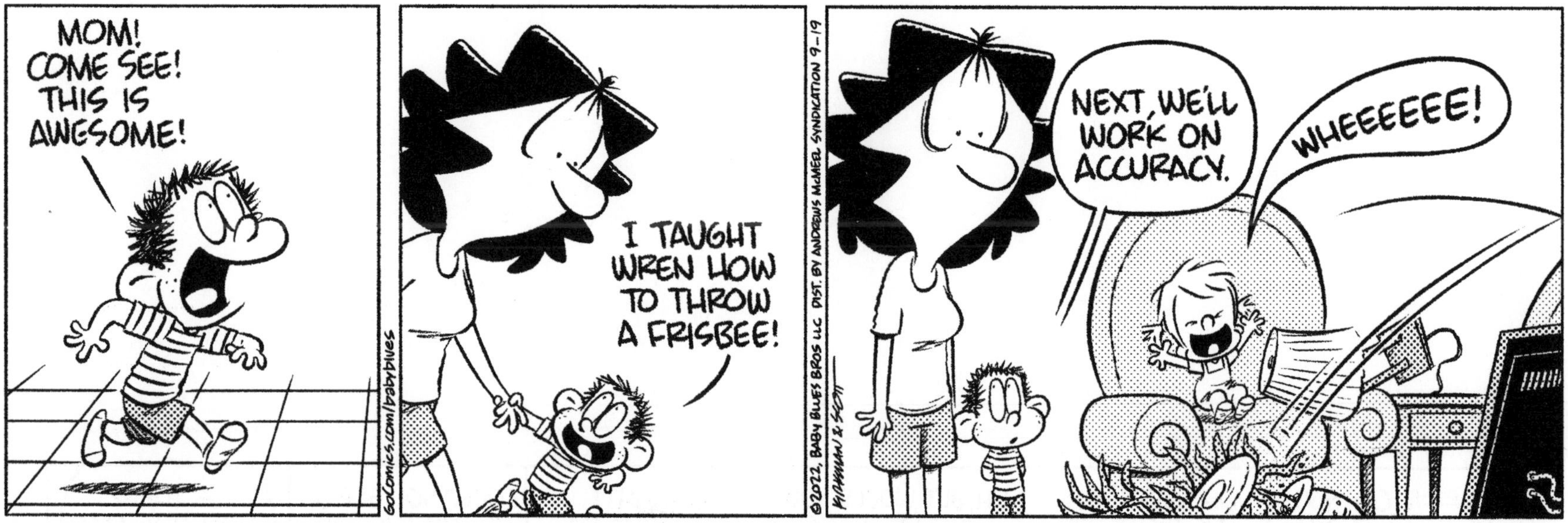
MOM! COME SEE! THIS IS AWESOME!
GoComics.com/babyblues
I TAUGHT WREN HOW TO THROW A FRISBEE!
©2022, BABY BLUES BROS LLC DIST. BY ANDREWS McMEEL SYNDICATION 9-19
KIRKMAN & SCOTT
NEXT, WE'LL WORK ON ACCURACY.
WHEEEEEEE!

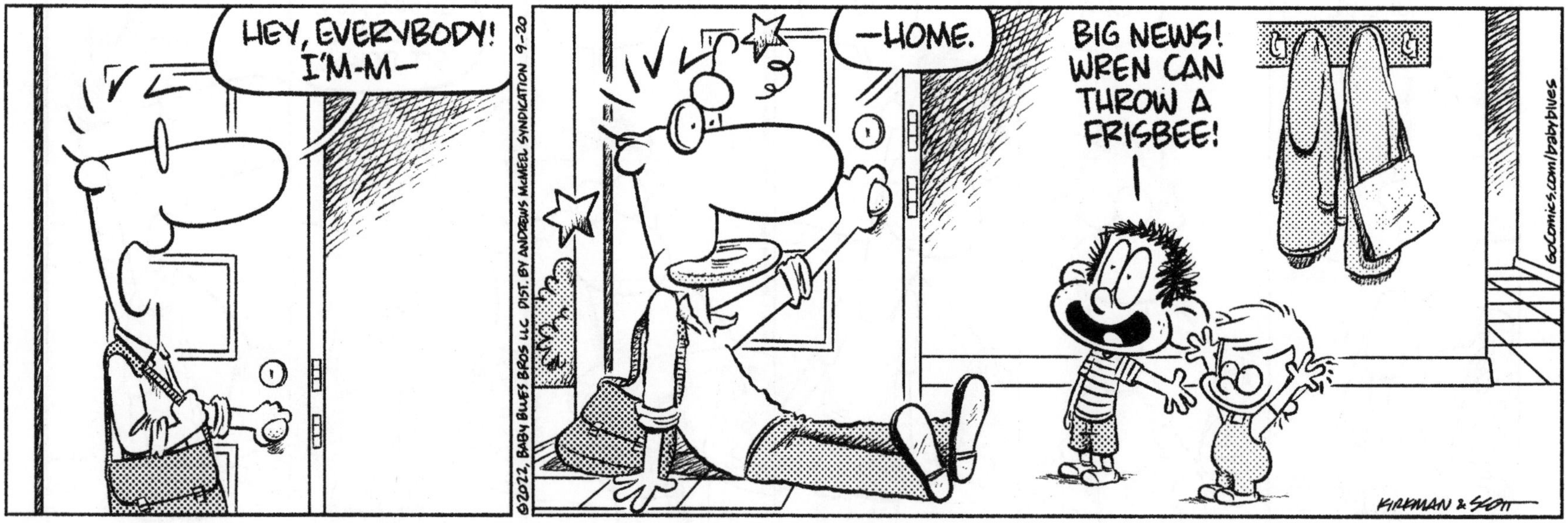
HEY, EVERYBODY! I'M-M—
©2022, BABY BLUES BROS LLC DIST. BY ANDREWS McMEEL SYNDICATION 9-20
—HOME.
BIG NEWS! WREN CAN THROW A FRISBEE!
GoComics.com/babyblues
KIRKMAN & SCOTT

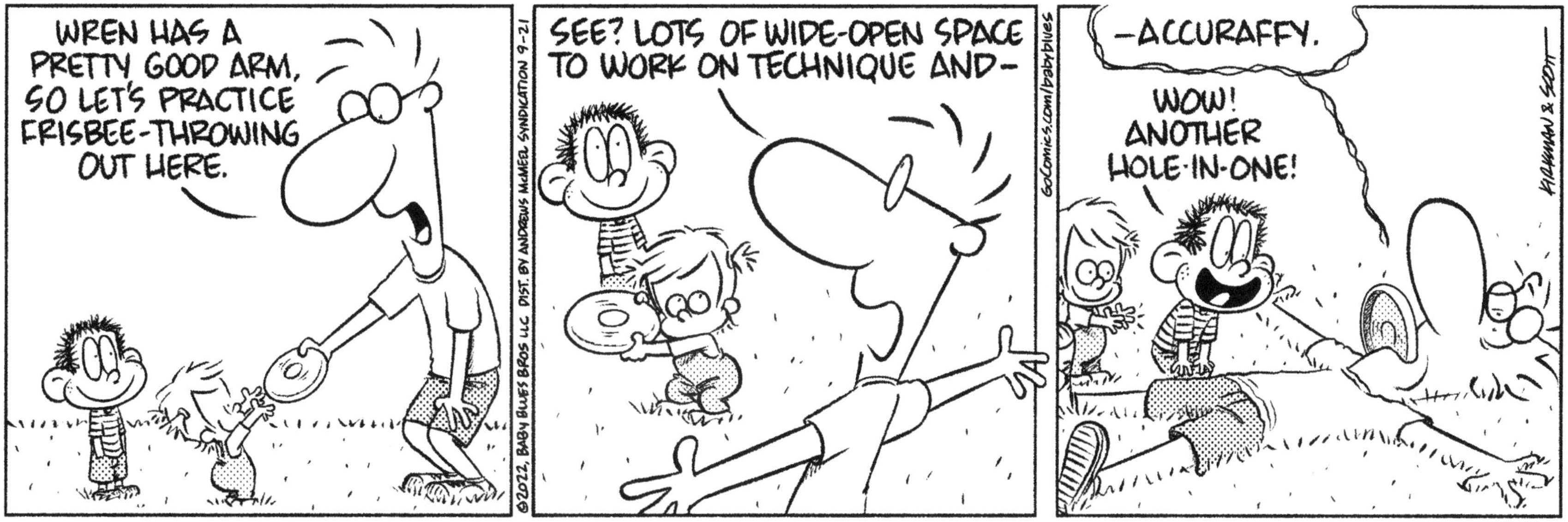
WREN HAS A PRETTY GOOD ARM, SO LET'S PRACTICE FRISBEE-THROWING OUT HERE.
SEE? LOTS OF WIDE-OPEN SPACE TO WORK ON TECHNIQUE AND—
—ACCURAFFY.
WOW! ANOTHER HOLE-IN-ONE!
©2022, BABY BLUES BROS LLC DIST. BY ANDREWS McMEEL SYNDICATION 9-21
GoComics.com/babyblues
KIRKMAN & SCOTT

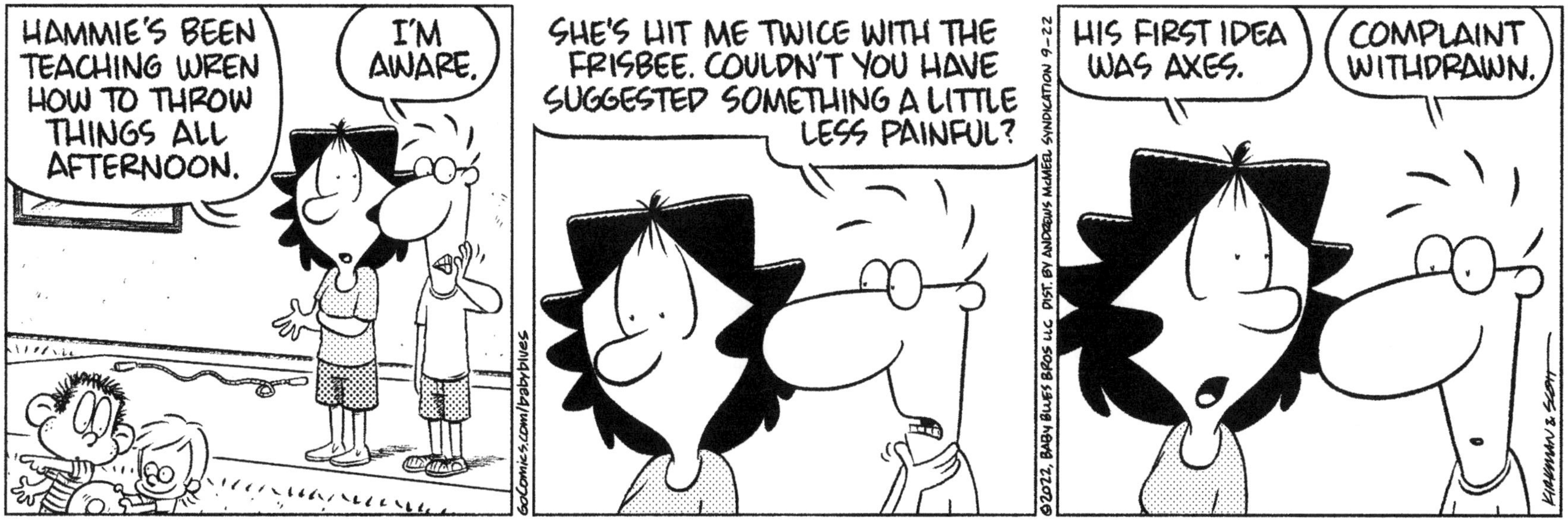
HAMMIE'S BEEN TEACHING WREN HOW TO THROW THINGS ALL AFTERNOON.
I'M AWARE.
SHE'S HIT ME TWICE WITH THE FRISBEE. COULDN'T YOU HAVE SUGGESTED SOMETHING A LITTLE LESS PAINFUL?
HIS FIRST IDEA WAS AXES.
COMPLAINT WITHDRAWN.
GoComics.com/babyblues
©2022, BABY BLUES BROS LLC DIST. BY ANDREWS McMEEL SYNDICATION 9-22
KIRKMAN & SCOTT

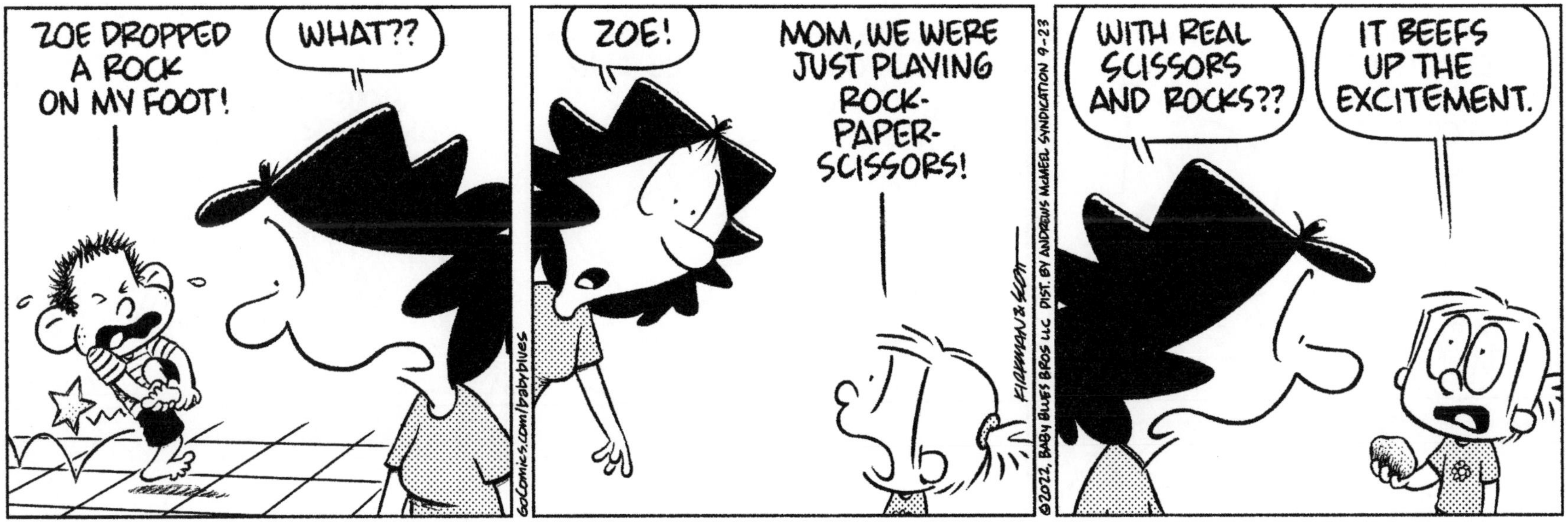
ZOE DROPPED A ROCK ON MY FOOT!
WHAT??
ZOE!
MOM, WE WERE JUST PLAYING ROCK-PAPER-SCISSORS!
WITH REAL SCISSORS AND ROCKS??
IT BEEFS UP THE EXCITEMENT.
GoComics.com/babyblues
KIRKMAN & SCOTT
©2022, BABY BLUES BROS LLC DIST. BY ANDREWS McMEEL SYNDICATION 9-23

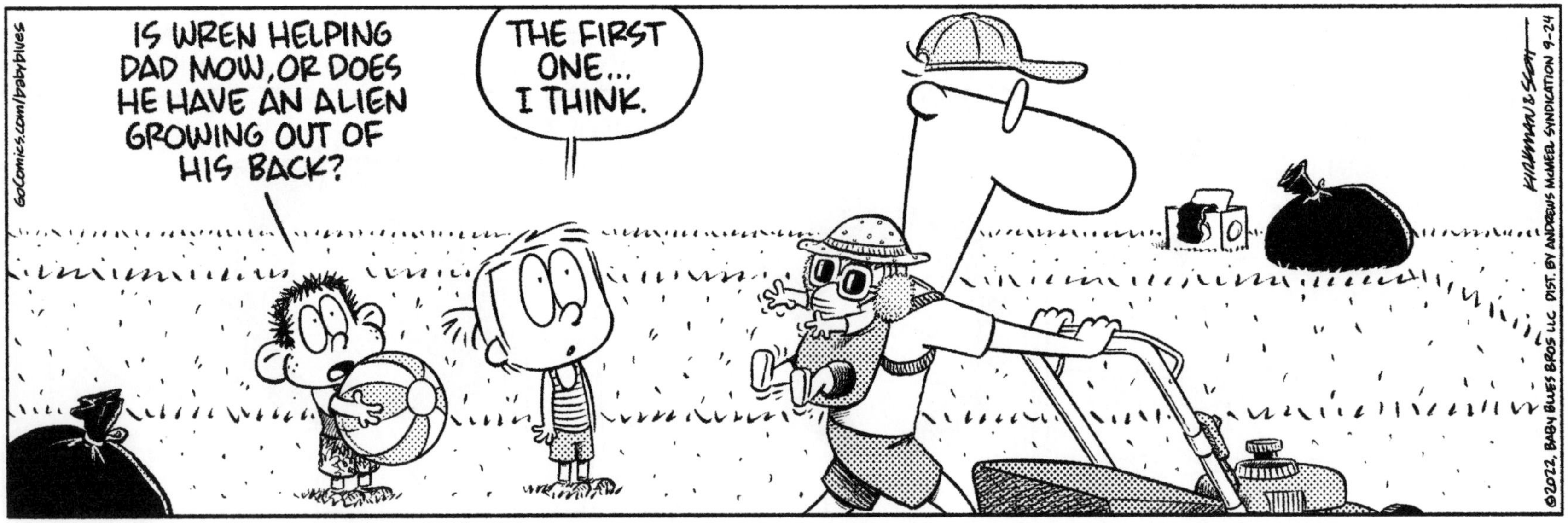
IS WREN HELPING DAD MOW, OR DOES HE HAVE AN ALIEN GROWING OUT OF HIS BACK?
THE FIRST ONE... I THINK.
GoComics.com/babyblues
KIRKMAN & SCOTT
©2022, BABY BLUES BROS LLC DIST. BY ANDREWS McMEEL SYNDICATION 9-24

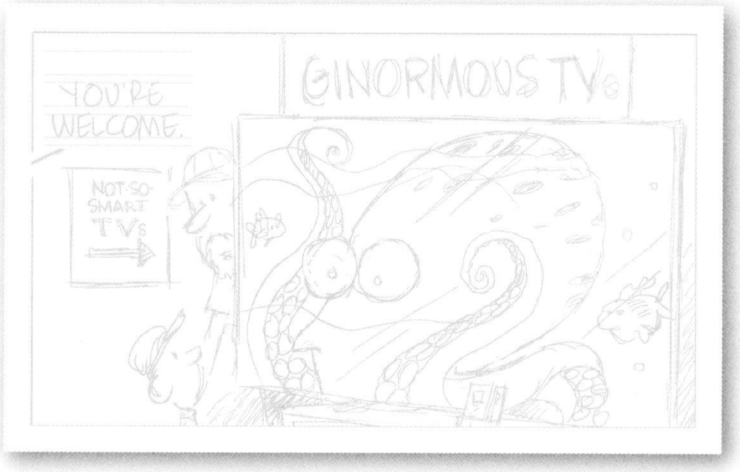
YOU'RE WELCOME.
GINORMOUS TVs
NOT-SO-SMART TVs

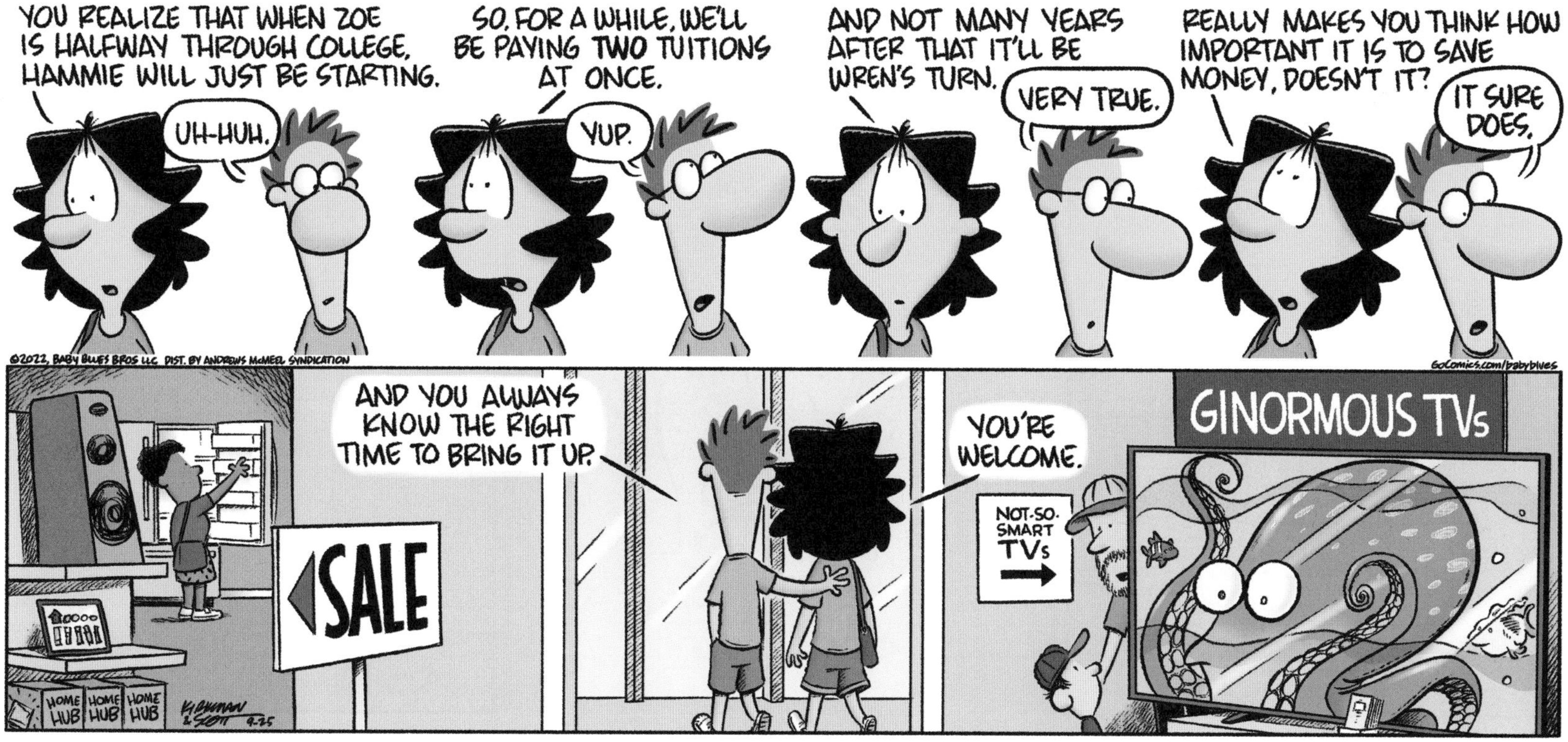
YOU REALIZE THAT WHEN ZOE IS HALFWAY THROUGH COLLEGE, HAMMIE WILL JUST BE STARTING.
UH-HUH.
SO, FOR A WHILE, WE'LL BE PAYING TWO TUITIONS AT ONCE.
YUP.
AND NOT MANY YEARS AFTER THAT IT'LL BE WREN'S TURN.
VERY TRUE.
REALLY MAKES YOU THINK HOW IMPORTANT IT IS TO SAVE MONEY, DOESN'T IT?
IT SURE DOES.
©2022, BABY BLUES BROS LLC DIST. BY ANDREWS McMEEL SYNDICATION
GoComics.com/babyblues
HOME HUB
HOME HUB
HOME HUB
SALE
KIRKMAN & SCOTT 9-25
AND YOU ALWAYS KNOW THE RIGHT TIME TO BRING IT UP.
YOU'RE WELCOME.
GINORMOUS TVs
NOT-SO-SMART TVs

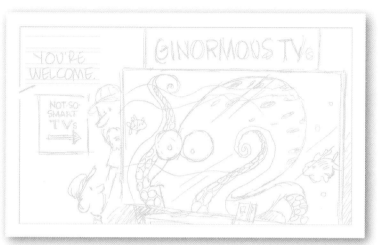

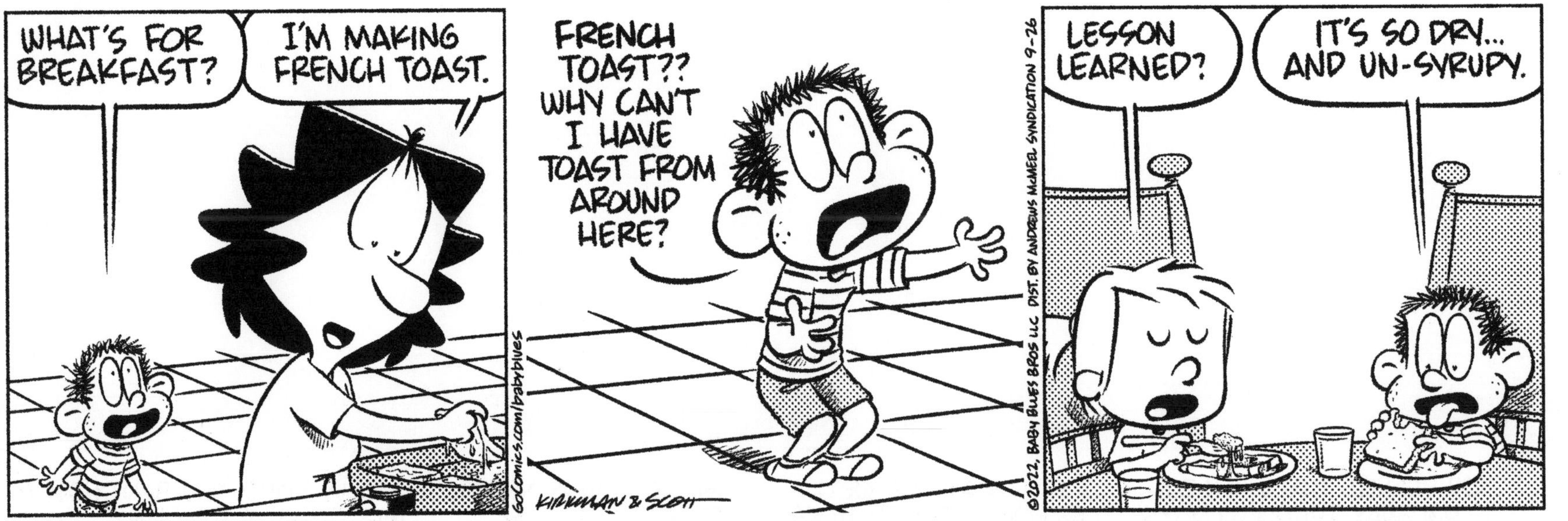
WHAT'S FOR BREAKFAST?
I'M MAKING FRENCH TOAST.
FRENCH TOAST?? WHY CAN'T I HAVE TOAST FROM AROUND HERE?
LESSON LEARNED?
IT'S SO DRY... AND UN-SYRUPY.
gocomics.com/babyblues
KIRKMAN & SCOTT
©2022, BABY BLUES BROS LLC DIST. BY ANDREWS McMEEL SYNDICATION 9-26

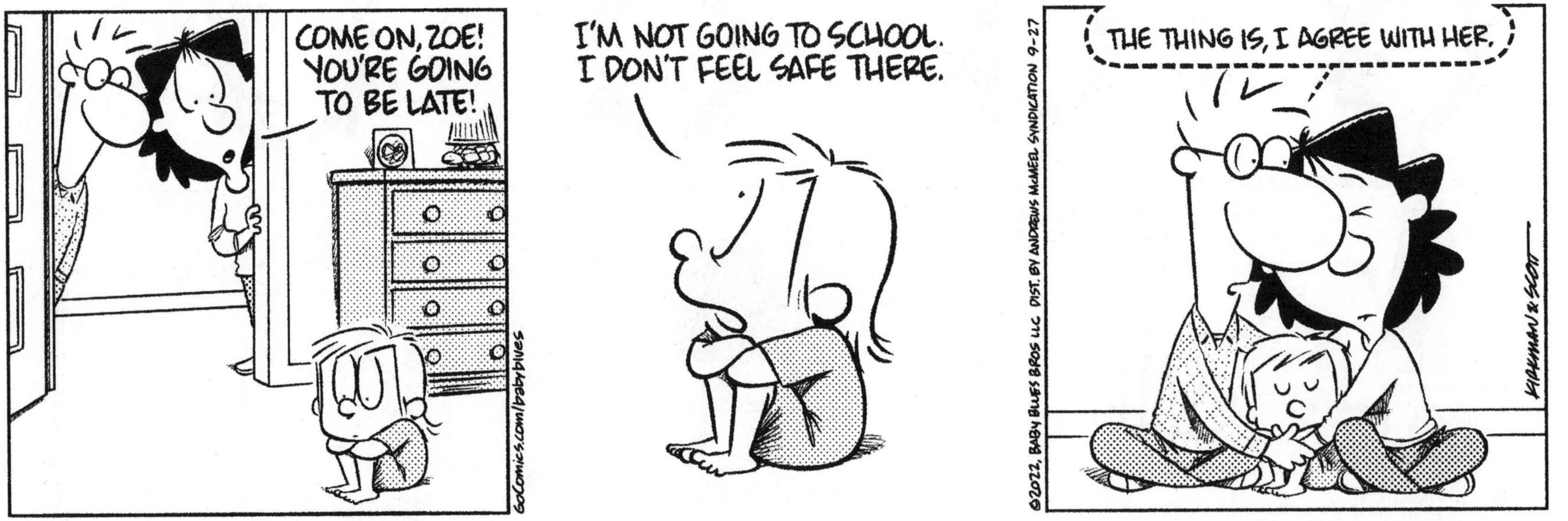
COME ON, ZOE! YOU'RE GOING TO BE LATE!
I'M NOT GOING TO SCHOOL. I DON'T FEEL SAFE THERE.
THE THING IS, I AGREE WITH HER.
gocomics.com/babyblues
©2022, BABY BLUES BROS LLC DIST. BY ANDREWS McMEEL SYNDICATION 9-27
KIRKMAN & SCOTT

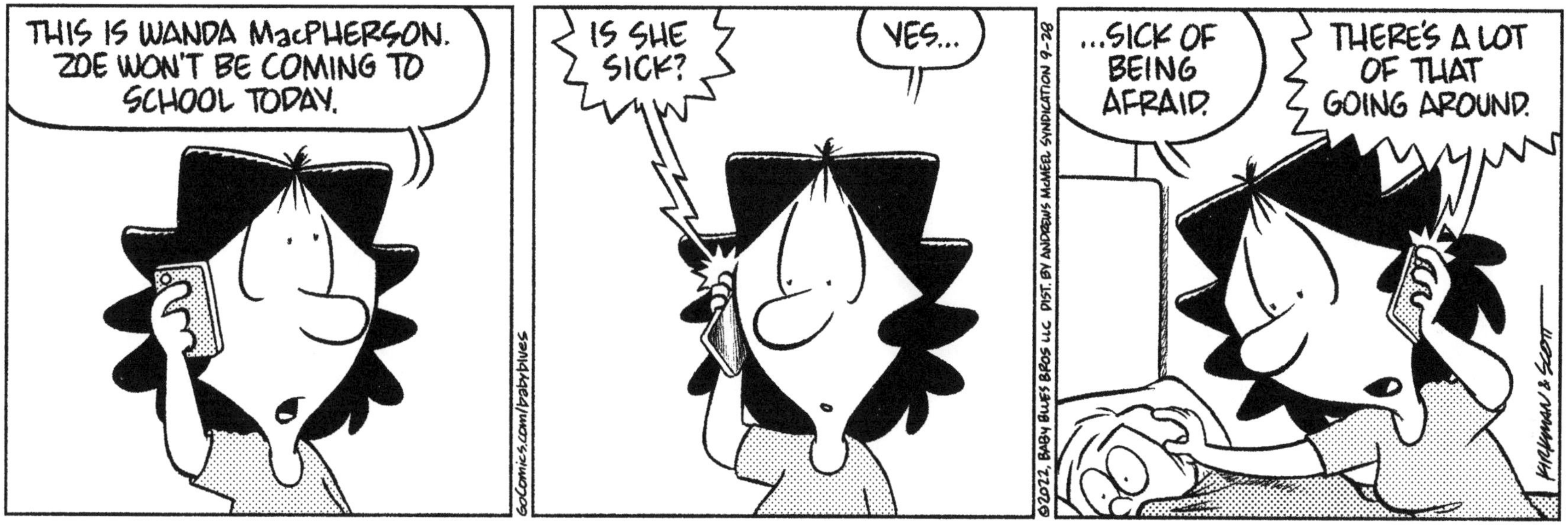
THIS IS WANDA MacPHERSON. ZOE WON'T BE COMING TO SCHOOL TODAY.
GoComics.com/babyblues
IS SHE SICK?
YES...
©2022, BABY BLUES BROS LLC DIST. BY ANDREWS McMEEL SYNDICATION 9-28
...SICK OF BEING AFRAID.
THERE'S A LOT OF THAT GOING AROUND.
KIRKMAN & SCOTT

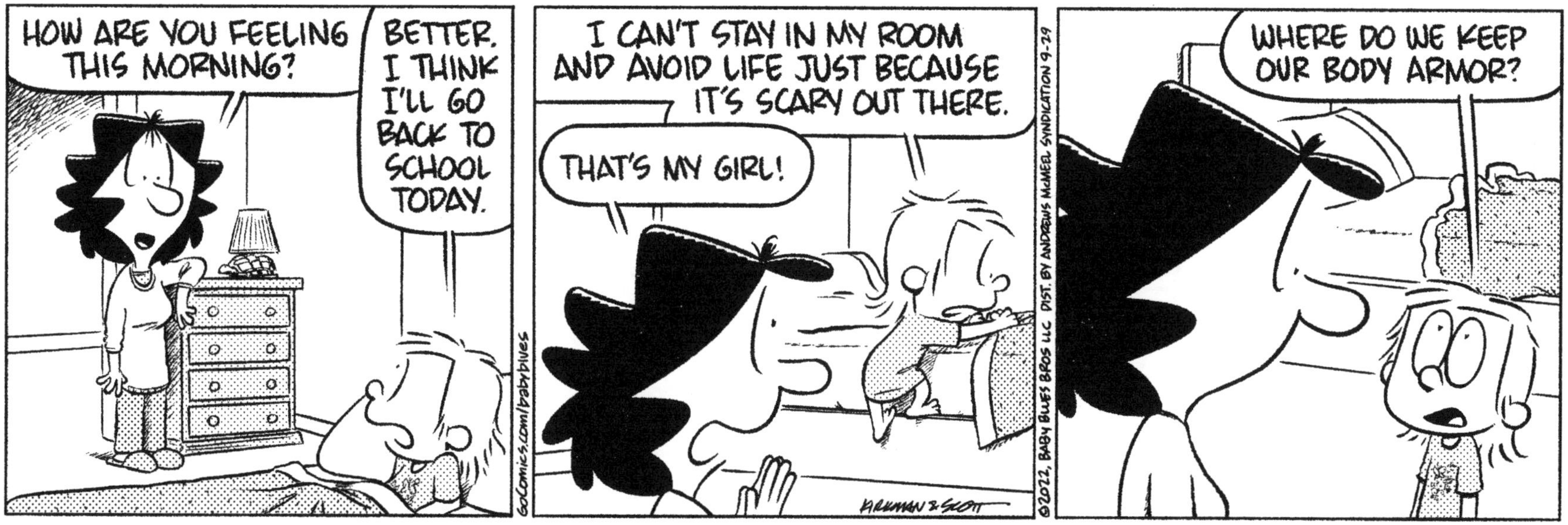
HOW ARE YOU FEELING THIS MORNING?
BETTER. I THINK I'LL GO BACK TO SCHOOL TODAY.
GoComics.com/babyblues
I CAN'T STAY IN MY ROOM AND AVOID LIFE JUST BECAUSE IT'S SCARY OUT THERE.
THAT'S MY GIRL!
KIRKMAN & SCOTT
©2022, BABY BLUES BROS LLC DIST. BY ANDREWS McMEEL SYNDICATION 9-29
WHERE DO WE KEEP OUR BODY ARMOR?

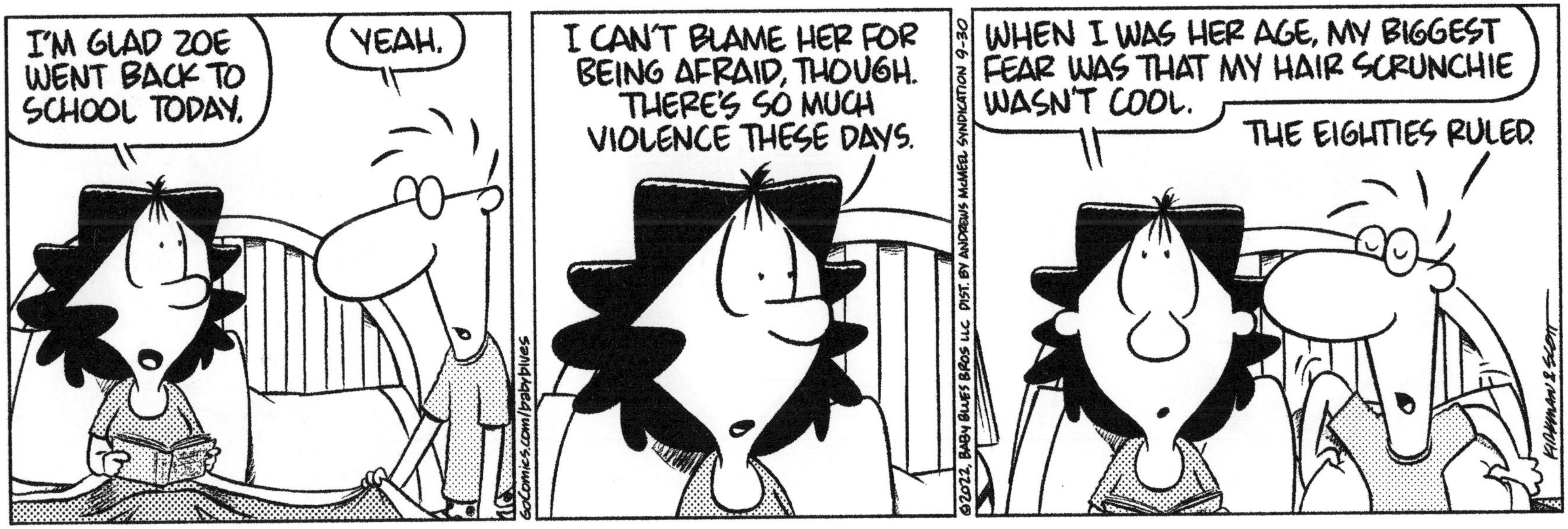
I'M GLAD ZOE WENT BACK TO SCHOOL TODAY.
YEAH.
GoComics.com/babyblues
I CAN'T BLAME HER FOR BEING AFRAID, THOUGH. THERE'S SO MUCH VIOLENCE THESE DAYS.
©2022, BABY BLUES BROS LLC DIST. BY ANDREWS McMEEL SYNDICATION 9-30
WHEN I WAS HER AGE, MY BIGGEST FEAR WAS THAT MY HAIR SCRUNCHIE WASN'T COOL.
THE EIGHTIES RULED.
KIRKMAN & SCOTT

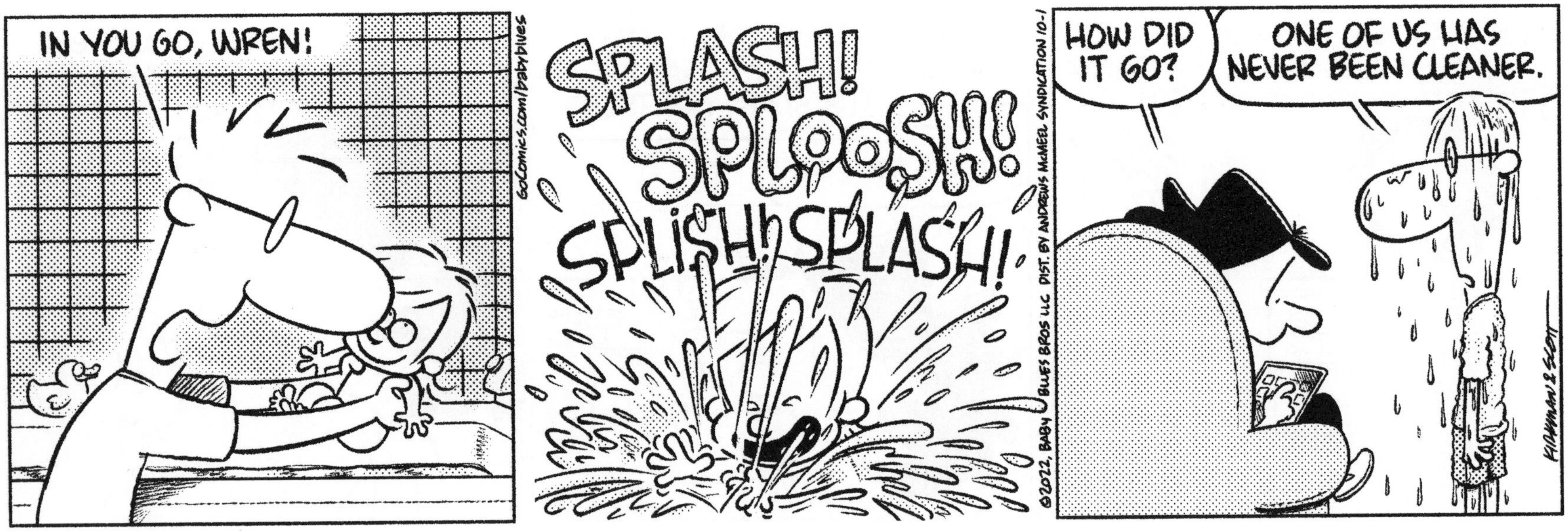
IN YOU GO, WREN!
GoComics.com/babyblues
SPLASH! SPLOOSH!
SPLISH! SPLASH!
©2022, BABY BLUES BROS LLC DIST. BY ANDREWS McMEEL SYNDICATION 10-1
HOW DID IT GO?
ONE OF US HAS NEVER BEEN CLEANER.
KIRKMAN & SCOTT

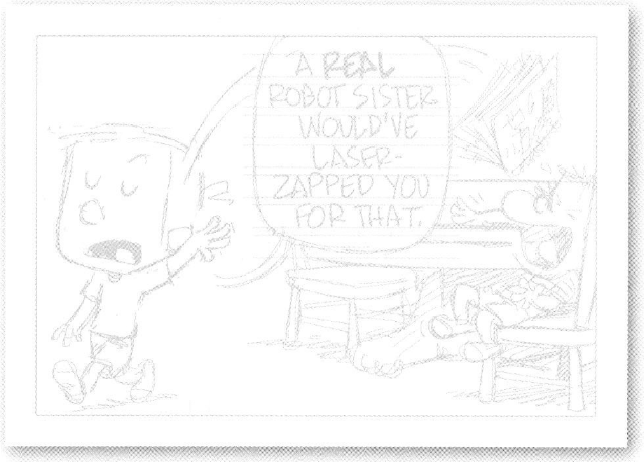
A REAL ROBOT SISTER WOULD'VE LASER-ZAPPED YOU FOR THAT.

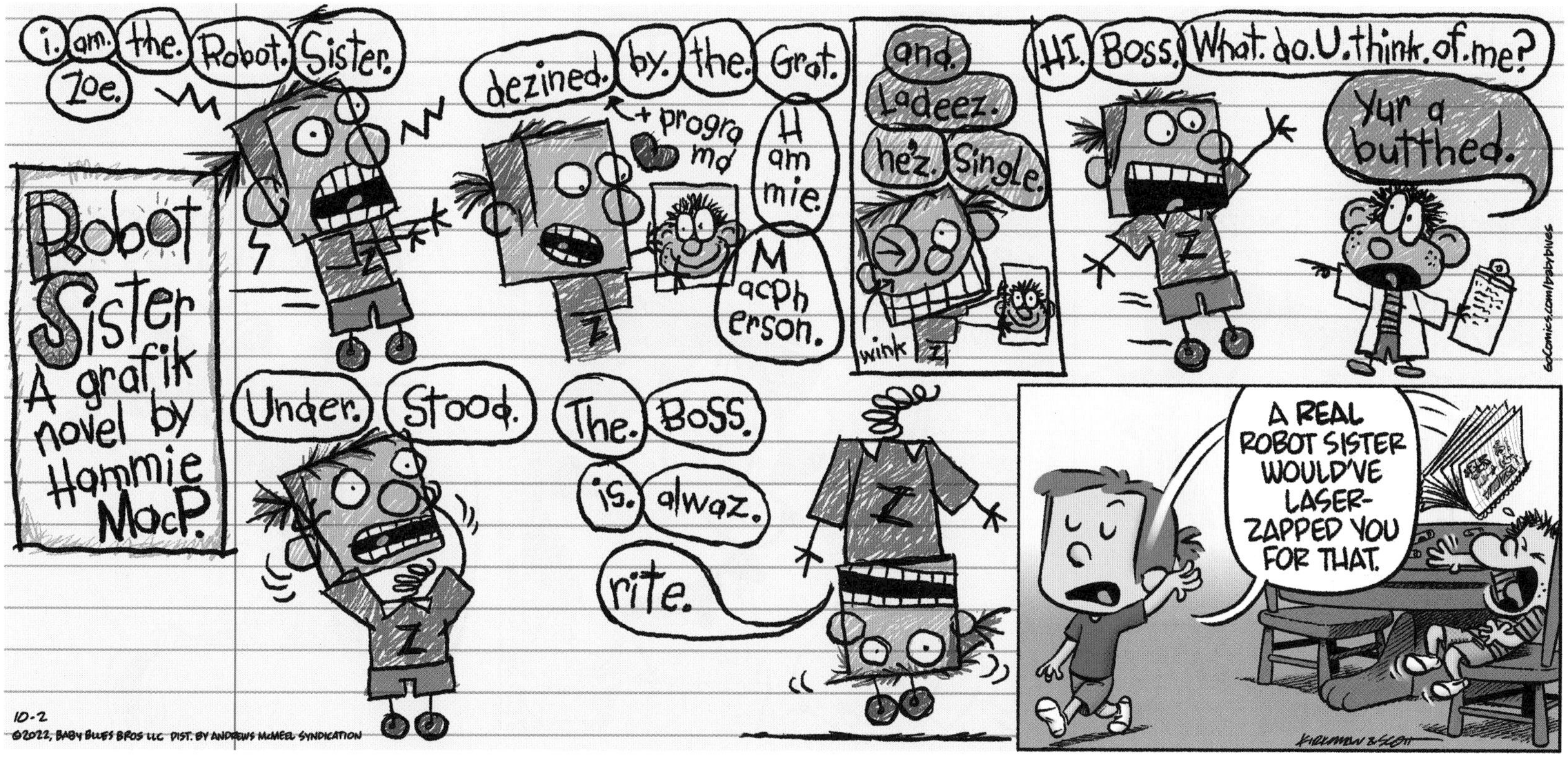
Robot Sister A grafik novel by Hammie MacP.
i. am. the. Robot. Sister.
Zoe.
dezined. by. the. Grat.
+ progra md
H am mie.
M acph erson.
and.
Ladeez.
he'z. Single.
wink
HI. Boss. What. do. U. think. of. me?
Yur a butthed.
Under. Stood.
The. BoSS.
is. alwaz.
rite.
A REAL ROBOT SISTER WOULD'VE LASER-ZAPPED YOU FOR THAT.
10-2
©2022, BABY BLUES BROS LLC DIST. BY ANDREWS MCMEEL SYNDICATION
GoComics.com/babyblues
KIRKMAN & SCOTT

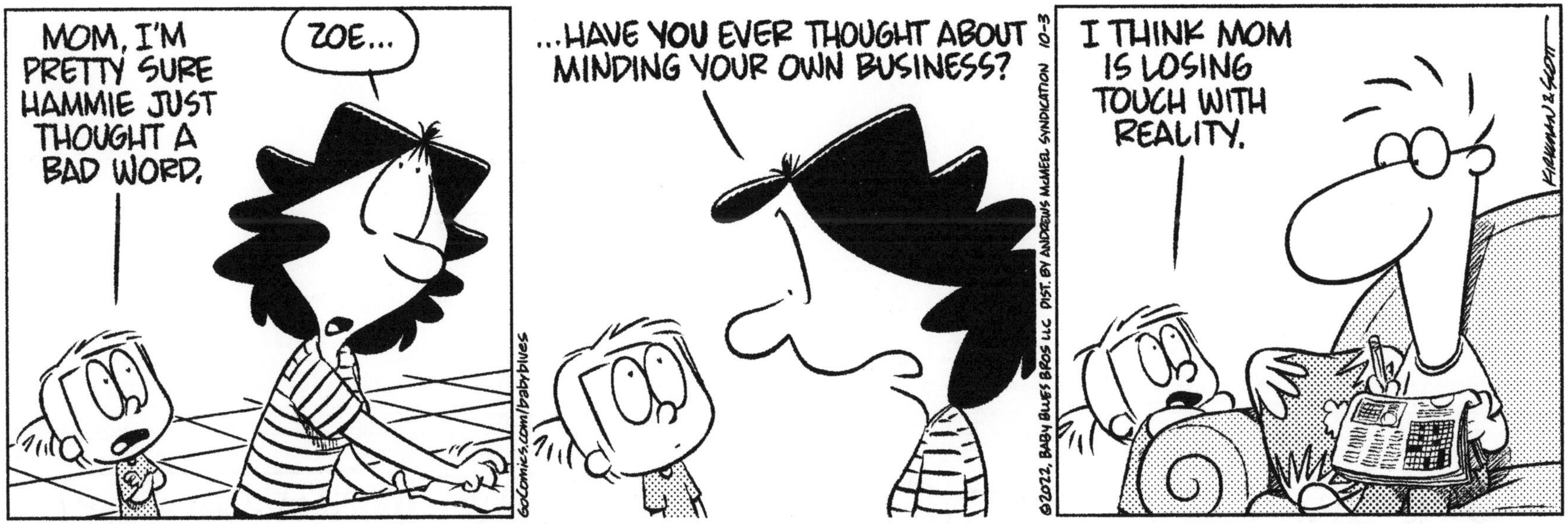
MOM, I'M PRETTY SURE HAMMIE JUST THOUGHT A BAD WORD.
ZOE...
...HAVE YOU EVER THOUGHT ABOUT MINDING YOUR OWN BUSINESS?
I THINK MOM IS LOSING TOUCH WITH REALITY.
GoComics.com/babyblues
©2022, BABY BLUES BROS LLC DIST. BY ANDREWS McMEEL SYNDICATION 10-3
KIRKMAN & SCOTT

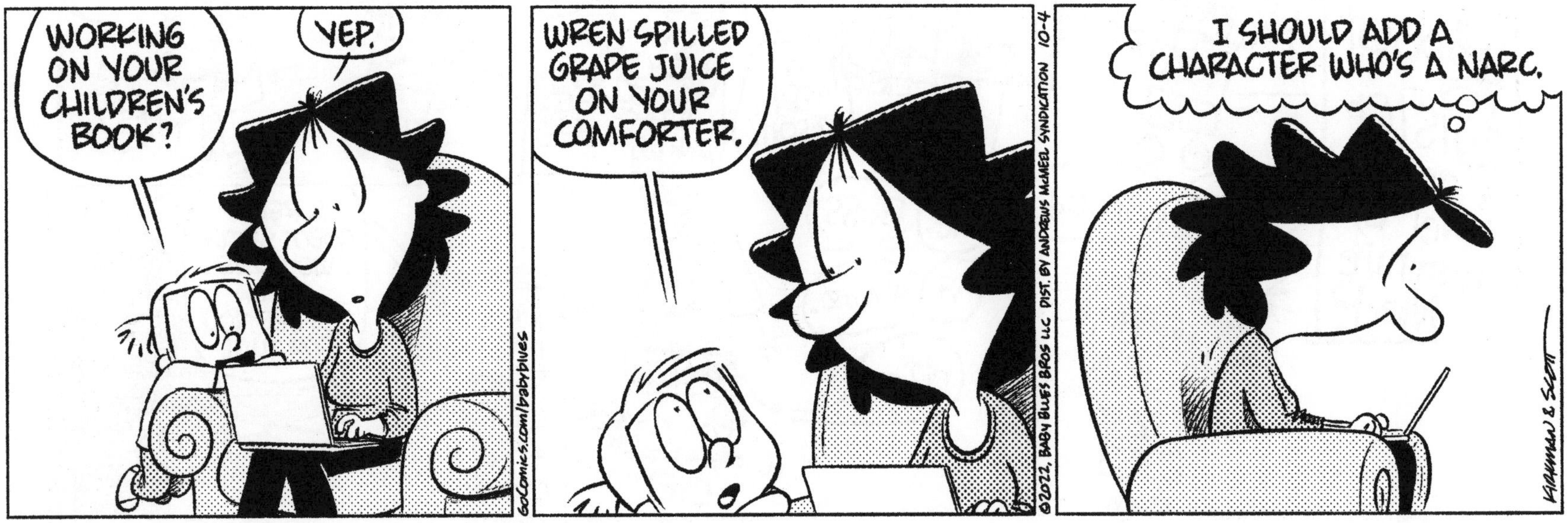
WORKING ON YOUR CHILDREN'S BOOK?
YEP.
WREN SPILLED GRAPE JUICE ON YOUR COMFORTER.
I SHOULD ADD A CHARACTER WHO'S A NARC.
GoComics.com/babyblues
©2022, BABY BLUES BROS LLC DIST. BY ANDREWS McMEEL SYNDICATION 10-4
KIRKMAN & SCOTT

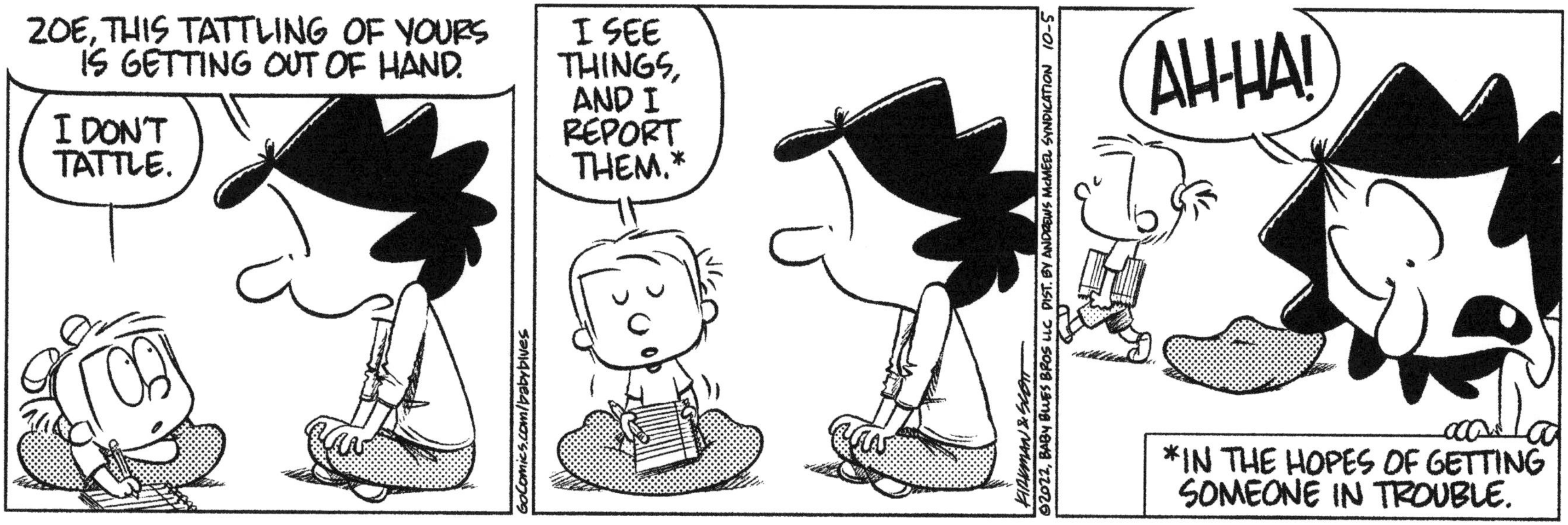
ZOE, THIS TATTLING OF YOURS IS GETTING OUT OF HAND.
I DON'T TATTLE.
GoComics.com/babyblues
I SEE THINGS, AND I REPORT THEM.*
KIRKMAN & SCOTT
©2022, BABY BLUES BROS LLC DIST. BY ANDREWS McMEEL SYNDICATION 10-5
AH-HA!
*IN THE HOPES OF GETTING SOMEONE IN TROUBLE.

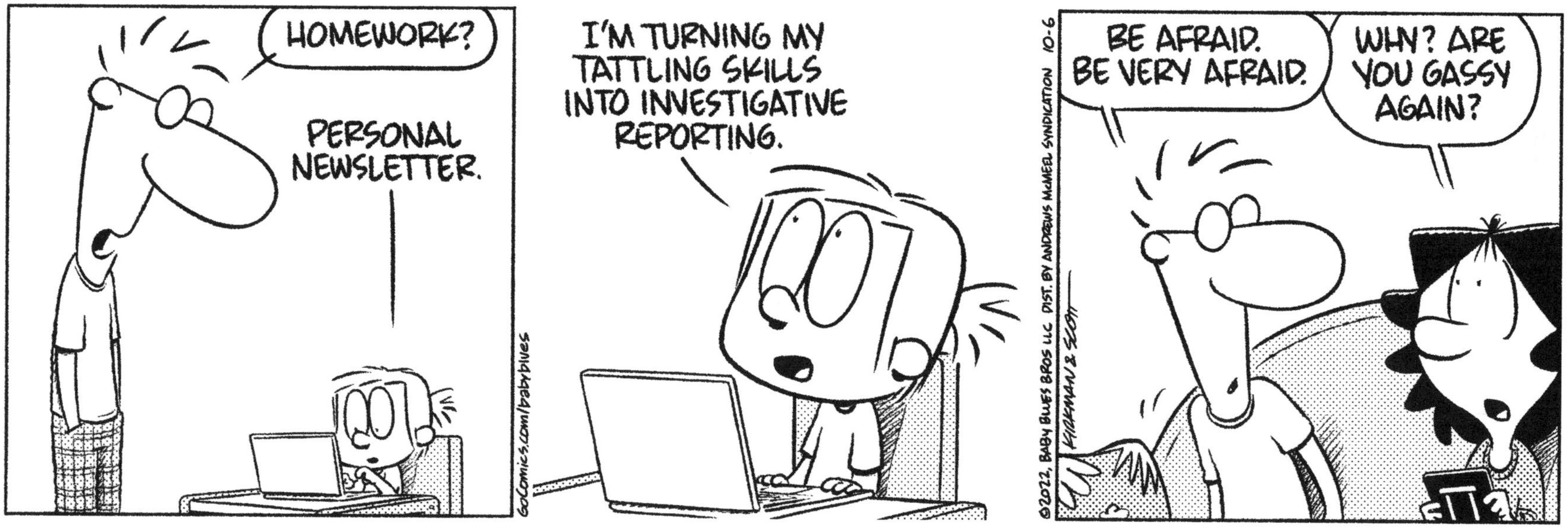
HOMEWORK?
PERSONAL NEWSLETTER.
GoComics.com/babyblues
I'M TURNING MY TATTLING SKILLS INTO INVESTIGATIVE REPORTING.
©2022, BABY BLUES BROS LLC DIST. BY ANDREWS McMEEL SYNDICATION 10-6
KIRKMAN & SCOTT
BE AFRAID. BE VERY AFRAID.
WHY? ARE YOU GASSY AGAIN?

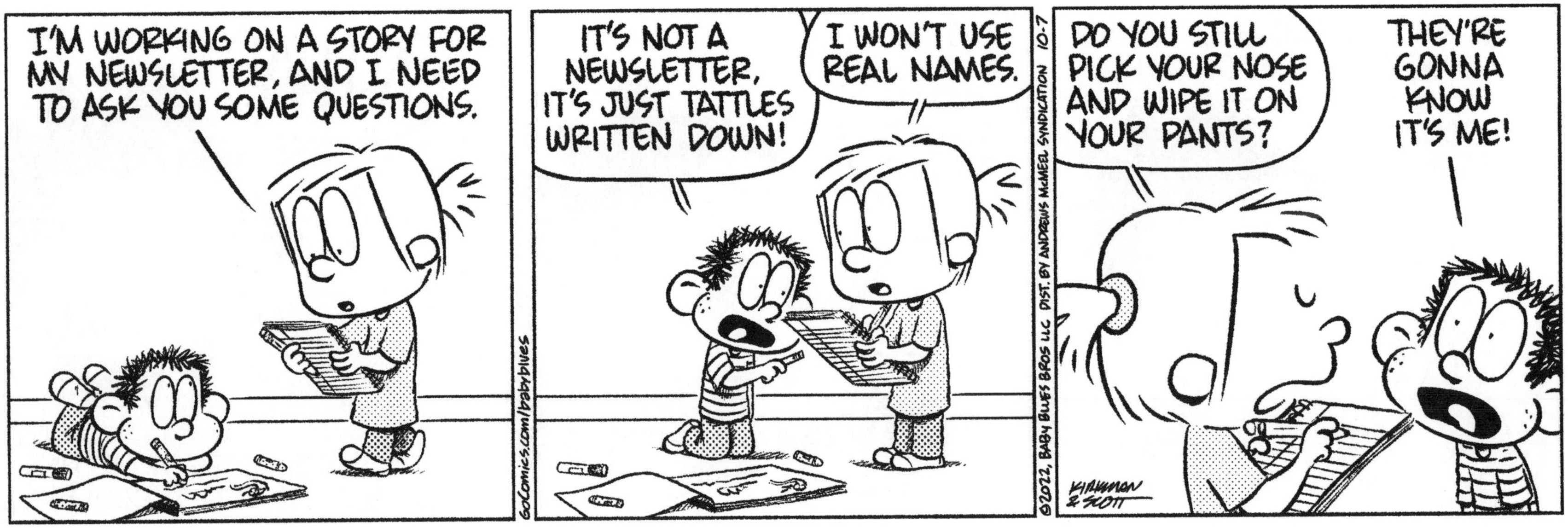
I'M WORKING ON A STORY FOR MY NEWSLETTER, AND I NEED TO ASK YOU SOME QUESTIONS.
GoComics.com/babyblues
IT'S NOT A NEWSLETTER, IT'S JUST TATTLES WRITTEN DOWN!
I WON'T USE REAL NAMES.
10-7
©2022, BABY BLUES BROS LLC DIST. BY ANDREWS McMEEL SYNDICATION
DO YOU STILL PICK YOUR NOSE AND WIPE IT ON YOUR PANTS?
THEY'RE GONNA KNOW IT'S ME!
KIRKMAN & SCOTT

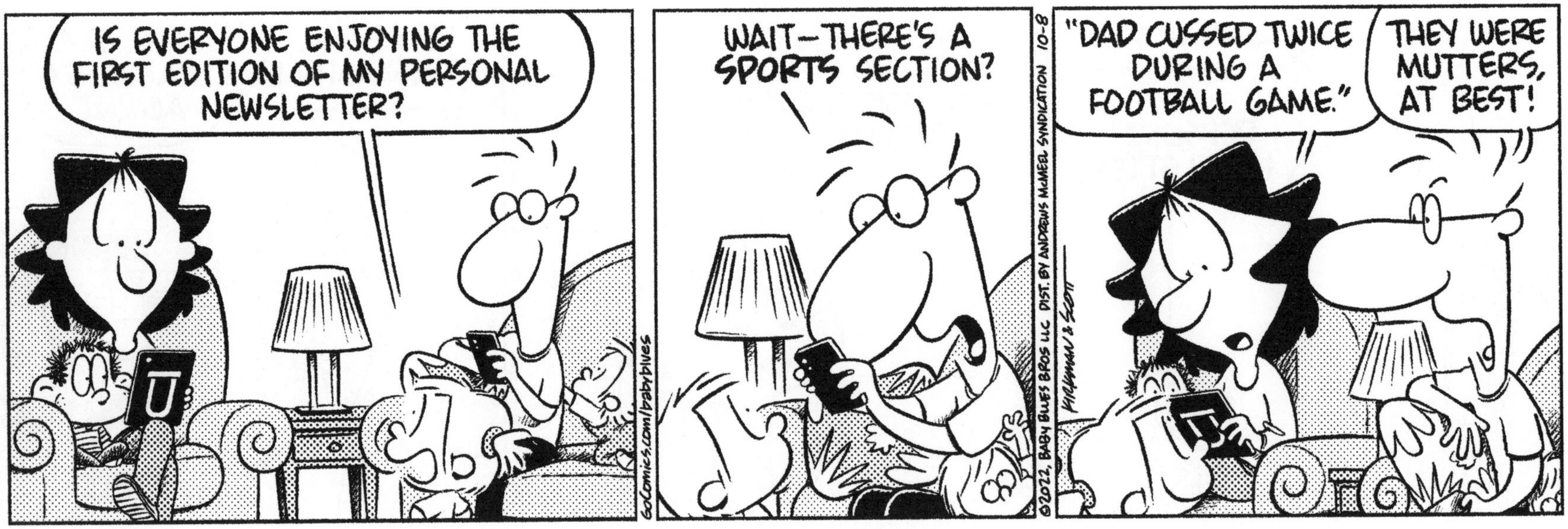
IS EVERYONE ENJOYING THE FIRST EDITION OF MY PERSONAL NEWSLETTER?
GoComics.com/babyblues
WAIT—THERE'S A SPORTS SECTION?
10-8
©2022, BABY BLUES BROS LLC DIST. BY ANDREWS McMEEL SYNDICATION
KIRKMAN & SCOTT
"DAD CUSSED TWICE DURING A FOOTBALL GAME."
THEY WERE MUTTERS, AT BEST!

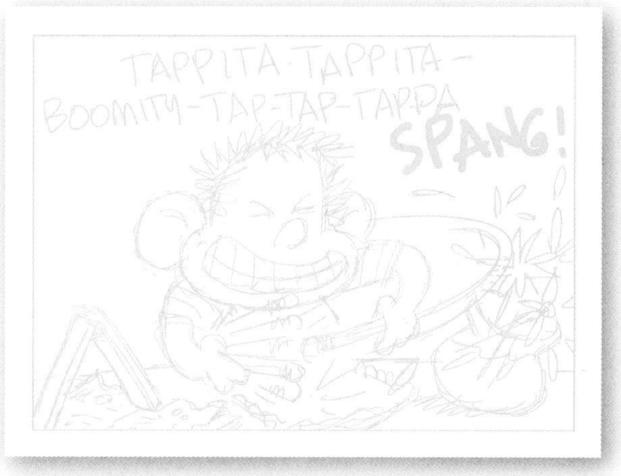
TAPPITA-TAPPITA-
BOOMITY-TAP-TAP-TAPPA
SPANG!

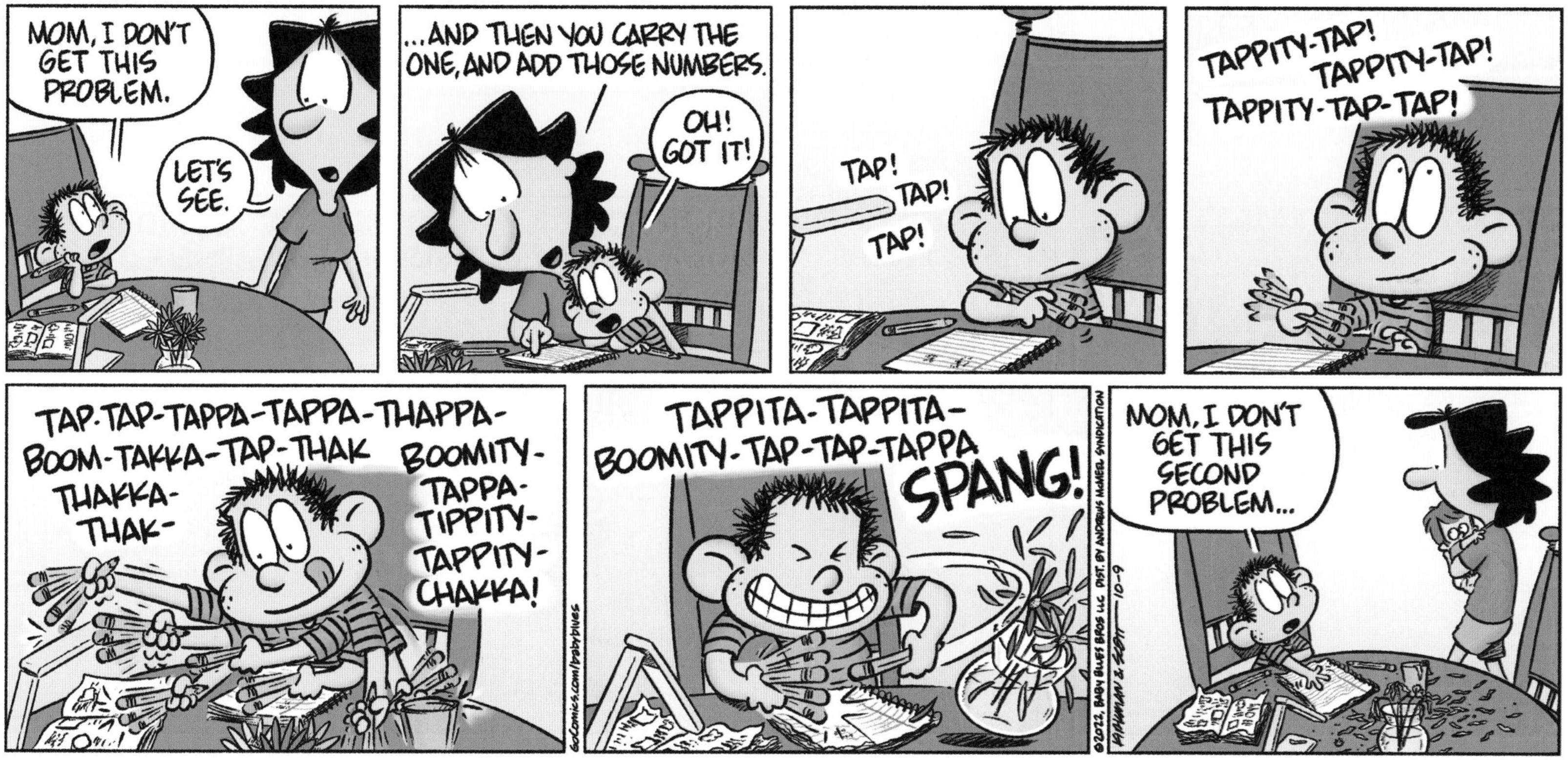
MOM, I DON'T GET THIS PROBLEM.
LET'S SEE.
...AND THEN YOU CARRY THE ONE, AND ADD THOSE NUMBERS.
OH! GOT IT!
TAP!
TAP!
TAP!
TAPPITY-TAP!
TAPPITY-TAP!
TAPPITY-TAP-TAP!
TAP-TAP-TAPPA-TAPPA-THAPPA-
BOOM-TAKKA-TAP-THAK
THAKKA-THAK-
BOOMITY-TAPPA-TIPPITY-TAPPITY-CHAKKA!
GoComics.com/babyblues
TAPPITA-TAPPITA-
BOOMITY-TAP-TAP-TAPPA
SPANG!
©2022, BABY BLUES BROS LLC. DIST. BY ANDREWS MCMEEL SYNDICATION
KIRKMAN & SCOTT 10-9
MOM, I DON'T GET THIS SECOND PROBLEM...

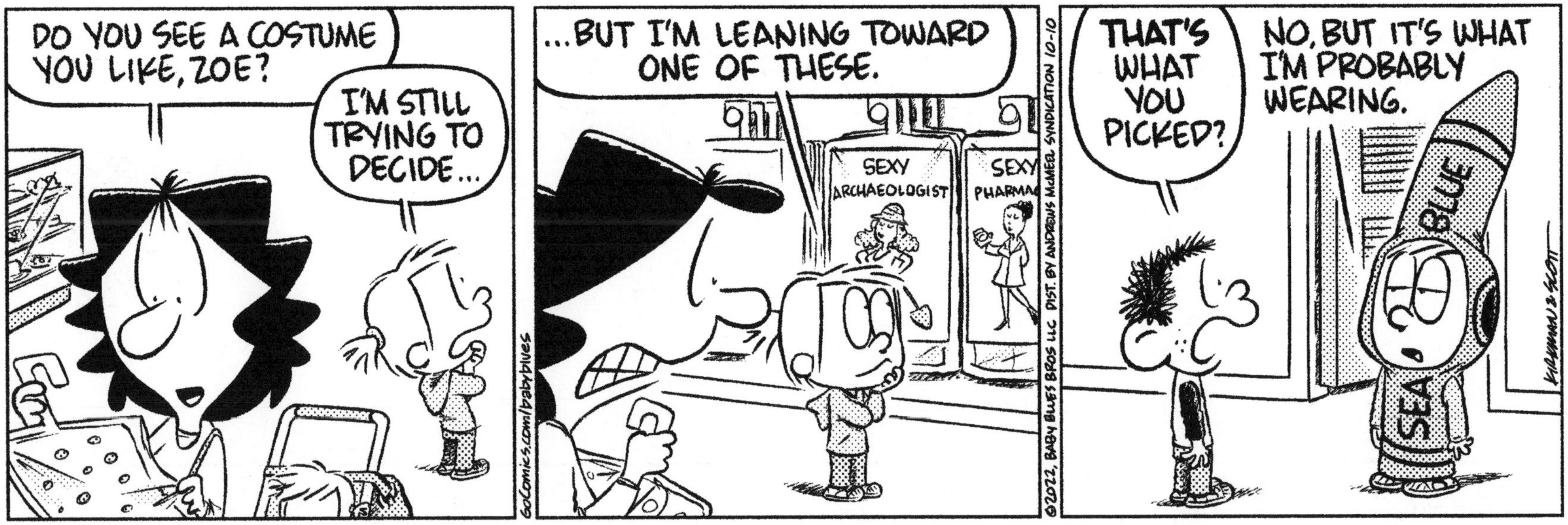
DO YOU SEE A COSTUME YOU LIKE, ZOE?
I'M STILL TRYING TO DECIDE...
GoComics.com/babyblues
...BUT I'M LEANING TOWARD ONE OF THESE.
SEXY ARCHAEOLOGIST
©2022, BABY BLUES BROS LLC DIST. BY ANDREWS McMEEL SYNDICATION 10-10
THAT'S WHAT YOU PICKED?
NO, BUT IT'S WHAT I'M PROBABLY WEARING.
SEA BLUE
KIRKMAN & SCOTT

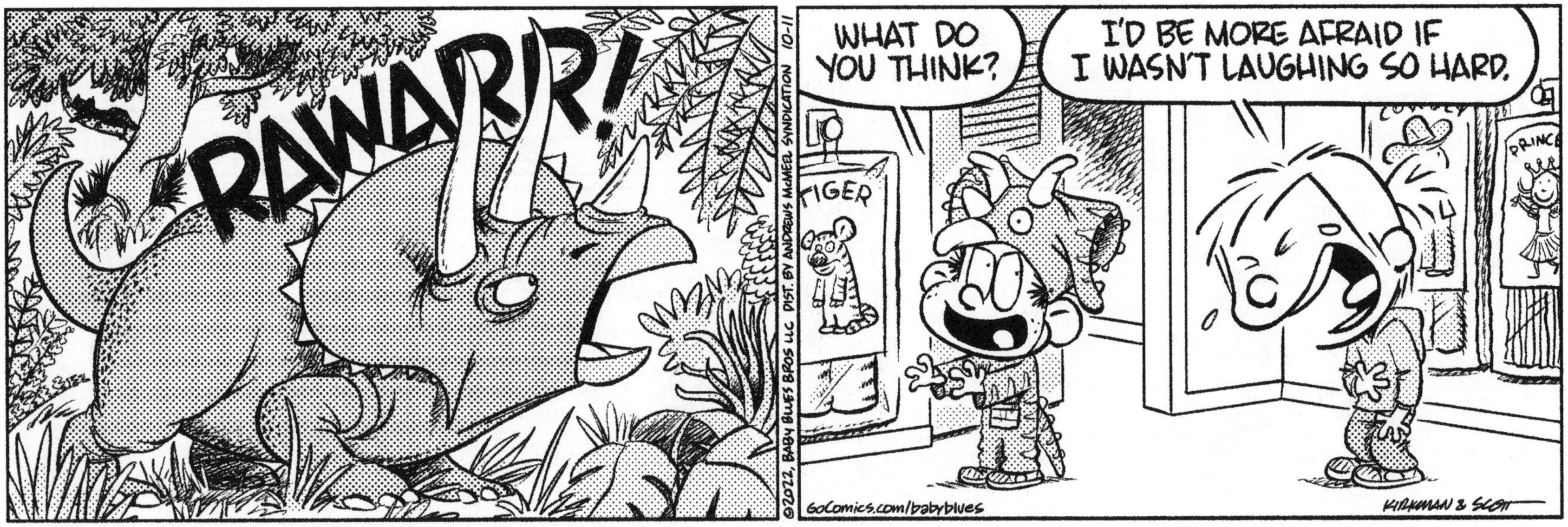
RAWARR!
©2022, BABY BLUES BROS LLC DIST. BY ANDREWS McMEEL SYNDICATION 10-11
WHAT DO YOU THINK?
I'D BE MORE AFRAID IF I WASN'T LAUGHING SO HARD.
TIGER
GoComics.com/babyblues
KIRKMAN & SCOTT

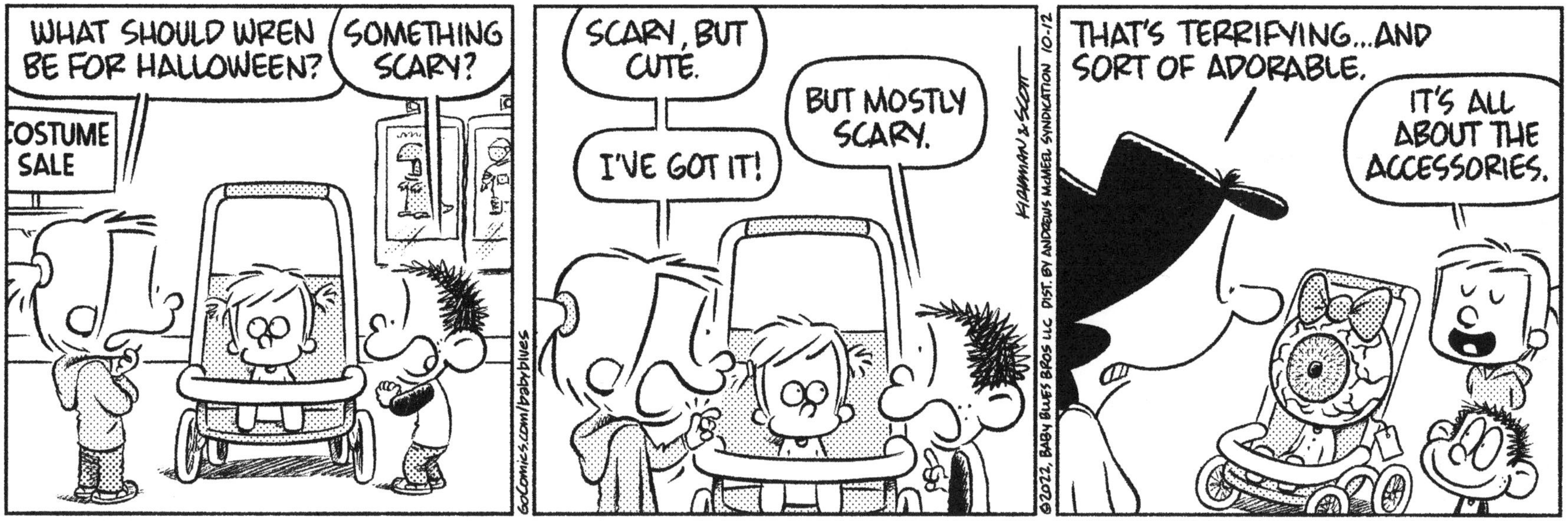

COSTUME SALE
WHAT SHOULD WREN BE FOR HALLOWEEN?
SOMETHING SCARY?
GoComics.com/babyblues
SCARY, BUT CUTE.
I'VE GOT IT!
BUT MOSTLY SCARY.
KIRKMAN & SCOTT 10-12
©2022, BABY BLUES BROS LLC DIST. BY ANDREWS McMEEL SYNDICATION
THAT'S TERRIFYING...AND SORT OF ADORABLE.
IT'S ALL ABOUT THE ACCESSORIES.

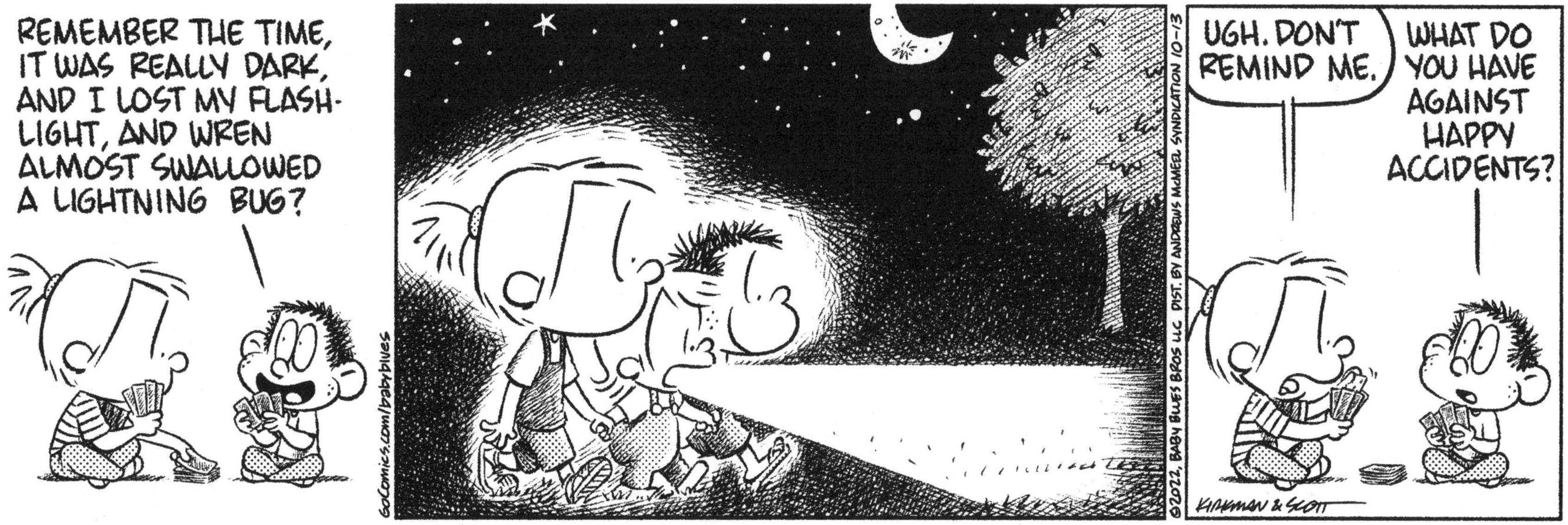

REMEMBER THE TIME, IT WAS REALLY DARK, AND I LOST MY FLASH-LIGHT, AND WREN ALMOST SWALLOWED A LIGHTNING BUG?
GoComics.com/babyblues
©2022, BABY BLUES BROS LLC DIST. BY ANDREWS McMEEL SYNDICATION 10-13
UGH. DON'T REMIND ME.
WHAT DO YOU HAVE AGAINST HAPPY ACCIDENTS?
KIRKMAN & SCOTT

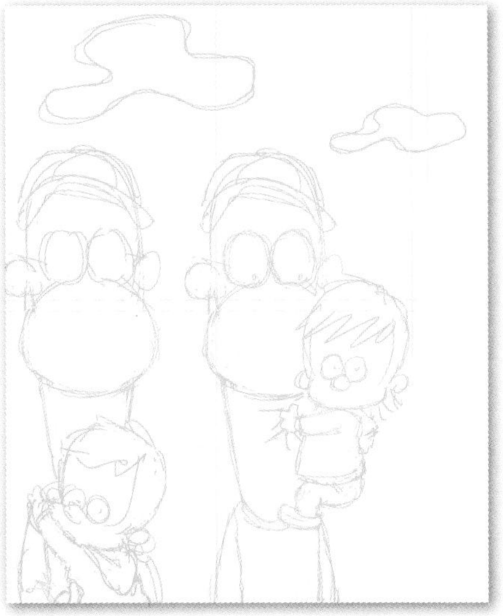

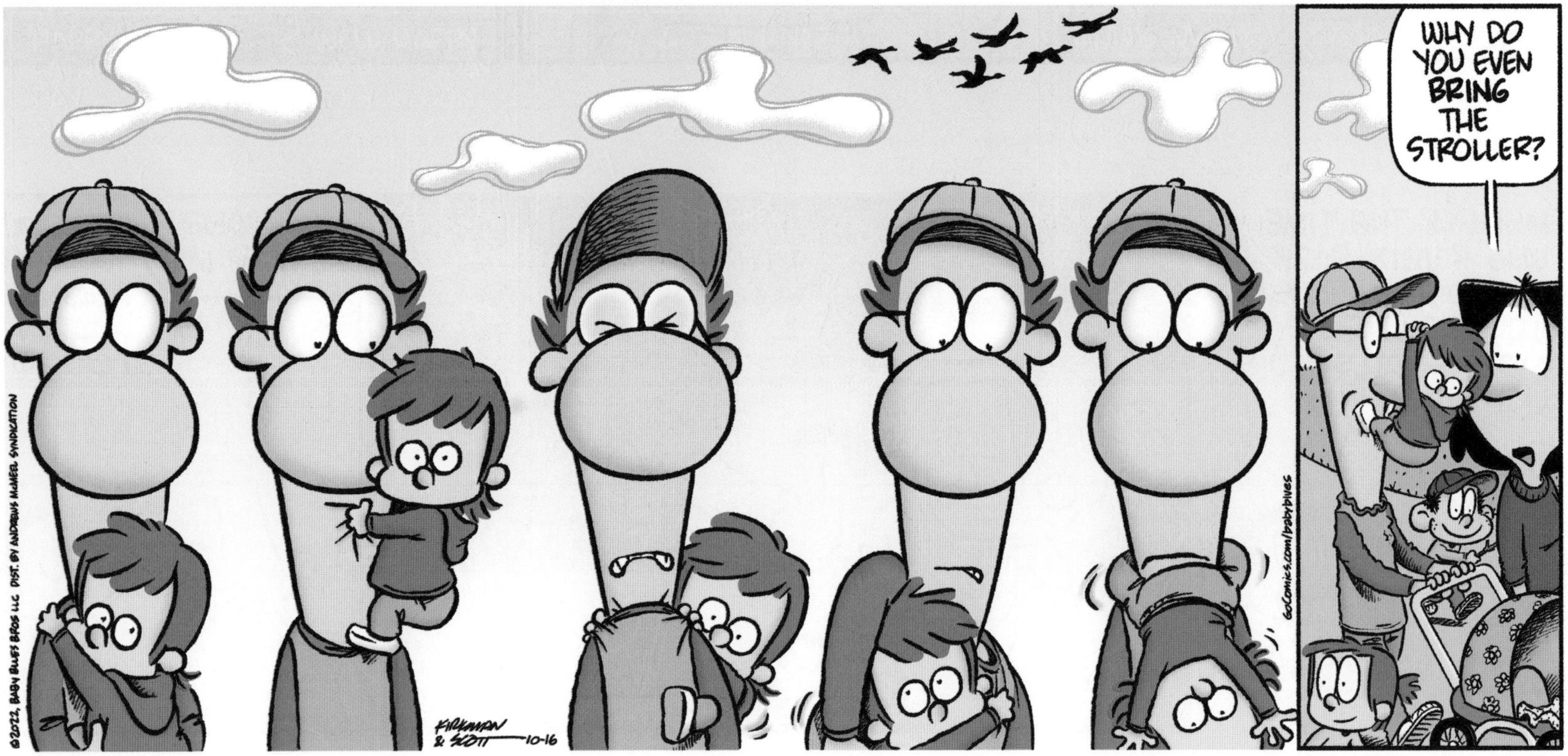
WHY DO YOU EVEN BRING THE STROLLER?
©2022, BABY BLUES BROS LLC DIST. BY ANDREWS MCMEEL SYNDICATION
KIRKMAN & SCOTT 10-16
GoComics.com/babyblues

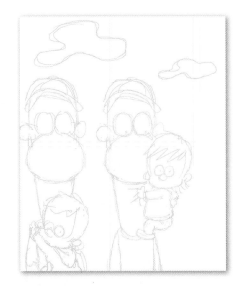

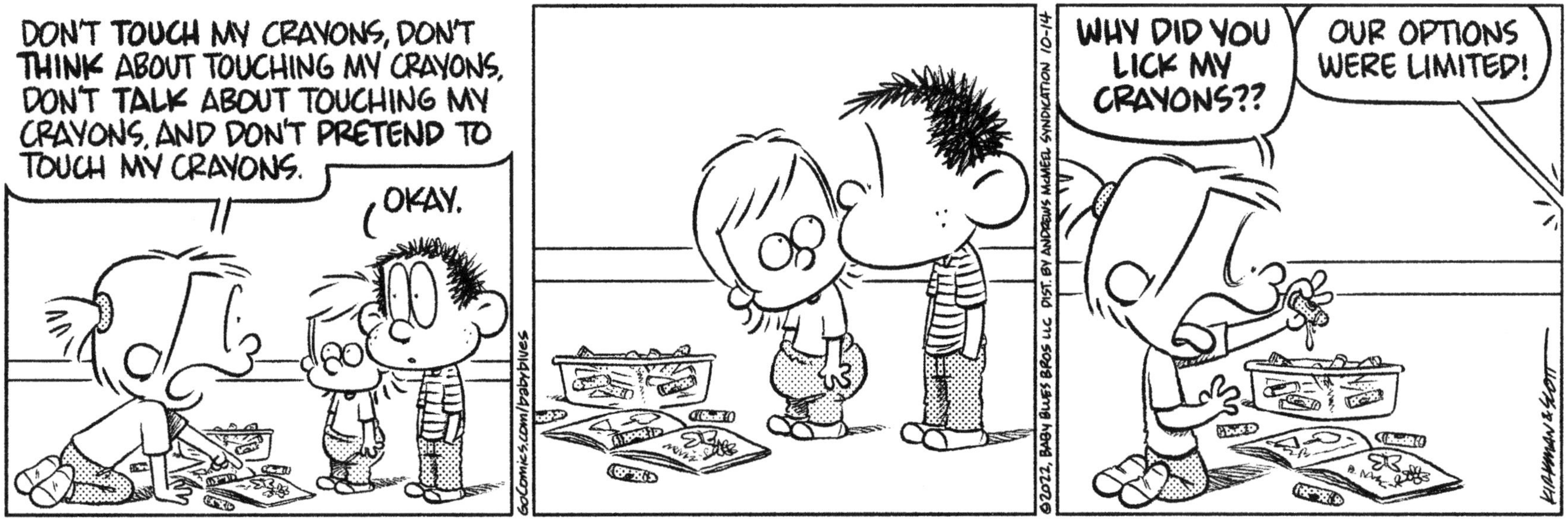
DON'T TOUCH MY CRAYONS, DON'T THINK ABOUT TOUCHING MY CRAYONS, DON'T TALK ABOUT TOUCHING MY CRAYONS, AND DON'T PRETEND TO TOUCH MY CRAYONS.
OKAY.
GoComics.com/babyblues
©2022, BABY BLUES BROS LLC DIST. BY ANDREWS McMEEL SYNDICATION 10-14
WHY DID YOU LICK MY CRAYONS??
OUR OPTIONS WERE LIMITED!
KIRKMAN & SCOTT

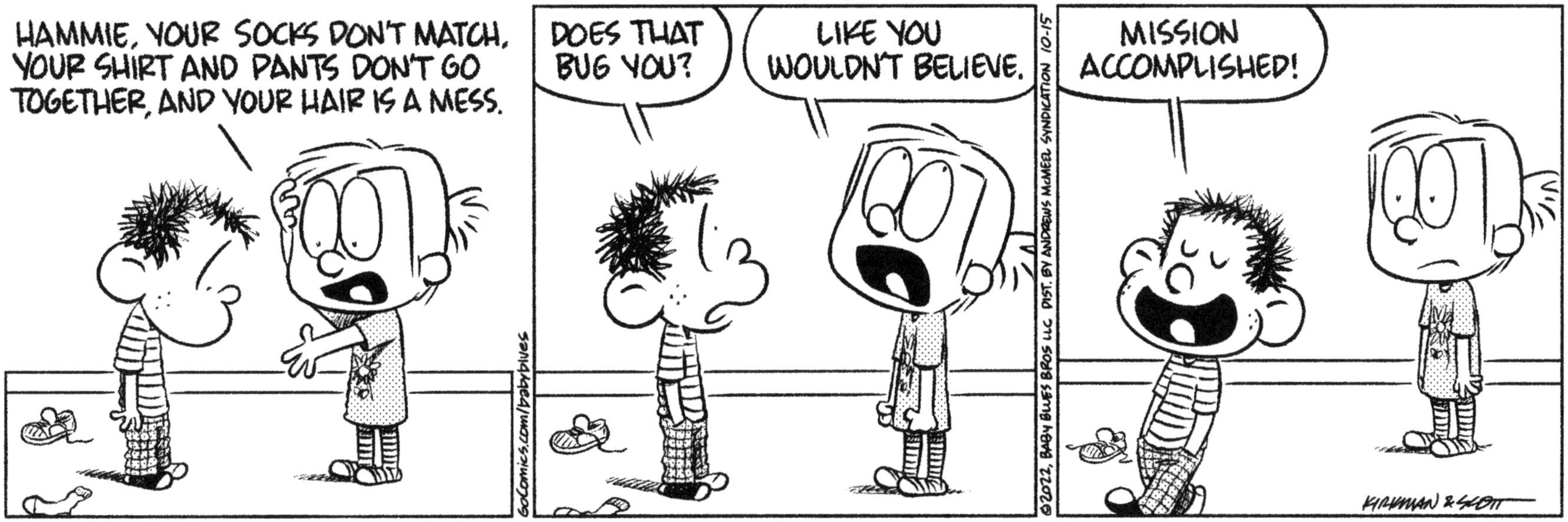
HAMMIE, YOUR SOCKS DON'T MATCH, YOUR SHIRT AND PANTS DON'T GO TOGETHER, AND YOUR HAIR IS A MESS.
GoComics.com/babyblues
DOES THAT BUG YOU?
LIKE YOU WOULDN'T BELIEVE.
©2022, BABY BLUES BROS LLC DIST. BY ANDREWS McMEEL SYNDICATION 10-15
MISSION ACCOMPLISHED!
KIRKMAN & SCOTT

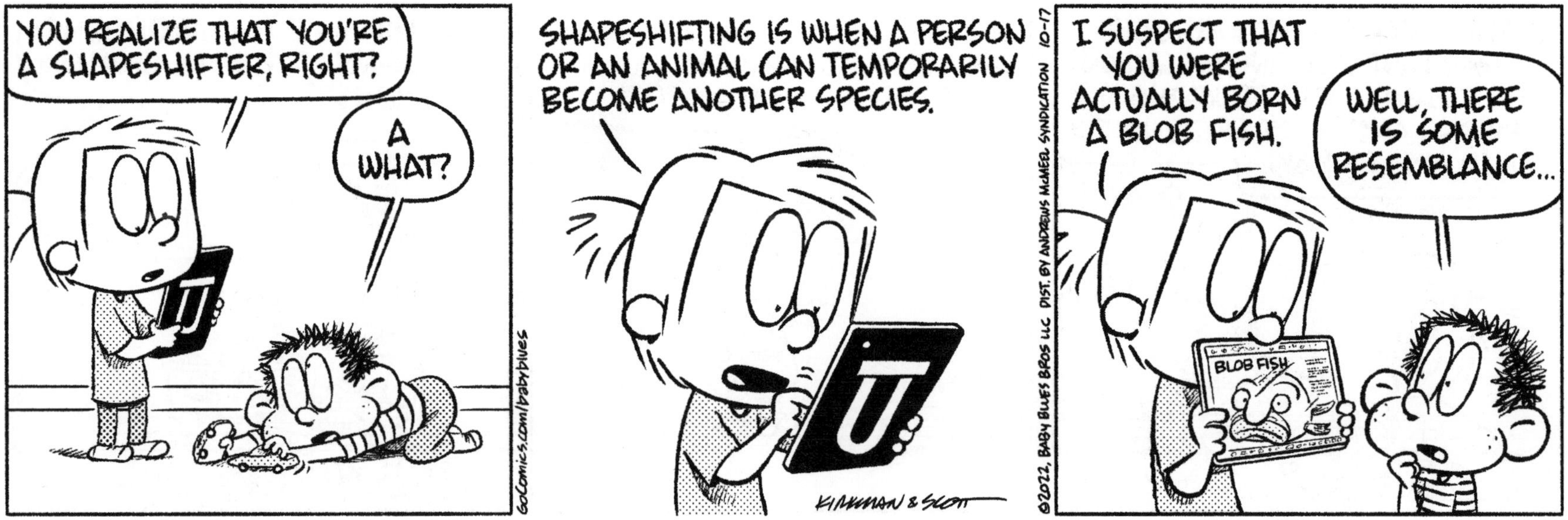
YOU REALIZE THAT YOU'RE A SHAPESHIFTER, RIGHT?
A WHAT?
GoComics.com/babyblues
SHAPESHIFTING IS WHEN A PERSON OR AN ANIMAL CAN TEMPORARILY BECOME ANOTHER SPECIES.
KIRKMAN & SCOTT
10-17
©2022, BABY BLUES BROS LLC DIST. BY ANDREWS McMEEL SYNDICATION
I SUSPECT THAT YOU WERE ACTUALLY BORN A BLOB FISH.
BLOB FISH
WELL, THERE IS SOME RESEMBLANCE...

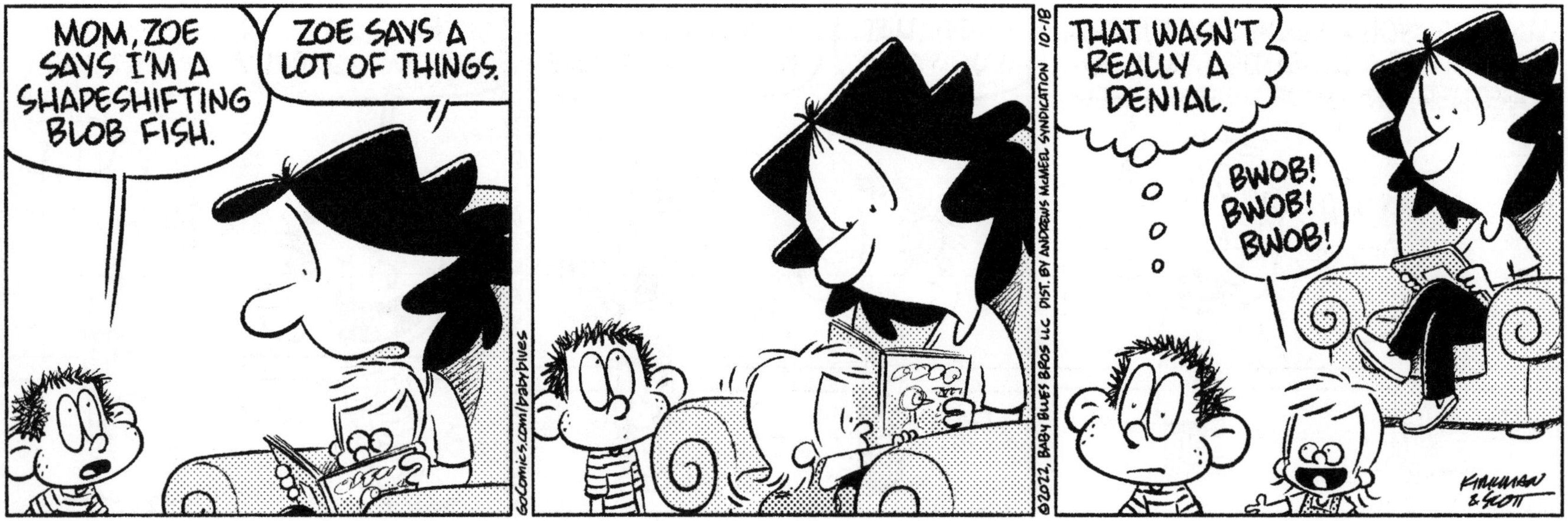
MOM, ZOE SAYS I'M A SHAPESHIFTING BLOB FISH.
ZOE SAYS A LOT OF THINGS.
GoComics.com/babyblues
10-18
©2022, BABY BLUES BROS LLC DIST. BY ANDREWS McMEEL SYNDICATION
THAT WASN'T REALLY A DENIAL.
BWOB! BWOB! BWOB!
KIRKMAN & SCOTT

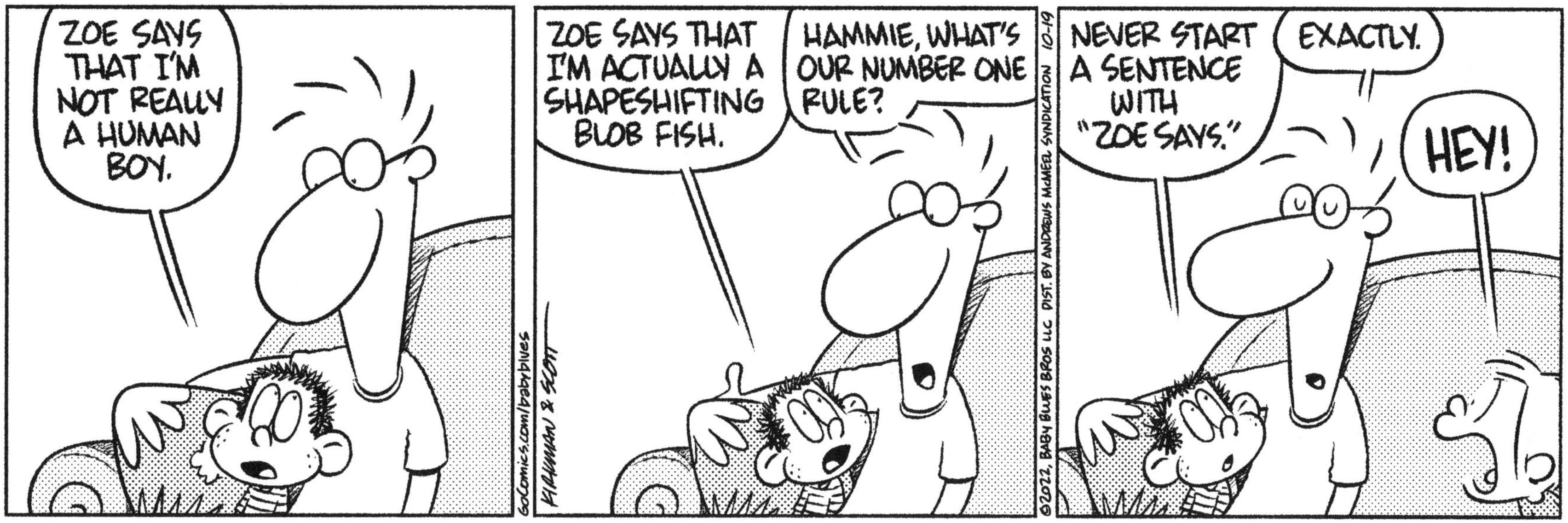
ZOE SAYS THAT I'M NOT REALLY A HUMAN BOY.
ZOE SAYS THAT I'M ACTUALLY A SHAPESHIFTING BLOB FISH.
HAMMIE, WHAT'S OUR NUMBER ONE RULE?
NEVER START A SENTENCE WITH "ZOE SAYS."
EXACTLY.
HEY!
GoComics.com/babyblues
KIRKMAN & SCOTT
10-19
©2022, BABY BLUES BROS LLC DIST. BY ANDREWS McMEEL SYNDICATION

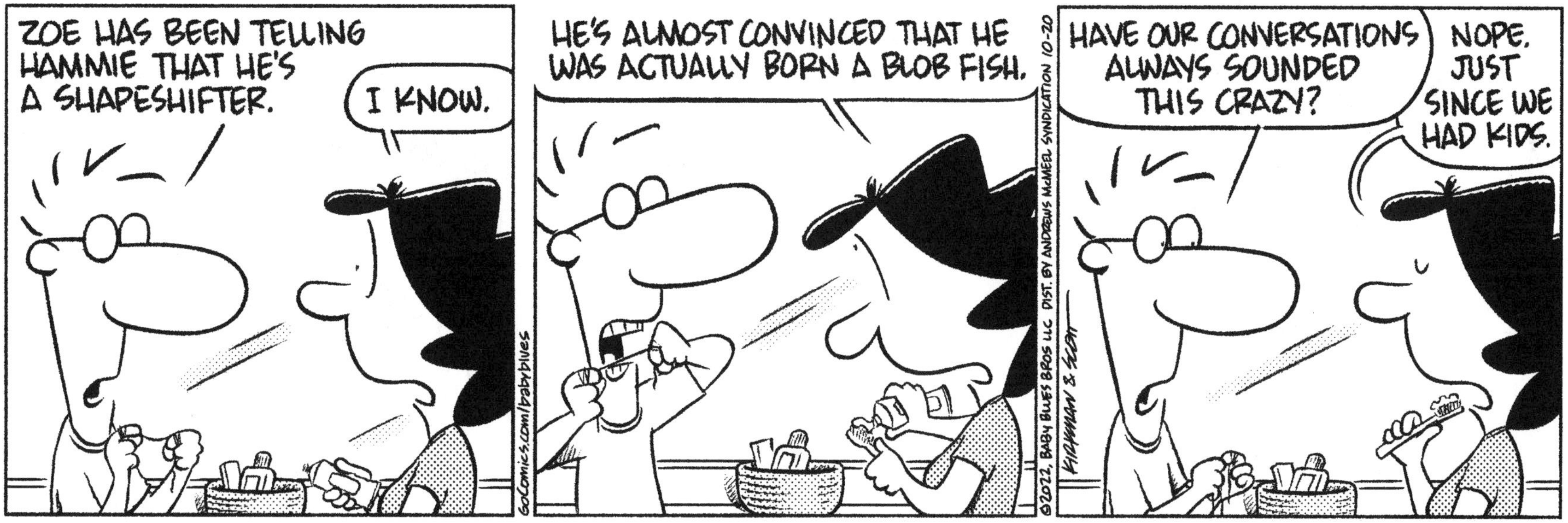
ZOE HAS BEEN TELLING HAMMIE THAT HE'S A SHAPESHIFTER.
I KNOW.
HE'S ALMOST CONVINCED THAT HE WAS ACTUALLY BORN A BLOB FISH.
HAVE OUR CONVERSATIONS ALWAYS SOUNDED THIS CRAZY?
NOPE. JUST SINCE WE HAD KIDS.
GoComics.com/babyblues
10-20
©2022, BABY BLUES BROS LLC DIST. BY ANDREWS McMEEL SYNDICATION
KIRKMAN & SCOTT

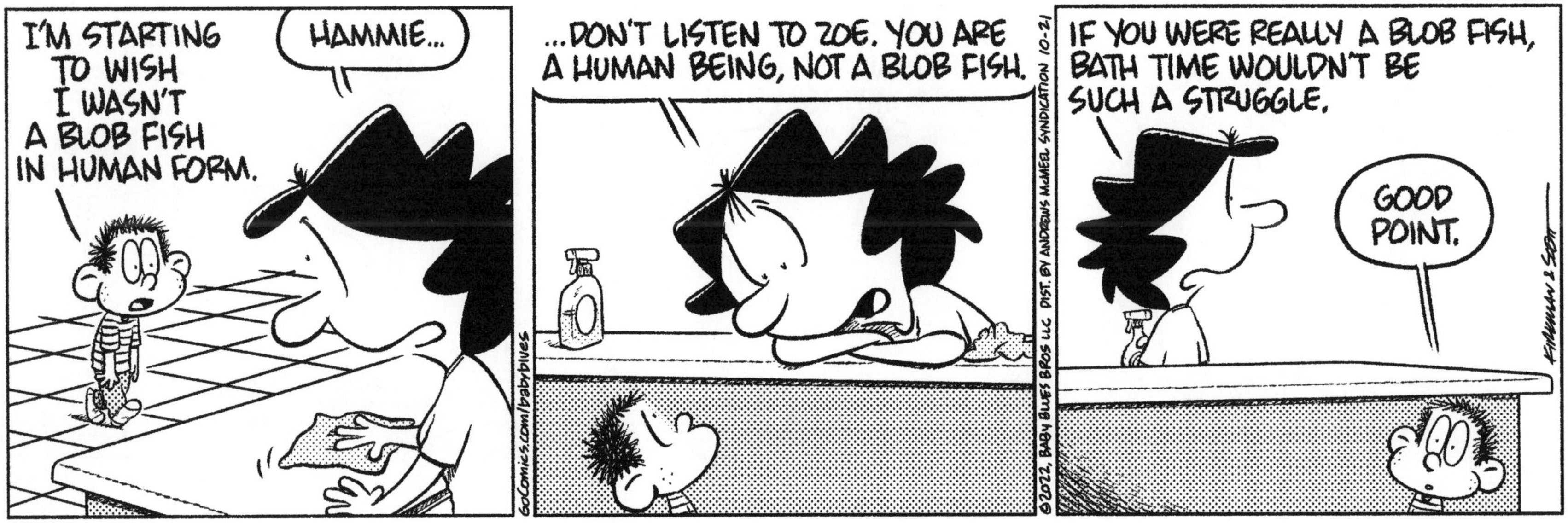
I'M STARTING TO WISH I WASN'T A BLOB FISH IN HUMAN FORM.
HAMMIE...
GoComics.com/babyblues
...DON'T LISTEN TO ZOE. YOU ARE A HUMAN BEING, NOT A BLOB FISH.
©2022, BABY BLUES BROS LLC DIST. BY ANDREWS MCMEEL SYNDICATION 10-21
IF YOU WERE REALLY A BLOB FISH, BATH TIME WOULDN'T BE SUCH A STRUGGLE.
GOOD POINT.
KIRKMAN & SCOTT

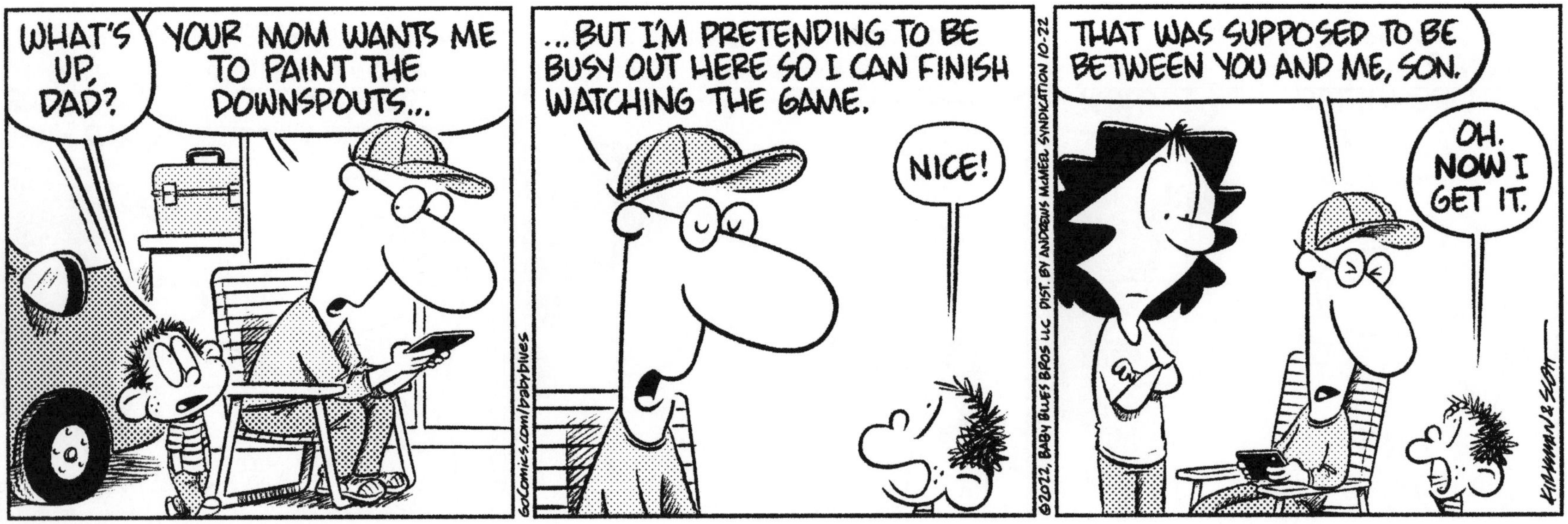
WHAT'S UP, DAD?
YOUR MOM WANTS ME TO PAINT THE DOWNSPOUTS...
GoComics.com/babyblues
...BUT I'M PRETENDING TO BE BUSY OUT HERE SO I CAN FINISH WATCHING THE GAME.
NICE!
©2022, BABY BLUES BROS LLC DIST. BY ANDREWS MCMEEL SYNDICATION 10-22
THAT WAS SUPPOSED TO BE BETWEEN YOU AND ME, SON.
OH. NOW I GET IT.
KIRKMAN & SCOTT

THUMP! THUMP!
THUMP!

GoComics.com/babyblues
THUMP! THUMP! THUMP!
THUMP! THUMP!
THUMP!
©2022, BABY BLUES BROS LLC DIST. BY ANDREWS McMEEL SYNDICATION
RAWWR
SPANG!
OW!
IT WASN'T A COMET THAT EXTINCTED THE DINOSAURS.
EXTINCTED?
10-23
KIRKMAN & SCOTT

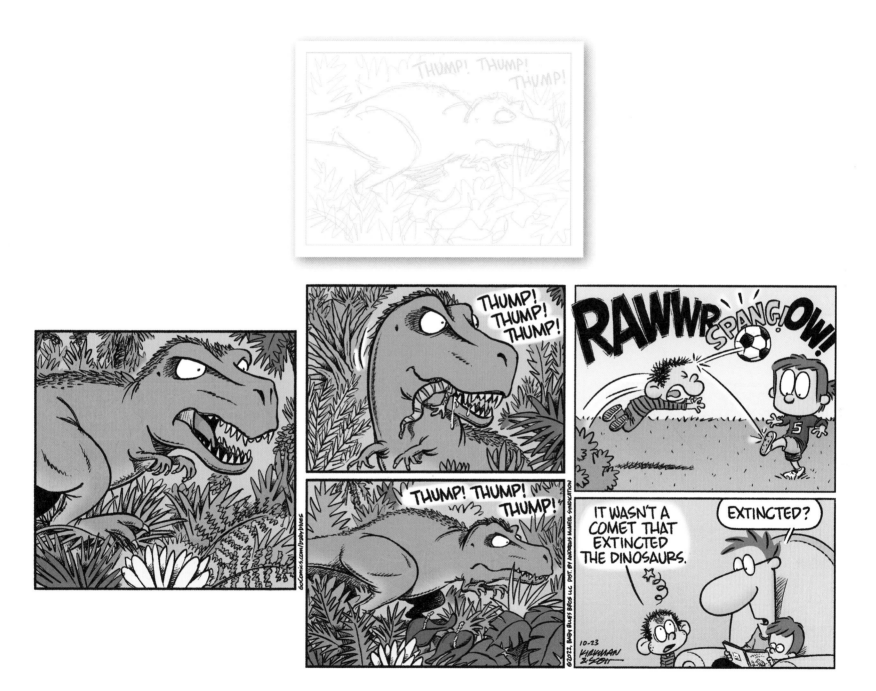

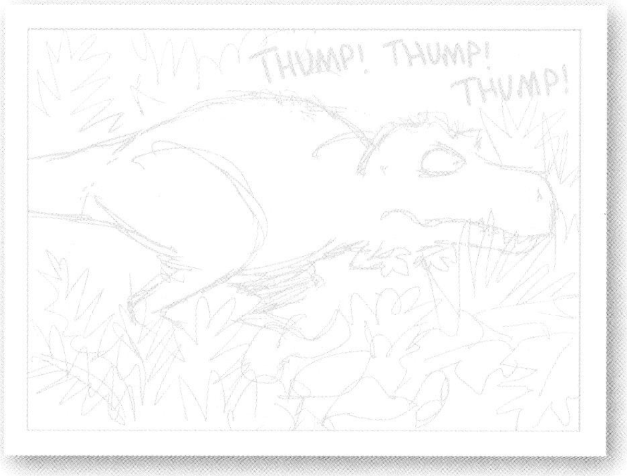

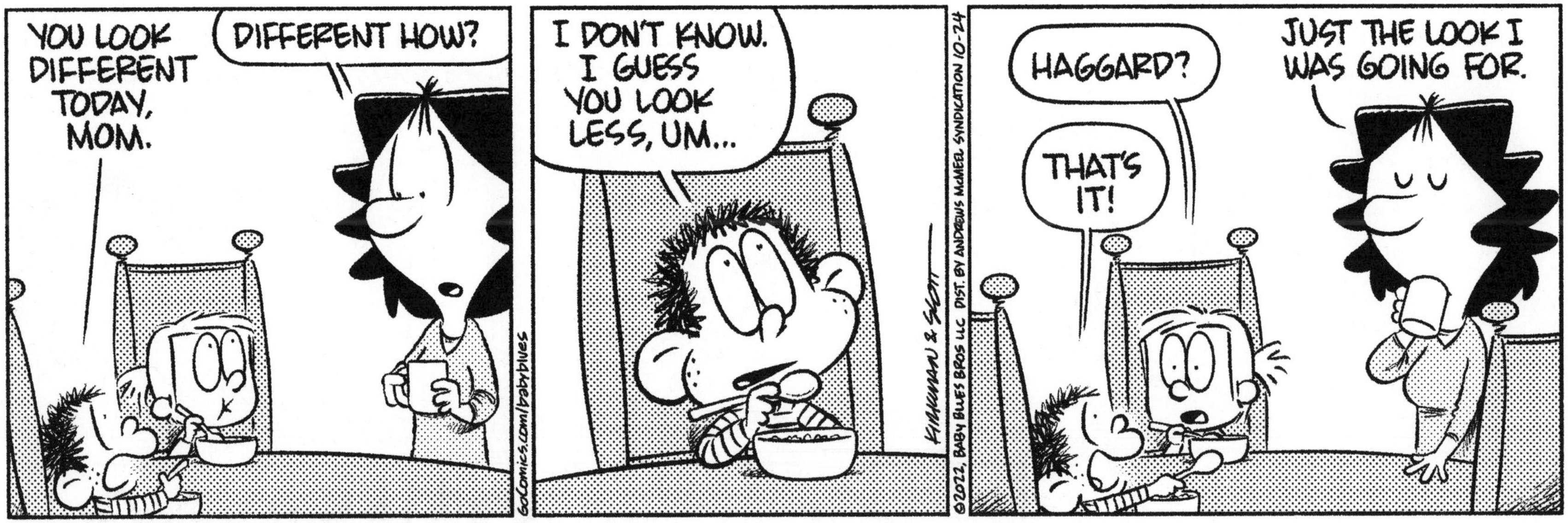
YOU LOOK DIFFERENT TODAY, MOM.
DIFFERENT HOW?
gocomics.com/babyblues
I DON'T KNOW. I GUESS YOU LOOK LESS, UM...
KIRKMAN & SCOTT
©2022, BABY BLUES BROS LLC. DIST. BY ANDREWS McMEEL SYNDICATION 10-24
HAGGARD?
THAT'S IT!
JUST THE LOOK I WAS GOING FOR.

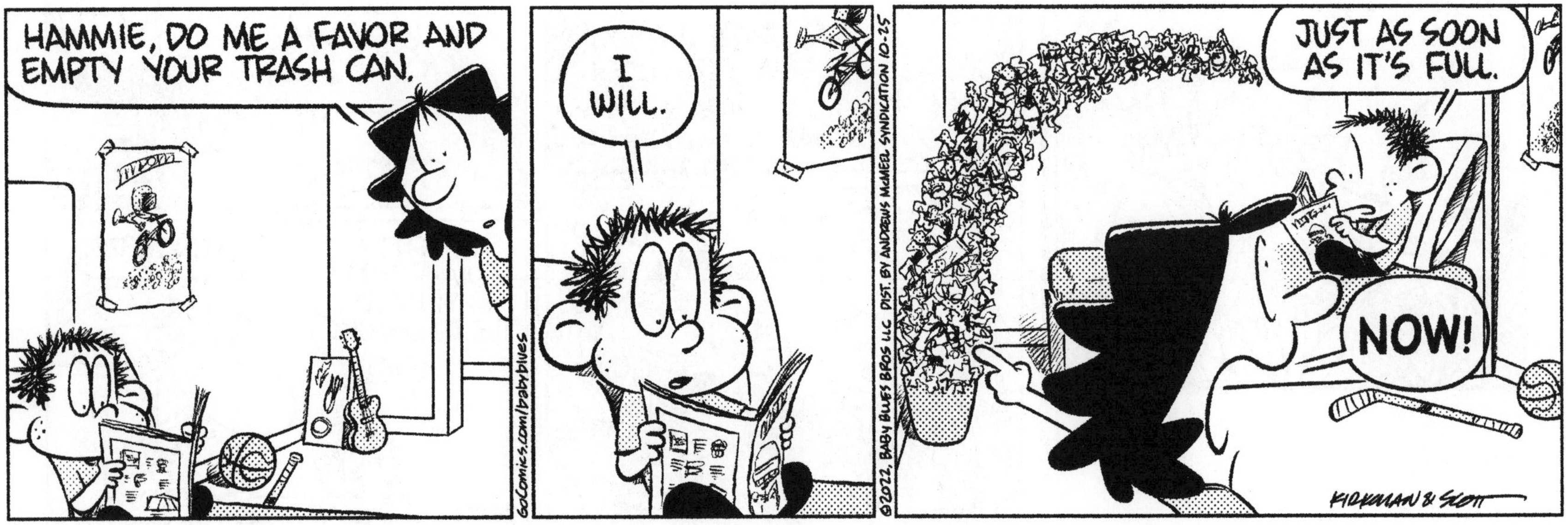
HAMMIE, DO ME A FAVOR AND EMPTY YOUR TRASH CAN.
gocomics.com/babyblues
I WILL.
©2022, BABY BLUES BROS LLC. DIST. BY ANDREWS McMEEL SYNDICATION 10-25
JUST AS SOON AS IT'S FULL.
NOW!
KIRKMAN & SCOTT

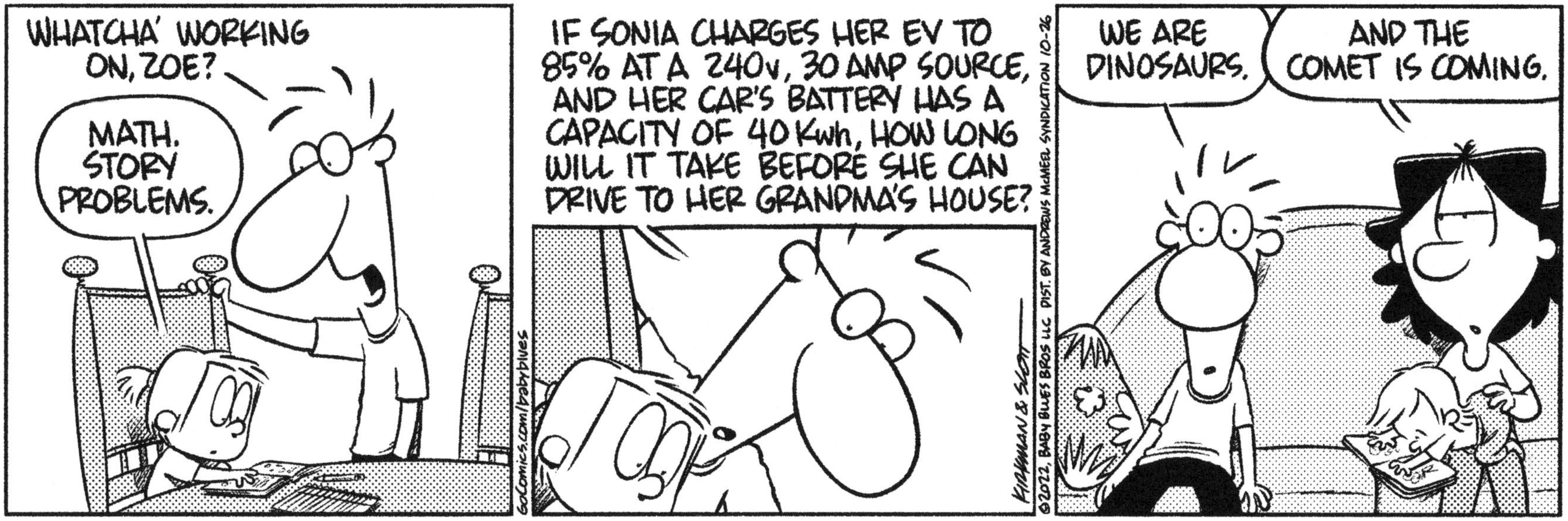
WHATCHA' WORKING ON, ZOE?
MATH. STORY PROBLEMS.
IF SONIA CHARGES HER EV TO 85% AT A 240v, 30 AMP SOURCE, AND HER CAR'S BATTERY HAS A CAPACITY OF 40 Kwh, HOW LONG WILL IT TAKE BEFORE SHE CAN DRIVE TO HER GRANDMA'S HOUSE?
WE ARE DINOSAURS.
AND THE COMET IS COMING.
gocomics.com/babyblues
KIRKMAN & SCOTT
©2022, BABY BLUES BROS LLC DIST. BY ANDREWS McMEEL SYNDICATION 10-26

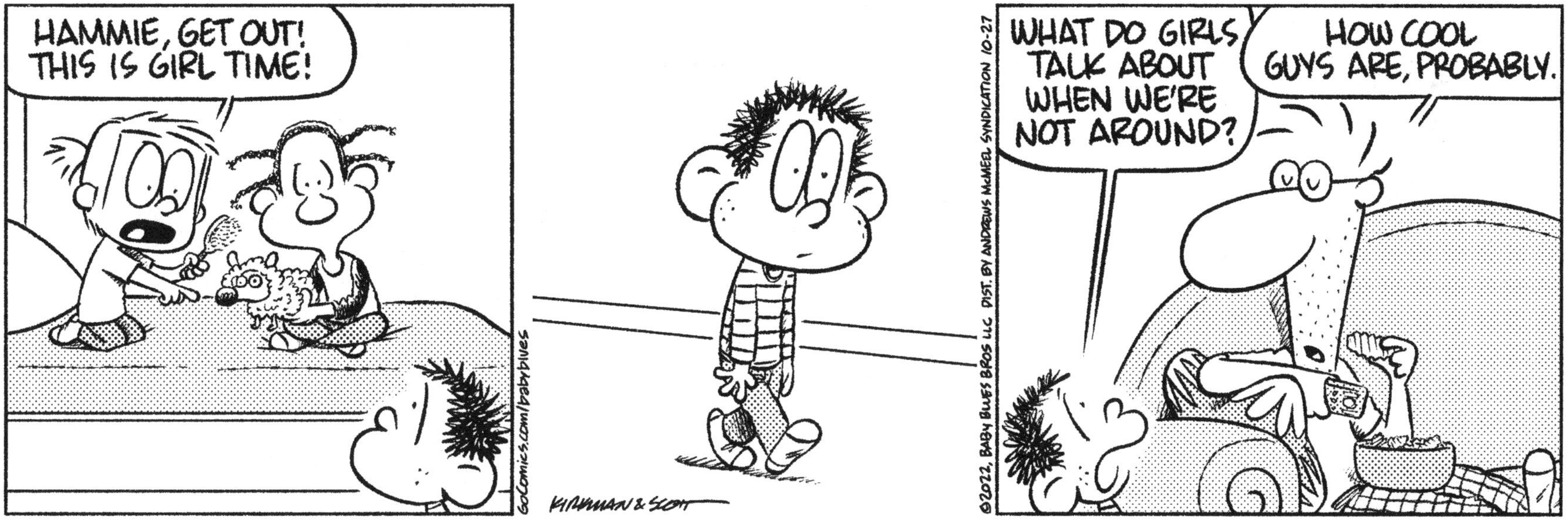
HAMMIE, GET OUT! THIS IS GIRL TIME!
WHAT DO GIRLS TALK ABOUT WHEN WE'RE NOT AROUND?
HOW COOL GUYS ARE, PROBABLY.
gocomics.com/babyblues
KIRKMAN & SCOTT
©2022, BABY BLUES BROS LLC DIST. BY ANDREWS McMEEL SYNDICATION 10-27

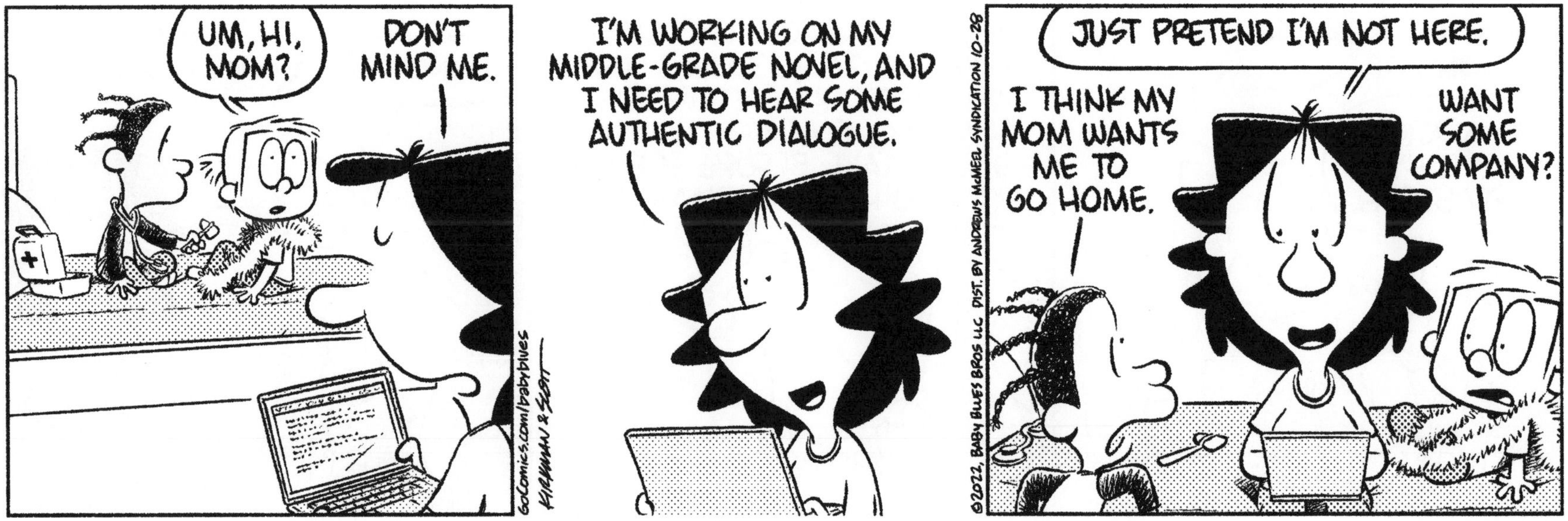
UM, HI, MOM?
DON'T MIND ME.
GoComics.com/babyblues
KIRKMAN & SCOTT
I'M WORKING ON MY MIDDLE-GRADE NOVEL, AND I NEED TO HEAR SOME AUTHENTIC DIALOGUE.
©2022, BABY BLUES BROS LLC DIST. BY ANDREWS McMEEL SYNDICATION 10-28
JUST PRETEND I'M NOT HERE.
I THINK MY MOM WANTS ME TO GO HOME.
WANT SOME COMPANY?

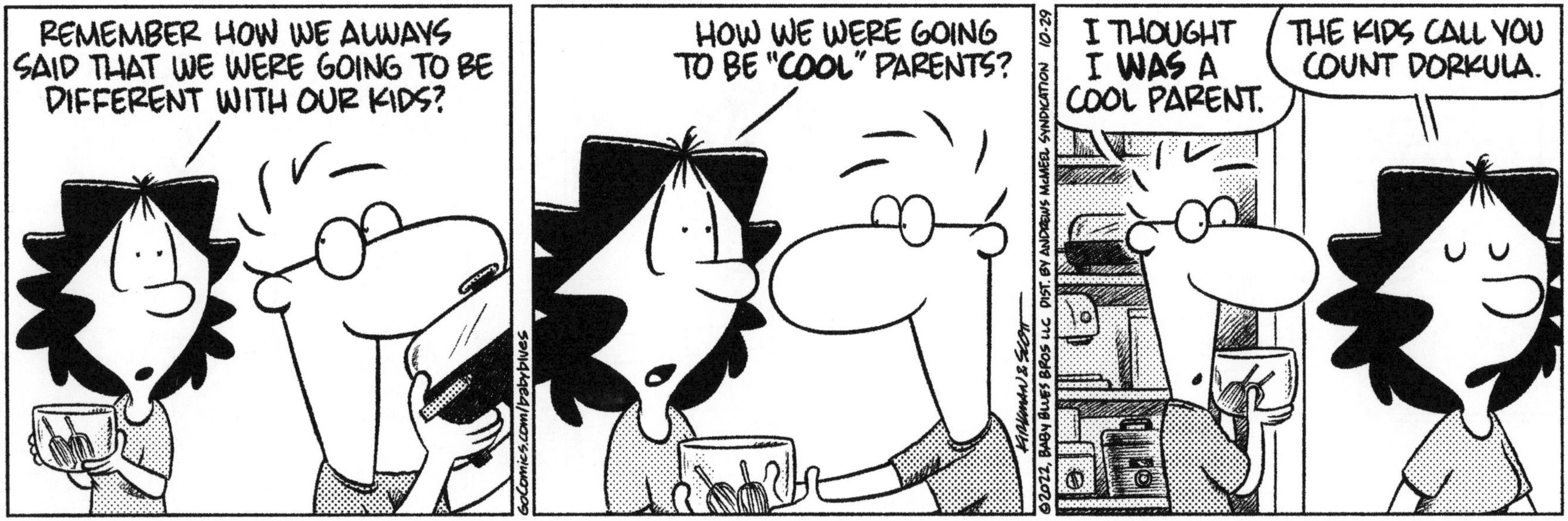
REMEMBER HOW WE ALWAYS SAID THAT WE WERE GOING TO BE DIFFERENT WITH OUR KIDS?
GoComics.com/babyblues
HOW WE WERE GOING TO BE "COOL" PARENTS?
KIRKMAN & SCOTT
©2022, BABY BLUES BROS LLC DIST. BY ANDREWS McMEEL SYNDICATION 10-29
I THOUGHT I WAS A COOL PARENT.
THE KIDS CALL YOU COUNT DORKULA.

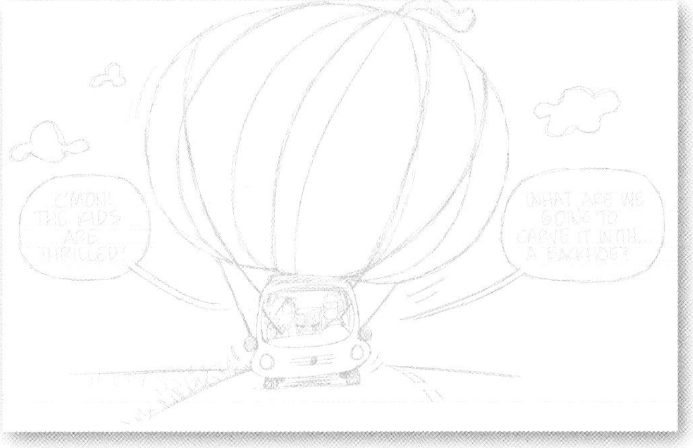
C'MON! THE KIDS ARE THRILLED!
WHAT ARE WE GOING TO CARVE IT WITH... A BACKHOE?

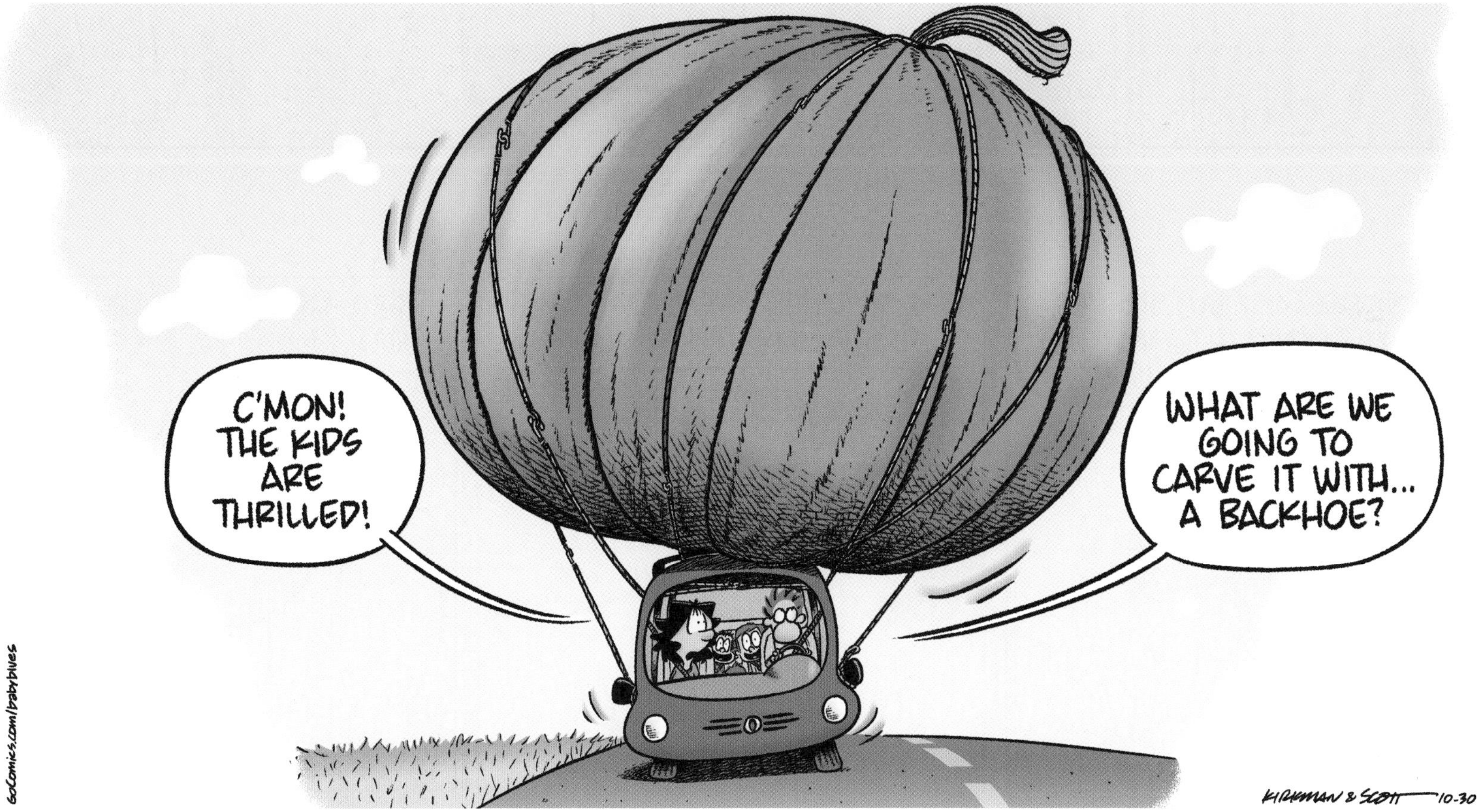
C'MON! THE KIDS ARE THRILLED!
WHAT ARE WE GOING TO CARVE IT WITH... A BACKHOE?
KIRKMAN & SCOTT 10-30

GoComics.com/babyblues

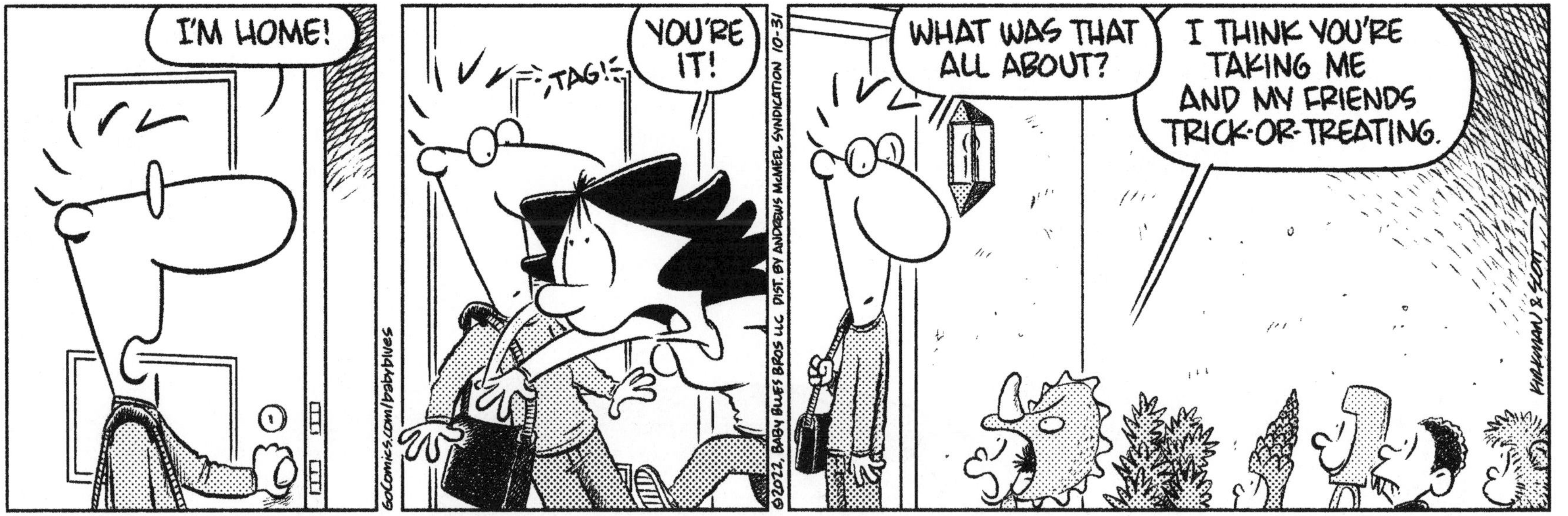
I'M HOME!
GoComics.com/babyblues
TAG!
YOU'RE IT!
©2022, BABY BLUES BROS LLC DIST. BY ANDREWS McMEEL SYNDICATION 10-31
WHAT WAS THAT ALL ABOUT?
I THINK YOU'RE TAKING ME AND MY FRIENDS TRICK-OR-TREATING.
KIRKMAN & SCOTT

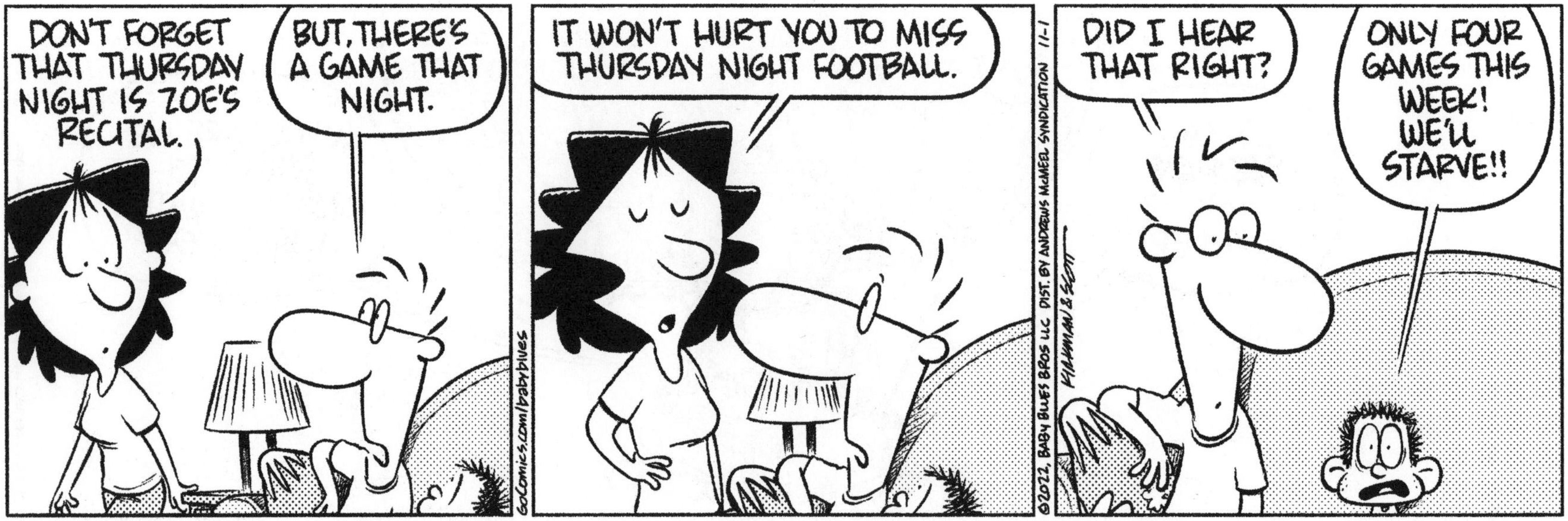
DON'T FORGET THAT THURSDAY NIGHT IS ZOE'S RECITAL.
BUT, THERE'S A GAME THAT NIGHT.
GoComics.com/babyblues
IT WON'T HURT YOU TO MISS THURSDAY NIGHT FOOTBALL.
©2022, BABY BLUES BROS LLC DIST. BY ANDREWS McMEEL SYNDICATION 11-1
KIRKMAN & SCOTT
DID I HEAR THAT RIGHT?
ONLY FOUR GAMES THIS WEEK! WE'LL STARVE!!

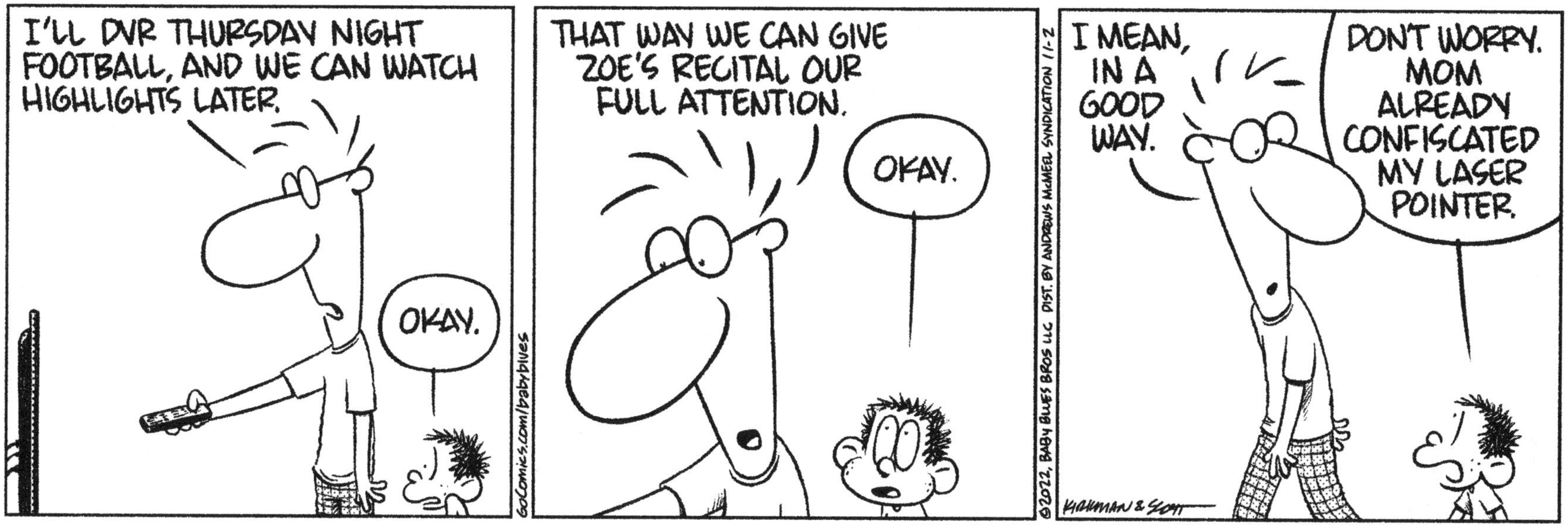
I'LL DVR THURSDAY NIGHT FOOTBALL, AND WE CAN WATCH HIGHLIGHTS LATER.
OKAY.
GoComics.com/babyblues
THAT WAY WE CAN GIVE ZOE'S RECITAL OUR FULL ATTENTION.
OKAY.
©2022, BABY BLUES BROS LLC DIST. BY ANDREWS McMEEL SYNDICATION 11-2
I MEAN, IN A GOOD WAY.
DON'T WORRY. MOM ALREADY CONFISCATED MY LASER POINTER.
KIRKMAN & SCOTT

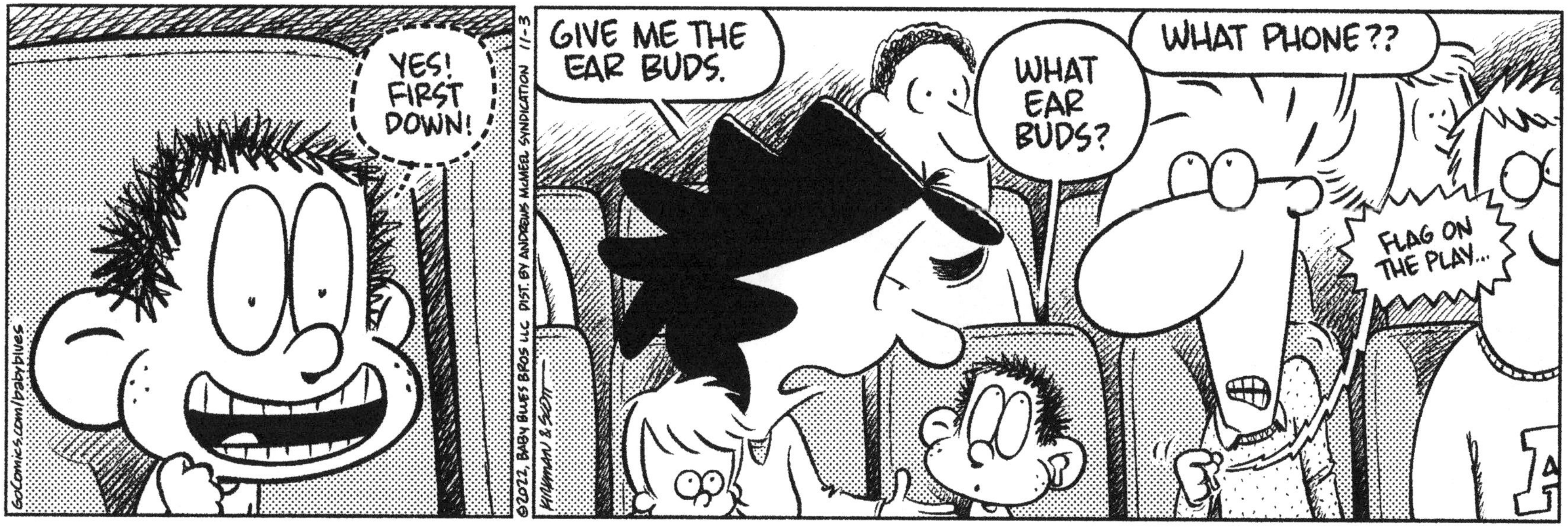
YES! FIRST DOWN!
GoComics.com/babyblues
©2022, BABY BLUES BROS LLC DIST. BY ANDREWS McMEEL SYNDICATION 11-3
KIRKMAN & SCOTT
GIVE ME THE EAR BUDS.
WHAT EAR BUDS?
WHAT PHONE??
FLAG ON THE PLAY...

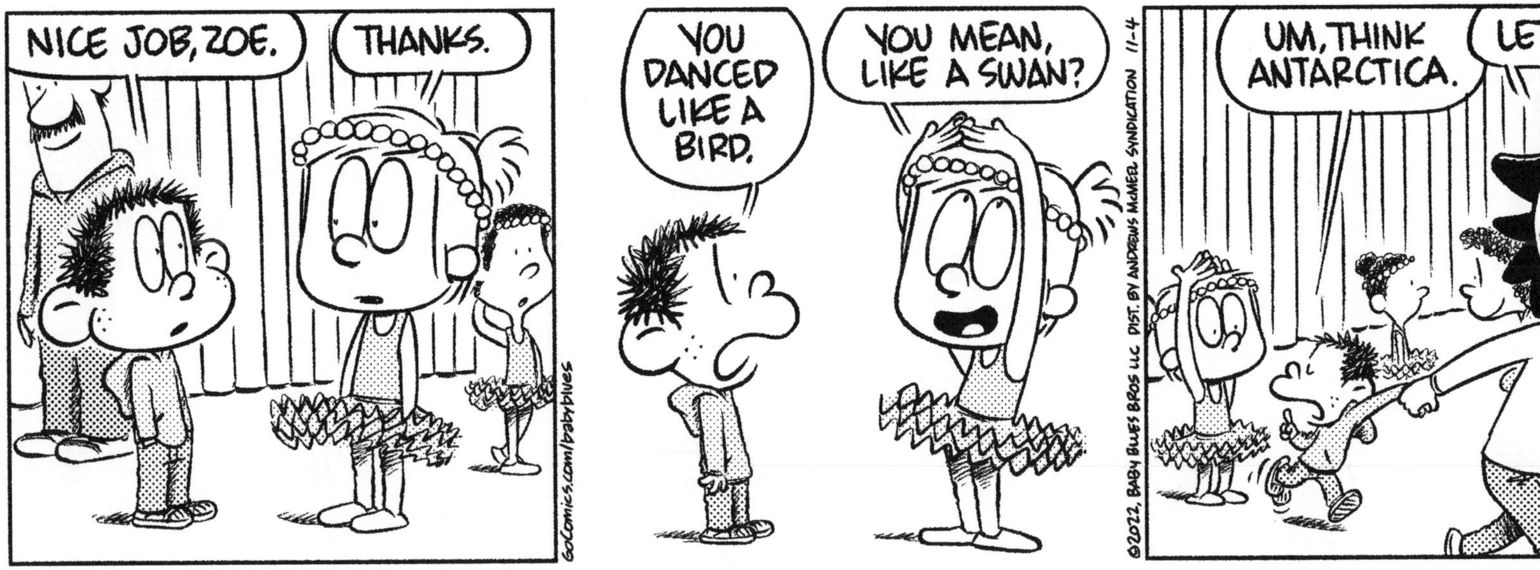
NICE JOB, ZOE.
THANKS.
GoComics.com/babyblues
YOU DANCED LIKE A BIRD.
YOU MEAN, LIKE A SWAN?
11-4
©2022, BABY BLUES BROS LLC DIST. BY ANDREWS McMEEL SYNDICATION
UM, THINK ANTARCTICA.
LET'S GO.
KIRKMAN & SCOTT

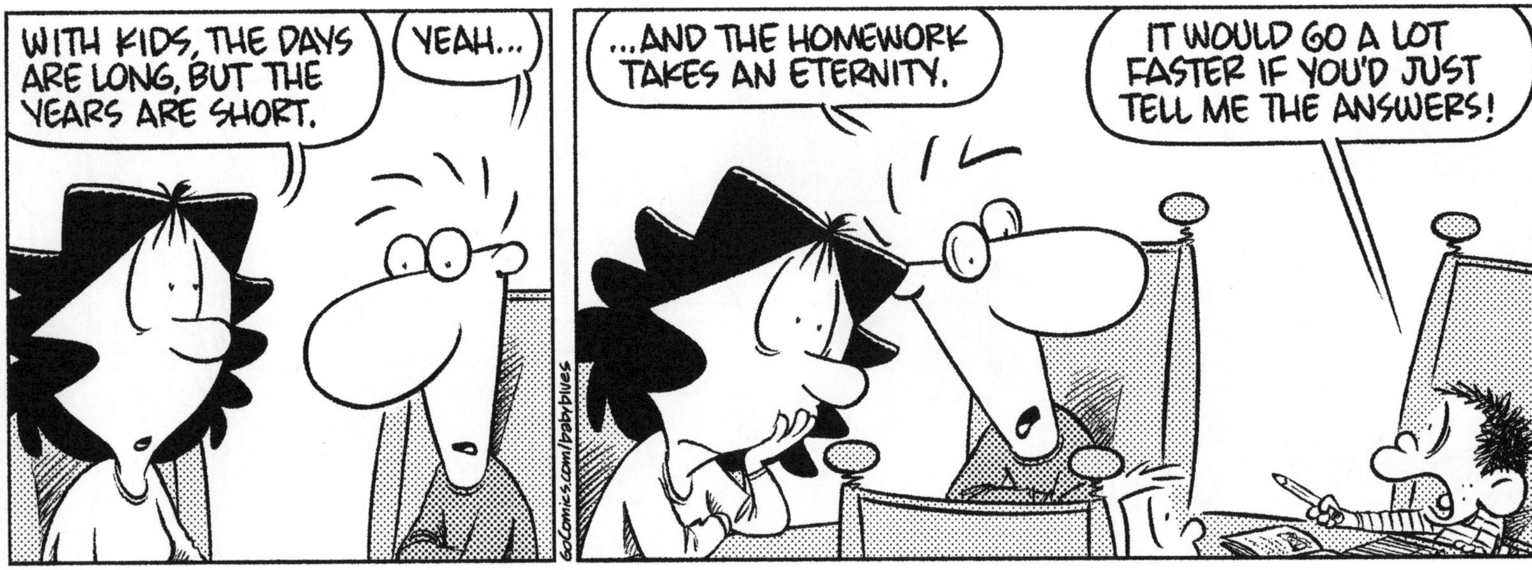
WITH KIDS, THE DAYS ARE LONG, BUT THE YEARS ARE SHORT.
YEAH...
GoComics.com/babyblues
...AND THE HOMEWORK TAKES AN ETERNITY.
IT WOULD GO A LOT FASTER IF YOU'D JUST TELL ME THE ANSWERS!
KIRKMAN & SCOTT
©2022, BABY BLUES BROS LLC DIST. BY ANDREWS McMEEL SYNDICATION 11-5

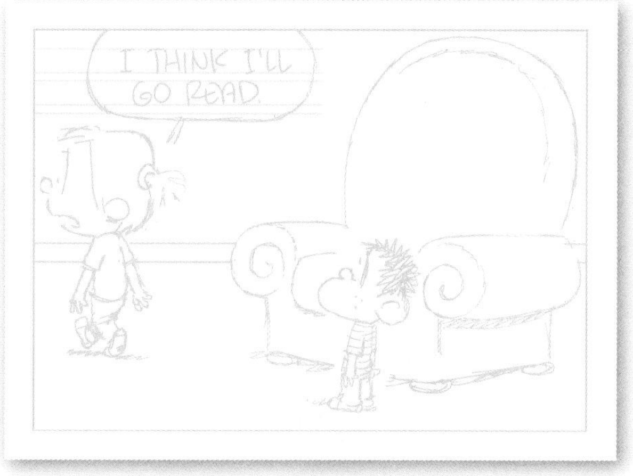
I THINK I'LL GO READ.

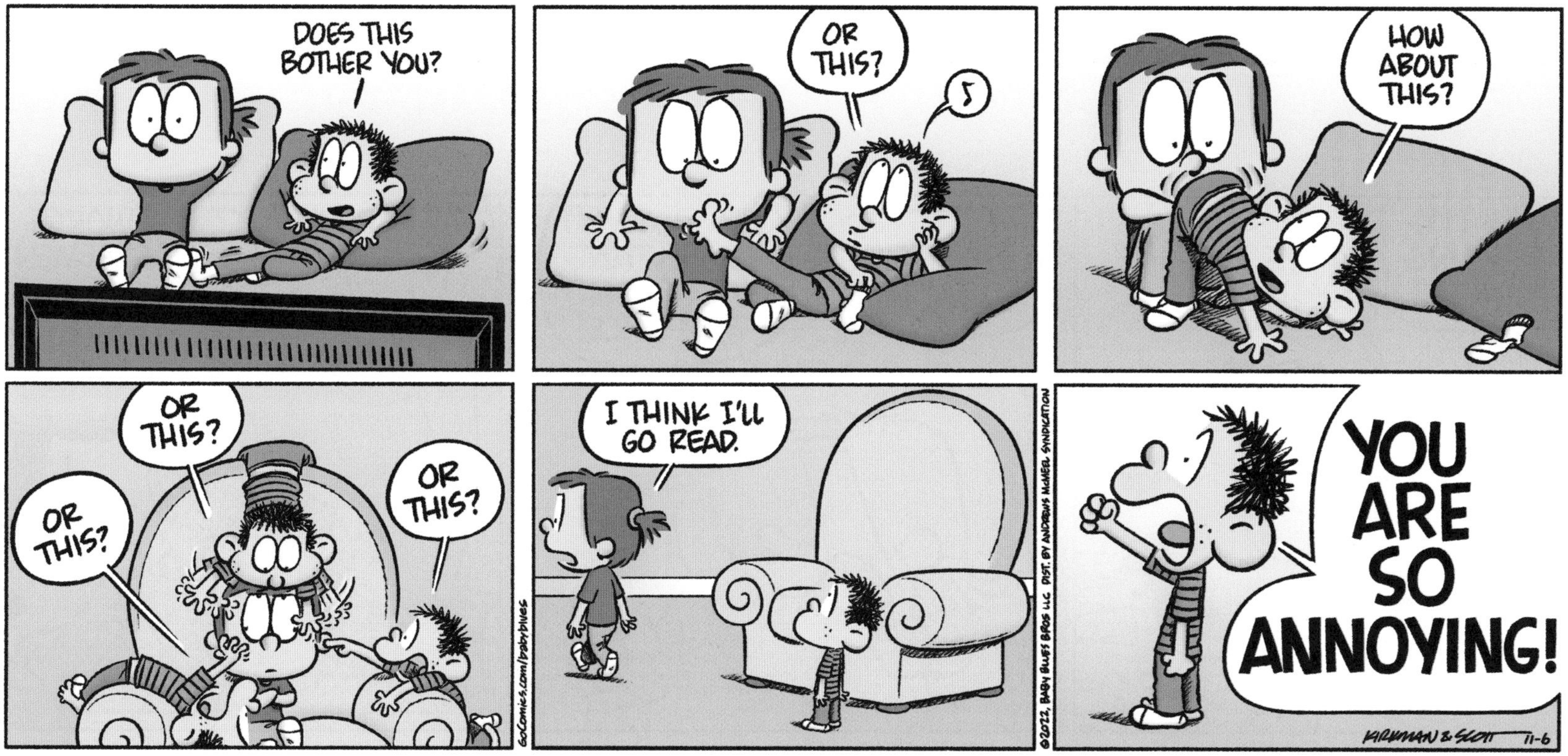
DOES THIS BOTHER YOU?
OR THIS?
HOW ABOUT THIS?
OR THIS?
OR THIS?
OR THIS?
GoComics.com/babyblues
I THINK I'LL GO READ.
©2022, BABY BLUES BROS LLC DIST. BY ANDREWS McMEEL SYNDICATION
YOU ARE SO ANNOYING!
KIRKMAN & SCOTT 11-6

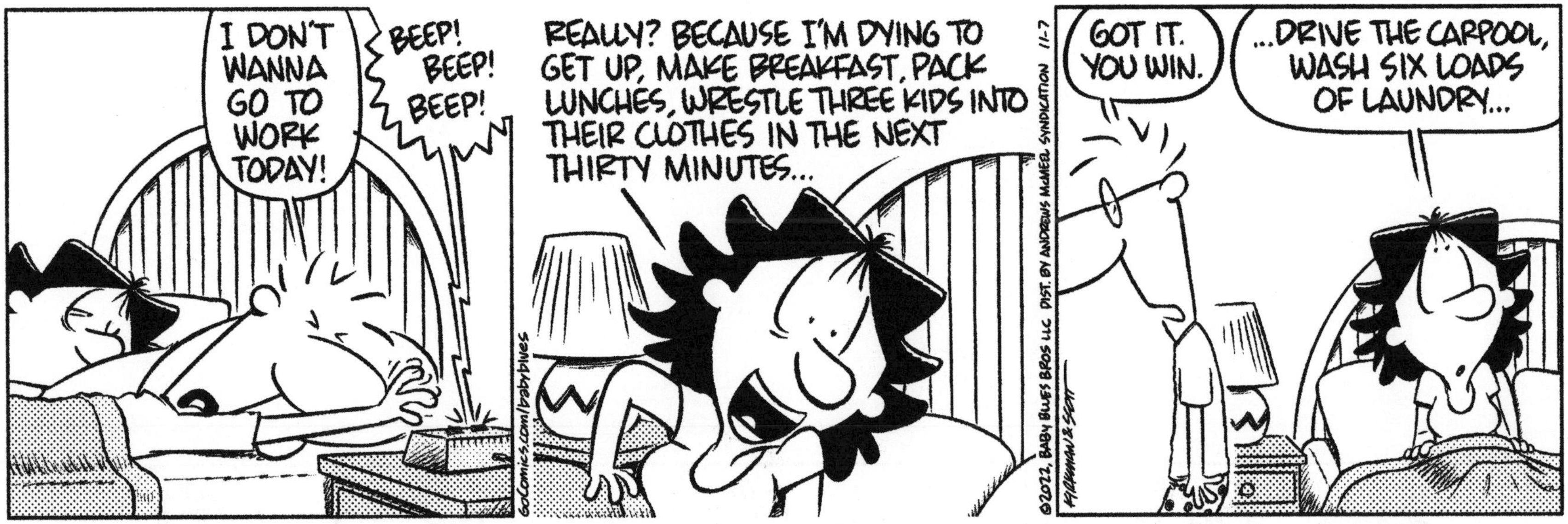
I DON'T WANNA GO TO WORK TODAY!
BEEP! BEEP! BEEP!
REALLY? BECAUSE I'M DYING TO GET UP, MAKE BREAKFAST, PACK LUNCHES, WRESTLE THREE KIDS INTO THEIR CLOTHES IN THE NEXT THIRTY MINUTES...
GOT IT. YOU WIN.
...DRIVE THE CARPOOL, WASH SIX LOADS OF LAUNDRY...
GoComics.com/babyblues
©2022, BABY BLUES BROS LLC DIST. BY ANDREWS McMEEL SYNDICATION 11-7
KIRKMAN & SCOTT

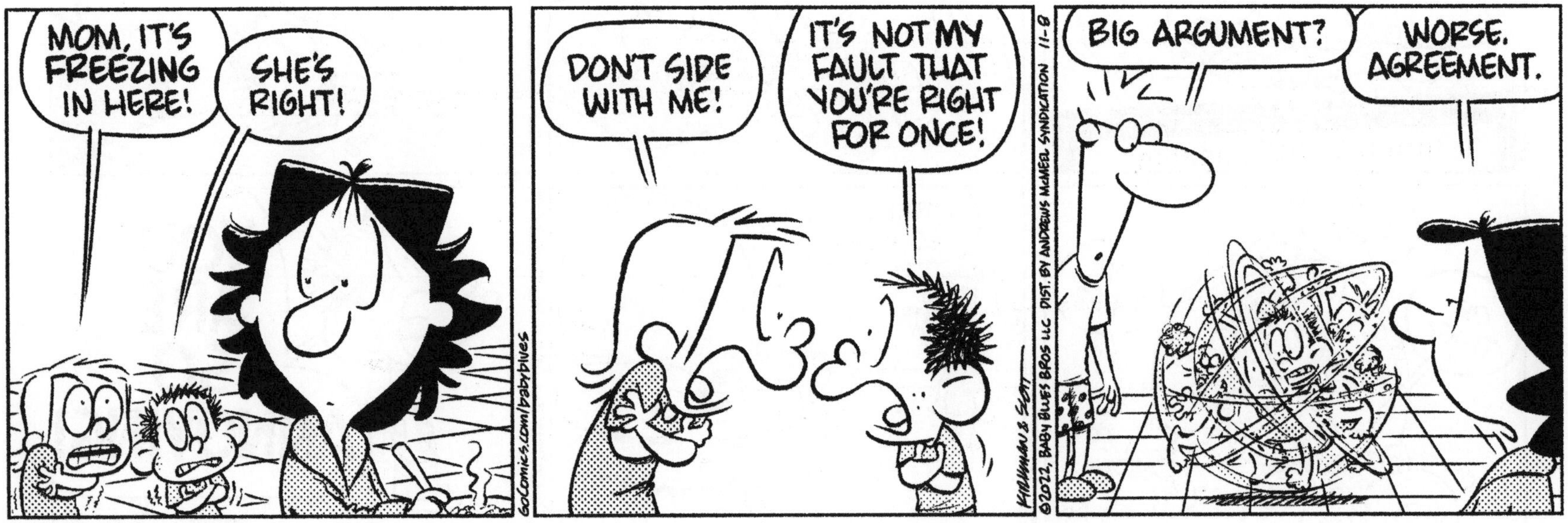
MOM, IT'S FREEZING IN HERE!
SHE'S RIGHT!
DON'T SIDE WITH ME!
IT'S NOT MY FAULT THAT YOU'RE RIGHT FOR ONCE!
BIG ARGUMENT?
WORSE. AGREEMENT.
GoComics.com/babyblues
©2022, BABY BLUES BROS LLC DIST. BY ANDREWS McMEEL SYNDICATION 11-8
KIRKMAN & SCOTT

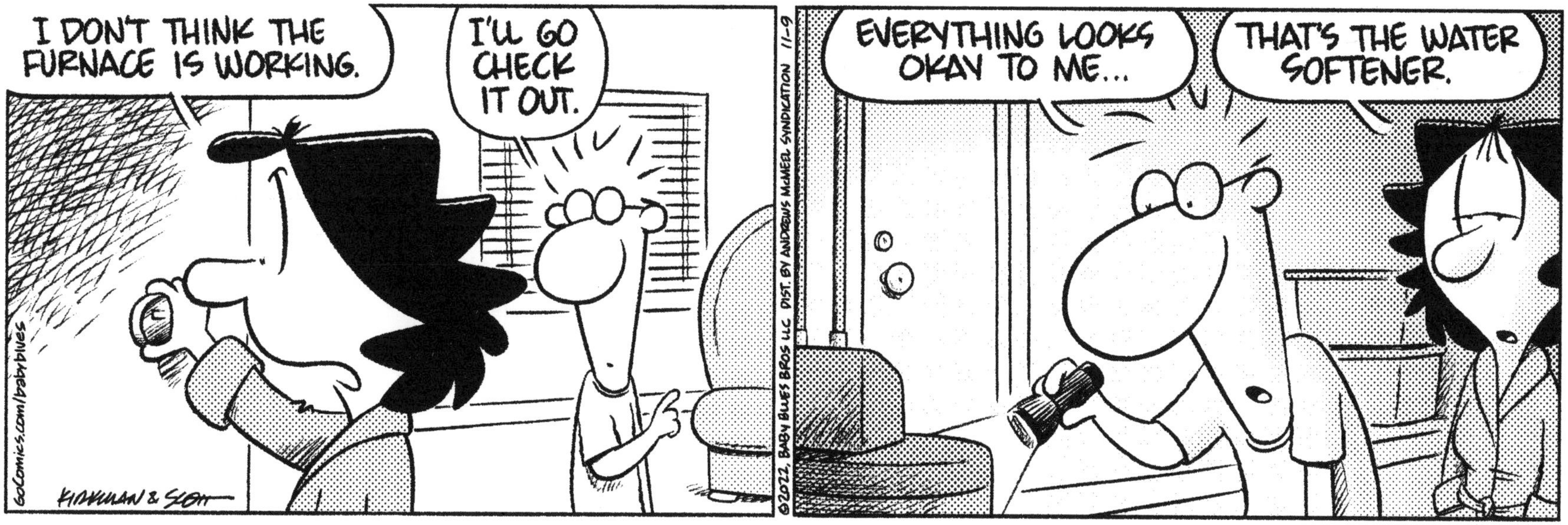
I DON'T THINK THE FURNACE IS WORKING.
I'LL GO CHECK IT OUT.
EVERYTHING LOOKS OKAY TO ME...
THAT'S THE WATER SOFTENER.
KIRKMAN & SCOTT
GoComics.com/babyblues
©2022, BABY BLUES BROS LLC DIST. BY ANDREWS McMEEL SYNDICATION
11-9

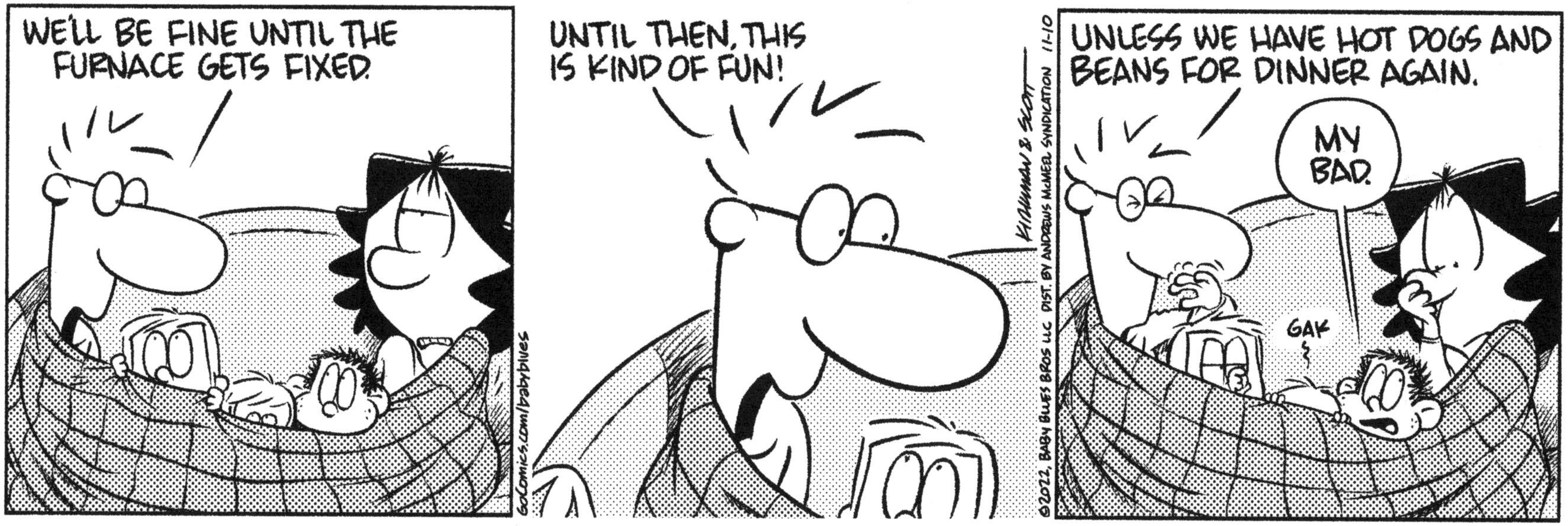
WE'LL BE FINE UNTIL THE FURNACE GETS FIXED.
UNTIL THEN, THIS IS KIND OF FUN!
UNLESS WE HAVE HOT DOGS AND BEANS FOR DINNER AGAIN.
MY BAD.
GAK
KIRKMAN & SCOTT
GoComics.com/babyblues
©2022, BABY BLUES BROS LLC DIST. BY ANDREWS McMEEL SYNDICATION
11-10

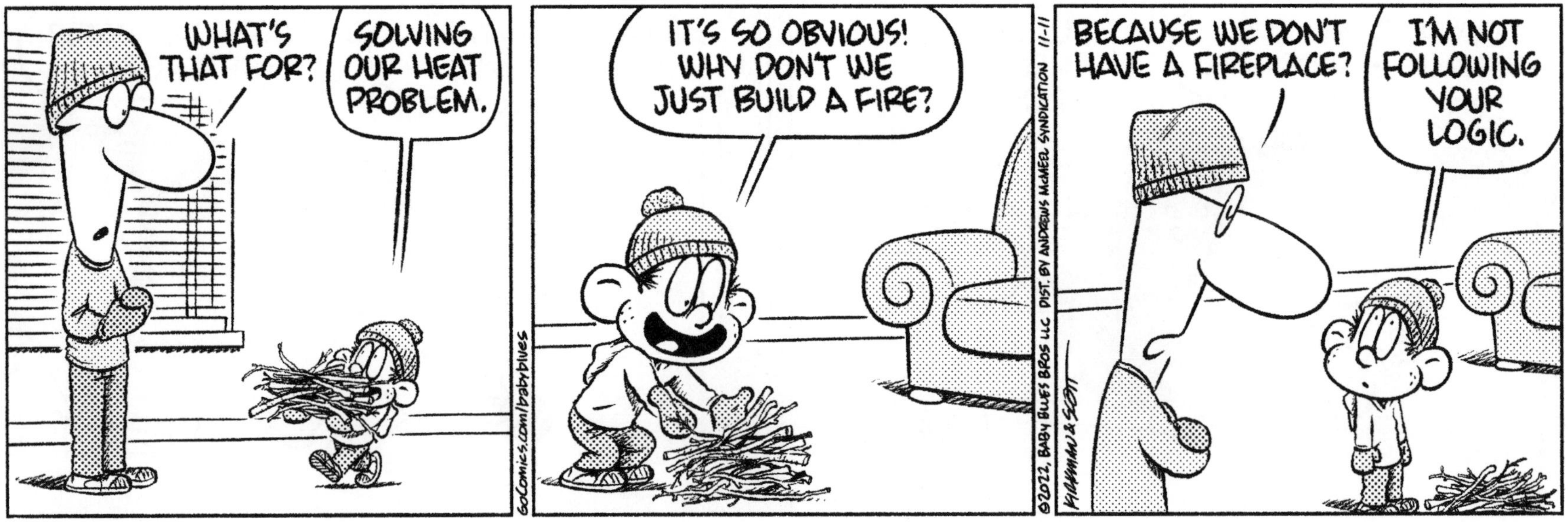
WHAT'S THAT FOR?
SOLVING OUR HEAT PROBLEM.
GoComics.com/babyblues
IT'S SO OBVIOUS! WHY DON'T WE JUST BUILD A FIRE?
©2022, BABY BLUES BROS LLC DIST. BY ANDREWS McMEEL SYNDICATION 11-11
KIRKMAN & SCOTT
BECAUSE WE DON'T HAVE A FIREPLACE?
I'M NOT FOLLOWING YOUR LOGIC.

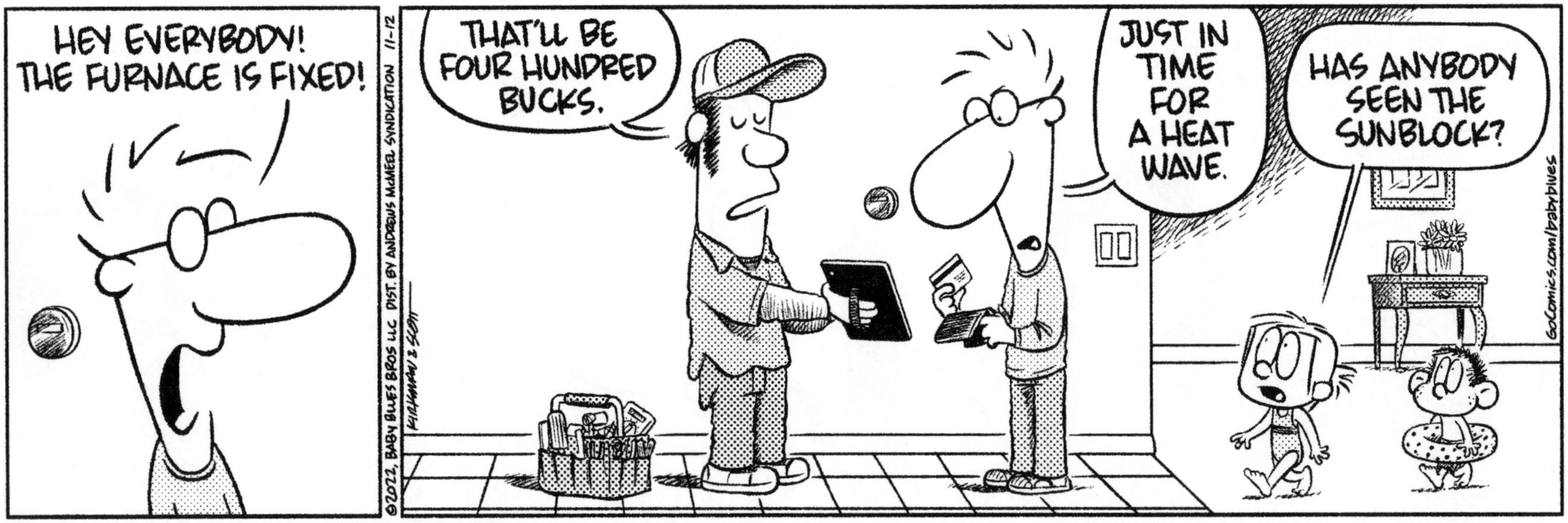
HEY EVERYBODY! THE FURNACE IS FIXED!
©2022, BABY BLUES BROS LLC DIST. BY ANDREWS McMEEL SYNDICATION 11-12
KIRKMAN & SCOTT
THAT'LL BE FOUR HUNDRED BUCKS.
JUST IN TIME FOR A HEAT WAVE.
HAS ANYBODY SEEN THE SUNBLOCK?
GoComics.com/babyblues

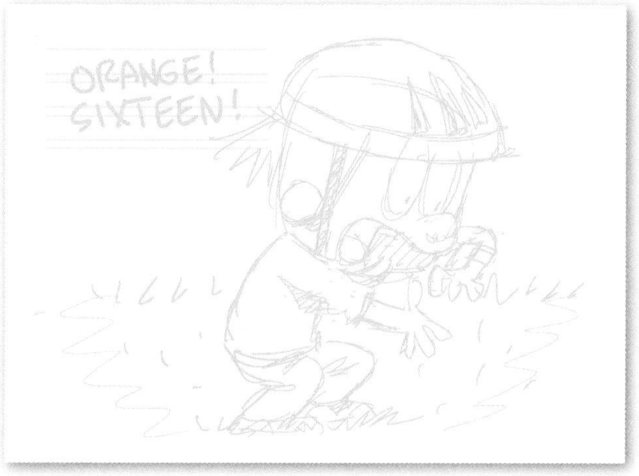
ORANGE! SIXTEEN!

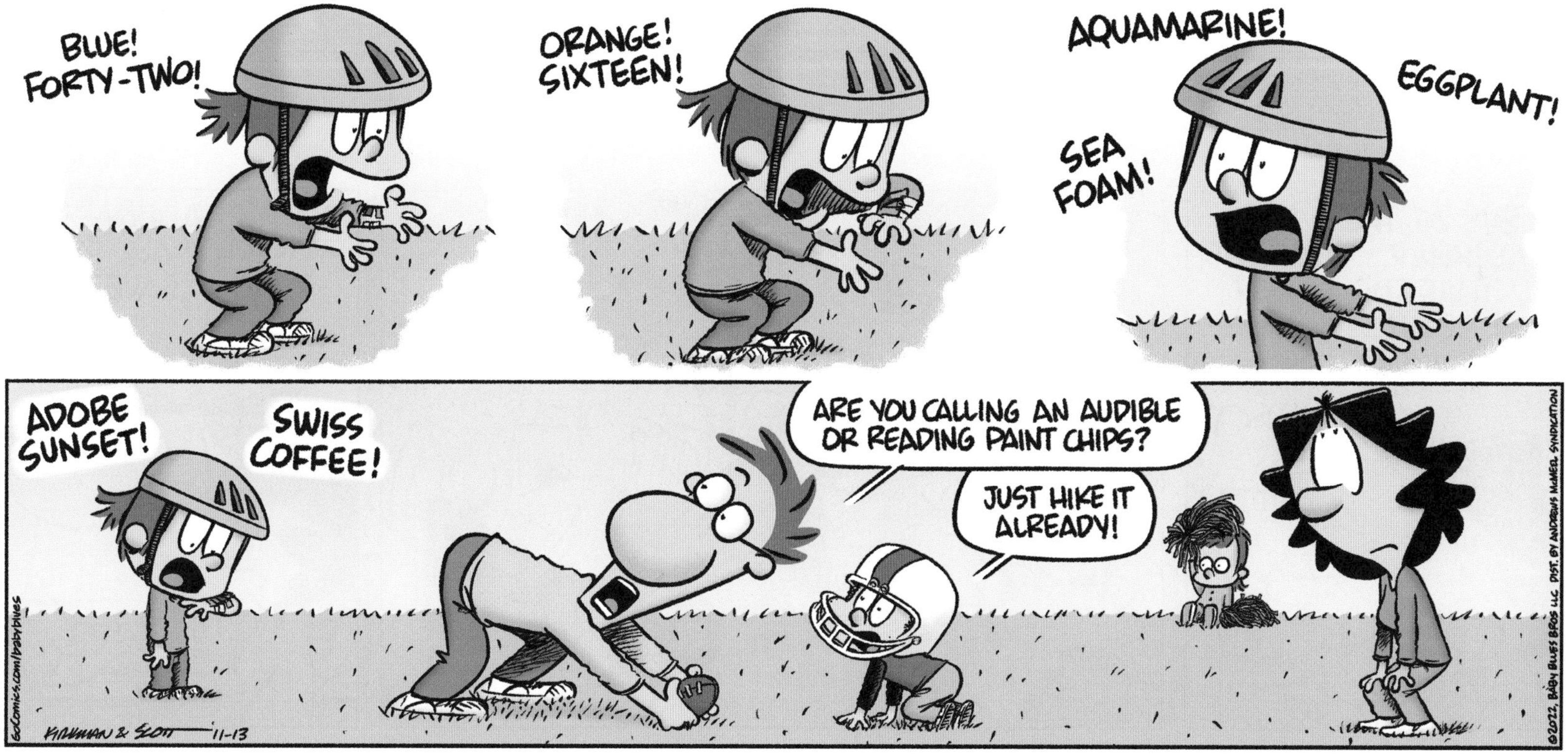
BLUE! FORTY-TWO!
ORANGE! SIXTEEN!
AQUAMARINE!
EGGPLANT!
SEA FOAM!
ADOBE SUNSET!
SWISS COFFEE!
ARE YOU CALLING AN AUDIBLE OR READING PAINT CHIPS?
JUST HIKE IT ALREADY!
GoComics.com/babyblues
KIRKMAN & SCOTT 11-13
©2022, BABY BLUES BROS LLC. DIST. BY ANDREWS McMEEL SYNDICATION

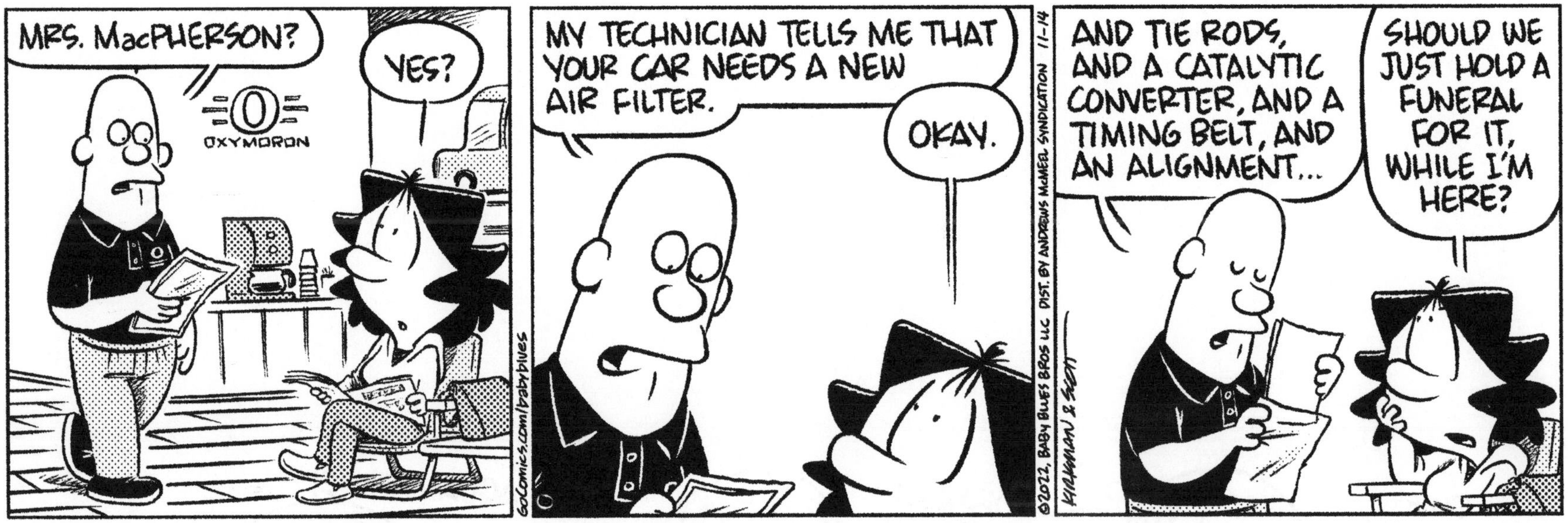
MRS. MacPHERSON?
YES?
OXYMORON
MY TECHNICIAN TELLS ME THAT YOUR CAR NEEDS A NEW AIR FILTER.
OKAY.
AND TIE RODS, AND A CATALYTIC CONVERTER, AND A TIMING BELT, AND AN ALIGNMENT...
SHOULD WE JUST HOLD A FUNERAL FOR IT, WHILE I'M HERE?
GoComics.com/babyblues
©2022, BABY BLUES BROS LLC DIST. BY ANDREWS McMEEL SYNDICATION 11-14
KIRKMAN & SCOTT

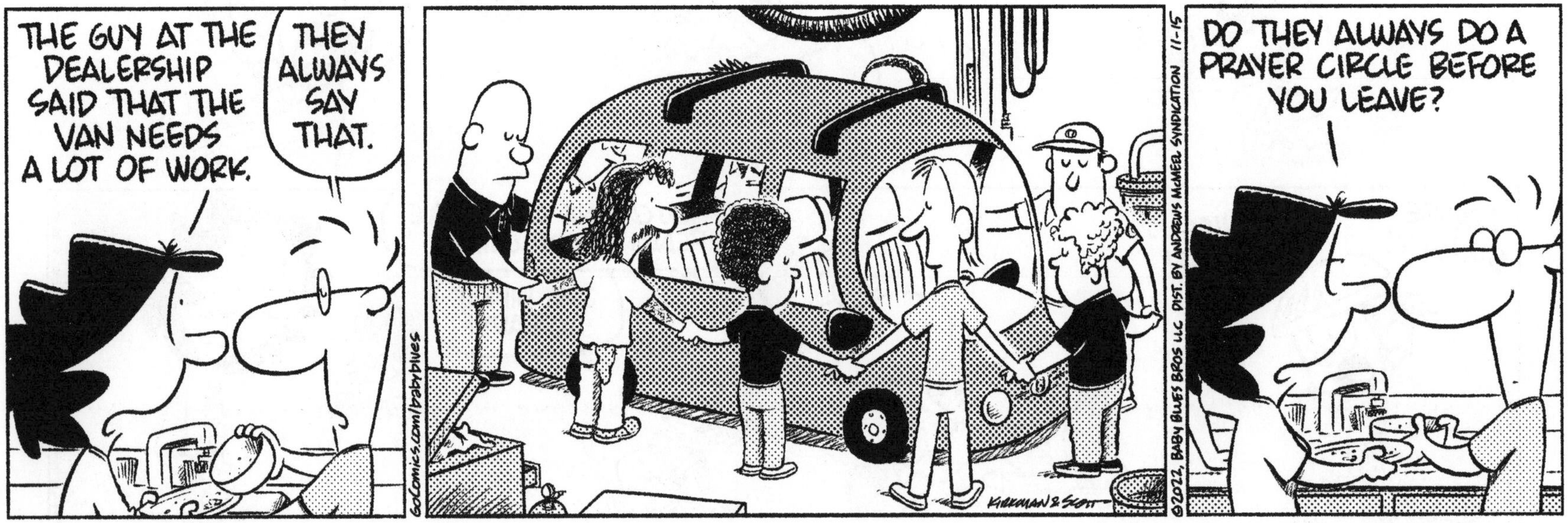
THE GUY AT THE DEALERSHIP SAID THAT THE VAN NEEDS A LOT OF WORK.
THEY ALWAYS SAY THAT.
GoComics.com/babyblues
KIRKMAN & SCOTT
©2022, BABY BLUES BROS LLC DIST. BY ANDREWS McMEEL SYNDICATION 11-15
DO THEY ALWAYS DO A PRAYER CIRCLE BEFORE YOU LEAVE?

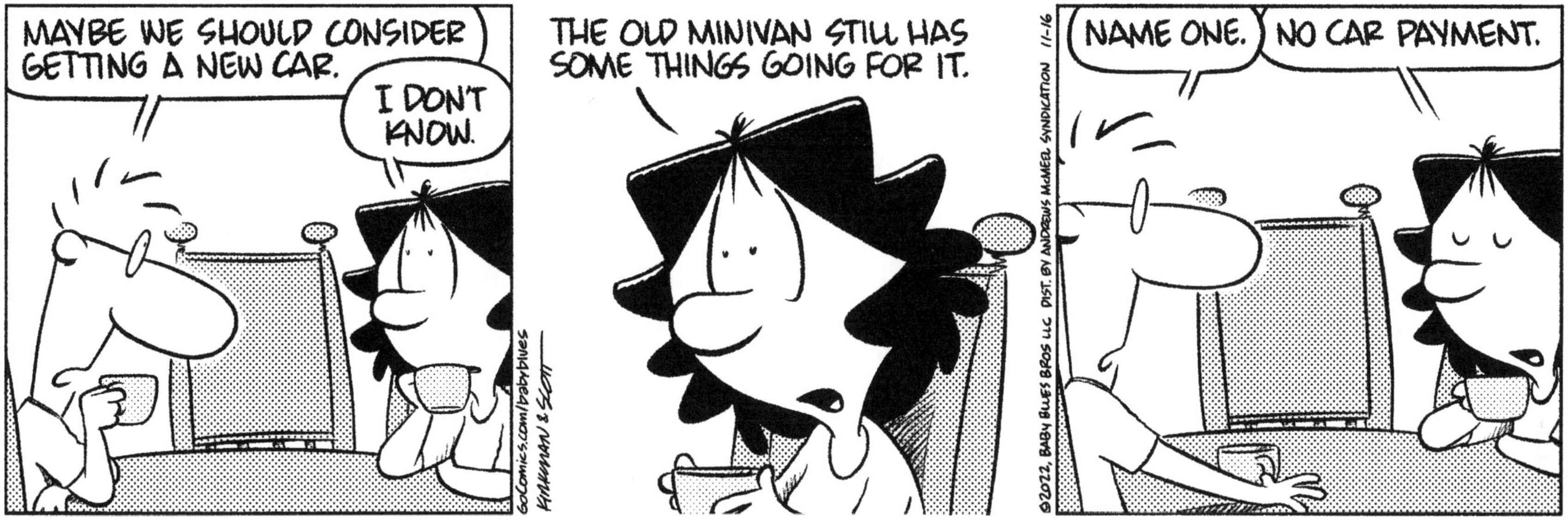
MAYBE WE SHOULD CONSIDER GETTING A NEW CAR.
I DON'T KNOW.
GoComics.com/babyblues
KIRKMAN & SCOTT
THE OLD MINIVAN STILL HAS SOME THINGS GOING FOR IT.
11-16
©2022, BABY BLUES BROS LLC DIST. BY ANDREWS McMEEL SYNDICATION
NAME ONE.
NO CAR PAYMENT.

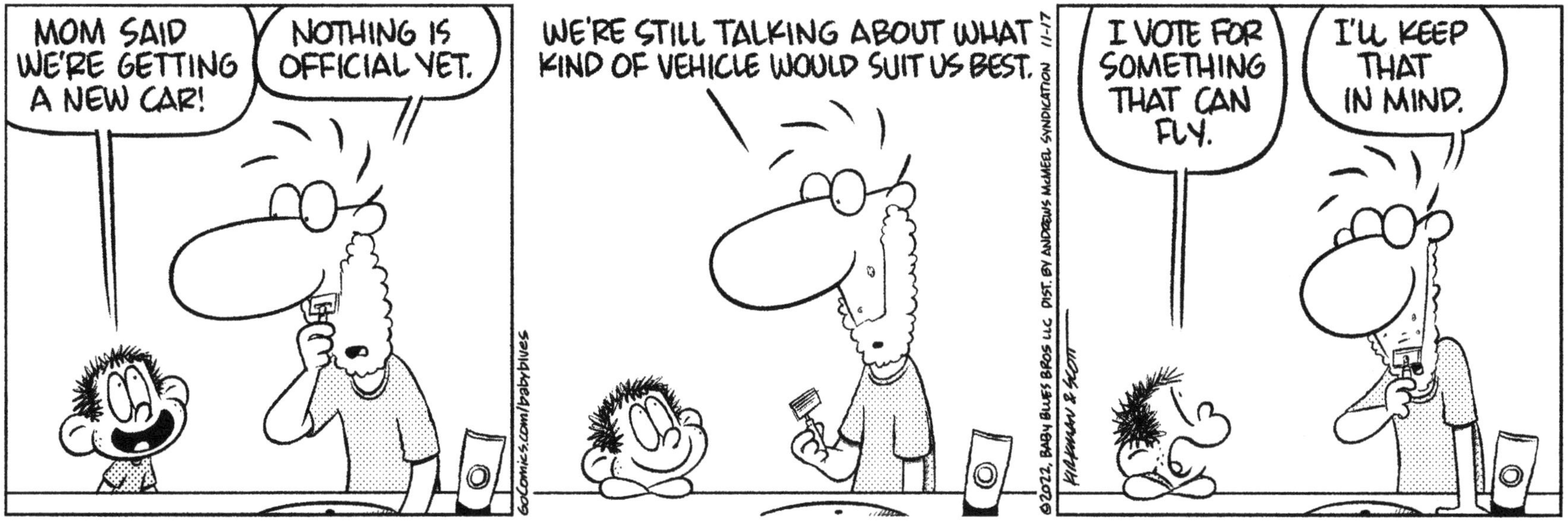
MOM SAID WE'RE GETTING A NEW CAR!
NOTHING IS OFFICIAL YET.
GoComics.com/babyblues
WE'RE STILL TALKING ABOUT WHAT KIND OF VEHICLE WOULD SUIT US BEST.
11-17
©2022, BABY BLUES BROS LLC DIST. BY ANDREWS McMEEL SYNDICATION
KIRKMAN & SCOTT
I VOTE FOR SOMETHING THAT CAN FLY.
I'LL KEEP THAT IN MIND.

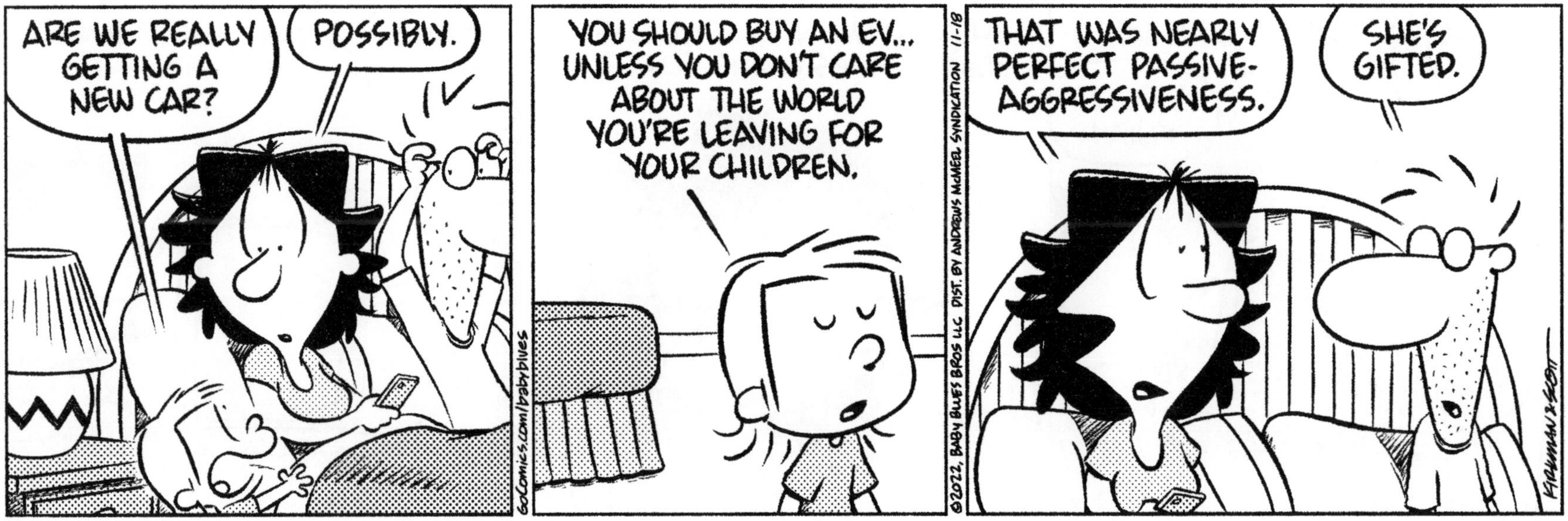

ARE WE REALLY GETTING A NEW CAR?
POSSIBLY.
GoComics.com/babyblues
YOU SHOULD BUY AN EV... UNLESS YOU DON'T CARE ABOUT THE WORLD YOU'RE LEAVING FOR YOUR CHILDREN.
11-18
©2022, BABY BLUES BROS LLC DIST. BY ANDREWS McMEEL SYNDICATION
THAT WAS NEARLY PERFECT PASSIVE-AGGRESSIVENESS.
SHE'S GIFTED.
KIRKMAN & SCOTT

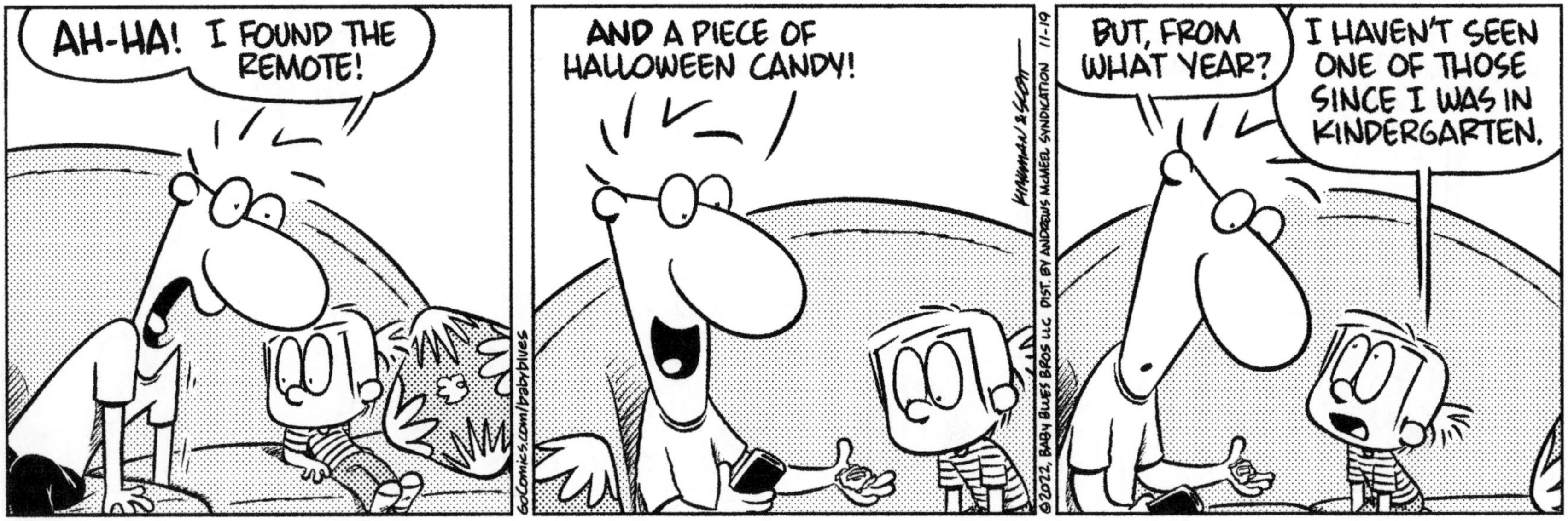

AH-HA! I FOUND THE REMOTE!
GoComics.com/babyblues
AND A PIECE OF HALLOWEEN CANDY!
11-19
KIRKMAN & SCOTT
©2022, BABY BLUES BROS LLC DIST. BY ANDREWS McMEEL SYNDICATION
BUT, FROM WHAT YEAR?
I HAVEN'T SEEN ONE OF THOSE SINCE I WAS IN KINDERGARTEN.

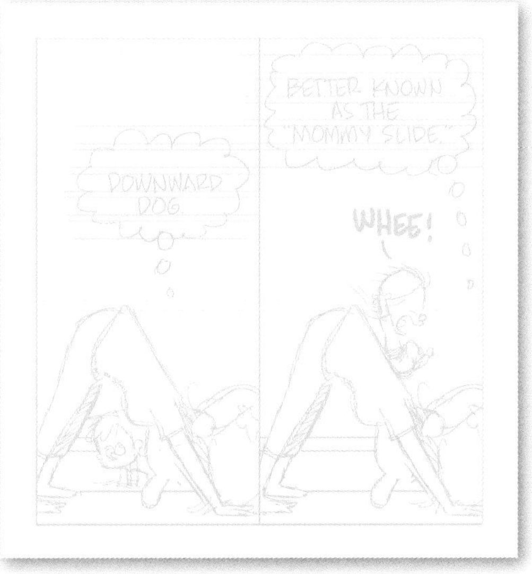
DOWNWARD DOG
BETTER KNOWN AS THE "MOMMY SLIDE."
WHEE!

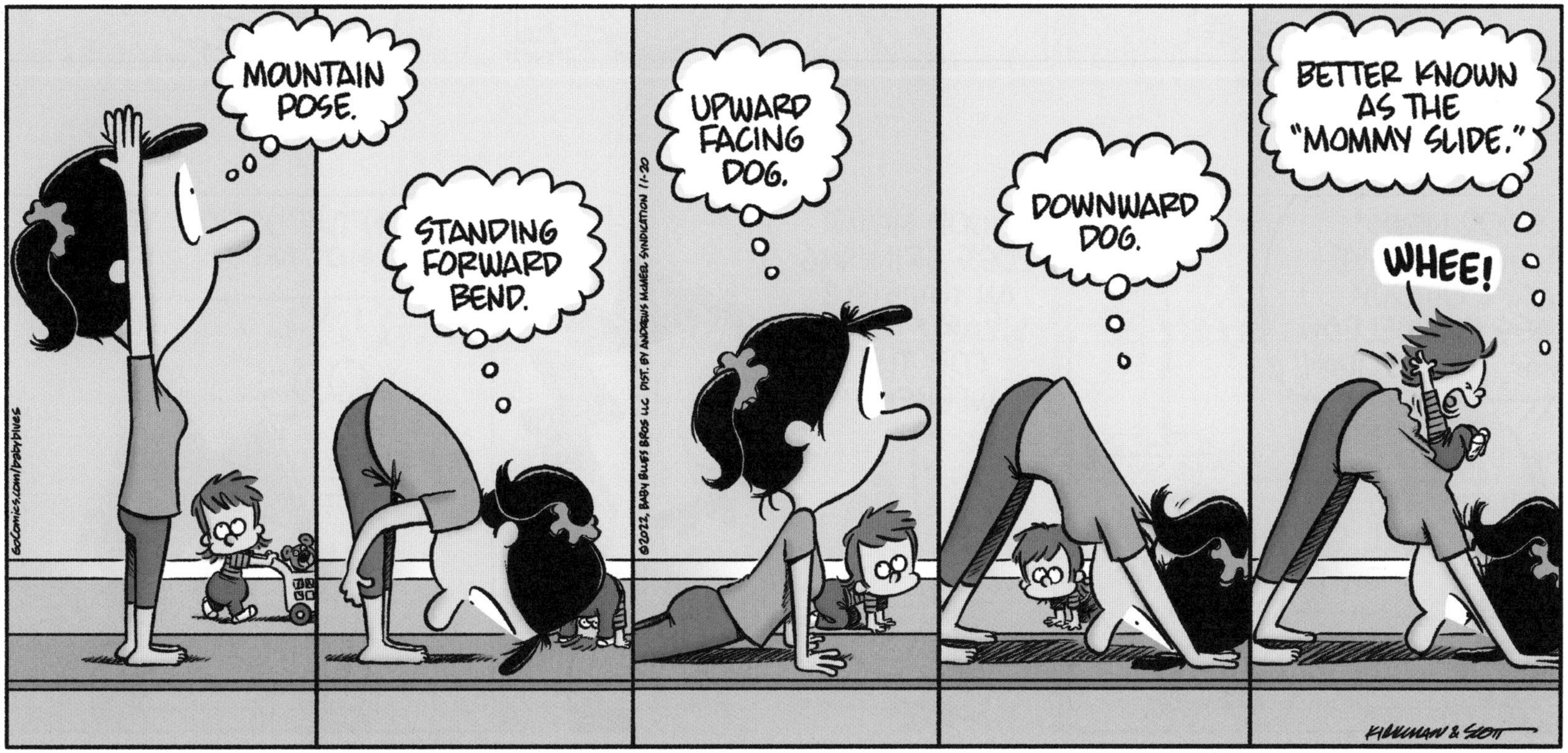
MOUNTAIN POSE.
GoComics.com/babyblues
STANDING FORWARD BEND.
©2022, BABY BLUES BROS LLC DIST. BY ANDREWS MCMEEL SYNDICATION 11-20
UPWARD FACING DOG.
DOWNWARD DOG.
BETTER KNOWN AS THE "MOMMY SLIDE."
WHEE!
KIRKMAN & SCOTT

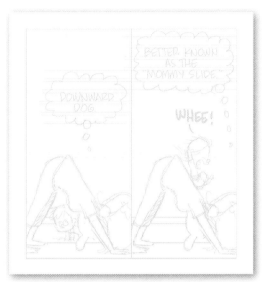

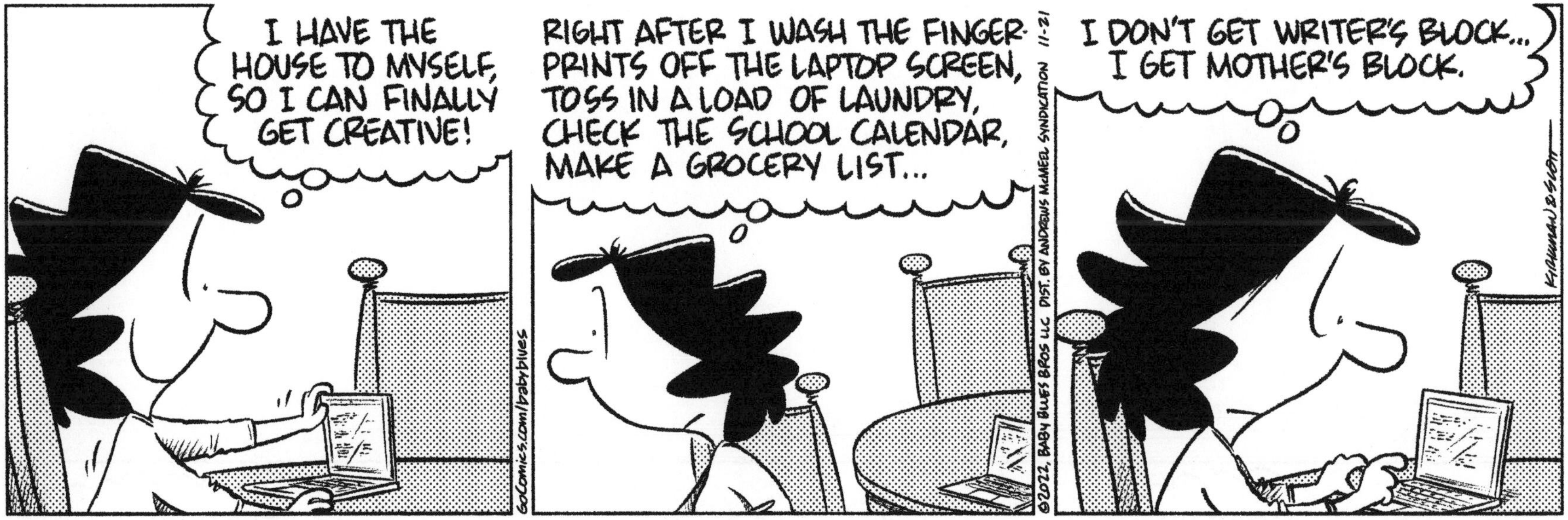
I HAVE THE HOUSE TO MYSELF, SO I CAN FINALLY GET CREATIVE!
GOCOMICS.COM/BABYBLUES
RIGHT AFTER I WASH THE FINGER-PRINTS OFF THE LAPTOP SCREEN, TOSS IN A LOAD OF LAUNDRY, CHECK THE SCHOOL CALENDAR, MAKE A GROCERY LIST...
©2022, BABY BLUES BROS LLC DIST. BY ANDREWS MCMEEL SYNDICATION 11-21
I DON'T GET WRITER'S BLOCK... I GET MOTHER'S BLOCK.
KIRKMAN & SCOTT

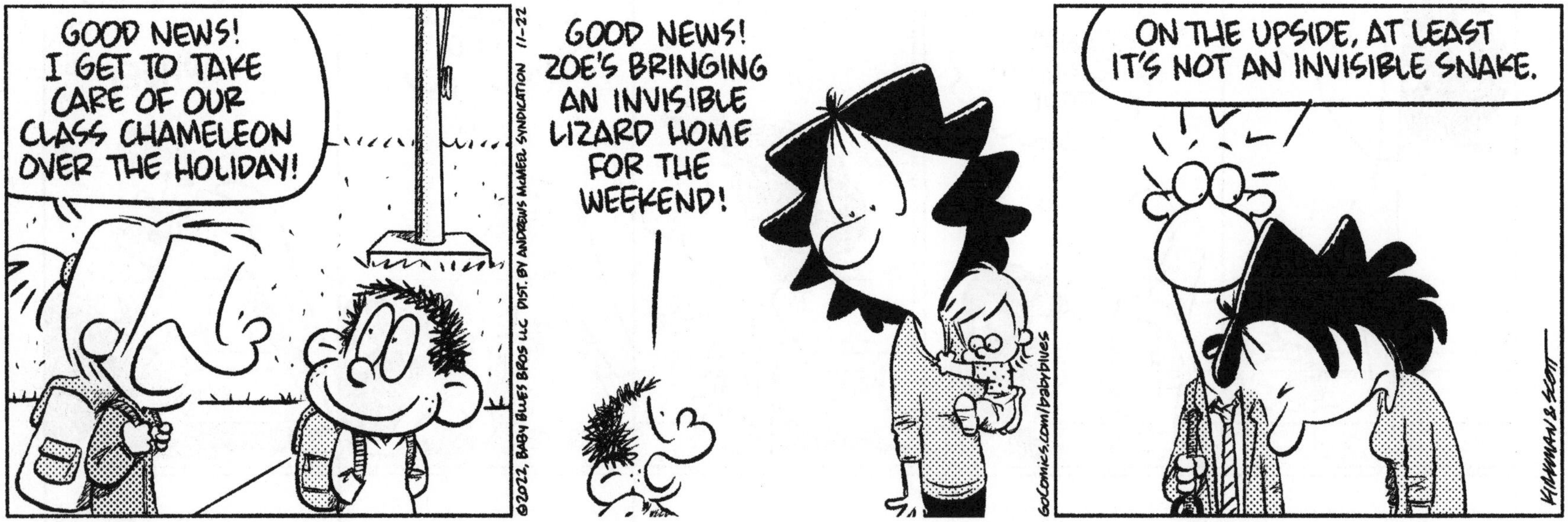
GOOD NEWS! I GET TO TAKE CARE OF OUR CLASS CHAMELEON OVER THE HOLIDAY!
©2022, BABY BLUES BROS LLC DIST. BY ANDREWS MCMEEL SYNDICATION 11-22
GOOD NEWS! ZOE'S BRINGING AN INVISIBLE LIZARD HOME FOR THE WEEKEND!
GOCOMICS.COM/BABYBLUES
ON THE UPSIDE, AT LEAST IT'S NOT AN INVISIBLE SNAKE.
KIRKMAN & SCOTT

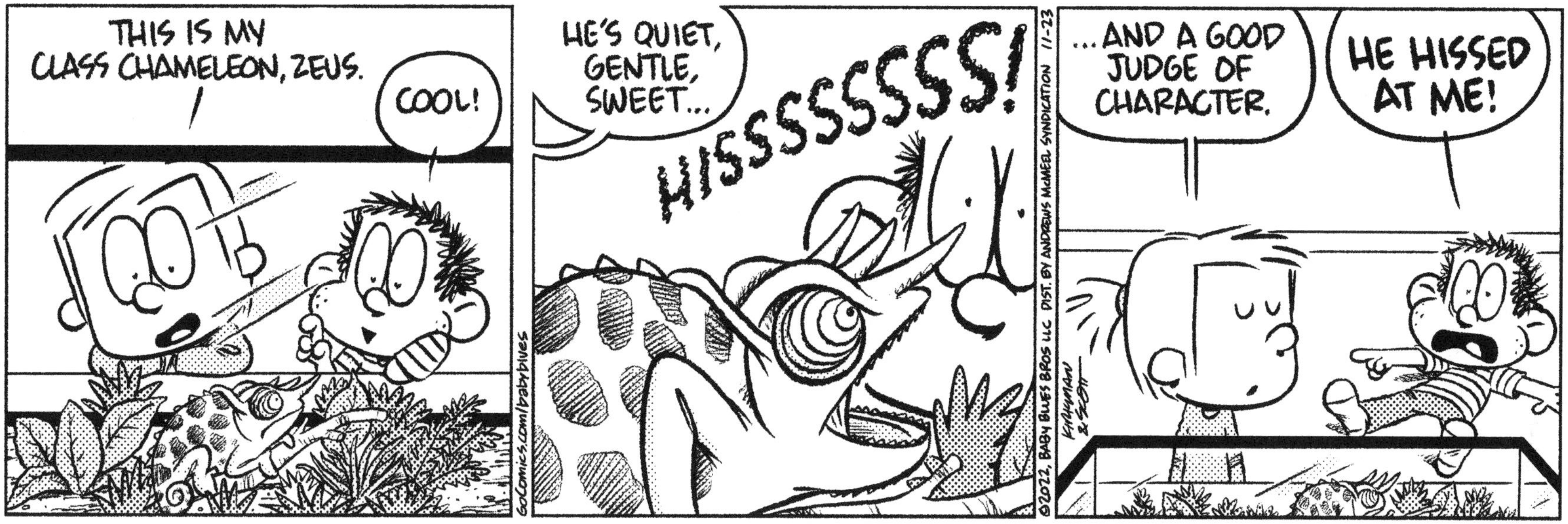
THIS IS MY CLASS CHAMELEON, ZEUS.
COOL!
HE'S QUIET, GENTLE, SWEET...
HISSSSSSSS!
...AND A GOOD JUDGE OF CHARACTER.
HE HISSED AT ME!
GoComics.com/babyblues
©2022, BABY BLUES BROS LLC DIST. BY ANDREWS McMEEL SYNDICATION 11-23
KIRKMAN & SCOTT

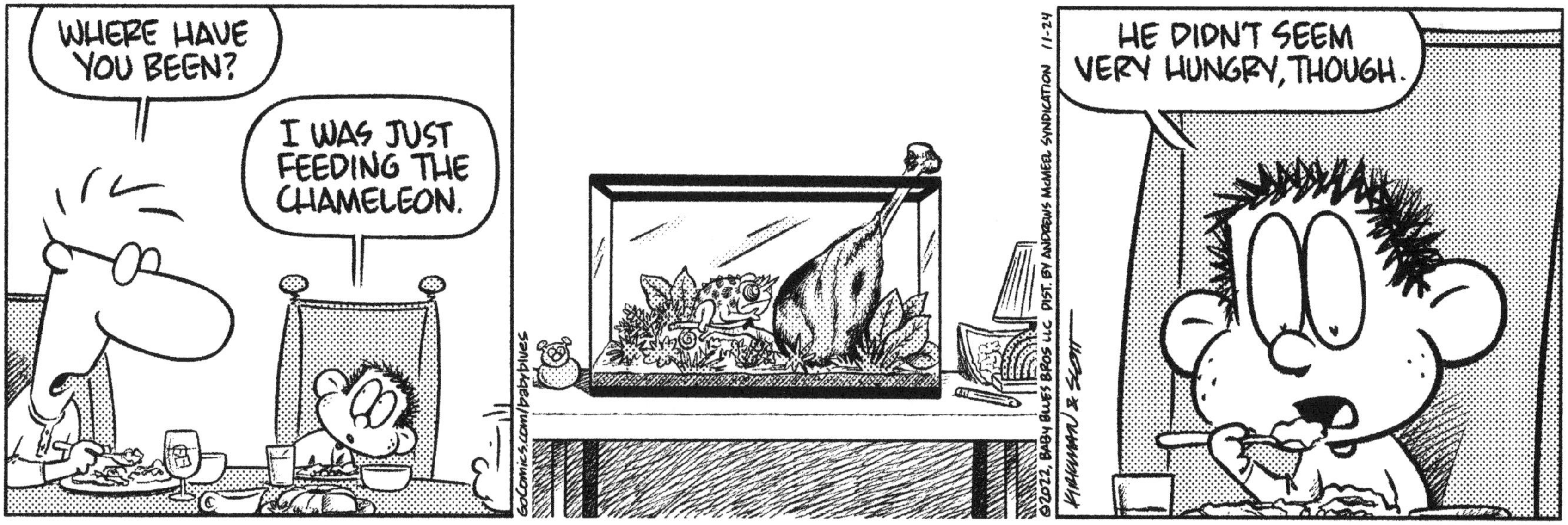
WHERE HAVE YOU BEEN?
I WAS JUST FEEDING THE CHAMELEON.
HE DIDN'T SEEM VERY HUNGRY, THOUGH.
GoComics.com/babyblues
©2022, BABY BLUES BROS LLC DIST. BY ANDREWS McMEEL SYNDICATION 11-24
KIRKMAN & SCOTT

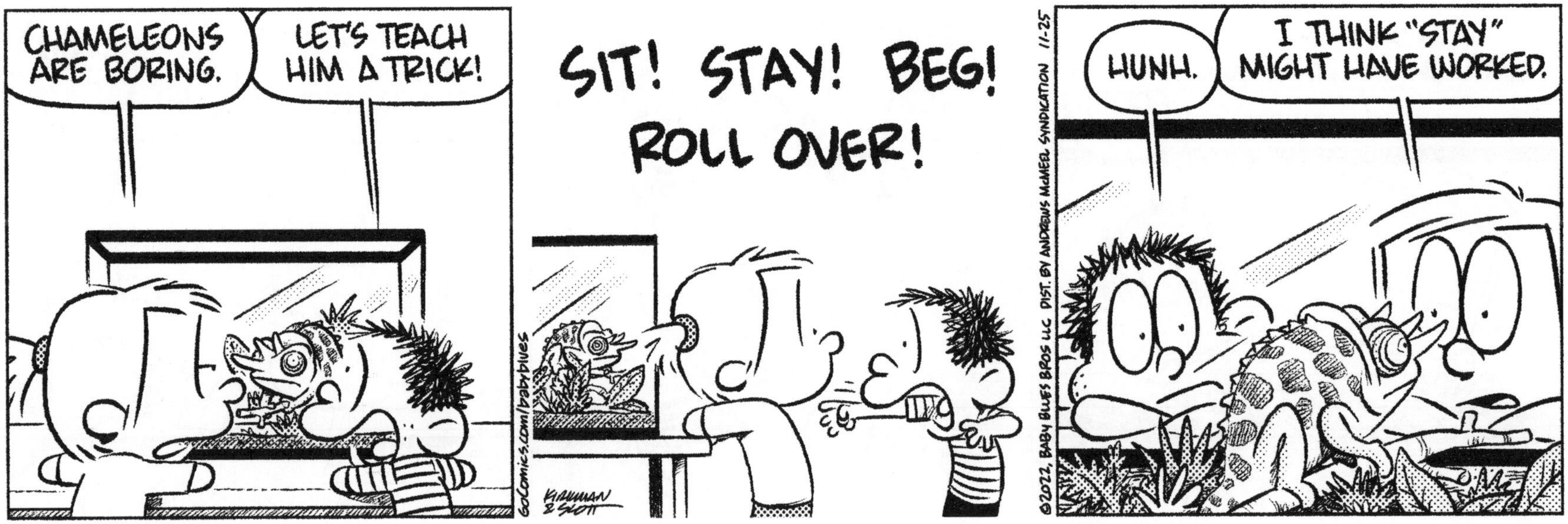
CHAMELEONS ARE BORING.
LET'S TEACH HIM A TRICK!
SIT! STAY! BEG! ROLL OVER!
GoComics.com/babyblues
KIRKMAN & SCOTT
©2022, BABY BLUES BROS LLC DIST. BY ANDREWS McMEEL SYNDICATION 11-25
HUNH.
I THINK "STAY" MIGHT HAVE WORKED.

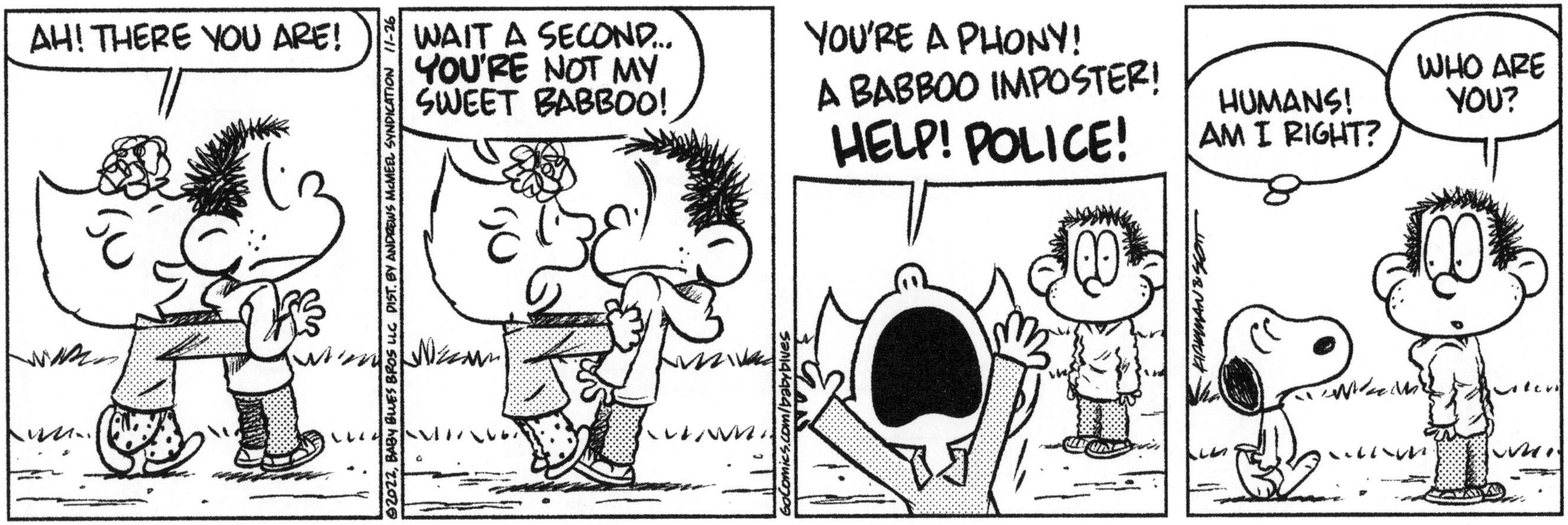
AH! THERE YOU ARE!
©2022, BABY BLUES BROS LLC DIST. BY ANDREWS McMEEL SYNDICATION 11-26
WAIT A SECOND... YOU'RE NOT MY SWEET BABBOO!
YOU'RE A PHONY! A BABBOO IMPOSTER! HELP! POLICE!
GoComics.com/babyblues
HUMANS! AM I RIGHT?
WHO ARE YOU?
KIRKMAN & SCOTT

YOU CAN'T RUIN A PAPER JUST BY DROPPING IT!

DID YOU GET YOUR MATH TEST BACK TODAY?
YES.
DID YOU BRING IT HOME WITH YOU?
YES.
IS IT IN THE HOUSE SOMEWHERE?
YES.
MAY I SEE IT?
NO. I ACCIDENTALLY DROPPED IT. IT'S RUINED.
KIRKMAN & SCOTT
9-18
©2022, BABY BLUES BROS LLC DIST. BY ANDREWS MCMEEL SYNDICATION
YOU CAN'T RUIN A PAPER JUST BY DROPPING IT!
GOCOMICS.COM/BABYBLUES
YOU CAN, IF YOU'RE CAREFUL WHERE YOU DROP IT.

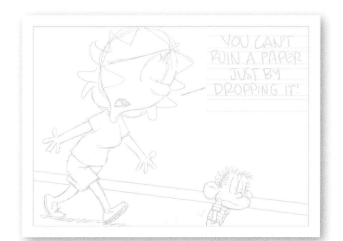

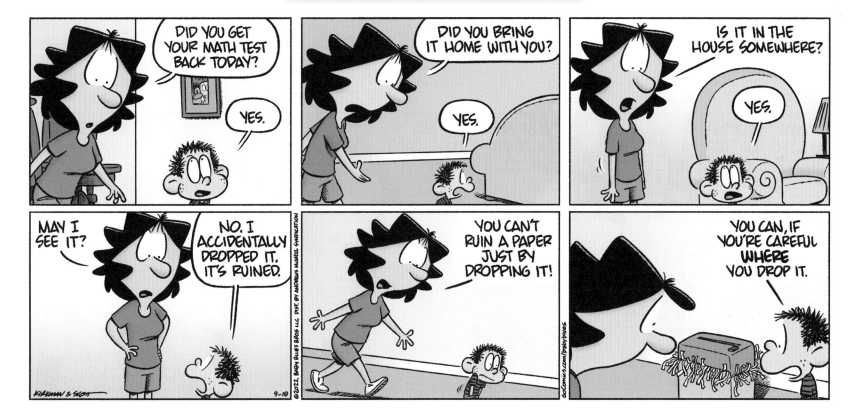

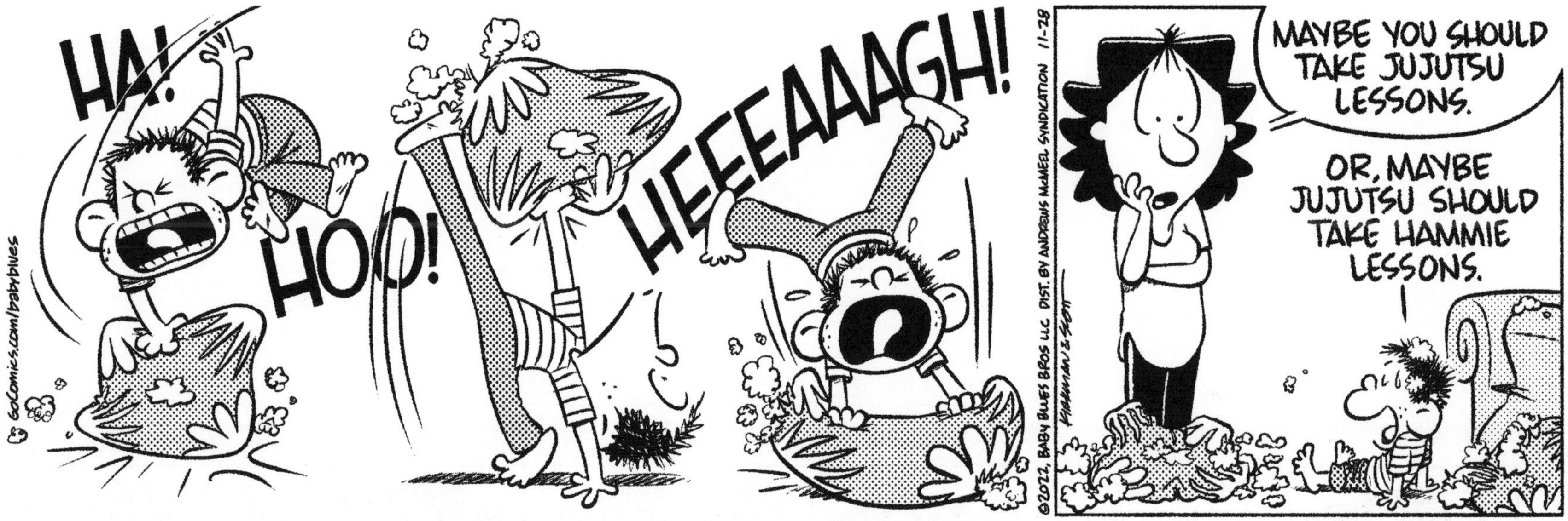
HA!
HOO!
HEEEAAAGH!
MAYBE YOU SHOULD TAKE JUJUTSU LESSONS.
OR, MAYBE JUJUTSU SHOULD TAKE HAMMIE LESSONS.
gocomics.com/babyblues
©2022, BABY BLUES BROS LLC DIST. BY ANDREWS McMEEL SYNDICATION 11-28
KIRKMAN & SCOTT

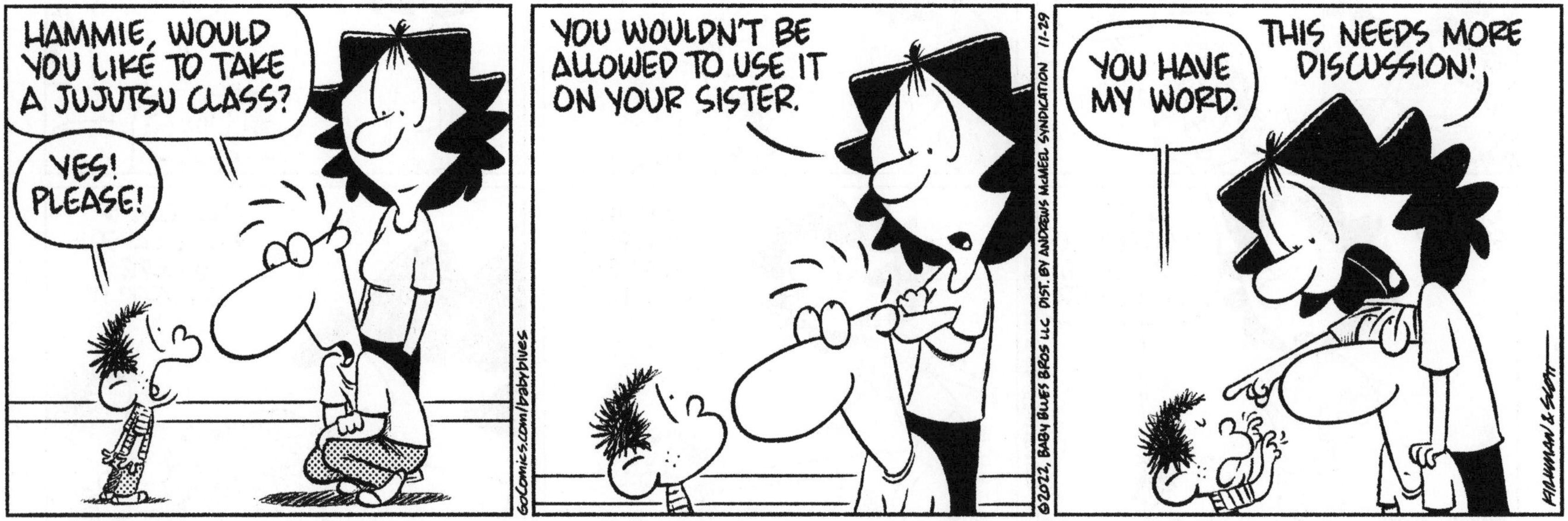
HAMMIE, WOULD YOU LIKE TO TAKE A JUJUTSU CLASS?
YES! PLEASE!
YOU WOULDN'T BE ALLOWED TO USE IT ON YOUR SISTER.
YOU HAVE MY WORD.
THIS NEEDS MORE DISCUSSION!
gocomics.com/babyblues
©2022, BABY BLUES BROS LLC DIST. BY ANDREWS McMEEL SYNDICATION 11-29
KIRKMAN & SCOTT

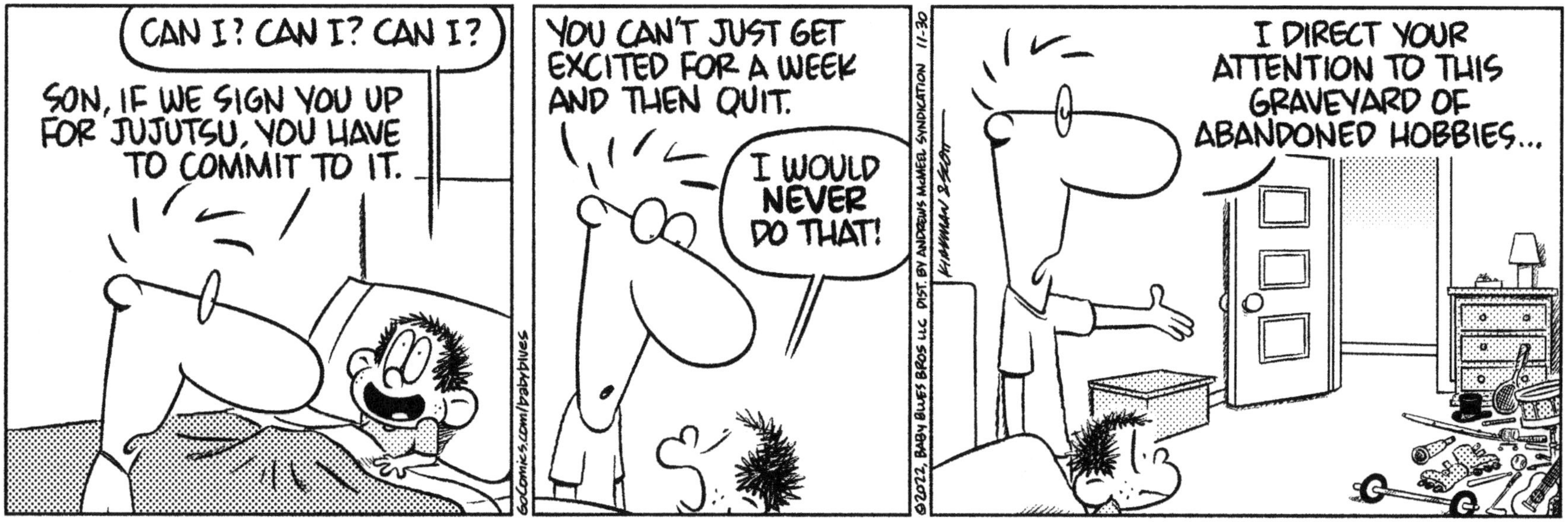
CAN I? CAN I? CAN I?
SON, IF WE SIGN YOU UP FOR JUJUTSU, YOU HAVE TO COMMIT TO IT.
GoComics.com/babyblues
YOU CAN'T JUST GET EXCITED FOR A WEEK AND THEN QUIT.
I WOULD **NEVER** DO THAT!
©2022, BABY BLUES BROS LLC DIST. BY ANDREWS McMEEL SYNDICATION 11-30
KIRKMAN & SCOTT
I DIRECT YOUR ATTENTION TO THIS GRAVEYARD OF ABANDONED HOBBIES...

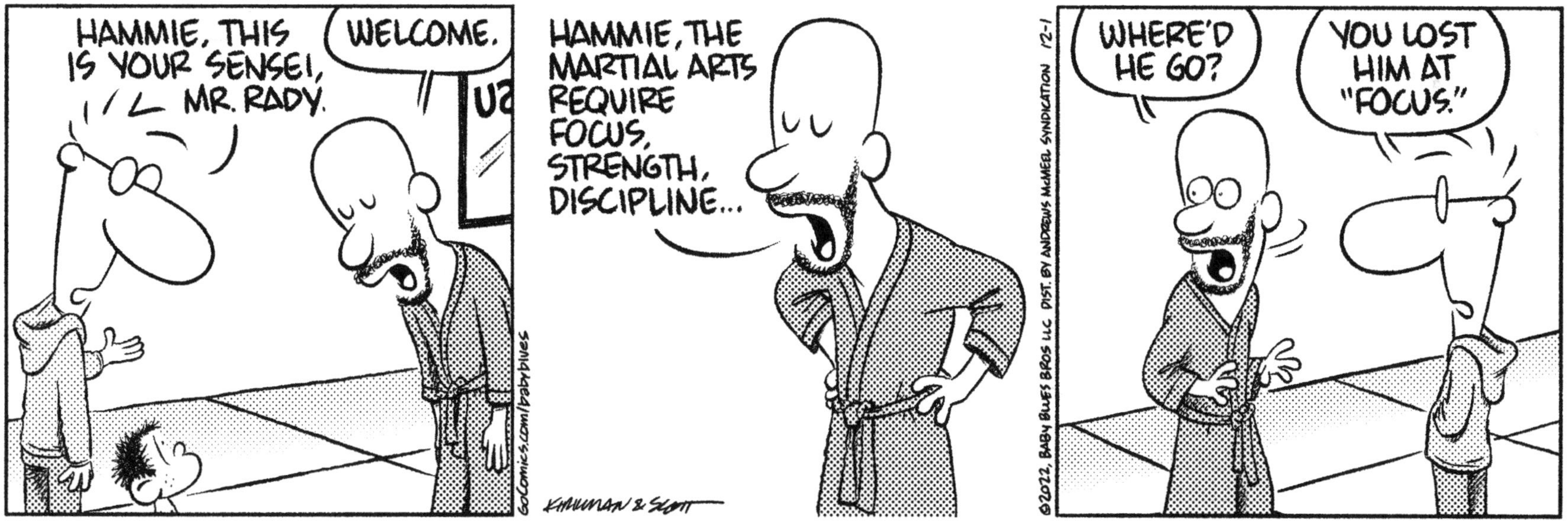
HAMMIE, THIS IS YOUR SENSEI, MR. RADY.
WELCOME.
GoComics.com/babyblues
HAMMIE, THE MARTIAL ARTS REQUIRE FOCUS, STRENGTH, DISCIPLINE...
KIRKMAN & SCOTT
©2022, BABY BLUES BROS LLC DIST. BY ANDREWS McMEEL SYNDICATION 12-1
WHERE'D HE GO?
YOU LOST HIM AT "FOCUS."

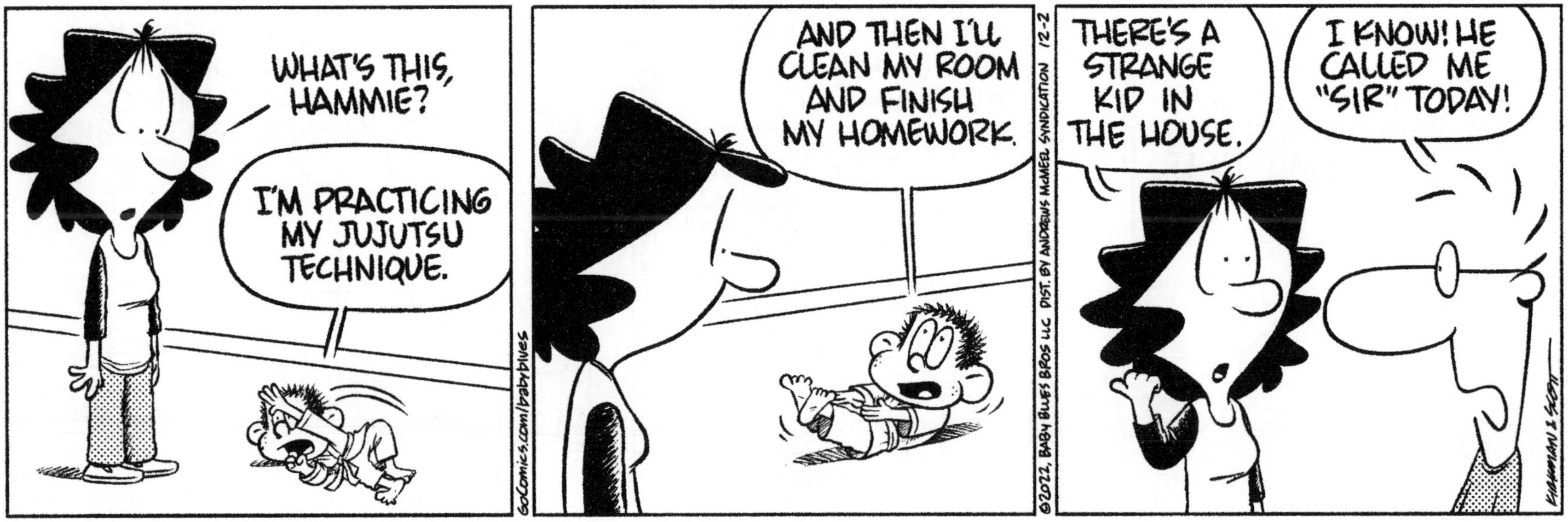
WHAT'S THIS, HAMMIE?
I'M PRACTICING MY JUJUTSU TECHNIQUE.
GoComics.com/babyblues
AND THEN I'LL CLEAN MY ROOM AND FINISH MY HOMEWORK.
©2022, BABY BLUES BROS LLC DIST. BY ANDREWS McMEEL SYNDICATION 12-2
THERE'S A STRANGE KID IN THE HOUSE.
I KNOW! HE CALLED ME "SIR" TODAY!
KIRKMAN & SCOTT

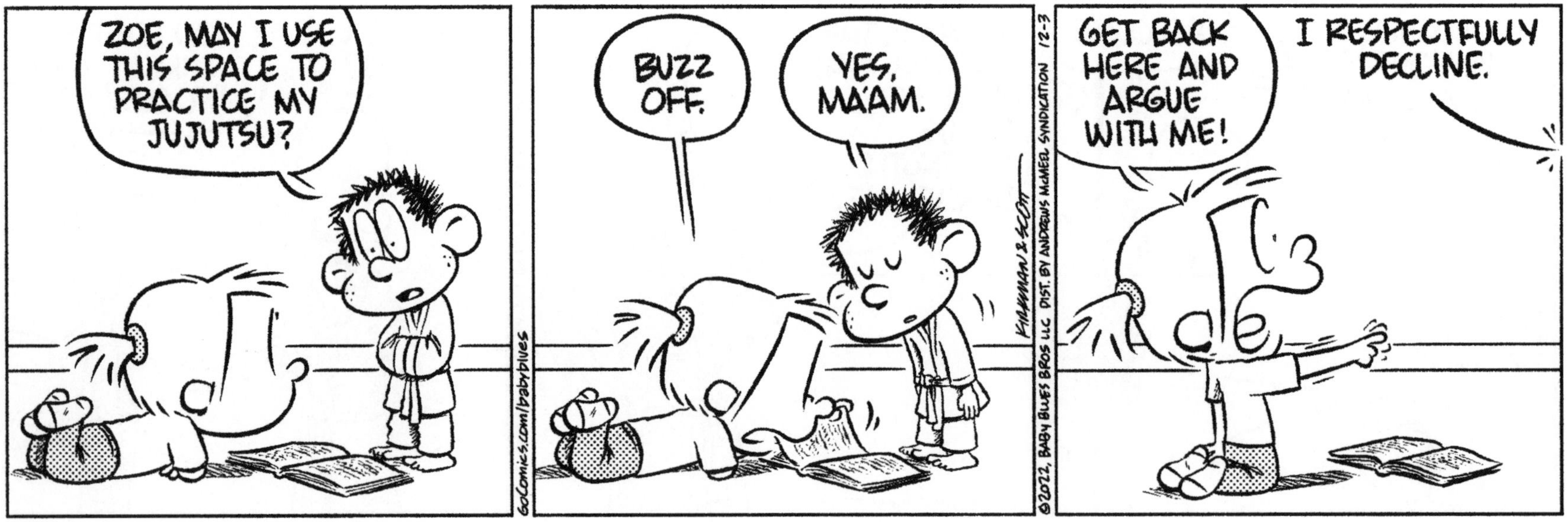
ZOE, MAY I USE THIS SPACE TO PRACTICE MY JUJUTSU?
GoComics.com/babyblues
BUZZ OFF.
YES, MA'AM.
KIRKMAN & SCOTT
©2022, BABY BLUES BROS LLC DIST. BY ANDREWS McMEEL SYNDICATION 12-3
GET BACK HERE AND ARGUE WITH ME!
I RESPECTFULLY DECLINE.

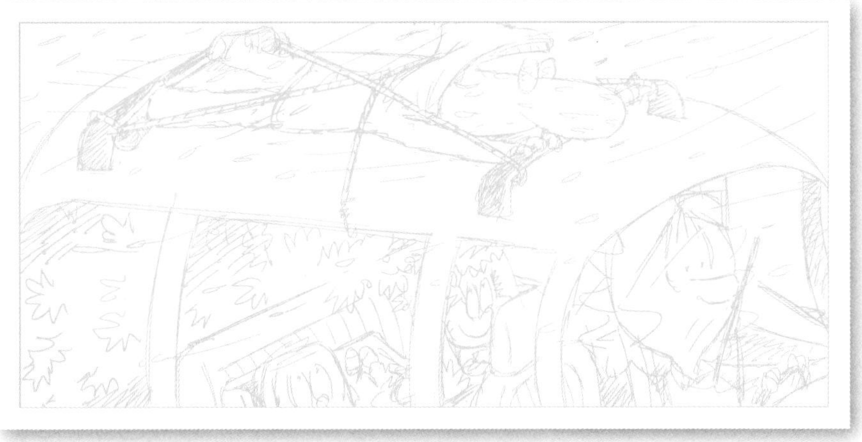

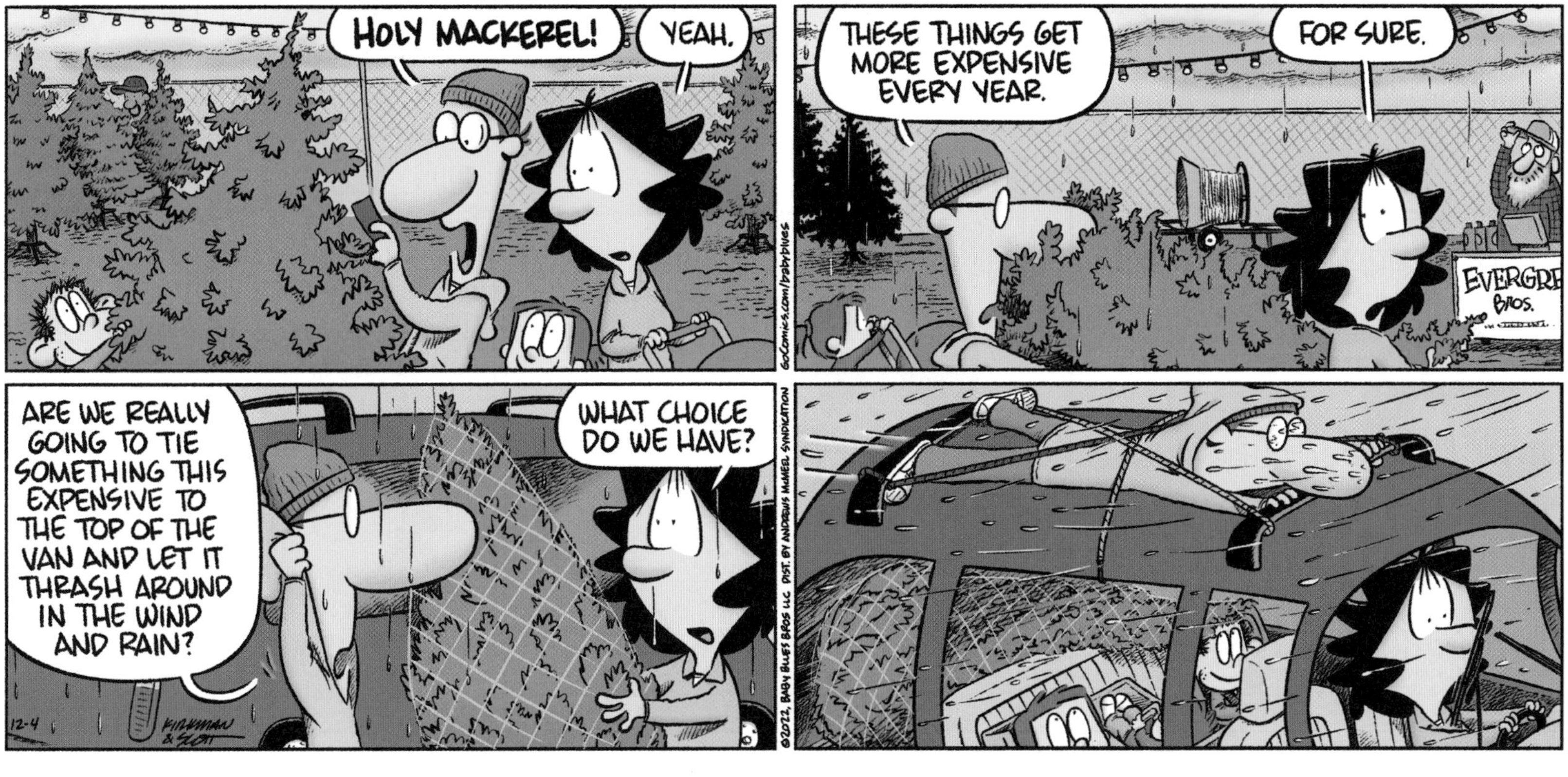

HOLY MACKEREL!
YEAH.
THESE THINGS GET MORE EXPENSIVE EVERY YEAR.
FOR SURE.
EVERGRE BROS.
GoComics.com/babyblues
©2022, BABY BLUES BROS LLC. DIST. BY ANDREWS MCMEEL SYNDICATION
ARE WE REALLY GOING TO TIE SOMETHING THIS EXPENSIVE TO THE TOP OF THE VAN AND LET IT THRASH AROUND IN THE WIND AND RAIN?
WHAT CHOICE DO WE HAVE?
12-4
KIRKMAN & SCOTT

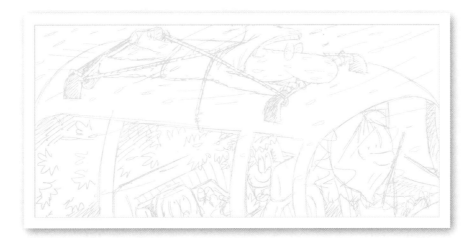

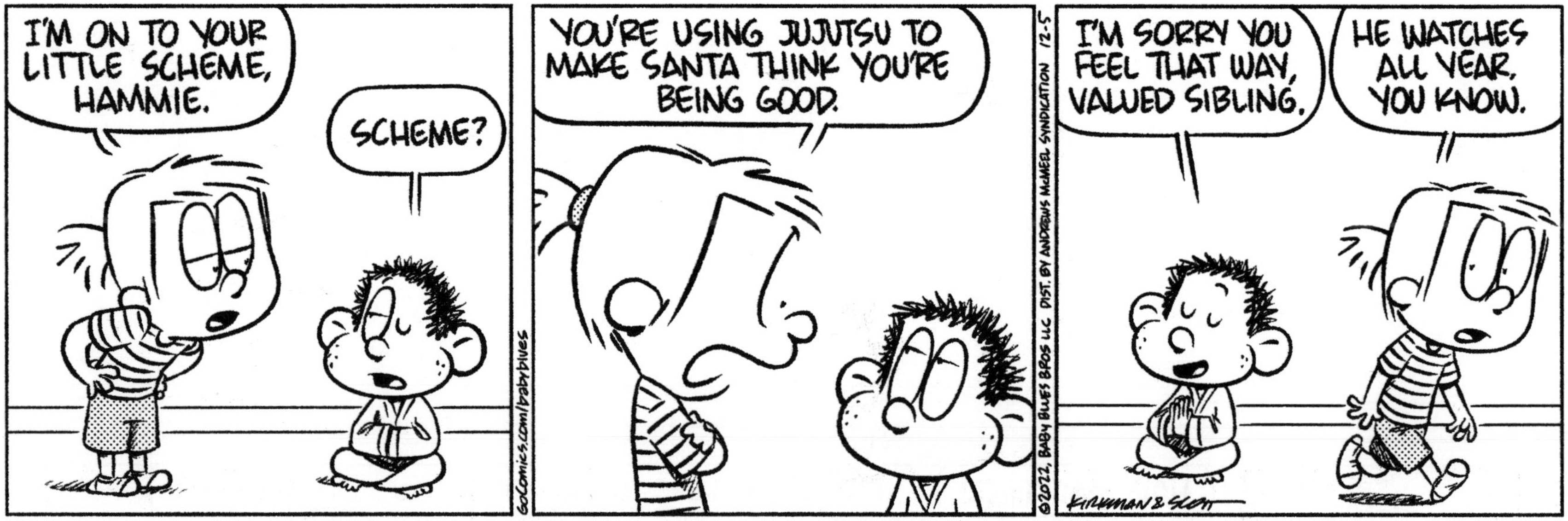
I'M ON TO YOUR LITTLE SCHEME, HAMMIE.
SCHEME?
YOU'RE USING JUJUTSU TO MAKE SANTA THINK YOU'RE BEING GOOD.
I'M SORRY YOU FEEL THAT WAY, VALUED SIBLING.
HE WATCHES ALL YEAR, YOU KNOW.
GoComics.com/babyblues
©2022, BABY BLUES BROS LLC DIST. BY ANDREWS McMEEL SYNDICATION 12-5
KIRKMAN & SCOTT

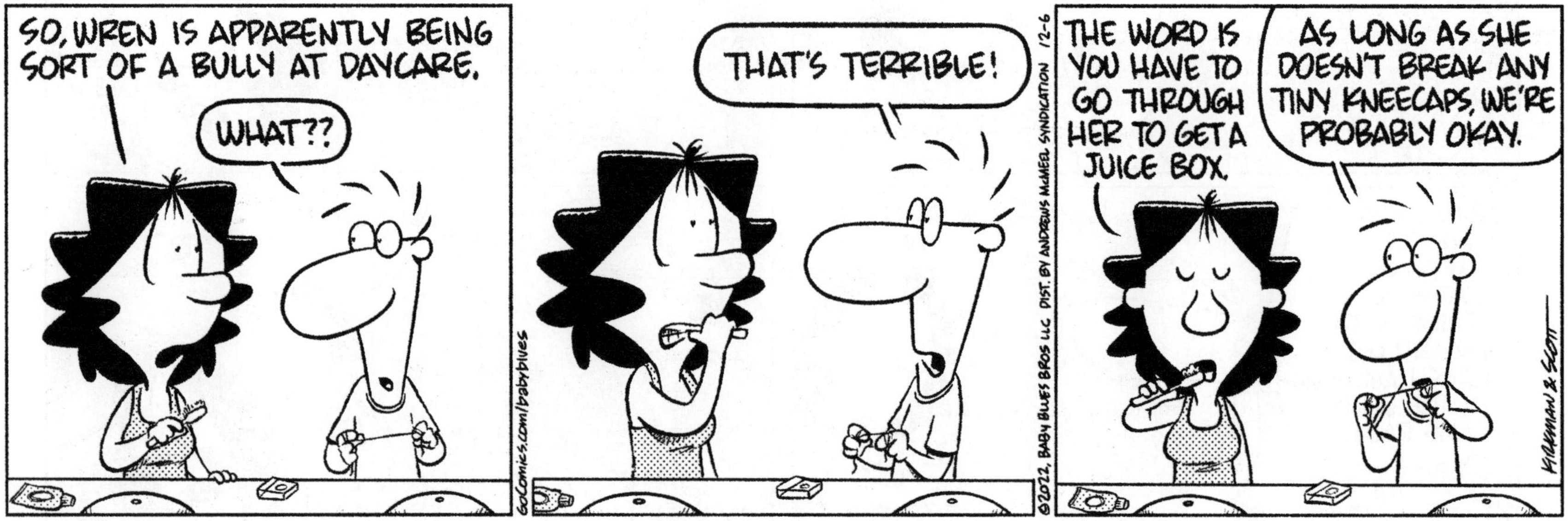
SO, WREN IS APPARENTLY BEING SORT OF A BULLY AT DAYCARE.
WHAT??
THAT'S TERRIBLE!
THE WORD IS YOU HAVE TO GO THROUGH HER TO GET A JUICE BOX.
AS LONG AS SHE DOESN'T BREAK ANY TINY KNEECAPS, WE'RE PROBABLY OKAY.
GoComics.com/babyblues
©2022, BABY BLUES BROS LLC DIST. BY ANDREWS McMEEL SYNDICATION 12-6
KIRKMAN & SCOTT

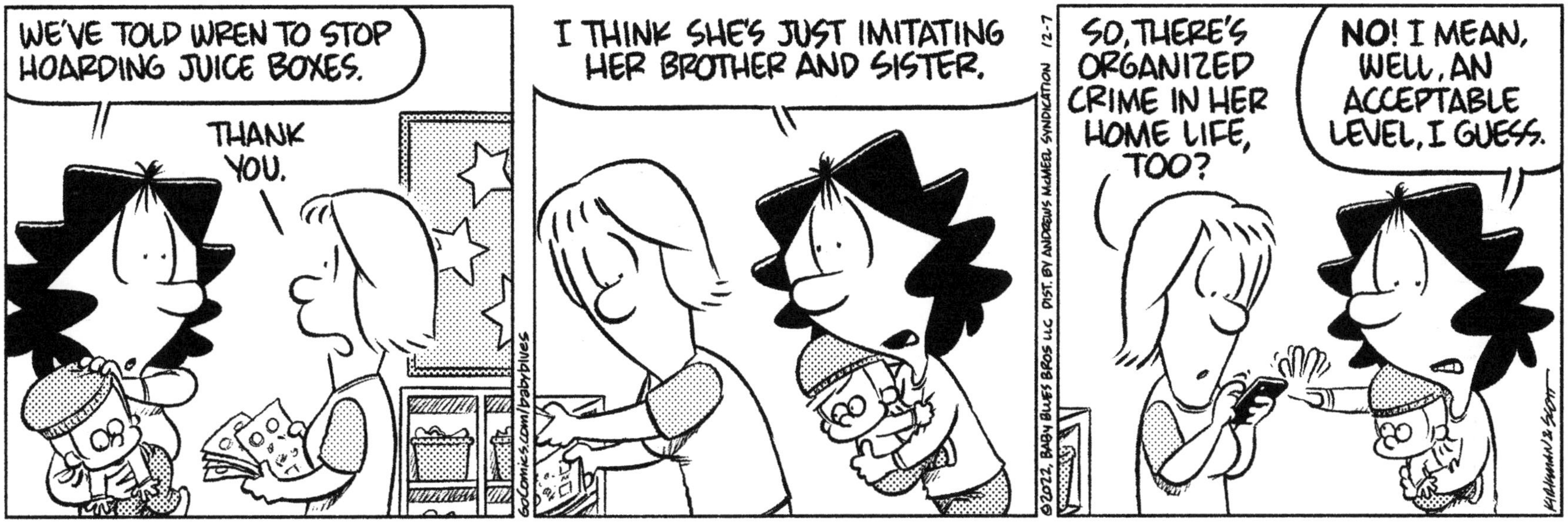
WE'VE TOLD WREN TO STOP HOARDING JUICE BOXES.
THANK YOU.
GoComics.com/babyblues
I THINK SHE'S JUST IMITATING HER BROTHER AND SISTER.
12-7
©2022, BABY BLUES BROS LLC DIST. BY ANDREWS McMEEL SYNDICATION
SO, THERE'S ORGANIZED CRIME IN HER HOME LIFE, TOO?
NO! I MEAN, WELL, AN ACCEPTABLE LEVEL, I GUESS.

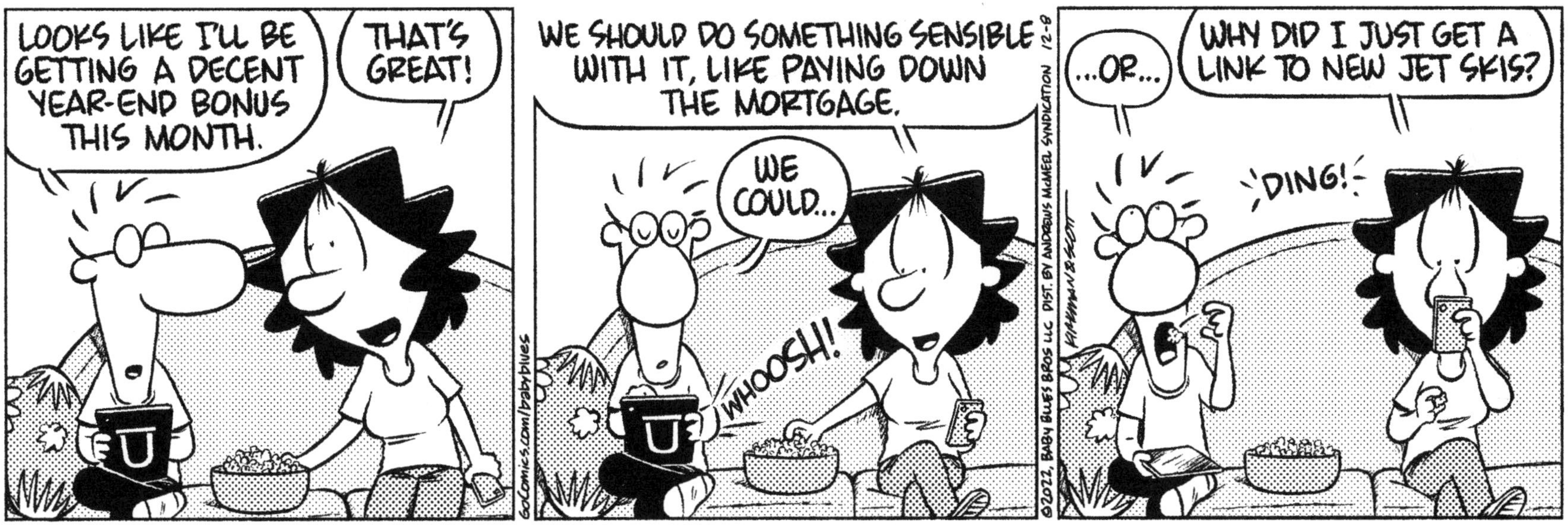
LOOKS LIKE I'LL BE GETTING A DECENT YEAR-END BONUS THIS MONTH.
THAT'S GREAT!
GoComics.com/babyblues
WE SHOULD DO SOMETHING SENSIBLE WITH IT, LIKE PAYING DOWN THE MORTGAGE.
WE COULD...
WHOOSH!
12-8
©2022, BABY BLUES BROS LLC DIST. BY ANDREWS McMEEL SYNDICATION
...OR...
WHY DID I JUST GET A LINK TO NEW JET SKIS?
DING!

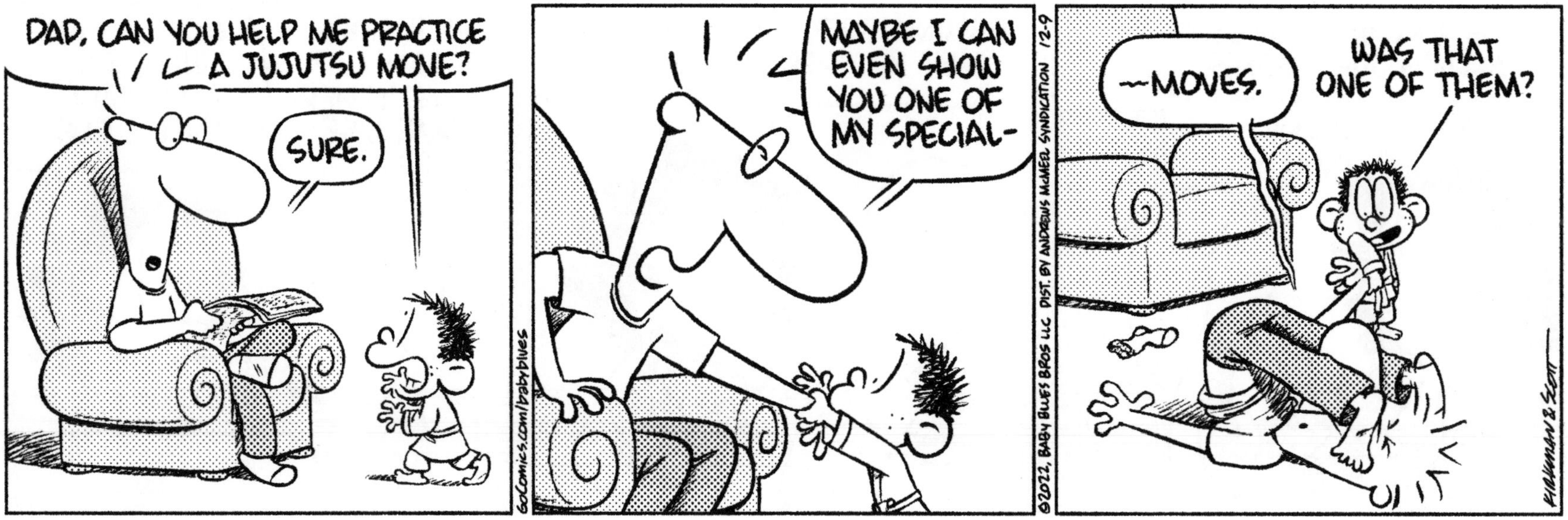
DAD, CAN YOU HELP ME PRACTICE A JUJUTSU MOVE?
SURE.
GoComics.com/babyblues
MAYBE I CAN EVEN SHOW YOU ONE OF MY SPECIAL-
©2022, BABY BLUES BROS LLC DIST. BY ANDREWS McMEEL SYNDICATION 12-9
--MOVES.
WAS THAT ONE OF THEM?
KIRKMAN & SCOTT

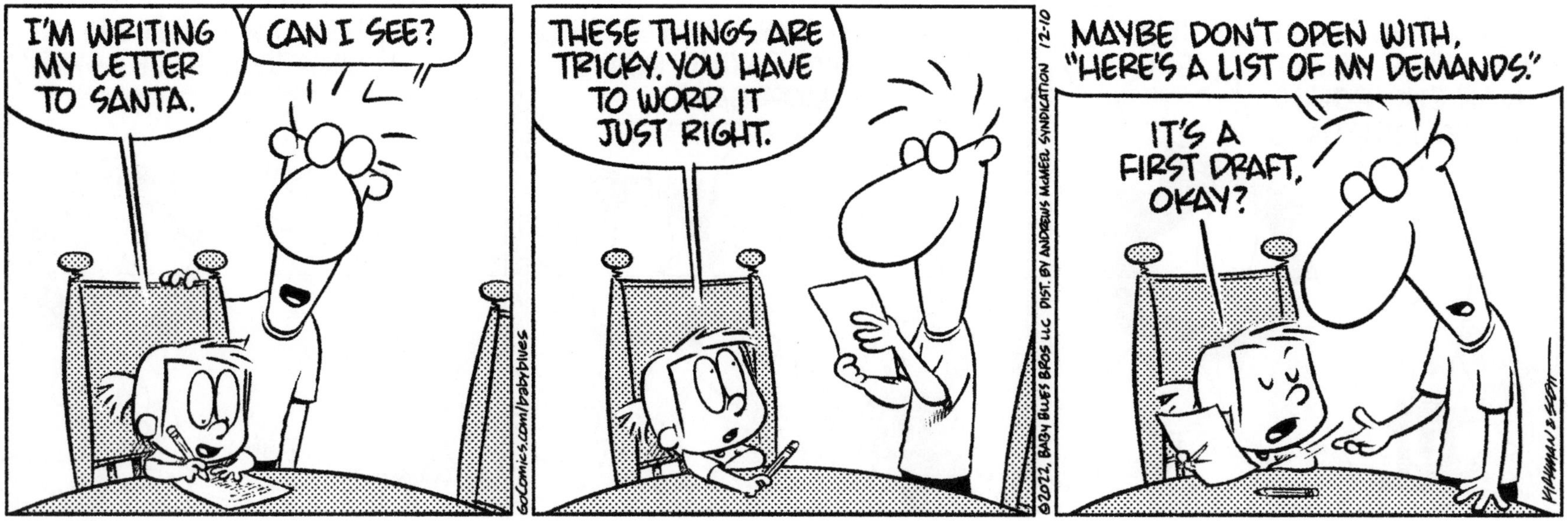
I'M WRITING MY LETTER TO SANTA.
CAN I SEE?
GoComics.com/babyblues
THESE THINGS ARE TRICKY. YOU HAVE TO WORD IT JUST RIGHT.
©2022, BABY BLUES BROS LLC DIST. BY ANDREWS McMEEL SYNDICATION 12-10
MAYBE DON'T OPEN WITH, "HERE'S A LIST OF MY DEMANDS."
IT'S A FIRST DRAFT, OKAY?
KIRKMAN & SCOTT

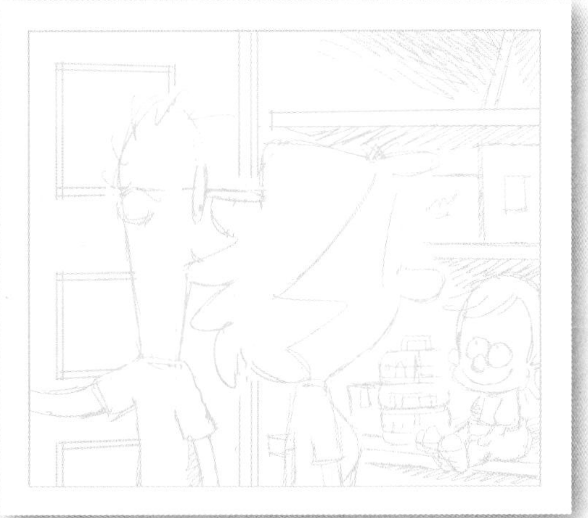

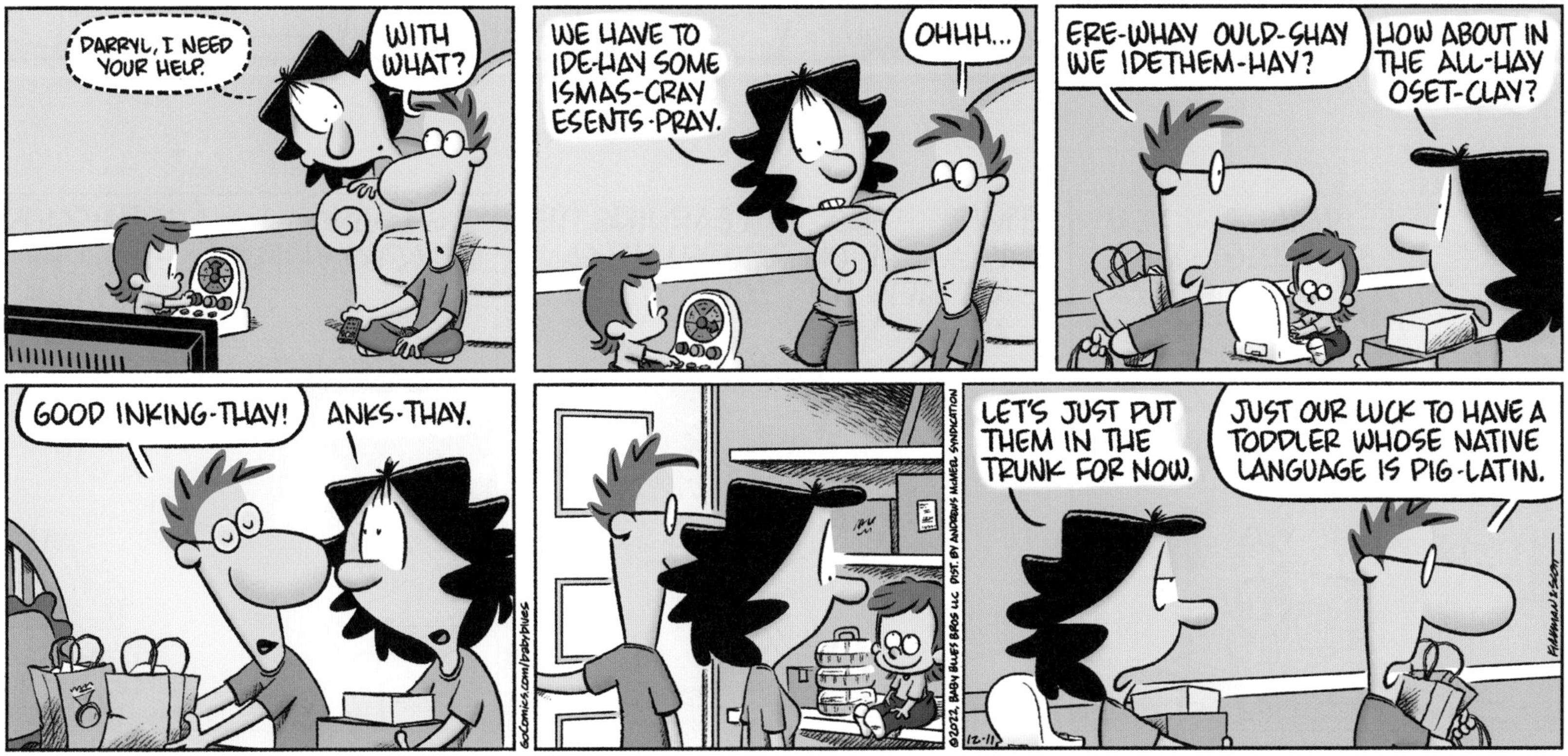
DARRYL, I NEED YOUR HELP.
WITH WHAT?
WE HAVE TO IDE-HAY SOME ISMAS-CRAY ESENTS-PRAY.
OHHH...
ERE-WHAY OULD-SHAY WE IDETHEM-HAY?
HOW ABOUT IN THE ALL-HAY OSET-CLAY?
GOOD INKING-THAY!
ANKS-THAY.
GoComics.com/babyblues
©2022, BABY BLUES BROS LLC DIST. BY ANDREWS MCMEEL SYNDICATION
12-11
LET'S JUST PUT THEM IN THE TRUNK FOR NOW.
JUST OUR LUCK TO HAVE A TODDLER WHOSE NATIVE LANGUAGE IS PIG-LATIN.
KIRKMAN & SCOTT

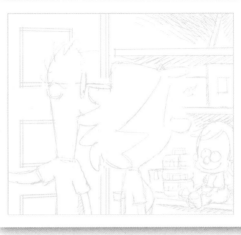

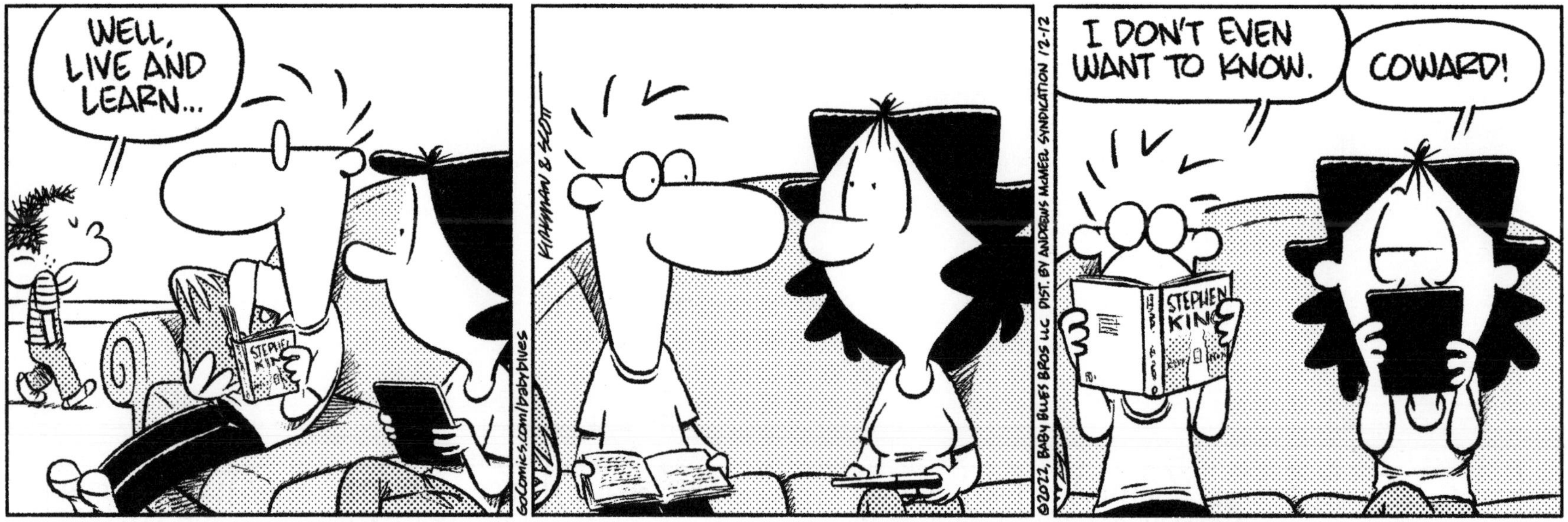
WELL, LIVE AND LEARN...
KIRKMAN & SCOTT
GoComics.com/babyblues
©2022, BABY BLUES BROS LLC DIST. BY ANDREWS McMEEL SYNDICATION 12-12
STEPHEN KING
I DON'T EVEN WANT TO KNOW.
COWARD!

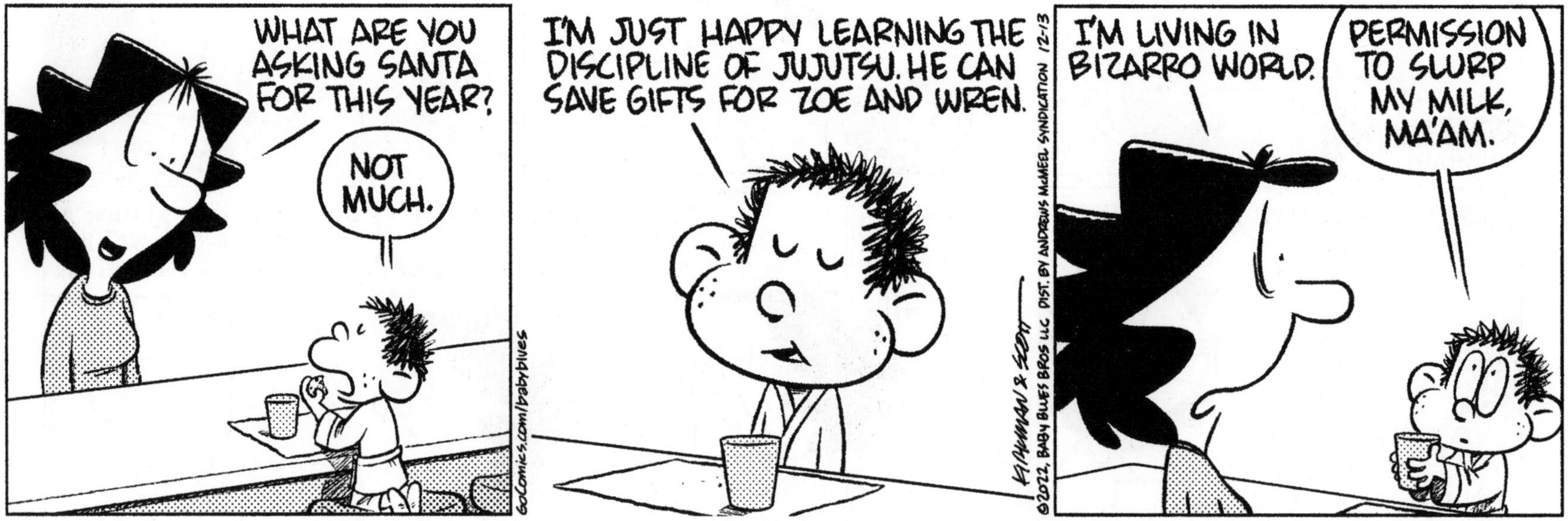
WHAT ARE YOU ASKING SANTA FOR THIS YEAR?
NOT MUCH.
GoComics.com/babyblues
I'M JUST HAPPY LEARNING THE DISCIPLINE OF JUJUTSU. HE CAN SAVE GIFTS FOR ZOE AND WREN.
KIRKMAN & SCOTT
©2022, BABY BLUES BROS LLC DIST. BY ANDREWS McMEEL SYNDICATION 12-13
I'M LIVING IN BIZARRO WORLD.
PERMISSION TO SLURP MY MILK, MA'AM.

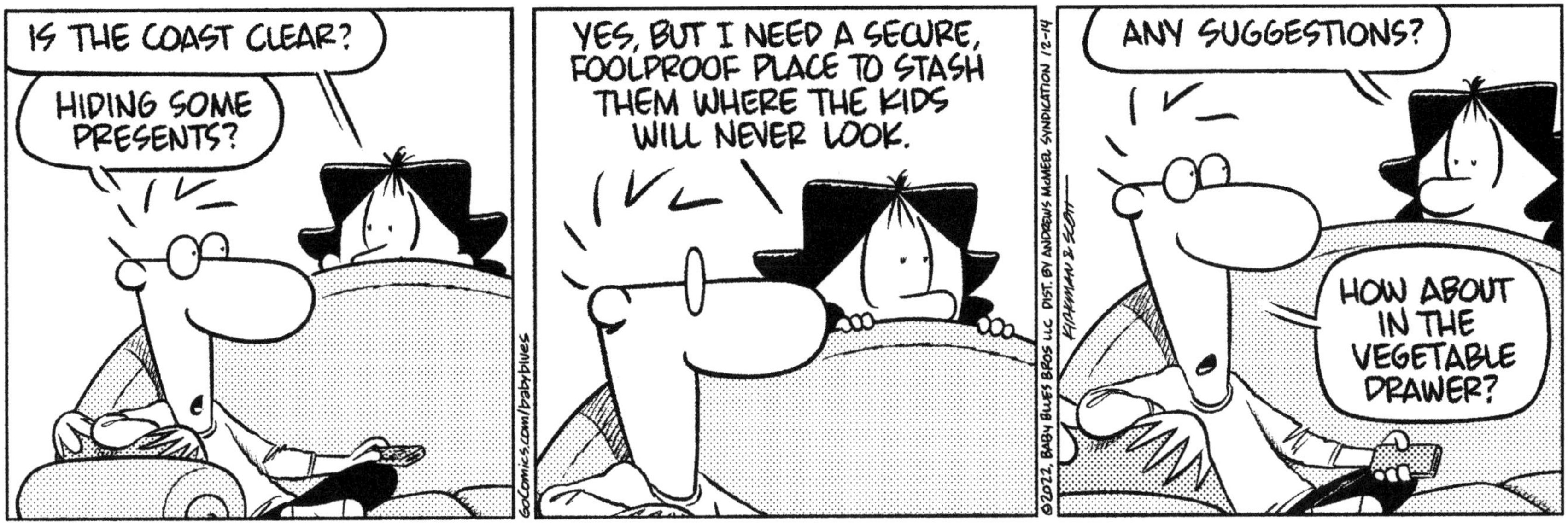
HIDING SOME PRESENTS?
IS THE COAST CLEAR?
YES, BUT I NEED A SECURE, FOOLPROOF PLACE TO STASH THEM WHERE THE KIDS WILL NEVER LOOK.
ANY SUGGESTIONS?
HOW ABOUT IN THE VEGETABLE DRAWER?
GoComics.com/babyblues
©2022, BABY BLUES BROS LLC DIST. BY ANDREWS McMEEL SYNDICATION 12-14
KIRKMAN & SCOTT

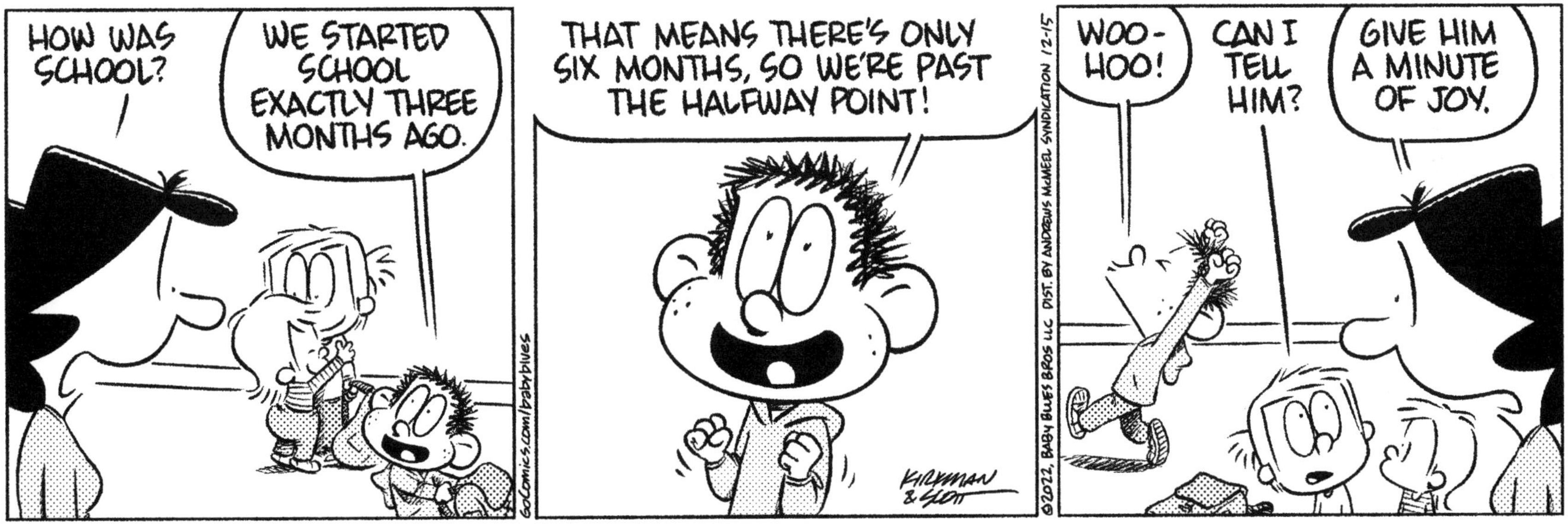
HOW WAS SCHOOL?
WE STARTED SCHOOL EXACTLY THREE MONTHS AGO.
THAT MEANS THERE'S ONLY SIX MONTHS, SO WE'RE PAST THE HALFWAY POINT!
WOO-HOO!
CAN I TELL HIM?
GIVE HIM A MINUTE OF JOY.
GoComics.com/babyblues
©2022, BABY BLUES BROS LLC DIST. BY ANDREWS McMEEL SYNDICATION 12-15
KIRKMAN & SCOTT

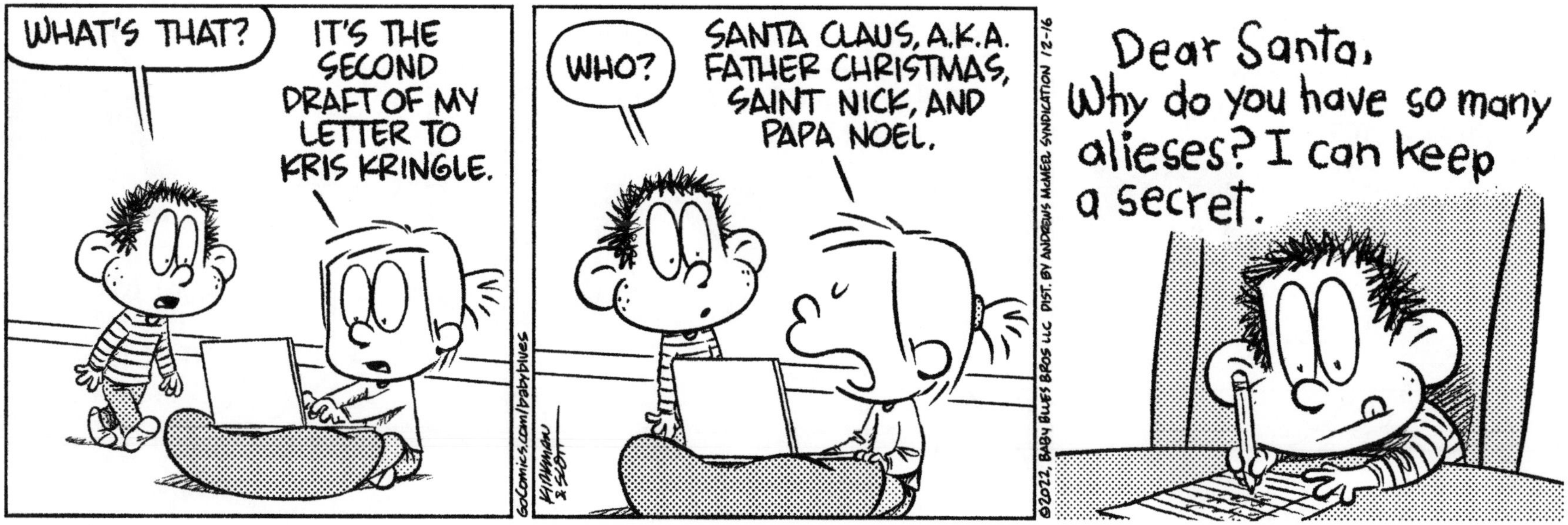
WHAT'S THAT?
IT'S THE SECOND DRAFT OF MY LETTER TO KRIS KRINGLE.
GoComics.com/babyblues
WHO?
SANTA CLAUS, A.K.A. FATHER CHRISTMAS, SAINT NICK, AND PAPA NOEL.
©2022, BABY BLUES BROS LLC DIST. BY ANDREWS McMEEL SYNDICATION 12-16
Dear Santa,
Why do you have so many alieses? I can keep a secret.

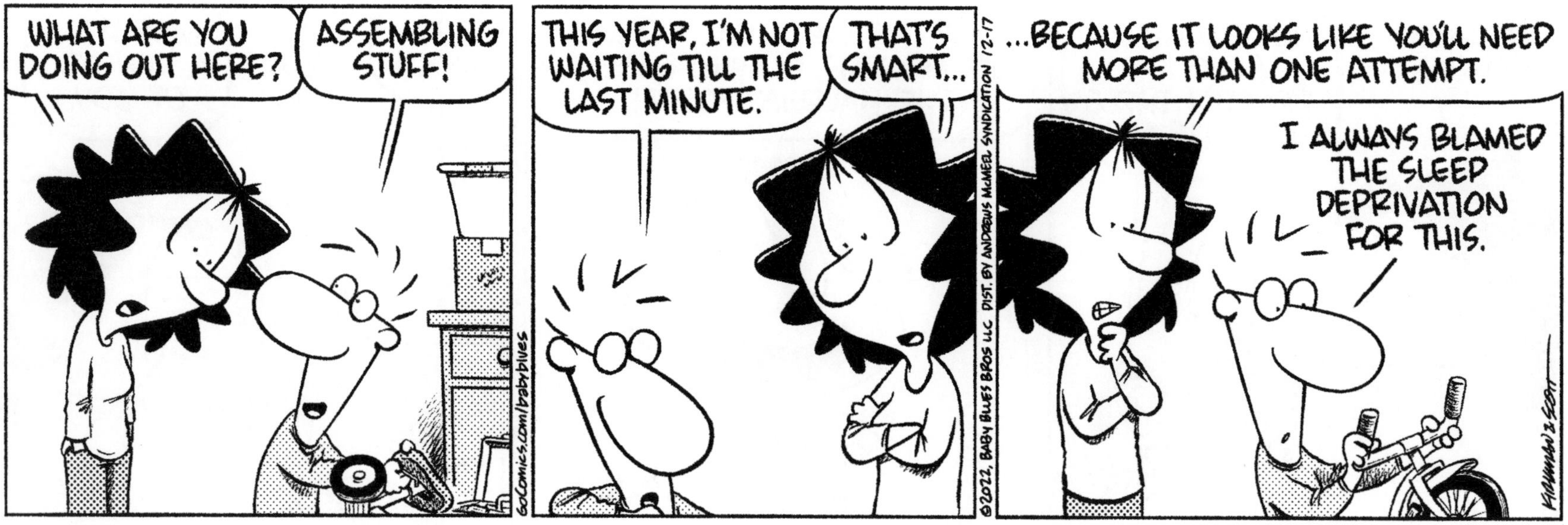
WHAT ARE YOU DOING OUT HERE?
ASSEMBLING STUFF!
GoComics.com/babyblues
THIS YEAR, I'M NOT WAITING TILL THE LAST MINUTE.
THAT'S SMART...
©2022, BABY BLUES BROS LLC DIST. BY ANDREWS McMEEL SYNDICATION 12-17
...BECAUSE IT LOOKS LIKE YOU'LL NEED MORE THAN ONE ATTEMPT.
I ALWAYS BLAMED THE SLEEP DEPRIVATION FOR THIS.

AND THE SNOWMAN IS FROM THE YEAR WE ALL GOT FOOD POISONING AND SPENT CHRISTMAS DAY BARFING

OOH! I LOVE THIS ONE!
GoComics.com/babyblues
WE GOT THAT ORNAMENT FROM THE HOSPITAL GIFT SHOP THE YEAR YOU HAD TO GET STITCHES.
©2022, BABY BLUES BROS LLC DIST. BY ANDREWS McMEEL SYNDICATION
THIS ONE IS FROM THE CHRISTMAS I BURNED THE TURKEY, AND WE ATE PIZZA FOR DINNER.
12-18
AND THE SNOWMAN IS FROM THE YEAR WE ALL GOT FOOD POISONING AND SPENT CHRISTMAS DAY BARFING.
WE DON'T HAVE ORNAMENTS, WE HAVE CHRISTMAS DISASTER KEEPSAKES.
WAS THIS FROM THE YEAR I FELL OFF THE LADDER, OR THE FENDER BENDER AT THE MALL?
KIRKMAN & SCOTT

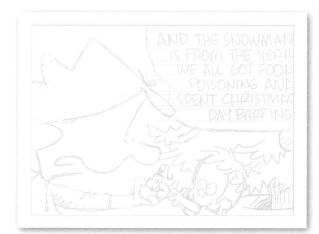

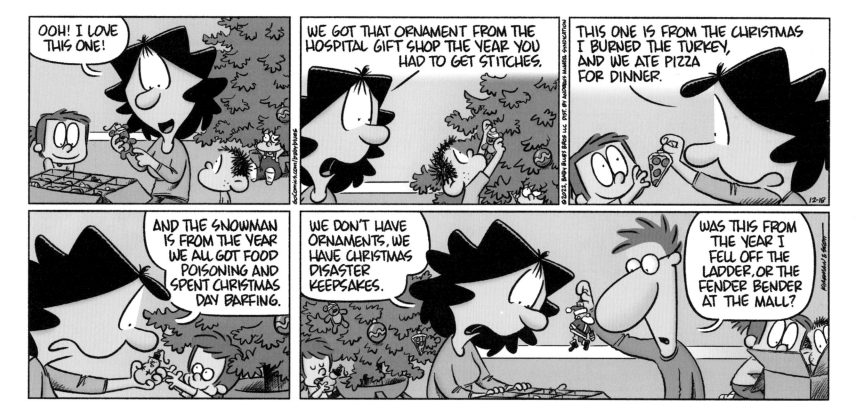

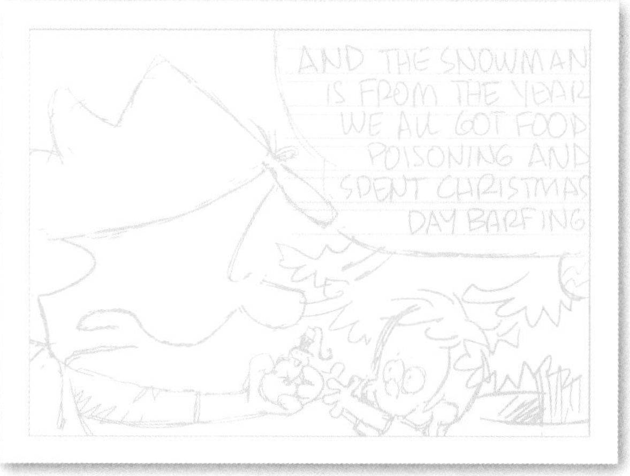

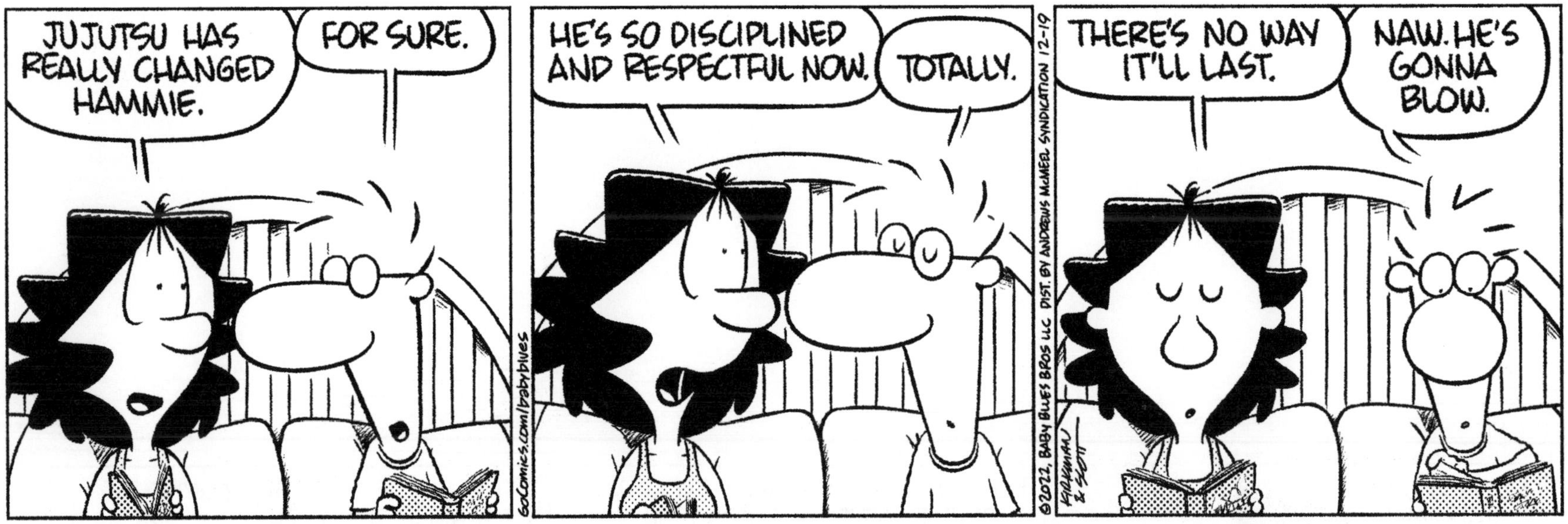
JUJUTSU HAS REALLY CHANGED HAMMIE.
FOR SURE.
GoComics.com/babyblues
HE'S SO DISCIPLINED AND RESPECTFUL NOW.
TOTALLY.
©2022, BABY BLUES BROS LLC DIST. BY ANDREWS McMEEL SYNDICATION 12-19
THERE'S NO WAY IT'LL LAST.
NAW. HE'S GONNA BLOW.

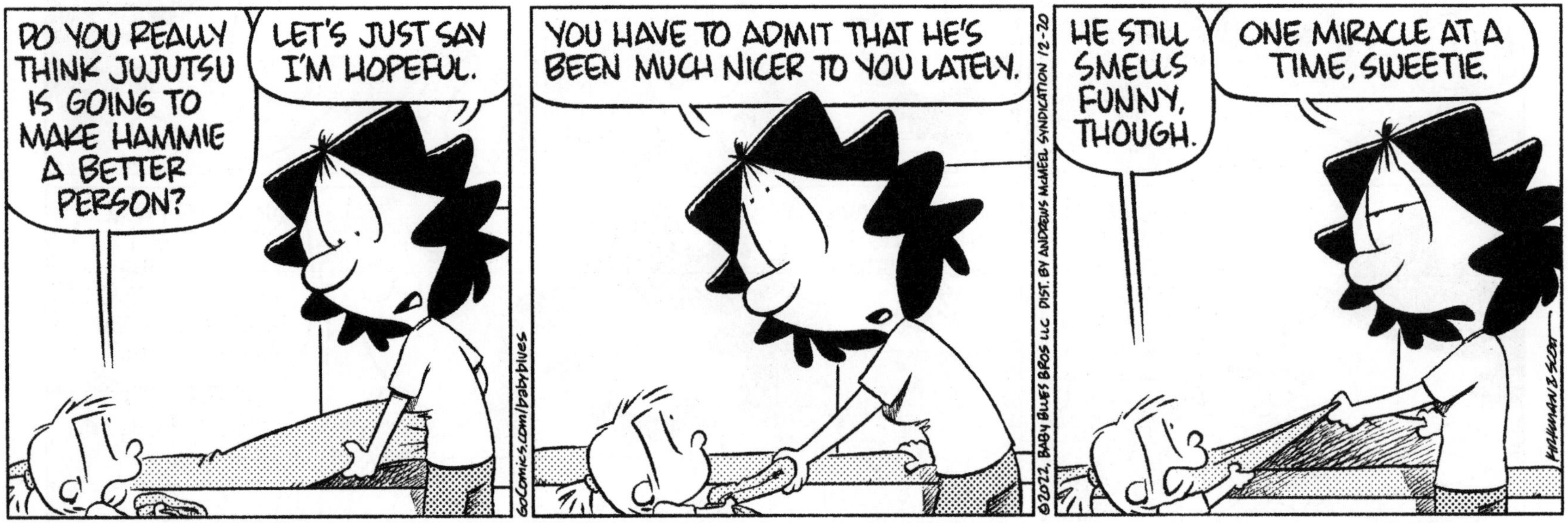
DO YOU REALLY THINK JUJUTSU IS GOING TO MAKE HAMMIE A BETTER PERSON?
LET'S JUST SAY I'M HOPEFUL.
GoComics.com/babyblues
YOU HAVE TO ADMIT THAT HE'S BEEN MUCH NICER TO YOU LATELY.
©2022, BABY BLUES BROS LLC DIST. BY ANDREWS McMEEL SYNDICATION 12-20
HE STILL SMELLS FUNNY, THOUGH.
ONE MIRACLE AT A TIME, SWEETIE.

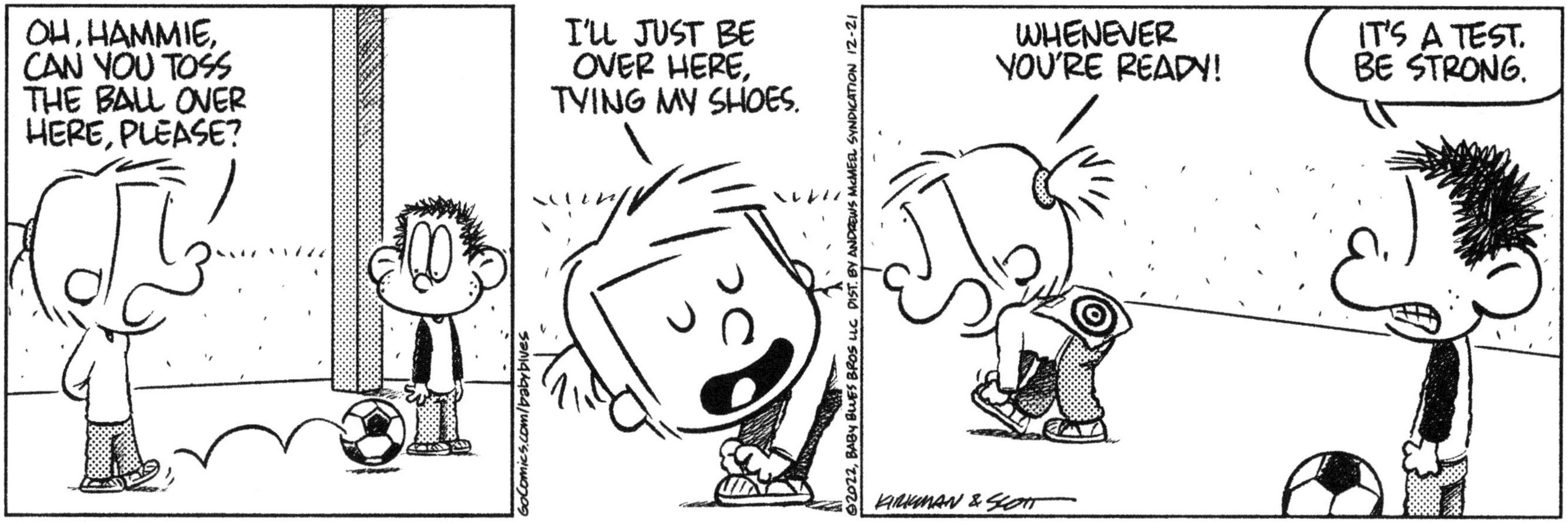
OH, HAMMIE, CAN YOU TOSS THE BALL OVER HERE, PLEASE?
GoComics.com/babyblues
I'LL JUST BE OVER HERE, TYING MY SHOES.
©2022, BABY BLUES BROS LLC DIST. BY ANDREWS McMEEL SYNDICATION 12-21
WHENEVER YOU'RE READY!
IT'S A TEST. BE STRONG.
KIRKMAN & SCOTT

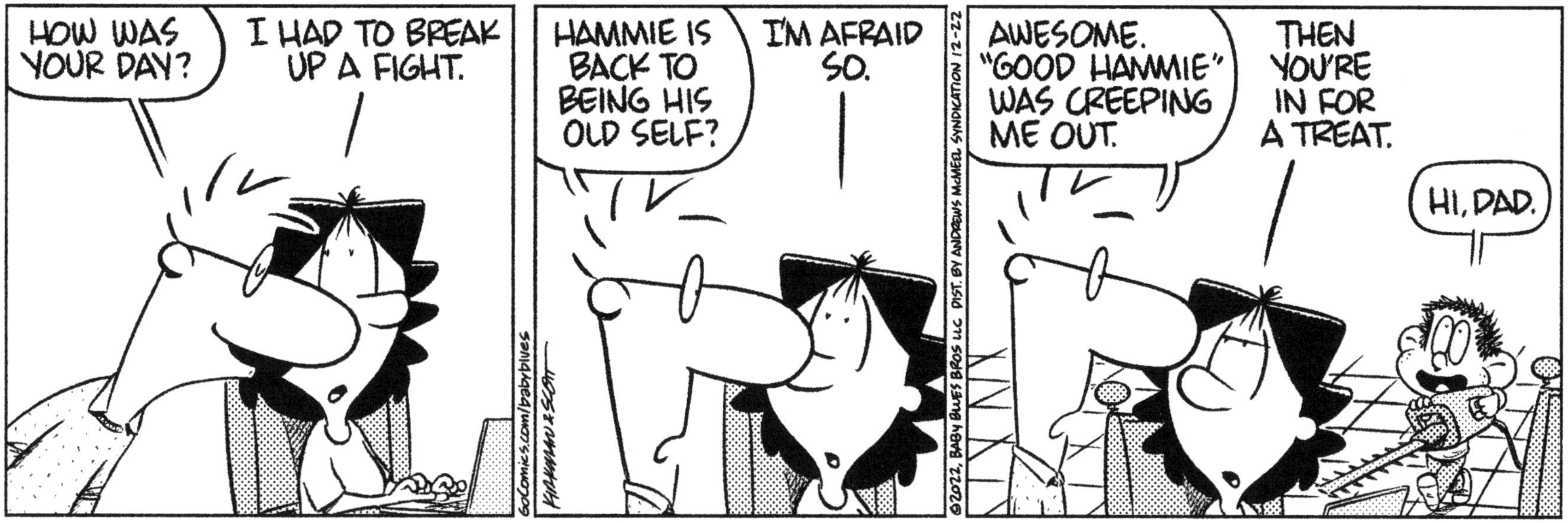
HOW WAS YOUR DAY?
I HAD TO BREAK UP A FIGHT.
GoComics.com/babyblues
KIRKMAN & SCOTT
HAMMIE IS BACK TO BEING HIS OLD SELF?
I'M AFRAID SO.
©2022, BABY BLUES BROS LLC DIST. BY ANDREWS McMEEL SYNDICATION 12-22
AWESOME. "GOOD HAMMIE" WAS CREEPING ME OUT.
THEN YOU'RE IN FOR A TREAT.
HI, DAD.

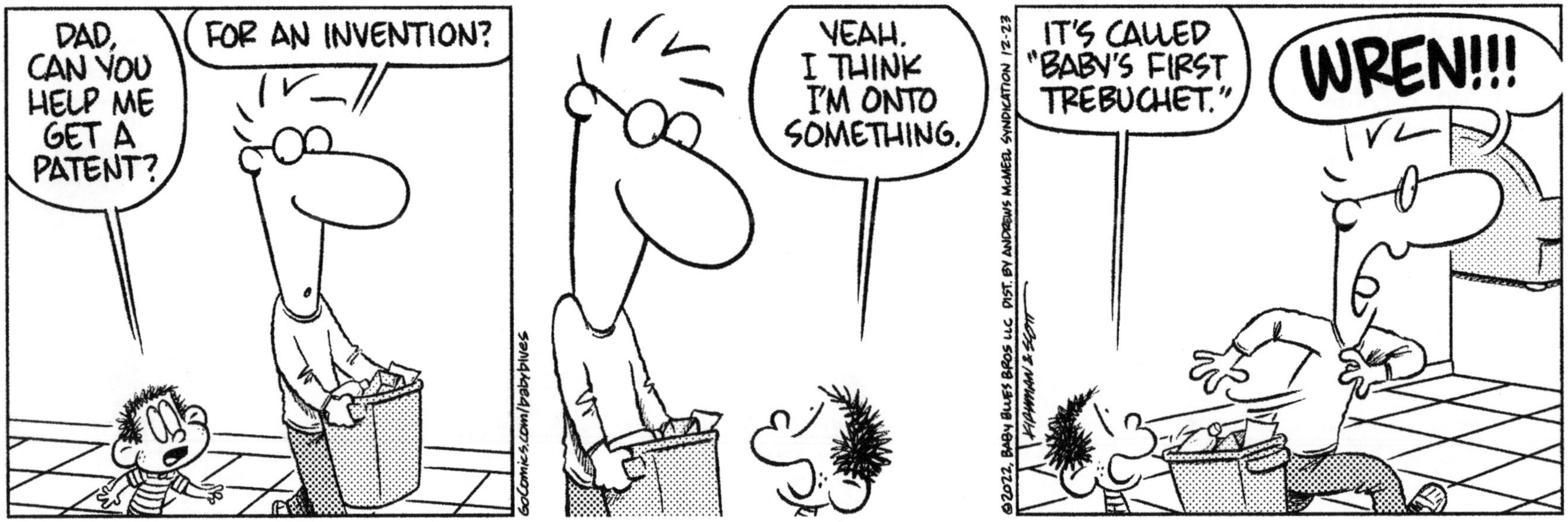
DAD, CAN YOU HELP ME GET A PATENT?
FOR AN INVENTION?
GoComics.com/babyblues
YEAH. I THINK I'M ONTO SOMETHING.
©2022, BABY BLUES BROS LLC DIST. BY ANDREWS McMEEL SYNDICATION 12-23
KIRKMAN & SCOTT
IT'S CALLED "BABY'S FIRST TREBUCHET."
WREN!!!

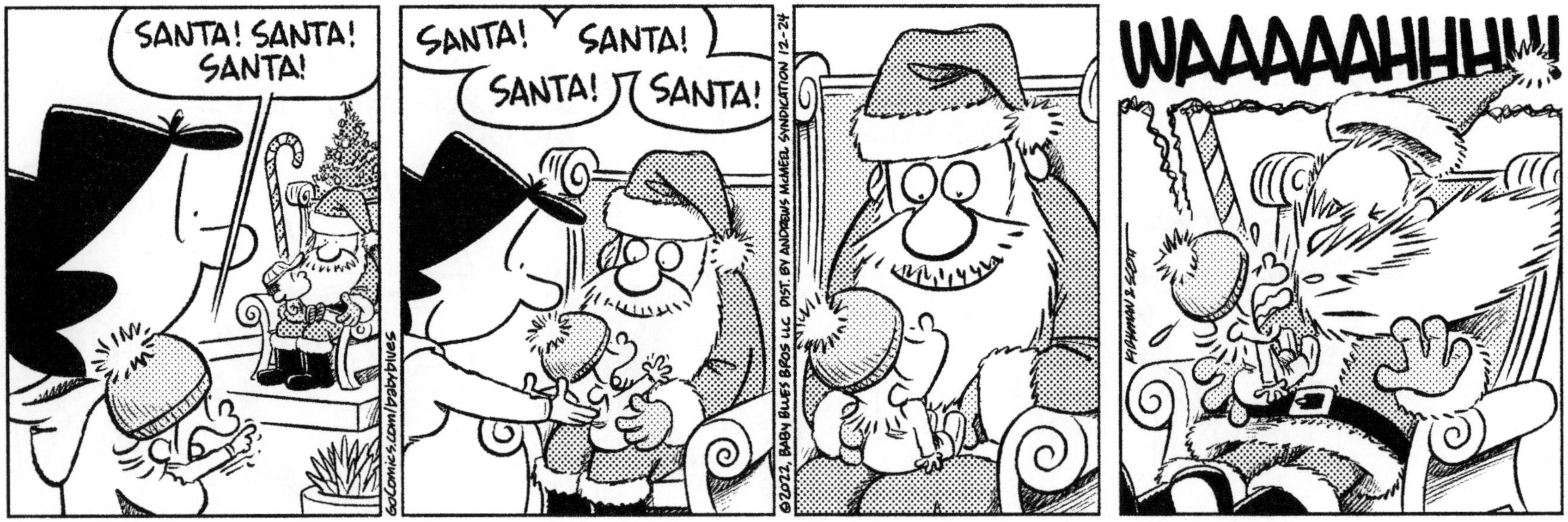
SANTA! SANTA! SANTA!
GoComics.com/babyblues
SANTA!
SANTA!
SANTA!
SANTA!
©2022, BABY BLUES BROS LLC DIST. BY ANDREWS McMEEL SYNDICATION 12-24
WAAAAAHHHH!
KIRKMAN & SCOTT

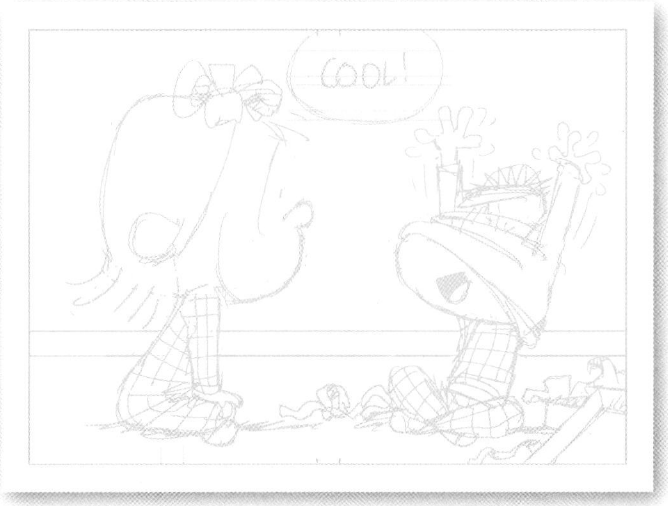
COOL!

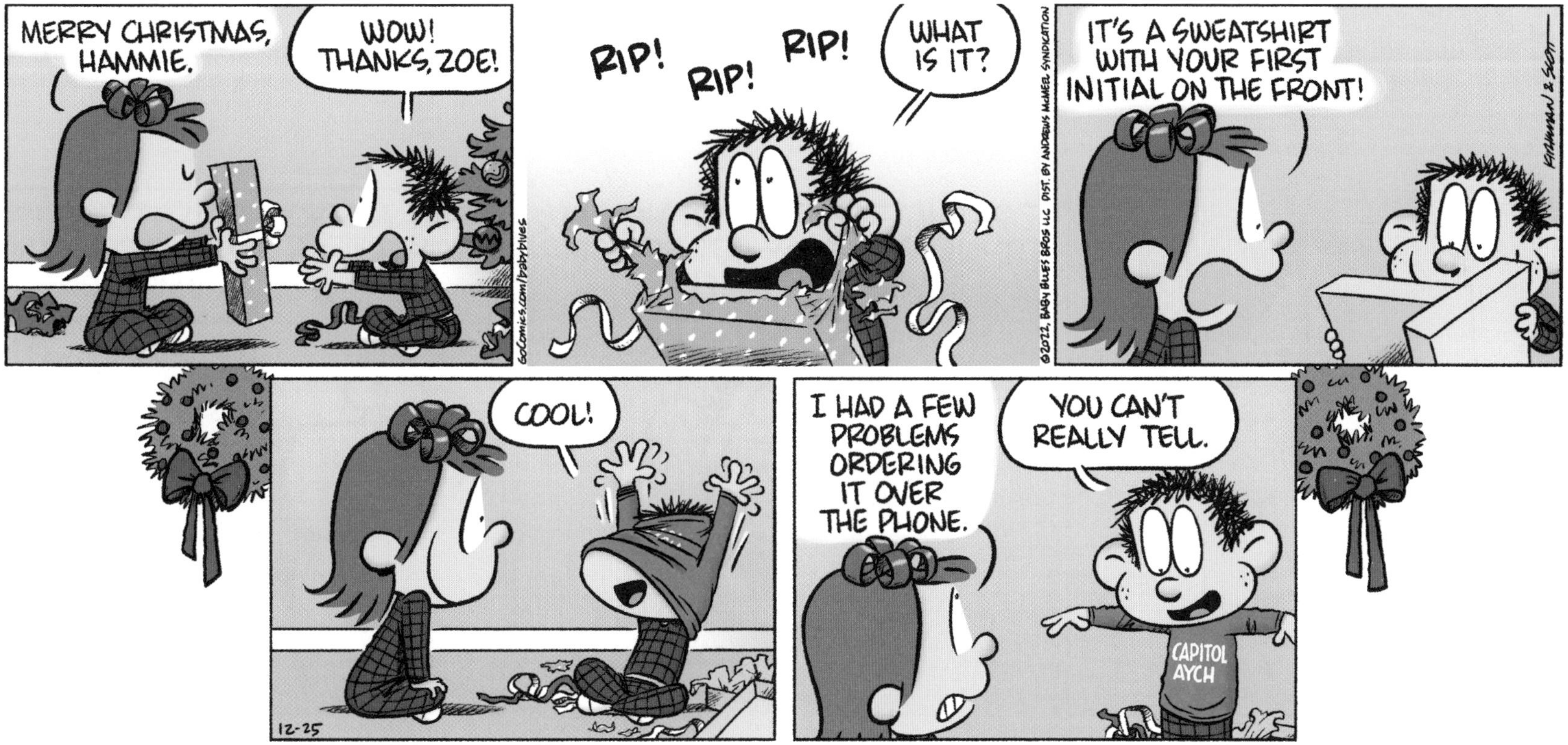
MERRY CHRISTMAS, HAMMIE.
WOW! THANKS, ZOE!
GoComics.com/babyblues
RIP!
RIP!
RIP!
WHAT IS IT?
©2022, BABY BLUES BROS LLC DIST. BY ANDREWS McMEEL SYNDICATION
IT'S A SWEATSHIRT WITH YOUR FIRST INITIAL ON THE FRONT!
KIRKMAN & SCOTT
COOL!
12-25
I HAD A FEW PROBLEMS ORDERING IT OVER THE PHONE.
YOU CAN'T REALLY TELL.
CAPITOL AYCH

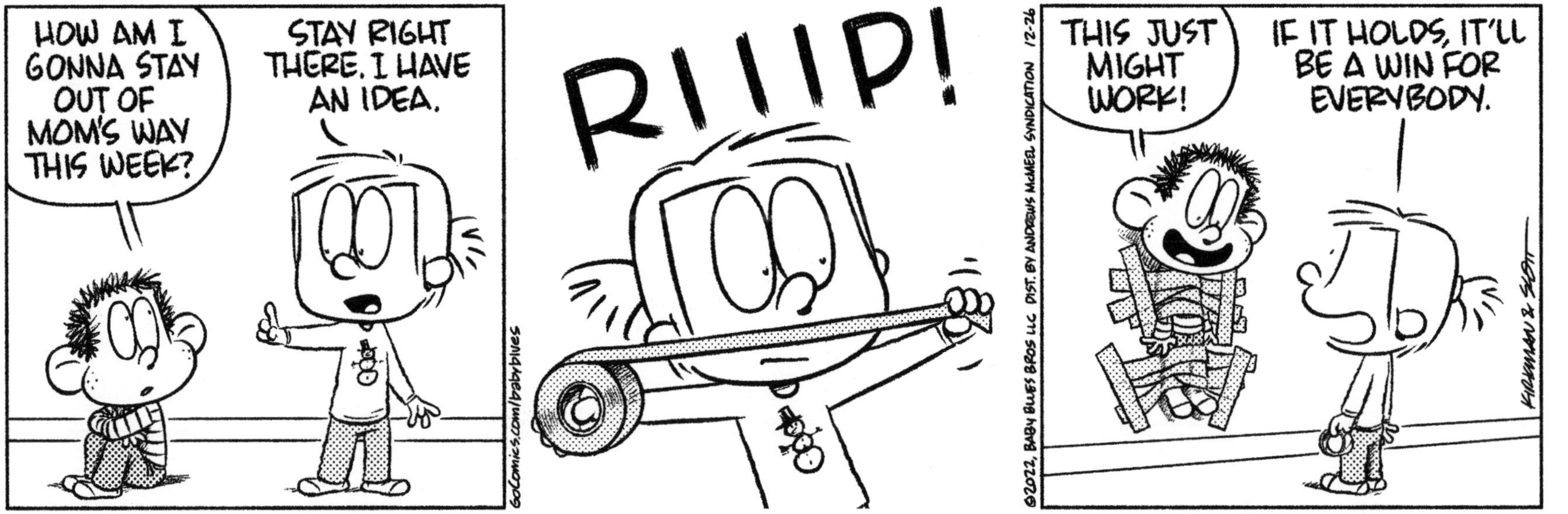
HOW AM I GONNA STAY OUT OF MOM'S WAY THIS WEEK?
STAY RIGHT THERE. I HAVE AN IDEA.
GoComics.com/babyblues
RIIIP!
©2022, BABY BLUES BROS LLC DIST. BY ANDREWS MCMEEL SYNDICATION 12-26
THIS JUST MIGHT WORK!
IF IT HOLDS, IT'LL BE A WIN FOR EVERYBODY.
KIRKMAN & SCOTT

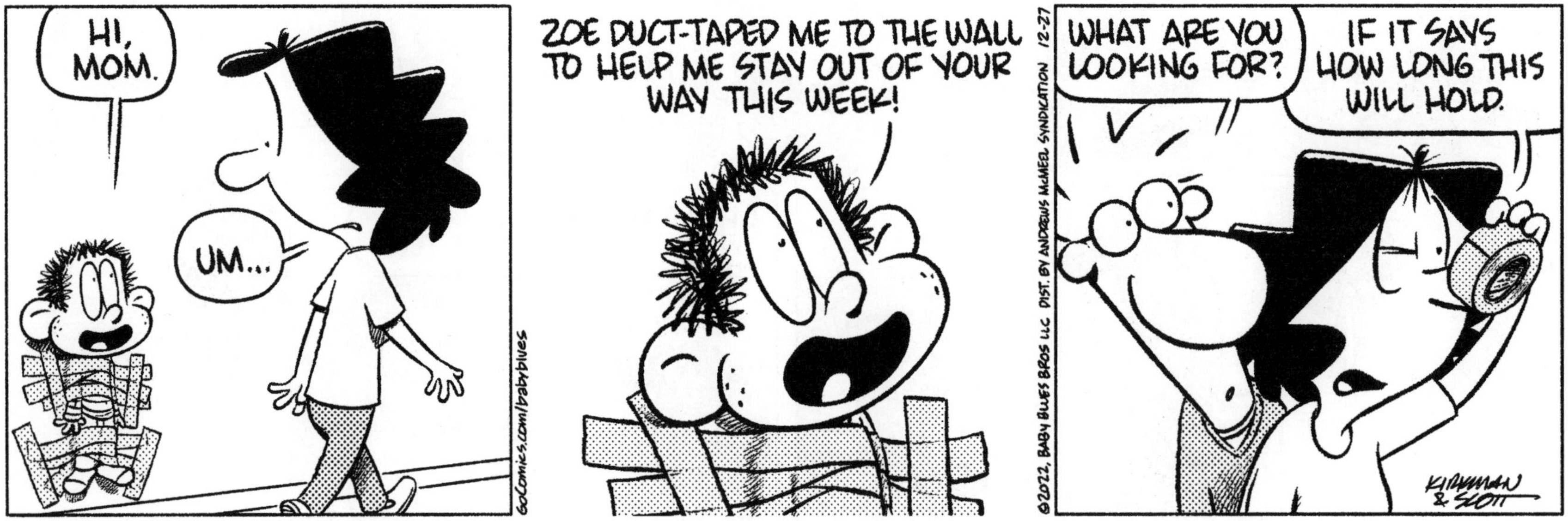
HI, MOM.
UM...
GoComics.com/babyblues
ZOE DUCT-TAPED ME TO THE WALL TO HELP ME STAY OUT OF YOUR WAY THIS WEEK!
©2022, BABY BLUES BROS LLC DIST. BY ANDREWS MCMEEL SYNDICATION 12-27
WHAT ARE YOU LOOKING FOR?
IF IT SAYS HOW LONG THIS WILL HOLD.
KIRKMAN & SCOTT

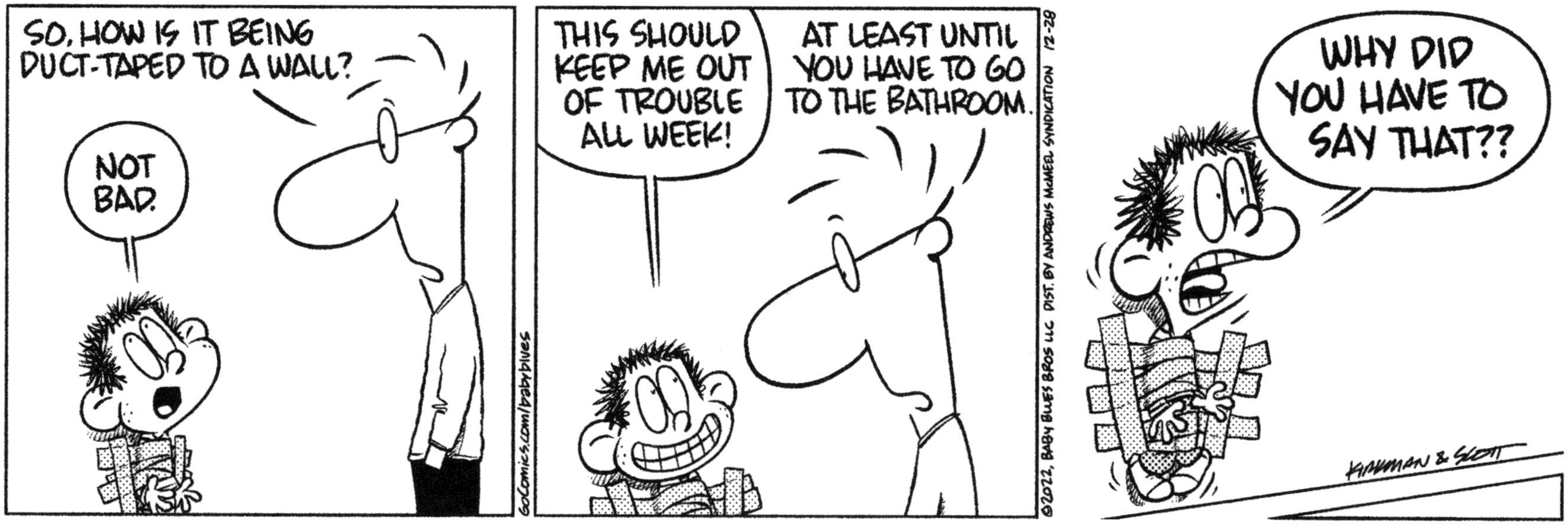
SO, HOW IS IT BEING DUCT-TAPED TO A WALL?
NOT BAD.
GoComics.com/babyblues
THIS SHOULD KEEP ME OUT OF TROUBLE ALL WEEK!
AT LEAST UNTIL YOU HAVE TO GO TO THE BATHROOM.
©2022, BABY BLUES BROS LLC DIST. BY ANDREWS McMEEL SYNDICATION 12-28
WHY DID YOU HAVE TO SAY THAT??
KIRKMAN & SCOTT

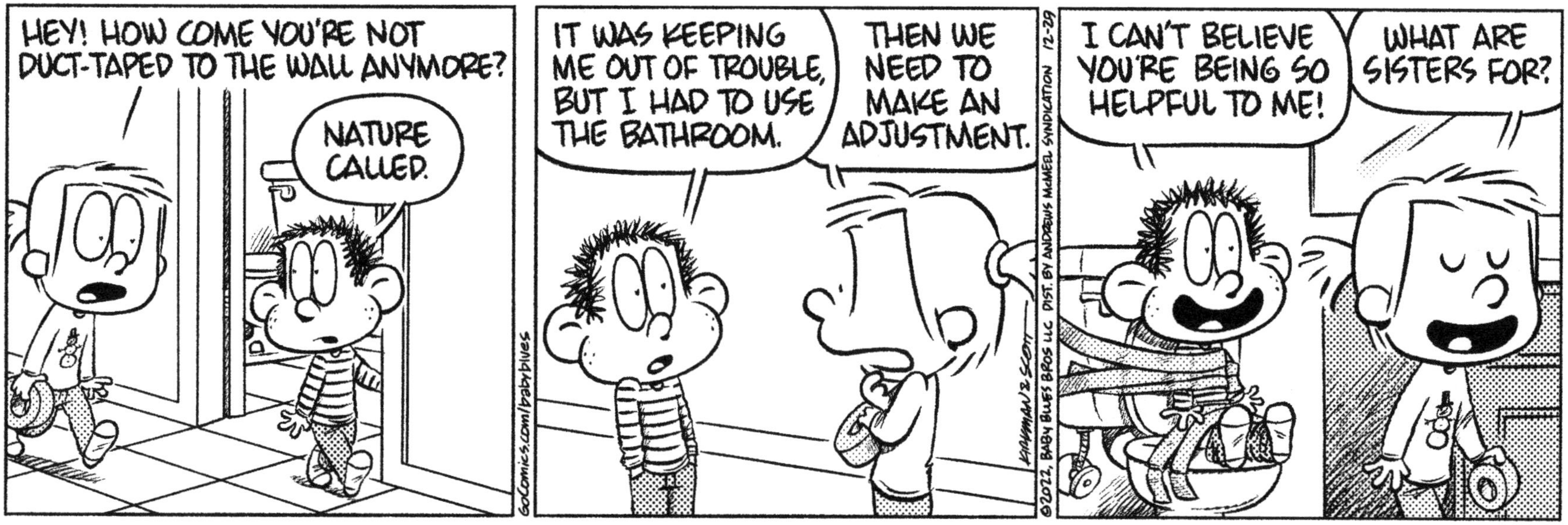
HEY! HOW COME YOU'RE NOT DUCT-TAPED TO THE WALL ANYMORE?
NATURE CALLED.
GoComics.com/babyblues
IT WAS KEEPING ME OUT OF TROUBLE, BUT I HAD TO USE THE BATHROOM.
THEN WE NEED TO MAKE AN ADJUSTMENT.
KIRKMAN & SCOTT
©2022, BABY BLUES BROS LLC DIST. BY ANDREWS McMEEL SYNDICATION 12-29
I CAN'T BELIEVE YOU'RE BEING SO HELPFUL TO ME!
WHAT ARE SISTERS FOR?

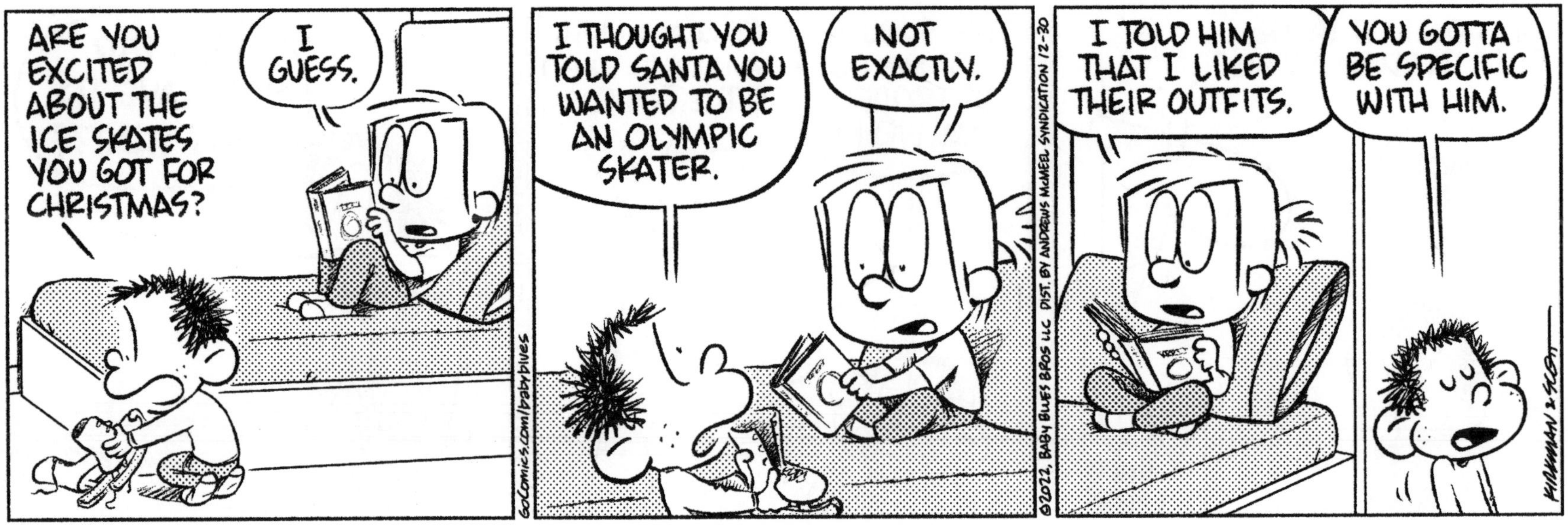
ARE YOU EXCITED ABOUT THE ICE SKATES YOU GOT FOR CHRISTMAS?
I GUESS.
GoComics.com/babyblues
I THOUGHT YOU TOLD SANTA YOU WANTED TO BE AN OLYMPIC SKATER.
NOT EXACTLY.
©2022, BABY BLUES BROS LLC DIST. BY ANDREWS McMEEL SYNDICATION 12-30
I TOLD HIM THAT I LIKED THEIR OUTFITS.
YOU GOTTA BE SPECIFIC WITH HIM.
KIRKMAN & SCOTT

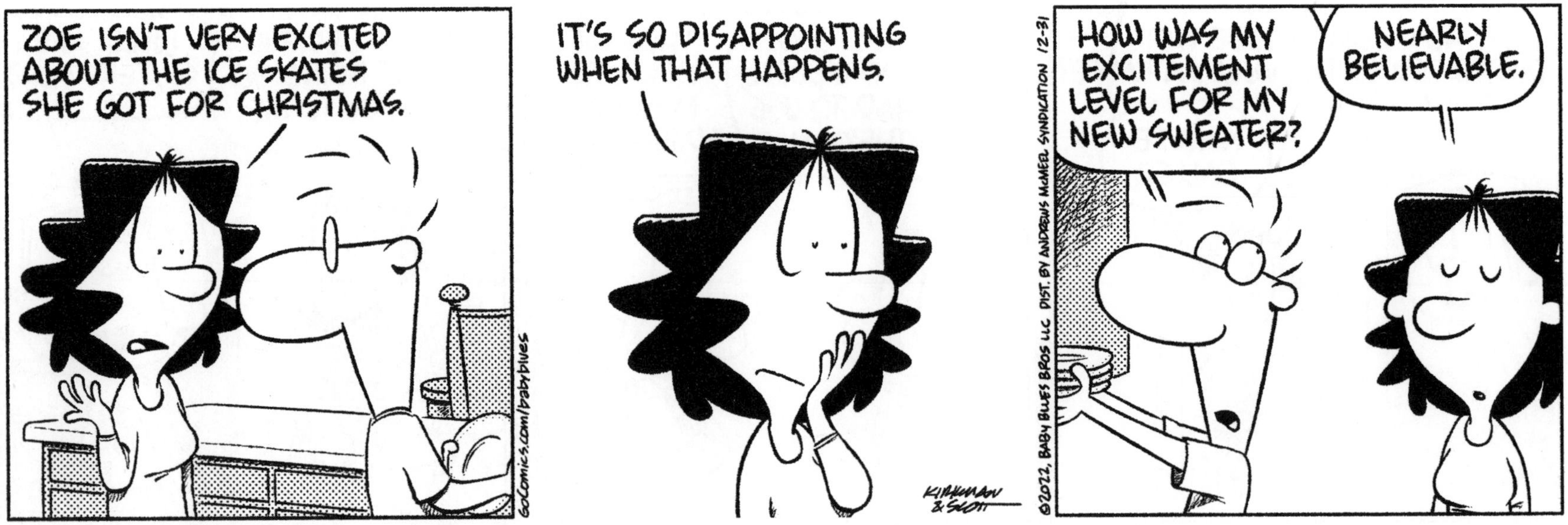
ZOE ISN'T VERY EXCITED ABOUT THE ICE SKATES SHE GOT FOR CHRISTMAS.
GoComics.com/babyblues
IT'S SO DISAPPOINTING WHEN THAT HAPPENS.
KIRKMAN & SCOTT
©2022, BABY BLUES BROS LLC DIST. BY ANDREWS McMEEL SYNDICATION 12-31
HOW WAS MY EXCITEMENT LEVEL FOR MY NEW SWEATER?
NEARLY BELIEVABLE.